D1271363

Catalogue of Choral Music Arranged in Biblical Order

compiled by James Laster

The Scarecrow Press, Inc.
Metuchen, N.J., & London 1983

Library of Congress Cataloging in Publication Data

Laster, James, 1934-
    Catalogue of choral music arranged in Biblical order.

    1. Church music--Bibliography.   2. Choral music--
Bibliography.   I. Title.
ML128.C54L4   1983   016.7834   82-16745
ISBN 0-8108-1592-3

TABLE OF CONTENTS

L I S T   O F   A B B R E V I A T I O N S

S	Soprano
A	Alto
T	Tenor
B	Bass
C	Cambiata
SATB/SATB	Double Choir
SA(T)B	Voice part in parenthesis is optional
kro	Keyboard Rehearsal Only
n.d.	No date
n.#.	No number
AMSI	Art Masters Studio
GIA	Gregorian Institute of America
RSCM	Royal School of Church Music

PREFACE

The CATALOGUE OF CHORAL MUSIC ARRANGED IN BIBLICAL ORDER is designed as an aid for the church musician and/or pastor seeking to plan unified worship services. It will also be of use to those church musicians who follow the Liturgical Calendar and plan music appropriate to the appointed lessons. It will be a source to choir directors of non-church positions who would like to locate choral settings based on a particular Scripture text.

Anthems are arranged in the CATALOGUE in Biblical order, from Genesis to Revelation, according to the Biblical passage -- book, chapter and verse(s). Anthems based upon texts from the Apocrypha are placed as a group between the Old and the New Testament. Multiple settings of the same Scripture passage are listed alphabetically by composer under the appropriate Scripture entry. Books of the Bible for which no musical settings were found are omitted from the CATALOGUE.

The CATALOGUE began as a small project which was to list only the few hundred titles based on Biblical texts found in the Choral Library of the Shenandoah College and Conservatory of Music, and the libraries of two or three Winchester, Virginia, churches. When it was decided that it might be a worthwhile venture to expand the contents and to make the CATALOGUE as complete as possible, letters were sent to about thirty-five music publishers requesting single copies of anthems for examination and cataloging. The response from the publishers was most favorable. Along with their packets of music, some sent personal letters of encouragement and support. Others offered helpful suggestions.

Grateful appreciation is expressed to the following publishers for either sending music, or for opening their offices so that their choral music files could be examined on the premises: Abingdon Press, Augsburg Publishing House, Belwin/Mills, Boosey & Hawkes, Broadman Press, Alexander Broude, Broude Brothers, Cambiata Press, Choristers Guild, Concordia Publishing House, Carl Fischer, Mark Foster, Galaxy, Gregorian Institute of America, F. Harris (Canada), Hope Publishing Company, Novello Publishing House, Oxford University Press, Plymouth Music Company, and E. C. Schirmer.

In addition to the publishers mentioned, The Choral Library of Westminster Choir College, Princeton, New Jersey, was a major source for locating music. Included in this CATALOGUE, one will find titles from Westminster's 'Collection' (multiple copy files), as well as music from their large single-copy reference holdings. My thanks to Sheri Clausin, Choral Librarian, and her assistant, Beth Sherfi, for their help and support in this endeavor. Titles from the Choral Library of the National Cathedral, Washington, D.C. were also included in this CATALOGUE. Appreciation is expressed to Douglas Major, Assistant Organist of the Cathedral, for opening the Library, and for sharing his work on a similar project, which is included in this CATALOGUE.

Very early in the cataloging, the problem of how to treat the Book of Psalms was encountered. All Psalms are entered in the CATALOGUE according to the King James numbering. This will account for the few instances where the title of the anthem uses the Vulgate numbering, but it is filed according to the King James numbering.

For the most part, items found in the CATALOGUE are published as separate octavos. Where anthem collections are included, titles are entered separately, with the name of the collection given along with the publisher at the end of the citation.

There has been no attempt to include the music of the Anglican Services. Settings of the Magnificat, Nunc Dimittis, Jubilate Deo, etc., are included when they are published as separate titles, rather than as Services.

There are two types of entries found in the CATALOGUE: a Main Entry, and a SEE Reference. An annotated Main Entry is as follows:

(1) PROVERBS 3:5,6   (2) PSALM 121:7,8
        (3) WETZLER, ROBERT
        (4) HE SHALL DIRECT YOUR PATHS
        (5) SATB   ORGAN, OR PIANO
        (6) AMSI (1981) 414

(1) Biblical Reference -- Book, Chapter, Verse(s).

(2) Additional Scripture used in the anthem; or the name of the author of a paraphrased text, or a translator of a text will appear here.

(3) Composer's Name, including arranger and editor, if appropriate.

(4) Title. All texts are assumed to be in English unless otherwise indicated.

(5) Voicing, solos (if any), accompaniment.

   A) When an anthem has the voice parts reduced for keyboard playing, but the work is intended for unaccompanied singing, it is listed as 'kro' (keyboard rehearsal only).

   B) When an anthem is printed in open score with no keyboard reduction and is intended for unaccompanied singing, it is listed as No Accompaniment.

   C) When an anthem uses accompaniment, it will be listed as Keyboard, Organ, or Piano. Optional or additional instrumentation will be indicated here.

(6) The name of the Publisher, the most recent date of publication, and the octavo number appear at the end of each citation. Information concerning instrumental parts, other versions of the same title, and the name of the collection also appear after the publisher's information. Items where no date is given are listed as (n.d.) or left blank. Items for which there is no octavo number are listed as (n.#.) or left blank.

An Annotated SEE Reference is as follows:

(1) PSALM 121:7,8
        (2) SEE: PROVERBS 3:5, 6
        (3) WETZLER, ROBERT
        (4) HE SHALL DIRECT YOUR PATHS

(1) Biblical Reference -- Book, Chapter, Verse(s).

(2) The SEE Reference which refers to the Main Scripture Heading where the complete citation is located.

(3) and (4) Composer and Title for the Main Heading are repeated in the SEE Reference.

The Biblical reference which appears on the printed music has been used as the reference for cataloging. When there were obvious errors, they were corrected. There are variations in the way publishers list scripture sources, which accounts for irregularities in listings. Many anthems give as their text source, 'The Psalms,' or 'from the Bible,' or 'from Scripture.' Every effort was made to locate the specific passages in these cases, but some texts were too jumbled or mixed to locate. Whenever the text could be located, it is included in the CATALOGUE. By the same token, there are anthems which use Biblical texts which have been omitted because the exact Scripture reference and the text could not be located.

A very special expression of gratitude is extended to the Shenandoah College and Conservatory of Music for the Faculty Development Grant which provided funding for the beginning of this project. Appreciation is also extended to Dr. Thomas Layne, professor of mathematics and director of the Computer Services of Shenandoah and his assistant, Leslie Watada, for the development of a program which allowed for a computer-sort of the data, and a working printout of the CATALOGUE. A word of gratitude is expressed to Lois Hoffman for her work on the Composer Index. Finally, sincere thanks to Mrs. Marjorie Edmondson for her typing skills in providing the final copy.

A work such as this is always out of date. Due to the vast amount of choral music, it is obvious that many titles will have been overlooked, and the latest publications omitted. It is hoped that a supplement or a revision of the CATALOGUE will be brought out from time to time in order to keep it as current as possible, and thereby continue to be of assistance to those who will find a use for it.

JHL

CATALOGUE

OF

CHORAL MUSIC

ARRANGED IN

BIBLICAL ORDER

THE OLD TESTAMENT

GENESIS

1:00 (based on)
   Wink, Sue Karen
   Good, Good, Good
   SATB   Piano
   Broadman (1976) 4555-13

1:1-3
   Hunnicutt, Judy
   God, Creator
   SATB   Handbells
   Augsburg (1974) 11-3011

1:1-3
   Pinkham, Daniel
   In the Beginning of Creation
   SATB   Tape
   E. C. Schirmer (1970) 2902

1:1-4 (John 1:1-5)
   Kauffman, Ronald
   In the Beginning
   SATB   Keyboard   Narrator
   Elkan-Vogel (1978) 362-03258

1:1 - 2:7
   Copland, Aaron
   In the Beginning
   SATB   (S-solo)   kro
   Boosey & Hawkes (1947) n.#.

2:1-3
   Gottlieb, Jack
   Vay'Chulu (The Heaven and the Earth Were
       Finished) (Hebrew)
   TB   Organ
   Presser (1971) 312-40781

4:9-10
   Aichinger, Gregor
   Ubi Est Abel Frater Tuus? (Latin only)
   SAB   No accompaniment
   Arista (1977) AE 269

4:9-10
   Aichinger, Gregor (ed. R. Proulx)
   Where is Now Abel?
   SAB   kro
   GIA (1974) G-1854

8:22 (Psalm 27:7; Zechariah 8:12; Psalm 65:9,
       11; I Chronicles 29:13)
   Simper, Caleb
   While the Earth Remaineth
   SATB   Organ
   Weekes [Galaxy] (n.d.) W.4088

12:2, 3
   Adler, Samuel
   God's Promise
   SSA   Keyboard
   Oxford (1972) 94.404

22:1-13
   Capello, Giovanni (ed. & arr. Lloyd
       Pfautsch)
   Abraham and Isaac
   SATB   Keyboard
   Abingdon (1961) APM 143

28:16, 17
   Burnell, J.
   Surely the Lord is in This Place
   SATB   Organ ad lib.
   Novello (1959) 29.0357.01

28:16, 17
   Burnell, J.
   Surely the Lord is in This Place
   SATB   Organ ad lib.
   Novello (1931) 264 (in Short and Easy
       Anthems, Set I); (also in The
       Novello Anthem Book)

28:16, 17
   Burroughs, Bob
   Surely the Lord is in This Place
   SAB   kro
   Kjos (1981) ED-GC 101

28:16, 17 (Psalm 134)
   Clokey, Joseph
   The House of God
   SATB   Organ
   Flammer (1956) 84469

28:16-17 (Micah 6:8; Isaiah 54:13, 14;
       Isaiah 60:18)
   Fannon, Daniel Stephen
   Surely The Lord is in This Place
   SATB   kro
   Concordia (1973) 98-2149

28:16, 17
   Hurford, Peter
   Truly the Lord is in This Place (Two
       Sentences)
   SATB   Organ
   Novello (1972) MW29

28:16-17
  Lorenz, Ellen Jane
  The Gate of Heaven
  SATB   Organ and/or Handbells
  Abingdon (1976) APM-774

28:16-17 (Psalm 137:4; Psalm 95)
  Pfautsch, Lloyd
  The Lord Is In This Place
  SATB   Congregation, Reader, Brass
  Abingdon (1975) APM-963 (Brass APM-964)

28:16-17
  Powell, Robert J.
  Surely The Lord Is In This House
  SATB   kro
  Lorenz (1967) E-71

28:16-17
  SEE: I Corinthians 3:9, 16-17, 23
  Sowerby, Leo
  For We Are Laborers Together With God

28:17 (Psalm 84:1)
  Rubbra, Edmund
  This Is Truly The House Of God, Op. 95
  SATB   kro
  Lengnick (1959) 4000

28:17
  SEE: Psalm 122:1
  Thompson, Randall
  The Gate Of Heaven

31:49
  Horman, John
  May The Lord Watch (from Two Benedictions)
  4-part round   Keyboard
  Hinshaw (1981) HMC-487

32:24-26 (Wesley)
  Williamson, Malcolm
  Wrestling Jacob
  SATB   (S-solo)   Organ
  Novello (1962) 29.0389.10

32:24, 26-27, 29b-30 (Wesley)
  Routley, Erik
  Come O Thou Traveler Unknown
  SATB   Organ
  Agape [Hope] (1981) ER 1920

37:33-35
  Senfl, Ludwig (ed. James Erb)
  When Jacob Had Beheld The Cloak (English/
      German)
  SATB   kro
  Lawson Gould (1959) 798

49:10-11
  Schütz, Heinrich (ed. C. Buell Agey)
  Lo, The Scepter From Judah Shall Not Be
      Removed (German/English)
  SATTB   Organ
  Concordia (1961) 98-1559

49:25-26
  SEE: Ezekiel 34:13-16
  Parker, Tom
  Lead Us On, Good Shepherd

E X O D U S

2:00 (based on)
  Lockwood, Normand
  The Birth Of Moses
  SSA   Piano   Flute
  Merrymount [Mercury] (1949) MC 140

3:00 (based on)
  Krapf, Gerhard (arr.)
  The God Of Abraham Praise
  2-part mixed   Organ
  Augsburg (1971) 11-1824

4:21-23
  Kennedy, Mike & Ann Cadwallander, (arr.)
  Go Down Moses
  2 mixed voices   Piano or Guitar
  GIA (1972) G-1770

9:16
  SEE: James 4:10
  Pethel, Stan
  He Shall Lift You Up

12:2
  SEE: Isaiah 25:1-9
  Sisler, Hampson
  Let Us Exalt Him

13:17 (Exodus 16:23; Isaiah 11:10)
  Gregor, Christian (ed. Ewald Nolte)
  In Slumber, Peaceful Slumber (English/
      German)
  SSAB or SATB   Organ
  Boosey & Hawkes (1969) 5701

13:22
  SEE: Isaiah 33:20-21
  Kauffman, Ronald (arr.)
  Glorious Things Of Thee Are Spoken

15:00 (based on)
  Thiman, Eric
  Come Ye Faithful Raise The Strain
  SATB   Organ
  Novello (1971) MW 10

15:1-2
  Felciano, Richard
  I Will Sing To The Lord (Songs For
      Darkness And Light)
  3 part equal voices   No accompaniment
  E. C. Schirmer (1971) 2803

15:1-2
  Pethel, Stan
  I Will Sing Unto The Lord
  SATB   2 Trumpets; 1 Horn; 2 Trombones
  Broadman (1978) 4562-53

15:1-2, 11
  Reynolds, William J.
  I Will Sing Unto The Lord
  Unison with descant   Keyboard
  Broadman (1965) (found in The Junior
          Choir Sings, #3)

15:1-6, 11, 18
  Adler, Samuel
  A Song Of Exaltation
  SATB   Organ
  Abingdon (1966) APM-249

15:1-6, 11-13, 17-18
  Wyton, Alec
  I Will Sing To The Lord
  Unison   Organ
  Hinshaw (1977) HMC-260

15:1-6, 15
  Pulkingham, Betty Carr
  The Song Of Moses
  2 mixed voices   Piano or Guitar
  GIA (1972) G-1771

15:2
  Handel, G. F. (ed. Don Craig and Harold
      Maxon)
  And I Will Exalt Him
  SATB   Piano or Organ
  Plymouth (1972) FS-103

15:2 (plus additional)
    Hopson, Hal
    The Lord Is My Strength and My Song
    Unison   Keyboard   Optional Bells
        and Percussion
    Choristers Guild (1972) A-101

15:4, 21
    Baristow, E. C.
    Sing Ye To the Lord
    SATB   Organ
    H. W. Gray (n.d.) 2123

15:4, 21
    Baristow, Edward
    Sing Ye To the Lord
    SATB   Organ
    Novello (n.d.) 2132

15:11
    Berger, Jean
    Who is Like Unto Thee, O Lord
    SATB   Organ ad lib.
    Augsburg (1966) ACL-1482

15:11
    Gottlieb, Jack
    Mi Chamochah (Who Is Like Unto You)
        (Hebrew)
    SATB   Organ, Cantor, Percussion
    Presser (1971) 312-40776

15:11
    Pergolesi, G. B. (ed. & arr. Walter Ehret)
    Who Is Like Unto Thee O God?
    SATB   Piano or Organ
    GIA (1976) G-1978

15:11, 18
    Weisgall, Hugo
    Who Is Like Unto Thee (English/Hebrew)
    SATB   (B-solo)   Piano or Organ
    Presser (1961) 312-40514

15:20-21
    Fromm, Herbert
    Song of Miriam
    SSA   (B or S solo)   Piano, Percussion
        ad lib.
    Carl Fischer (1946) CM-6181

15:20-22 (based on)
    Dett, R. Nathaniel
    The Song of Miriam
    SSA   (S-solo)   Keyboard
    J. Fischer (1965) 9978

16:23
    SEE: Exodus 13:17
    Gregor, Christian (ed. & arr. Ewald Nolte)
    In Slumber, Peaceful Slumber

19:1, 16-17 (and other)
    Lee, T. Charles
    The Face of Moses Shone
    SATB   Organ
    H. W. Gray (1949) CMR-2092

19:5-6
    Schalit, Heinrich
    The Sacred Covenant
    SATB   Organ
    Transcontinental (1963) 144

20:2-17
    Haydn, Joseph
    The Holy Ten Commandments (English/German)
    Canon 3-5 voices   No accompaniment
    Mercury (1942) MC-10

33:14 (Isaiah 60:19)
    Haan, Raymond H.
    My Presence Shall Go With Thee
    SATB   Organ (Optional TTBB section)
    Sacred Music Press (1980) S-252

34:6
    SEE: Psalm 69:29
    Brahms, Johannes
    Ich aber bin Elend

34:6, 7 (Acts 1:24; Psalm 95:7)
    Gregor, Christian (arr. E. V. Nolte)
    Lord, God, Merciful and Gracious (Two
        Anthems From The Moravians)
    SATB   kro
    Abingdon (1965) APM-525

34:6, 7
    Norris, Kevin
    Offertory/Maundy Thursday (Verses and
    Offertories/Lent)
    Unison   Organ
    Augsburg (1980) 11-9545

L E V I T I C U S

25:9
    Moore, Undine Smith
    Lord We Give Thanks To Thee
    SATB   kro
    Warner Brothers (1973) CH0620

N U M B E R S

6:24-26
    Fryxell, Regina Holmen
    Benediction (from Seven Choral Service
        Settings)
    SATB   No accompaniment
    Abingdon (1963) APM-242

6:24-26
    Lutkin, Peter
    The Lord Bless You and Keep You
    SATB   Organ ad lib.
    Concordia (1959) (found in The Church
        Choir Book, 97-6320)

6:24-26
    Lutkin, Peter
    The Lord Bless You and Keep You
    SATB   optional organ
    Presser (1959) 312.40420

6:24-26
    Mueller, Carl F.
    The Lord Bless You
    SATB   kro
    G. Schirmer (1934) 8069

6:24-26
    Nystedt, Knut
    The Benediction
    SATB   kro
    Associated (1966) A-500 (also found in
        AMP Contemporary Choral Collection)

6:24-26
    Shaw, Kirby
    Benediction
    SATB   kro
    Schmitt, Hall, McCreary (1971) 6224

6:24-26
    Smith, Gregg
    The Lord Bless Thee And Keep Thee
    SSA   (S-solo)   Organ
    G. Schirmer (1969) 11160

6:24-26
    Willan, Healey
    The Aaronic Benediction
    SATB   No accompaniment
    C. F. Peters (1958) 6099

10:29 (Psalm 34:3, 11)
    Clokey, Joseph
    Come Thou
    SATB   Organ
    J. Fischer (1958) 9067

15:40
    SEE: Deuteronomy 6:5-9
    Sowerby, Leo
    Thou Shalt Love The Lord Thy God

24:5 (Psalm 5:8; Psalm 26:8; Psalm 69:14)
    Gottlieb, Jack
    Mah Tovu (English/Hebrew)
    SATB   Cantor, Organ
    Presser (1971) 312-40772

24:5
    Ouseley, F. A. Gore
    How Goodly Are Thy Tents
    SATB   optional Organ
    Oxford (found in Anthems For Choirs,
        Volume I)

24:5-6
    Ouseley, Frederick A. Gore
    How Goodly Are Thy Tents
    SATB   Organ
    C. T. Wagner Reprint (n.d.) C-067005

24:17 (Psalm 2:9)
    Mendelssohn, Felix (ed. Don Razey)
    A Star Shall Rise Up Out Of Jacob
    SATB   Organ or Piano
    Carl Fischer (1977) CM-8047

24:17
    Mendelssohn, Felix
    Behold A Star From Jacob Shining
    SATB   Organ
    E. C. Schirmer (1936) (also in Second
        Concord Anthem Book - Grey)

24:17
    SEE: Matthew 2:1
    Mendelssohn, Felix
    Say Where Is He Born & There Shall A Star

D E U T E R O N O M Y

4:7, 9
    Brahms, Johannes
    Where Is Such A Nation, Op. 109, #3
        (English/German)
    SATB/SATB   kro
    C. F. Peters (1964) 6567

4:29, 31
    Powell, Robert J.
    Seek The Lord Your God
    SA   Keyboard
    Abingdon (1976) APM-512 (in Anthems For
        Treble Voices)

4:30-31
    SEE: Matthew 5:4
    Crandell, Robert
    The Second Beatitude

6:4, 5
    Nelson, Ron
    Hear O People (Four Anthems For Young
        Choirs)
    Unison   Piano or Organ
    Boosey & Hawkes (1965) 5576

6:5-9
    Amram, David
    Thou Shalt Love The Lord Thy God
    SATB   kro
    C. F. Peters (1964) 6684A

6:5-9 (Numbers 15:40)
    Sowerby, Leo
    Thou Shalt Love The Lord Thy God
    SATB   Organ
    H. W. Gray (1966) CMR 2928

6:13
    SEE: Joshua 24:15
    Mueller, Carl F.
    Choose You This Day

8:10
    SEE: Psalm 67:5-7
    Harwood, Basil
    Let The People Praise Thee, O God

11:14 (Psalm 65:10-13
    Rowley, Alec
    I Will Give You Rain In Due Season
    SATB   Organ
    Thompson (1958) 540

16:15
    SEE: Psalm 67:5-7
    Harwood, Basil
    Let The People Praise Thee, O God

28:9-10
    Geisler, Johann (ed. E. Nolte)
    The Lord Keepeth Thee (English/German)
    SSAB   Piano
    Boosey & Hawkes (1965) 5608

30:15-16
    Wells, Dana F.
    The New Covenant (Four Modern Anthems)
    SATB   Piano
    Abingdon (1970) APM-619

30:19
    Winslow, R. K.
    I Call Heaven and Earth
    SATB & SAT   No accompaniment
    Elkan-Vogel (1965) 1216

32:1-4
    Felciano, Richard
    Give Ear O Heavens (Songs For Darkness
        and Light)
    3 Part   No accompaniment
    E. C. Schirmer (1971) 2803

32:1-4
    Powell, Robert J.
    Give Ear, O Ye Heavens
    SATB   Organ or Piano
    Kjos (1963) 5364

32:1-4
    Shirfin, Seymour
    Give Ear, O Ye Heavens
    SATB   Organ
    C. F. Peters (1960) 6206

32:1-4
    Wood, Dale
    Give Ear O Ye Heavens
    SATB   Organ
    Schmitt,Hall & McCreary (1960) SD6007

32:1-10 (paraphrase)
    Hruby, Dolores
    The Apple of Your Eye
    2 Part   Keyboard
    Augsburg (1980) 1971

33:2-3
    West, John E.
    The Lord Came From Sinai
    SATB   Organ
    Novello (1907) 906

33:2-4
    Karlin, Robert
    Dialogue
    SATB   Tape
    Art Masters (1970) AMS 175

33:13-16
    Holman, Derek
    Blessed Be the Lord for His Land
    SATB   Organ
    RSCM (1963) (found in Harvest Festival
        Music)

33:26-27
    Williams, David H.
    The Eternal God is Thy Refuge
    SATB   Organ
    Carl Fischer (1968) CM-7648

33:27-29
    West, John E.
    The Eternal God is Thy Refuge
    SATB   Organ
    Novello (1911) 303

37:7-43
    Mechem, Kirke
    The Song of Moses (from Songs of Wisdom)
    SATB   kro
    E. C. Schirmer (1970) 2737

JOSHUA

1:9 (Joshua 3:4-5; I Kings 8:57-58, 60-61)
    Darke, Harold
    Be Strong And Of A Good Courage
    SATB   Organ
    Oxford (1964) A-206

3:4-5
    SEE: Joshua 1:9
    Darke, Harold
    Be Strong and of a Good Courage

6:1-21
    Kennedy, Mike & Ann Cadwallader, (arr.)
    Joshua Fit de Battle of Jericho
    2 mixed voices   Piano or Guitar
    GIA (1972) G-1772

6:1-21
    Knight, Clarence (arr.)
    Battle of Jericho
    SACB   Piano
    Cambiata Press (1974) S9740

24:15 (Psalm 65:4; Deuteronomy 6:13)
    Mueller, Carl F.
    Choose You This Day
    SATB   kro
    Carl Fischer (1961) CM-7227

JUDGES

11:39
    Carissimi, G.
    Plorate Fili (English/Latin)
    SSAATB   Organ
    Baltimore Music (n.d.) 357

11:40 (based on)
    Carissimi, G. (ed. Norman Grayson)
    Lament Ye Children of Israel (Plorate
        Filii Israel) (English/Latin)
    SSATBB   Organ
    Bourne (1959) E-34

11:40 (based on)
    Carissimi, Giacomo
    Plorate Filii Israel (Latin)
    SSAATB   Optional keyboard
    Kjos (1947) ED. 29

RUTH

00:0
    Castelnuovo-Tedesco, Mario
    Naomi and Ruth, Op. 137
    SSA   (S-solo)   Piano or Organ
    Mills (1950) n.#.

00:0
    Spies, Claudio
    Verses from the Book of Ruth
    SSA   Piano   Narrator
    Presser (1961) 312-40516

1:00
    Kosakoff, Reuven
    Ruth and Naomi
    SA   (Baritone solo)   Keyboard
    Transcontinental (1965) TCL 370

1:16
    Berlinski, Herman
    Entreat Me Not
    SATB   (A-solo)   Organ or Piano
    Merrymount (1963) MC 380

1:16
    Goldman, Maurice
    Entreat Me Not to Leave Thee
    SATB   (S-solo)   Keyboard
    Transcontinental (1970) TCL-611

1:16
    Ludlow, Joseph
    The Words of Ruth
    SATB   Organ or Piano
    Associated (1967) A-576

1:16
    Slater, Jean
    Entreat Me Not to Leave Thee
    SATB   kro
    Galaxy (1944) GM 1463

1:16-17
    Howe, Mary
    Song of Ruth
    SATB   (S-solo)   Organ
    G. Schirmer (1940) 8487

1:16-17
    Peeters, Flor
    Wedding Song (English/German)
    SATB   (S-solo)   Organ
    C. F. Peters (1962) 6191

I S A M U E L

2:10
    SEE: Psalm 84:9
    Blow, John
    Behold O God Our Defender

15:22
    SEE: Hosea 6:3, 6
    Dailey, William
    As The Rain of Early Spring

15:22
    Gates, Crawford
    To Obey is Better than Sacrifice, Op. 49,
        #3
    SATB   Piano or Organ
    Sonos (1975) CSW 204

II S A M U E L

1:17
    Tomkins, Thomas (ed. Denis Stevens)
    Then David Mourned
    SSATB   Organ
    C. F. Peters (1961) 6069

1:19
    SEE: Lamentations 1:4
    Handel, G. F. (ed. Max Seiffert)
    Funeral Anthem on the Death of Queen
        Caroline

1:19-28
    Pinkham, Daniel
    The Lament of David
    SATB   Tape
    E. C. Schirmer (1974) 2939

1:25
    SEE: Lamentations 1:4
    Handel, G. F. (ed. Max Seiffert)
    Funeral Anthem on the Death of Queen
        Caroline

1:25-26
    Weelkes, Thomas
    David's Lament for Jonathan
    SSAATB   kro
    Novello (1964) 1435

1:25-26
    Weelkes, Thomas (ed. Walter Collins)
    O Jonathan
    SSAATB   kro
    Associated (1960) NYPM 12

18:24-27, 31-33
    Sanders, Robert L.
    The Death of Absalom
    SATB   kro
    Broude Brothers (1960) BB 2039

18:33
    Billings, William (ed. Lee Kjelson)
    David's Lamentation
    SATB   kro
    Belwin (1971) 2264

18:33
    Billings, William
    David's Lamentation
    SATBB   kro
    C. F. Peters (1971) 66336

18:33
    Billings, William (arr. Elie Siegmeister)
    David's Lamentation
    SATB   kro
    Carl Fischer (1950) CM 6572

18:33
    Billings, William (ed. James R. Wilson)
    David's Lamentation
    SATB   kro
    G. Schirmer (1965) 11270

18:33
    Billings, William
    David's Lamentation
    SATB   kro
    Walton (1968) 2203

18:33
    Chorbajian, John
    When David Heard That His Son Was Slain
    SATB   kro
    G. Schirmer (1974) 11997

18:33
    Deering, Richard (ed. C. F. Simkins)
    And the King Was Moved
    SSATB   keyboard
    Oxford (1965) A-222

18:33
    Deering, Richard (ed. C. F. Simkins)
    Contristatus est Rex David (English/Latin)
    SSATB   kro
    C. F. Peters (1969) 1513

18:33
    Dinerstein, Norman
    When David Heard
    SSAATTBB   kro
    Boosey & Hawkes (1979) 6014

18:33
    Easte, Michael (ed. C. F. Simkins)
    When David Heard that Absalom was Slain
    SSATTB   kro
    C. F. Peters (1967) 1557

18:33
    Josquin des Pres (ed. Arnold Payson)
    Absalom, O My Son (English/Latin)
    SATB   kro
    Frank (1963) F 445

18:33
    Josquin des Pres (ed. Theodore Marier)
    Absalom, Fili Mi (Latin only)
    SATB   Brass Quartet (no accompaniment)
    Robert King (1958) 605

18:33 (Based on)
  Lockwood, Normand
  David Mourneth For Absalom
  SSAATTBB   kro
  Kjos (1937) 12

18:33
  Pfautsch, Lloyd
  David's Lamentation
  SATB   No accompaniment
  Lawson Gould (1974) 51800

18:33
  Tomkins, Thomas (ed. Kurt Stone)
  Absalom
  SSAATB   kro
  Broude Brothers (1975) BB 5034

18:33
  Tomkins, Thomas
  When David Heard
  SAATB   Organ
  Oxford (1978) (also in Oxford Book of
        Tudor Anthems)

18:33
  Tomkins, Thomas (ed. Cyril Simkins)
  When David Heard That Absalom Was Slain
  SAATB   kro
  G. Schirmer (1965) 11287

18:33
  Weelkes, Thomas
  When David Heard
  SSAATB   kro
  Arista (1981) AE 438

18:33
  Weelkes, Thomas (ed. Walter Collins)
  When David Heard
  SSAATB   kro
  Associated (1960) NYPMA 11

18:33
  Weelkes, Thomas (ed. John A. Parkinson)
  When David Heard
  SSAATB   kro
  Novello (1956) Anth. 1316

18:33
  Weelkes, Thomas
  When David Heard
  SSAATB   kro
  Oxford (1978) (also in Oxford Book of
        Tudor Anthems)

22:00 (adapted)
  Trued, S. Clarence
  The Lord Is My Rock
  SATB   Piano or Organ
  Boonin (1975) B-190

22:2-3, 7
  Kirk, Theron
  The Lord Is My Rock
  SATB   Keyboard
  Carl Fischer (1981) CM 8136

22:7, 17, 18 (John 6:51)
  Gieseke, Richard W.
  I Called To My God For Help
  SAB   No accompaniment
  Concordia (1978) 97-5481

23:3, 4
  Thompson, Randall
  The Last Words of David
  SATB   Piano
  E. C. Schirmer (1950) 2294

23:3, 4
  Thompson, Randall
  The Last Words Of David
  TTBB   Piano
  E. C. Schirmer (1950) 2154

I KINGS

1:38-40
  Handel, G. F. (ed. William Herrmann)
  Zadok the Priest (Coronation Anthem, #1)
  SSAATBB   Keyboard
  G. Schirmer (1969) 2772

1:39-40
  Handel, G. F.
  Zadok the Priest (Coronation Anthem, #1)
  SSAATBB   Keyboard
  H. W. Gray (n.d.) 2646

1:39, 40
  Handel, G. F. (ed. E. Silas)
  Zadok the Priest
  SATB   Organ
  Novello (n.d.) 29.0217.06

1:39, 40
  Handel, G. F.
  Zadok the Priest
  SSAATBB   Keyboard
  Novello (n.d.) 29.0209.05

3:9
  Ford, Virgil T.
  Give Thy Servant an Understanding Heart
  SATB   kro
  Carl Fischer (1963) CM 7365

8:0 (words suggested by)
  Wesley, S. S. (ed. H. Watkins Shaw)
  O Lord My God
  SATB   Keyboard
  RSCM (found in Festival Service Book, #8)

8:0
  Wesley, S. S. (arr. Vincent Knight)
  O Lord, My God (Solomon's Prayer)
  SAB   Organ
  Curwen (1963) 11198

8:12-13 (I Kings 9:3)
  Whettam, Graham
  Then Spake Solomon, Op. 49b
  SATB   Organ
  G. Schirmer (1963) 11264

8:13, 27-28 (Psalm 84:1-4; Psalm 26:8-11;
        Psalm 134:1-3
  Milner, Anthony
  I Have Surely Built Thee
  SATB   Organ
  Novello (1959) 1373

8:13, 27-30
  SEE: Nehemiah 9:5, 6
  Bliss, Arthur
  Stand Up And Bless The Lord Your God

8:27-30 (Acts 7:48-50; I Corinthians 3:16;
        II Corinthians 6:16)
  Kirk, Theron
  The Temple Of The Living God
  SATB   Brass and Percussion
  Carl Fischer (1972) CM 7788

8:27-30, 37-39 (I Kings 9:3)
    Sowerby, Leo
    Will God Indeed Dwell on the Earth?
    SATB   (B-solo)   Organ
    H. W. Gray (1963) 2796

8:28-30
    Tallis, Thomas (ed. William Hermann)
    Heare The Voyce and Prayer of Thy Servant
    SSAA   kro
    Concordia (1966) 98-1855

8:28-30
    Tallis, Thomas (ed. Walter Ehret)
    Hear the Voice and Prayer of Thy Servants
    SATB   kro
    Elkan-Vogel (1970) 362-01310

8:28-30
    Tallis, Thomas (ed. John West)
    Hear the Voice and Prayer
    SATB   Organ ad. lib.
    H. W. Gray (n.d.) 2868

8:28-30
    Tallis, Thomas (ed. Paul Doe)
    Hear the Voice and Prayer
    SATB   Optional Organ
    Novello (1972) NECM 18

8:28-30
    Tallis, Thomas
    Hear the Voice and Prayer
    AATB   No accompaniment
    Oxford (1965) (found in Anthems for
        Men's Voices, Volume I)

8:28, 30
    Wesley, Samuel S.
    O Lord My God
    SATB   No accompaniment
    Oxford (1933) (found in Church Anthem
        Book)

8:57-58, 60-61
    SEE: Joshua 1:9
    Darke, Harold
    Be Strong and of a Good Courage

9:3
    SEE: Nehemiah 9:5, 6
    Bliss, Arthur
    Stand Up and Bless the Lord Your God

9:3
    SEE: I Kings 8:27-30, 37-39
    Sowerby, Leo
    Will God Indeed Dwell on the Earth?

9:3
    SEE: I Kings 8:12-13
    Whettam, Graham
    Then Spake Solomon, op. 49b

10:1-13
    Castelnuovo-Tedesco, Mario
    The Queen of Sheba
    SSA   (S-solo)   Piano
    Affiliated Music [Mills] (1953) n.#.

18:20-46 (adapted)
    Wood, Dale
    Elijah! (text - Stephen Lazicki)
    Unison treble or SATB   Piano, optional
        Percussion, Guitar, Bass
    Choristers Guild (1970) A-99

18:36-37
    Mendelssohn, Felix (arr. Earl Willhoite)
    Lord God of Abraham
    SATB   (B-solo)   Organ or Piano
    Shawnee (1952) n.#.

II KINGS

19:24-26
    SEE: Psalm 104:14-15
    Browne, Richmond
    Chortos I

I CHRONICLES

1:16, 23-25, 29-31
    Mead, Edward
    Sing unto the Lord All the Earth
    SATB   Piano or Organ
    Carl Fischer (1966) 7543

16:00 (Psalm 145)
    Huston, John
    A Canticle of Thanksgiving
    SATB   Organ
    H. W. Gray (1959) CMR 2624

16:00
    Krause, Ken
    His Love is Eternal
    SATB   Keyboard
    Broadman (1982) 4563-72

16:8-12, 14, 23-25
    Price, Milburn
    O Give Thanks Unto the Lord
    SATB   3 trumpets, 2 trombones, tuba
    Broadman (1979) 4566-03

16:23-24
    Wells, Dana F.
    Sing Unto the Lord (Four Modern Anthems)
    SATB   Keyboard
    Abingdon (1970) APM 619

16:28-29, 34
    Schalk, Carl
    Offertory/Pentecost 13 (Verses and Offer-
        tories - Pentecost 12-20)
    Unison   Organ
    Augsburg (1978) 11-9539

16:31
    Byrd, William
    Laetentur Coeli (Be Glad, Ye Heavens)
        (Latin/English)
    SATBB   kro
    Oxford (1973) TCM 29

16:35
    Harper, Marjorie
    Deliver Us
    SATB   Organ or Piano
    Beekman (1957) MC 282

17:36
    Antes, John (ed. & arr. Karl Kroeger)
    All Praise Be to the Lord (English/German)
    SATB   Organ
    Boosey & Hawkes (1976) 5938

28:20
    Campbell, Sidney
    Be Strong and of Good Courage
    SATB   Organ
    RSCM (found in Festival Service Book,
        Volume VII)

28:20 (Psalm 132)
    Oxley, Harrison
    Be Strong And Of A Good Courage
    SATB   Organ
    Oxford (1962) A-174

29:00
SEE: Psalm 115:1
Gore, Richard T.
Not Unto Us, Lord

29:10-13
Yancey, Thomas
The Song of David
SATB   Organ
Flammer (1972) A-5596

29:11 (Psalm 29:11; Isaiah 26:3; Psalm 5:11)
Simper, Caleb
Shout for Joy
SATB   Organ
Weekes [Harris] (1935) W.5485

29:13
SEE: Psalm 96:4, 9
Hollins, Alfred
O Worship the Lord

29:13
SEE: Genesis 8:22
Simper, Caleb
While the Earth Remaineth

II   CHRONICLES

5:13
Matthews, Thomas
The Trumpeters and Singers Were As One
SATB   Organ
H. T. Fitzsimons (1959) 2167

5:13
Miller, Thomas A.
The Trumpeters and Singers Were As One
SATB   Organ, 2 trumpets
Broadman (1968) 4562-08

5:13
Powell, Robert J.
The Trumpeters and Singers Were As One
SATB   Organ, 2 Trumpets, 2 Trombones,
    Timpani
Abingdon (1964) APM-346 (Parts APM-358)

5:13-14
Poston, Elizabeth
Antiphon and Psalm - - Laudate Dominum
SATB   Organ
Boosey & Hawkes (1956) 5122

6:2, 18-20, 41
Ferguson, Edwin Earle
I Have Built an House
SATB   Organ
Lawson Gould (1964) 51161

7:1-3 (Psalm 73:1; Psalm 72:18-19)
Elmore, Robert
The Fire Came Down
SSA   (A-solo)   Organ
H. W. Gray (1950) 2151

7:16
Hillert, Richard
Verse/Dedication (Verses and Offertories -
    Lesser Festivals)
Unison   Organ
Augsburg (1980) 11-9543

20:21
Roesch, Robert A.
Give Thanks to Him
SATB   Keyboard
Flammer (1980) A-5893

N E H E M I A H

9:5, 6 (Isaiah 63:15; I Kings 8:13, 27-30;
    I Kings 9:3)
Bliss, Arthur
Stand Up and Bless the Lord Your God
SATB   (S-B Solos)   Organ
Novello (1960) 1387

9:5-9, 11-12
Stevens, Halsey
Blessed Be Thy Glorious Name
SATB   kro
Mark Foster (1968) MF 114

9:6 (Neander)
Wolff, S. Drummond
Praise To The Lord
SATB   Organ (Optional Brass)
Concordia (1974) 98-2208

J O B

0:0
Jergenson, Dale
The Lament of Job
SATB   No accompaniment
G Schirmer (1975) 12030

1:21
SEE: Job 2:10
Seele, Thomas
Si bona suscepimus

2:10 (Job 1:21)
Seele, Thomas
Si bona suscepimus (Latin)
TTBB   Continuo
Hanssler FH 1.347

3:3, 4, 20-21, 23-24 (Psalm 43:3; Psalm 97:
    11; Psalm 119:130; Psalm 27:1;
    Psalm 139:12, and others)
Cook, Melville
Antiphon
SATB   Organ
Novello (1975) MT 1586

3:3, 23-26 (and other) (Job 14:7, 9, 11-12,
    and other)
Mechem, Kirke
The Protest of Job (from Songs of Wisdom)
SATB   kro
E. C. Schirmer (1970) 2739

3:11, 13, 18-21a (taken from)
Herder, Ronald
The Job Elegies
SATB   (A-solo)   kro
Associated (1966) (found in The AMP Con-
    temporary Choral Collection)

3:20-23 (Lamentations 3:41; James 5:11)
   Brahms, Johannes
   Why Then Has The Light Been Given, Op. 74,
      #1 (English/German)
   SATB   kro
   C. F. Peters (1968) 66135

5:8-9
   SEE: Job 23:3
   Baumgartner, H. Leroy
   In Him We Live

11:7
   SEE: Job 23:3
   Baumgartner, H. Leroy
   In Him We Live

13:10, 13
   SEE: Job 23:3
   Baumgartner, H. Leroy
   In Him We Live

14:1-2
   Bach, Johann Christoph
   A Man Born of a Woman (from Three Songs of
      Mourning) (English/German)
   SSATB   Piano
   Broude Brothers (1952) 126

14:1-2
   Berger, Jean
   Man Born of Woman (Two Laments)
   SATB   kro
   Carl Fischer (1975) CM 7929

14:1-2 (Joel 2:12-13; Psalm 117)
   Lidholm, Ingvar
   Laudi (Latin only)
   SATB   No accompaniment
   Carl Gehrmans [Walton] (1948) 2718

14:1-2
   Purcell, Henry (ed. Anthony Lewis & Nigel
      Fortune)
   Man That is Born of Woman (Funeral
      Sentences)
   SATB   Organ continuo
   Novello (1960) PSR 6

14:1-2
   Purcell, Henry (ed. Thurston Dart)
   Man That Is Born of Woman
   SATB   Organ
   Stainer & Bell (1961) 689

14:1, 2
   Wesley, Samuel S.
   Man That Is Born Of A Woman
   SATB   Organ
   Oxford (1933) (found in Church Anthem
      Book)

14:1-2
   Wilbye, John (translated and edited David
      Brown)
   Homo natus de muliere   (Latin only)
   SSAATB   kro
   Oxford (1976) A 312

14:7, 14
   Berger, Jean
   If A Man Dies
   SATB   kro
   Carl Fischer (1973) CM 7809

14:7, 9, 11-12 (and other)
   SEE: Job 3:3, 23-26
   Meechem, Kirke
   The Protest of Job (from Songs of Wisdom)

19:25
   SEE: Romans 6:9
   Diemer, Emma Lou
   Alleluia! Christ is Risen

19:25 (based on)
   Hopson, Hal H.
   I Know That My Redeemer Lives (Duke Street)
   SATB   Organ, Congregation
   GIA (1978) G-2344

19:25
   Peeters, Flor
   I Know That My Redeemer Liveth
   SATB   Organ
   C. F. Peters (1962) 6346

19:25-26 (I Corinthians 15:20)
   Handel, G. F. (arr. William Webber)
   I Know That My Redeemer Liveth
   SATB   Keyboard
   H. W. Gray (1930) 1081 (Also available
      in an SSA arrangement)

19:25, 26, 27
   Bach, Johann Michael
   I Know That My Redeemer Liveth
   SATBB   kro
   Oxford (1933) (found in Church Anthem Book)

19:25-27
   Bach, Johann Michael
   I Know That My Redeemer Liveth (English/
      German)
   SATBB   Continuo
   Concordia (1974) (found in Second Motet
      Book, 97-5205)

19:25-27
   Bach, Johann Michael
   I Know That My Redeemer Lives
   SATBB   kro
   Oxford (n.d.) OM 13

19:25-27
   Bach, Johann Michael
   Ich weiss dass mein Erloser lebt (German)
   SATBB   No accompaniment
   Merserburger (1977) (in Motetten alter
      Meister)

19:25-27
   Lassus, Orlandus
   Scio enim (Latin only)
   SATB   kro
   J. & W. Chester (1977) JWC 55103 (in Fifth
      Chester Book of Motets)

19:25-27
   Morley, Thomas (ed. Cyril Simkins)
   I Know That My Redeemer Liveth
   SATB   Optional Organ
   Concordia (1978) 98-2393

19:25-27
   Schütz, Heinrich (ed. C. Buell Agey)
   I Know That My Redeemer Lives (English/
      German)
   SSAATBB   Organ or piano ad lib.
   G. Schirmer (1967) 11386

21:22-23, 25-26, 28-29 (Job 22:29)
   Haines, Edmund
   Dialogues from the Book of Job
   SSAA (S-A solos)   Piano
   Tetra [Alexander Broude] (1965) AB 119

22:21
   SEE: Proverbs 3:5-6
   Freestone, G. S.
   Trust In The Lord

22:21-30 (Free Paraphrase)
    Greene, Maurice (edited H. Diack Johnstone)
    Acquaint Thyself With God
    SATB   (A or T solo)   Organ
    Novello (1971) NECM 23

22:29
    SEE: Job 21:22-23, 25-26, 28-29
    Haines, Edmund
    Dialogue from the Book of Job

23:3 (Job 5:8-9; Psalm 10:1; Job 11:7; Job 36:
        26; Job 13:10, 13; Acts 17:24-28)
    Baumgartner, H. Leroy
    In Him We Live
    SATB   Organ
    Oliver Ditson (1925) 332-13905

23:3, 8-9 (John 20:29)
    Bennett, W. Sterndale
    O That I Knew Where I Might Find Him
    SATB   Optional accompaniment
    Oxford (1933) (found in Church Anthem Book)

28:1, 5, 12-13, 20, 23-28
    Wells, Dana F.
    Where Shall Wisdom Be Found?
    SATB   kro
    Abingdon (1975) APM 503

28:12-13, 15, 23-28
    Boyce, William
    Oh, Where Shall Wisdom Be Found?
    SATB   Organ
    E. C. Schirmer (1955) 2631

    28:12-15, 18, 20-28
    Boyce, William
    O Where Shall Wisdom Be Found?
    SSATB   Organ
    Novello (n.d.) 29.0106.04

28:20-21, 23-28
    Newbury, Kent
    Wisdom and Understanding
    SATB   No accompaniment
    Somerset Press [Hope] (1974) SP 722

28:20-21, 23-28
    Newbury, Kent
    Wisdom and Understanding
    SSA   kro
    Somerset Press [Hope] (1970) SP 692

29:11
    SEE: Lamentations 1:4
    Handel, G. F. (ed. Max Seiffert)
    Funeral Anthem On The Death Of Queen
        Caroline

36:26
    SEE: Job 23:3
    Baumgartner, H. Leroy
    In Him We Live

38:1-11, 16-17 (Job 40:7-10, 14)
    Vaughan Williams, Ralph
    The Voice Of The Whirlwind
    SATB   Organ
    Oxford (1947) 40.012

38:4-7
    Barker, Ken
    Where Were You
    SATB   Piano
    Word (1981) CS-3001

38:7 (Luke 2:11-14)
    Steel, Christopher
    The Morning Stars Sang Together, Op. 31
    SATB   Organ
    Novello (1967) 1469

40:7-10, 14
    SEE: Job 38:1-11, 16-17
    Vaughan Williams, Ralph
    The Voice Out Of The Whirlwind

P S A L M S

1:00 (Psalm 91)
    Baumgartner, H. Leroy
    His Delight Is In The Law Of The Lord
    SATB   Organ
    Abingdon (1968) APM-454

1:00
    Bourgeois, Louis (C. Goudimel) (ed. A.
        Couper)
    Psalm 1 (Two Versions) (English/French)
    SATB   kro
    Presser (1975) 312-41098

1:00
    Butler, Eugene (adapted Bill Rich)
    Blessed Is The Man
    CCBB   kro
    Cambiata Press (1975) C-97564

1:00
    Butler, Eugene
    Blessed Is The Man
    SACB   kro
    Cambiata Press (1972) C-97203

1:00
    Calvin, Susan
    Psalm 1
    SATB   Organ
    Fine Arts Music (1967) CM-1051

1:00 (paraphrase)
    Kirkland, Terry
    Blessed Is The Man
    Unison   Keyboard
    Broadman (1979) 4560-91

1:00 (based on)
    Lasso, Orlando (ed. Bliss)
    Blest Is The Man
    SSA   kro
    Augsburg (1962) PS603

1:00
    Leef, Henry Granville (arr. Edwin E.
        Ferguson)
    Psalm 1
    SATB   Piano or Organ
    Lawson Gould (1966) 51240

1:00
    Lekberg, Sven
    Blessed Is The Man
    SATB   kro
    Galaxy (1963) GMC-2255

1:00
    Marshall, Jane
    Blessed Is The Man
    SATB   Organ
    Abingdon (1960) APM-106

1:00
    Pascal de l'Estocart
    Psalm 1
    SATB   kro
    Leeds [MCA] (1965) L-468

1:00
    Pinkham, Daniel
    Happy Is The Man (from Passion of Judas)
    SATB   Organ
    E. C. Schirmer (1978) 3033

1:00   (based on)
    Proulx, Richard
    Happy Is The Man Who Fears the Lord
    Unison   Organ, oboe and flute
    Augsburg (1969) 11-0312

1:00
    Schütz, Heinrich (ed. Robert E. Wunderlich)
    Blessed Is He Who Walks Not In The Path Of
        The Wicked
    SA   Organ
    Concordia (1969) 98-1920

1:00
    Schütz, Heinrich   (ed. George Lynn)
    Psalm 1
    SATB   Organ
    Mercury (1952) 352-00143

1:00
    Schwoebel, David
    Psalm 1
    SATB   Keyboard
    Broadman (1981) 4563-82

1:00
    Stevens, Halsey
    Psalm 1: Beatus Vir
    SATB   kro
    Mark Foster (1966) MF 112

1:00
    Waring, Peter
    Blessed Is The Man
    SATB   Organ
    E. C. Schirmer (1966) 2677

1:00   (adapted)
    Williams, Frances
    Blessed Is The Man
    SATB   Piano or Organ
    Flammer (1946) 2526

1:1, 2
    Hassler, Hans Leo (ed. Clifford Richter)
    Blest Be The Man (Beatus vir qui non
        abiit) (English/Latin)
    SATB   kro
    Tetra [Alexander Broude] (1967) AB-157

1:1-3
    Holmboe, Vagn
    Beatus vir   Op. 96A   (Latin)
    SSATB   No accompaniment
    Walton (1968) n.#.

1:1-3
    Schütz, Heinrich
    Blessed Is He Who Walks Not In The Paths
        Of Godliness (English/German)
    SA   Organ
    Brodt (1960) W. C. 1

1:1-3
    Young, Gordon
    Blessed Is The Man
    Unison mixed   Organ
    Presser (1960) 312-40467

2:00
    Diercks, John
    Why Do the Nations Rage
    Unison   Keyboard
    Abingdon (1967) APM-572

2:1, 2
    SEE: Psalm 2:7
    Ferris, William
    The Lord Said to Me

2:1-4
    SEE: Psalm 23
    Bernstein, Leonard
    Chichester Psalms (Second Movement)

2:1-12
    Mendelssohn, Felix
    Why Rage Fiercely the Heathen
    SATB/SATB   kro
    Augsburg (n.d.) 11-0647

2:4
    LaLande, Michael de (arr. Robert Hines)
    He That Sitteth in the Heavens
    SA   Piano or Organ
    Elkan-Vogel (1971) 362-01327

2:7   (Psalm 2:1-2)
    Ferris, William
    The Lord Said to Me
    SATB   Organ, 2 trumpets, 2 trombones,
                                    timpani
    GIA (1968) G-1389

2:7-8
    Wetzler, Robert
    Offertory/Christmas Eve (Verses and
        Offertories - Advent I - The Baptism
        of Our Lord)
    2-part   Organ
    Augsburg (1979) 11-9541

2:7-8
    Wetzler, Robert
    Verse/Christmas Day (Verses and Offertories
        Advent I - The Baptism of Our Lord)
    SATB   Organ
    Augsburg (1979) 11-9541

2:7-8   (Psalm 110:3)
    Wetzler, Robert
    Offertory/Christmas Day (Verses and
        Offertories - Advent I - The Baptism
        of Our Lord)
    SATB   Organ
    Augsburg (1979) 11-9541

2:9
    SEE: Numbers 24:17
    Mendelssohn, Felix (ed. Don Razey)
    A Star Shall Rise Up Out Of Jacob

2:9
    SEE: Matthew 2:1
    Mendelssohn, Felix
    Say Where Is He Born and There Shall a
        Star

2:9-11
    Sullivan, Arthur (arr. George B. Nevin)
    Turn Thy Face from My Sins
    TTBB   Accompanied
    Presser (1931) 21038

2:10-13
    Moevs, Robert
    Et nunc, reges
    SSA   Flute, Clarinet, Bass Clarinet
        (optional piano)
    E. C. Schirmer (1964) 2569

3:00   (paraphrased George Herbert)
  Joubert, John
  How Are My Foes Increased Lord!   Op. 61
  SATB   Organ
  Novello (1970) NCM 29

3:00
  Lee, T. Charles
  Psalm III
  SATB   Organ
  H. W. Gray (1957) 2454

3:00
  Purcell, Henry (ed. Anthony Lewis & Nigel
      Fortune)
  Jehova, quam multi sunt hostes (Latin only)
  SSATB   Organ continuo
  Novello (1978) RSR.19

3:00
  Purcell, Henry
  O Lord God How Many Are They That Hate Me
      (Latin/English)
  SSATB   (T-B solos)   Keyboard
  Bayley-Ferguson (1929) 1434

3:00
  Tuthill, Burnett
  Psalm 3
  TTBB   kro
  Carl Fischer (1956) CM 6865

3:00   (adapted)
  Wesley, Samuel S. (arr. C. Upshur)
  Hear My Prayer
  Unison   Keyboard
  Flammer (1960) (found in Unison Anthems
      With Descants)

3:1-3
  Clarke, Thomas (ed. Mason Martens)
  I Will Magnify Thee, O Lord
  Unison   Organ
  Concordia (1965) 98-1796

3:1-4
  Jeppesen, Knud
  O Lord How Numerous Are My Foes
  SATB   kro
  Broude Brothers (1975) BB-5022

3:1, 4, 7-9
  Wetzler, Robert
  Praise the Lord, All the People
  SATB   Organ
  H. W. Gray (1968) CMR 3019

3:6
  Kent, James (ed. Elwyn Wienandt and
      Robert Young)
  Salvation Belongeth Unto The Lord
  SATB   Keyboard
  J. Fischer (1970) 10009

3:8
  Baker, Richard C.
  Salvation Belongeth Unto The Lord
  SATB   kro
  F. Harris (1974) HC 4057

3:8   (Matthew 21:9)
  Copley, Evan
  Salvation Belongeth Unto The Lord
  SATB   No accompaniment
  Abingdon (1961) APM-145

4:00
  Arcadelt, Jacques (arr. C. Mueller)
  Give Ear Unto My Prayer
  SAB   Piano or Organ
  Carl Fischer (n.d.) CM 7336

4:00
  Arcadelt, Jacques
  Give Ear Unto My Prayer (Ave Maria)
      (Latin/English)
  SATB   kro
  Novello (n.d.) 29.0304.00

4:00
  Parker, Alice and Robert Shaw (arr.)
  Psalm 4
  SATB   No accompaniment
  G. Schirmer (1955) 584

4:00   (paraphrase by J. Patrick)
  Purcell, Henry (ed. Anthony Lewis & Nigel
      Fortune)
  Hear Me, O Lord the Great Support
  ATB or TTB   Organ continuo
  Novello (1966) PSR.9

4:1   (Psalm 5:2)
  Schütz, Heinrich
  Give Ear, O Lord   (Erhöre mich) (English/
      German)
  SA or TB   Organ or Piano (optional
      cello)
  Mercury (1941) 352-00013

4:1   (Psalm 5:2)
  Schütz, Heinrich (arr. Don McAfee)
  Hear Me, O Lord
  2 voices   Keyboard
  Capella Music (1971) n.#.

4:1
  Schütz, Heinrich (ed. Robert Wunderlich)
  O Hear Me, Lord
  SS   Organ
  Augsburg (1967) ACL-1512

4:1, 7, 9
  Hall, King
  Hear Me When I Call
  SATB   Organ
  B. F. Wood (1934) 320

4:7   (Psalm 31:1, 3)
  Copley, R. Evan
  In Thee O God Do I Put My Trust
  SATB   kro
  Flammer (1962) 84751

4:8
  Gadsby, Henry (arr. Carl F. Mueller)
  I Will Lay Me Down in Peace
  SAB   Organ
  G. Schirmer (1940) 8693

4:8   (adapted)
  Yardumian, Richard (Harmonized)
  In Peace I Lay Me Down (from Eleven Easter
      Chorales)
  SATB   No accompaniment
  Elkan-Vogel (1978) 362.03280

4:9
  SEE: Psalm 5:8
  Wesley, Samuel S.
  Lead Me Lord

4:9
  Willan, Healey
  I Will Lay Me Down in Peace
  SATB   kro
  Concordia (1950) 98-1231

5:00
  Butler, Eugene
  Give Ear, O Lord
  SATB   Organ
  Carl Fischer (1973) CM 7836

5:00
    Kelly, Bryan
    Ponder My Words, O Lord
    SATB   No accompaniment
    Novello (1966) 1480

5:00
    Lassus, Orlandus
    Verba mea auribus (English/German)
    3 part women   No accompaniment
    Mercury (1942) DCS-21

5:1
    Fetler, Paul
    Give Ear To My Words, O Lord (A Morning
        Prayer)
    SATB   kro
    Augsburg (1957) 1200

5:1
    Schütz, Heinrich (ed. W. Stanton)
    Ponder My Words, O Lord
    SATB   kro
    Hinrichsen (1950) 111

5:1-2
    Schütz, Heinrich (ed. Walter Ehret)
    Harken Unto My Cry (Virba mea auribus
        percipe) (English/Latin)
    SATB   kro
    Tetra [Alexander Broude] (1972) AB 715-6

5:1-3, 7-8, 11-12 (Psalm 25:4-5)
    Schubert, Franz (edited Daniel Pinkham)
    O Hear Me When I Call On Thee
        (English/German)
    SATB   Organ
    E. C. Schirmer (1966) 2684

5:1-3, 7, 12-13
    Walmisley, Thomas
    Ponder My Words
    SSAA   Organ
    RSCM (n.d.) 211

5:1-3, 11
    Adler, Samuel
    Listen To My Words, Lord
    2 part   Organ or Piano
    Augsburg (1974) 11-0658

5:1-7
    Kay, Ulysses
    Give Ear To My Words, O Lord (from Choral
        Triptych)
    SATB   Organ or Piano
    Associated (1967) A-495

5:2
    SEE: Psalm 4:1
    Schütz, Heinrich
    Give Ear, O Lord

5:2-3
    Elgar, Edward
    O Hearken Thou
    SATB   Organ
    Novello (1911) 03.0134.05 (found in Seven
        Anthems of Edward Elgar)

5:3
    Corfe, Joseph (ed. Derek Holman)
    My Voice Shalt Thou Hear (from Ponder My
        Words, O Lord)
    Unison Treble   Organ or Piano
    Novello (1961) 29.0196.10

5:3
    Tomkins, Thomas
    My Voice Shalt Thou Hear
    TTBB   Organ
    Oxford (1965) (in Anthems for Men's
        Voices, Volume II)

5:3, 8
    SEE: Psalm 16:1
    Manz, Paul
    Preserve Me, O Lord

5:8
    SEE: Numbers 24:5
    Gottlieb, Jack
    Mah Tovu

5:8 (Psalm 4:9)
    Wesley, S. S.
    Lead Me Lord
    SATB   (S-solo)   Organ
    RSCM (1975) (found in Twelve Easy Anthems)

5:8 (Psalm 4:9)
    Wesley, S. S.
    Lead Me Lord
    SATB   (S-solo)   Organ
    Novello (n.d.) 29.0305.09

5:8 (Psalm 4:9)
    Wesley, S. S.
    Lead Me Lord
    SATB   (S-solo)   Organ
    Oxford (also in Church Anthem Book and in
        Anthems for Choirs, Volume I)

5:8 (Psalm 4:9)
    Wesley, S. S.
    Lead Me Lord
    SATB (S-solo)   Organ
    E. C. Schirmer (1925) 166 (also in
        Concord Anthem Book, - Red)

5:8 (Psalm 4:9)
    Wesley, S. S.
    Lead Me Lord
    SATB   (S-solo)   Organ
    G. Schirmer (n.d.) 300

5:8 (Psalm 4:9)
    Wesley, S. S.
    Lead Me Lord
    SATB   (S-solo)   Organ
    B. F. Wood (1933) n.#.

5:11
    Haan, Raymond H.
    A Song of Joy
    Unison   Organ
    AMSI (1975) AMSI-277

5:11
    SEE: I Chronicles 29:11
    Simper, Caleb
    Shout for Joy

5:11, 12
    Graun, Karl H. (ed. Arthur Hilton)
    Let All That Put Their Trust in Thee
    SATB   kro
    Mercury (1970) 352-00397

6:00
    Byrd, William (ed. Noah Greenberg)
    Lord in Thy Rage
    SAB   kro
    Associated (1956) NYPM 5 (also available
        in TTB voicing)

6:00
    Freestone, G. S.
    O Lord, Rebuke Me Not
    SATB   kro
    Elkan-Vogel (1969) 1292

6:00
    Gabrieli, Andrea
    Domine, ne in furore (Latin)
    SSATTB   No accompaniment
    Barenreiter (1969) 921

6:00
    Purcell, Henry (ed. Anthony Lewis & Nigel
        Fortune)
    Lord, I Can Suffer
    SATB or SSAB   Organ continuo
    Novello (1966) RSR.10

6:1-3
    Byrd, William (ed. G. E. P. Arkwright)
    Lord In Thy Rage
    SAT   kro
    Broude (n.d.) OEE 4

6:1-4
    Gibbons, Orlando
    O Lord, In Thy Wrath
    SSAATB   kro
    Oxford (1966) (also found in Oxford Book of
        Tudor Anthems)

6:1-4
    Locke, Matthew
    Lord Rebuke Me Not
    TTB   Keyboard
    Oxford (1965) (found in Anthems for Men's
        Voices, Volume II)

6:2-3
    Erbach, Christian (ed. William Haldeman)
    Have Compassion Now On Me, O Lord (English/
        Latin)
    SATB   kro
    Concordia (1968) 98-1935

6:3   (Jeremiah 7:14)
    Victoria, Tomas (ed. B. Rainbow)
    Miserere mei Domine (Latin)
    SATB   kro
    Novello (n.d.) MV 138

6:4
    Croft, William (ed. Adrian Carpenter)
    Turn Thee, O Lord (from O Lord Rebuke Me Not)
    SSATTB   Optional Organ
    Novello (1971) MT 1537

6:6
    Caldara, Antonio
    Laboravi in gemitur meo (Latin only)
    ATB   continuo
    Oxford (1965) (found in Anthems for Men's
        Voices, Volume I)

7:1
    Beebe, Hank
    In Thee Do I Put My Trust
    2 part   Piano or Organ
    Hinshaw (1976) HMC 188

7:1-2
    Marcello, Benedetto (ed. Richard Wienhorst)
    O Lord, Deliver Me
    SA   Keyboard
    Concordia (1954) 98-1044

8:00
    Beck, John Ness
    The Apollo Psalm
    SAB   Piano or Organ
    Choristers Guild (1969) A-83

8:00
    Bennett, Ronald C.
    What is Man?
    SATB   kro
    Alexander Broude (1982) AB-892

8:00   (adapted)
    Butler, Eugene
    How Excellent Is Thy Name
    SATB   Keyboard
    Bourne (1967) 837

8:00
    Corigliano, John
    Psalm 8
    SATB   Organ
    G. Schirmer (1977) 12098

8:00
    Diemer, Emma Lou
    How Majestic Is Thy Name
    Unison   Organ
    H. W. Gray (1962) CMR 2729

8:00
    Donato, Anthony
    How Excellent Is Thy Name
    SATB   Organ
    Southern (1966) 1030

8:00
    Hillert, Richard
    Psalm 8
    Unison   Keyboard, Choir, Congregation
    Augsburg (1978) (found in Seasonal Psalms
        For Congregation And Choir) 11-9376

8:00   (paraphrased)
    Hopson, Hal H.
    God of All Creation
    2 part mixed   Keyboard
    GIA (1978) G-2168

8:00
    Hopson, Hal H.
    O Lord, Our Lord, Majestic Is Thy Name
    SA   Piano or Organ
    Flammer (1971) E-5152

8:00
    Joubert, John
    O Lord Our Lord   Op. 45
    SATB   Organ
    Novello (1964)   Anth. 1441

8:00
    Kalmanoff, Martin
    O Lord How Glorious Is Thy Name
    SATB   Piano
    Choral Art (1960) R-155

8:00   (adapted)
    Kreutz, Robert
    How Glorious Your Name, O Lord
    SATB   kro
    World Library (1979) 7602-8

8:00
    Latrobe, Christian (ed. Henry B. Ingram,
        Jr.)
    The Name of Christ Be Praised
    2 part   Keyboard
    Abingdon (1977) APM-731

8:00   (paraphrased by Fred Kaan)
    Lovelace, Austin
    Lord, How Majestic Is Your Name
    Unison   Keyboard
    Broadman (1979) 4560-89

8:00
    McAfee, Don
    Psalm 8 (Three Psalm-Hymns for Juniors)
    Unison   Keyboard
    Canyon Press (1967) 6703

8:00 (Paraphrased by John Patrick - 1674)
    Purcell, Henry (transcribed by Anthony
        Lewis & Nigel Fortune)
    O Lord, Our Governor
    SSAB or SSTB   Organ continuo
    Novello (1966) PSR.14

8:00
    Schmutz, Albert D.
    O Lord, Our God
    SATB   kro
    Abingdon (1972) APM-920

8:00
    York, David Stanley
    O Lord, How Excellent Is Thy Name
    SATB   Organ
    Golden Music (1963) G7

8:1a
    SEE: Isaiah 6:3a
    Martens, Edmund
    Holy Is The Lord (Four Introits - Set I)

8:1
    Handel, G. F.
    How Excellent Thy Name, O Lord
    SATB   Organ
    E. C. Schirmer (1936) (also in Second Con-
       cord Anthem Book - Grey)

8:1
    Handel, G. F. (arr. Elwood Coggin)
    O Lord, How Excellent Thy Name
    SAB   Organ or Piano
    Kjos (1971) 5727

8:1
    Marcello, Benedetto (ed. R. Wienhorst)
    O Lord Our Governor
    Solo and Unison   Keyboard
    Concordia (1955) 98-1045

8:1
    Marcello, Benedetto (ed. & arr. Walter Ehret)
    O Lord How Excellent Is Thy Name
    SATB   Piano or Organ
    Shawnee (1967) A-891

8:1
    Telemann, Georg Philipp
    Oh Lord, Our Master, How Glorious Is Thy
       Name
    2-part canon   No accompaniment
    Concordia (found in Second Morning Star
       Book, 97-4702)

8:1   (Psalm 84:9; Psalm 17:5: Psalm 61:6;
        Psalm 21:6; Psalm 29:9)
    Willan, Healey
    O Lord, Our Governor
    SATB   Organ
    Novello (1953) 315

8:1, 2
    Marcello, Benedetto (ed. Wienhorst)
    O Lord, Deliver Me
    TTBB   Accompanied
    Concordia   98-1044

8:1, 3, 4
    Cram, James D.
    Lord, Our Lord
    SATB   Keyboard
    Broadman (1975) 4545-86

8:1a, 3-5
    Stanton, Kenneth W.
    O Lord, How Excellent Is Thy Name
    Unison   Keyboard
    Broadman (1974) 4551-65

8:1, 3-6
    Morgan, Haydn
    How Excellent Is Thy Name
    SATB   kro
    Belwin (1972) 2267

8:1, 3-6
    Englert, Eugene
    How Glorious Is Your Name
    SATB (S-solo)   Keyboard
    GIA (1977) G-2109

8:1, 3-6
    Hanson, Howard
    How Excellent Thy Name
    SATB   Organ
    Carl Fischer (1956) CM 6806

8:1, 3-6
    Hanson, Howard
    How Excellent Thy Name
    SSAA   Piano
    Carl Fischer (1953) CM 6706

8:1-4
    Causey, C. Harry
    Psalm 8
    SA   Piano
    Fred Bock (1980) B-G 0140

8:1-5
    MacMillan, Alan
    How Excellent Is Thy Name
    SATB   Organ (optional brass and timpani)
    Rock Harbor Press (1980) RMO-805

8:1-5
    Young, Robert
    Psalm 8
    SATB   3 Trombones, Tuba, Timpani
    Broadman (1978) 4565-86

8:1-9
    Frackenpohl, Arthur
    Psalm VIII
    SATB   Organ
    Rongwen [Broude] (1955) RM 398

8:1-9
    Wilson, John F.
    O Lord, How Majestic Is Thy Name
    SATB   Keyboard
    Hope (1969) A-400

8:3-9 (Psalm 9:1-2)
    Dalby, Martin
    When I Consider Thy Heavens
    SATB   Organ
    Novello (1967) MT 1490

8:4 (Psalm 100, and other)
    Peloquin, C. Alexander
    Lord Jesus Come
    SATB   Organ
    GIA (1974) G-1880

8:5-6
    SEE: Luke 24:5-7
    Nelson, Ronald
    Introit for Easter

8:9 (Psalm 9:2, adapted)
    Marcello, Benedetto (ed. Paul Chase)
    O Lord, How Excellent Is Thy Name
    SSA   Keyboard
    Flammer (1980) B-5161

9:00 (adapted)
    Barrett-Ayres, Reginald
    I Will Praise Thee O God
    SATB   Organ
    Novello (1973) 29.0266.04

9:00
    Blakley, Duane
    With My Whole Heart
    SATB   Organ or Piano (optional brass)
    Bourne (1969) 873

9:00 (based on)
    LeJeune, Claude (ed. A. B. Couper)
    With My Whole Heart, O God (English/French)
    SATB   kro
    Presser (1971) 352-00445

9:00   (based on)
    Lockwood, Normand
    I Will Give Thanks With All My Heart
    SATB   No accompaniment
    Augsburg (1966) PS-622

9:00   (adapted)
    Pote, Allen
    I Will Give Thanks
    SATB   Optional Piano and Trumpets
    Fortress Press (1975) 3-75001

9:1-2
    SEE: Psalm 8:3-9
    Dalby, Martin
    When I Consider Thy Heavens

9:1-2   (Psalm 19:7-8)
    Hruby, Dolores
    I Will Give Thanks
    SA   Keyboard
    Concordia (1978) 98-2405

9:1, 2
    McCray, James
    I Will Give Thanks To the Lord
    SATB   Handbells (No accompaniment)
    Alexander Broude (1980) AB 888

9:1, 2
    Nystedt, Knut
    I Will Praise Thee, O Lord
    SSATB   kro
    Augsburg (1958) 1217

9:1-2
    Rohlig, Harald
    I Will Praise You
    Unison   Keyboard
    Concordia (1973) 97-5165 (also found in
        Explode With Joy)

9:1-2
    Smith, Charles David
    Confitebor Tibi
    SATB   kro
    Carl Fischer (1957) CM 6979

9:1-2
    SEE: Psalm 13:5
    Willan, Healey
    I Have Trusted In Thy Mercy

9:1, 2, 3, 5
    Berger, Jean
    I Will Praise Thee, O Lord
    SATB   2 Trumpets   kro
    Associated (1968) A-560

9:1, 2, 4, 19, 20
    Baker, Robert C.
    I Will Praise Thee, O Lord
    SATB   Organ
    F. Harris (1979) HC.4083

9:1-2, 9
    Butler, Eugene
    I Will Give Thanks
    SATB   Organ or Piano
    Carl Fischer (1974) CM 7851

9:1-4
    Pinkham, Daniel
    Celebrabro te, Domine (Three Motets)
        (Latin)
    SSA   Organ
    C. F. Peters (1979) 66709

9:1-8
    Silvester, Frederick C.
    I Will Give Thanks Unto Thee, O Lord
    SATB   Organ
    F. Harris (1949) F.H. 4038

9:1, 9-11   (1912 Psalter)
    Mozart, W. A. (arr. G. Track)
    O Lord Most High, With All My Heart
    SAB   Organ
    GIA (1972) G-1751

9:1, 9-11   (1912 Psalter)
    Mozart, W. A. (arr. G. Track)
    O Lord Most High, With All My Heart
    SATB   Organ
    GIA (1973) G-1825

9:2
    SEE: Psalm 8:9
    Marcello, Benedetto
    O Lord, How Excellent Is Thy Name

9:3, 19
    Kreutz, Robert
    Rise, O Lord
    SAB   No accompaniment
    GIA (1979) G-2249

9:4, 20
    Burroughs, Bob
    Rise, O Lord
    2 mixed voices   Organ
    Presser (1973) 312-41007

9:10-11
    Powell, Robert J.
    They That Know Thy Name
    SA(T)B   Organ
    Schmitt, Hall, McCreary (1962) 8011

9:10-11, 19-20
    Jenkins, Joseph Willcox
    A Stronghold In Times of Distress   Op. 66
    Unison   Organ
    World Library (1970) EMP-1588-1

9:11
    LeJeune, Claude
    Canon
    SATB   kro
    Tetra [Alexander Broude] (1967) AB 139

9:11-12
    Schütz, Heinrich, (ed. C. Buell Agey)
    Praise Ye Jehovah   (English/German)
    SA or TB   Organ
    Abingdon (1962) APM-170

9:12-13
    Schütz, Heinrich (ed. Don McAfee)
    Praise To The Lord
    2 part   Organ
    Capella Music (1971)

9:15
    Levy, Marvin David
    Prayer (May the Words of My Mouth)
    SATB   Organ
    Boosey & Hawkes (1966) 5602

10:1
    SEE: Job 5:8
    Baumgartner, H. Leroy
    In Him We Live

10:1-2, 7, 12
    Elmore, Robert
    Why Standest Thou Afar Off, O Lord
    Unison   Organ
    Galaxy (1966) GMC-1994

10:1, 10, 17-18
    Cooley, John C.
    Psalm 10
    SATB   Keyboard or String Quartet
    Abingdon (1980) APM-786 (String Parts,
        APM-974)

11:4
    Boberg, Robert
    The Lord Is In His Holy Temple (Introits,
        Benedictions and Responses)
    SATB   No accompaniment
    Boston Music (1981) 13959

11:1-2
    Victoria, Tomas
    As titerunt regas   (Latin)
    SATB   No accompaniment
    J. W. Chester (1960) #16

12:00
    Goodman, Albert G.
    Psalm XII
    SSA   (baritone solo)   Organ
    Mercury (1955) MC 230

12:00   (Luther)
    Praetorius, Michael
    O God From Heaven Look Below
    TTB   No accompaniment
    Oxford (1965) (found in Anthems for Men's
        Voices, Volume II)

12:1, 6
    Hovhaness, Alan
    Help, Lord; For The Godly Man Ceaseth
        (Four Motets) Op. 268, #2
    SATB   kro
    Associated (1973) A-692

13:00
    Altman, Ludwig
    Psalm 13
    SATB (A-solo)   Organ
    Lawson Gould (1967) 51347

13:00
    Berger, Jean
    The 13th Psalm
    SATB   kro
    J. Fischer (1952) 8673

13:00
    Brahms, Johannes
    Psalm 13   Op. 27
    SSA   Organ
    Marks (1965) 104   (string parts on hire)

13:00
    Brahms, Johannes
    Psalm 13   Op. 27
    SSA   Organ
    Oxford (1973)   (found in Anthems For Choirs,
        Volume 3)

13:00   (paraphrased)
    SEE: Psalm 19 (paraphrased)
    Hopson, Hal H.
    God's Glory Echoes Through The Skies

13:00
    Kay, Ulysses
    How Long Wilt Thou Forget Me, O Lord
        (Choral Triptych)
    SATB   Organ
    Associated (1967) A-496

13:00
    Korte, Karl
    Psalm 13
    SATB   Tape
    E. C. Schirmer (1974) 2926

13:00
    Lekberg, Sven
    How Long Wilt Thou Forget Me, O Lord
    SATB   kro
    Galaxy (1963) GMC-2260

13:00
    London, Edwin
    Three Settings of the 13th Psalm
    SSA/TTBB
    Modern Jazz Quartet (1969)

13:00
    Martin, Warren
    Psalm XIII
    SATB   kro
    Rongwen [Broude] (1955) RM 397

13:00
    Powell, Robert J.
    Psalm 13
    SATB   Keyboard
    Lorenz (1967) E-83

13:00
    Ratcliffe, Desmond
    How Long Wilt Thou Forget Me?
    SATB   Organ
    Novello (1967) 1472

13:00
    Starer, Robert
    A Psalm of David (The Thirteenth Psalm)
    SATB   Organ or Piano
    Presser (1961) 312-40477

13:00
    Young, Gordon
    How Long Wilt Thou Forget Me
    SATB   Organ
    Galaxy (1962) GMC-2233

13:00
    Zimmermann, Heinz Werner
    Psalm 13
    SATB   Organ and Bass
    Carl Fischer (1974) CM 7888

13:1
    Pflueger, Carl (revised H. L. Heartz)
    How Long Wilt Thou Forget Me
    SATB (A-solo)   Keyboard
    Edwin Morris (1914) 380

13:1-2a, 3, 5-6
    Root, Georg Frederick (ed. Mason Martens)
    How Long Wilt Thou Forget Me, O Lord
    SATB   Keyboard
    McAfee (1975) (in Bicentennial Edition of
        American Choral Music)

13:1-6
    Rorem, Ned
    How Long Wilt Thou Forget Me, O Lord
        (Psalm and a Proverb)
    SATB   Piano or String Quartet
    E. C. Schirmer (1965) 2674

13:3-4
    DiLasso, Orlando
    Illumina occulos meos   (Latin)
    SATB   No accompaniment
    Arista (1976) AE-307

13:3, 5, 6
    Roff, Joseph
    Lighten Mine Eyes
    SATB   kro
    Abingdon (1975) APM-482

13:3-6
    Hemingway, Roger
    Consider And Hear Me, O Lord My God
    SSA   Organ
    Novello (1976) 29.0378.04

13:5   (Psalm 9:1-2)
    Willan, Healey
    I Have Trusted In Thy Mercy
    Unison   Keyboard
    Concordia (1953) (found in We Praise Thee,
        Volume I, 97-7564)

13:5-6
    Antes, John (ed. Karl Kroeger)
    My Heart Shall Rejoice In His Salvation
    SATB   Keyboard
    Boosey & Hawkes (1976) 5940

13:5-6
    Johnson, David N.
    Offertory/Epiphany VIII (Verses and Offer-
        tories - Epiphany II - The Trans-
        figuration of Our Lord)
    Unison   Organ
    Augsburg (1980) 11-9544

13:5-6
    Schütz, Heinrich (ed. Don McAfee)
    Lord, My Hope Is In Thee   (Herr, ich hoffe)
        (English/German)
    SS or any 2 parts   Keyboard
    Belwin (1971) DMC-8093

13:5-6
    Schütz, Heinrich (ed. Don McAfee)
    Lord My Hope Is In Thee
    2 part   Organ or Piano
    Capella Music (1971) n.#.

13:6   (adapted)
    Marcello, Benedetto (ed. Richard Wienhorst)
    And With Songs I Will Celebrate
    SA   Keyboard
    Concordia (1955) 98-1047

13:6
    Telemann, G. P.
    Ich hoffe darauf   (English/German)
    SAB or SS   Organ continuo, 2 violins
    Hanssler (1977) HE 29.023

14:1-2
    Hovhaness, Alan
    The Fool Hath Said In His Heart (Four
        Motets) Op. 268, #4
    SATB   kro
    Associated (1973) A-694

14:7
    Geisler, Johann C.   (ed. & arr. Ewald
        Nolte)
    O That Salvation For Israel Would Come
        (English/German)
    SS(A)TB   Piano or Organ
    Boosey & Hawkes (1969) 5706

15:00
    Whyte, Robert (ed. Judith Blezzard)
    Lord Who Shall Dwell In Thy Tabernacle
    SSAAB or SSATB   No accompaniment
    Novello (1974) MT 1581

15:00
    Wood, Frederic
    Whoso Doeth These Things   Op. 52, #1
    SATB   kro
    Francis Day (1952) 228

15:1-2
    Bevin, Elway (ed. Maurice Bevan)
    Lord Who Shall Dwell In Thy Tabernacle?
    SAB   Optional Organ
    Oxford (1963) A-178

15:1, 2   (Psalm 122:1, 2, 6-9)
    Bliss, Arthur
    Lord, Who Shall Abide In Thy Tabernacle?
    SATB   Organ
    Novello (1968) Anth. 1475

15:1-2   (Psalm 24:3-5)
    Darst, W. Glenn
    Lord, Who Shall Abide
    SATB   Organ
    Elkan-Vogel (1971) 362-03121

15:1-2
    Hovhaness, Alan
    Lord, Who Shall Abide In Thy Temple
        (Four Motets) Op. 268, #3
    SATB   kro
    Associated (1973) A-693

15:1-2
    Pelz, Walter
    Who Shall Abide
    SAB   Guitar and Flute
    Augsburg (1965) 11-0617

15:1-2
    Pergolesi, G. B. (ed. & arr. W. Ehret)
    Who Shall Abide In Thy Tabernacle
    SATB   Keyboard
    Augsburg (1980) 11-1965

15:1-2, 4-5
    Park, Chai Hoon
    O Lord, Who Shall Abide in Thy Tabernacle
    SATB   Organ
    F. Harris (1974) HC 4060

15:1-3, 5
    Pinkham, Daniel
    Who May Lodge In Thy Tabernacle? (from
        The Passion of Judas)
    SATB   Organ
    Ione Press [E. C. Schirmer] (1978) 3034

15:1-3, 7
    Diggle, Roland
    Lord, Who Shall Dwell In Thy Tabernacle
    SATB   Piano
    Witmark (1945) W-3216

15:7-9
    Hruby, Dolores
    Blessed Be The Lord, Who Schools Me
        (from Three Sacred Songs)
    SA   Organ
    Concordia (1973) 98-2098

16:00
    Schuff, Albert
    Preserve Me, O God
    SATB   kro
    Schmitt, Hall, & McCreary (1958) 1764

16:1   (Psalm 5:3, 8)
    Manz, Paul O.
    Preserve Me, O Lord
    SATB   kro
    Augsburg (1958) 1228

16:1
    Marcello, Benedetto (ed. Robert S. Hines)
    Preserve Me, O Lord
    SATB   Keyboard
    Concordia (1979) 98-2433

16:1-2, 12
    Ossewaarde, Jack H.
    Preserve Me O God
    SATB   kro
    H. W. Gray (1962) CMR-2777

16:1, 10-11
    Goodman, Joseph
    Preserve Me O God
    SATB   kro
    Merrymount (1963) MC 417

16:5-7
    Asola, Giovanni (adapted Edward Diemente)
    Make My Steps Steadfast (Four Short Anthems
        for Lent and Easter)
    SATB   Organ
    Lawson Gould (1969) 51523

16:5-9, 11
    White, Jack Noble
    O Lord You Are My Portion and My Cup
    SATB   Organ
    H. W. Gray (1981) GCMR 3446

16:7 (Psalm 81:1-3; Psalm 21:1, 4; Psalm 122:
        3, 6-7; Psalm 125:2)
    Phillips, John C.
    The Lot is Fallen Unto Me
    SATB   Organ
    Novello (1975) 86.0043.00

16:8
    SEE: (Psalm 55:22)
    Bass, Claude
    Cast Thy Burden Upon the Lord

16:10-12
    SEE: Psalm 57:8
    Sowerby, Leo
    My Heart Is Fixed, O God

17:00
    Marcello, Benedetto (ed. Vincent Novello)
    Give Ear Unto Me
    SS   Keyboard
    Concordia (found in Second Morning Star
        Choir Book, 97-4702)

17:00
    Marcello, Benedetto
    Give Ear Unto Me
    2 part   Organ
    Novello (n.d.) 29.0320.02

17:1-2
    Sweelinck, J. P. (ed. Donald Colton)
    O Lord, Attend My Cry
    SATB   kro
    Concordia (1973) 98-2202

17:5
    Marcello, Benedetto (ed. Richard Wienhorst)
    Oh, Hold Thou Me Up
    SA   Keyboard
    Concordia (1954) 98-1046 (also found in
        The Morning Star Choir Book, 97-6287)

17:5
    SEE: Psalm 8:1
    Willan, Healey
    O Lord, Our Governor

17:6-8
    Roff, Joseph
    I Have Called Upon Thee
    SATB   Organ
    Pallma (1963) 716

17:6-9
    Williamson, Malcolm
    Evening Air Psalm (from Psalms of the
        Elements)
    Unison Choir   Organ, congregation
    Boosey & Hawkes (1976) 5950

18:00
    Hovland, Egil
    How Long, O Lord
    SATB   kro
    Walton (1968) 2901

18:00
    Rogers, Bernard
    Psalm 18
    TTBB (T-solo) Piano
    Presser (1964) 312-40600

18:1-2, 6-7, 17, 29, 47
    Sowerby, Leo
    I Will Love Thee, O Lord
    SATB   Organ
    H. W. Gray (1956) 2421

18:1-2, 25-28
    Sellew, Donald
    I Will Love Thee, O Lord
    SATB   Piano ad lib.
    Hall & McCreary (1954) 1178

18:1-3 (1912 Psalter)
    Peninger, David (arr.)
    I Love The Lord, His Strength Is Mine
    SACB   Keyboard
    Cambiata Press (1973) C-17314

18:2
    Wells, Dana F.
    The Lord Is My Rock (Four Modern Anthems)
    SATB   Piano
    Abingdon (1970) APM-619

18:6-18
    Williamson, Malcolm
    I Will Call Upon The Lord (from Psalms
        of the Elements)
    Unison   Organ, Congregation
    Boosey & Hawkes (1976) 5962

18:28
    SEE: Psalm 138:7
    Fryxell, Regina Holmen
    The Lord Is My Light (from Seven Choral
        Service Settings)

19:00
    Beethoven, Ludwig (arr. C. P. Scott)
    The Heavens Are Declaring
    SATB   Organ
    Carl Fischer (1917) CM 150

19:00 (paraphrase)
    Beethoven, Ludwig
    The Heavens Are Telling
    SATB   Organ
    E. C. Schirmer (n.d.) 303 (also found in
        Concord Anthem Book - Red)

19:00
    Billings, William (ed. Leonard Van Camp)
    The Heavens Declare
    SATB   Keyboard
    Concordia (1973) 98-2188

19:00 (Addison)
    Graves, John
    The Spacious Firmament on High
    SATB & Unison   Organ
    Novello (1969) 1478

19:00
    Haydn, Franz J. (arr. Charles Phillips)
    The Heavens Are Telling
    SATB (S-T-B solos) Organ (optional
        instruments)
    Carl Fischer (1920) CM 127

19:00 (adapted)
    Haydn, Franz J.
    The Heavens Are Telling (from Creation)
    SATB   Piano
    Novello (n.d.) 29.0210.09

19:00 (paraphrased) (Psalm 13 paraphrased)
    Hopson, Hal H.
    God's Glory Echoes Through the Skies
    Unison   Organ
    Hinshaw (1980) HMC-410

19:00
    Lewis, Anthony
    The Heavens Proclaim The Glory of God
    SATB   Organ
    Novello (1965) 1459

19:00
    Marcello, B. (arr. C. Alexander Peloquin)
    The Heavens Declare   (English/Italian)
    SATB (T-solo)   Keyboard
    McLaughlin & Reilly (1964) 2463

19:00
    Salibury, Sonny
    Psalm 19 (from The Electric Church)
    2 part   Keyboard
    Word (1968) CS-2454

19:00
    Schütz, Heinrich (ed. Walter Ehret)
    The Heavens Declare the Glory of God
         (English/German)
    SSATBB   Optional accompaniment
    Abingdon (1980) APM-700

19:00
    Schütz, Heinrich (ed. C. Buell Agey)
    The Heavens Declare The Glory of the Lord
         (English/German)
    SSATTB   Organ or Piano
    G. Schirmer (1967) 11400

19:00
    Wyton, Alec
    The Heavens Declare
    Unison   Organ or Piano
    Calvary Press (1974) n.#.

19:1
    SEE: Isaiah 45:8a
    Cassler, G. Winston
    Drop Down, Ye Heavens from Above

19:1
    Marcello, Benedetto (arr. Don Razey)
    The Glory of the Lord
    SAB   Piano/Organ
    Carl Fischer (1979) CM 7978

19:1
    Marcello, Benedetto (arr. Don Razey)
    The Glory of the Lord
    SATB   Piano/Organ
    Carl Fischer (1979) CM 8091

19:1
    SEE: Psalm 121
    Muro, Don
    I Will Lift Up Mine Eyes

19:1
    Thiman, Eric
    The Heavens Declare (Six Introductory Sen-
         tences)
    SATB   Organ
    Novello (1973) MW-25

19:1-4
    Haydn, Franz Joseph
    The Heavens Are Telling (from Creation)
    SATB   Piano
    E. C. Schirmer (1931) 496

19:1-4
    Haydn, Franz Joseph
    The Heavens Are Telling (from Creation)
    SATB   Piano
    Lawson Gould (1963) 51147

19:1-4
    Hunnicutt, Judy
    A Psalm of Praise
    Unison   Flute and Piano
    Choristers Guild (1976) A-175

19:1-4
    Marcello, Benedetto (arr. Hal Hopson)
    Psalm Nineteen
    SATB   No accompaniment
    Agape [Hope] (1979) HH3912

19:1-4
    Tomkins, Thomas (ed. Denis Stevens)
    The Heavens Declare The Glory of God
    TTBB   No accompaniment
    Concordia (1959) 98-1432

19:1-6   (Addison)
    Haydn, F. J. (Descant by K. K. Davis)
    The Spacious Firmament
    2 part   Piano
    E. C. Schirmer (1938) 1130

19:1-6   (Addison)
    Tallis Canon (arr. Irvin Cooper)
    The Spacious Firmament on High
    SCC(B)   Piano
    Cambiata Press (1979) 1979132

19:2-7 and Doxology
    Schütz, Heinrich
    Die Himmel erzählen die Ehre Gottes
    SSATTB   Continuo
    Hanssler   H.E. 20.386

19:4
    Wills, Arthur
    Their Sound is Gone Out   (from Two Anthems)
    ATB   Organ
    Novello (1966) M.V. 148

19:4
    Wills, Arthur
    Their Sound is Gone Out
    SSA   Organ
    Novello (1966) MV 148

19:7-8
    SEE: Psalm 9:1-2
    Hruby, Dolores
    I Will Give Thanks

19:7-8
    Mathias, William
    The Law of the Lord   Op. 61, #2
    SATB   No accompaniment
    Oxford (1973) A 301

19:7-9
    Lynn, George
    The Law of the Lord Is Perfect
    SATB   kro
    Carl Fischer (1976) CM 7948

19:8-11
    Peloquin, C. Alexander
    Lord, You Have the Words
    SATB   Solo   Organ
    GIA (1971) G-1663 (also in Songs of Israel
         G-1666)

19:8-11
    Proulx, Richard
    Lord, You Have the Words
    2 part   4 Handbells   Percussion
    GIA (1973) G-1804

19:14
    Altman, Ludwig
    Choral Meditation
    SATB   Organ
    Transcontinental (1963) TCL 147

19:14
    Bloch, Ernest
    Silent Devotion and Response (English/
         Hebrew)
    SATB   Piano
    Broude Brothers (1962) BB 179

19:14
Persichetti, Vincent
Prayer (from Hymns and Responses for the
    Church Year)
SATB   No accompaniment
Elkan-Vogel (1956) 463-00001

19:14
Purcell, Henry
Let The Words Of My Mouth (from Lord, Who
    Can Tell?)
TTB   Keyboard
Oxford (1965) (found in Anthems for Men's
    Voices, Volume II)

19:14
Rodgers, John
May The Words Of My Mouth (from Seven
    Choral Sentences)
SATB   Organ
H. W. Gray (1981) GCMR 3453

19:14
Starer, Robert
May The Words (English/Hebrew)
SATB (S-solo) Organ
MCA (1971) n.#.

19:14
Titcomb, Everett
Let The Words Of My Mouth
SATB   Organ ad lib.
H. W. Gray (1959) 2601

19:14
Weisgall, Hugo
May The Words (English/Hebrew)
SATB   kro
Presser (1961) 312-40507

19:14, 15
Pears, James R.
Let The Words Of My Mouth
SATB (S-solo) Organ
Flammer (1937) (found in Flammer Collection
    of Anthems, II)

19:15
Amram, David
May The Words Unto Thee, O Lord
SATBB   kro
C. F. Peters (1964) 6684a

19:15
Gottlieb, Jack
Silent Meditation
SATB   Organ
Presser (1971) 312-40780

20:00
Butler, Eugene
A Psalm Of Assurance
SATB   Keyboard
Hinshaw (1976) HMC-175

20:00
Schütz, Heinrich (ed. Paul Boepple)
The Lord Shall Hear (Four Psalms)
    (English/German)
SATB   No accompaniment
Mercury (1941) 352-00006

20:1-2
Sweelinck, Jan P. (ed. Percy Young)
In The Troublesome Day The Lord Will Hearken
SATB   kro
Broude (1978) MGC 28

20:1-2
Taverner, John
In Trouble And Adversity
SATB   kro
Broude (1980) CR-5

20:1-4
Schütz, Heinrich (ed. John Kingsbury)
May God Attend In Thy Distress (Three
    Chorales) (English/German)
SATB   kro
Music 70 (1975) M70-153

20:5-7
Croft, William (ed. Percy Young)
We Will Rejoice
SATB   (A-T-B-solos)   Organ
Broude (1975) MGC 9

20:5, 9
SEE: Psalm 33:11-12
Willan, Healey
In The Name Of Our God

20:7
SEE: Psalm 43:3, 5
Gounod, Charles
Send Out Thy Light

20:9
SEE: Psalm 8:1
Willan, Healey
O Lord Our Governor

21:00 (Tailour's Version, 1615)
Thiman, Eric
Thy Church, O God, Her Heart To Thee
    Upraiseth
SATB   Organ
Novello (1940) 29.0246.10

21:1
Handel, G. F. (ed. Denys Darlow)
The King Shall Rejoice
SATB   Keyboard
RSCM (found in Festival Service Book, VIII)

21:1-4
SEE: Psalm 16:7
Phillips, John C.
The Lot Is Fallen Unto Me

21:1, 3, 5
Handel, G. F.
The King Shall Rejoice (Coronation Anthem,
    #2)
SAATBB   Organ
G. Schirmer (1971) ED. 2821

21:1-7
MacMillan, Ernest
The King Shall Rejoice In Thy Strength
SATB   Organ
F. Harris (1935) n.#.

21:9
SEE: Psalm 8:1
Willan, Healey
O Lord Our Governor

21:13
Purcell, Henry (arr. Walter Ehret)
Be Thou Exalted Lord
SSATB   Keyboard
Carl Fischer (1979) CM 8085

22:00 (adapted)
SEE: Psalm 96 (adapted)
Clausen, Rene
All That Hath Life And Breath, Praise Ye
    The Lord

22:00
Near, Gerald
My God, My God, Why Hast Thou Forsaken Me?
SATB   Organ
H. W. Gray (1971) CMR 3208

22:00 (based on)
    Wetzler, Robert
    My God, Why Hast Thou Forsaken Me? (Two
        Lenten Meditations)
    SATB   Organ
    Abingdon (1964) APM-347

22:1
    Blow, John (ed. Robert Hickok)
    My God, My God, Look Upon Me
    SATB   kro
    Broude Brothers (1954) BB-903

22:1
    SEE: Psalm 96:1
    Clausen, Rene
    All That Hath Life And Breath Praise Ye
        The Lord

22:1, 2, 7-8, 14, 17-19 (Psalm 38:21, 22)
    Greene, Maurice (ed. Percy M. Young)
    My God, My God, Look Upon Me
    SSATB   (T-solo)   Organ
    Broude Brothers (1978) MGC 29

22:1-5
    Swenson, Warren
    My God, Why Hast Thou Forsaken Me?
    SSATBB   kro
    Galaxy (1971) GMC 2475

22:1, 19, 20 (adapted)
    Yardumian, Richard (Harmonized)
    My God, My God (from Eleven Easter Chorales)
    SATB   No accompaniment
    Elkan-Vogel (1978) 362.03280

22:2
    Reynolds, John
    O My God, I Cry In The Daytime
    SA   Organ
    Oxford (1973) (found in Anthems for Choirs,
        Volume 2)

22:5, 6 (Psalm 29:11)
    Brahms, Johannes
    Yea, Our Forefathers   Op. 109, #1
    SATB/SATB   kro
    C. F. Peters (1964) 6565

22:8-9
    Peloquin, C. Alexander
    My God, My God
    SATB   Solo   Organ
    GIA (1971) G-1658 (also in Songs of
        Israel, G-1666)

23:00 (Becker Psalter 1561)
    Angell, Warren
    The Lord My Shepherd Is
    SATB   Piano
    Kickapoo [Carl Fischer] (1956) 111

23:00
    Aschaffenburg, Walter
    The 23rd Psalm
    SATB   (T-solo)   Organ, Oboe
    Presser (1968) 312-40692

23:00
    Bain, James Leith (arr. E. T. Davies)
    Brother James Air
    TTBB   kro
    Oxford (1949) 681

23:00
    Bain, James Leith (arr. Gordon Jacob)
    Brother James's Air
    Unison & SATB   Keyboard
    Oxford (1958) 40P914

23:00
    Bass, Claude
    Psalm Twenty-Three
    SATB   Organ or Piano
    Broadman (1961) 4561-08

23:00 (Watts)
    Bass, Claude
    The Lord My Shepherd Is
    SATB   Keyboard (optional Flute)
    Broadman (1982) 4563-74

23:00 (Wesley)
    Beck, Theodore (arr.)
    My Shepherd Will Supply My Need
    SA   Guitar
    Concordia (1974) (found in Seven Anthems
        for Treble Choirs, Volume I, 97-5218)

23:00 (Rous)
    Beck, Theodore
    The Lord's My Shepherd
    SATB   kro
    Concordia (1968) 98-1931

23:00 (Baker)
    Beck, Theodore (arr.)
    The King Of Love My Shepherd Is (based on
        St. Columba)
    SSA   2 Recorders   (no accompaniment)
    Concordia (1974) (found in Seven Anthems
        for Treble Choirs, Volume I, 97-5218)

23:00
    Beeson, Jack
    Psalm 23 (from Three Settings From The
        Bay Psalm Book)
    SATB   Optional Piano
    Oxford (1969) 94.324

23:00
    Berger, Jean
    The Lord Is My Shepherd
    SATB   kro
    Broude Brothers (1965) BB 3053

23:00
    Berger, Jean
    The Lord To Me A Shepherd Is (from The
        Bay Psalm Book)
    SATB   No accompaniment
    Shawnee Press (1964) A-729

23:00
    Berkeley, Lennox
    The Lord Is My Shepherd Op. 91, #1
    SATB   (S-solo)   Organ
    Chester [Alexander Broude] (1976) JWC 55057

23:00 (Psalm 2:1-4)
    Bernstein, Leonard
    Chicester Psalms, Second Movement
        (Hebrew)
    SATB   Solo   Piano (Orchestra)
    G. Schirmer (1965) 2656

23:00 (Addison)
    Billings, William (ed. Leonard Van Camp)
    The Lord My Pasture Shall Prepare
    SATB   Keyboard
    Concordia (1973) 98-2193

23:00 (New English Bible)
    Binkerd, Gordon
    Psalm 23
    SATB   (T-solo)   Organ
    Boosey & Hawkes (1972) 5820

23:00 (Baker)
    Blakley, Duane (arr.)
    The King Of Love My Shepherd Is
    SATB   Organ, optional Flute, Oboe, Clarinet
    Shawnee (1982) A-5978

23:00
Burroughs, Bob (arr.)
The Lord's My Shepherd (Crimond)
SAB   two octaves of Handbells
Agape [Hope] (1980) RS 7704

23:00
Cain, Noble
The Lord Is My Shepherd
SATB   Optional accompaniment
Flammer (1944) A-5028

23:00
Caldwell, Mary E.
The Shepherd's Psalm
SATB   Youth Choir   Organ
H. W. Gray (1962) 2736

23:00
Cartford, Gerhard M.
Psalm 23
Unison   Choir & Congregation   Keyboard
Augsburg (1978) (found in Seasonal Psalms
      for Congregation and Choir, 11-9376)

23:00
Creston, Paul
Psalm XXIII   Op. 37
SATB   (S-solo)   Piano
G. Schirmer (1953) 10145

23:00
Creston, Paul
Psalm XXIII   Op. 37
TTBB   Piano
G. Schirmer (1953) 10157

23:00
Daniels, M. L.
I Will Dwell In The House Of The Lord
SATB   kro
Flammer (1971) A-5563

23:00
Davis, Katherine K. (arr.)
The Twenty-third Psalm
SA   Piano or Organ
Remick (1966) TMK-4453

23:00
Dietterich, Philip
Psalm 23
SAB   Keyboard
Agape [Hope] (1975) AG-7164

23:00
Dupuis, Thomas
The Lord Is My Shepherd
SATB   (extended Soprano solo)   Organ
St. Mary's Press (1955) n.#.

23:00 (adapted)
Dvorak, Anton (arr. Francis Snow)
God Is My Shepherd
SA Keyboard
Charles Homeyer [Carl Fischer] (1941) 461

23:00 (adapted)
Dvorak, Anton (arr. Francis Snow)
God Is My Shepherd
SSA   Keyboard
Charles Homeyer [Carl Fischer] (1941) 462

23:00
Dvorak, Anton (arr. J. J. Baird)
God Is My Shepherd
SA   Piano
G. Schirmer (1945) 9458

23:00
Dvorak, Anton
God Is My Shepherd
SATB   Organ
Summy-Birchard (1934) B-949

23:00
Dvorak, Anton (arr. Jeffrey Van)
God Is My Shepherd, Op. 99, #4
Unison   Guitar
Augsburg (1976) 11-0663

23:00
Elmore, Robert
The Lord Is My Shepherd
TB   Organ or Piano
Flammer (1963) 85074

23:00
Franck, Cesar (arr. Charles Black)
The Lord's My Shepherd
SATB   Organ
H. W. Gray (1961) 2901

23:00
Fromm, Herbert
The 23rd Psalm
SA   Organ (flute ad lib.)
Transcontinental (1960) TCL 331

23:00
Fromm, Herbert
The 23rd Psalm
SATB   Organ (flute ad lib.)
Transcontinental (1949) TCL-108

23:00
Gardiner, William (arr. A. Avalos)
The Lord's My Shepherd (based on Belmont)
SAB   Keyboard
Pro Art (1953) 1463

23:00 (and antiphon)
Gelineau, Joseph (arr. J. G. Phillips)
My Shepherd Is The Lord
SATB   Accompaniment ad lib.
McLaughlin & Reilly (1962) 2348

23:00
German tune (arr. C. H. Upshur)
The Lord's My Shepherd
Unison   Keyboard
Flammer (1960) (found in Unison Anthems
      With Descant)

23:00
Gibbs, C. Armstrong (arr.)
Brother James Air
SAB   Organ
Oxford (1953) 42.954

23:00 (Watts)
Goemanne, Noel
My Shepherd Will Supply My Need
SATB   Organ or Cello and Flute
GIA (1972) G-1738

23:00
Goudimel, Claude (ed. Ronald Herder)
Two Settings of the 23rd Psalm (English/
      French)
SATB   kro
Continuo [Alexander Broude] (1972) AB 713

23:00 (Metrical)
Grant, David
Crimond
SATB   Organ faux bourdan
Paterson (1936) #32

23:00 (Metrical)
Grant, David
Crimond with descant
SATB   Organ
Paterson (1947) n.#.

23:00 (Paraphrased)
Hamill, Paul (arranger)
My Shepherd
SATB   kro
Abingdon (1969) APM-608

23:00 (George Herbert)
    Handel, G. F. (arr. Reginald Jacques)
    The God of Love My Shepherd Is (melody from
        Solomon)
    SA   Keyboard
    Oxford (1963) E 102

23:00 (Addison)
    Harris, William H.
    The Lord My Pasture Shall Prepare
    SATB   Organ
    Novello (1944) MT 1222 (also in The
        Novello Anthem Book)

23:00
    Harter, Harry H.
    The Twenty-Third Psalm (based on Crimond)
    SATB   kro
    Shawnee (1955) A-348

23:00
    Hennagin, Michael
    Psalm 23
    SATB   Organ
    Walton (1969) 2807

23:00 (Scottish Psalter)
    Hillert, Richard
    The Lord's My Shepherd
    SATB   kro
    Concordia (1979) 98-2439

23:00 (Baker)
    Hillert, Richard
    The King of Love My Shepherd Is
    SATB   Organ, flute
    Concordia (1981) 98-2523

23:00
    Homilius, Gottfried August (ed. Percy Young)
    The Lord Is My Shepherd (German/English)
    SATB   kro
    Broude Brothers (1976) MGC 16

23:00
    How, Martin
    Psalm 23
    Unison (or Baritone Solo) Optional descant
        Keyboard
    Boosey & Hawkes (1981) W.180

23:00 (Bay Psalter)
    Hunnicutt, Judy
    The Lord To Me a Shepherd Is
    SATB   No accompaniment
    GIA (1978) M-2181

23:00
    Hustad, Don (arr.)
    The Lord's My Shepherd (Crimond)
    SATB   No accompaniment
    Hope (1960) HA 110

23:00
    Hutcheson, Charles (arr. Eric Smith)
    The Lord's My Shepherd (based upon the
        tune Stracathro)
    SA or SATB   Piano
    Boosey & Hawkes (1956) 5170

23:00
    Hytrek, Sister Theophane
    Psalm 22
    Unison   Organ (optional flute)
    GIA (1971) G-1608

23:00
    Jacob, Gordon (editor)
    Bro. James Air
    Unison   Organ
    Oxford (1932) 44P 047

23:00
    Jacob, Gordon (editor)
    Bro. James Air
    SATB   Organ
    Oxford (1932) 763

23:00
    Jacob, Gordon (editor)
    Bro. James Air
    2 part   Organ
    Oxford (1960) 44P 047

23:00
    Jacob, Gordon (editor)
    Bro. James Air
    SSA   Organ
    Oxford (1935) 44.029

23:00
    James, Philip
    The 23rd Psalm
    SATB (S-solo) Organ
    H. W. Gray (1927) 864

23:00
    Jenkins, Cyril
    The Lord Is My Shepherd
    SATB   Organ
    Harris (1961) FH 3068

23:00 (Watts)
    Johnson, David N.
    My Shepherd Will Supply My Need
    SAB   Keyboard
    Concordia (1967) (found in Gloria Deo)

23:00
    Jones, David Hugh
    Psalm XXIII
    SATB   Organ
    Flammer (1939) 84155

23:00
    Kemmer, George W.
    The Lord Is My Shepherd
    SATB (S & T solo, or Junior Choir) Organ
    H. W. Gray (1950) 2134

23:00
    Kemp, John S. C.
    Psalm 23
    Children's Choir or Soprano solo   Organ
    Golden Music (1963) G-12

23:00
    Kimberling, Clark
    The King of Love
    Unison   Keyboard (optional flute)
    University of Evansville Press (1981) A1205

23:00
    Klusmeier, R. T.
    The Lord Is My Shepherd
    SATB   Piano or Organ
    Harmuse [F. Harris] (1975) HC 4063

23:00
    Koshat, Thomas (arr. Newell Dayley)
    The Lord Is My Shepherd
    TTBB   No accompaniment
    Sonos Music Resources (1975) CSW 154

23:00
    Lawrence, Darlene
    Psalm 23
    SATB   45 Handbells
    Gentry (1981) G-437

23:00
    Leaf, Robert
    The Lord Is My Shepherd
    Unison   Keyboard
    Choristers Guild (1980) A-231

23:00
    Leighton, Kenneth
    The Lord Is My Shepherd (from Three Psalm,
        Op. 54)
    TTBB   No accompaniment
    Novello (1974) NCM 34

23:00
    Lekberg, Sven
    The Lord Is My Shepherd
    SATB (S-solo)   kro
    Galaxy (1963) GMC 2257

23:00
    Lockwood, Normand
    The Lord Is My Shepherd
    2 part mixed   Organ
    Merrymount (1956) MC279

23:00
    Malotte, Albert Hay (arr. Kenneth Downing)
    The Twenty-third Psalm
    TTBB   Piano
    G. Schirmer (1947) 9612

23:00
    Marshall, Jack
    David's Song
    SATB   Piano (optional guitar, string
        bass, and drums)
    Flammer (1972) A-5601 (parts for instru-
        ments available from publisher)

23:00
    Martin, Warren
    Psalm 23
    2 choruses of 2 parts each   2 pianos
    Hinshaw (1981) HMC 411

23:00
    Matthews, Thomas
    The Lord Is My Shepherd
    SATB   Organ
    H. T. Fitzsimmons (1956) 2137

23:00
    Matthews, Thomas
    The Lord Is My Shepherd
    SA   Organ
    H. T. Fitzsimons (1971) 5026 (A three-part
        treble arrangement is also available.)

23:00
    Mechem, Kirke
    Psalm 23   Op. 41, #1
    SATB (Passacaglia) Keyboard with cello or
        bassoon
    Carl Fischer (1975) CM 7897

23:00   (adapted)
    Morgan, Haydn
    My Shepherd Is The Lord Most High
    SATB   kro
    Remick (1959) R-3324

23:00
    Mueller, Carl F.
    The Lord Is My Shepherd
    SATB   Organ
    Carl Fischer (1951) CM 6616

23:00
    Mueller, Carl F.
    The Lord's My Shepherd (Crimond)
    SA   Piano or Organ
    Carl Fischer (1952) CM 6673

23:00
    Mueller, Carl F.
    The Lord's My Shepherd (Crimond)
    SAB   Keyboard
    Carl Fischer (1970) CM 7719

23:00
    Mueller, Carl F.
    The Lord's My Shepherd (Crimond)
    TTBB   Piano or Organ
    Carl Fischer (1952) CM 6681

23:00   (Baker)
    Nolte, Ewald V.
    The King of Love   (St. Columba)
    SATB   kro
    Concordia (1958) 98-1415

23:00
    Owens, Jimmy (ed. Charles Brown)
    The Lord Is My Shepherd
    SAB   Keyboard
    Word (1972) CS.2549

23:00   (Eric Johnson)
    Page, Sue Ellen
    The Lord Is Like A Shepherd
    Unison   Keyboard and Recorder
    Hinshaw (1978) HMC-432

23:00   (Scottish Psalter 1650)
    Penhorwood, Edwin
    A Psalm Folksong
    SATB   Keyboard
    Hinshaw (1981) HMC-534

23:00   (Watts)
    Pooler, Marie (arr.)
    My Shepherd Will Supply My Need
    Unison or two parts   Keyboard
    Augsburg (1963) 11-0609

23:00   (Addison)
    Powell, Robert J.
    The Lord My Pasture Shall Prepare
    SA   Organ
    Abingdon (1976) APM-512   (found in Anthems
        For Treble Voices)

23:00   (F. Rous)
    Reinagle, Alexander R. (setting by S. Drum-
        mond Wolff)
    The Lord's My Shepherd
    SAB   Organ
    Concordia (1975) 98-2253

23:00
    Rochberg, George
    Psalm 23
    SATB   kro
    Presser (1956) 312-40297

23:00
    Rodby, Walter & Joseph Roff
    Air for Brother James
    2 part mixed   Piano or Organ
    Hope (1980) A-518

23:00
    Rozsa, Miklos
    The Twenty-third Psalm, Op. 34
    SATB   kro
    Broude (1974) BB 5005

23:00
    Rutter, John
    The Lord Is My Shepherd
    SATB   Organ, Oboe solo
    Oxford (1978) 94.216

23:00
    Schack, David
    The Lord Is My Shepherd
    Unison   Keyboard
    Concordia (1973) 98-2145

23:00   (Watts)
      Schalk, Carl
      My Shepherd Will Supply My Need
      2 part mixed   Keyboard   (optional treble
           instrument)
      Concordia (1969) 98-2286

23:00
      Schack, David
      The Lord Is My Shepherd
      Unison   Keyboard
      Concordia (1973) 98-2145

23:00
      Schubert, Franz (arr. Louis V. Saar)
      The 23rd Psalm
      SSA   Piano
      Carl Fischer (1915) CM 5106

23:00
      Schubert, Franz (arr. Carl Deis)
      The Lord Is My Shepherd
      SATB   Organ
      G. Schirmer (1954) 10130

23:00
      Schubert, Franz (arr. Percy Higgs)
      Psalm 23
      2 part treble   Organ
      Oxford (1943) 1655

23:00
      Schubert, Franz
      The Lord Is My Shepherd
      SA   Keyboard
      Novello (n.d.) 29.0328.08

23:00
      Schubert, Franz (arr. John Stainer)
      The Lord Is My Shepherd   op. 132
      SATB   Organ
      Allan [F. Harris] (1909)   343

23:00
      Schubert, Franz (arr. John Stainer)
      The Lord Is My Shepherd
      SATB   Organ
      Novello (1898) 20.0120.10

23:00
      Schubert, Franz (ed. Ivan Trusler)
      The Twenty-third Psalm   Op. 132
      SSA   Organ
      Marks (1960) 4186

23:00
      Schubert, Franz (arr. John Stainer)
      The Lord Is My Shepherd
      SATB   Organ
      H. W. Gray (n.d.) 1622

23:00
      Schubert, Franz (arr. W. G. Whittaker)
      The Lord Is My Shepherd
      SSAA   Keyboard
      Oxford (1928) 1405

23:00   (based on)
      Schumann, George (ed. Paul Christiansen)
      Yea Though I Wander
      SATB   kro
      Augsburg (1948) 1063

23:00
      Schütz, Heinrich
      The Lord My Faithful Shepherd Is
      SATB   Organ ad.lib.
      Schmitt, Hall, McCreary (1951) (found in
           Rare Choral Masterpieces)

23:00
      Schütz, H. (ed. Ulrich S. Leopold)
      The Lord My Pasture Shall Prepare (Four
           Psalms)
      SATB   Keyboard
      Chantry (1959) n.#.

23:00
      Shaw, Oliver (ed. Mason Martens)
      The Lord Is My Shepherd
      SATB   Keyboard
      McAfee (1975) (found in Bicentennial
           Collection of American Choral Music)

23:00   (paraphrased)
      Shelly, Harry Rowe (ed. Ivan Trusler)
      The King of Love My Shepherd Is
      SATB   Organ or Piano
      Plymouth (1963) (also found in Anthems
           For The Church Year, Volume I)

23:00
      Sleeth, Natalie
      The Lord Is My Shepherd
      Unison   Keyboard
      Broadman (1979) 4560-93

23:00   (paraphrased)
      Smart, Henry
      The Lord Is My Shepherd
      SA   Piano
      Novello (n.d.) 29.0319.09

23:00
      Smart, Henry (arr. Ralph H. Bellairs)
      The Lord Is My Shepherd
      SATB   Organ
      Novello (1980) (found in In The Beauty
           Of Holiness)

23:00
      Stanford, C. Villiers
      The Lord Is My Shepherd
      SATB   Organ
      Novello (1975) (found in King of Glory)

23:00
      Taylor, Noxie (arr.)
      The Twenty-third Psalm
      SAC(B)   Piano
      Cambiata Press (1975) U-17556

23:00
      Thompson, Randall
      The Lord Is My Shepherd
      SATB   Piano or Harp
      E. C. Schirmer (1966) 2688

23:00
      Thompson, Randall
      The Lord Is My Shepherd
      SSAA   Piano or Harp
      E. C. Schirmer (1964) 2578

23:00   (Watts)
      Thomson, Virgil
      My Shepherd Will Supply My Need
      SATB   kro
      H. W. Gray (1947) 2046 (also available in
           SAB version)

23:00   (Watts)
      Thomson, Virgil
      My Shepherd Will Supply My Need
      SA   Keyboard
      H. W. Gray (1959) 2562 (also available in
           SSA, and SSAA versions)

23:00   (Watts)
      Thomson, Virgil
      My Shepherd Will Supply My Need
      TTBB   Keyboard
      H. W. Gray (1949) 2108

23:00   (Scottish Psalter 1650)
Titcomb, Everett
The Lord's My Shepherd (based on Crimond)
SATB   Organ
H. W. Gray (1963) 2809

23:00   (Sternhold and Hopkins)
Tomkins, Thomas (ed. Denis Stevens)
My Shepherd Is The Living Lord
SATB   (A-T solos)   Organ
Concordia (1958) 98-1416

23:00   (Sternhold and Hopkins)
Tomkins, Thomas (ed. Bernard Rose)
My Shepherd Is The Living Lord
SATB   (A-solo)   Organ
Stainer & Bell (1957) 581

23:00
Trew, Arthur (arr.)
Brother James Air
Unison   Piano
Oxford (1938) OCS-1139

23:00
Vaughan Williams, Ralph
The Twenty-third Psalm
SATB (S-solo)   kro
Oxford (1953) 43L 913

23:00
Vermulst, Jean
Psalm 22
2 part   Organ, flute
World Library (1964) ESA-7452   (Also versions
      for SATB and for 3 equal voices.)

23:00
Vree, Marion (arr.)
Psalm 23
Unison   Keyboard and flute
Schmitt, Hall, McCreary (1969) 2583

23:00   (Watts)
Walker, David S.
Good Shepherd, May I Sing Thy Praise
4 voices   Flute, Metallophones in Soprano,
      Alto and Bass, Drum, Triangle
Concordia (1978) 98-2374   (flute part,
      97-5468)

23:00
Waterman, Frances
Twenty-third Psalm - An Adaptation
Unison   Keyboard
Choristers Guild (1973) A-144

23:00
Webber, W. S. Lloyd
The Lord Is My Shepherd
SATB   Organ
Novello (1978) (found in Into His Courts
      With Praise)

23:00
Wesley, Samuel Sebastian
The Lord Is My Shepherd
SATB (B-solo)   Organ
Oxford (1933) (found in Church Anthem Book)

23:00   (George Herbert)
Wesley, S. S. (arr. Kenneth J. Eade)
The God Of Love My Shepherd Is
SATB   Organ
Novello (1977) 29.0436.05

23:00
Whitehead, Alfred
Psalm XXIII
SSATB   kro
Carl Fischer (1935) CM 452

23:00
Williams, David H.
Psalm 23
SATB   (S-solo)   Organ
H. W. Gray (1953) 2295

23:00   (Baker)
Williams, David H.
The King of Love
SATB   Organ
H. W. Gray (1959) CMR 2600

23:00
Williamson, Malcolm
The King Of Love (Carols of King David)
Unison   Organ
Boosey & Hawkes (1972) W.005

23:00
Wilson, Harry Robert
The Twenty-third Psalm
SATB   kro
Bourne (1949) 2228

23:00   (Baker)
Wolff, S. Drummond (setting by)
The King of Love My Shepherd Is (on tune,
      St. Columba)
SAB   Organ
Concordia (1981) 98-2527

23:00   (Rouss)
Young, Gordon
The Lord's My Shepherd
SATB   Keyboard
Lorenz (1966) E-61

23:00
Young, Gordon
The Lord Is My Shepherd
SATB   Organ
Flammer (1970) A-5536

23:00
Young, Gordon
God Is My Shepherd
SATB   Keyboard
Flammer (1974) A-5664

23:00
Zimmermann, Heinz W.
Psalm 23
SATB   Organ, Double Bass
Augsburg (1970) 11-0638   (bass part,
      11-0639)

23:1b
Telemann, G. P.
Der Herr ist mein Hirte (English/German)
SSB or SS   Organ, 2 violins
Hanssler   H.E. 39.012

23:1-2
Haydn, F. J.
Lo, My Shepherd's Hand Divine (Adapted
      from Mass in G)
SATB   Organ
E. C. Schirmer   (found in second Concord
      Anthem Book - Grey)

23:1-2, 4, 6
Wise, Michael (ed. Michael J. Smith)
The Lord Is My Shepherd
SATB (S-S solos)   Organ
Novello (1975) 88.0027.08

23:1-3
Greene, Maurice
The Lord Is My Shepherd
SS   Organ
Oxford (1973) (found in Anthems for Choirs,
      Volume 2)

23:1-4
    Dvorak, Anton (arr. Marion Vree)
    God Is My Shepherd
    SA   Keyboard, Oboe or Flute
    Presser (1968) 312.40702

23:1-4
    Herder, Ronald
    From The Twenty-third Psalm
    SATB   kro
    Associated (1967) (also found in Contem-
        porary Settings of the Psalms)

23:1-4, 6
    MacFarren, G. A.
    The Lord's My Shepherd
    SATB   Piano or Organ
    G. Schirmer (n.d.) 5097

23:1-4, 6
    Wesley, S. S.
    The Lord Is My Shepherd
    SATB (S & B solos)   Organ
    W. T. Wagner Reprint (n.d.) C-567006

23:3-6
    Hillert, Richard
    Offertory/Common of Saints Not Martyrs
        (Verses and Offertories - Lesser
        Festivals)
    Unison   Organ
    Augsburg (1980) 11-9542

23:4
    SEE: Isaiah 54:10
    Wagner, Douglas
    For The Mountains Shall Depart

23:6   (John 6:51-57; Matthew 26:26-28)
    Peloquin, Alexander
    Holy Communion
    SATB   Organ
    GIA (1979) G-2248

24:00
    Adler, Samuel
    Psalm 24
    SATB   Organ and Brass
    Presser (1961) 312-40476 (Brass parts
        available on rental from publisher.)

24:00
    Altman, Ludwig
    Lift Up Your Heads
    SATB   Organ
    Transcontinental (1963) TCL 148

24:00
    Benson, Warren
    Psalm XXIV
    SSA   Piano (or strings)
    Carl Fischer (1977) CM 7982

24:00
    Boulanger, Lili
    Psaume 24 (French/English)
    SATB   Organ
    Durand (1924) n.#.

24:00
    Bush, Geoffrey
    Psalm 24
    SATB   Organ or Brass (2 Trumpets,
        2 Trombones, Timpani)
    Novello (1969) NCM 28

24:00
    Davidson, Charles
    Lift Up Your Heads, O Ye Gates
    SATB   Organ
    Beekman (1963) MC 433

24:00
    Diercks, Louis H.
    The Earth Is The Lord's
    SATB   kro
    Witmark (1952) 5-W3453

24:00
    Freudenthal, Josef
    The Earth Is The Lord's
    SATB   Keyboard
    Transcontinental (1962) TCL-139

24:00
    Held, Wilbur
    Psalm 24
    SAB   Congregation   Keyboard
    Augsburg (1978) (found in Seasonal Psalms
        for Congregation and Choir, 11-9376)

24:00 (and Scriptural paraphrase)
    Hopson, Hal
    Introit and Procession
    Unison Antiphonal Choirs   Organ
        Brass Quartet
    Choristers Guild (1971) A-107

24:00
    Ives, Charles
    Psalm XXIV
    SATB   kro
    Presser (1955) 352-00385

24:00
    Lasso, Orlando (ed. Bliss)
    Who Shall Ascend Unto His Hill
    SSA   kro
    Augsburg (1962) PS 605

24:00
    Lockwood, Normand
    The Earth Is The Lord's
    SATBB   kro
    Presser (1950) 312.40064

24:00
    Martin, Warren
    Psalm 24
    2 choruses of 2 parts   2 pianos
    Hinshaw (1981) HMC-412

24:00
    Nelson, Ronald A.
    Lift Up Your Heads
    SAB   Organ
    Augsburg (1971) 11-1635

24:00
    Rhea, Arthur
    Psalm 24
    SATB   Organ
    Chantry (1971) n.#.

24:00
    Sowerby, Leo
    Ad te Levavi animam meam
    SATB   kro
    Summy Birchard (1959) 5293

24:00 (adapted)
    Stevens, Halsey
    God Is My Strong Salvation
    SATB   kro
    Mark Foster (1969) MF 118

24:00 (based on)
    Walker, Alan
    Lift Up Your Heads, Ye Mighty Gates
    Unison   Keyboard
    H. W. Gray (1957) 2452

24:00
Wheelock, Larry L
Psalm 24
SATB   Keyboard
Augsburg (1979) 11-0676

24:00
Williams, David H.
Lift Up Your Heads
Unison   Keyboard, Trumpet, Tambourine
Art Masters (1971) 190

24:00
Williamson, Malcolm
Who Is The King Of Glory (Carols Of King
      David)
Unison   Organ
Boosey & Hawkes (1972) W.004

24:1
Jenni, Donald
Ad te Levani (Latin/English)
SSAATTBB   kro
Associated (1981) A-708

24:1-2
Beebe, Hank
The Earth Is The Lord's
Unison   Organ or Piano
Carl Fischer (1972) CM 7820

24:1-2
Beebe, Hank
The Earth Is The Lord's (The Twenty-Fourth
      Psalm)
Unison   Organ and/or Piano
      Optional Flute
Carl Fischer (1973) CM 7820

24:1-2, 3-6, 7-10
Bevans, William
Psalm 24
SATB   Organ
Abingdon (1970) APM-677

24:1, 2, 7-10
Newbury, Kent
He Is The King Of Glory
SATB   Keyboard
Flammer (1974) A-5672

24:1-2, 7-10 (paraphrased)
Powell, Robert J.
The Earth Is The Lord's
SA   Organ
Abingdon (1976) APM-512 (found in Anthems
      For Treble Voices)

24:1-4
Kirk, Theron
The Earth Is The Lord's
SATB   No accompaniment
Elkan-Vogel (1978) 362-03267

24:1-4, 9, 10
Pratt, George
The Earth Is The Lord's
Unison   Organ
RSCM (1973) 251

24:1-5
Mueller, Carl F.
The Earth Is The Lord's
SA   Piano or Organ
Flammer (1935) 86031

24:1-5, 7
McCormick, Clifford
The Earth Is The Lord's
SATB   Organ
Shawnee (1953) A-208 (also found in
      Anthems From Scripture)

24:3-5
Beebe, Hank
Who Shall Ascent? (The Twenty-Fourth
      Psalm)
2 part mixed   Piano or Organ
Carl Fischer (1972) CM 7863

24:3-5
SEE: Psalm 15:1-2
Darst, W. Glen
Lord, Who Shall Abide

24:6
Beebe, Hank
This Is The Generation (The Twenty-Fourth
      Psalm)
SATB   Organ and Piano
Carl Fischer (1972) CM 7819

24:7-8
Coleridge-Taylor, S. (arr. Carl F. Mueller)
Lift Up Your Heads
SAB   Organ
Carl Fischer (1951) CM 6885

24:7-8
Hammerschmidt, Andreas (ed. Robert Field)
Lift Up Your Heads, O Ye Gates
SAB   Keyboard
Presser (1978) 312-41211

24:7-8
Hammerschmidt, Andreas (ed. Robert Field)
Lift Up Your Heads, O Ye Gates
SSATBB   Keyboard
Presser (1975) 312-41080

24:7, 8
Pote, Allen
Lift Up Your Heads
SATB   Keyboard (Optional 2 Trumpets,
      2 Trombones, Flute)
Hinshaw (1978) HMC-344

24:7-9
Beebe, Hank
Lift Up Your Heads (The Twenty-Fourth
      Psalm)
SAATB   Piano or Organ
Carl Fischer (1972) CM 7973

24:7-9 (and additional)
Lovelace, Austin
The King Of Glory
SATB and Unison   Keyboard
Choristers Guild (1978) A-198

24:7, 8a, 10b
Amner, John (ed. M. Bevan)
Lift Up Your Heads O Ye Gates
SATB   kro
Oxford (1960) (found in Sixteenth Century
      Anthem Book)

24:7-8, 10
Gibbons, Orlando
Lift Up Your Heads
SSAATB   Optional Organ
Oxford (1966) TCM 41

24:7-10
Amner, John (ed. Anthony Greening)
Lift Up Your Heads
SSATB   Organ
Oxford (1972) A-291

24:7-10 (Georg Weissel)
Beck, Theodore
Lift Up Your Heads, You Mighty Gates (based
      on Macht Hoch die Tür)
SA   Organ   (Optional Handbells)
Concordia (1980) 98-2475

24:7-10
Berger, Jean
Lift Up Your Heads
SATB/SATB   Organ, 3 Trumpets
Carl Fischer (1974) CM-7866

24:7-10
Blow, John (ed. Watkins Shaw)
Lift Up Your Heads
SATB   Organ and Strings
Novello (1970) NECM 17

24:7-10
Croft, William
Lift Up Your Heads
SATB   Keyboard
Abingdon (1965) APM-306 (in Select Anthems
     for Mixed Voices, Volume 2)

24:7-10
Glarum, L. Stanley
The King of Glory
SATB   kro
Abingdon (1973) APM-466

24:7-10
Hammerschmidt, Andreas (ed. Donald Rotermund)
Lift Up Your Heads, Ye Gates
SSATBB   Continuo
Concordia (1976) 98-2279

24:7-10
Hammerschmidt, Andreas
Macht die Tür weit (English/German)
SATB   Keyboard
Hanssler H.E. 1.007

24:7-10
Mathias, William
Lift Up Your Heads O Ye Gates   Op. 44, #2
SATB   Organ
Oxford (1973) 42.380 (also in Anthems for
     Choirs, Volume I)

24:7-10
Michael, Tobias
Lift Up Your Heads
SSATB   Organ, 3 Violins, Viola, Cello
Concordia (1968) 97-4815 (Parts 97-4816)

24:7-10
Westra, Evert
Lift Up Your Heads O Ye Gates
SSATTB   Optional Organ
Chantry (1965) n.#.

24:7-10
Willan, Healey
Lift Up Your Heads O Ye Gates
SSA   Keyboard
Concordia (1962) 97-7160 (found in We Praise
     Thee, Volume II)

24:7-10   (Georg Weissel)
Willan, Healey
Lift Up Your Heads, Ye Mighty Gates (based
     on Macht hoch die Tür)
SATB   Organ
Concordia (1950) 98-2003

24:9-10
Berger, Jean
Lift Up Your Heads
SATB   No accompaniment
Summy Birchard (1961) SUMCO 5484

24:9-10
Leighton, Kenneth
Lift Up Your Heads O Ye Gates
SATB   kro
Novello (1966) ANTH 1463

24:10
Beebe, Hank
Who Is The King Of Glory? (The Twenty-
     Fourty Psalm)
SATB and Children's Choir   Organ and Piano
Carl Fischer (1972) CM-7979

24:10   (Ephesians 4:10; John 14:18; Luke 24:
     49)
Marenzio, Luca
O Rex Gloriae   (Latin)
SATB   kro
J. & W. Chester (1977) JWC 55096 (found in
     First Chester Book of Motets)

25:00
SEE: Isaiah 40
Beebe, Hank
I Wait For The Lord

25:00
Binkerd, Gordon
Ad te Levavi (Unto The Father) (English/
     Hebrew)
SATB   kro
Associated (1962) (also in Contemporary
     Settings Of The Psalms)

25:00
Ford, Virgil T.
Unto Thee O Lord
SATB   kro
G. Schirmer (1963) 11101

25:00   (paraphrase)
Goudimel, Claude (arr. Alinda Couper)
To Thee O Lord My Heart Rises
Two part   Keyboard
J. Fischer (1958) 9098 (found in The Chapel
     Choir For Junior Chorus)

25:00
Jams-de-Fer, Philibert
Psalm XXV
SATB   kro
MCA (1965) L469

25:00
Lassus, Orlandus
Judica me, Domine (Latin/English)
TT(B)B   No accompaniment
Mercury (n.d.) #21

25:00   (Psalm 100; Psalm 101)
Muro, Don
O Be Joyful In The Lord
SATB   Organ and Tape
H. W. Gray (1974) GCS 21

25:00
Pote, Allen
Prayer For Guidance
Unison or Two Part   Keyboard
Hinshaw (1977) HMC-244

25:00
Waters, James L.
Psalm 25
SATB   kro
Golden Music (1967) H-6

25:00
Willaert, Adrianus (ed. Zanon-Vene)
Lead Me In Ways Of Truth
SATB   kro
Ricordi (1957) NY-1888

25:1   (Psalm 26:1)
Arcadelt, Jacques
O Lord My God To Thee
SATB   No accompaniment
Oxford (1933) (found in Church Anthem
     Book)

25:1
    Jenni, D.
    Ad te Levavi   (English/Latin)
    ATB   kro
    Associated (1974) A-708

25:1
    Rachmaninoff, S.
    To Thee O Lord
    SATB   kro
    Baley & Ferguson (1915) (found in Oxford's
        Anthems for Choirs, Volume I)

25:1 (paraphrased J. Garth)
    Marcello, Benedetto
    To Thee, O Lord My God
    TB   Continuo
    Oxford (1965) (found in Anthems for Men's
        Voices, Volume II)

25:1-2
    SEE: Psalm 61:1
    Kopyloff, Alexander
    Hear My Cry, O God

25:1, 3-4
    Aulbach, Francis E.
    Unto Thee O Lord
    SATB (S-solo) Keyboard
    Carl Fischer (1956) CM 6824

25:1, 3, 4
    Ford, Virgil T.
    Unto Thee O Lord
    SAB   kro
    G. Schirmer (1967) 11506

25:1, 4a
    Beston, Charles
    Unto Thee Do I Lift Up My Soul
    SATB   kro
    Elkan-Vogel (1964) 1192

25:1, 4
    Goode, Jack C.
    Unto Thee O Lord (Prayer Intonations)
    Unison   Organ
    Abingdon (1974) APM-516

25:1-2, 4-5   (Psalm 19:8)
    Englert, Eugene
    I Lift Up My Soul
    SATB   Organ and Flute
    Augsburg (1977) 11-1797

25:1, 4-5, 8-9, 10, 14
    Peloquin, C. Alexander
    To You O Lord
    SATB   Solo   Organ
    GIA (1971) G-1654 (also in Songs of Israel,
        G-1666)

25:2
    SEE: Psalm 141:1
    Arcadelt, Jacob
    O Lord I Cry To Thee

25:3
    SEE: Psalm 55:8
    Mendelssohn, Felix
    Cast Thy Burden Upon The Lord

25:3
    SEE: Psalm 55:22
    Mendelssohn, Felix
    Cast Thy Burden Upon The Lord

25:4, 5
    Pelz, Walter
    Show Me Thy Ways
    SATB   Oboe, Guitar
    Augsburg (1970) 11-0642

25:4-5
    Rohlig, Harald
    Teach Me Your Ways Lord
    Unison or SA   Keyboard
    Concordia (1973) 98-2358 (also found in
        Explode With Joy, 97-5165)

25:4-5
    SEE: Psalm 5:1-3, 7-8, 11-12
    Schubert, Franz (ed. Daniel Pinkham)
    O Hear Me When I Call On Thee

25:5, 6
    Farrant, Richard (ed. M. Shaw)
    Call To Remembrance
    SATB   kro
    H. W. Gray (n.d.) CMR 1751

25:5-6
    Farrant, Richard (ed. Walter Collins)
    Call To Remembrance
    SATB   Optional Organ
    Hinshaw (1981) HMC-492

25:5, 6
    Farrant, Richard
    Call To Remembrance
    SATB   kro
    Oxford (1978) (found in Oxford Book Of
        Tudor Anthems)

25:5, 6
    Farrant, Richard
    Call To Remembrance
    SATB   kro
    Oxford (1978) TCM 60B (also found in Church
        Anthem Book)

25:5-6
    Hilton, John (The Elder)
    Call To Remembrance
    SSAATTBB   Organ ad lib.
    Oxford (1964) TCM 97

25:5, 6, 7
    Farrant, Richard (ed. Norman Greyson)
    Call To Remembrance
    SATB   kro
    Bourne (1957) ES 17

25:6
    Battishill, Jonathan (ed. Giles Bryant)
    Call To Remembrance
    SATB   Optional Organ
    Leeds (1968) #4

25:6-7
    Farrant, Richard (ed. & arr. S. Drummond
        Wolff)
    Call To Remembrance, O Lord
    TTBB   kro
    Concordia (1975) 98-2246

25:15-16, 19
    Boyce, William
    Turn Thee To Me
    SSATB   Keyboard
    Oxford (1933) CMS #14 (also found in Church
        Anthem Book)

25:16-17
    Boyce, William
    The Sorrows Of My Heart (from Turn Thee
        Unto Me)
    SS   Keyboard
    Concordia (1956) 98-1380

25:16-17
    Boyce, William
    The Sorrows Of My Heart (from Turn Thee
        Unto Me)
    SS or SA or TT or TB   Keyboard
    Concordia (1956) (found in Lift Up Your
        Hearts, 97-6219)

25:16-17
Boyce, William
The Sorrows Of My Heart
SS   Organ
Oxford (1966) CMSR 14a (also found in
    Anthems for Choirs, Volume II)

26:00
Lassus, Orlandus
Judica me, Domine   (English/German)
Three part women   No Accompaniment
Mercury (1942) DES 21

26:00
Schütz, Heinrich (ed. Maynard Klein)
They That Sow In Tears (English/Latin)
SSATB   kro
G. Schirmer (1977) 12101

26:1
SEE: Psalm 25:1
Arcadelt, Jacques
O Lord My God To Thee

26:1, 4-5   (Psalm 28:2)
Malotte, Albert Hay
Unto Thee O Lord
SATB   Piano or Organ
G. Schirmer (1942) 8816

26:2-3
Boyce, William (arr. Watkins Shaw)
Examine Me, O Lord (from Be Thou My Judge)
SS   Organ or Piano
Novello (1957) 29.0195.01

26:5-8 (Metrical version)
Haydn, F. Joseph (ed. H. C. Robbins-Landon)
How Oft, Instinct With Warm Divine
SA(T)B   kro
Broude Brothers (1980) CR 1

26:7
Battishill, Jonathan
O Remember Not
SAB   Organ
E. C. Schirmer (1955) 2615

26:8
SEE: Numbers 24:5
Gottlieb, Jack
Mah Tovu

26:8
Near, Gerald
Lord, I Have Loved Thy Habitations (Three
    Introits)
SATB   kro
Calvary Press (1975) 1-009

26:8-11
SEE: I Kings 13:27-28
Milner, Anthony
I Have Surely Built Thee

26:8-9, 12
Tomkins, Thomas (ed. Denis Stevens)
O Lord, I Have Loved
SAATB   Organ
C. F. Peters (1961) 6068

27:00
Beebe, Hank
The Lord Is My Light
SATB   Keyboard
Hindon [Hinshaw] (1980) HPC-7016

27:00 (based on J. Montgomery)
Powell, Robert J.
God Is My Strong Salvation
SAB   kro
Augsburg (1964) 1378

27:00
Speaks, Oley (arr. Lucien Chaffin)
The Lord Is My Light
SATB (S & T solos)   Organ
G. Schirmer (1913) n.#.

27:00 (adapted)
Upshur, Claire H.
Chorale
Unison   Keyboard
Flammer (1960) (Found in Unison Anthems
    With Descant)

27:00 (taken from)
Wienhorst, Richard
Hear O Lord
SATB   kro
Associated (1963) A-430 (also in Contem-
    porary Settings of the Psalms, AMP-
    6910)

27:1
SEE: Job 3:3, 4, 20, 21, 23, 24
Cook, Melville
Antiphon

27:1
Englert, Eugene
The Lord Is My Light And My Salvation
SATB   Organ
GIA (1980) G-2348

27:1
Schütz, Heinrich (ed. & arr. Douglas Wagner)
The Lord Is My Light And My Salvation
2 part mixed   Keyboard   2 Trumpets
Belwin (1980) DMC 1208

27:1-2, 5, 7, 9, 13, 14
Bender, Jan
The Lord Is My Light And My Salvation
SATB/SATB   kro
Concordia (1961) 97-6339

27:1, 3, 5
Allitsen, Frances (arr. Sumner Salter)
The Lord Is My Light
SATB   Organ
Boosey & Hawkes (1924) 1339

27:1, 3, 5
Allitsen, Frances (arr. Noble Cain)
The Lord Is My Light
SSA   Piano
Boosey & Hawkes (1946) 1759

27:1, 3, 5
Allitsen, Frances (arr. V. E. Wright)
The Lord Is My Light
SATB   Organ or Piano
Flammer (1955) A-5049

27:1, 3, 5
Pfautsch, Lloyd
The Lord Is My Light
SATB   Keyboard
Sacred Music Press (1968) NOS-24

27:1-3, 8, 11, 16
Parker, Horatio
The Lord Is My Light
SATB   Organ
G. Schirmer (1918) 3552

27:1-3, 8, 11, 16
Parker, Horatio
The Lord Is My Light
SATB   Organ
F. Harris (n.d.) 1336

27:1, 4, 7
Wyton, Alec
The Lord Is My Light
SATB   Organ
Presser (1977) 312-41171

27:1, 5
Cram, James D.
The Lord Is My Light
SATB   Keyboard
Broadman (1973) 4545-64

27:4
Jeppesen, Knud
One Thing Have I Desired Of The Lord
SATB   kro
Broude Brothers (1975) BB 5020

27:4
Lucky, Harrell C.
One Thing Have I Desired Of The Lord
SATB (S & T solos) Organ   Bells ad lib.
GIA (1976) G-2045

27:4
Schütz, Heinrich (ed. Don McAfee)
One Thing I Ask Of The Lord
2 part   Organ or Piano
Capella Music (1971) n.#.

27:4
Schütz, Heinrich (ed. Ulrich S. Leupold)
One Thing Have I Desired (Eins bitten ich
    von Herren) (English/German)
SA or TB   Keyboard
Concordia (1957) 98-1369

27:4-6
Butler, J. Melvin
One Thing Have I Asked Of The Lord
SATB   Organ
Hinshaw (1977) HMC-211

27:4-7
Howells, Herbert
One Thing Have I Desired
SATB   kro
Novello (1968) 29.0406.03

27:7
SEE: Genesis 8:22
Simper, Caleb
While the Earth Remaineth

27:7-8
Roff, Joseph
Hide Not Thy Face From Me
SATB   Organ
GIA (1978) G-2206

27:8-14
Sherman, Roger
Be Strong
2 mixed voices   Handbells
GIA (1979) G-2198

27:10
Farrant, Richard (arr. John Holler)
Hide Not Thou Thy Face
TTBB   kro
H. W. Gray (1973) CMR 3292

27:10 (based on)
Farrant, Richard
Hide Not Thou Thy Face
SATB   No accompaniment
Novello (1975) 88.0032.04

27:10
Farrant, Richard
Hide Not Thou Thy Face
SATB   Organ
Oxford (1978) TCA 60A (also found in
    Oxford Book of Tudor Anthems)

27:10
Farrant, Richard (ed. Gerald Knight)
Hide Not Thou Thy Face
SATB   kro
RSCM (1957) 217

27:14
SEE: Isaiah 40:31
Roff, Joseph
Wait On The Lord

28:00
Hovhaness, Alan
Psalm 28   op. 162
SATB   Organ
C. F. Peters (1958) 6149

28:1 (adapted)
Titcomb, Everett
Praised Be The Lord
SATB   Optional Organ
C.C. Birchard (1952) 2057

28:1
Fitschel, James
Be Not Silent
SATB   kro
Boonin (1976) 256

28:2 (Psalm 56:9)
Diercks, John
Lord, I Cry Unto Thee
SATB   Keyboard
Abingdon (1963) APM-303

28:7 (Psalm 31:24)
Berger, Jean
The Lord Is My Strength
SATB   2 Trumpets
Augsburg (1979) 11-1911

28:7
SEE: Isaiah 55:12
Diemer, Emma Lou
For Ye Shall Go Out With Joy

29:00
Cartford, Gerhard M.
Psalm 29
Unison or SATB   Keyboard
Augsburg (1979) 11-0672

29:00
SEE: Psalm 148 (words from)
Fromm, Herbert
Anthem Of Praise

29:00
Leaf, Robert
Festal Anthem
SATB   Organ, Trumpet in B-flat
Augsburg (1977) 11-1795 (trumpet part
    on the music)

29:00
Richter, Willy
The 29th Psalm - O Ye Mighty Give Unto The
    Lord Glory and Strength
SATB   Organ
G. Schirmer (1943) 9216

29:00
Schütz, Heinrich (arr. George Lynn)
Psalm 29
SATB   kro
Presser (1950) 312.40072

29:00
Schütz, Heinrich (ed. C. Buell Agey)
The Voice Of The Lord Sounds Upon The
    Waters (English/German)
SATB   Organ or Piano
Mercury (1963) MC-407

29:00
Sweelinck, J. P.
Psalm 29   (English/French)
SSATB   Keyboard
Ed. Musico (1961) G-539

29:00
Weisgall, Hugo
Psalm 29   (English/Hebrew)
2 part   Solo   Organ   (Optional brass)
Presser (1973) 312-40958

29:1-2
Palestrina, G. P. (ed. H. Elliot Button)
Exaltabo te, Domine
SSATB   kro
Novello (n.d.) 1135

29:1-2
Schütz, Heinrich (ed. C. Buell Agey)
Give Unto The Lord, O Ye Mighty   (English/
    German)
Unison   Organ
Abingdon (1961) APM-135

29:1-2
Schütz, Heinrich
Give To Jehovah
Unison   Keyboard
Concordia   (found in Second Morning Star
    Choir Book, 97-4702)

29:1-3
Landgrave, Phillip
Give Unto The Lord
SATB   Keyboard or Brass
Broadman (1964) 451-648

29:1, 2, 3, 11
Seay, M. Berry
Give Unto The Lord The Glory
SATB   Organ
Flammer (1956) 84466

29:1-4, 10-11
Daniels, M. L.
Psalm of David
SATB   kro
Elkan-Vogel (1966) 1230

29:1-5
Rocherolle, Eugenie
Give To The Lord
SATB   Keyboard
Warner Music (1970) WB 129

29:2-4
Wetzler, Robert
Offertory/The Baptism of Our Lord
    (Verses and Offertories - Advent I -
    The Baptism of Our Lord)
Unison   Organ
Augsburg (1979) 11-9541

29:5, 7
Hovhaness, Alan
The God Of Glory Thundereth
SATB   Organ
C. F. Peters (1962) 6440

29:11
SEE: Psalm 22:5, 6
Brahms, Johannes
Yea Our Father

29:11
SEE: I Chronicles 29:11
Simper, Caleb
Shout For Joy

30:00
Isaacson, Michael
Psalm 30   (English/Hebrew)
SATB   Percussion and Brass
Music 70 (1979) M70-247

30:00
Pisk, Paul
Psalm XXX
TTBB   No accompaniment
Southern (n.d.) ME 1012

30:00
Tye, Christopher
I Will Exalt Thee
SATB   kro
Oxford (1936) 59

30:00   (adapted)
Wagner, Douglas
Joy In The Morning Shall Be Mine
SATB   Handbells
GIA (1979) G-2278

30:1
Corfe, Joseph (edited & realized by
    Derek Holman)
I Will Magnify Thee, O Lord
SS   Keyboard
Novello (1960) 29.0197.08

30:1-3
Erbach, Christian (ed. William Halderman)
I Will Extol Thee O Lord (Exaltabo te,
    Domine)   (English/Latin)
SATB   kro
Concordia (1968) 98-1936

30:1, 3
Young, Gordon
I Will Extol Thee
SATB   Organ, 3 Trumpets
Flammer (1969) A-5083

30:1-4, 11-13
Tye, Christopher (ed. John Langdon)
I Will Exalt Thee
SATB   Organ
Novello (1970) NECM-10

30:4-5
Newbury, Kent A.
Sing Praises, Sing Praises
SSA   kro
Music 70 (1979) M70-238

30:4, 5
Schütz, Heinrich (ed. William Herrmann)
Sing O Ye Saints   (English/German)
SS   Organ
Concordia (1958) 98-1414

30:4, 5, 12
Baker, Richard C.
Sing Unto The Lord (from Three Short
    Introits)
SATB   kro
F. Harris (1974) HC 54057

30:4, 11-13
Tye, Christopher (ed. A. Ramsbottham)
Sing Unto The Lord
SATB   kro
Oxford (1936) (found in Sixteenth Century
    Anthem Book)

30:5-6
Schütz, Heinrich (ed. Don McAfee)
Praise Ye The Lord (Ihr Heiligen Lobsinget)
    (English/German)
SS or any 2 parts   Keyboard
Belwin (1980) DMC 8090

30:5-6
Schütz, Heinrich (ed. Don McAfee)
Praise Ye The Lord
2 part   Organ or Piano
Capella (1971)

30:5a
    SEE: Psalm 95:1-3a
    Kimball, Jacob (ed. Mason Martens)
    O Come Sing Unto The Lord

30:10
    Parker, Alice
    Hear O Lord   (from Sunday Rounds)
    3 part round   No accompaniment
    Hinshaw (1975) HMC-106

30:12-13
    Droste, Doreen
    Hear My Prayer
    SATB   Organ
    Associated   (1958) A-301

31:00
    Waters, James
    Psalm 31
    SATB   kro
    G. Schirmer (1974) 12006

31:1
    Buxtehude, Dietrich (ed. Piet Kiel, Jr.)
    In te Domine speravi (Latin only)
    SAB   Continuo
    Harmonia Uitgave   [C. F. Peters] (1964)
        HU 1900

31:1
    Gaburo, Kenneth
    Psalm
    SATB   No accompaniment
    World Library (1965) ESA 961-8

31:1-2
    Handel, G. F.   (ed. Arthur Hilton)
    In Thee, O Lord, Have I Trusted
    SAB   Piano or Organ
    Presser (1971) 352-00439

31:1-2
    Schütz, Heinrich (ed. Maynard Klein)
    In te, Domine (Lord In Thee Do I Put My
        Trust   (English/Latin)
    SATB   kro
    G. Schirmer (1973) 11971

31:1, 3
    SEE: Psalm 4:7
    Copley, R. Evan
    In Thee, O God Do I Put My Trust

31:1, 2, 3
    Bender, Jan
    In Thee, O Lord Do I Put My Trust
    Unison   Keyboard
    Augsburg (n.d.) PS 611

31: 1a, 2a, 3
    Glarum, L. Stanley
    In Thee Lord
    SATB   kro
    Bourne (1959) SG-1

31:1-3
    Roff, Joseph
    In Thee, O Lord, Do I Put My Trust
    SATB   Accompanied
    Pallma (1963) 742

31:1, 3, 23
    Milner, Arthur
    O Lord, In Thee Do I Put My Trust
    SATB   kro
    Novello (1980) (found in Into His Courts
        With Praise)

31:1-6, 17-18, 26-27
    Stevens, Halsey
    In Thee O Lord Have I Put My Trust
    SATB   Organ
    C. F. Peters (1962) 6520

31:6
    SEE: Psalm 140:7
    Brewer, A. H.
    O Lord God Thou Strength Of My Health

31:6-7, 16, 20
    Hillert, Richard
    Offertory/Common of Martyrs (Verses and
        Offertories - Lesser Festivals)
    Unison   Organ
    Augsburg (1980) 11-9542

31:16, 19
    Johnson, David N.
    Offertory/Epiphany IV (Verses and Offer-
        tories - Epiphany II - The Trans-
        figuration Of Our Lord)
    Unison   Organ
    Augsburg (1980) 11-9544

31:21-24   (metrical)
    Haydn, F. Joseph (ed. H. C. Robbins Landon)
    Blest Be The Name of Jacob's God
    SA(T)B   kro
    Broude Brothers (1980) CR 13

31:24
    SEE: Psalm 28:7
    Berger, Jean
    The Lord Is My Strength

32:00
    Fuller, Jeanne Weaver
    Exsultate Justi   (Latin)
    SATB   kro
    Associated (1967) A-550   (also found in
        The AMP Contemporary Choral Collection
        A-642)

32:00   (adapted)
    MacMillan, Alan
    Whom The Lord Hath Forgiven
    TTBB   Organ
    Rock Harbor Press (1980) RMO 802

32:00   (adapted)
    Satie, Erik (arr. Luigi Zaninelli)
    Give Thanks To The Lord   (2nd Gymnopedies)
    SATB   Piano or Harp
    Walton (1971) 3403

32:00
    Weber, Paul
    Psalm 32
    SST or SAB Congregation   Organ
    Augsburg (1979) 11-0682

32:1, 2
    SEE: Isaiah 53:4, 5
    Bender, Jan
    A Little Lenten Cantata

32:1, 2
    Tomkins, Thomas
    Blessed Is He Whose Unrighteousness Is
        Forgiven
    ATB   No accompaniment
    Oxford (1965) (found in Anthems for Men's
        Voices, Volume I)

32:1-6
    Padilla, Juan Gutierrez (ed. Roger Wagner)
    Exsultate justi in Domino   (Latin)
    SATB/SATB   kro
    Lawson Gould (1962) 51118

32:11
    Coggin, Elwood
    Be Ye Glad and Rejoice, O Ye Righteous
    SATB   Organ or Piano
    G. Schirmer (1968) 11558

32:11
    Fritschel, James
    Be Glad
    SSAATTBB   kro
    Augsburg (1974) 11-0549

32:12
    Powell, Robert J.
    Be Glad, You Righteous
    SAB   Piano
    Carl Fischer (1981) CM-8139

32:12   (Psalm 65:9, 11-14)
    Statham, Heathcote
    Be Glad and Rejoice
    SAB   Organ
    RSCM (1963)   (found in Harvest Festival
        Music)

33:00
    Butler, Eugene
    A Festive Psalm
    SATB   (optional Junior Choir)   Organ
        2 Trumpets, 2 Trombones, Timpani
    Carl Fischer (1979) CM-8078 (parts CM-8078A)

33:00   (Wesley)
    Hill, Nancy
    Rejoice!
    Unison or 2 part   Piano   24 Handbells
    Broadman (1976) 4560-59

33:00   (adapted by Myrtle Wilson)
    Hovdsven, E. A.
    Blessed Is The Nation
    SATB   Keyboard
    J. Fischer (1972) FEC 10064

33:00   (adapted)
    Lenel, Ludwig
    Rejoice In The Lord
    SATB   Optional accompaniment
    Presser (1968) 312-40693

33:00
    Lenel, Ludwig
    Rejoice In The Lord
    SSAATTBB   Optional Piano
    Westminster Choir College (1949) WCC 13

33:00
    Marshall, Jane
    Our Soul Waits For The Lord   (from Two
        Quiet Psalms)
    SATB   Keyboard
    Sacred Music Press (1980) S-271

33:00
    Neff, James
    Shout For Joy Before The Lord
    SATB   kro
    Augsburg (1974) 11-0655

33:00
    Titcomb, Everett
    Rejoice In The Lord, O Ye Righteous
    SATB   Organ
    Flammer (1966) 84863

33:1   (Psalm 118:15)
    Nares, James (ed. Derek Holman)
    Rejoice In The Lord O Ye Righteous
    Unison Treble   Organ
    RSCM (1960) 220

33:1
    Steffani, Agostino (ed. Austin Lovelace)
    Rejoice In The Lord
    SAB   Keyboard
    Concordia (1975) 98-2217

33:1-2
    Viadana, Lodovico
    Exultate Justi in Domino   (English/Latin)
    SATB   Organ
    Walton (1964) 2153

33:1-2, 4-5, 20
    Simper, Caleb
    Our Help and Shield
    SATB   Organ
    Weeks [Harris] (n.d.) n.#.

33:1-3
    Banchieri, Adriano (ed. Ronald Anderson)
    Exultate justi in Domino (English/Latin)
    SA(TB)   Keyboard
    Concordia (1979) 98-2445

33:1-3
    Rohlig, Harald
    God Is Here Let's Celebrate
    Unison   Keyboard
    Concordia (1973) 97-5165 (found in Explode
        With Joy)

33:1-3
    Viadana, Ludovico (ed. M. Klein)
    Exsultate justi   (English/Latin)
    SATB   Keyboard
    GIA (1978) G-2140

33:1-3
    Viadana, Ludovico (ed. B. Rainbow)
    Exsultate justi (Praise Your God Ye
        Righteous) (Latin/English)
    SATB   Organ ad.lib.
    Oxford (1960)   (found in Sixteenth Century
        Anthem Book)

33:1-3
    Viadana, Ludovico
    Exultate justi   (Latin only)
    SATB   No accompaniment
    Arista (1972) AE 211

33:1-3
    Viadana, Ludovico (ed. Nino Borucahia)
    Exultate justi   (Latin)
    SATB   kro
    McLaughlin & Reilly (1961) 2304

33:1-3
    Viadana, Lodovico (ed. & arr. Leland Sateren)
    Sing Ye Righteous
    SATB   kro
    Concordia (1960) 98-1527

33:1-4
    Humfrey, Pelham (edited Watkins Shaw)
    Rejoice In The Lord, O Ye Righteous
    SATB   Organ
    Oxford (1958) CMS 35

33:1-4
    Kirk, Theron
    Rejoice In The Lord
    SATB   Organ, 2 Trumpets
    Marks (1967) 4428

33:1-4
    Vaughan Williams, Ralph
    A Choral Flourish
    SATB   kro
    Oxford (1956) 43.934

33:1, 3-4, 6, 13, 16-18   (adapted)
    Lockwood, Normand
    Rejoice In The Lord
    SATB   2 Horns, 2 Trombones, Timpani
    World Library (1970) ESA 1916

33:1, 5b, 6a
    Cassler, C. Winston
    The Earth Is Full Of Goodness
    SATB   kro
    Augsburg (1963) ACL-1344

33:1, 5, 6a
    Proulx, Richard
    Of The Kindness Of The Lord
    2 part   Organ
    Augsburg (1968) 11-1539

33:1-5, 20-22
    Schmutz, Albert D.
    Rejoice In The Lord
    SATB   Piano or Organ
    Abingdon (1976) APM 439   (found in Anthems
        From The Psalms)

33:1-6, 8
    Eidsvoog, John
    Psalm 33
    SATB   Keyboard
    AMSI (1979) AMSI 372

33:2-3
    Seele, Thomas
    Benedicam Dominum (Latin)
    TTBB   Continuo
    Hanssler #349

33:3, 4
    Goode, Jack C.
    Sing To The Lord
    SATB   Organ
    Abingdon (1962) APM-218

33:6   (adapted)
    SEE: Hebrews 11:1, 3-8, 23-31
    Lockwood, Normand
    A Cloud of Witnesses

33:11-12
    SEE: Psalm 48:1
    Willan, Healey
    Great Is The Lord

33:11-12 (Psalm 20:5, 9; Psalm 60:12)
    Willan, Healey
    In The Name Of Our God
    SATB   Organ
    H. W. Gray (1917) 466

33:20-22
    Heussenstamm, George
    Our Soul Waits For The Lord
    SATB   kro
    Concordia (1965) 98-1753

33:21
    SEE: Isaiah 2:3, 5
    Crowe, John F.
    The Light Of The World

33:21
    Wesley, Charles
    Like As We Do Put Our Trust In Thee
    SS   Organ
    Novello (1957) 95

34:1
    Copley, R. Evan
    I Will Bless The Lord
    Unison Treble   Organ
    Abingdon (1965) APM-341 (found in Seven
        General Anthems for Unison Treble
        Choir)

34:1
    King, Charles
    I Will Alway Give Thanks
    SA   Organ
    Oxford (1973) (in Anthems for Choirs,
        Volume II)

34:1, 3
    Titcomb, Everett
    I Will Alway Give Thanks
    SATB   Organ
    Flammer (1962) 84701

34:1-3
    King, Robert (ed. Mason Martens)
    I Will Alway Give Thanks
    SAB or ATB   Organ
    Concordia (1964) 98-1659 (also found in
        Sing For Joy, 97-5046)

34:1-3
    Roff, Joseph
    I Will Bless The Lord
    SATB   Organ
    GIA (1980) G 2367

34:1, 3-5
    James, Allen
    Look To Him And Be Radiant
    SATB   kro
    H. W. Gray (1971) CMR 3221

34:1-8, 13-14
    Hytrek, Sister Theophane
    Psalm 33
    SSA or SATB   Organ
    GIA (1971) G-1607

34:1-9, 11-12, 14
    Cram, James D.
    In Praise of God's Goodness
    SSA or SSATTB   Keyboard
    Flammer (1973) B-5157

34:2-9
    Peloquin, C. Alexander
    Taste and See
    SATB   Solo   Organ
    GIA (1971) G-1664 (also found in Songs of
        Israel, G-1666)

34:3, 11
    SEE: Numbers 10:29
    Clokey, Joseph
    Come Thou

34:3-4
    Mueller, Carl F.
    O Magnify The Lord With Me
    SA   Piano or Organ
    Carl Fischer (1953) 6684

34:4-6
    Johnson, David N.
    Offertory/Epiphany III (Verses and Offer-
        tories - Epiphany II - The Trans-
        figuration Of Our Lord)
    Unison   Organ
    Augsburg (1980) 11-9544

34:6
    SEE: Psalm 105:4
    Herbst, Johannes
    See Ye His Countenance In All Places

34:8
    Copley, R. Evan
    O Taste and See
    Unison   Organ
    Augsburg (1964) 11-0681

34:8
    Copley, R. Evan
    O Taste and See
    Unison treble   Organ
    Abingdon (1964) APM-341 (found in Seven
        General Anthems for Unison Treble Choir)

34:8
  Hastings, Thomas
  O Taste And See
  SATB   Organ
  Mark Foster (1976) MF276 (also in Anthem
      Book, I MF 211)

34:8
  Issac, Heinrich
  Gustate et Videto (Latin only)
  SATB   kro
  J. & W. Chester (1977) JWC 55127 (in Fifth
      Chester Book of Motets)

34:8   (plus Latin Hymn)
  Kreutz, Robert
  Jesu dulcis: The Taste of Goodness
  SATB   Congregation   Organ
  GIA (1980) G-2304

34:8
  Nikolsky, A.
  O Taste and See How Gracious Is The Lord
  SSATB   kro
  J. Fischer (1916) 4171

34:8
  Vaughan Williams, Ralph
  O Taste and See
  SATB (S-solo)   Organ
  Oxford (1933) (also found in A First Motet
      Book, 97-4845, Concordia)

34:8
  Wolff, S. Drummond
  O Taste and See
  SATB (S-solo)   Organ
  Concordia (1956) (found in Lift Up Your
      Hearts, 97-6219)

34:8-10
  Ford, Virgil T.
  O Taste and See
  SATB   kro
  Flammer (1962) 84714

34:8-10
  Goss, John
  O Taste and See
  SATB   Organ
  Novello (n.d.) 29.0101.03

34:8-10
  Schalk, Carl
  Offertory Pentecost 20   (Verses and Offer-
      tories 12-20)
  Unison   Organ
  Augsburg (1978) 11-9539

34:8-10
  Vaughan Williams, Ralph
  O Taste and See
  SATB (S-solo)   Organ
  Oxford (1953) (found in Oxford Easy Anthem
      Book, and Anthems for Choirs, Volume IV)

34:8-10
  Vaughan Williams, Ralph
  O Taste and See
  SSA (S-solo)   Organ
  Oxford (1935) n.#.

34:11
  Steffani, Agostino (ed. Richard Wienhorst)
  Come Ye Children and Harken To Me
  SS   Keyboard
  Concordia (1962) 98-1593

34:18
  SEE: Psalm 96:4, 9
  Hollins, Alfred
  O Worship The Lord

34:18
  Sullivan, Arthur S.
  The Lord Is Nigh (from The Prodigal Son)
  SATB   Organ
  E. C. Schirmer (1955) 2628

36:00
  DiLasso, Orlando (ed. Lundquist)
  Hear O Lord My Prayer
  SATB   Keyboard
  Elkan-Vogel (1956) 1110

36:00   (S. Medley)
  Herman, Nikolaus (setting by S. Drummond
      Wolff)
  Awake My Soul
  SAB   kro
  Concordia (1965) 98-1749

36:5-7
  SEE: Psalm 66:1-3, 7
  Willan, Healey
  O Be Joyful In God

36:5-7, 9 (paraphrased J. Garth)
  Marcello, Benedetto
  Thy Mercy, Jehovah
  TB   Continuo
  Oxford (1965) (found in Anthems for Men's
      Voices, Volume II)

36:5-9
  Cram, James D.
  Lord Your Constant Love
  SSA or SSATTB   No accompaniment
  Flammer (1973) B-5157

36:7
  Haan, Raymond
  Oh How Precious
  2 part mixed   Organ
  Hinshaw (1978) HMC-305

36:7-9
  Pinkham, Daniel
  How Precious Is Thy Loving Kindness
  SATB   Organ or Piano
  C. F. Peters (1968) P-66100

36:8-11
  Adler, Samuel
  How Precious Is Thy Lovingkindness
  SATB (S or T solo)   Keyboard
  Oxford (1960) 94P 202

37:00   (adapted)
  Morgan, Haydn
  Fret Not Thyself
  SATB   accompaniment ad lib.
  J. Fischer (1972) 10060

37:00
  Young, Gordon
  Fret Not Thyself
  SATB   Organ
  Flammer (1970) A-5540

37:1
  SEE: Psalm 104:14-15
  Browne, Richmond
  Chortos I

37:1, 5, 7
  Hopson, Hal
  O Rest In The Lord
  SATB   Keyboard
  Flammer (1979) A-5834

37:1, 5, 7
  Mendelssohn, Felix (arr. L. Stanley Glarum)
  O Rest In The Lord
  SATB   Piano ad lib.
  Hall & McCreary (1948) 1657

37:1-6
 Bernhard, Christopher (ed. David Streetman)
 Habe deine Lust an dem Herrn (English/
   German)
 SATB   Organ
 Lawson Gould (1974) 51830

37:3-6
 Roff, Joseph
 Trust In The Lord And Do Good
 SATB   Piano or Organ
 Carl Fischer (1964) CM-7433

37:5
 Liebhold (c. 1725)
 Commit Your Life To The Lord
 SATB   Optional Organ
 Concordia (1974) 98-2541 (also found in The
   Second Motet Book, 97-5205)

37:7
 Mendelssohn, Felix (arr. Clarice Knight)
 O Rest In The Lord (Elijah)
 SSCB   Piano
 Cambiata Press (1975) M117567

37:11, 18, 22
 SEE: Psalm 87:17
 Seele, Thomas
 In me transierunt

37:30-31
 Bruckner, Anton (ed. John Finley Williamson)
 Os Justi (English/Latin)
 SSAATTBB   kro
 G. Schirmer (1937) 8121

38:1-2, 21-22
 Blow, John (ed. Heathcote Statham)
 Put Me Not To Rebuke
 SATB   Organ ad lib.
 Oxford (1925) A-204

38:9-10
 SEE: Job 4, 20-21, 23-24
 Cook, Melville
 Antiphon

38:10
 DiLasso, Orlando (ed. Eric Dawson)
 Cor Meum   (Latin)
 SSA or TTB   kro
 National Music Publisher (1973) WHC-33

38:19
 Lassus, Orlandus (ed. Archibald T. Davison)
 Inimici Autem
 TTBB   kro
 E. C. Schirmer (1935) 954

38:19
 Lassus, Roland da
 Inimici Autem   (English/Latin)
 SATB   kro
 E. C. Schirmer (1976) ECS 2981 (also found
   in The Renaissance Singer)

38:21 (Ecclesiastes 12:1-7)
 Mechem, Kirke
 Forsake Me Not, O Lord
 SATB   kro
 E. C. Schirmer (1972) 2733

38:21-22
 SEE: Psalm 22:1-2, 7-8, 14, 17-19
 Greene, Maurice (ed. Percy M. Young)
 My God Look Upon Me

38:21-22
 SEE: Isaiah 53:4-6
 Pasquet, Jean
 A Lenten Meditation

39:00
 DiLasso, Orlando (ed. Lindquist)
 Hear O Lord Hear My Prayer
 SATB   kro
 Elkan-Vogel (1956) 1110

39:00 (taken from)
 Milford, Robin
 Lord, Let Me Know Mine End
 SATB   No accompaniment
 Oxford (1935) A-289

39:1
 DiLasso, Orlando
 Expectans expectavi
 SATB   No accompaniment
 Arista (1976) AE 305

39:5-8, 12-15
 Locke, Matthew (ed. Giles Bryant)
 Lord Let Me Know Mine End
 SSATB (S-S-A-T-B solos)   Organ
 Leeds (1967) #1

39:5-8, 13, 15
 Greene, Maurice (ed. Alfred Davis)
 Lord Let Me Know Mine End
 SATB   Piano
 Music 70 (1972) M70-106

39:5-8, 13, 15
 Greene, Maurice (ed. E. Bullock)
 Lord Let Me Know Mine End
 SATB   Organ
 Oxford (1938) 42.208 (score and string
   parts on hire)

39:12
 SEE: Psalm 61:1
 Kopyloff, Alexander
 Hear My Cry O God

39:12-13
 Young, Gordon
 Hear My Prayer
 Unison Treble   Organ
 Presser (1960) 312-40467

39:13-14
 SEE: Hebrews 11:1, 3-8, 23-31
 Lockwood, Normand
 A Cloud Of Witnesses

40:00 (H. Lute)
 Burroughs, Bob
 Praise The Lord His Glories Show
 SATB   kro
 Abingdon (1972) APM-654

40:00
 Kraft, Leo
 I Waited Patiently
 TTB   No accompaniment
 Mercury (1964) MC 443

40:1
 Mendelssohn, Felix
 I Waited For The Lord (from Hymn of Praise)
 SATB   Piano
 Carl Fischer (1947) CM 6250

40:1-5
 Adler, Samuel
 Psalm 40
 SATB   Organ
 Oxford (1968) 94.209

40:1-5
 SEE: Psalm 96:1-3
 Zimmermann, Heinz Werner
 Psalm Konzert

40:1-7, 10, 19-21
    Arnatt, Ronald
    I Waited Patiently For The Lord
    2 part treble   Organ
    Mercury (1962) 352.00344

40:1, 16, 26
    Young, Philip M.
    Psalm 40
    2 part   Organ
    Augsburg (1969) (found in Music For The
        Contemporary Choir, Volume I)

40:7   (based on)
    SEE: Hebrews 10:7
    Brandon, George (arr.)
    Carol of the Baptism

40:13-17
    Shepherd, John
    Haste Thee, O God
    SATB   Organ
    Oxford (1969) TCM 77

41:7
    SEE: Jeremiah 11:19
    Vittoria, Tomas
    I Was Like An Innocent Lamb

41:12-16   (metrical)
    Haydn, F. Joseph (ed. H. C. Robbins Landon)
    Maker Of All Be Thou My Guard
    SA(T)B   kro
    Broude Brothers (1980) CR-2

42:00
    Betts, Donald
    As The Hart Panteth After The Water Brooks
    SATB   kro
    Associated (1972) A-674

42:00
    Bourgeous, Louis (arr. C. Goudimel)
    As A Hart Longs For The Brooklet   (English/
        French)
    SATB   kro
    Presser (1971) 352.00436

42:00
    Diemer, Emma Lou
    As A Hart Longs
    SATB   Accompaniment ad lib.
    H. W. Gray (1960) CMR 2642

42:00
    Diggle, Richard
    As Pants The Wearied Hart
    SATB   kro
    Hall & McCreary (1946) 1632

42:00
    DiLasso, Orlando (ed. Carolyn Bliss)
    As Pants The Hart
    SSA   kro
    Augsburg (1962) PS 604

42:00
    Hawkins, Gordon
    As The Hart Panteth
    SATB   No accompaniment
    Oxford (1963) A-195

42:00
    Mechem, Kirke
    Why Art Thou Cast Down   Op. 41, #2
    SAB   Piano or Organ
    Carl Fischer (1975) CM-7898

42:00
    Mendelssohn, Felix (arr. Warner Imig)
    As The Hart Longs
    SATB   Piano
    Choral Art (1962) R-167

42:00
    Mendelssohn, Felix
    As The Hart Longs
    SATB   Piano
    G. Schirmer (n.d.) 2081

42:00
    Mendelssohn, Felix (adapted Dale Barker)
    Trust Thou In God
    SATB   Organ or Piano
    G. Schirmer (1962) 10916

42:00   (Tate & Brady)
    Powell, Robert J.
    As Pants The Hart
    SATB   kro
    Jack Spratt (1961) 579

42:00   (adapted)
    Purifoy, John (arr.)
    Psalm 42
    2 part   Accompanied
    Word (1981) CS 2999

42:00
    Shepherd, Arthur
    Psalm XLII
    SSAATTBB   Organ
    C. C. Birchard (1950) n.#.

42:00
    Smith, Larry A.
    Psalm 42 Op. 9
    Unison   Piano or Organ
    Marks (1978) MC 4664

42:00   (Tate and Brady)
    Thiman, Eric
    As Pants The Hart
    SATB   Optional keyboard
    Witmark (1931) 2546

42:00   (Tate and Brady)
    Tye, Christopher (ed. Cyril F. Simkins)
    As Pants The Hart
    SATB   Keyboard
    Concordia (1976) 98-2297

42:00   (based on)
    Warner, Richard
    As Pants The Hart
    SATB   No accompaniment
    H. W. Gray (1961) CMR 2702

42:00   (Tate and Brady)
    Wilson, Hugh (arr. David Herman)
    As Pants The Hart
    SATB   Organ (optional instrument in
        C or B-flat)
    Augsburg (1980) 11-0689

42:1
    Palestrina, G. P.
    Sicut cervus (Latin only)
    SATB   No accompaniment
    Arista (1969) AE 165

42:1
    Palestrina, G. P.
    Sicut cervus (Latin/English)
    SATB   kro
    E. C. Schirmer (1976) (found in The
        Renaissance Singer)

42:1
    Palestrina, G. P.
    Sicut cervus (Latin only)
    SATB   kro
    J. & W. Chester (1977) JWC 55096 (found in
        First Chester Book of Motets)

42:1-2
   Goudimel, Claude (ed. George Lynn)
   Ainsi qu'on oit le cert bruire (English/
        French)
   SATB   kro
   G. Schirmer (1971) 11805

42:1-2
   Lombardo, Robert
   As The Hart Panteth
   SATB   kro
   C. F. Peters (1963) 6455

42:1-2
   Spohr, L. (arr. James Stimpson)
   As Pants The Hart (from Crucifixion)
   SAATB (S-solo)   Organ
   Novello (n.d.) 175

42:1-2
   Willan, Healey
   Like As The Hart
   SATB (S-solo)   Organ
   Concordia (1950) 98-1230 (also found in
        The Parish Choir Book, 97-7574)

42:1-2, 5, 7-8, 11
   Imbrie, Andrew
   Psalm 42
   TBB   Organ
   C. F. Peters (1965) 6888

42:1-3
   Handel, G. F. (arr. Hal Hopson)
   As The Deer For Water Longs
   2 part mixed   Organ
   Agape [Hope] (1980) HH 3914

42:1-3
   Howells, Herbert
   Like As The Hart Desireth The Waterbrooks
   SATB   Organ
   Oxford (1943) 109 (also in Anthems for
        Choirs, Volume IV)

42:1-3
   Palestrina, G. P. (ed. Percy Young)
   Sicut cervus (Just As The Hart) (English/
        Latin)
   SATB   kro
   Broude (1976) MGC 19

42:1-3
   Palestrina, G. P.
   Sicut cervus
   SATB   Unaccompanied
   E. C. Schirmer (found in Concord Anthem
        Book - Red)

42:1-3
   Palestrina, G. P.
   Sicut cervus (Latin/English)
   SATB   Keyboard
   GIA (1978) G-2141

42:1-3
   Palestrina, G. P. (ed. Robert Hufstader)
   Sicut cervus (Like As The Hart)
   SATB   Keyboard
   Mercury (1946) n.#.

42:1-3
   Pierre de la Rue
   Sicut cervus
   SATB   No accompaniment
   Mercury (1947) DCS-36

42:1, 2, 4
   Somary, Johannes
   As The Hart Longs For Running Water
   SATB   No accompaniment
   Galaxy (1970) 1.2476.1

42:1-3, 6, 12-13, 15
   Leighton, Kenneth
   Like As The Hart (from Three Psalms,
        Op. 56)
   TTBB   No accompaniment
   Novello (1974) NCM 34

42:1-4
   Harker, F. Flaxington
   Like As The Hart Desireth The Water Brooks
   SATB   Piano or Organ
   G. Schirmer (1944) 8637

42:1-5
   Kent, Richard
   As The Hart Panteth
   SATB   kro
   Lawson-Gould (1979) 52024

42:1-5
   Williamson, Malcolm
   Like As The Hart (from Psalms of the
        Elements)
   Unison Choir   Congregation,   Organ
   Boosey & Hawkes (1976) 5953

42:1-5
   Young, Gordon
   As A Hart Longs For Flowing Streams
   Unison mixed   Organ
   Presser (1960) 312-40467

42:1-7
   Fitzgerald, Mike (arr. M. Armstrong)
   Psalm 42:   As A Doe
   SATB   Piano
   GIA (1973) G-2032

42:1, 15
   Marcello, B.
   As The Hart Panteth
   SS   Keyboard
   H. W. Gray (n.d.) CMR 3091

42:2-4
   Felciano, Richard
   As The Hind Longs For The Running Water
        (from Songs for Darkness and Light)
   3 part   No accompaniment
   E. C. Schirmer (1971) 2803

42:3
   Ferrabosco II, Alphonso
   Fuerunt mihi lacrimae (Latin only)
   TTBB   kro
   Oxford (1965) (found in Anthems For Men's
        Voices, Volume II)

42:4
   Handel, G. F. (ed. Douglas McEwen)
   With The Voice Of Praise And Thanksgiving
        (from Chandos Anthem, #6)
   SATB   Keyboard
   Carl Fischer (1969) ZCM-106 (oboe and
        string parts   ZCM-106A)

42:4-7
   Aston, Peter
   For I Went With The Multitude
   SATB   Organ
   Novello (1971) 29.0012.02

42:5
   Gibbons, Orlando (ed. Robert Hickok)
   Why Art Thou So Heavy, O My Soul?
   SATB   kro
   Broude Brothers (1954) BB 902

42:5
   Mendelssohn, Felix (ed. Robert S. Hines)
   Hope Thou In God
   SAB   Keyboard
   Schmitt, Hall, McCreary (1966) 5522

42:6
   Gibbons, Orlando (ed. Arnold Payson)
   Why Art Thou So Heavy O My Soul
   SATB   kro
   Franck Music Co.   (1963) F 444

42:11
   Pinkham, Daniel
   Why Art Thou Cast Down
   SATB   Organ ad lib.
   C. F. Peters (1962) 6366

42:11
   Schein, Johann H. (ed. John R. Scholten)
   Why Art Thou Cast Down, My Spirit?
   SSATB   kro
   Concordia (1966) 98-1852

42:11
   Schütz, Heinrich (ed. Paul Boepple)
   Why Afflict Thyself O My Soul   (English/
       German)
   2 voices   Continuo and 2 instruments
   Mercury (1942) MC-20

43:00   (adapted)
   Butler, Eugene
   The Sanctuary of God
   SATB   Organ, 2 Trumpets, Timpani
   Agape (1979) EB-9207

43:00
   Lassus, Orlandus (ed. Paul Boepple)
   Deus auribus nostris (Latin/English)
   TT(B)B   No accompaniment
   Mercury   #21

43:00
   Mendelssohn, Felix
   Judge Me O God
   SATB   kro
   Oxford (1933) (in Church Anthem Book)

43:00
   Mendelssohn, Felix
   Judge Me, O God
   SATB   Piano
   Presser (n.d.) 10406

43:00
   Mendelssohn, Felix
   Richte mich, Gott   (German only)
   SSAATTBB   No accompaniment
   Breitkopf (n.d.) 3564

43:00
   Purcell, Henry (ed. Eric Van Tassel and
       Edward Higginbottom)
   Give Sentence With Me O God
   SATB (T-T-B solos)   Organ
   Novello (1977) 29.0438.01

43:00
   Rochberg, George
   Psalm 43
   SSATBB   kro
   Presser (1956) 312-40298

43:1-3
   Gorczycki, G. G. (ed. J. A. Herter)
   Judica Me Deus (English/Latin)
   SATB   Organ
   GIA (1976) G-1973

43:3
   SEE: Job 3:3-4, 21, 23-24
   Cook, Melville
   Antiphon

43:3   (Psalm 51:9-10)
   Freylinghausen, J. A. (arr. Paul
       Christiansen)
   Create In Me A Clean Heart
   SATB   No accompaniment
   Augsburg (1976) 11-1793

43:3-4
   Latrobe, Christian (ed. Karl Kroeger)
   O Send Out Thy Light And Thy Truth
   SAB   (S-solo)   Keyboard
   Boosey & Hawkes (1979) 6017

43:3-4
   Willan, Healey
   Oh Send Out Thy Light
   SA   Keyboard
   Concordia (1962) 97-7160   (found in We
       Praise Thee, Volume II)

43:3, 5
   Balakireff (ed. Wallace Gillman)
   O Send Thy Light Forth
   SATB   kro
   Presser (1959) G-4002

43:3, 5
   Balakirew, Milya
   Send Out Thy Light
   SSA   kro
   Boosey & Hawkes (1953) 1924

43:3, 5
   Balakirev, M. A. (ed. Nobel Cain)
   Send Forth Thy Light
   SATB   kro
   Hall & McCreary (1933) 1554

43:3, 5
   Balakireff, M. A. (ed. Robert Hallagin)
   Send Out Thy Light
   SATB   kro
   Presser (1960) 312-40444

43:3-5
   Farrell, Michael F.
   Send Out Thy Light
   SACB   kro
   Cambiata Press (1980) C980149

43:3, 5   (Psalm 20:7)
   Gounod, Charles
   Send Out Thy Light
   SATB   Keyboard
   Carl Fischer (1946) CM 6256

43:4-5
   Williams, Frances
   Hope Thou in God
   SATB   Organ or Piano
   Flammer (1967) 84908

43:5
   Berger, Jean
   Why Art Thou Cast Down, O My Soul?
   SATB   kro
   Augsburg (1964) 11-0616

43:5-6
   Loosemore, Henry (ed. Cyril F. Simkins)
   Why Art Thou So Heavy, O My Soul?
   SATB   kro
   Concordia (1979) 98-2437

44:00
   Lassus, Orlandus
   Deus, Auribus Nostris (English/German)
   3 part women   No accompaniment
   Mercury (1942) DCS-21

44:00
   Sweelinck, J. P. (ed. Harold Aks)
   We Have Heard The Words
   SATB   kro
   Marks (1959) 86

44:1-5
   Sullivan, Arthur (ed. Percy Young)
   We Have Heard With Our Ears, O God
   SSATB   Organ
   Broude (1978) MGC-26

44:1-9
   Howells, Herbert
   We Have Heard With Our Ears (#2 of Four
         Anthems)
   SATB   Organ
   Oxford (1943) A 108

44:23   (plus ancient Hebrew poem)
   Adler, Samuel
   Awake, Do Not Cast Us Off!
   SATB   Organ
   Oxford (1969) 94.208

44:23-24
   Byrd, William
   Exsurge, Domine   (Latin)
   SSATB   Optional Accompaniment
   Oxford (1963) TCM-25

45:00   (words from)
   Jackson, Francis
   Audi, filia (Hearken O Daughters)(English)
   SATB   Organ
   Oxford (1961) A-172

45:00   (based on, P. Nicolai)
   Lenel, Ludwig
   O Morning Star So Pure, So Bright
   Unison   Organ or Piano
   Concordia (1958) 98-1452

45:00   (based on, P. Nicolai)
   Nicolai, Philip (setting by Jan Bender)
   How Lovely Shines The Morning Star
   SATB (S-solo) Organ, trumpet, congregation
   Concordia (1975) 98-2260

45:00   (based on, P. Nicolai)
   Praetorius, Michael (ed. Charles Fischmann)
   O Morning Star, How Fair and Bright
   SSATB   kro
   Concordia (1972) 98-2096

45:00   (based on, P. Nicolai)
   Rohlig, Harald
   How Lovely Shines The Morning Star
   SAB   Organ, Trumpets
   Concordia (1965) 97-4687 (trumpets,
         97-4688; choir 98-1795)

45:1, 9, 11
   Handel, G. F.
   My Heart Is Inditing (Coronation Anthem, #3)
   SAATBB   Organ
   G. Schirmer (1970) ED 2836

45:2
   Johnson, David N.
   Verse/The Transfiguration (Verses and
         Offertories - Epiphany II - The Trans-
         figuration of Our Lord)
   Unison   Organ
   Augsburg (1980) 11-9544

45:2, 4, 6
   Pinkham, Daniel
   Grace Is Poured Abroad
   SATB   Optional Organ
   C. F. Peters (1971) 66297

45:2, 8
   SEE: Song of Songs 8:10
   Gregor, Christian (ed. E. Nolte)
   Lord In Thy Presence

45:2, 8
   Nanino, Giovanni Maria
   Diffusa est gratia (English/Latin)
   SATB   kro
   E. C. Schirmer (1976) ECS 2984 (also found
         in The Renaissance Singer)

45:2, 8
   Nanino, G. M. (arr. Archibald T. Davison)
   Diffusa est gratia   (Latin)
   TTBB   kro
   E. C. Schirmer (1935) 949

45:7, 17
   Pinkham, Daniel
   Thou Hast Loved Righteousness
   SATB   Organ ad lib.
   C. F. Peters (1964) 6841

45:14-15
   Bruckner, Anton (ed. Richard Peek)
   Affrentur regi virgines
   SATB   Organ or 3 Trombones
   Augsburg (1968) 11-0626

45:14, 15
   Bruckner, Anton
   Offertorium (from Two Motets)
   SATB   3 Trombones
   C. F. Peters (1959) 6037

45:15, 17
   Bruckner, Anton (ed. Richard Peek)
   Let Us Celebrate God's Name
   SATB   Organ or 3 Trombones
   Augsburg (1968) 11-0626

45:16-17
   Wesley, Samuel S. (ed. John Marsh)
   Constitues eos principes (from Two Motets)
   SSATB   No accompaniment
   Novello (1974) NECM 28

46:00   (adapted)
   Bach, J. S. (ed. & arr. Hal H. Hopson)
   The Lord Is Our Refuge
   SATB   Piano or Organ
   Carl Fischer (1979) CM 8087

46:00   (adapted)
   Beebe, Hank
   Be Still
   2 part choir   Keyboard
   Hindon [Hinshaw] (1979) HPC 7012

46:00
   Bender, Jan
   God Is Our Refuge
   SATB   Keyboard
   Augsburg (1963) PS 608

46:00
   Buck, Dudley (ed. Leonard Van Camp)
   The Lord of Hosts Is With Us
   SATB   Piano
   European American (1978) EA 380

46:00   (Ainsworth Psalter)
   Malin, Don (arr.)
   An Hopeful Shelter and a Strength
   SATB   kro
   B. F. Wood (1963) 829

46:00
   Pachelbel, Johann (ed. Hans Eggebrecht)
   God Is Our Refuge And Strength (English/
         German)
   SATB/SATB   Continuo
   Concordia (1968) 97-6244   (Barenreiter 2872)

46:00   (Carlyle)
   Praetorius, Michael
   A Safe Stronghold Our God Is Still
   TTB   No accompaniment
   Oxford (1965) (found in Anthems for Men's
         Voices, Volume II)

46:00   (Luther)
     Schalk, Carl
     A Mighty Fortress
     SATB   Organ
     Concordia (1966) 98-1842

46:00   (Luther)
     Schein, Johann
     A Mighty Fortress
     2 part treble   Keyboard
     Concordia (1966) 98-1859

46:00   (Paraphrase)
     Schreiber, Frederick C.
     God Is Our Very Hope and Strength
     SATB   Organ
     H. W. Gray (1955) 2391

46:00
     Spayde, Luther T.
     Psalm 46
     SATB   Organ or Piano
     Abingdon (1978) APM-651

46:00
     Wood, Dale
     Psalm 46
     SAB   Congregation   Organ
     Augsburg (1978) (found in Seasonal Psalms
          for Congregation and Choir 11-9376)

46:00
     Zimmermann, Heinz Werner
     God Is Our Defense and Strength
     SSATB   Vibraphone, Harpsichord, Bass
     Agape [Hope] (1975) n.#.

46:00
     Zimmermann, Heinz Werner
     Gott ist unser zu Versicht (German)
     SSATB   No accompaniment
     Barenreiter (1962)   4354

46:1
     Mozart, W. A.
     God Is Our Refuge   K. 20
     SATB   kro
     Concordia (1975) (found in Mozart Anthem
          Book, Volume I 97-5230)

46:1
     Mozart, W. A.
     God Is Our Refuge and Strength   K. 20
     SATB   kro
     Schmitt, Hall, McCreary (1951)   (found in
          Rare Choral Masterpieces)

46:1
     Mozart, W. A. (ed. Kurt Stone)
     God Is Our Refuge   K. 20
     SATB   kro
     Tetra [Alexander Broude] (1965) AB 129

46:1
     Ridout, Alan
     God Is Our Hope and Strength
     SATB   No accompaniment
     Williams School of Church Music [Alexander
          Broude] (1978)   n.#.

46:1-2
     Preston, Simon
     God Is Our Hope and Strength
     SSAATTBB   No accompaniment
     Oxford (1966) A 238

46:1-2, 4
     Distler, Hugo
     God Is Now Our Sure Defense
     SSA   kro
     Concordia (1968) 97-4846   (in Der Jahrkreis)

46:1, 2, 4, 10
     McCormick, Clifford
     Be Still and Know
     SATB   Organ
     Shawnee (1959) A 528   (also found in
          Anthems from Scripture, G-34)

46:1, 3
     Buck, Dudley
     God Is Our Refuge   Op. 57
     SATB   Piano
     Oliver Ditson (1914)   1206

46:1-3, 5-7
     Ouchterlony, David
     God Is Our Refuge and Strength
     SATB   Organ
     F. Harris (1970) HC 1001

46:1-5
     SEE: Psalm 47:1-2, 5-7
     Steel, Christopher
     O Clap Your Hands

46:1-7
     Pool, Kenneth
     God Is Our Refuge and Strength
     SATB   Organ or Piano
     Brodt (1965) 564

46:1-9
     Anders, Charles
     God Is For Us A Refuge and Strength
     Unison   Organ
     Augsburg (1969) 11-0630

46:1, 9-10
     Bard, Vivien
     Be Still and Know That I Am God
     SATB   Piano
     Carl Fischer (1940) CM 585

46:4
     Marcello, Benedetto
     There Is A River
     Unison   Piano
     E. C. Schirmer (1940) 1894

46:4
     Powell, Robert J.
     There Is A River
     SATB   kro
     Abingdon (1966) APM-535   (also in Festival
          Anthems for SAB)

46:4-5, 10
     Lynn, George
     There Is A River
     SATB   kro
     Presser (1973) 312-41013

46:4-7
     Lewis, John Leo
     There Is A River
     SATB   kro
     Lorenz (1966) E-62

46:10
     Fitschel, James
     Be Still
     SATB   Keyboard
     Walton (1974) 2920

46:10
     Glarum, L. Stanley
     Be Still and Know
     SATB   kro
     Bourne (1958)   3G-2

46:10 (adapted) (Ezekial 18:4-9, adapted)
    Morgan, Haydn
    Be Still and Know That I Am God
    SATB   Optional keyboard
    Carl Fischer (1962) CM 7327

46:10
    SEE: Psalm 47:1-2, 5-7
    Woodward, Henry
    O Clap Your Hands

46:10-11
    Wetherill, Edward
    Be Still and Know That I Am God
    SSATBB   No accompaniment
    Flammer (1975) A-5693

46:16-17
    Wesley, S. S. (ed. John Marsh)
    Constitues Eos Principes (Latin)
    SSATB   No accompaniment
    Novello (1974) NECM 28

47:00
    Altman, Ludwig
    Psalm 47
    SATB   Organ
    Transcontinental (1971) TCL-614

47:00
    Beck, John Ness
    The God of Abraham Praise
    SATB   Organ or Piano   Brass
    Beckenhorst Press (1972) BP 1012 (Brass
        parts 1012A)

47:00
    Beeson, Jack
    Psalm 47 (from Three Settings From The Bay
        Psalm Book)
    SATB   Optional piano
    Oxford (1969) 94.332

47:00
    Berger, Jean
    Clap Hands All People   (from Bay Psalm
        Book, Set I)
    SATB   No accompaniment
    Shawnee (1964) A-729

47:00
    Couperin, Francois (arr. Kenneth W. Jewell)
    O Clap Your Hands
    SA   Organ or Piano
    Concordia (1966) 98-1821

47:00
    Couperin, Francois (arr. Kenneth W. Jewell)
    O Clap Your Hands
    SAB   Organ or Piano
    Concordia (1966) 98-1822

47:00   (adapted)
    Cousins, M. Thomas
    O Clap Your Hands
    SATB   Keyboard accompaniment
    Brodt (1959)   527

47:00   (adapted)
    Diercks, John H.
    Clap Your Hands
    SATB   Piano or Organ
    Abingdon (1960) APM-103

47:00   (adapted)
    Diercks, John
    Clap Your Hands
    Unison (optional SATB)   Keyboard
    Choristers Guild (1978) A-199

47:00   (adapted)
    Dunford, Benjamin
    Clap Your Hands
    SATB   Piano   Optional Guitar and Bass
    Belwin (1972) FEC 10061

47:00   (adapted)
    Eddleman, David
    Clap Your Hands
    SATB   No accompaniment   Bongos,
        Cowbells
    Carl Fischer (1978) CM 8039

47:00
    Gabrieli, Giovanni (ed. Paul Winter)
    Omnes gentes   (Latin only)
    SSAT/SATB/ATBB/SATB   kro
    C. F. Peters (1960) 4813

47:00
    Gibbons, Orlando
    O Clap Your Hands
    SSAATTBB   kro
    Oxford (1966) (also found in Oxford Book
        of Tudor Anthems)

47:00
    Gomolka, Mikolaj (arr. Johannes Riedel)
    Let Us Clap Our Hands
    SATB   kro
    Schmitt, Hall, McCreary (1962) 1411

47:00
    Harris, J. W.
    Clap Your Hands, Ye People, Praise the
        Lord
    SATB   Hand clapping   kro
    Pallma Music (1971) PC-796

47:00   (taken from)
    Hopson, Hal
    Antiphonal Praise
    Antiphonal Unison Choir   Organ
    Sacred Music Press (1980) S-255

47:00   (with Doxology)
    Hopson, Hal
    O Clap Your Hands
    SATB   (Optional hand clapping)   Organ
    Flammer (1972) A-5594

47:00   (based on)
    Hunnicutt, Judy
    Clap Your Hands All Ye Children
    Unison   Keyboard
    Augsburg (1971) 11-1632

47:00
    King, Alvin
    Psalm 47
    SATB   Narrator, Organ,   Brass
    Augsburg (1969) 11-9335)

47:00
    Lindh, Jody
    Psalm 47
    SATB   Organ and Trumpet
    Broadman (1974) 4563-02

47:00
    Nelson, Ronald
    Clap Your Hands Stomp Your Feet
    Unison   Keyboard
    Augsburg (found in Music for the Contem-
        porary Choir, Volume 2, 11-9285)

47:00
    Nelson, Ronald
    Clap Your Hands Stomp Your Feet
    Unison   Keyboard
    Augsburg (1971) 11-0649

47:00
    Pelz, Walter
    Psalm 47
    SAB   Organ and Congregation
    Augsburg (1978) (found in Seasonal Psalms
        for Congregation and Choir, 11-9376)

47:00   (taken from)
    Pfautsch, Lloyd
    Sing Praises
    SATB   kro
    Lawson Gould (1967) 51367

47:00
    Powell, Robert J.
    O Clap Your Hands
    2 part   Organ
    GIA (1977) G-2088

47:00   (based on)
    Price, Milburn
    Praise God With A Shout
    SATB   Organ
    Carl Fischer (1973) CM 7815

47:00   (paraphrased by John Patrick, 1679)
    Purcell, Henry (ed. Anthony Lewis and
        Nigel Fortune)
    O All Ye People Clap Your Hands
    SSTB   Organ continuo
    Novello (1966) PSR 11

47:00   (adapted)
    Reynolds, Gordon
    Alleluia! God Is Gone Up With A Merry
        Noise
    SSA   kro
    Novello (1970) CS 127

47:00
    Roff, Joseph
    All You People Clap Your Hands
    Unison   Organ
    GIA (1971) G 1618

47:00
    Schmutz, Albert D.
    O Clap Your Hand
    SATB   Organ
    Abingdon (1976) APM 439   (found in
        Anthems from the Psalms)

47:00
    Shaw, Martin
    O Clap Your Hands Together, All Ye People
    SATB   Organ
    Novello (1967) 03.0137.10 (found in With
        A Joyful Noise)

47:00
    Vaughan Williams, Ralph
    O Clap Your Hands
    SATB   Organ (or Organ, Brass and
        Percussion, or Orchestra)
    Galaxy (1920) 1.5000.1

47:00   (adapted)
    Webb, Charles H.
    Psalm 47
    2 part   Keyboard (optional finger
        cymbals and triangle)
    Choristers Guild (1979) A-207

47:1
    SEE: Acts 1:11
    Martens, Edmund
    You Men of Galilee (from Four Introits,
        Set I)
47:1
    Rohlig, Harald
    O Clap Your Hands
    SATB   No accompaniment
    Augsburg (1963) 11-0607

47:1-2   (Psalm 48:1
    Goode, Jack
    God Has Gone Up
    SATB   Organ
    H. W. Gray (1975) 3332

47:1-2, 4-6
    Shaw, Martin
    O Clap Your Hands Together All Ye People
    SATB   Organ
    Novello (1967) 29.0141.02

47:1-2, 5-6
    Young, Gordon
    O Clap Your Hands
    SATB   Organ
    Oxford (1969) 94.206

47:1-2, 5-7   (Psalm 46:1-5; Psalm 149:1, 3;
        Psalm 145:3)
    Steel, Christopher
    O Clap Your Hands Together   Op. 50
    SATB   Organ or Brass
    Novello (1971) MW 15

47:1-2, 5-7   (Psalm 46:10)
    Woodward, Henry
    O Clap Your Hands
    SATB   kro
    Summy Birchard (1951) B-1568

47:1-2, 5-7
    Wyton, Alec
    Clap Your Hands
    Unison   Keyboard
    Gemini [Alexander Broude] (1977) GP 101

47:1-2, 5-8
    Lynn, George
    Clap Your Hands
    SATB   kro
    Presser (1971) 312-40745

47:1-2, 6
    Cousins, M. Thomas
    O Clap Your Hands
    SSAATTBB   Organ
    Brodt Music (1959) 527

47:1-2, 6, 8
    Lindh, Jody
    Psalm 47
    SATB   Organ, Trumpet
    Broadman (1974) 4563-02

47:1-3, 6
    Bullis, Thomas
    O Clap Your Hands Together
    SATB   Organ
    Novello (1973) 29.0268.00

47:1-3, 6-7
    Gram, James D.
    Praise God With Loud Songs (from Psalms
        of Praise)
    SSA or SSATTB   Keyboard
    Flammer (1973) B-5157

47:1-3, 6-7
    Green, Maurice (transcribed and edited
        C. F. Simkins)
    O Clap Your Hands
    SSATB   Keyboard
    Concordia (1974) 98-2224

47:1, 4-5   (Acts 1:11)
    Titcomb, Everett
    God is Gone Up
    SATB   Organ
    H. W. Gray (1952) CMR 2192

47:1, 5-6
    Weelkes, Thomas (ed. Walter Collins)
    All People Clap Your Hands
    SAATB   Organ
    Oxford (1963) A 193

47:1, 5-8
    Hallock, Peter
    O Clap Your Hands
    2 part choir   Congregation   Percussion
    Walton (1971) 2194

47:1, 5-8
    Newbury, Kent A.
    God Reigns Over The Nation
    SATB   kro
    Flammer (1971) A 5557

47:1-6
    Hewitt-Jones, Tony
    O Clap Your Hands Together
    SATB   Organ   (optional 3 trumpets)
    Novello (1966) MT 1486

47:1, 6
    Roberts, Nancy M.
    Clap Your Hands
    SATB   Keyboard
    Broadman (1967) 4561-69

47:1, 6-8
    Glover, Robert F.
    O Clap Your Hands
    SAB   Organ
    Canyon (1954) n.#.

47:1, 7   (Psalm 48:1)
    Falling, Wilfred
    Clap Your Hands
    SAB   Piano
    Shawnee (1971) D-129

47:1-7
    Milner, Arthur
    O Clap Your Hands
    SAB   Organ
    Novello (1965) 1443

47:1, 7
    Moe, Daniel
    Psalm Concerto (Part III)
    SATB   2 Trumpets, 2 Trombones, String Bass
    Augsburg (1970) 11-0634

47:1-7
    Rutter, John
    O Clap Your Hands
    SATB   Organ
    Oxford (1973) 42.378 (also in Anthems For
        Choirs, Volume 4)

47:1-7
    Vaughan Williams, Ralph
    O Clap Your Hands
    SATB   Organ and Brass
    Galaxy (1920) 222

47:1, 7 (Psalm 95:4, 5)
    Young, Carlton R.
    Clap Your Hands
    Unison and 2 part   Keyboard, Tape
    Broadman (1976) 4560-62

47:1, 8
    Rohlig, Harald
    Clap Your Hands
    Unison   Keyboard
    Concordia (1973) (in Explode With Joy,
        97-5165)

47:2-3, 6-7, 8-9
    Peloquin, C. Alexander
    God Mounts His Throne
    SATB (solo)   Organ (Optional percussion)
    GIA (1971) G-1661 (also in Songs Of Israel,
        G-1666)

47:5
    Byrd, William
    Alleluia, Ascendit Deus
    SSATB   No accompaniment
    Stainer & Bell (1938) 416

47:5
    Byrd, William (arr. & ed. John Kingsbury)
    Alleluia: Our Lord Is Risen (Ascendit
        Deus) (Latin/English)
    SSATB   kro
    Tetra [Broude] (1979) AB 844

47:5
    Clement, Jacques (ed. Carl Deis)
    Ascendit Deus (English/Latin)
    SAATB   kro
    G. Schirmer (1934) 7754

47:5
    Philips, Peter
    Ascendit Deus
    SSATB   kro
    Oxford (1965) 43.452 (also in Oxford Book
        of Tudor Anthems)

47:5-6 (Psalm 68:18)
    Hutchings, Arthur
    God Is Gone Up With A Merry Noise
    SATB   kro
    Novello (1967) 29.0311.03 (also in Short
        and Easy Anthems, Set 2; also in The
        Novello Anthem Book)

47:5-7
    Croft, William (ed. Giles Bryant)
    God Is Gone Up
    SATB   Organ
    Leeds Music (1971) #6

47:5-7
    Croft, William
    God Is Gone Up With A Merry Noise
    SSAATB   Organ
    Novello (1978) NECM 34

47:5-7
    Croft, William
    God Is Gone Up With A Merry Noise
    SSAATB   Organ
    RSCM (found in Festival Service Book,
        Volume 2)

47:6-7 (adapted)
    Glarum, L. Stanley
    Sing Praises
    S(S)AB   kro
    Hall & McCreary (1962) 8013

47:6-7 (adapted)
    Glarum, L. Stanley
    SATB   kro
    Hall & McCreary (1948) 1656

47:6-7 (adapted)
    Glarum, L. Stanley
    Sing Praises
    SSAA   kro
    Hall & McCreary (1956) 2557

47:6-7 (adapted)
    Glarum, L. Stanley
    Sing Praises
    TTBB   kro
    Hall & McCreary (1956) 3510

47:7
   Vaughan Williams, Ralph
   O Clap Your Hands
   SATB   Organ   (optional Brass)
   Galaxy (1920)   1.5000.1

48:00
   Sowerby, Leo
   Great Is The Lord
   SATB   Organ
   H. W. Gray (1933) n.#.

48:00
   Whitcomb, Robert
   Great Is The Lord
   SATB   kro
   Associated (1974) A 699

48:1
   SEE: Psalm 47:1-2
   Goode, Jack
   God Has Gone Up

48:1
   Kirk, Theron
   Great Is The Lord (A Triptych of Psalms)
   SATB   kro
   Kjos (1968) 5489A

48:1   (Psalm 148:1-4)
   Newbury, Kent A.
   Great Is The Lord
   SATB   Organ or Piano
   G. Schirmer (1971) 11813

48:1   (Psalm 84:4; Psalm 33:11-12; Psalm
       89:19)
   Willan, Healey
   Great Is The Lord
   SATB   kro
   Oxford (1952) 43L 322

48:1
   SEE: Psalm 47:1, 7
   Falling, Wilfred
   Clap Your Hands

48:1
   SEE: Psalm 121
   Muro, Don
   I Will Lift Up Mine Eyes

48:1   (based on)
   Williams, Paul and Donna
   Psalm 48
   Unison   Keyboard
   Broadman (1977) 4558-89

48:5 (Psalm 108:5; Psalm 110:3a)
   Lovelace, Austin
   God Is Gone Up
   SATB   kro
   Carl Fischer (1957) CM 6992

48:8
   Elvey, Stephen
   We Wait For Thy Lovingkindness, O God
   SS   Organ
   Oxford (1972) E 131

50:00
   Christiansen, F. Melius
   Psalm 50
   SSAATTBB   kro
   Augsburg (n.d.) 82

50:00
   LeJeune, Claude
   Psalm 50
   SAB   No accompaniment
   Mercury (1945) MC 56

50:1, 3-4
   Marcello, Benedetto (ed. & arr. Robert S.
       Hines)
   The Mighty God
   SAB   Keyboard
   Concordia (1977) 98-2314

50:1, 3, 22
   Stonard, William (ed. John Morehen)
   Harken, All Ye People
   SAATB   Organ and Instruments
   Concordia (1966) 98-1856

50:1-4, 6, 23
   Gibbs, Alan
   God Hath Spoken
   SATB   Organ
   RSCM (1967) 229

50:1-6   (metrical)
   Haydn, F. Joseph
   The Lord Th' Almighty Monarch Spoke
   SA(T)B   kro
   Broude Brothers (1980) CR 14

50:2-3, 5
   Kreutz, Robert E.
   From Zion Perfect In Beauty
   SATB   Organ
   GIA (1976) G-2005

50:2-3, 5
   Track, Gerhard
   From Zion's Beauty (Ex Sion Speoies)
   SATB/SATB and Treble Choir   kro
   McLaughlin & Reilly (1964) 2514

50:3, 8
   Casciolini, Claudio (ed. A. Kaplan)
   Asperges Me
   SATB   Keyboard
   Tetra [Alexander Broude] (1966) n.#.

50:14-15, 23
   Glarum, L. Stanley
   Offer Unto God Thanksgiving
   SATB   kro
   Augsburg (1959) 1242

50:14, 23
   Hillert, Richard
   Offertory/Presentation (Verses and Offer-
       tories - Lesser Festivals)
   Unison   Organ
   Augsburg (1980) 11-9543

51:00
   Allegri, Gregorio (arr. Ivor Atkins)
   Miserere (English)
   SSATB   kro
   Novello (1979) 29.0291.05

51:00
   Hasse, Johann A. (ed. Hugo Leichtentritt)
   Miserere
   SSAA   Piano (strings)
   G. Schirmer (1937) 1580

51:00
   Josquin des Prez
   Miserere Mei Deus
   STTTB   No accompaniment
   Merseburger (1956) EM 550

51:00
   Lekberg, Sven
   Have Mercy Upon Us
   SATB   kro
   G. Schirmer (1968) 11582

51:00
    Leo, Leonard (ed. H. Wiley Hitchcock)
    Miserere
    SATB/SATB   Organ
    Concordia (1961) 97-6371

51:00   (paraphrased)
    McAfee, Don
    A Hymn of Supplication
    SATB   Keyboard
    H. W. Gray (1968) CMR 3033

51:00
    McAfee, Don
    Psalm 51
    SATB   Organ
    McAfee (1974) M 1039

51:00
    Mendelssohn, Felix (arr. Hal H. Hopson)
    Hear, O Lord   (from Christus)
    2 part mixed   Organ
    Sacred Music Press (1981) S-265

51:00
    Pergolesi, G. B. (arr. Hal Hopson)
    O My God Bestow Thy Tender Mercy (arr.
        from Stabat Mater)
    2 part mixed   Organ
    Carl Fischer (1976) CM 7974

51:00
    Wolff, S. Drummond
    Turn Thy Face From My Sins
    SATB   Accompaniment ad lib.
    Concordia (1963) 98-1691

51:1
    Byrd, William
    Miserere mei (Latin only)
    SATBB   kro
    Oxford (1973) (also found in Oxford Book
        of Tudor Anthems)

51:1
    Byrd, William
    Miserere mei   (Latin/English)
    SATBB   kro
    Oxford (1973) TCM 26

51:1
    diLasso, Orlando (ed. Robert E. Wunderlich)
    Lord, O Lord, Have Mercy
    SATB   kro
    Augsburg (1964) 1422

51:1
    Tomkins, Thomas (ed. M. Bevan)
    Have Mercy Upon Me, O God
    SAB   Optional Organ
    Oxford (1963) A-179

51:1
    Tomkins, Thomas
    Have Mercy Upon Me, O God
    TBB   No accompaniment
    Oxford (1965) (found in Anthems for Men's
        Voices, Volume II)

51:1-2
    Byrd, William
    Have Mercy Upon Me O God
    SAATTB   Organ or Strings
    Stainer [Galaxy] (1964) n.#.

51:1-2
    Tomkins, Thomas (ed. R. Proulx)
    Have Mercy Upon Me
    SAB   kro
    GIA (1974) G-1899

51:1-2
    Pinkham, Daniel
    Be Gracious To Me, O God (from The
        Passion of Judas)
    SATB (S-A-T-B-solos)   Organ
    E. C. Schirmer (1978) 3035

51:1, 2, 6
    Vaet, Jacobus
    Miserere mei (from Sechs Motetten)
        (Latin/German)
    SATTB   No accompaniment
    Kalmus (n.d.) n.#.

51:1-2, 10-12
    Kirk, Theron
    Psalm 51
    SATB   kro
    Summy Birchard (1956) 4916

51:1-3, 6, 8-10, 12, 15, 17-18
    SEE: Isaiah 26:9
    Yardumian, Richard
    Create In Me A Clean Heart

51:1-3, 4a
    Oliver, Stephen
    The Elixir
    SATB S-B solos) No accompaniment
        Melody instrument
    Novello (1976) 29.0435.07

51:1, 10, 11, 12
    LeLacheur, Rex
    Create In Me A Clean Heart
    SATB (T-solo)   Organ
    F. Harris (1975) HC 4062

51:2
    Handel, G. F. (ed. Donald Plott)
    Wash Me Throughly From My Wickedness
    TB   Piano or Organ
    Brodt (1960) DC 7

51:2
    Handel, G. F. (ed. Austin Lovelace)
    Wash Me Throughly From My Wickedness
    SA or TB   Keyboard
    Hinshaw (1981) HMC 496

51:2
    Handel, G. F.
    Wash Me Throughly
    SA   Organ
    Oxford (1973) (found in Anthems for Choirs,
        Volume 2)

51:2-3
    Pergolesi, Giovanni (ed. Robert S. Hines)
    Wash Me O Lord God (English/Latin)
    SA   Piano or Organ
    Elkan-Vogel (1973) 362-03146

51:2-3
    Wesley, Samuel S.
    Wash Me Throughly From My Wickedness
    SATB (S-solo)   Organ
    Concordia (1974) (found in The Second
        Motet Book, 97-5205)

51:2, 3
    Wesley, Samuel S.
    Wash Me Throughly From My Wickedness
    SAT (S-solo)   Organ
    E. C. Schirmer (1926) 321

51:2, 3
    Wesley, Samuel S.
    Wash Me Throughly From My Wickedness
    SATB (S-solo)   Organ
    Novello (n.d.) 29.0111.00

51:2, 3
    Wesley, Samuel S.
    Wash Me Throughly From My Wickedness
    SATB (S-solo)   Organ
    Oxford (found in Church Anthem Book)

51:3-6, 12-14, 17
    Peloquin, C. Alexander
    Have Mercy On Me
    SATB   (S-solo)   Organ
    GIA (1971) G-1657 (also found in Songs of
        Israel, G-1666)

51:7
    Haydn, Michael (ed. T. Donley Thomas)
    Asperges me   (English/Latin)
    SATB   Organ ad lib.
    C. F. Peters (1962) 6298

51:8, 11-12, 17
    Wesley, Samuel S.
    Cast Me Not Away From Thy Presence
    SSATTB   Organ
    Novello (n.d.) 29.0127.07

51:8, 11-12, 17
    Williams, C. Lee
    Cast Me Not Away
    SATB   kro
    Novello (1906) 841

51:9
    Casciolini, Claudio (ed. A. Kaplan)
    Cleanse Me, O Lord
    SATB   Keyboard
    Tetra [Alexander Broude] (1966) n.#.

51:9-10
    Davis, Katherine K.
    Renew A Right Spirit Within Me
    SA   (S-solo)   kro
    G. Schirmer (1962) 11017

51:9-10
    Davis, Katherin K.
    Renew A Right Spirit Within Me
    SATB (T-solo)   kro
    G. Schirmer (1962) 11016

51:9-10
    SEE: Psalm 43:3
    Freylinghausen, J. H. (arr. Paul
        Christiansen)
    Create In Me A Clean Heart

51:9-10
    Ruffo, Vincenzo
    Hide Not Thy Face From My Sins (English/
        Latin)
    TTBB   kro
    E. C. Schirmer (1938) 632

51:9, 10, 11
    Attwood, Thomas
    Turn Thy Face From My Sins
    SATB   Organ
    Novello (n.d.) 29.0221.04

51:9, 10, 11
    Attwood, Thomas
    Turn Thy Face From My Sins
    SATB   Organ
    Oxford (found in Church Anthem Book)

51:9-11
    Atwood, Thomas
    Turn Thy Face From My Sin
    SATB (S-solo)   Keyboard
    RSCM [Hinshaw] (1974)   RSCM 503

51:9, 10, 11
    Attwood, Thomas
    Turn Thy Face From My Sins
    SATB   Organ
    RSCM (found in Twelve Easy Anthems)

51:9-11
    Sullivan, Arthur
    Turn Thy Face From My Sins
    SATB   Organ
    Boston Music (1912) (found in The
        Parishonal Choir, Volume 2)

51:10
    Brahms, Johannes, (ed. John Finley
        Williamson)
    Create In Me O Lord, Op. 29, #2 (English/
        German)
    SATBB   kro
    G. Schirmer (1931) 7504

51:10   (Matthew 5:8)
    Larson, Edward L.
    Invocation   (Messenger of Peace)
    SATB with spoken sentences No accompaniment
    Roger Dean (1977) CE 109

51:10, 11
    Sullivan, Arthur
    Turn Thy Face From My Sins
    SATB   Organ
    E. C. Schirmer (n.d.) 171 (also found in
        Concord Anthem Book - Red)

51:10-12
    Attwood, Thomas
    Turn Thy Face
    SATB   Organ
    H. W. Gray (n.d.) 155

51:10, 11, 12
    Brahms, Johannes (ed. John Finley
        Williamson
    Motet from Psalm LI, Op. 29, #2 (English/
        German)
    SAATBB   kro
    G. Schirmer (1931) 2089

51:10, 11, 12
    Bouman, Paul
    Create In Me A Clean Heart O God
    2 part   Organ
    Concordia (1956) 98-1143

51:10, 11, 12
    Burroughs, Bob
    Create In Me A Clean Heart
    2 part   Keyboard
    Broadman (1975) 4551-90

51:10, 11, 12
    Copes, V. Earle
    Create In Me A Clean Heart
    SATB   No accompaniment
    J. Fischer (1956) 8924

51:10-12
    Fryxell, Regina Holmen (adapted)
    Create In Me A Clean Heart
    SATB   No accompaniment
    Abingdon (1963) APM-242 (found in Seven
        Choral Service Settings)

51:10, 11, 12
    Glarum, L. Stanley
    Create In Me A Clean Heart O God
    SATB   kro
    Bourne (1958) SG-4

51:10-12
    Katz, David (ed. Gerald R. Mack)
    Create In Me O God
    SSATB   kro
    Carl Fischer (1980) CM 8112

51:10, 11, 12
    Lahmer, Reuel
    Create In Me A Clean Heart
    SSATBB   kro
    Presser (1964) 312.40575

51:10, 11, 12
    Morgan, Haydn
    Create In Me A Clean Heart O God
    2 part treble   Keyboard
    B. F. Wood (1964) 651

51:10-12
    Norris, Kevin
    Offertory/Ash Wednesday (Verses and
        Offertories - Lent)
    Unison   Organ
    Augsburg (1980) 11-9545

51:10, 11, 12
    Pasquet, Jean
    Create In Me A Clean Heart
    SAB   Keyboard
    Augsburg (1968) 11-0627

51:10-12
    Schalk, Carl
    Create In Me A Clean Heart, O God
    2 part mixed   Keyboard
    Concordia (1969) 98-2543

51:10, 11, 12
    Schütz, Heinrich (ed. Don McAfee)
    Lord Create In Me A Cleaner Heart (English/
        German
    SS or an 2 voices   Continuo
    Belwin (1980) DMC 8091

51:10-12
    Willan, Healey
    Create In Me A Clean Heart O God
    SATB   Organ
    Concordia (1959) (found in The Church Choir
        Book 97-6320)

51:10-12
    Willan, Healey
    Create In Me A Clean Heart O God (in the
        key of E-flat)
    SATB   Keyboard
    Concordia (1959) 98-2238

51:10, 11, 12
    Willan, Healey
    Create In Me A Clean Heart O God
    Unison   Keyboard
    Concordia (found in The Second Morning
        Star Choir Book 97-4702)

51:10-12
    Willan, Healey
    Create In Me A Clean Heart O God
    Unison   Keyboard
    Concordia (1959) 98-2544

51:10, 11, 12, 13
    Mueller, Carl F.
    Create In Me A Clean Heart
    SAB   Organ
    G. Schirmer (1948) 9707

51:10, 11, 12, 13
    Mueller, Carl F.
    Create In Me A Clean Heart
    SATB   Organ
    G. Schirmer (1941) 8682

51:10-13
    Muskrat, Nancy and Bruce
    Create In Me
    SATB   Organ
    Concordia (1977) 98-2311

51:11
    Brahms, Johannes (ed. John Finley
        Williamson)
    O Cast Me Not Away From Thy Countenance
        Op. 29, #2 (English/German)
    SATB   kro
    G. Schirmer (1931) 7505

51:11
    Williams, Ralph E.
    Take Not Thy Holy Spirit From Me
    SATB   unaccompanied
    Kjos (1947) 5095

51:11, 12, 13, 14
    Brahms, Johannes
    Make Thou In Me God, Op. 29 (English/
        German)
    SATBB   kro
    C. F. Peters (1968) 66134

51:12
    Brahms, Johannes (ed. John Finley
        Williamson)
    Grant Unto Me The Joy Of Thy Salvation
        Op. 29, #2 (English/German)
    SSATBB   kro
    G. Schirmer (1931) 7506

51:12
    Lully, J. B. (ed. Ron Nelson)
    Restore Unto Me (from Miserere mei Deus)
    SS   Continuo and 2 violins
    Augsburg (1969) TI-307

51:12-14
    Anonymous
    Schaffe in mir Gott ein reines Herz
        (German only)
    SSAB   No accompaniment
    Merseburger (1977) (found in Motetten
        Alter Meister)

51:12-14
    Hammerschmidt, Andreas
    Schaffe in mir, Gott, ein reines Herz
        (German)
    SSATBB   No accompaniment
    Hanssler (1961) 1.004

51:17
    Greene, Maurice (ed. Richard Graves)
    The Sacrifice of God is a Troubled Spirit
    SSATB   Organ ad lib.
    Summy Birchard (1955) 5306

51:17
    Powell, Robert J.
    The Sacrifices Of God
    SAB   kro
    Abingdon (1966) APM-535 (found in Festival
        Anthems For SAB)

52:11 (German text only)
    Freydt, Johann Ludwig (ed. & arr. Karl
        Kroeger)
    Forever I Praise Thee (Ich danket dir
        Ewiglich) (English/German)
    SATB   Organ or Piano
    Boosey & Hawkes (1981) 6048

53:00 (adapted)
    Lenel, Ludwig
    Rejoice In The Lord
    SATB   Optional accompaniment
    Presser (1968) 312-40693

53:15
    Battishill, Jonathan
    O Lord, Look Down From Heaven
    SATB   Organ
    Novello (n.d.) Anth 184

54:00
    Ives, Charles (Ed. John Kirkpatrick and
            Gregg Smith)
    Psalm 54
    SATB   kro
    Presser (1973) 342.40026

54:00
    Lewis, John Leo
    Save Me, O God, By Thy Name
    SATB   Organ or Piano
    G. Schirmer (1962) 10994

54:00
    Rogers, Benjamin (ed. J. Perry White)
    Save Me, O God
    SATB   Organ
    Concordia (1975) 98-2248

54:1-2
    Hovhaness, Alan
    Save Me, O God   Op. 105
    SATB   Organ   2 Trumpets, 2 Trombones
    C. F. Peters (1968) 66192A

54:1-2, 4, 6
    Hovhaness, Alan
    Behold God Is My Help   Op. 26
    SATB   (B-solo)   Organ
    C. F. Peters (1968) 66190

54:1-2, 7
    Lalande, Michael de (arr. Robert Hines)
    Save Me, O God By Thy Name
    SA   Piano
    Lawson Gould (1967) 51306

54:1-3
    Boyce, William (ed. John R. Van Nice)
    Save Me O God
    SATB   Piano or Organ
    Lawson Gould (1976) 51913

54:1-3
    Willis, Richard
    Hear My Prayer
    SATB   Optional keyboard
    Word (1973) CS 2628

54:1-7
    Purcell, Henry
    Save Me, O God   (English/German)
    SSATB   No accompaniment
    found in Das Chorwerk, #17 (Purcell Funf
            Geistliche Chore)

54:4, 6-7
    Johnson, David N.
    Offertory/Epiphany VI (Verses and Offer-
            tories - Epiphany II - The Trans-
            figuration of Our Lord)
    Unison   Organ
    Augsburg (1980) 11-9544

54:11-13
    Peterson, Wayne
    Psalm 54
    SATB   kro
    Lawson Gould (1959) 818

55:00
    Lekberg, Sven
    Give Ear To My Prayer, O God
    SATB   kro
    Galaxy (1963) GMC 2258

55:00 (based on)
    Mueller, Carl F.
    If Thou But Suffer God To Guide Thee
    SATB   Keyboard
    Broadman (1975) 4565-52

55:00 (based on)
    Neumark, Georg (arr. Jody Lindh)
    If Thou But Suffer God To Guide Thee
    SATB   Organ
    Concordia (1971) 98-2081

55:1-4
    Arcadelt, Jacques
    Give Ear Unto My Prayer   (English/Latin)
    SATB   Organ
    H. W. Gray (n.d.)   60

55:1-4
    Arcadelt, Jacques
    Give Ear Unto My Prayer   (English/Latin)
    SATB   Organ
    Novello (1951) (found in Short and Easy
            Anthems, Set 2)

55:1-5, 22
    Kroeger, Karl
    Hear My Prayer, O Lord
    SATB   kro
    Boosey & Hawkes (1974) 5905

55:1-6
    Greene, Maurice (ed. Percy Young)
    Hear My Prayer
    SATB   (A-T-B solos)   Organ
    Broude (1974) MGC 3

55:1-7
    Mendelssohn, Felix
    Hear My Prayer
    SATB   (s-solo)   Keyboard
    Novello (n.d.) 29-0117-0

55:1-7
    Mendelssohn, Felix (ed. James McKelvy)
    Hear My Prayer
    SATB   (S-solo)   Organ (optional strings)
    Mark Foster (1981) MF 222

55:1, 17, 19
    Jeppesen, Knud
    Hear My Prayer, O God   (from Five Motets)
    SATB   kro
    Broude (1975) BB 5019

55:6
    SEE: Psalm 120:4-5
    Amner, John (ed. Mason Martens)
    Woe Is Me

55:6, 7, 8
    Smieton, J. More
    If That I Had Wings Like A Dove
    SATB   (S-solo)   Organ
    F. Harris (n.d.) FH 2619

55:8   (Psalm 108:4; Psalm 25:3)
    Mendelssohn, Felix
    Cast Thy Burden Upon The Lord
    SATB   No accompaniment
    Concordia (1959) (found in The Church Choir
            Book, 97-6320)

55:22   (based on)
    Anderson, William H.
    If Thou But Suffer God To Guide Thee
    SATB   Piano or Organ
    Carl Fischer (1953) CM 6676

55:22   (Psalm 16:8)
    Bass, Claude
    Cast Thy Burden Upon The Lord
    SATB   Organ or Piano
    Broadman (1961) 4561-07

55:22 (Psalm 108:4; Psalm 25:3)
    Mendelssohn, Felix
    Cast Thy Burden Upon The Lord
    SATB   Organ
    Oxford (1933) (found in Church Anthem Book)

55:23 (adapted)
    Aulbach, Francis E.
    O Cast Thy Burden Upon The Lord
    SATB   kro
    Carl Fischer (1954) CM 6741

55:23
    Mendelssohn, Felix (arr. M. Farrell)
    Cast Thy Burden   (Elijah)
    SACB   kro
    Cambiata Press (1980) M980143

56:9
    SEE: Psalm 28:2
    Diercks, John
    Lord, I Cry Unto Thee

56:10, 11
    Purcell, Henry
    In God's Word Will I Rejoice
    ATB   Continuo
    Oxford (1965) (found in Anthems for Men's
        Voices, Volume I)

56:12-13 (Psalm 93:1, 3; Psalm 111:1, 9-10)
    Lynn, George
    The Lord Is King
    SATB   Optional Keyboard
    Presser (1963) 312-40548

57:00 (taken from)
    Silvester, Frederick C.
    Be Merciful Unto Me, O Lord
    SATB   kro
    F. Harris (1949) n.#.

57:00 (adapted)
    Webb, Charles H.
    Psalm 57
    Unison   Keyboard
    Choristers Guild (1979) A 219

57:1, 8-10
    Diemer, Emma Lou
    Awake My Glory
    SATB   Keyboard (Optional Guitar)
    Abingdon (1976) APM-962

57:1-2
    Perry, Julia
    Be Merciful Unto Me, O God
    SATB (S and B solos)   Organ
    Galaxy (1953) GMC 1947

57:1-2, 8-10
    Schmutz, Albert D.
    Be Merciful Unto Me
    SATB   Piano or Organ
    Abingdon (1976) APM-439 (found in Anthems
        From The Psalms)

57:1, 3
    Glarum, L. Stanley
    Be Merciful Unto Me, O God
    S(S)AB   kro
    Augsburg (1957) 1201

57:5, 7-11
    Butler, Eugene
    My Heart Is Steadfast O God
    SAB   Organ/piano
    Hope (1966) A-378

57:5-11
    Roff, Joseph
    Be Thou Exalted, O God
    SATB   Organ
    Mercury (1965) MC-491

57:6
    SEE: Psalm 66:1-3, 7
    Willan, Healey
    O Be Joyful In God

57:7 (Psalm 103:1-8)
    Harrer, Johann Gottlob (ed. Percy Young)
    My Heart Is Prepared (German/English)
    SATB   kro
    Broude (1976) MGC 18

57:7, 9 (and other)
    Bitgood, Roberta
    My Heart Is Ready, O God
    Unison   Keyboard and flute
    Broadman (1980) 4560-98

57:8   (Psalm 16:10-12)
    Sowerby, Leo
    My Heart Is Fixed, O God
    SATB   Organ
    H. W. Gray (1956) 2414

57:8-11
    Rogers, James H.
    Awake Up, My Glory
    SATB   Organ
    G. Schirmer (1936) 5197

57:9 (Psalm 118:24; I Corinthians 15:20, 57)
    Barnby, J.
    Awake Up, My Glory
    SATB   Piano or Organ
    Pro Art (n.d.) 1209

57:10, 11, 12
    Rossini, G. (adapted E. J. Fitzhugh)
    I Will Give Thanks Unto Thee, O Lord
    SATB (S-solo)   Piano or Organ
    Flammer (1905) A-5046

57:11, 14
    Cousins, M. Thomas
    Glorious Everlasting
    SATB   Keyboard
    Brodt (1959) 504

59:1-2 (Psalm 60:11)
    Parsons, Robert
    Deliver Me From Mine Enemies
    SSAATB   kro
    Novello (1954) 1297

59:17
    Glarum, L. Stanley
    Unto Thee Will I Sing
    SATB   kro
    G. Schirmer (1963) 11053

60:11
    SEE: Psalm 59:1-2
    Parsons, Robert
    Deliver Me From Mine Enemies

60:12
    SEE: Psalm 33:11-12
    Willan, Healey
    In The Name of Our Lord

61:1 (Psalm 39:12; Psalm 25:1-2; Psalm 103:1;
        Psalm 108:5)
    Kopyloff, Alexander
    Hear My Cry O God
    SATB   Organ
    Ditson (1929) 332-13804

61:1
    Tallis, Thomas (ed. Paul Doe)
    O sacrum convivium (I Call and Cry to Thee)
        (Latin/English)
    SAATB   Optional keyboard
    Novello (1972) NECM 26

61:1-2
   Weldon, John (ed. Henry Ley)
   Hear My Crying
   SSATBB   Organ
   Oxford (1960) CMSR 39

61:1-4
   Boatwright, Howard
   Hear My Cry, O God
   SATB   kro
   E. C. Schirmer (1959) 2440

61:1-4
   Hovhaness, Alan
   From The End Of The Earth   Op. 187
   SATB   Organ
   C. F. Peters (1961) 6255

61:1-8
   Lekberg, Sven
   Hear My Cry, O God
   SATB (S-solo)   kro
   Witmark (1948) 5W3331

61:1-48   (Bay Psalm Book)
   Noss, Luther
   Hackney Tune
   TBB   kro
   Associated (1956) AMP 95567

61:5
   SEE: Psalm 8:1
   Willan, Healey
   O Lord Our Governor

61:6-8   (metrical)
   Haydn, F. Joseph (ed. H. C. Robbins Landon)
   Long Life Shall Israel's King Behold
   SA(T)B   kro
   Broude Brothers (1980) CR 15

61:6-8
   Weelkes, Thomas
   O Lord, Grant The King A Long Life
   SSAATB   Organ
   Oxford (1975) TCM 88

62:00
   Pascal de l'Estocort
   Psalm LXII
   SATB   kro
   MCA (1965) L 464

62:1
   Hooper, William L.
   My Soul Waiteth In Silence
   SATB   kro
   Carl Fischer (1972) CM 7785

62:1, 2, 7a
   Willan, Healey
   Truly My Soul Waiteth Upon God
   SA   Keyboard
   Concordia (1953) (found in We Praise Thee,
      Volume I, 97-7564)

62:1, 2, 7, 8
   Sanders, Robert L.
   Truly My Soul Waiteth Upon God
   SATB   kro
   Galaxy (1954) 1.2015.1

62:1, 7
   Wood, John
   My Soul, Truly Waiteth Still Upon God
      (from Two Introits)
   SATB   kro
   Novello (1961) 1388

62:1-8
   Nelson, Ronald A.
   For God Alone My Soul Awaits (from Three
      Psalms)
   SATB   Brass or Woodwind Quintet
   Augsburg (1976) 11-0560   (parts 11-0561)

62:1-8
   Sacco, P. Peter
   Truly My Soul Waiteth Upon God
   SATB   kro
   Foster & Hall (1968) FH 110

62:5-7
   Roff, Joseph
   My Soul, Wait Thou Only Upon God
   SATB   Piano or Organ
   Abingdon (1965) APM-432

62:7-8
   Pfohl, Henry
   In God Is My Salvation
   TB   Organ or Piano
   Flammer (1961) C-5022

63:00 (Paraphrased by John Patrick - 1679)
   Purcell, Henry (ed. Anthony Lewis and Nigel
      Fortune)
   Early O Lord My Fainting Soul
   SATB or SSAB   Organ continuo
   Novello (1966) PSR 8

63:1-4
   Nelson, Ronald A.
   O God, Thou Art My God (from Three Psalms)
   SATB   Brass or Woodwind Quintet
   Augsburg (1976) 11-0560 (parts 11-0561)

63:1, 2, 5
   Weelkes, Thomas (ed. John A. Richardson)
   Early Will I Seek Thee
   SATB   Keyboard ad lib.
   Sacred Songs (1967) CS 316

63:1, 3, 4 (Isaiah 40:31, paraphrase)
   Handel, G. F. (ed. H. Hopson)
   Blest Are They Whose Spirits Long   (from
      Israel in Egypt)
   2 part mixed   Organ
   Choristers Guild (1977) A-183

63:1-5
   Hall, Kay H.
   Psalm 63
   SATB   Keyboard
   Broadman (1976) 4546-06

63:1-5, 8
   Purcell, Henry (ed. Anthony Lewis and Nigel
      Fortune)
   O God Thou Art My God
   SATB   Organ continuo
   Novello (1959) 46.0005.03

63:1-8
   Lekberg, Sven
   O God, Thou Art My God
   SATB   kro
   Kjos (1955) 5192

64:00
   Bassett, Leslie
   Hear My Prayer, O Lord
   2 part children's choir   Organ
   C. F. Peters (1967) 66121

64:00
   Harter, Harry H.
   The Righteous Shall Rejoice
   SATB   Timpani   kro
   Belwin (1964) 2053

64:10
   Lewis, John Leo
   The Righteous Shall Rejoice
   SATB   kro
   Concordia (1957) 98-1391

65:00 (based on)
    Blake, Leonard
    Sing to the Lord of Harvest
    SATB   Organ
    RSCM (1965) 215

65:00
    Goudimel, Claude
    Psalm 65 (The Ainsworth Psalter)
    SATB   kro
    New York Public Library Edition [C. F.
        Peters] (1938) n.#.

65:00 (selections)
    Hare, Ian
    Thou, O God, Art Praised in Zion
    SATB   Organ
    Oxford (1973) A-300 (also found in Anthems
        For Choirs, Volume 4)

65:00
    Steel, Christopher
    Thou, O God Art Praised In Zion
    SATB   Organ
    Novello (1966) 1479

65:1
    Corfe, Joseph (arr. C. Harlar)
    Thou, O God, Art Praised in Sion
    2 part   Organ
    Oxford (1953) OM.1

65:1-2
    Cassler, Winston
    Thou, O God, Art Praised
    SATB   kro
    Concordia (1952) CH-1024

65:1-2
    MacPherson, Charles (arr. C. H. Trevor)
    Thou, O God, Art Praised In Sion
    SS   Organ
    Novello (1971) Chor. Series 126

65:1, 2, 5-14
    Steel, Christopher
    Thou, O God, Art Praised In Zion
    SATB   Organ
    Novello (1966) 11465

65:1-4
    Latrobe, Christian (ed. Karl Kroeger)
    Praise Waiteth For Thee, O God, In Zion
    SATB (T-solo)   Organ or Piano
    Boosey & Hawkes (1981) 6050

65:1-8
    Williamson, Malcolm
    Thou Art Praised In Zion
    Unison Choir   Congregation, Organ
    Boosey & Hawkes (1976) 5924

65:4
    SEE: Joshua 24:15
    Mueller, Carl F.
    Choose You This Day

65:9-10   (and other)
    Rowley, Alec
    Thou Visitest The Earth
    2 part treble   Keyboard
    Boosey & Hawkes (1952) 1912

65:9-11
    Greene, Maurice (arr. Paul Thomas)
    Thou Visitest The Earth
    SS or SA   Keyboard
    Concordia (1957) 98-1817 (also found in
        Morning Star Choir Book, 97-6237)

65:9-11
    Greene, Maurice
    Thou Visitest The Earth
    SATB (T-solo)   Organ
    Oxford (1933) (found in Church Anthem
        Book)

65:9, 11
    Lefanu, Nicola
    The Little Valleys (from The Valleys
        Shall Sing)
    SSSS   No accompaniment
    Novello (1975) 29.0367.09

65:9, 11
    SEE: Genesis 8:22
    Simper, Caleb
    While The Earth Remaineth

65:9, 11-13
    Bullock, Ernest
    Thou Visitest The Earth
    Unison or 2 part   Organ
    Oxford (1954) E 66

65:9, 11-14
    SEE: Psalm 67:5
    Shaw, Martin
    Let All The People Praise Thee

65:9, 11-14
    SEE: Psalm 32:12
    Statham, Heathcote
    Be Glad and Rejoice

65:9, 12
    Greene, Maurice (ed. Watkins Shaw)
    Thou Visitest The Earth
    SATB (S or T solo)   Organ
    Novello (1970) NECM 13

65:9-12
    Greene, Maurice (arr. Henry Ley)
    Thou Visitest The Earth
    SS   Organ
    Oxford (1945) E 41

65:9, 12
    Greene, Maurice (arr. Derek Holman)
    Thou Visitest The Earth
    SAB   Organ
    RSCM (1963) (found in Harvest Festival
        Music)

65:9-14
    Williamson, Malcolm
    Farmer's Earth Psalm (from Psalms of the
        Elements)
    Unison   Congregation, Organ
    Boosey & Hawkes (1976) 5957

65:10-13
    SEE: Deuteronomy 11:14
    Rowley, Alec
    I Will Give You Rain In Due Season

65:14
    SEE: Psalm 104:24
    Barnby, Joseph
    O Lord, How Manifold

65:14
    SEE: Psalm 118:12-13
    Maunder, J. H.
    Praise The Lord Of Jerusalem

65:14
    SEE: Psalm 147:12, 13
    Maunder, J. H.
    Praise The Lord, O Jerusalem

65:14
    Powell, Robert J.
    God's Joyful Harvest
    Unison   2 recorders, Alto metallophone
    Choristers Guild (1978) R-28

65:14
    SEE: Psalm 104:24-28, 33
    Shaw, Martin
    O Lord, How Manifold Are Thy Works

65:14
    SEE: Psalm 103:1, 2
    Smart, Roland
    Praise The Lord, O My Soul

66:00
    Fissinger, Edwin
    O Make A Joyful Noise
    SATB   kro
    Associated (1966) A-515

66:00   (Bay Psalm Book)
    Harter, Harry H.
    O, All Ye Lands, A Joyful Noise
    SATB   Piano
    Belwin (1963) 2026

66:00   (Becker Psalter)
    Schütz, Heinrich (arr. Fred L. Precht)
    Praise God, Ye Lands
    TTBB   No accompaniment
    Concordia (1963) 98-1681

66:00
    Sweelinck, Jan Pieters (ed. M. N. Lundquist)
    Glorify The Lord
    SSATB   kro
    Summy (1939) 1348

66:1
    SEE: Revelation 7:12
    Wagner, C. G.
    Blessing, Glory and Wisdom and Thanks

66:1, 2 (I Corinthians 5:7; I Peter 1:3)
    Gieseke, Richard W.
    Sing Praise To The Lord
    SAB   No accompaniment
    Concordia (1978) 97-5481

66:1, 2 (Isaiah 48:20b)
    Jennings, Kenneth
    With A Voice of Singing
    SATB   kro
    Augsburg (1964) 11-1379

66:1-2, 4
    Beethoven, Ludwig (arr. John Pattinson)
    Make A Joyful Noise Unto God (from Ode to
        Joy)
    SATB (T-solo)   Keyboard
    Carl Fischer (1924) CM 146

66:1, 2, 4
    Fetler, Paul
    Make A Joyful Noise
    SATB   kro
    Augsburg (1966) 1476

66:1-3
    Hovland, Egil
    Jubilate
    SATB (T-solo)   Organ
    Lycke [Augsburg] (1966) ACL 1529

66:1-3
    Zimmerman, Heinz Werner
    Make a Joyful Noise Unto God
    SSATB   No accompaniment
    Chantry (1966) n.#.

66:1-3, 7 (Psalm 36:5-7; Psalm 57:6; Psalm
       145:13)
    Willan, Healey
    O Be Joyful In God
    SATB (S-solo)   Organ
    C. F. Peters (1957) 6073

66:1-4   (adapted)
    Kreutz, Robert
    Let All The Earth Worship You
    SATB   Organ
    GIA (1978) G-2165

66:1-4
    Milner, Arthur
    O Be Joyful In God
    SATB   Organ
    Novello (1964) 1426

66:1, 4, 8
    Rogers, Benjamin (ed. J. Perry White)
    O Be Joyful   (English/Latin)
    2 part mixed   Keyboard
    Augsburg (1977) 11-0667

66:1, 8
    Greene, Maurice (arr. George Brandon)
    Loudly Shout His Praise
    TBB   Keyboard
    Concordia (1976) 98-2301

66:1, 16
    Halmos, Laszlo (ed. Erik Routley)
    Jubilate Deo   (English)
    SATB   No accompaniment
    Hinshaw (1976) HMC 164

66:2-4
    SEE: Galatians 6:14
    Anerio, Felice
    Nos autem gloriari

66:2, 4, 8
    Mueller, Carl F.
    Sing Forth
    SATB   kro
    Carl Fischer (1956) 6876

66:4
    SEE: Psalm 103:1, 2
    Smart, Roland
    Praise The Lord, O My Soul

66:7-13
    Williamson, Malcolm
    The Voice of His Praise (from Psalms of the
       Elements)
    Unison   Congregation, Organ
    Boosey & Hawkes (1976) 5961

66:14-18
    Amner, John
    O Come Hither And Hearken
    SSATB   Keyboard
    Novello (1969) NECM 2

66:14, 17
    Greene, Maurice
    O Come Hither
    SS   Organ
    Oxford (1973) (found in <u>Anthems For Choirs</u>,
       Volume 2)

67:00
    Arnatt, Ronald
    Festival Psalm
    SATB   Organ
    H. W. Gray (1961) CMR 2684

67:00
    Aston, Peter
    God Be Merciful Unto Us
    SATB   Organ
    Novello (1967) MT.1494

67:00
Berger, Jean
Let The People Praise Thee, O God
SATB   2 Trumpets   kro
Tetra [Alexander Broude] (1964) 754
        Trumpet parts sold separately

67:00   (Lyte)
Burroughs, Bob
God of Grace, God of Mercy
SAB   Keyboard
Broadman (1976) 4552-10

67:00
Cartford, Gerhard
Psalm 67
Unison   Keyboard
Augsburg (1979) 11-0673

67:00
Diemer, Emma Lou
Awake, My Glory
SATB   Organ or Piano   (optional guitar)
Abingdon (1976) APM-962

67:00
Fraser, Shena
God Be Merciful Unto Me
SATB   Organ
Sam Fox (1966) 129

67:00
Fryxell, Regina
Psalm 67
Unison   (optional second part)   Organ
H. W. Gray (1954) 2337

67:00
Gordon, Philip
The Sixth-seventh Psalm
SATB   Organ or Piano
Mercury (n.d.) MC 259

67:00   (Psalm 100)
Green, Jane R.
Poetry and Praise   (Two Psalms)
Unison   Handbells
Choristers Guild (1977) A-181

67:00   (based on)
Gumpelzhaimer, Adam (ed. R. Proulx)
O Praise The Lord
SAB   No accompaniment
GIA (1980) G-2294

67:00
Hallstrom, Henry
Psalm 67
SATB   Organ
H. W. Gray (1948) 2045

67:00
Ives, Charles
The Sixth-seventh Psalm
SATB   kro
Associated (1939) A-274   (also in Con-
        temporary Settings of Psalm Texts)

67:00
King, Alvin
Psalm 67
SSATB   kro
Summy-Birchard (1955) 4766

67:00
Martin, Warren
Psalm 67
2 choruses (2 part)   2 pianos
Hinshaw (1981) HMC-414

67:00
Mathais, William
Let The People Praise Thee, O God
SATB   Organ
Oxford (1981) A-331

67:00
McGlohon, Loonis
Lord, Bless and Pity Us
SATB   Keyboard   (optional guitar)
Malcolm Music [Flammer] (1980) A-5892

67:00
Means, Claude
God Be Merciful Unto Me
SATB   Organ
H. W. Gray (1971) CMR-3218

67:00   (based on)
Moe, Daniel
God Be Merciful
SATB   Organ
Augsburg (1956) 1176

67:00   (based on)
Monhardt, Maurice
Let The People Praise Thee
SATB   No accompaniment
Augsburg (1963) 11-0610

67:00
Naylor, Bernard
Deus misereatur
2 part treble   Organ
Oxford (1971) n.#.

67:00
Rogers, Benjamin (ed. J. Perry White)
God Be Gracious To Us   (English/Latin)
TB or 2 part mixed   Keyboard
Augsburg (1976) 11-0665

67:00   (Lyte)
Schalk, Carl F.
God of Mercy, God of Grace
SATB   Keyboard
Concordia (1960) 98-1526

67:00
Schmutz, Albert D.
God Be Merciful Unto Us
SATB   Piano or Organ
Abingdon (1976) APM-549   (found in Anthems
        From The Psalms)

67:00
Schoen, Frank A.
May God Have Pity On Us
Unison   Cantor, Congregation, Organ
GIA (1971) G-1711

67:00
Schütz, Heinrich (ed. Maynard Klein)
Deus, misereatur nostri   (English/Latin)
SATB   kro
G. Schirmer (1973) 11969

67:00
Smith, A. G. Warren
God Be Merciful Unto Us
SATB   Accompanied
Stainer & Bell (1960) 594

67:00
Smith, William (ed. John Whitworth)
Psalm 67
SAATB   Organ
Oxford (1966) A-235

67:00
Staley, F. Broadus
God Be Merciful Unto Us
SATB   Organ
Abingdon (1963) APM-247

67:00
Tchesnokoff, Paul (arr. James Allan Dash)
God Be Merciful
SATB   No accompaniment
Summy Birchard (1962) J5525

67:00   (adapted)
Van Dyke, Paul C.
Prayer for God's Blessing
SATB   Organ
G. Schirmer

67:00
Waring, Peter
God Be Merciful Unto Us
SATB   Organ
E. C. Schirmer (1962) 2494

67:00
Willan, Healey
God Be Merciful Unto Us
SSA   Keyboard
Concordia (1962) 97-7160 (found in We
    Praise Thee, Volume 2)

67:00
Wood, Dale
Psalm 67
SAB   Congregation   Organ
Augsburg (1978) (found in Seasonal Psalms
    For Congregation and Choir, 11-9376)

67:00
Zimmermann, Heinz Werner
Psalm 67
SATB   Organ, Glockenspiel, String Bass
Carl Fischer (n.d.) CM 7857

67:1
Schütz, Heinrich (ed. Walter Ehret)
O God Be Merciful Unto Us   (English/Latin)
SATB   Optional keyboard
Tetra [Alexander Broude] (1975) AB 742

67:1
Tye, Christopher (ed. M. Klein)
O God Be Merciful
SATB   Organ
GIA (1978) G-2142

67:1
Tye, Christopher
O God Be Merciful To Us
SATB   Optional Organ
Oxford (1971) TCM 73b

67:1
Tye, Christopher (ed. P. C. Buck)
O God Be Merciful
SATB   kro
Oxford (1934) (found in Sixteenth Century
    Anthem Book)

67:1, 2, 3, 6-7
Bouman, Paul
God Be Merciful
SS or SA   Organ
Concordia (1980) 98-2471

67:1-3, 7
Fryxell, Regina Holmen
Psalm 67
Unison   Organ
H. W. Gray (1954) CMR 2337

67:1-7
Hovhaness, Alan
God Be Merciful Unto Us   (from Three Motets)
    Op. 259, #2
SATB   kro
Rongwen [Broude Brothers] (1974) RM 3527

67:1-7
Pulsifer, Thomas R.
Psalm 67
SATB   Organ or Piano
Abingdon (1974) APM-820

67:3-4
Powell, Robert J.
Let All The People Praise Thee
SA   Organ
Concordia (1969) 98-1973

67:3, 4   (adapted)
Roesch, Robert
O Make A Joyful Noise To God
SATB   Keyboard
Broadman (1975) 4545-93

67:3-5
Willan, Healey
Let The People Praise Thee, O God
SS   Keyboard
Concordia (1953) (found in We Praise Thee,
    Volume 1, 97-7564)

67:3, 6, 7
Frith, Michael
Let The People Praise Thee, O God
SATB   Organ
RSCM (found in Festival Service Book, #8)

67:4-7
Hammerschmidt, Andreas (ed. Fritz Oberdoerf-
    fer)
Let The People Praise Thee, O God
Unison   Continuo and 2 violins
Concordia (1965) 98-1826

67:5 (Psalm 65:9, 11, 12, 14)
Shaw, Martin
Let All The People Praise Thee, O God
SAT or SAB   Organ
Novello (1947) 85079

67:5-7
Couper, Alinda
Let The People Praise Thee
SATB   kro
Abingdon (1969) APM-854

67:5-7 (Psalm 104:13-15; Deuteronomy 8:10;
    Deuteronomy 16:15)
Harwood, Basil
Let The People Praise Thee, O God
SATB   Organ
Novello (1933) 1187

68:1, 3
Locke, Matthew
Let God Arise
ATB   kro
Oxford (1965) (found in Anthems for Men's
    Voices, Volume 1)

68:1, 3
SEE: Wisdom 1:7a
Martens, Edmund R.
The Spirit of the Lord (from Four Introits,
    Set 1)

68:1-3, 24-26, 34-35
Wills, Arthur
Let God Arise
SATB   No accompaniment
G. Schirmer (1965) 11360

68:1-4
    Williamson, Malcolm
    Let God Arise (from Psalms of the Elements)
    Unison   Congregation   Organ
    Boosey & Hawkes (1976) 5965

68:11, 12
    Crook, Arthur (arr. H. A. Chambers)
    Teach Me The Way
    SA   Piano
    Allan (1956) 280

68:18
    SEE: Psalm 47:5-6
    Hutchings, Arthur
    God Is Gone Up With A Merry Noise

68:18, 32-34
    Pinkham, Daniel
    Thou Art Ascended On High (from Easter
        Cantata)
    SATB   Piano or Brass
    C. F. Peters (1962) 6393

68:20
    SEE: Psalm 135:1
    Nares, James
    O Praise The Lord

68:20   (Psalm 69:16)
    Williams, Frances
    Canticle from the Psalms
    SATB   Organ or Piano
    Harold Flammer (1969) 85523

68:21-22
    Dowland, John (adapted Edward Diemente)
    Insult Has Broken My Heart (from Four Short
        Anthems for Lent and Easter)
    SATB   Organ
    Lawson Gould (1969) 51523

68:28-29
    Aichinger, Gregor (ed. Mason Martens)
    Confirma hoc, Deus   (English/Latin)
    SATB   kro
    Walton (1967) 6016

68:28, 29
    SEE: Acts 2:2
    Aichinger, Gregor
    Factus est repente

68:28, 29
    Byrd, William (ed. Joseph Kerman)
    Confirma hoc, Deus   (Latin/English)
    SSATB   kro
    Novello (1973) 29.0271.00

68:28-29
    Handl, Jacob (ed. Mason Martens)
    Confirma hoc, Deus   (English/Latin)
    TTBB   kro
    Concordia (1962) 98-1655

68:32-33
    Roff, Joseph
    Sing Unto God
    SATB   Accompanied
    F. Pallma (1964) 759

68:32, 33, 34
    Fetler, Paul
    Sing Unto God
    SATB   Optional Keyboard
    Augsburg (1959) 11-1244

68:32-35
    Lewis, John Leo
    Sing Unto God
    SATB   Keyboard
    Lorenz (1965) E.35

69:00
    Cockshott, Gerald
    Psalmus
    SSATBB   kro
    Choral Art (1962) R-168

69:3
    Rameau, Jean Philippe
    Laboravi clamans (Latin)
    SSATB or SATBB   Continuo
    C. F. Peters (1972) 66276

69:14
    SEE: Numbers 24:15
    Gottlieb, Jack
    Mah Tova

69:16
    SEE: Psalm 68:20
    Williams, Frances
    Canticle from the Psalms

69:20
    diLasso, Orlando
    Imporperium expectavit
    SATBB   No accompaniment
    Arista (1973) AE 227

69:29   (Exodus 34:6, 7)
    Brahms, Johannes (ed. Maynard Klein)
    Ich aber bin Elend Op. 110, #1 (English/
        German)
    SATB/SATB   kro
    G. Schirmer (1972) 11950

69:30   (Psalm 92:1, 5)
    Newbury, Kent A.
    I Will Praise God With A Song
    SATB   kro
    Hope (1970) A-420

69:30-33
    Cain, Noble
    I Will Praise The Name Of God
    SATB   Keyboard
    Flammer (1971) A-5576

69:31, 34-36
    Blow, John (ed. Heathcote Statham)
    I Will Praise The Name Of God
    SATB   Organ
    Oxford (1925) A-200

70:00   (Bay Psalm Book)
    Noss, Luther
    Cambridge Short Tune
    TBB   kro
    Associated (1956) AMP-95567

70:00
    Sowerby, Leo
    Psalm 70
    TTBB   Organ
    H. W. Gray (1967) 2995

70:00
    Stevenson, Robert
    Make Haste O God
    SATB   kro
    Associated (1951) 312-40100

70:1
    Hovhaness, Alan
    Make Haste   Op. 86
    SATB   No accompaniment
    C. F. Peters (1961) 6288

70:1
    Martini, G. B.
    Domine, ad adjuvandum in festina
    SATB   Keyboard
    Concordia (1958) 97-6304

70:1
    Pachelbel, Johann (ed. Henry Woodward)
    Deus in adjutorium (English/Latin)
    SSATB   Organ
    Piedmont [Marks] (1969) 15331

70:1-3
    Senfl, Ludwig
    Deus in adjutorium (Latin)
    SATB   kro
    J. W. Chester (1977) JWC 55106 (found in
        Fourth Chester Book of Motets)

70:1-4
    Batten, Adrian
    Haste Thee, O God
    SATB   Organ
    Oxford (1970) TCM 78 (also found in Anthems
        For Choirs, Volume 1)

70:1-6
    Rorem, Ned
    The Seventieth Psalm
    SATB   Organ (instruments available on
        rental from publisher)
    H. W. Gray (1966) CCS-20

70:2
    Lande, Michael de la (ed. Philip Brunelle)
    Lord, Confound them (from Deus in adjutorium)
    SATBB   Organ or Piano
    Salabert (1976) n.#.

70:2
    Zimmermann, Heinz Werner
    Hurry, God, To My Aid
    SSATB   Vibraphone, Harpsichord, Bass
    Barenreiter (1962) also Agape [Hope]
        (1975) n.#.

71:00   (based on)
    Heussenstamm, George
    In Thee, O Lord Do I Hope
    SSA   kro
    Augsburg (1970) 11-1586

71:00
    Van Hulse, Camil
    In Thee, O Lord, Do I Put My Trust
    SATB (S or T solo) Organ
    H. W. Gray (1953) 2314

71:1-3
    Marshall, Jane
    In Thee, O Lord
    SATB   No accompaniment
    Augsburg (1980) 11-0686

71:1-3a
    Schütz, Heinrich
    Herr, auf dich Traus ich (German/English)
    SSATB   Organ
    Hanssler (1971) HE 20.377.02

71:7-8, 10
    Zingarelli, N.
    Go Not Far From Me, O God
    SAB   Organ or Piano
    G. Schirmer (1955) 10335

71:7-8, 10
    Zingarelli, N.
    Go Not Far From Me, O God
    SATB   kro
    G. Schirmer (1935) 4889

71:7-8, 10
    Zingarelli, Nicola (ed. Wallingford
        Riegger)
    Go Not Far From Me, O God
    SATB   Organ
    Flammer (1956) A-5215

71:8, 10
    Zingarelli, Nicola
    Go Not Far From Me, O God
    SAB   Organ
    Flammer (1956) 88586

71:8, 11
    Burroughs, Bob
    He Shall Rule From Sea to Sea
    SATB   Organ or Piano
    Presser (1974) 312-41014

72:00   (Montgomery)
    Bingham, Seth
    Hail To The Lord's Annointed
    SATB   Organ
    Flammer (1967) 84910

72:00   (Watts Paraphrase)
    Dressler, John (arr.)
    Jesus Shall Reign (Duke Street)
    SATB   Keyboard
    Abingdon (1962) APM-165

72:00
    Hatton, John (Setting by Carl Schalk)
    Jesus Shall Reign Where'er The Sun
    SATB   No accompaniment
    Concordia (1965) 98-1797

72:00   (Watts)
    Hopson, Hal (arr.)
    Jesus Shall Reign Where'er The Sun
    SATB   Congregation   Organ
    GIA (1978) G-2135

72:00   (Watts)
    SEE: Psalm 95
    Fetler, David
    Sing Unto The Lord

72:00   (based on)
    Hruby, Dolores
    Alleluia, Sing it, Alleluia
    SSA or SSC   Keyboard
    Augsburg (1980) 1971

72:00   (Watts)
    Thiman, Eric
    Jesus Shall Reign
    SATB   Organ
    Paterson (1936) 1642

72:00
    SEE: Matthew 28:16-20
    Peeks, Richard
    Lo, I Am With You Always

72:2, 7-8, 10-11, 12-13
    Peloquin, C. Alexander
    Lord Every Nation On Earth
    SATB (solo)   Organ (optional brass)
    GIA (1971) G-1656 (also found in Songs of
        Israel, G-1666)

72:3, 18-19   (Psalm 100:1-2)
    Moe, Daniel
    Blessed Be The Lord God
    SATB   No accompaniment
    Augsburg (1962) ACL-1310

72:6-8, 19
    Buck, Dudley
    He Shall Come Down Like Rain   Op. 53, #4
    SATB (S-A-T-B solos)   Organ
    Presser (1913) 332.00465

72:6, 11, 18
    McCormick, Clifford
    He Shall Come Down Like Rain
    SATB   kro
    Shawnee (1953) A-285 (also found in
        Anthems From Scripture, G-34)

72:12   (Isaiah 61:1, 2, 3, 11)
    Parry, C. Hubert
    He Delivered The Poor (from Hear My Words,
        Ye People)
    S   Organ
    RSCM (1971) 239

72:18-19
    Amner, John
    Blessed Be The Lord God
    SATB   Keyboard
    Novello (1969) MT 1521

72:18-19
    Copley, R. Evan
    Blessed Be The Lord God (from Three Anthems
        Based on Canons)
    2 part   Keyboard
    Abingdon (1974) APM-448

72:18-19
    SEE: II Chronicles 7:1-3
    Elmore, Robert
    The Fire Came Down

72:18-19
    Mason, Lowell (ed. Elwyn Wienandt)
    Blessed Be The Lord God of Israel (from
        Two Thanksgiving Anthems)
    SATB   No accompaniment
    Hope (1974) US-1772

73:1
    SEE: II Chronicles 7:1-3
    Elmore, Robert
    The Fire Came Down

73:25, 26
    Marshall, Jane
    Whom Have I
    SAB   No accompaniment
    Augsburg (1978) 11-0677

73:25-26, 28
    Bender, Jan
    Whom Have I In Heaven But Thee? Op. 24, #1
    SATB   kro
    Concordia (1962) 98-1637

74:1, 2
    Child, William (ed. Peter le Huray)
    O God, Wherefore Art Thou Absent From Us
    SATB   Optional accompaniment
    Blandford [Alexander Broude] (1965) AB 218

74:1, 21
    Hovhaness, Alan
    Why Hast Thou Cut Us Off
    SATB   kro
    Associated (1955) AMP-95511

74:2, 4 (Psalm 76:4, 5)
    Wienhorst, Richard
    O Lord Thine Enemies Roar
    SATB   kro
    Associated (1961) AMP-345 (also found in
        Contemporary Settings of Psalms)

74:4, 8-9, 14
    Purcell, Henry (ed. F. Blume)
    Lord, How Long Wilt Thou Be Angry
    SSATB   No accompaniment
    Arista (n.d.) AE 115

74:12
    SEE: Psalm 135:1-3
    Willan, Healey
    O Praise The Lord

75:00
    Campra, Andre (ed. M. Couraud)
    Tibi confegit (Latin only)
    SATBB   Organ
    Mark Foster (1974) MF 194

75:00
    Glarum, L. Stanley
    We Give Thanks To Thee
    SAB   Optional Organ or Piano
    G. Schirmer (1965) 11292   (also available
        in SATB, and SSA)

75:00
    Sweelinck, J. P. (ed. Thomas Dunn)
    O Lord God, To Thee Be Praise (English/
        French)
    SATB   Organ
    E. C. Schirmer (1971) 2792

75:1
    Hovhaness, Alan
    Unto Thee O God
    SATB   kro
    Associated (1955) (also found in Contempo-
        rary Settings Of Psalm Texts, APM-6910)

75:1
    Parker, Alice
    Give Thanks (from Sunday Rounds)
    4 part round   No accompaniment
    Hinshaw (1973) HMC 106

75:1, 9
    Sweelinck, J. P.
    O Lord God To Thee Be Praise (English/
        French)
    SATB   kro
    G. Schirmer (1926) 2620

75:3
    SEE: Isaiah 57:1-2
    Handl, Jacob
    Ecce quomodo moritur justus (Arista Edition)

75:9-10
    Anerio, Felice (adapted Edward Diemente)
    The Earth Feared
    SATB   Organ
    Lawson Gould (1969) 51523

76:2
    SEE: Isaiah 57:1-2
    Handl, Jacob
    Ecce quomodo moritur justus (E. C. Schirmer)

76:4, 5
    SEE: Psalm 75:2, 4
    Wienhorst, Richard
    O Lord, Thine Enemies Roar

76:15, 16
    Reisberg, Horace
    Quinquagesima Sunday, Gradual, Tract
    Unison   Organ
    World Library (1968) EMP-1512

77:00
    Buck, Dudley
    He Shall Come Down Like Rain
    SATB   Organ
    Oliver Ditson

77:1, 2, 7, 9, 12, 13 (adapted)
    Land, Lois
    I Cry Aloud To God
    SATB (A-solo)   Organ
    Plymouth (1978) SC-53

77:2
    Guami, Giuseppi
    In die tribulationis (Latin)
    SATTB   No accompaniment
    Oxford (1980) (found in Ten Venetian Motets)

77:18b   (Psalm 84:1, 2a)
    Martens, Edmund
    The Lightnings Lightened The World (from
        Four Introits, Set II)
    Unison   Handbells
    Concordia (1979) 97-5467

78:1-3
    McCormick, Clifford
    As Smoke Is Driven Away
    SATB   No accompaniment
    Shawnee (1954) (also found in <u>Anthems</u> <u>From</u>
        <u>Scripture</u> G-34)

78:32
    SEE: Matthew 29:1-2, 5-6
    Vincent, Charles
    As It Began To Dawn

79:2
    Binkerd, Gordon
    From Your Throne, O Lord
    Unison   Organ
    Boosey & Hawkes   5826

79:5, 8, 9, 13
    Purcell, Henry (ed. Paul Boepple)
    Lord, How Long Wilt Thou Be Angry
    SSATB   Organ <u>ad lib.</u>
    Mercury (1946) MC-35

79:5, 8, 9, 14
    Purcell, Henry (ed. J. A. Westtrap)
    Lord How Long Wilt Thou Be Angry?
    SSATB   Organ <u>ad lib.</u>
    Novello (1944) 29.0144.07

79:8
    Purcell, Henry
    O Remember Not
    ATB   No accompaniment
    Oxford (1965) (found in <u>Anthems</u> <u>For</u> <u>Men's</u>
        <u>Voices</u>, Volume I)

79:14
    Greene, Maurice (ed. Mason Martens)
    So We That Are Thy People (from Sing We
        Merrily)
    SATB   Keyboard
    Walton (1972) M-122

80:00
    Christiansen, Paul
    Bread of Tears
    SSAATB   kro
    Augsburg (1948) 1058

80:00
    Diercks, John
    How Long, O Lord
    SATB   Organ
    Dow (1960) W 304

80:1
    Bach, J. S.
    Kantate #104 Du Hirte Israel Höre
        (German)
    SATB   Keyboard
    Breitkopf & Hartel (n.d.) 6370

80:1-2
    Ierley, Merritt
    Hear, O Thou Shepherd Of Israel
    SATB   Keyboard
    Concordia (1973) 98-2162

80:1-3
    Palestrina, G. P. (ed. Henry Washington)
    Exsultate Deo (Latin)
    SAATB   kro
    J. & W. Chester (1958) JWC 8794

80:1-3
    Proulx, Richard
    Advent Anthem
    SATB   Organ
    Augsburg (1969) 11-1559

80:1-3
    Proulx, Richard
    From Thy Throne O Lord
    SATB   Organ
    GIA (1969) G-2404

80:1-4, 6-7
    SEE: Psalm 103:10-16
    Sowerby, Leo
    A Liturgy Of Hope

80:4-7, 18
    Purcell, Henry (ed. Anthony Lewis and Nigel
        Fortune)
    O Lord God Of Hosts
    SSAATTBB   Organ
    Novello (1958) 46.0002.09

80:16
    Byrd, William
    Cibavit eos (Latin)
    SATB   kro
    J. & W. Chester (1977) JWC 55103 (found in
        <u>Second</u> <u>Chester</u> <u>Book</u> <u>of</u> <u>Motets</u>)

80:19 (John 15:4-5, 10, 12)
    Wyatt, Noel
    Turn Us Again, O Lord God Of Hosts
    SATB   Piano or Organ
    Flammer (1962) 84702

81:00
    Effinger, Cecil
    Sing We Merrily
    SATB   Organ (or Organ & Strings, or
        Full Orchestra)
    H. W. Gray (1949) #6

81:00
    Hassler, Hans Leo
    Exsultate Deo (Latin)
    SSATB   No accompaniment
    Arista (1978) AE 291

81:00
    Howells, Herbert
    Exultate Deo (English)
    SATB   Organ
    Oxford (1977) A-322

81:00
    Ives, Grayston
    Sing Joyfully
    SATB   Organ
    Banks (1980)

81:00 (taken from)
    Moe, Daniel
    Sing Aloud To God Our Strength
    SATB   Organ & 2 Trumpets
    J. Fischer (1964) 9579

81:00
    Najera, Edmund
    Exultate Deo (Latin)
    SATB   Piano
    G. Schirmer (1974) 12011

81:00
    Parker, Alice and Robert Shaw (arr.)
    Psalm 81
    SATB   No accompaniment
    G. Schirmer (n.d.) 585

81:00
    Poulenc, Francis
    Exultate Deo (Latin)
    SATB   No accompaniment
    Salabert (1941) n.#.

81:00
    Sweelinck, Jan P. (ed. T. A. Anderson)
    Psalm 81: O Sing With Full Voice (English/
        French)
    SSATTB   No accompaniment
    Mark Foster (1972) MF 127

81:00
    Wyton, Alec
    Sing Joyfully
    2 part treble   Organ
    Beekman (1964) MC 457

81:1
    Greene, Maurice (ed. Mason Martens)
    Sing We Merrily
    SATB   Keyboard
    Walton (1972) 2300

81:1
    Greene, Maurice (ed. Mason Martens)
    Sing We Merrily (from Sing We Merrily)
    SATB (S-A-T solos)   Keyboard
    Walton (1972) M-122

81:1
    Greene, Maurice (ed. Mason Martens)
    Sing We Merrily (first chorus from Sing We
        Merrily)
    SSATB   Keyboard
    Walton (1972) W 2300

81:1
    Palestrina, G. P. (ed. John F. Williamson)
    Exultate Deo (Sing and Praise Jehovah)
        (English/Latin)
    SAATB   kro
    G. Schirmer (1933) 7672

81:1
    Scarlatti, Alessandro
    Exsultate Deo
    SATB   No accompaniment
    Arista (1968) AE 113

81:1
    Scarlatti, Alessandro (ed. C. Buell Agey)
    Exultate Deo (Latin/English)
    SATB   kro
    G. Schirmer (1963) 11001

81:1
    Scarlatti, Alessandro (ed. Fritz Rikko)
    Exultate Deo (Latin)
    SATB   kro
    Marks (1955) MC 76

81:1
    Scarlatti, Alessandro (ed. Maurits Kesnar)
    Exultate Deo (Latin)
    SATB   kro
    Elkan Vogel (1943) n.#.

81:1
    Scarlatti, Alessandro (ed. Robert McDowell)
    Sing Aloud With Gladness (Latin/English)
    SATB   kro
    RSCM (1973) 252

81:1-2 (Psalm 92:1, 4)
    Powell, Robert J.
    Sing We Merrily (from Anthems for Treble
        Voices)
    SA   Organ
    Abingdon (1976) APM-512

81:1-2
    Wesley, Samuel
    Sing Aloud With Gladness (English/Latin)
    SSATB   Organ
    Worldwide Music (n.d.) n.#.

81:1-3 (adapted)
    Clawson, Donald
    Sing We Merrily Unto God
    2 part youth   Organ
    H. W. Gray (1966) CMR 2938

81:1-3
    Hackenberger, Andreas (ed. Dennis Sparger)
    Exultate Deo (Latin)
    SATB/SATB   No accompaniment
    Mark Foster (1982) MF 418

81:1-3
    King, Gordon
    Sing We Merrily
    SATB   Organ
    Mark Foster (1980) MF 196

81:1-3 (Psalm 84:1, 4)
    Kirk, Theron
    A Psalm Of Joy
    SATB   Keyboard
    Carl Fischer (1981) CM 8137

81:1-3 (Psalm 148:12)
    Lefebvre, Channing
    Sing We Merrily
    SATB   Organ
    H. W. Gray (1960) 2677

81:1-3
    Marsh, John
    Sing We Merrily
    SATB   Organ and 3 Trumpets
    Oxford (1980) A-328

81:1-3
    Ossewaarde, Jack H.
    Sing We Merrily
    SATB   Organ
    H. W. Gray (1969) CMR 3074

81:1-3
    SEE: Psalm 16:7
    Phillips, John C.
    The Lot Is Fallen Unto Me

81:1-3 (Psalm 84:4-7)
    Shaw, Martin
    Sing We Merrily Unto God Our Strength
    SATB/SATB   kro
    Novello (1960) Anth 1181

81:1-3
    Symons, Christopher
    Sing We Merrily
    SS   Organ
    Oxford (1968) E-114 (also found in Anthems
        For Choirs, Volume 2)

81:1-3, 5, 13, 14-16, 18
    Hedges, Anthony
    Hold Not Thy Tongue, O God
    SATB   Organ
    Novello (1959) Anth 1364

81:1, 2, 3, 14, 15   (Psalm 98: 6, 7)
    Orr, Robin
    Sing Aloud Unto God
    SATB   Organ
    Oxford (1968) A-261

81:1-4
    Batten, Adrian (ed. John E. West)
    Sing We Merrily Unto God
    SATB   Keyboard
    Novello (1906) Anth 856

81:1-4
    Batten, Adrian (ed. M. Bevan)
    O Sing Joyfully
    SATB   kro
    Oxford (1960) (found in Sixteenth Century
        Anthem Book)

81:1-4
Byrd, William
Sing Joyfully
SSAATB   Organ
Stainer & Bell (1948) #559

81:1-4
Byrd, William
Sing Joyfully
SSAATB   Organ
Oxford (1978) (found in Oxford Book Of
    Tudor Anthems)

81:1-4
Batten, Adrian (ed. John Morehan)
O Sing Joyfully
SATB   Keyboard
RSCM (1967) 228

81:1-4
Byrd, William (ed. George J. Bennett)
Sing Joyfully Unto God
SSATTB   Organ ad lib.
Novello (n.d.) 29.0132.03

81:1-4
Campbell, Sidney
Sing We Merrily Unto God Our Strength
SATB   Organ
Novello (1962) 29.0253.02

81:1-4
Carpenter, Adrian
Sing We Merrily
SSATB   kro
Oxford (1972) A 298

81:1-4
Jones, Howard
Sing Aloud
SATB   Organ
Novello (1976) 29.0380.06

81:1-4
Mundy, John (ed. Edmund H. Fellowes)
Sing Joyfully
SSATB (B-solo)   Organ or Strings
Oxford (1975) TCM 92

81:1-4
Proulx, Richard
Sing We Merrily
SATB   Organ   2 Trumpets, 2 Trombones
GIA (1971) G-2403

81:1-4
Rimmer, Frederick
Sing We Merrily
SATB   Organ
Novello (1963) MT 1443

81:16
Mozart, W. A.
Cibavit eos (He Fed Them Also) K. 44
    (English/Latin)
SATB   kro
Concordia (1974) (found in Mozart Anthem
    Book, Volume 1, 97-5230)

83:1
Goode, Jack C.
O God Do Not Keep Silence (Prayer Intona-
    tions)
Unison   Organ
Abingdon (1974) APM-516

83:1
Hovhaness, Alan
Keep Not Thou Silence
SATB   kro
Associated (1950) A-207 (also found in
    AMP Contemporary Choral Collections)

83:1   (Psalm 86:10)
Pergolesi, Giovanni (ed. Roger Forester)
Be Not Silent Unto Us
SATB   kro
Schmitt (1965) 1421

83:1-3, 5, 13-16, 18
Hedges, Anthony
Hold Not Thy Tongue, O God
SATB   Organ
Novello (1959) Anth   1364

84:00
Berger, Jean
How Amiable Are Thy Tabernacles
SATB/SATB   Organ (optional Handbells)
Abingdon (1969) APM-695

84:00   (adapted)
Dieterich, Milton
Psalm Eighty-four
SATB   Piano ad lib.
Pro Art   (1956) 1643

84:00   (paraphrased)
Faure, Gabriel (arr. Hal H. Hopson)
Psalm 84: Cantique de Jean Racine
SATB   Organ or Piano
Carl Fischer (1978) CM 8042

84:00
Gideon, Miriam
How Goodly Are Thy Tents
SATB   kro
Merrymount (1959) MC 350

84:00   (taken from)
Greene, Maurice (ed. Richard Craves)
The Lord God Is A Light
SS   Piano
G. Schirmer (1956) 10491

84:00
Hammerschmidt, Andreas (ed. Don Malin)
How Lovely Is Thine Own Dwelling Place
SSATB   Keyboard
Belwin Mills (1981) OCT 2436

84:00   (adapted)
Hunter, Ralph
O Lord Of Hosts
SSAA   Organ
Marks (1970) 4507

84:00
Kirk Theron
How Lovely Are Thy Dwellings
SATB   Piano
G. Schirmer (1980) 12406

84:00
Kubik, Gail
How Lovely Thy Place
SATB   Unaccompanied
H. W. Gray (1953)

84:00
Maslen, Benjamin
The House of God
SATB   Organ
Novello (1969) MW 9

84:00
Mason, Lowell (arr. Leonard Van Camp)
How Lovely Are Thy Dwellings
SATB (S-S-solos)   kro
Boonin (1976) 289

84:00   (Paraphrase Watts)
Noble, T. Tertius
Lord Of The Worlds Above
SATB   Organ
Galaxy (1940) 1047

84:00   (Scottish Psalter)
     Powell, Robert J.
     How Lovely Is Thy Dwelling Place
     SAB   Piano
     Choristers Guild (1972) A-113

84:00   (John Milton)
     Proulx, Richard
     Psalm 84
     SATB   kro
     GIA (1976) G-1706

84:00   (Becker Psalter)
     Schütz, Heinrich (arr. Fred L. Precht)
     How Lovely Is Thy Dwelling
     TTBB   No accompaniment
     Concordia (1963) 98-1681

84:00
     Schütz, Heinrich (ed. Paul Boepple)
     To Me In Joy Returning (English/German)
     SATB   No accompaniment
     Mercury (1941) 352-00006

84:00   (edited)
     Sowerby, Leo
     Behold, O God Our Defender
     SATB   Organ
     H. W. Gray (1966) CMR 2919

84:00   (adapted)
     Standford, Patric
     How Amiable Are Thy Dwellings
     SATB   Organ
     Novello (1971) NCM 30

84:00   (Milton)
     Thiman, Eric
     How Lovely Are Thy Dwellings Fair
     SS   Organ
     Novello (1939) Chor. Ser. 78

84:00   (adapted)
     Thiman, Eric
     Lord Of The Worlds Above
     SATB   Organ
     H. W. Gray (1958) CMR 2555

84:00   (Psalm 90)
     Vaughan Williams, Ralph
     O How Amiable
     SATB   Organ
     Oxford (1940) 42P 056 (also found in
          Anthems for Choirs, Volume 4; and
          Oxford Easy Anthem Book)

84:00
     Widor, Charles-Marie (ed. Philip Brunelle)
     How Lovely Are Thy Temples
     SATB   Organ
     Salabert (1976) n.#.

84:00
     Willan, Healey
     Oh How Amiable Are Thy Dwellings
     SS   Keyboard
     Concordia (1953) (found in We Praise Thee,
          Volume I, 97-7564)

84:00   (Milton)
     Williams, David H.
     How Lovely Are Thy Dwellings Fair
     SATB   Organ
     Broadman (1964) 453-739

84:1, 2
     Campra, Andre
     Quam dilecta tabernacula
     SAB   Organ
     Arista (1977) AE 266

84:1, 2   (based on)
     Latrobe, Christian (ed. V. Nolte)
     How Sweet Thy Dwellings Lord
     ST   Keyboard
     Brodt (1968) 1007

84:1, 2a
     SEE: Psalm 77:18b
     Martens, Edmund
     The Lightnings Lightened The World

84:1, 2
     SEE: Genesis 28:17
     Rubbra, E.
     This Is Truly The House Of God

84:1-2
     Tomkins, Thomas (ed. Maurice Bevan)
     O How Amiable Are Thy Dwellings
     ATBB   Organ
     Oxford (1961) CMS 38

84:1-2, 4
     Brahms, Johannes (arr. Ivor Atkins)
     We Love The Place Where Thine Honor Dwells
     SSA   Piano
     Oxford (1935) 1623

84:1, 2, 4
     Brahms, Johannes
     How Lovely Is Thy Dwelling Place (German
          Requiem)
     SATB   Piano
     G. Schirmer (n.d.) 5124   (also in Second
          Concord Anthem Book, Grey)

84:1, 2, 4
     Brahms, Johannes (ed. John E. West)
     How Lovely Are Thy Dwellings
     SATB   Organ
     Novello (1938) 29.0130.07

84:1, 2, 4
     Brahms, Johannes
     How Lovely Is Thy Dwelling Place
     SATB   Keyboard
     Carl Fischer (1953) CM 632

84:1, 2, 4
     Brahms, Johannes (arr. C. C. Palmer)
     We Love The Place   (Requiem)
     SATB   Keyboard
     Oxford (1933) (found in Church Anthem Book)

84:1-2, 4
     Gardner, John
     O How Amiable
     SATB   Organ
     Oxford (1965) A 225

84:1, 2, 4
     SEE: Luke 2:48, 49
     Schütz, Heinrich
     My Son, Wherefore Hast Thou Done This To
          Me?

84:1, 2, 13
     Weelkes, Thomas
     O How Amiable
     SAATB   Organ
     Oxford (1965) TCM-90

84:1-3
     Geisler, Johann C. (ed. E. V. Nolte)
     How Lovely Is Thy Dwelling Place (English/
          German)
     SSAB   Organ
     Boosey & Hawkes (1965) 5606

84:1-3
    West, John E.
    O How Amiable Are Thy Dwellings
    SATB   Organ
    G. Schirmer (1931) 4364

84:1-3, 8, 10
    Liddle, Samuel (arr. Kenneth Runkel)
    How Lovely Are Thy Dwellings
    3-choirs: Unison, SAB & SATB   Organ
    Boosey & Hawkes (1956) 5221

84:1-3, 8, 10
    Liddle, Samuel (arr. Noble Cain)
    How Lovely Are Thy Dwellings
    SSA   Keyboard
    Boosey & Hawkes (1946) 1758

84:1-3, 8, 10
    Liddle, Samuel (arr. W. Howorth)
    How Lovely Are Thy Dwellings
    SAB   Keyboard
    Boosey & Hawkes (1940) 1614

84:1-3, 8, 10
    Liddle, Samuel (arr. C. A. Rowley)
    How Lovely Are Thy Dwellings
    SATB   Organ
    Boosey & Hawkes (1941) H-15316

84:1-3, 8, 10
    Liddle, Samuel (arr. A. Samuelson)
    How Lovely Are Thy Dwellings
    2 part   Keyboard
    Boosey & Hawkes (1936) 1493

84:1, 4
    SEE: Psalm 81:1-3
    Kirk, Theron
    A Psalm Of Joy

84:1-4
    SEE: I Kings 8:13, 27-28
    Milner, Anthony
    I Have Surely Built Thee

84:1-4
    Sateren, Leland
    Lord God of Hosts, How Lovely
    SSAATTBB   kro
    Gamble Hinged Music (1955) 1734

84:1-9, 12, 13
    Leighton, Kenneth
    Quam Dilecta! (English)
    SATB (S-solo) kro
    Novello (1967) Anth 1471

84:1-13
    Williamson, Malcolm
    Morning Air Psalm (from Psalms of the
        Elements)
    Unison choir   Congregation, Organ
    Boosey & Hawkes (1976)   5949

84:2-3
    Telemann, G. P.
    Wie lieblich sind deine Wohnungen (English/
        German)
    SSB or SS   Organ continuo, 2 violins
    Hanssler (1972) HE 39.016

84:2-5, 13
    SEE: Psalm 122:1
    Arnatt, Ronald
    I Was Glad

84:4
    SEE: 48:1
    Willan, Healey
    Great Is The Lord

84:4
    SEE: Psalm 135:1-3
    Willan, Healey
    O Praise The Lord

84:4, 5, 12
    Glarum, L. Stanley
    Blessed Are They
    SATB   kro
    Carl Fischer (1964) CM 7431

84:4-7
    SEE: Psalm 81:1-3
    Shaw, Martin
    Sing We Merrily Unto God

84:4-8
    Berger, Jean
    How Lovely Are Thy Tabernacles
    SATB/SATB   kro
    Augsburg (1963) 11-9360

84:4-8, 10, 11
    Sumsion, Herbert
    Blessed Are They That Dwell In Thy House
    SATB/SATB   Organ
    Alfred Lengnick (1973) 4356

84:4, 10
    SEE: Psalm 122:1, 2
    Gustafson, Dwight
    The House Of Our Lord

84:5
    Geisler, Johann C.
    Blessed The People (English/German)
    SSAB or SATB   Organ
    Boosey & Hawkes (1968) 5659

84:5
    Thiman, Eric
    Blessed Is The Man (from Six Introductory
        Sentences)
    SATB   Organ
    Novello (1973) MW 25

84:8-12
    Sowerby, Leo
    Behold, O God, Our Defender
    SATB   Organ   (optional brass quartet
        and timpani)
    H. W. Gray (1966) 2919

84:9   (I Samuel 2:10)
    Blow, John
    Behold O God Our Defender
    SATB   Optional organ
    Stainer & Bell (1953) 5307

84:9
    SEE: Psalm 8:1
    Willan, Healey
    O Lord, Our Governor

84:9-10
    Howells, Herbert
    Behold, O God Our Defender
    SATB   Keyboard
    Novello (1953) SA 312

84:11
    Bach, J. S.
    God Is Ever Sun And Shield (from Cantata
        #29)
    Unison   Continuo with flute or oboe
        obligato
    Concordia (found in Third Morning Star Choir
        Book, 97-4972)

84:11
    SEE: Psalm 138:7
    Fryxell, Regina Holmen
    The Lord Is My Light (from Seven Choral
        Service Settings)

84:11
  Parker, Alice
  A Sun, A Shield
  1 or 2 parts   Autoharp, Bass, Percussion,
      Optional solo instrument
  E. C. Schirmer (1979) 2833

84:12
  Bach, J. S.
  Cantata #79, God Our Lord is Sun and Shield
  SATB   Piano 2 Flutes, 2 Oboes, 2 Horns
  Breitkopf and Hartel (1960) 7079

84:12
  Greene, Maurice (ed. Richard Graves)
  The Lord God Is A Light
  SS   Keyboard
  Curwen (1956) 10491

84:13
  Crotch, William
  Psalm 84 (O Lord God of Hosts)
  SATB   Organ
  St. Mary's Press (1955) n.#.

85:1
  SEE: Isaiah 45:8
  Byrd, William
  Rorate caeli desuper

85:1
  SEE: Jeremiah 29:11, 12, 14
  Wienhorst, Richard
  I Know The Thoughts I Think

85:1-2
  Gabrieli, Giovanni (ed. George Lynn)
  Benedixsti, Domine
  SSAATBB   Optional Organ
  G. Schirmer (1966) 11312

85:2
  SEE: Philippians 4:4-6
  Campbell-Watson, Franck
  Rejoice In The Lord Alway

85:6, 7
  Dietterich, Philip
  Wilt Not Thou Turn Again
  SATB   Organ
  Abingdon (1960) APM-134

85:7
  Wetzler, Robert
  Verse/Advent I (Verses and Offertories -
      Advent I - The Baptism Of Our Lord)
  SA   Organ
  Augsburg (1979) 11-9541

85:9, 12-13
  Wetzler, Robert
  Offertory/Advent I (Verses and Offertories -
      Advent I - The Baptism Of Our Lord)
  2 part   Organ
  Augsburg (1979) 11-9541

85:10, 11
  SEE: Isaiah 45:8
  Statham, H.
  Drop Down Ye Heaven

85:10-12
  Hillert, Richard
  Offertory/Peace (Verses and Offertories -
      Lesser Festivals)
  Unison   Organ
  Augsburg (1980) 11-9543

85:11
  Banchieri, Adriano (ed. Carl Bowman)
  Truth Has Risen (Veritas de terra) English/
      Latin)
  SATB   kro
  Music 70 (1972) M70-101

85:11, 13 (Milton)
  Tye, Christopher (arr. Gerald Knight)
  The Lord Will Come And Not Be Slow
  SATB   kro
  RSCM (1963)

86:00
  Berger, Jean
  Psalm 86
  SATB   2 Treble instruments in either
      B-flat or C
  Flammer (1975) A-5684

86:00
  Blow, John (ed. Heathcote Statham)
  Be Merciful Unto Me O Lord
  SATB   Organ ad lib.
  Oxford (1955) CMS 31

86:00
  Couper, Alinda
  Give Ear O Lord
  SATB   kro
  Abingdon (1969) APM-854

86:00 (paraphrase)
  Franck, Cesar (ed. Leo Sowerby)
  Bow Down Thine Ear (Domine non secundum)
  SATB   Organ
  H. T. Fitzsimons (1959) 2058

86:00 (paraphrase)
  Handel, G. F. (arr. Carl Fredrickson)
  Bow Down Thine Ear
  SATB   Organ or Piano
  Boston Music (1963) BMC-12907

86:00 (paraphrase)
  Handel, G. F. (ed. Walter Ehret)
  Bow Down Thine Ear
  SATB   Organ or Piano
  Boosey & Hawkes (1959) 5312

86:00
  Holst, Gustav
  Psalm 86
  SATB   Organ (or orchestra)
  Galaxy (1920) 1.5016.1

86:00
  Lully, Jean-Baptiste (arr. Robert Crandell)
  Thou O Lord, Art Lord God Alone
  SA or Unison   Organ
  H. W. Gray (1968) 3011 (also available in
      an SATB edition)

86:00 (adapted)
  McLaughlin, Marian
  O Turn Unto Me
  SAB   Organ
  Summy Birchard (1960) SUMCO 5328

86:00 (adapted)
  Palestrina, G. P.
  Bow Down Thine Ear O Lord (English/Latin)
  SATB   kro
  G. Schirmer (1933) 7729

86:00
  Piston, Walter
  Bow Down Thine Ear O Lord (from Psalm and
      Prayer of David)
  SATB   Piano
  Associated (1959) A 641 (also found in
      Contemporary Settings of the Psalms,
      APM-6910)

86:00
  Stoltzer, Thomas (ed. Otto Gombosi)
  Psalm 84   (English/German)
  SSATBB   kro
  Concordia (1953)   MS-1018

86:00   (adapted)
    Yeakle, Thomas
    Bow Down Thine Ear, O Lord
    SATB   kro
    H. W. Gray (1973) CMR 3275

86:1-2, 5
    Blow, John (ed. Heathcote Statham)
    Bow Down Thine Ear, O Lord
    SATB   Organ ad lib.
    Oxford (1925) A-201

86:1, 3, 5
    Arensky, A. S.
    Bow Down Before Thine Ear, O Lord
    SATB   kro
    J. Fischer (1944) 4162 (also found in
        Church Anthem Book)

86:1, 3, 5, 12
    Hayes, William
    Bow Down Thine Ear O Lord
    SATB   Organ
    Oxford (1973) A 294

86:1, 3-7, 12
    Dickinson, Clarence
    Bow Down Thine Ear O Lord
    SATB (B-solo)   Organ ad lib.
    H. W. Gray (1915) 41

86:1-4
    McLelland, Young Thomas
    Bow Down Thine Ear
    SATB (B-solo)   Organ
    Novello (1975) MW 42

86:1, 6
    Drozdof, I. (ed. and arr. I. Trasler)
    Incline Thine Ear O Lord
    SATB   Optional accompaniment
    Plymouth (1963) (found in Anthems For The
        Church Year)

86:1-6
    Mueller, Carl F.
    Bow Down Thine Ear
    SATB   Organ
    Carl Fischer (1950) 6561

86:1-7   (Bay Psalm Book)
    Berger, Jean
    Psalm 86 (I-Bow Down O Lord Thine Ear)
    SATB   Piano
    Concordia (1964) 98-1736

86:1-7
    Williams, Ralph
    Be Merciful Unto Me, O Lord
    SATB   Accompaniment ad lib.
    Schmitt, Hall, McCreary (1961) 877

86:2, 3
    McCormick, Clifford
    As Smoke Is Driven Away
    SATB   kro
    Shawnee (1954) n.#.

86:3, 4, 5
    Blow, John (ed. Heathcote Statham)
    Be Merciful Unto Me O Lord
    SATB   Organ ad lib.
    Oxford (1955) CMS 31

86:4
    Crotch, William
    Comfort O Lord The Soul Of Thy Servant
    SATB   Keyboard
    Carl Fischer (1968) HO 379

86:4
    Crotch, William
    Comfort, O Lord, The Soul Of Thy Servant
    SA   Organ
    E. C. Schirmer (1929) 1005

86:4
    Crotch, William (arr. John Goss)
    Comfort, O Lord The Soul Of Thy Servants
    SATB   Organ
    Novello (1943) 29.0229.10 (also found in
        Short Easy Anthems, Set I)

86:4
    Crotch, William
    Comfort O Lord The Soul Of Thy Servant
    SATB   Organ
    Oxford (1933) (found in Church Anthem Book)

86:4, 5
    Jenkins, Cyril
    Comfort Thy Servant
    SATB   kro
    F. Harris (1959) F.H.3029

86:4-5
    Snow, Francis W.
    Comfort The Soul Of Thy Servant
    SATB   kro
    Carl Fischer (1959) CM 6489

86:5-6
    Willan, Healey
    Give Ear O Lord Unto My Prayer
    SSA   No accompaniment
    Concordia (1953) (found in We Praise Thee,
        Volume I, 97-7564)

86:7-8, 10
    Blow, John (ed. Heathcote Statham)
    In The Time Of Trouble
    SATB   Organ ad lib.
    Oxford (1925) A 202

86:8-13
    Berger, Jean
    Psalm 86 (Amongst The Gods, O Lord)
    SATB   Piano
    Concordia (1964) 98-1737

86:9   (adapted)
    Thiman, Eric
    Let All The Nations   (from Six Introductory
        Sentences)
    SATB   Organ
    Novello (1973) MW 25

86:10
    SEE: Psalm 83:1
    Pergolesi, Giovanni (ed. Roger Forester)
    Be Not Silent Unto Us

86:11
    Hovhaness, Alan
    Teach Me Thy Ways
    SSA   No accompaniment
    Continuo [Alexander Broude] (1978) AB 446

86:11-12
    Fox, William
    Teach Me Thy Ways, O Lord
    SATB   No accompaniment
    RSCM (found in Service Book, Volume 7)

86:11, 12
    Fox, William
    Teach Me Thy Way O Lord
    SATB   No accompaniment
    Novello (1975) 03.0137.10 (also found in
        With A Joyful Noise)

86:11-12
    Hooper, Edmund (ed. Watkins Shaw)
    Teach Me Thy Way, O Lord
    SATB   Organ ad lib.
    Oxford (1961) 21A

86:11-12
    Roff, Joseph
    Teach Me Thy Ways, O Lord
    SATB   Keyboard
    Abingdon (1977) APM-626

86:12
    Moir, Franck (ed. Carl Deis)
    I Will Thank Thee O Lord
    SATB   Organ
    G. Schirmer (1939) 8397

86:14-17
    Berger, Jean
    Psalm 86 (O God, The Proud Rose 'Gainst)
    SATB   Piano
    Concordia (1964) 98-1738

87:1-7
    Williamson, Malcolm
    Psalm Of The City of David (from Psalms Of
        The Elements)
    Unison   Congregation, Organ
    Boosey & Hawkes (1976) 5956

87:2
    SEE: Psalm 93:11
    Geisler, Johann (ed. E. Nolte)
    The Lord Is Ruler   (English/German)

87:3
    SEE: Isaiah 33:20-21
    Kauffmann, Ronald (arr.)
    Glorious Things of Thee Are Spoken

87:4
    SEE: Psalm 150:4
    Schütz, Heinrich
    Jubilate deo in chordis

87:17   (Psalm 37:11, 18, 22)
    Seele, Thomas
    In me transierunt
    TTBB   Continuo
    Hanssler   #342

88:00   (Peter Cornelius)
    Bach, J. S. (Peter Cornelius, Op. 13, #1)
    Song of Repentence
    SATB   kro
    Broude Brothers (1952) BB 65

88:1
    Durante, Frances
    Misericordi es Domini in eternum cantabo
    SATB/SATB   kro
    G. Schirmer (1939) 5403

88:1, 2, 3, 13
    Croft, William (ed. Percy Young)
    O Lord God Of My Salvation
    SSAATB   (solos)   Organ
    Broude Brothers (1976) MGC 15

88:1, 2, 8
    Blow, John (ed. Watkins Shaw)
    O Lord Of My Salvation
    SSAATTBB   Organ ad lib.
    St. Michael's College, Tenbury (n.d.) n.#.

89:00   (based on)
    Frackenpohl, Arthur
    My Song Forever Shall Record
    SATB   kro
    Marks (1964) 4308

89:00
    Near, Gerald
    My Song Shall Be Alway Of The Lovingkindness
    SATB   Organ or Piano
    Calvary Press (1973) 1-002

89:00   (taken from)
    Rogers, Bernhard
    Lord God Of Hosts
    SATB   (B-solo)   Piano
    Presser (1964) 312-40601

89:00   (adapted)
    Warren, Elinor Remick
    Let The Heavens Praise Thy Wonders
    SATB   Organ
    H. W. Gray (1974) CMR 3313

89:1
    Mendelssohn, Felix (arr. C. Young)
    I Will Sing Of Thy Mercies)
    2 part   Accompanied
    Agape [Hope] (1978) AG-7228

89:1
    Near, Gerald
    I Will Sing Of The Mercies   (Three Introits)
    SATB   kro
    Calvary Press (1975) 1-009

89:1
    Sampson, Godfrey
    My Song Shall Be Alway of the Loving Kind-
        ness
    SATB   (S-solo)   Organ
    Novello (1937) MT 1153

89:1, 16-18
    Hallock, Peter
    You Love O Lord Forever Will I Sing
    SATB   Organ
    GIA (1977) G-2078

89:8-9, 11, 52
    Hovhaness, Alan
    O Lord God Of Hosts   Op. 27
    SATB   Organ   Brass quartet
    C. F. Peters (1968) 66188

89:13   (paraphrased)
    Handel, G. F. (arr. William Herrmann)
    Let Thy Hand Be Strengthened (from Coro-
        nation Anthem, #4)
    SSA   Organ or Piano
    G. Schirmer (1966) 11332

89:14, 15
    Blow, John (ed. Sydney Nicholson)
    Let Thy Hand Be Strengthened (for the
        Coronation of James II)
    SATB   Organ ad lib.
    Novello

89:13, 14   (paraphrased)
    Handel, G. F. (ed. William Herrmann)
    Let Thy Hand Be Strengthened (Coronation
        Anthem, #4)
    SAATB   Keyboard
    G. Schirmer (1967) 46204

89:15-18
    Wiscomb, Jeff
    Blessed Is The People
    SATB   kro
    Boston Music (1981) 13935

89:17
    Handel, G. F.
    Thou Art The Glory Of Their Strength
        (Chandos Anthem, #7)
    SATB   Organ
    Schmitt, Hall McCreary (1951) (found in
        Rare Choral Masterpieces)

89:19
    SEE: Psalm 48:1
    Willan, Healey
    Great Is The Lord

89:20-21
    Bruckner, Anton
    Inveni David (Latin)
    TTBB   4 Trombones
    C. F. Peters (1961) 6318

89:45-51
    Williamson, Malcolm
    How Long Wilt Thou Hide Thyself (from
        Psalms of the Elements)
    Unison   Congregation,   Organ
    Boosey & Hawkes (1976) 5964

90:00
    Beck, John Ness
    Thou Art God
    SATB   Organ or Piano
    Beckenhorst (1974) BP-1005

90:00 (Watts)
    Croft, William (arr. Jean Pasquet)
    O God Our Help In Ages Past
    SATB   Organ   (optional brass)
    Elkan Vogel (1972) 362.03137

90:00
    Fraser, Shena
    Lord, Thou Has Been Our Dwelling Place
    SATB   Organ
    Sam Fox (1966) PS 127

90:00
    Ives, Charles
    Psalm 90
    SATB   Organ and Bells
    Merion Music (1970) 342.40021

90:00
    Mendelssohn, Felix (ed. Arthur Hilton)
    Thou, Lord Our Refuge
    SATB   Optional organ or piano
    Mercury (1961) MC 400

90:00
    Monaco, Richard
    Lord, Thou Hast Been Our Dwelling Place
    SATB   Organ
    G. Schirmer (1965) 11228

90:00
    Norden, Hugo
    O Satisfy Us With Thy Mercy
    TTBB   No accompaniment
    Abingdon   APM 406

90:00 (Watts)
    Noss, Luther
    Highbridge
    TBB   kro
    Associated (1956 AMP 95581

90:00 (Psalm 100, paraphrased)
    Pfautsch, Lloyd
    Jubilate Deo
    SATB   Organ (3 Trumpets, 2 Trombones,
        cymbal)
    Lawson Gould (1971) 51624

90:00
    Porpora, Niccola
    Qui habitat in adjutorso (Latin only)
    SSA   Keyboard (or Strings)
    Marks (1976) MC 4647

90:00
    Sweelinck, J. P.
    Du warest alle Zeit Herr Unsre zu Flucht
        (German only)
    SATB   No accompaniment
    Merseburger (1977) (found in Motetten
        Alter Meister)

90:00
    Sweelinck, J. P.
    Psalm 90   (English/French)
    SATB   No accompaniment
    Mercury (1941) 352.00003

90:00
    SEE: Psalm 84
    Vaughan Williams, Ralph
    O How Amiable

90:00
    Young, Gordon
    A Canticle Of Creation
    SATB   Organ
    Flammer (1965) A 5045

90:1, 2
    Lahmer, Reuel
    O Lord You Have Been Our Refuge
    2 part mixed   Organ
    World Library (1958) EMP 1513

90:1, 2
    Mendelssohn, Felix
    Thou Lord Our Refuge
    SATB   No accompaniment
    Oxford (1933) (found in Church Anthem Book)

90:1, 2
    Monaco, Richard
    Lord Thou Hast Been Our Dwelling
    SATB   Organ
    G. Schirmer (1965) 11228

90:1, 2
    Sweelinck, J. P.
    Psalm 90
    SATB   kro
    Golden Music (1964) W-11

90:1, 2, 4
    Lefanu, Nicola
    Verses from Psalm 90
    SATB/SATB (S-solo)   No accompaniment
    Novello (1979) 29.0456.10

90:1, 2, 4, 12, 17
    Snyder, Wesley
    Lord Thou Hast Been Our Dwelling Place
    SACB   Piano
    Cambiata Press (1978) C 978108

90:1, 2, 10, 17
    Arnatt, Ronald
    Lord Thou Hast Been Our Dwelling Place
    SATB (T-solo)   Organ
    Mercury (1956) MC 266

90:1-4
    Young, Gordon
    Lord Thou Hast Been
    SATB   Keyboard, 3 Trumpets
    Hope (1980) F-962

90:1-5
    Vaughan Williams, Ralph
    Lord Thou Hast Been Our Refuge
    SATB/SATB   Organ
    G. Schirmer (1921) 9720

90:1-7, 9, 13, 17
    Joubert, John
    Lord Thou Hast Been Our Refuge
    SATB   Organ
    Novello (1967) NCM 1

90:1-10, 17
    Lekberg, Sven
    Lord Thou Hast Been Our Dwelling Place
    SATB   kro
    Kjos (1954) 5174

90:1-17
    Vaughan Williams, Ralph
    Lord Thou Hast Been Our Refuge
    SATB (S-A-T-B-solos)   Organ (orchestra)
    Curwen [G. Schirmer] (1921) 9720

90:5
    SEE: Psalm 104:14-15
    Browne, Richard
    Chortos I

90:13
    Atwood, Thomas
    Turn Thee Again, O Lord
    SATB   Organ
    E. C. Schirmer (1936) 1025 (also found in
        Second Concord Anthem Book - Grey)

90:13
    Atwood, Thomas
    Turn Thee Again O Lord
    SATB   Organ
    Oxford (found in Church Anthem Book)

90:14, 16
    Norden, Hugo
    O Satisfy Us Early With Thy Mercy
    TTBB   kro
    Abingdon (1965) APM-405

90:15
    SEE: Isaiah 2:3, 5
    Crowe, John F.
    The Light Of The World

90:16-17
    Beattie, Herbert
    Let Thy Work Appear (Six Choral Settings
        from the Psalms)
    SAB   Optional Organ
    G. Schirmer (1954) 510

90:17
    Lovelace, Austin C.
    The Beauty Of The Lord
    SATB   kro
    J. Fischer (1956) 8921

91:00
    SEE: Psalm 1
    Baumgartner, H. Leroy
    His Delight Is In The Law Of The Lord

91:00 (Psalm 105, based on)
    Brandon, George (arr.)
    Carol Of The Exodus
    SA or SAB   Keyboard
    Augsburg (1980) 1924

91:00
    SEE: Luke 24:29
    Distler, Hugo (ed. Larry Palmer)
    Christ, Who Alone Art Light Of Day

91:00
    Mendelssohn, Felix (ed. Morten J. Luvaas)
    Psalm 91
    SSAATTBB   kro
    C. C. Birchard (1935) 235

91:00
    Porpora, Niccola
    Psalm 90 (Qui habitat in adjutoria)
    SSAA   Keyboard (strings)
    Marks (1976) MC 4647

91:00
    Richter, Marga
    Psalm 91
    SATB   kro
    Elkan-Vogel (1965) 1209

91:00
    Scandrett, Robert
    Psalm 91
    SATB   Organ (optional 2 horns)
    J. Fischer (1971) FEC 10018

91:00
    Williamson, Malcolm
    Psalm Of God The Protector (from Psalms of
        the Elements)
    Unison   Congregation,   Organ
    Boosey & Hawkes (1976) 5946

91:1-2
    Broadhead, G. F.
    Whoso Dwelleth Under The Defence
    SATB   Organ
    Novello (1949) MT 1271 (also found in The
        Novello Anthem Book)

91:1-2
    Moore, Philip
    Whoso Dwelleth
    SATB   Organ
    H. W. Gray (1973) MCR 3278

91:1-2, 11
    McAfee, Don
    Psalm 91
    SATB   Keyboard
    Lorenz (1967) E 76

91:1-4, 9, 11, 16
    Glarum, L. Stanley
    He That Dwelleth
    SATB   kro
    Hall & McCreary (1957) 1755

91:1, 5, 11-12
    Lang, C. S.
    He Shall Give His Angels Charge Over Thee
    SSATB   kro
    Novello (1941) 1247

91:1, 11-12
    Jennings, Kenneth
    For He Shall Give His Angels Charge Over
        Thee
    SATB   kro
    Augsburg (1967) ACL-1499

91:1, 11-12
    Moe, Daniel
    He Shall Give His Angels Charge Over Thee
    SATB   kro
    Augsburg (1962) ACL-1306

91:2, 11, 12
    Peeters, Flor
    Canticum gaudii (Song of Joy) Op. 118
    SATB   Organ   Brass
    C. F. Peters (1973) 6642

91:4-5
    Binkerd, Gordon
    Scapulis suis   (Latin)
    SSAA   kro
    Associated (1964) A 428

92:00
  Christiansen, Paul
  Psalm 92
  SATB   Piano or Organ or Brass
  Schmitt, Hall, McCreary (1966) SD 6214

92:00
  Marshall, Jane
  It is Good to Give Thanks (from Two Quiet
       Psalms)
  SATB   Keyboard
  Sacred Music Press (1981) S-271

92:00   (paraphrase)
  Norden, N. Lindsay
  It Is A Good Thing
  SATB   Organ
  J. Fischer (1955) 8896

92:00
  Robertson, Ed
  Song of Thanksgiving and Praise
  SATB   Piano
  Jenson (1978) 404-19024

92:00
  Schubert, Franz (ed. Jan Meyerowitz)
  Psalm 92
  SATB (B-solo)   kro
  Alexander Broude (1978) AB 823

92:00   (adapted)
  Schweizer, Rolf
  How Good To Offer Thanks
  Unison   Keyboard
  Agape (1980) 939   (found in Choirbook For
       Saints and Sinners)

92:00   (based on)
  Sleeth, Natalie
  It Is Good
  2 part   Keyboard
  Hinshaw (1980) (in Laudamus, HMB 126)

92:1 (Psalm 93:4; Psalm 98:1)
  McCormick, Clifford
  It Is A Good Thing To Give Thanks
  SATB   kro
  Shawnee (1953) A-284 (also found in
       Anthems From Scripture, G-34)

92:1 (Psalm 104:10, 33)
  Mechem, Kirke
  I Will Sing Alleluia   Op. 40, #2
  SATB   Organ or Piano, flute, optional
       percussion
  Carl Fischer (1974) CM 7861

92:1
  Palestrina, G. P. (ed. John F. Williamson)
  Bonum est confiteri (It is a Good Thing)
  SATBB   kro
  G. Schirmer (1945) 9391

92:1-2
  Berger, Jean
  It Is Good To Give Thanks
  SATB   kro
  Transcontinental (1968) TCL 606

92:1-2
  Studen, Johann (ed. T. P. Klammer)
  It Is A Good Thing
  SSA   kro
  Concordia (1950) CTS 41

92:1-4
  Dirksen, Richard
  Give Thanks Unto The Lord
  SA or TB   Organ
  Flammer (1974) E 5166

92:1-4
  SEE: James 1:17
  Hancock, Gerre
  In Thanksgiving

92:1-4
  Hurd, Michael
  It Is A Good Thing To Give Thanks
  SATB   Organ
  RSCM (1973) (found in Five Anthems for
       Today)

92:1-4
  Lekberg, Sven
  It Is A Good Thing To Give Thanks
  SATB   kro
  G. Schirmer (1968) 11562

92:1-4
  Mueller, Luise
  A Song For The Sabbath
  SSATB   No accompaniment
  Abingdon (1975) APM-476

92:1, 4
  SEE: Psalm 81:1-2
  Powell, Robert J.
  Sing We Merrily (in Anthems For Treble
       Voices)

92:1-4
  Schwartz, Paul
  It Is A Good Thing To Give Thanks
  TTBB   kro
  Rongwen (1959) RM 20289

92:1-4
  Mechem, Kirke
  It Is Good To Give Thanks   Op. 41, #3
  Unison   Keyboard
  Carl Fischer (1975) CM 7896

92:1-5
  Hatch, Owen Andrews
  It Is A Good Thing To Give Thanks
  SA   Keyboard (optional guitar and two
       flutes)
  Concordia (1977) 98-2317

92:1, 5
  SEE: Psalm 69:30
  Newbury, Kent A.
  I Will Praise God With A Song

92:1, 12, 13
  Proulx, Richard
  The Just Man Shall Flourish
  Unison   Organ, with Flute and Oboe
  Augsburg (1970) 11-0637

92:5
  Gaul, A. R.
  Great And Marvelous Are Thy Works (from
       The Holy City)
  SATB   Keyboard
  Carl Fischer (1946) CM 6255

92:5
  Parker, Alice
  O Lord, How Great Are Thy Words (Sunday
       Rounds)
  4 part Round   No accompaniment
  Hinshaw (1975) HMC 106

92:6
  Peter, Johann F. (ed & arr. Karl Kroeger)
  Lord, Thy Creations, How Great They Are
       English/German
  SATB   Organ or Piano
  Boosey & Hawkes (1978) 5918

92:12, 13   (Psalm 93:1, 4)
    Butler, Eugene
    The Lord Reigneth
    SAB   Piano or Organ
    Hope (1967) A-381

93:00
    Binkerd, Gordon
    The Lord Is King
    SATB   Organ
    C. F. Peters (1961) 6260

93:00
    Cruft, Adrian
    The Lord Reigneth (from Two Psalms of
        Praise) Op. 48
    Unison   Piano Duet
    Leeds (1969) n.#.

93:00 (paraphrased by Woodward)
    Dacques, Pierre (arr. Charles Wood)
    God Omnipotent Reigneth
    SATB   Organ
    E. C. Birchard (1927) 1160

93:00   (paraphrased by Woodward)
    Dacques, Pierre (arr. Charles Wood)
    God Omnipotent Reigneth
    SATB   Organ
    RSCM (found in Festival Service Book, #6)

93:00
    Elmore, Robert
    Psalm 93
    SATB   Organ
    H. W. Gray (1953) 2303

93:00
    Lockwood, Normand
    The Lord Reigneth
    SSATBB   kro
    Galaxy (1938) 891

93:00
    Lynn, George
    The Lord Doth Reign
    SATB   kro
    Abingdon (1962) APM-245

93:00
    Nystedt, Knut
    Dominus Regnat
    SATB   No accompaniment
    C. F. Peters (1963) 6540

93:00
    Sowerby, Leo
    The Lord Is King
    SATB   Organ
    H. W. Gray (1964) 2816

93:00 (words taken from)
    Titcomb, Everett
    The Lord Reigneth
    SATB   Organ
    H. W. Gray (1956) 2446

93:1   (Psalm 87:2)
    Geisler, Johann (ed. E. Nolte)
    The Lord Is Ruler   (English/German)
    SSAB   Piano
    Boosey & Hawkes (1965) 5607

93:1-2a
    Greene, Maurice (ed. Mason Martens)
    It Is A Good Thing (from Sing We Merrily)
    SATB (T-solo)   Keyboard
    Walton (1972) M-122

93:1, 2, 3
    Josquin des Pres (ed. Royal Stanton)
    God Reigns
    SATB   kro
    Flammer (1974) A-5656

93:1-3
    SEE: Psalm 56:12-13
    Lynn, George
    The Lord Is King

93:1, 4
    SEE: Psalm 92:12, 13
    Butler, Eugene
    The Lord Reigneth

93:1a, 5
    Manz, Paul O.
    The Lord Reigneth
    SATB   Organ
    Augsburg (1961) 1372

93:1-5
    Walter, Samuel
    The Lord Reigneth
    SATB or SA   Keyboard
    Abingdon (1962) APM-203

94:1-7   (Psalm 111:10)
    Baker, Robert
    O Lord God Unto Whom Vengeance Belongeth
    SATB (B-solo)   Organ
    H. W. Gray (1941) CMR 1741

93:4
    SEE: Psalm 92:1
    McCormick, Clifford
    It Is A Good Thing

94:6-7
    Wapen, Francis
    Come, Let Us Bow Down   Op. 12, #3
    SB   or TB   Organ
    GIA (1970) G-1550

94:7-10
    Baristow, Edward
    If The Lord Had Not Helped Me
    SATB   Organ
    Novello (1910) 979

95:00
    Berger, Jean
    O Come Let Us Sing Unto The Lord
    SATB   kro
    Broude Brothers (1957) BB 1027

95:00
    Croce, Giovanni (ed. Maynard Kline)
    Cantate Domino (English/Latin)
    SATB   kro
    G. Schirmer (1966) 11419

95:00   (1912 Psalter)
    Englert, Eugene
    O Come And Sing Unto The Lord
    SATB   Keyboard (optional trumpet)
    GIA (1980) G-2342

95:00
    Englert, Eugene
    Psalm 95
    SAB   Congregation, Organ
    Augsburg (1978) (found in Seasonal Psalms
        For Congregation and Choir, 11-9376)

95:00 (Psalm 72, Watts)
    Fetler, David
    Sing Unto The Lord
    SATB   Organ (optional Junior Choir and
        Handbells)
    Carl Fischer (1976) CM 7951

95:00   (Ainsworth Psalter)
    Finney, Ross Lee
    Come Let Us To The Lord Shout Joyfully
    SATB (S-T-solos)   Organ or Piano
    Carl Fischer (1951) CM 6834

95:00   (based on)
Francis, J. Henry
O Come Let Us Sing
SATB   kro
Presser (1952) 312.40115

95:00   (adapted)
Gabrieli, Giovanni
Come Let Us Sing A Song of Joy
SATB/SATB   (optional Brass or Woodwinds or
       Strings)
Shawnee (1974) A-1243

95:00
Gehrig, Philip
Come Let Us Sing To The Lord
Unison   Organ
Augsburg (1980) 1999

95:00
George, Earl
Cantate Domino   (Latin)
SATB divsi   kro
Summy Birchard (1959) 5253

95:00
Gibbons, Orlando (ed. & transcribed by
       Cyril F. Simkins)
O Come, Let Us Sing Unto The Lord (from The
       Short Service)
SATB   kro
Concordia (1975) 98-2233

95:00
Gore, Richard T.
O Come Let Us Sing Unto The Lord
SSAA   Organ ad lib.
J. Fischer (1951) 8594

95:00
Harris, David
O Come, Let Us Sing Unto The Lord
SATB   Organ
Oxford (1968) A 255

95:00
Josquin des Pres (ed. Royal Stanton)
God Reigns
SATB   kro
Flammer (1974) A 5656

95:00   (adapted)
Kirk, Theron
O Come Loud Anthems Let Us Sing
SATB   kro
Shawnee (1956) A 397

95:00   (taken from)
Krul, Eli
O Come, Let Us Sing
SATB   Organ
C. F. Peters (1961) 6245

95:00
LeJeune, Claude
Psalm 95
SAB   No accompaniment
Mercury (1945) MC 56

95:00
Mendelssohn, Felix
The Lord Is A Mighty God
SATB   Piano or Organ
Flammer (n.d.) A-5393

95:00
Mendelssohn, Felix (arr. O. C. Christiansen)
The Lord Is A Mighty God
SATB   Piano or Organ
Kjos (1963) #9

95:00
Moyer, J. Harold
Let Us Sing To The Lord
SSAATTBB   kro
Golden Music (1946) G-18

95:00
McKinney, Mathilde
Psalm 95
SATB   kro
Golden Music (1967) G-34

95:00
Nelson, Ron
Psalm 95: Come, Let Us Praise Yahweh
SATB (solos)   Organ and instruments
Boosey & Hawkes (1975) 758

95:00
SEE: Genesis 28:16-17
Pfautsch, Lloyd
The Lord Is In This Place

95:00
Rodby, John
Chorale
SATB   kro
Somerset [Hope] (1971) CE 4325

95:00
Schütz, Heinrich (ed. Ulrich S. Leopold
Come Ye Now Make A Joyful Noise
SATB   Keyboard
Chantry Press (1959) n.#.

95:00
Schütz, Heinrich (ed. Daniel G. Reuning)
O Come Let Us Praise God (from Five Psalms)
   (English/German)
SATB   No accompaniment
GIA (1973) G-1790

95:00
Steel, Christopher
O Come, Let Us Sing Unto The Lord
SATB   Organ
Novello (1967) 1467

95:00
Swann, Donald
O Come Let Us Sing Unto The Lord
2 part   Piano
Curwen (1970) 11792   (also available in
       SATB setting)

95:1
SEE: Psalm 105:1-3
Geisler, Johann
Thank Ye The Lord

95:1
Zimmermann, Heinz Werner
Come Let Us Praise
SATB   Keyboard
Carl Fischer (1976) CM 7936

95:1-2 (paraphrase)
Amner, John
Come, Let's Rejoice
SATB or SSTB   Keyboard
Oxford (1971) A 279

95:1, 2
Amner, John (arr. Anthony Gruning)
Come Let's Rejoice
SATB   Keyboard
RSCM (found in Festival Service Book, #7)

95:1-2
Schalit, Heinrich
Sing Unto The Lord
SATB   Organ
Transcontinental (1964) TCL 602

95:1-3a (Psalm 117:2; Psalm 30:5a)
    Kimball, Jacob (ed. Mason Martens)
    O Come Sing Unto The Lord
    SATB   kro
    McAfee (1975) (found in Bicentennial
        Collection of American Choral Music)

95:1-3
    Page, Robert
    Venite exsultemus Domino
    Three Choirs: SSA/SATB/TBB
        No accompaniment
    Standard Music (1971) A6MX1

95:1-3
    Sweelinck, J. P. (ed. Donald Colton)
    Venite, Exultemus Domino (Come Priase Him)
    SSATB   kro
    Concordia (1969) 98-1938

95:1-3
    Sweelinck, J. P. (ed. Dennis Kudlawiec)
    Venite Exsultemus Domino (English/Latin)
    SSATB   Optional accompaniment
    Summy Birchard (1962) 5517

95:1-3a
    Track, Gerhard
    O Come Let Us Sing To The Lord
    SATB   Organ or Piano
    GIA (1972) G-1715

95:1-5
    Mawby, Colin
    O Come Let Us Sing
    2 part treble   Organ
    GIA (1964) G-1098

95:1-6
    Carter, John
    O Come Let Us Sing
    SATB   Piano
    Broadman (1975) 4545-94

95:1-6 (Psalm 96:1, 3)
    Hopson, Hal H.
    Festival Psalm
    SATB   Organ (2 Trumpets, Horn, 2 Trom-
        bones)
    Agape [Hope] (1979) HH 3911

95:1-6
    Scott, Kayron Lee
    O Come Let Us Sing Unto The Lord
    SATB   Organ or Brass
    Augsburg (1970) 11-0671

95:1, 6 (Psalm 98:1)
    Smith, Charles W.
    O Sing Unto The Lord
    SATB   Piano, Tambourine, Triangle
    Broadman (1974) 4545-83

95:1-7
    Berger, Jean
    O Come Let Us Sing Unto The Lord
    SATB   kro
    Broude Brothers (1957) BB 1027

95:1-7 (Psalm 96:9, 13)
    Diemer, Emma Lou
    O Come Let Us Sing Unto The Lord
    TTBB   Keyboard
    Carl Fischer (1977) CM 8014

95:1-7a
    Hunnicutt, Judy
    Psalm 95
    SA   Handbells
    Augsburg (1979) 11-0674

95:1-7
    Hurd, Michael
    O Come Let Us Sing
    SATB   Organ
    Novello (1972) MW 20

95:1-7 (Psalm 96:9, 13)
    Kirk, Theron
    O Come Let Us Sing
    SSATBB   Brass and Percussion
    Summy Birchard (1959) 5295 (Brass parts
        sold separately)

95:1-7 (based on)
    Leaf, Robert
    Rejoice Be Glad In The Lord
    2 part   Organ
    Augsburg (1971) 11-9285 (also found in
        Contemporary Choir, Volume 2)

95:1-7
    Piccolo, Anthony
    O Come, Let Us Sing Unto The Lord
    SATB   Organ
    Oxford (1980) A329

95:1-7
    Pote, Allen
    Psalm 95
    SATB   Keyboard (optional percussion and
        guitar)
    Choristers Guild (1977) A-189

95:1-7
    Young, Gordon
    O Come Let Us Sing Unto The Lord
    SATB   Keyboard
    H. W. Gray (1965) CMR 2913

95:3
    SEE: Psalm 98:1
    Kirk, Theron
    Sing A New Song To The Lord

95:3-8, 12-15
    SEE: Psalm 96:2, 3, 5, 7-10
    Wesley, Samuel S.
    Ascribe Unto The Lord

95:4, 5
    SEE: Psalm 47:1, 7
    Young, Carlton
    Clap Your Hands

95:6
    Persichetti, Vincent
    Introit (from Hymns and Responses For The
        Church Year)
    SATB   Keyboard
    Elkan Vogel (1956) 463.00001

95:6, 7
    Palestrina, G. P.
    O Come Let Us Worship
    SATB   kro
    E. C. Schirmer #145 (also found in
        Concord Anthem Book - Red)

95:7
    SEE: Exodus 34:6, 7
    Gregor, Christian (arr. E. V. Nolte)
    Lord God, Merciful and Gracious

95:11, 13
    Berkeley, Michael
    Laetentur coeli (Latin)
    SATB   kro
    G. Schirmer (1979) 12359

95:11-13
    Hassler, Hans Leo (ed. Peter Gram Swing)
    Laetentur Coeli (English/Latin)
    TTBB   kro
    Concordia (1957) 98-1339

96:00   (adapted)
    Bortniansky, Dimitri S.
    O Let Us Sing A New Song
    SATB   kro
    Abingdon (1963) APM-278   (found in Select
        Anthems For Mixed Voices, Volume 1)

96:00   (Watts)
    Brandon, George (arr.)
    Advent Carol
    SA or Unison   Organ
    GIA (1972) G-1719

96:00 (Joel 2:13)
    Butler, Eugene
    Sing To The Lord A Marvelous Song
    SATB   Piano or Organ
    Hope (1973) A-451

96:00   (Joel 2:13)
    Butler, Eugene
    Sing To The Lord A Marvelous Song
    SSA   Piano or Organ
    Hope (1976) A-483

96:00 (adapted) (Psalm 22, adapted)
    Clausen, Rene
    All That Hath Life And Breath, Praise Ye
        The Lord
    SATB   kro
    Mark Foster (1981) MF 223

96:00
    Cooke, Arnold
    O Sing Unto The Lord A New Song
    SATB   Organ
    Novello (1961) 1412

96:00
    Copley, R. Evan
    O Sing Ye To The Lord (Three Anthems Based
        On Canons)
    2 part   Keyboard
    Abingdon (1974) APM-448

96:00
    Copley, R. Evan
    O Sing Unto The Lord A New Song
    SATB   kro
    Abingdon (1977) APM-521

96:00 (selections)
    Daniels, M. L.
    Let The Heavens Rejoice
    SATB   kro
    Flammer (1971) A-5564

96:00
    Gabrieli, Giovanni (ed. Karl-Heinz Schnee)
    Cantate domine   (English/Latin)
    SSATTB   kro
    Walton (1978) 6048

96:00
    Gottlieb, Jack
    Shiru Ladonai   (Hebrew)
    SATB   Organ and Percussion
    Presser (1971) 312-40774

96:00
    Handel, G. F. (ed. & arr. Robert S. Hines)
    Let The Whole Earth Stand In Awe
    SAB   Keyboard
    Concordia (1980) 98-2473

96:00
    Handel, G. F. (ed. Richard Peek)
    O Sing Unto The Lord (from 4th Chandos
        Anthem)
    SAB (S-solo)   Organ, oboe obligato
    Concordia (1973) 98-2200

96:00
    Hassler, Hans Leo
    Cantate Domino (English/German)
    SATB   kro
    Hanssler   H.E. 1.125

96:00
    Held, Wilbur
    Psalm 96
    SAB   Congregation,   Organ
    Augsburg (1978) (found in Seasonal Psalms
        for Congregation and Choir, 11-9376)

96:00   (paraphrase)
    Hopson, Hal H.
    Sing A New Song To The Lord
    Unison   Keyboard (optional Handbells)
    Choristers Guild (1979) A-204

96:00
    Kirk, Theron
    O Sing Unto The Lord (from Triptych of
        Psalms)
    SATB   kro
    Kjos (1968) 5489c

96:00
    Kreutz, Robert
    Sing A New Song
    SATB   kro
    Summy Birchard (1959) 5256

96:00 (based on)
    Mozart, W. A. (arr. Elwood Coggin)
    Praise Him! Declare His Glory
    SAB   Organ or Piano
    Flammer (1974) D-5227

96:00   (Psalm 126)
    Naylor, Peter
    O Sing Unto The Lord
    SATB   Organ
    Novello (1970) NCM 27

96:00
    Powell, Robert J.
    Sing All The Earth
    SAB (S-T solos)   Piano
    Carl Fischer (1973) CM 7822

96:00
    Purcell, Henry (ed. Watkins Shaw)
    O Sing Unto The Lord A New Song
    SATB   Organ and Strings
    Novello (1956) 29.0146.03

96:00
    Schein, J. H. (ed. Ronald A. Nelson)
    Sing To The Lord
    SAB   Organ
    Calvary Press (1977) n.#.

96:00
    Schütz, Heinrich (ed. Ulrich S. Leopold)
    In Joyous Psalms Praise Ye The Lord
    SATB   Keyboard
    Chantry Music Press (1959) n.#.

96:00
    Sweelinck, J. P. (ed. Donald Colton)
    Cantate Domino (O Sing Ye To The Lord
        (Latin/English)
    SSATB   kro
    Concordia (1969) 98-1937

96:00
    Sweelinck, J. P. (ed. Walter Ehret)
    Cantate Domino   (English/Latin)
    SSATB   kro
    Walton (1969) 6029

96:00
    Sweelinck, J. P. (ed. Maynard Klein)
    O Sing Ye To The Lord   (English/Latin)
    SSATB   kro
    G. Schirmer (1977) 12102

96:00
    Sweelinck, J. P.
    Psalm 96
    SATB   No accompaniment
    Mercury (1941) MC 4

96:00
    Vecchi, Orazio (ed. Roger Wilhelm)
    Cantate Domino   (Latin)
    SATB   Optional organ
    Lawson Gould (1972) 51633

96:00
    Viadana, Lodovico (ed. John Cramer)
    Cantate Domino (English/Latin)
    SATB   kro
    Marks (1964) 4291

96:00   (based on)
    Watson, Walter
    Sing A New Song
    Unison children   Piano or Organ, Oboe
    Ludwig (1974) C-1163

96:1 (adapted) (Psalm 22:1, adapted)
    Clausen, Rene
    All That Hath Life And Breath, Praise Ye
       The Lord
    SATB   kro
    Mark Foster (1981) MF 223

96:1 (Psalm 98:1; Psalm 100:1)
    Gallus, Jacob (ed. Dwight E. Woldy)
    Alleluia Sing A New Song
    SATB/SATB/SATB   No accompaniment
    Augsburg (1964) 11-0613

96:1
    Haydn, Michael (arr. Hal H. Hopson)
    Sing A New Song
    SAB   Keyboard
    Flammer (1980) D-5306

96:1
    Pachelbel, Johann
    Singet dem Herrn ein neues Lied (German)
    SATB/SATB   No accompaniment
    Hanssler (1967) HE1.008

96:1
    Purcell, Henry
    O Sing Unto The Lord
    SATB   Organ
    E. C. Schirmer   #155 (also found in Concord
       Anthem Book - Red)

96:1   (Psalm 100:1)
    Track, Gerhard
    Sing To The Lord A New Song
    SATB   kro
    Schmitt, Hall & McCreary (1966) 8024

96:1-2
    Berger, Jean
    Cantate Domino   (Latin)
    SATB   kro
    Concordia (1961) 98-1557

96:1, 2
    Bolt, Conway A.
    Psalm 96
    SATB   Piano or Organ, Percussion
    Agape [Hope] (1972) WS 1402

96:1-2   (Psalm 100:2-3)
    Geisler, Johann Christian (ed. E. Nolte)
    Sing To The Lord A New-Made Song
    SSAB/SSAB or SATB/SATB   Piano or Organ
    Boosey & Hawkes (1968) 5682

96:1-2
    Staden, Johann (ed. Paul Thomas)
    Sing To The Lord A New Song
    SAB   Organ and 2 Flutes
    Concordia (1966) 98-1886

96:1-2, 4, 9, 11
    Glarum, L. Stanley
    O Sing Unto The Lord A New Song
    SSAATTBB   kro
    Schmitt, Hall & McCreary (1959) 1791

96:1-3
    Bender, Jan
    O Sing Unto The Lord A New Song
       Op. 43, #2
    SATB   kro
    Concordia (1967) 98-1876

96:1-3   (Psalm 100:1-2, 4)
    Couperin, Francois (ed. Kenneth Jewell)
    Sing Unto The Lord A New Song
    SA   Keyboard
    Concordia (1963) 98-1709

96:1-3
    Croce, Giovanni
    Cantate Domino omnis terra
    SATB   No accompaniment
    Arista (1971) AE 199

96:1-3
    Hassler, Hans Leo
    Cantate Domino (English/Latin)
    SATB   kro
    E. C. Schirmer (1976) 2979 (also found in
       The Renaissance Singer)

96:1-3
    Hassler, Hans Leo
    Cantate Domine
    SATB   kro
    J. & W. Chester (1977) JWC 55107 (found in
       Fourth Chester Book of Motets)

96:1, 2, 3
    Hassler, Hans Leo
    O Sing Unto The Lord
    SAB   kro
    E. C. Schirmer (n.d.) 2240

96:1, 2, 3
    Hassler, Hans Leo
    O Sing Unto The Lord
    SATB   kro
    E. C. Schirmer   #154 (also found in
       Concord Anthem Book - Red)

96:1, 2, 3
    Hassler, Hans Leo
    O Sing Unto The Lord
    SSA   No accompaniment
    E. C. Schirmer (n.d.) 821

96:1, 2, 3
    Hassler, Hans Leo
    O Sing Unto The Lord
    TTBB   No accompaniment
    E. C. Schirmer (n.d.) 68

96:1, 2, 3
    Hassler, Hans Leo
    O Sing Unto The Lord   (Latin/English)
    SATB   No accompaniment
    Flammer (1938) A-5553

96:1-3
  Morley, Thomas (ed. Anthony Greening)
  O Sing Unto The Lord A New Song
  SAB   Optional organ
  RSCM (1978) (found in Six Easy Three-Part
      Anthems)

96:1-3
  SEE: Psalm 95:1-6
  Hopson, Hal
  Festival Psalm

96:1-3
  Rohlig, Harald
  Sing A New Song To The Lord
  Unison   or SA   Keyboard
  Concordia (1973) 98-2357 (also found in
      Explode With Joy, 97-5165)

96:1-3 (Psalm 40:1-5; Psalm 103:8-11;
      Psalm 107:1-22, 43)
  Zimmermann, Heinz Werner
  Psalm Konzert
  SSATB   Bass, 3 Trumpets, Vibraphone
  Concordia (1965) 97-4854

96:1, 3, 10
  Stern, Theodore
  Sing Unto The Lord A New Song
  SATB   Organ
  Augsburg (1974) 11-0657

96:1-3, 6, 9, 11-13
  Copes, V. Earle
  A New Song
  SATB   Organ or Piano
  Abingdon (1962)   APM-195

96:1-4
  Aston, Peter
  O Sing Unto The Lord A New Song
  SATB   Organ
  RSCM (1978) (found in Anthems From
      Addington, Volume I)

96:1-4
  Aston, Peter
  O Sing Unto The Lord A New Song
  SATB   Organ
  RSCM [Hinshaw] (1978) (published by Hinshaw
      as separate octavo)

96:1, 4 (Psalm 98:1, 5)
  Smith, Stanley
  Sing Unto The Lord
  Unison   Optional percussion and Piano
  Choristers Guild (1969)   A-70

96:1-4
  Buxtehude, Dietrich (ed. Bruno Crusnick)
  Sing To The Lord   (English/German)
  SAB   Organ
  Concordia (1956) 97-6246

96:1-4, 6, 8, 9 (Psalm 98:5, 6, 9)
  Mathias, William
  O Sing Unto The Lord   Op. 29
  SATB   Organ
  Oxford (1965) A-228

96:1-4, 9, 11-13
  Adler, Samuel
  Psalm 96
  SATB   Organ
  G. Schirmer (1967) 11491 (also found in
      20th Century Choral Music)

96:1-5
  Pool, Kenneth
  O Sing Unto The Lord A New Song
  SATB   Organ
  Brodt (1965) 533

96:1-9
  Pachelbel, J.
  Singet dem Herrn ein neues Lied (German)
  SATB/SATB   kro
  Hanssler   H.E. 1.008

96:2, 3, 5, 7-10 (Psalm 115:3-8, 12-15)
  Wesley, Samuel S.
  Ascribe Unto The Lord
  SATB   Organ
  Novello (n.d.) 109

96:2, 3, 5, 7-10 (Psalm 95:3-8, 12-15)
  Wesley, Samuel S.
  Ascribe Unto The Lord
  SATB   Organ
  Novello (n.d.) 29.0105.06

96:2-4, 6
  Hillert, Richard
  Offertory/Common of Apostles, Evangelists
      (Verses and Offertories - Lesser
      Festivals)
  Unison   Organ
  Augsburg (1980) 11-9542

96:2, 6, 9
  SEE: Habakkuk 2:20
  Simper, Caleb
  The Lord Is In His Holy Temple

96:3
  Handel, G. F.
  Declare His Honor
  SAB   Organ
  Concordia (1968) 98-1957

96:3-4
  Handel, G. F.
  Declare His Honor (from Chandos Anthem, #4,
      O Sing Unto The Lord)
  SAB   Continuo, 2 violins, oboe
  Concordia (1976) (found in The SAB Choir
      Goes Baroque, 97-4232)

96:3-6, 9-10
  Purcell, Henry
  Declare His Honour
  SATB (B-solo)   Organ
  Oxford (1933) (found in Church Anthem Book)

96:4   (Psalm 97:1, 6, 8, 12)
  Brandon, George
  The Lord Is King! Let The Earth Rejoice
  SAB   Organ
  Concordia (1980) 98-2477

96:4, 9   (Psalm 34:18; Psalm 145:8;
      I Chronicles 29:13)
  Hollins, Alfred
  O Worship The Lord
  SATB   Organ
  Novello (1903) MT 731 (also found in The
      Novello Anthem Book)

96:6
  SEE: Revelation 7:12
  Wagner, C. G.
  Blessing Glory and Wisdom and Thanks

96:6, 10
  Purcell, Henry
  Glory and Worship are Before Him
  SATB   Organ
  E. C. Schirmer   #146 (also found in The
      Concord Anthem Book - Red)

96:7-13
  Travers, John
  Ascribe Unto The Lord
  SATB (T-B solos)   Organ
  Novello (n.d.) 29.0109.09

96:9
    Travers, John
    O Worship The Lord (from Ascribe Unto The
        Lord)
    Unison   Organ
    RSCM (n.d.) 245

96:9, 13
    SEE: Psalm 95:1-7
    Diemer, Emma Lou
    O Come, Let Us Sing Unto The Lord

96:9, 13
    SEE: Psalm 95:1-7
    Kirk, Theron
    O Come Let Us Sing

96:11-13
    Hassler, Hans Leo
    Laetentur caeli (Latin)
    SATB   kro
    J. & W. Chester (1977) JWC 55107 (found in
        Fourth Chester Book Of Motets)

96:11-13
    Pinkham, Daniel
    Laetentur caeli (from Three Motets)
        (Latin)
    SSA   Organ
    C. F. Peters (1979) 66709

97:00 (Jerusalem Bible)
    Peloquin, C. Alexander
    Shout For Joy
    SATB   Organ (optional congregation)
    GIA (1971) G 1624

97:00
    Schütz, Heinrich (ed. Ulrich S. Leopold)
    The Earth Is King (Four Psalms)
    SATB   Keyboard
    Chantry Music (1959) n.#.

97:00
    Schütz, Heinrich
    The Lord Is King (Four Psalms) (English/
        German)
    SATB   No accompaniment
    Presser (1941) 352.00006

97:00 (based on)
    Wapen, Francis
    The Lord Reigns
    SATB   Organ, Brass Quartet with Timpani
    Concordia (1973) 97-5128 (parts 97-5129)

97:1 (based on)
    SEE: Isaiah 9:6 (based on)
    Anonymous (ed. Albert Seay)
    Born To Us Is The Christ Child

97:1
    Ossewaarde, Jack H.
    Alleluia (from Two Short Motets or Introits)
    SATB   kro
    H. W. Gray (1965) CMR 2894

97:1, 6, 8, 12
    SEE: Psalm 96:4
    Brandon, George
    The Lord Is King!   Let The Earth Rejoice

97:10
    Ouseley, F. A. G.
    O Ye That Love The Lord
    SATB   Organ
    Novello (1953) (also found in Short And
        Easy Anthems, Set 2)

97:11
    SEE: Job 3:3-4, 20-21, 23-24
    Cook, Melville
    Antiphon

98:00
    Alexander, Josef
    O Sing Unto The Lord
    SATB   Organ
    Abingdon (1970) APM-562

98:00
    Archer, Violet
    Sing A New Song To The Lord
    SATB   Organ
    Waterloo (1974) n.#.

98:00   (Wesley)
    Beck, John Ness
    O For a Thousand Tongues
    SATB (S & B solos)   Organ or Brass
        Quartet
    Gentry (1976) G-308

98:00   (Smith-Goodspeed)
    Bitgood, Roberta
    A Song of Triumph
    SATB and Treble Choir   Keyboard
    Hope (1968) F-924

98:00 (Geneva Psalter)
    Bourgeois, Louis (arr. Dick L. Van Halsema)
    Psalm 98
    SATB   kro
    Carl Fischer (1957) CM 6982

98:00
    Clark, K. C.
    Sing Unto The Lord
    SATB   kro
    Lawson Gould (1954) 51238

98:00
    Crandell, Robert
    O Sing Unto The Lord A New Song
    SATB   Organ
    Witmark (1952) 5-W-3444

98:00
    Crawford, John
    Psalm 98
    TBB   Piano, or Brass Quintet
    Oxford (1971) 94.102   (parts sold separately)

98:00
    Dello Joio, Norman
    O Sing Unto The Lord
    TBB   Organ
    Carl Fischer (1959) CM 7138

98:00
    Dickau, David C.
    Sing To The Lord A New Song
    SATB   Piano
    Shawnee (1979) A-1566

98:00
    Distler, Hugo
    Psalm 98
    SATB   No accompaniment
    Arista (1965) AE 110

98:00
    Distler, Hugo
    Singet Dem Herren   Op. 12, #1
    SATB   kro
    Boonin (1975) 243

98:00
    Fromm, Herbert
    Psalm 98
    SATB (T-solo)   Organ
    Transcontinental (1964) TCL 603

98:00
    Gallus, Jacobus
    Psaume XCVIII
    SSATB   No accompaniment
    Les Editions Ouvrieres [Galaxy] (1960) n.#.

98:00   (adapted Routley)
    Geneva Psalter Tune (arr. Carlton Young)
    New Songs Of Celebration
    2 part mixed   Organ, 2 Trumpets, 2 Trom-
       bones
    Agape [Hope] (1977) AG 7226

98:00   (Wesley)
    Glaser, Carl (arr. James H. Laster)
    O For A Thousand Tongues
    SATB   Organ (Optional brass quartet)
    Hinshaw (1981) HMC 533

98:00   (Watts)
    Handel, G. F. (arr. Lee Turner)
    Joy To The World! The Lord Is Come
    Unison with descant   Keyboard
    Broadman (1978) 4560-75

98:00
    Hartley, Walter S.
    O Sing A New Song
    SSATB   kro
    MCA (1968) n.#.

98:00
    Hughes, Howard
    Sing To The Lord
    2 voices   Organ
    GIA (1976) G-2011

98:00
    Huston, John
    O Sing Unto The Lord
    SATB   Organ
    H. W. Gray (1953) 2301

98:00
    Kraft, Leo
    A New Song
    TBB   No accompaniment
    Mercury (1966) MC 500

98:00
    Lekberg, Sven
    O Sing Unto The Lord A New Song
    SATB   kro
    Summy Birchard (1964) 5703

98:00
    Ludlow, Ben
    Let The Floods Clap Their Hands
    3 part speech choir   Percussion
    Flammer (1974) A 5673

98:00
    Lynn, George
    Cantate Domino   (English)
    SATB   kro
    Golden Music Press (1963) H-3

98:00   (adapted)
    McCray, James
    Come Sing Unto The Lord
    SAB   Organ
    H. W. Gray (1980) GCMR 3422

98:00
    Nelson, Ronald A.
    Psalm 98   Joy To The World
    SA   Organ
    Augsburg (1971) 11-1634

98:00
    Peloquin, C. Alexander
    All The Ends Of The Earth
    2 part choir   solo   Organ
    GIA (1971) G-1655 (also found in Songs Of
      Israel, G-1666)

98:00
    Rohlig, Harald
    Sing Unto The Lord
    SATB   kro
    Abingdon (1963) APM-277

98:00
    Schütz, Heinrich
    Der 98 Psalm   (German only)
    SATB/SATB   No accompaniment
    Barenreiter (1962) 2398

98:00
    Schütz, Heinrich (ed. Abraham Kaplan)
    Psalm 98
    SATB/SATB   kro
    Mills (1968) 60829

98:00
    Schütz, Heinrich (ed. Franz Wullner)
    Sing To The Lord A New Song
    SATB/SATB   kro
    G. Schirmer (1901) 5962

98:00
    Schütz, Heinrich (ed. Daniel Reuning)
    Sing To The Lord A Brand New Song (from
      Five Psalms, op. 5) (English/German)
    SATB   No accompaniment
    GIA (1973) G-1790

98:00
    Sinzheimer, Max
    Cantate Domino
    SATB   Organ
    Flammer (1967) 84918

98:00
    Sjostrand, Gene
    O Sing Unto The Lord
    SATB   Piano or Organ
    Flammer (1969) A-5555

98:00
    Strickling, George F.
    A New Song
    SSATBB   Keyboard
    Abingdon (1979) APM-826

98:00
    Taylor, Clifford
    Sing To The Lord A New Song
    SATB   Organ
    Lawson Gould (1959) 803

98:00
    Van Iderstine, A. P.
    Sing Unto God A New Song
    SATB   Organ, Bongos
    The New Music (1975) NMA 120

98:00
    Williamson, Malcolm
    Cantate Domino
    SATB   Organ
    Boosey & Hawkes (1970) 312.40793

98:00
    Willan, Healey
    O Sing Unto The Lord A New Song
    SATB (B-solo) Organ, 2 Trumpets, 2 Trom-
      bones
    C. F. Peters (1966) 6016

98:00   (paraphrase - Walser)
    Wills, Arthur
    Sing A New Song To The Lord
    Unison   Piano or Organ
    Novello (1965) A-1453

98:00
    Wood, Dale
    Sing A Joyful Song In Praise
    SSATBB (B-solo)   Organ
    Hall & McCreary (1951) 1710

98:00   (taken from)
    Wycisk, Kurt J.
    O Sing
    SATB   kro
    Augsburg (1948) 1054

98:1
    SEE: Psalm 96:1
    Gallus, Jacob
    Alleluia Sing A New Song

98:1 (Psalm 95:3; and others)
    Kirk, Theron
    Sing A Song To The Lord
    SSCB   Piano (optional percussion)
    Cambiata (1978) C978107

98:1
    SEE: Psalm 92:1
    McCormick, Clifford
    It Is A Good Thing

98:1a
    SEE: Isaiah 9:6
    Martens, Edmund
    Unto Us A Child Is Born (from Four Introits,
        Set II)

98:1
    SEE: Psalm 95:1, 6
    Smith, Charles, W.
    O Sing Unto The Lord

98:1-2
    Haan, Raymond
    Rejoice In The Lord
    SATB   Organ
    Augsburg (1979) 11-0675

98:1, 2
    Willan, Healey
    Oh Sing Unto The Lord A New Song
    SA   Keyboard
    Concordia (1962) 97-9760 (found in We
        Praise Thee, Volume 2)

98:1-2
    Zimmermann, Heinz Werner
    O Sing Unto The Lord
    SATB   Double Bass
    Chantry Music (1962) n.#.

98:1-3 (adapted)
    Rotermund, Donald
    Sing A New Exultant Song, Alleluia!
    SAB   No accompaniment
    Augsburg (1978) 11-1900

98:1-3
    Weinhorst, Richard
    Sing Ye
    SAB   kro
    Concordia (1971) 98-2074

98:1-3, 9
    Pachelbel, Johann (ed. Leland Sateren)
    Sing A New Song (English/German)
    SATB/SATB   No accompaniment
    AMSI (1977) 329

98:1-3, 9
    Pachelbel, Johann (ed. Walter Ehret)
    Sing To The Lord A New Song
    SATB/SATB   kro
    Hinshaw (1978) HMC 297

98:1, 4-6
    Mechem, Kirke
    Sing Unto The Lord A New Song, Op. 27
    ST and SAB   kro   solo Trumpet
    Mark Foster (1965) MF 403

98:1, 5
    SEE: Psalm 96:1, 4
    Smith, Stanley
    Sing Unto The Lord

98:1, 5, 6
    Haan, Raymond H.
    Break Forth Into Song
    SATB   Organ
    Broadman (1980) 4451-51

98:1-10
    Bender, Jan
    Psalm 98
    SATB   Keyboard and Clarinet, or Viola
    Bethel Lutheran Church, Madison, Wisconsin
        (1964) BM 102

98:2, 3, 4
    Binkerd, Gordon
    Third Mass of Christmas
    SATB   Organ
    Boosey & Hawkes (1967) 5829

98:3
    Wetzler, Robert
    Verse/Christmas II (Verses and Offertories -
        Advent I - Baptism Of Our Lord)
    Unison   Organ
    Augsburg (1979) 11-9541

98:3b
    Zielenski, Mikolaj (ed. J. Herter)
    Viderunt omnes fine terrae (English/Latin)
    SATB   Organ ad lib.
    GIA (1976) G-2001

98:4
    Kirk, Theron
    Make A Noise
    SATB   No accompaniment (optional finger
        cymbals and tambourine)
    Hope (1982) A-533

98:4, 6
    Newbury, Kent A.
    Break Forth Into Joyous Song
    SATB   Keyboard
    Hope (1977) A-488

98:4-6
    Newbury, Kent A.
    Make A Joyful Noise To The Lord
    SATB   Organ
    Lawson Gould (1962) 51069

98:4, 6, 7 (adapted)
    Sindlinger, Maureen
    Make A Joyful Noise To The Lord
    Unison   Keyboard (optional recorder or
        flute)
    Choristers Guild (1967) A-47

98:4-7
    SEE: Psalm 100:1-2
    Mezzagori, Giovanni (ed. Ronald Anderson)
    Jubilate deo (Latin/English)

98:5, 6, 9
    SEE: Psalm 96:1-4, 6, 8-9
    Mathias, William
    O Sing Unto The Lord

98:6-7
    SEE: Psalm 81:1-3, 14-15
    Orr, Robin
    Sing Aloud Unto God

98:7-10
   SEE: Psalm 149:1-3
   Leighton, Kenneth
   O Sing Unto The Lord A New Song (Three
      Psalms)

98:8
   Ludlow, Ben
   Let The Floods Clap Their Hands
   3 part speech choir
   Flammer (1974) A-5673

99:00
   DeMille, Robert
   Make A Joyful Noise
   SSATB   kro
   Plymouth (1967) JR 124

99:00
   Goemanne, Noel
   Entrata
   SATB   Organ
   World Library (1965) ESA 955-8

99:00
   Pachelbel, Johann
   Der Herr ist König (The Lord God Reigneth)
        English/German)
   SATB/SATB   Continuo
   Concordia (1954) 97-7568

99:00 (The Grail)
   Walker, Christopher
   Cry Out With Joy
   Unison   Keyboard
   Oxford (1975) E 136

99:00 (based on)
   Wapen, Francis
   The Lord Is King   Op. 44, #1
   SAB   Organ
   GIA (1979) G-2219

99:5
   Thiman, Eric
   Exalt Ye The Lord   (from Six Introductory
        Sentences)
   SATB   Organ
   Novello (1973) MW 25

100:00
   Agazzari, Agostino
   Jubilate Deo (English/Latin)
   SAB   Continuo and 2 violins
   Concordia (1976) 98-2362 (also found in
        The SAB Choir Goes Baroque, 97-5232)

100:00
   Allured, Donald
   Psalm 100
   SATB   Organ (4 or 5 octave handbells)
   Agape [Hope] (1981) RS-7711

100:00
   Arnatt, Ronald
   O Be Joyful
   Antiphonal Unison Voices   Keyboard
   Walton (1971) 2254

100:00
   Arnold, Malcolm
   Two Ceremonial Psalms
   SSA   No accompaniment
   Patersons (1952) 1863

100:00
   Bales, Gerald
   Jubilate Deo
   SATB   Organ   3 Trumpets, 3 Trombones,
        Percussion
   Waterloo Music (1966) n.#.

100:00
   Berger, Jean
   Make Ye A Joyful Noise (from Bay Psalm
        Book, Set II)
   SATB   No accompaniment
   Shawnee (1980) A-1597

100:00 (based on)
   Berger, Jean
   O Sing All Ye Lands
   SATB   kro
   Augsburg (1962) 1337

100:00
   SEE: Psalm 108:2
   Bernstein, Leonard
   Chichester Psalms   Chorus #1

100:00
   Blair, Dallas
   Make A Joyful Noise
   SATB   Keyboard
   Broadman (1975) 4545-87

100:00
   Bristol, Lee Hastings, Jr.
   Psalm 100
   SATB   Organ
   Presser (1976) 312.41126

100:00
   Britten, Benjamin
   Jubilate Deo
   SATB   Organ
   Oxford (1961) S-551 (also found in Anthems
        For Choirs, Volume 4)

100:00
   Cabena, Barrie
   Jubilate Deo
   SATB   Organ or Piano
   Huron Press [Oxford] (1967) HSS-5

100:00
   Cain, Noble
   Make A Joyful Sound
   SSAATTBB   Keyboard
   Flammer (1946) A-5318

100:00
   Cope, Cecil
   Jubilate
   SATB   Organ
   Boosey & Hawkes (1969) 5761

100:00
   Couperin, Francois (arr. Kenneth Jewell)
   Make A Joyful Noise
   SAB   Organ or Piano
   Concordia (1970) 98-2041 (also found in
        Sing For Joy, 97-5046)

100:00 (adapted)
   Cox, Ainslee
   O Be Joyful In The Lord
   SATB   kro
   Presser (1954) 312.40216

100:00
   Croft, William (ed. Rebecca Harrison)
   O Be Joyful In The Lord All Ye Lands
   SATB   Organ
   Concordia (1979) 98-2397

100:00
   Cruft, Adrian
   Jubilate Deo   Op. 51
   SATB   Organ (optional brass ensemble)
   Boosey & Hawkes (1969) CCS 85

100:00
diLasso, Orlando
Jubilate Deo
SATB   No accompaniment
Arista (1972) AE 219

100:00 (adapted)
diLasso, Orlando (ed. & arr. Robert Fields)
Jubilate Deo
SATB   kro
Boosey & Hawkes (1964) 5490

100:00
Dirksen, Richard
Jubilate Deo
2 part mixed   Organ
Lawson Gould (1960) 894

100:00
Donato, Anthony
Make A Joyful Noise
Unison children   Organ (optional brass
    quartet)
Kjos (1964) 6099 (brass parts BR 6099)

100:00
Dorste, Doreen
O Be Joyful In The Lord
2 part   Organ or Piano
Associated (1960) A 337

100:00 (adapted)
Eddlemann, David
Be Joyful In The Lord
SATB   Optional keyboard (trumpet trio
    and bass)
Carl Fischer (1981) CM 8129

100:00
Ellsworth, A. Eugene
O Be Joyful
SATB   No accompaniment
Abingdon (1971) APM-500

100:00
Faustini, J. Wilson
Hail The Lord
SATB   Organ or Piano
Golden Music (1963) G-9

100:00
Fetler, Paul
Sing and Rejoice (Jubilate Deo)
SATB 3 Trumpets, 2 Horns, 3 Trombones
Augsburg (1965) 11-9235

100:00
Fink, Michael
Jubilate Deo (O Be Joyful)
SATB   Organ (optional brass sextet)
E. C. Schirmer (1976) 2948

100:00
Ford, Virgil T.
Make A Joyful Noise
SATB   Keyboard or Handbells
Flammer (1967) A-5144

100:00
Frackenpohl, Arthur
Make A Joyful Noise
SATB   Organ (optional brass)
Elkan Vogel (1954) 1187 (score and parts
    on rental)

100:00
Freed, Isadore
Make A Joyful Noise
SATB   Optional accompaniment
Transcontinental (n.d.) TCL 112

100:00
Fruch, Armin Leberecht
Psalm 100
SATB   kro
Hall & McCreary (1951) 1706

100:00
Gabrieli, Giovanni
Jubilate Deo (Latin)
SSAATTBB   No accompaniment
Arista (1978) AE 296

100:00
Gabrieli, Giovanni (ed. Norman Grayson)
Jubilate Deo
SSAATTBB   No accompaniment
Bourne (1963) ES 72

100:00
Gabrieli, Giovanni (ed. C. Grayson)
Jubilate Deo
SSAATTBB   No accompaniment
Kjos (1940) 7007

100:00
Gardner, John
Jubilate Deo   Op. 37, #2
SATB   No accompaniment
Oxford (1960) n.#.

100:00
Glarum, L. Stanley
O Be Joyful
SATB   No accompaniment
Carl Fischer (1950) CM 6550

100:00
Glarum, L. Stanley
O Be Joyful
TTBB   No accompaniment
Carl Fischer (1950) CM 7249

100:00
Greenhill, Harold
Make A Joyful Noise
SATB   Organ
Novello (1933) 1088

100:00
Gustafson, Dwight
All People That On Earth Do Dwell
SATB   Organ or Brass
J. Fischer (1968) 9857 (parts for brass
    available from publisher)

100:00
Hallock, Peter
Antiphon on Psalm 100
SATB   Trumpet
GIA (1977) 5-2082

100:00 (paraphrase)
Hancock, Vicki
Make A Noise Unto The Lord!
Unison or 2 part   18 Handbells
Broadman (1977) 4560-66

100:00
Harrison, Julius
Psalm C
SATB   Organ
Lengnick (1953) 3803

100:00
Hassler, Hans Leo
Jubilate Deo
SATB   No accompaniment
Anni Bank (1950 40

100:00
   Hillert, Richard
   Psalm 100
   Unison   Congregation   Organ
   Augsburg (1978) (found in Seasonal Psalms
        For Congregation and Choir, 11-9376)

100:00
   Hoag, Charles K.
   O Be Joyful
   SSATBB   kro
   G. Schirmer (1972) 11859

100:00   (Ulrik Koren)
   Hoff, Erik (setting by S. Drummond Wolff)
   Ye Lands, To The Lord Make A Jubilant Noise
   SATB   Organ
   Concordia (1977) 98-2309

100:00   (Ravenscroft)
   Holst, Gustav (editor)
   All People That On Earth Do Dwell
   SATB   Organ
   Stainer & Bell (1970) #7

100:00
   Howells, Herbert
   Jubilate Deo
   SATB   Organ
   Novello (1967)   1438

100:00
   Humfrey, Pelham (transcribed & edited,
        Cyril F. Simkins)
   O Be Joyful
   SSATB   kro
   Concordia (1970) 98-2051

100:00
   Hunnicutt, Judy
   Make A Joyful Noise
   SATB   Keyboard
   Augsburg (1977) 11-1810

100:00
   Hunnicutt, Judy
   Sing For Joy To The Lord
   2 part treble   Piano or Handbells
   Augsburg (1976) 11-1772

100:00
   Huston, John
   O Be Joyful In The Lord
   SATB   Organ
   H. W. Gray (1955) CMR 2371

100:00
   Ives, Grayston
   Jubilate (O Be Joyful In The Lord)(English)
   SATB   Organ
   Novello (1975) NCM 44

100:00
   Ives, Charles (ed. John Kirkpatrick and
        Gregg Smith
   Psalm 100
   SA & SATB   Organ
   Merion [Presser] (1975) 342.40113

100:00
   Jacob, Gordon
   O Be Joyful In The Lord
   SATB   Organ
   Novello (1958) Anth. 1372

100:00
   James, Philip
   O Be Joyful In The Lord
   SATB   Keyboard
   Galaxy (1951) GMC 1904

100:00
   Johnson, Allen (ed. Don Neuen)
   Christmas Triology
   SA   Piano
   Lawson Gould (1978) 52052

100:00
   Jolley, Florence (arr.)
   All People That On Earth Do Dwell
   SATB   Organ
   G. Schirmer (n.d.) 623

100:00
   Jones, W. Bradwen
   O Be Joyful In The Lord
   Unison (boys)   Piano or Organ
   Novello (1955) 1321

100:00
   Joubert, John
   O Be Joyful   Op. 100
   SATB   Organ
   ABI   #1061

100:00
   Kelly, Brian
   O Be Joyful In The Lord
   SATB   Organ
   Novello (1970)   29.0156.00

100:00   (adapted)
   Krapf, Gerhard
   Sing Ye To The Lord
   SAB   kro
   Abingdon (1966) APM-527

100:00
   Kroeger, Karl
   Make A Joyful Noise
   SATB   Piano
   Carl Fischer (1978) CM 8044

100:00
   Lacey, David T.
   O Be Joyful In The Lord
   SATB   Organ
   H. W. Gray (1971) CMR 3229

100:00
   Laverty, John Timothy
   Psalm 100
   SATB   kro
   Hall & McCreary (1954) 1719

100:00
   Lawes, William (ed. Gordon Dodd)
   All People That On Earth Do Dwell
   SATB (T-B-solos)   Organ
   Stainer & Bell [Galaxy] (1966) n.#.

100:00
   Leaf, Robert
   With A Jubilant Song
   SATB   Organ, 3 Trumpets
   Augsburg (1971) 11-1621

100:00
   Leighton, Kenneth
   O Be Joyful In The Lord
   SATB   Organ
   Oxford (1967) A 240

100:00
   Lekberg, Sven
   Make A Joyful Noise Unto The Lord
   SATB   kro
   Galaxy (1952) 1.1873.1

100:00
   Ley, Henry G.
   O Be Joyful In The Lord
   SSS (boys or women)   Organ
   Oxford (1951) n.#.

100:00
    Longthorne, Brian
    O Be Joyful
    SATB   Organ
    Oxford (1967) A-244

100:00 (text by Brooke)
    Lovelace, Austin
    All Lands and Peoples
    2 part mixed   Organ
    Augsburg (1964) 1397

100:00
    Lynn, George
    The Lord Is Good
    SATB   kro
    Presser (1971)   312-40746

100:00
    LeJeune, Claude
    Psalm 100   (English/French)
    SAB   No accompaniment
    Mercury (1945) MC 56

100:00
    Marshall, Jane
    Make A Joyful Noise
    2 part treble   Piano
    Carl Fischer (1956) CM 7322

100:00
    Martin, Gilbert
    O Be Joyful In The Lord
    SATB   Organ
    Carl Fischer (1976) CM 7949

100:00
    Martin, Gilbert
    O Be Joyful In The Lord (A Morning Canticle)
    SATB   Organ
    H. W. Gray (1975) 3336

100:00
    Mathias, William
    Make A Joyful Noise Unto The Lord, Op. 26,
        #2
    SATB   Organ
    Oxford (1965) A-220 (also found in Anthems
        For Choirs, Volume 4)

100:00
    Mathias, William
    Make A Joyful Noise Unto The Lord, Op. 26,
        #2
    SATB   Organ
    RSCM (found in Festival Service Book, #5)

100:00
    Mayfield, Larry
    Make A Joyful Noise To The Lord
    SATB   Piano
    Broadman (1979) 4566-09

100:00
    Mechem, Kirke
    Make A Joyful Noise Unto The Lord
    SATB   kro
    E. C. Schirmer (1961) ECS 1773

100:00
    Mendelssohn, Felix (ed. Robert Hines)
    The Hundredth Psalm (Der Hundertste Psalm)
        (English/German)
    SATB   kro
    Concordia (1975) 98-2215

100:00
    Miller, Thomas A.
    Make A Joyful Noise
    SATB   Organ or Piano
    New Music (1973) NM A 101

100:00
    Mozart, W. A. (ed. Boyd Bacon)
    Jubilate Deo (Latin/English)
    SATB   kro
    G. Schirmer (1980) 12394

100:00
    Mueller, Carl F.
    All People That On Earth Do Dwell
    SATB   kro
    Carl Fischer (1950) CM 6588

100:00
    Mueller, Carl F.
    The One Hundredth Psalm
    SA   Organ
    Flammer (1935) 86032

100:00
    Mueller, Carl F.
    The One Hundredth Psalm
    SAB   Piano
    Flammer (1942) D-5005

100:00
    SEE: Psalm 25
    Muro, Don
    O Be Joyful

100:00
    McCray, James
    Jubilate Deo
    SATB   13 or 19 Handbells   kro
    Tetra [Alexander Broude] (1981) n.#.

100:00
    Naylor, Bernard
    O Be Joyful In The Lord
    SATB   Organ
    Novello (1966)   1462

100:00   (with other texts)
    Nelson, Ron
    For Freedom Of Conscience
    SATB   Organ   2 or 3 Trumpets, Narrator
    Boosey & Hawkes (1980) 6037

100:00
    Nelson, Ronald A.
    Make A Joyful Noise (Three Psalms)
    SATB   Brass or Woodwind Quartet
    Augsburg (1976) 11-0560 (parts 11-0561)

100:00
    Nourse, John
    Jubilate Deo
    SATB   Organ
    Oxford (1968)   A-243

100:00   (1611 Version)
    Orr, Robin
    Make A Joyful Noise Unto The Lord
    2 part treble   Organ
    Oxford (1970) E-123

100:00
    SEE: Psalm 150
    Ouchterlony, David
    A Psalm Of Praise

100:00
    Ouchterlony, David
    O Be Joyful In God
    SATB and Junior Choir   Organ
    F. Harris (1977) HC 4073

100:00
    Pachelbel, Johann
    Jauchzet dem Herrn (Shout to the Lord)
        (English/German)
    SATB/SATB   Continuo
    Concordia (1954) 97-7570

100:00
    Peeters, Flor
    Jubilate Deo, Op. 40b (Latin/English)
    SATB   Organ
    McLaughlin & Reilly (1955) M 2096

100:00
    Peeters, Flor
    Jubilate Deo, Op. 40 (English/Latin)
    TTB   Organ
    McLaughlin & Reilly (1954) 2370

100:00
    SEE: Psalm 8:4
    Peloquin, C. Alexander
    Lord Jesus Come

100:00
    Peloquin, C. Alexander
    Psalm One Hundred
    SATB   Organ (optional brass, strings,
        percussion)
    GIA (1974) G-1861

100:00
    SEE: Psalm 90
    Pfautsch, Lloyd
    Jubilate Deo

100:00
    Pinkham, Daniel
    Jubilate Deo
    Unison and SSA and SATB   Organ
    E. C. Schirmer (1966) 2003

100:00
    Porter, Ewell
    Psalm 100
    SATB   kro
    Broadman (1965) 4537-65

100:00
    Powell, Robert J.
    O Be Joyful In The Lord
    SATB   Organ
    H. W. Gray (1972) CMR 3248

100:00
    Pritchard, Arthur J.
    O Be Joyful In The Lord
    SATB   Organ
    H. W. Gray (1973) CMR 3276

100:00 (and Sarum Antiphon)
    Proulx, Richard
    Behold Now The House Of God
    SATB   Organ
    Augsburg (1969) 11-1572

100:00
    Purcell, Henry
    Jubilate Deo (English)
    SATB   Organ
    Schmitt, Hall, McCreary (1951) (found in
        Rare Choral Masterpieces)

100:00
    Purvis, Richard
    Jubilate Deo
    Unison   Organ
    MCA (1943) 02089-064

100:00 (adapted)
    Ramsfield, Jerome K.
    Make A Joyful Sound!
    SATB   Piano
    Shawnee (1971) A-5559

100:00   (Kethe)
    Roberts, Nancy M.
    All People That On Earth Do Dwell
    SATB   Keyboard
    Broadman (1971) 4562-28

100:00
    Roff, Joseph
    Sing Joyfully To The Lord
    Unison   Organ
    GIA (1971) G-1617

100:00
    Rohlig, Harald
    Sing For Joy To The Lord
    Unison or SA   Keyboard
    Concordia (1973) 97-5165 (found in Explode
        With Joy)

100:00
    Roman, Johann Helmich (ed. S. Drummond
        Wolff)
    Jubilate Deo (English/Latin)
    SATB   Keyboard
    Concordia (1972) 98-2291

100:00
    Roman, Johann H. (ed. S. Drummond Wolff)
    Jubilate Deo (English/German)
    SATB   Keyboard
    Concordia (1972) 97-5025 (optional instru-
        ments, 97-5026)

100:00
    Roth, Robert N.
    Psalm 100
    Unison   Accompanied
    Canyon (1958) 5801

100:00 (based on)
    Russell, Carlton
    O Be Joyful In The Lord!
    SATB   Organ
    H. W. Gray (1980) GCMR 3430

100:00
    Schütz, Heinrich
    Der 100 Psalm
    SATB   No accompaniment
    Barenreiter (n.d.) 480

100:00
    Schütz, Heinrich (ed. Walter Ehret)
    Praise Ye The Father
    SATB/SATB   Optional brass
    Presser (1976) 312.41124

100:00
    Schütz, Heinrich
    Psalm 100
    SATB, or SATB and Brass   No accompaniment
    Gordon Thompson (1973) E.I.2002

100:00
    Schütz, Heinrich (ed. George Lynn)
    Psalm 100
    SATB/SATB   kro
    Presser (1951) 312-40084

100:00
    Schütz, Heinrich (ed. Daniel Reuning)
    Sing To Jehovah (from Five Psalms) Op. 5
        (English/German)
    SATB   No accompaniment
    GIA (1973) G-1790

100:00
    Sellars, James
    Psalm 100
    SATB   Optional accompaniment
    Carl Fischer (1970) CM 7739

100:00
    Shaw, Geoffrey
    O Be Joyful In The Lord
    SATB   Organ
    Novello (1962) AP 24

100:00
  Simper, Caleb
  Make A Joyful Noise
  SATB   Organ
  Presser (1907) 5953

100:00
  Smart, David
  Make A Joyful Noise Unto The Lord
  SA   Organ or Piano and Percussion
  Hope (1968) F-931

100:00
  Sweelinck, J. P.
  All People That On Earth Do Dwell (English)
  SATB   Organ
  E. C. Schirmer (1971) 2791

100:00
  Tallis, Thomas
  All People That On Earth Do Dwell
  SATB   kro
  E. C. Schirmer (n.d.) 1012 (also found in
      Second Concord Anthem Book - Grey)

100:00
  Thalben-Ball, George
  O Be Joyful In The Lord
  SATB   Organ
  Novello (1958) MT 1581   (also found in King
      Of Glory)

100:00 (metrical paraphrase)
  Tomblings, Philip
  All From The Sun's Uprise
  SAB   Organ
  Oxford (1936) E-18 (also found in Oxford
      Easy Anthem Book)

100:00
  Vaughan, Roger
  Psalm 100
  SATB   kro
  Oxford (1963) 94.319

100:00   (Kethe)
  Vaughan Williams, Ralph
  The Hundredth Psalm (O Be Joyful In The
      Lord)
  SATB   Organ
  Galaxy (1929) 1.5022.1

100:00   (Kethe)
  Vaughan Williams, Ralph
  The Old Hundredth Psalm Tune
  SATB   Congregation   Organ (Orchestra)
  Oxford (1953) 42P953

100:00
  Walton, William
  Jubilate Deo
  SATB/SATB   Organ
  Oxford (1973) 42.373

100:00
  Weaver, John B.
  Psalm 100
  SATB   Organ
  Boosey & Hawkes (1960) 5336

100:00
  White, Louie L.
  Jubilate Deo (English)
  SATB   Keyboard
  Abingdon (1962) APM-177

100:00
  Wickens, Dennis
  Jubilate Deo (English)
  SATB   Organ
  Oxford (1968) S 587

100:00
  Willan, Healey
  Make A Joyful Noise Unto The Lord
  SA   Keyboard
  Concordia (1962) 97-7610 (found in We
      Praise Thee, Volume II)

100:00
  Willan, Healey
  O Be Joyful
  SATB   Organ
  Chanteclair [Gordon Thompson] (1973) G-591

100:00
  Williams, David
  Make A Joyful Noise
  SATB   Organ
  H. W. Gray (1974) CMR 3305

100:00
  Williams, David H.
  Psalm 100
  SATB   Organ
  C. C. Birchard (1952) 2047

100:00
  Wood, Charles
  O Be Joyful In The Lord
  SATB   Organ
  Novello (1980) (found in Into His Courts
      With Praise)

100:00   (based on)
  Wood, Dale
  Call To Worship (in Choral Sentences for
      Worship)
  SATB   No accompaniment
  Sacred Music Press (1973) S-141

100:00
  Wood, Dale
  Jubilate Deo
  2 part   Organ (optional percussion)
  Augsburg (1971) 11-9285 (found in Music for
      the Contemporary Choir, Volume 2)

100:00
  Wood, Dale
  Jubilate Deo
  SATB   Organ (optional percussion)
  Augsburg (1970) 11-1603

100:00
  Young, Carlton
  Jubilate Deo
  Unison   Piano, Bass, Drums
  Agape (1973) AG-7129 (found in Fourteen
      Canticles and Responses)

100:00
  Young, Philip
  Sing Ye Joyfully To The Lord
  SA   Organ
  Augsburg (1966) PS 620

100:00
  Zimmermann, Heinz Werner
  Psalm 100
  SATB   Organ, Bass
  Augsburg (1970) 11-0640

100:1   (and other)
  Gabrieli, G. (ed. Dale Jergenson and Daniel
      Wolfe)
  Plaudit
  SSAT/SATB/TTBB   Organ and instruments
  G. Schirmer (1972) 11895

100:1
  SEE: Psalm 96
  Gallus, J.
  Alleluia! Sing A New Song

100:1   (Psalm 150:3)
    Ramsfield, Jerome K.
    O Be Joyful
    SATB   Piano or Organ
    Flammer (1971) A 5558

100:1
    Titcomb, Everett
    O Be Joyful In The Lord
    SATB   kro
    Carl Fischer (1954) CM 6708

100:1
    SEE: Psalm 96:1
    Track, Gerhard
    Sing To The Lord A New Song

100:1, 2
    Hunnicutt, Judy
    In Praise To God
    SATB   Organ and Handbells
    Augsburg (1973) 11-0652

100:1-2   (Psalm 98:4-7)
    Mezzogorri, Giovanni (ed. Ronald Anderson)
    Jubilate Deo   (Latin/English)
    SS or SA or TT or TB   Keyboard
    Concordia (1980) 98-2470

100:1-2
    SEE: Psalm 72:3, 18-19
    Moe, Daniel
    Blessed Be The Lord God

100:1-2, 4
    SEE: Psalm 96:1-3
    Couperin, Francois (arr. & ed. Kenneth
        Jewell)
    Sing Unto The Lord A New Song

100:1-3
    di Lasso, Orlando (arr. Robert Field)
    Jubilate Deo   (English/Latin)
    SATB   kro
    Boosey & Hawkes (1964) 5490

100:1-3
    diLasso, Orlando (ed. C. Buell Agey)
    Jubilate Deo   (English/Latin)
    SATB   kro
    G. Schirmer (1973) 11987

100:1-3
    diLasso, Orlando (ed. Maynard Klein)
    Jubilate Deo omnis terra (Latin/English)
    SATB   kro
    G. Schirmer (1967) 11410

100:1-3
    Hassler, Hans Leo (ed. Walter Ehret)
    Jubilate Deo (Latin/English)
    SATB/SATB   kro
    Concordia (1978) 98-2348 (parts for Brass,
        Choir II, 98-2366)

100:1-3
    Lassus, Orlandus
    Jubilate Deo   (Latin only)
    SATB   kro
    J. & W. Chester (1977) JWC 55103 (found in
        Fifth Chester Book of Motets)

100:1-3
    Lassus, Orlandus
    Jubilate Deo   (Latin only)
    SATB   kro
    Mercury (1947) 352.00080

100:1-4   (Psalm 105:1-2)
    Berk, Adele
    Alleluia Is Our Song
    SA   Piano
    H. W. Gray (1981) GCMR 3436

100:1, 4
    Hanlon, Kevin
    Psalm 100 (Two Choral Introits)
    SATB   No accompaniment
    Alexander Broude (1982) AB 962

100:2
    Handel, G. F. (arr. Lloyd Pfautsch)
    Know That The Lord Is God
    2 part mixed   Organ
    Lawson Gould (1960) 872

100:2
    Handel, G. F. (ed. Walter Barrie)
    Serve The Lord With Gladness
    SATB   Piano or Organ
    Lawson Gould (1959) 794

100:2-3
    SEE: Psalm 96:1-2
    Geisler, J. C. (ed. E. V. Nolte)
    Sing To The Lord A New-Made Song

100:2, 3, 5
    Peloquin, C. Alexander
    We Are His People
    SATB   Solo   Organ
    GIA (1971) G-1665 (also found in Songs of
        Israel, G 1666)

100:4
    Hennagin, Michael
    Enter Into His Gates (from Four Responses)
    Unison mixed   Organ
    Walton (1974) 2809

100:4
    Proulx, Richard
    Processional Psalm
    2 equal voices   4 Handbells
    GIA (1972) G-1750

100:4, 5
    Posegate, Maxcine Woodbridge
    Fanfare For Thanksgiving
    SATB   Piano or Organ, 3 Trumpets
    Flammer (1965) A-5052

100:4-5   (adapted)
    Savage, Howard S.
    Enter Into His Gates
    SATB   Accompanied
    Hall & McCreary (1941) 1567

100:5
    SEE: Philippians 4:4
    Rickard, Jeffery (ed. & arr.)
    Rejoice In The Lord

101:00
    Diemer, Emma Lou
    I Will Sing Of Mercy And Judgment
    SATB   Piano
    Carl Fischer (1970) CM 7804

101:00
    SEE: Psalm 25
    Muro, Don
    O Be Joyful

101:1-4
    Mawby, Colin
    My Song Shall Be Of Mercy And Judgment
    2 treble voices   Organ
    GIA (1964) G-1098

102:00
    Dimeo, John J.
    Hear My Prayer, O Lord
    SATB   Organ
    H. W. Gray (1967) CMR 2969

102:00
    Sweelinck, J. P.
    Psalm 102
    SATB   No accompaniment
    Mercury (1941) MC 5

102:1 (adapted from)
    diLasso, Orlando (ed. C. Buell Agey)
    Domine exaudi orationem meam (Lord Hear My
        Prayer) (English/Latin)
    SATB   kro
    G. Schirmer (1966) 11422

102:1
    diLasso, Orlando (ed. John Kingsbury)
    Lord Hear My Prayer   (English/Latin)
    SATB   kro
    Presser (1976) 312-41149

102:1
    Purcell, Henry
    Hear My Prayer, O Lord
    SSATTBB   Optional Organ
    Blandford [Alexander Broude] (1965) AB 221

102:1
    Purcell, Henry (ed. Watkins Shaw)
    Hear My Prayer, O Lord
    SSAATTBB   Organ
    Novello (1969) 88.0009.10

102:1, 2 (Psalm 103:1, 13, 14)
    Kopylof, A. (ed. Carl Engel)
    Hear My Prayer
    SATB   kro
    Boston Music (1917) 1294

102:1, 2
    Locke, Matthew
    O Lord Hear My Prayer
    ATB   Continuo
    Oxford (1965) (found in Anthems for Men's
        Voices, Volume I)

102:1-2
    Newbury, Kent A.
    Hear My Prayer, O Lord
    SATB   kro
    G. Schirmer (1969) 11578

102:1-2
    Tomkins, T.
    Hear My Prayer, O Lord
    ATBB   kro
    Oxford (1965) (found in Anthems for Men's
        Voices, Volume I)

102:2
    Morgan, Haydn
    Hide Not Thy Face
    SATB   kro
    Carl Fischer (1957) CM 6296

102:11, 12, 13
    Blow, John (ed. Heathcote Statham)
    My Days Are Gone Like A Shadow
    SATB   Organ ad lib.
    Oxford (1955) n.#.

102:12, 25-27 (and other)
    Sateren, Leland
    O God, The Rock of Ages
    SATB   Organ
    Augsburg (1971) 11-1642

102:13
    diLasso, Orlando (ed. Eric Dawson)
    Tu exsurgens   (Latin)
    SSA or TTB   kro
    National Music (1973) WHC 33

102:16 (Psalm 122:6, 7; Psalm 132:15)
    Cole, John (ed. Mason Martens)
    When The Lord Shall Build Up Zion
    SATB (T-solo)   Organ
    McAfee (1975) (in Bicentennial Collection
        Of American Choral Music)

102:24
    Thiman, Eric
    O Lord, How Manifold Are Thy Works (from
        Six Introductory Sentences)
    SATB   Organ
    Novello (1973) MW 25

102:25-27   (I Corinthians 3:9, 11, 16;
        John 4:24;   Hebrews 12:1-2; Isaiah 58:
        11-12)
    DeTar, Vernon
    The Glory Of The Lord
    SATB   Organ
    H. W. Gray (1940) 1410

102:25-27
    Locke, Matthew
    In The Beginning, O Lord
    ATB   kro
    Oxford (1965) (found in Anthems for Men's
        Voices, Volume I)

103:00 (Lyte)
    Andrews, Mark
    Praise My Soul The King of Heaven
    TTBB   Organ
    G. Schirmer (1933) 7734

103:00 (adapted from)
    Bach, J. S. (arr. Hal H. Hopson)
    Bless The Lord My Soul
    SA   Accompanied
    Flammer (1979) E 5201

103:00
    Beethoven, L. (arr. A. B. Couper)
    Praise My Soul The King Of Heaven
    SA with descant   Keyboard
    J. Fischer (1958) 9098 (found in The
        Chapel Choir For Juniors)

103:00 (Watts paraphrase)
    Brandon, George
    Bless The Lord
    SATB   kro
    GIA (1975) G-1931

103:00 (Bay Psalm Book)
    Brandon, George (arr.)
    O My Soul, Jehovah Bless
    SATB   Organ
    Concordia (1968) 98-1923

103:00
    Cain, Noble
    Psalm 103
    SATB   Organ or Piano
    Flammer (1967) A-5033

103:00
    Child, William (ed. Gerald Knight)
    Praise The Lord O My Soul
    SATB   Keyboard
    Carl Fischer (1965) CM 7509

103:00
    Child, William (ed. C. F. Simkins)
    Praise The Lord O My Soul
    SATB   Keyboard
    RSCM (1963) 227

103:00
    Dirksen, Richard
    Bless The Father, O My Soul
    SATB   No Accompaniment
    Flammer (1971) A 5725

103:00
    Freed, Isadore
    Bless The Lord O My Soul
    SATB   Optional Accompaniment
    Transcontinental Music (n.d.) TCL 113

103:00
    Frith, Michael
    Bless The Lord All His Angels
    SATB   Keyboard
    RSCM (found in Festival Service Book, #7)

103:00 (Lyte)
    Gilbert, Norman
    Praise My Soul The King Of Heaven
    SSA or Unison   Piano
    Oxford (1963) 44.212

103:00   (Psalm 150)
    Goemanne, Noel
    Praise To The Lord
    SATB   Organ, 1 or 2 Trumpets
    GIA (1979) G-2224

103:00
    Greene, Maurice
    O Praise The Lord   (from Praise The Lord O
        My Soul)
    Unison   Organ
    Bosworth [RSCM] (1910) 13691

103:00 (adapted by John Moment)
    Ippolitof-Ivanof, M. (arr. Peter J.
        Wilhousky)
    Bless Ye The Lord
    SATB   kro
    Carl Fischer (1943) CM 636

103:00   (Lyte)
    Livingston, Hugh, Jr.
    Praise My Soul The King Of Heaven
    SATB   Keyboard
    Broadman (1973) 4540-64

103:00   (adapted)
    Lotti, Antonio (ed. Walter Ehret)
    Blessed The Lord O My Soul
    SAB   Piano or Organ
    Ludwig Music (1969) L9138

103:00
    Proulx, Richard and J. Gelineau
    My Soul Give Thanks To The Lord
    SATB   Organ, Cantor, Congregation,
        Handbells
    GIA (1975) G-1921

103:00   (adapted)
    Russian Air (arr. Clarice Knight)
    Psalm 103
    SC(B)   Piano
    Cambiata Press (1980) T180137

103:00   (B. Rees)
    Webber, Lloyd
    Unite To Praise Thy Maker's Name
    SATB   Organ
    Novello (1961) MT 1419

103:1
    Beck, John Ness
    Canticle Of Praise
    SATB   Piano or Organ
    Presser (1964) 312-40588

103:1 (plus additional)
    Dirksen, Richard
    Bless The Father O My Soul
    SATB   No accompaniment
    Flammer (1976) A 5725

103:1
    SEE: Psalm 61:1
    Kopyloff, Alexander
    Hear My Cry, O God

103:1, 2
    Hanlon, Kevin
    Psalm 103 (Two Choral Introits)
    SATB   No accompaniment
    Alexander Broude (1982) AB 962

103:1, 2
    Moe, Daniel
    Psalm Concerto - Part II
    SATB   2 Trumpets, 2 Trombones, Bass
    Augsburg (1970) 11-0633

103:1, 2 (Psalm 66:4; Psalm 65:14)
    Smart, Richard
    Praise The Lord O My Soul
    SATB   Organ
    Novello (n.d.) 29.0142.00

103:1-2
    Tomkins, Thomas
    Praise The Lord, O My Soul
    SSTB   Organ
    Oxford (1969) TCM 49

103:1-2, 8
    Young, Carlton
    Bless The Lord
    SATB   Organ
    Hope (1977) CY 3347

103:1-2, 8, 13, 18
    Ippolitoff-Ivanoff, M. (ed. Carl F.
        Mueller)
    Bless The Lord O My Soul
    SATB   kro
    G. Schirmer (1963) (found in Five Centuries
        Of Choral Music)

103:1-2, 8, 13, 18 (adapted)
    Ippolitoff-Ivanoff, M.
    Bless The Lord
    SATB   Organ ad lib.
    H. W. Gray (1920) 200

103:1-2, 8, 13, 18
    Ippolitoff-Ivanoff, Michael (arr. H. Clough-
        Leighter)
    Bless The Lord
    SATB   Organ ad lib.
    Oliver Ditson (1934) 332.13770

103:1-2, 11
    Pasquet, Jean
    Bless Thou The Lord
    SAB   kro
    Augsburg (1962) 11-0602

103:1-3
    Clarke, Jeremiah (ed. Mason Martens)
    Praise The Lord, O My Soul
    SAB   Organ
    Concordia (1965) 98-1785

103:1-3 (Psalm 146:1)
    Tomkins, Thomas (ed. John Morehen)
    Praise The Lord, O My Soul
    SATB   Organ
    Novello (1970) NECM 12

103:1, 3, 6, 11
    Bach, J. S. (arr. Hal Hopson)
    Bless The Lord My Soul (from Cantata #196)
    SA or TB   Keyboard
    Flammer (1975) A-5696

103:1-4
     Burroughs, Bob
     Bless His Holy Name
     SATB   kro
     Presser (1971) 312-40950

103:1-4
     Clatterbuck, Robert C.
     Psalm 103
     SATB   Keyboard
     Hope (1982) A-541

103:1-4
     Corelli, Arcangelo (arr. Benjamin J. Stone)
     Bless The Lord, O Bless His Holy Name
     SAB   Organ or Piano
     Boston Music (1964) 13133

103:1-4
     Greene, Maurice
     Praise The Lord O My Soul
     Unison   Organ
     RSCM (1974)   (found in Twelve Easy Anthems)

103:1-4
     Schütz, Heinrich (ed. Walter Ehret)
     Praise Ye The Lord My Soul (Lobet den
          Herren) (English/German)
     SATB/SATB   Organ or Piano
     Presser (1974) 312-41056

103:1-4, 10, 12
     Landgrave, Phillip
     Bless The Lord O My Soul
     SATB   Keyboard
     Broadman (1978) 4563-09

103:1-4, 22
     Child, William (ed. C. F. Simkins)
     Praise The Lord O My Soul
     SATB   Keyboard
     RSCM (1963) 227

103:1-5
     Geisler, Johann (ed. E. Nolte)
     Bless The Lord, O My Soul   (English/German)
     SS duet   Piano
     Boosey & Hawkes (1968) 5693

103:1-5
     Lovelace, Austin
     Bless Thou The Lord, O My Soul
     SATB   kro
     Canyon (1960) 6011

103:1-5
     Lovelace, Austin
     Bless The Lord O My Soul
     Unison/SATB   Keyboard
     Choristers Guild (1980) A 225

103:1-5
     Marshall, Jane
     Bless The Lord O My Soul
     Unison   Organ
     Broadman (1979) 4560-92

103:1-6   (Neander)
     Bunjes, Paul
     Praise To The Lord, The Almighty
     SATB   Congregation   Organ and Trumpet
     Concordia (1959) 97-4450

103:1-5, 8-9, 14
     Bush, Geoffrey
     Praise The Lord, O My Soul
     SATB   (S & T solos)   Organ
     Novello (1956) Anth. 1344

103:1-6   (based on)
     Distler, Hugo
     Praise Ye The Lord   (English/German)
     SATB   kro
     Barenreiter (1965) 134

103:1-6   (Neander)
     Krapf, Gerhard
     Praise To The Lord, The Almighty
     SSA   (S-solo)   Organ and Flute
     Concordia (1972) 97-5107   (flute part,
          97-5231)

103:1-6   (Neander)
     Manz, Paul
     Praise To The Lord   Op. 13
     SATB   Congregation, Organ (Brass)
     Concordia (1975) 97-5297

103:1-6   (Neander)
     Rohlig, Harald
     Praise To The Lord
     SATB   Congregation, Organ, Flute, Trum-
                    pet
     Concordia (1958) 97-4423   (Trumpet part -
          97-4430;   Flute part 97-4431)

103:1-6   (Neander)
     Spar, Otto
     Praise To The Lord, The Almighty
     SAB   kro
     Concordia (1955)   98-1080

103:1-6
     Stein, Carl   (arr. Walter Wismar)
     Bless The Lord, O My Soul
     TTBB   kro
     Schmitt, Hall & McCreary (1959) 3513

103:1-8
     SEE: Psalm 57:7
     Harrer, J. G.
     My Heart Is Prepared

103:1, 13, 14
     SEE: Psalm 102:1, 2
     Kopylof, A.
     Hear My Prayer

103:2
     SEE: Psalm 104:24
     Barnby, J.
     O Lord How Manifold

103:2
     Gregor, Christian (ed. Jeannine Ingram)
     Praise Ye The Lord, O My Soul
     SATB   Keyboard
     Carl Fischer (1978)   CM 8067

103:2-4
     Schütz, Heinrich
     Lobe den Herren, Meine Seele (from Psalmen
          David, 1619)
     SATB/SATB (S-A-T-B-solos)   Continuo
     Hanssler   H.E. 1.040

103:2-5
     Jeppesen, Knud
     Praise God My Soul
     SATB   kro
     Broude Brothers (1975)   BB 5023

103:8, 10   (Psalm 138:1-5)
     Martin, Reginald W.
     I Will Praise Thee
     SATB   Organ or Piano
     Mercury (1957)   MC 290

103:8-11
     SEE: Psalm 96:1-3
     Zimmermann, Heinz Werner
     Psalm Konzert

103:10-16 (Psalm 80:1-4, 6-7; Psalm 119:18-20)
     Sowerby, Leo
     A Liturgy Of Hope
     SATB   (S-solo)   Organ
     Boston Music (1928)   8065

103:13
    Cherubini, Luigi (arr. Austin Lovelace)
    Like As A Father
    3 part canon for children and adult choirs
        with Piano
    Choristers Guild (1974) A-156

103:13
    Cherubini, Luigi
    Like As A Father
    3 part canon   Keyboard
    Summy Birchard (1959) 5297

103:13
    Cherubini, Luigi
    Like As A Father
    Canon for 3 voices with Keyboard
    Summy Birchard (1959) SUMCO 5297

103:13-14, 17-18
    Geisler, J. C. (ed. & arr. E. Nolte)
    Like As A Father Doth Pity His Children
    SS Duet   Organ
    Boosey & Hawkes (1968) 5678

103:13-16
    Kay, Ulysses
    Like As A Father (part of A New Song - from
        Three Psalms For Chorus)
    SATB   Keyboard
    C. F. Peters (n.d.) 6222

103:20
    Hillert, Richard
    Verse/St. Michael and All Angels (Verses
        and Offertories - Lesser Festivals)
    Unison   Organ
    Augsburg (1980) 11-9542

103:30
    Felciano, Richard
    Pentecost Sunday - Double Alleluia
    Unison Male Choir   Organ, Tape
    WLSM (1967) EMP 1532

104:00
    SEE: Psalm 145
    Darke, Harold
    A Psalm of Thanksgiving

104:00 (adapted)
    Goode, Jack C.
    The Glory Of The Lord
    SATB   Organ
    H. W. Gray (1973) CMR 3294

104:00
    Gretchaninoff, A. (ed. Winfred Douglas)
    Praise The Lord O My Soul (from Vespers,
        Op. 59, #1)
    SATB   Keyboard
    H. W. Gray (n.d.) n.#.

104:00 (Grant setting of Kethe paraphrase)
    Haydn, J. Michael (arr. Robert Shaw)
    O Worship The King
    SATB   Organ
    G. Schirmer (1952) 10096

104:00 (paraphrase)
    Kay, Ulysses
    O Worship The King (Hanover)
    SATB   Organ
    C. F. Peters (1960) 6223

104:00
    Mathias, William
    Bless The Lord, O My Soul   Op. 51
    SATB   Organ
    Oxford (1972) A 284

104:00
    McAfee, Don
    Psalm 104 (Three Psalm-Hymns for Juniors)
    Unison   Keyboard
    Canyon Press (1967) 6703

104:00 (paraphrase)
    Rubbra, Edmond
    Up O My Soul   Op. 108
    SATB   kro
    Lengnick (1960) 4015

104:00 (taken from)
    Tuffs, A.
    O Lord Thou Art Very Great
    SATB   Accompanied
    Golden Music (1970) G-36

104:00 (Robert Grant)
    Wolff, S. Drummond
    Oh, Worship The King (Hanover)
    SATB   Organ, 2 Trumpets, Congregation
    Concordia (1977) 98-2323

104:1-4, 10-12, 14, 15
    Gibbs, C. Armstrong
    Bless The Lord O My Soul
    SA(T)B   Organ
    Oxford (1934) E-14 (also found in Oxford
        Easy Anthem Book)

104:1-4, 32-35
    Cassells-Brown, Alastair
    Praise The Lord O My Soul
    SATB or TTBB   Organ
    H. W. Gray (1955) 2393

104:1-5
    Mathias, William
    Bless The Lord, O My Soul   Op. 51
    SATB   Organ
    Oxford (1972) A 284

104:1, 10-11, 13-15, 24, 35
    Ferguson, Barry
    Praise The Lord, O My Soul
    SATB or Unison   Organ
    Novello (1975) MW 35

104:1, 24, 29-31, 34
    Peloquin, C. Alexander
    Lord Send Out Your Spirit
    SATB (solo) Organ (optional percussion)
    GIA (1971) G-1662 (also found in Songs of
        Israel, G-1666)

104:10, 33
    SEE: Psalm 92:1
    Mechem, Kirke
    I Will Sing Alleluia   Op. 40, #2

104:13-15
    SEE: Psalm 67:5-7
    Harwood, Basil
    Let The People Praise Thee, O God

104:13-15
    Schalk, Carl
    Offertory/Pentecost 12 (Verses and Offer-
        tories - Pentecost 12--20)
    Unison   Organ
    Augsburg (1978) 11-9539

104:14-15   (Psalm 37:1; Psalm 90:5; Isaiah 40:6;
        II Kings 19:24-26; Nahum 3:17, plus
        others)
    Browne, Richard
    Chortos I
    Speech Choir
    Flammer (1973) A-5629

104:16-18, 21-22, 24, 35
Beck, John Ness
The Young Lion
SATB   Piano or Organ
Beckenhorst (1972) BP 1001

104:24 (Psalm 65:14; Psalm 103:2)
Barnby, J.
O Lord How Manifold Are Thy Works
SATB   Organ
Novello (n.d.) 29.0228.01

104:24-26
Krenek, Ernst
Leviathan (Three Motets)
SSA   kro
Rongwen (1961) RM 3506

104:24-28, 33   (Psalm 65:14)
Shaw, Martin
O Lord, How Manifold Are Thy Works
Unison   Organ
Novello (1954) Anth. 1310

104:31-34
Goode, Jack
The Glory Of The Lord
SATB   Organ
H. W. Gray (1973) CMR 3294

104:31, 33-35
Goss, John
The Glory Of The Lord
SATB   Organ
Novello (n.d.) 177

104:31-33
Jeffreyes, George (ed. & realized Francis
     Grubb)
Erit Gloria Domini (English/Latin)
SS   Continuo
Oxford (1963) E 99

104:33, 34
Neff, James
I Will Sing To The Lord
2 part mixed   Keyboard
Augsburg (1973) 11-0635

104:33-35
Amner, John
I Will Sing Unto The Lord
SSATB (T-solo)   Organ
Oxford (1968) A-249

105:00
SEE: Psalm 91
Brandon, George
Carol Of The Exodus

105:00 (adapted)
Emig, Lois Myers
Be Happy! Rejoice!
2 part   Keyboard
Flammer (1978) E 5187

105:00
Glarum, L. Stanley
Fanfare For Thanksgiving
SAB   kro
G. Schirmer (1966) 11347

105:00
Glarum, L. Stanley
Fanfare For Thanksgiving
SATB   kro
G. Schirmer (1962) 10893

105:00
Glarum, L. Stanley
Fanfare For Thanksgiving
SSA   kro
G. Schirmer (1966) 11348

105:00 (adapted)
Pooler, Frank
The Face Of God
SATB   kro
Augsburg (1966) 1465

105:00 (based on)
Scarlatti, Domenico (arr. Helen Clair Lowe)
We Will Sing For Joy
Unison   Keyboard
Choristers Guild (1978) A-202

105:00
Schütz, Heinrich (ed. Daniel Reuning)
Thanks Be To Yahweh (from Five Psalms) Op. 5
     (English/German)
SATB   No accompaniment
GIA (1973) G-1790

105:00
Tomkins, Thomas
O Give Thanks Unto The Lord
ATTB   Optional Organ
Oxford (1964) TCM 19

105:1-2
SEE: Psalm 100:1-4
Berk, Adele
Alleluia Is Our Song

105:1-2
Croft, William (ed. Mason Martens)
O Give Thanks Unto The Lord
SAB   Organ
Concordia (1965) 98-1788

105:1-2
Titcomb, Everett
O Give Thanks Unto The Lord
SATB   kro
Carl Fischer (1964) CM 7407

105:1-3
Berger, Jean
O Give Thanks Unto The Lord
SATB   kro
Hinshaw (1979) HMC 387

105:1-3 (Psalm 95:1; Psalm 135:3)
Geisler, Johann C.
Thank Ye The Lord (Danket dem Herrn)
     (English/German)
SSAB   Piano or Organ
Boosey & Hawkes (1965) 5601

105:1-5
Hassler, Hans Leo (ed. Elwood Coggin)
Sing Unto Him With Psalms
SATB   kro
General Music (1979) n.#.

105:4 (Psalm 34:6)
Herbst, Johannes (ed. & arr. Karl Kroeger)
Seek Ye His Countenance In All Places
     (Suchet sein antliz) (English/German)
SATB   Keyboard, 2 violins)
Carl Fischer (1977) CM 8009

105:7
SEE: Psalm 135:1
Nares, James
O Praise The Lord

105:14, 15
SEE: Psalm 136:1
Krenek, Ernst
Thanksgiving

106:1
Beattie, Herbert
O Give Thanks (part of Six Choral Settings)
SAB   Optional Organ
G. Schirmer (1954) 510

106:1
 Hovhaness, Alan
 Praise Ye The Lord
 SATB   kro
 Associated (1955) A-208

106:1-3, 46
 Bliss, Arthur
 O Give Thanks Unto The Lord
 SATB   Organ
 Novello (1965) MT 1471

106:1-4
 Humphreys, Don (arr. William Stickles)
 Praise Ye The Lord
 SATB   Organ or Piano
 Willis (1966) 7391

106:1, 4, 48
 Purcell, Henry
 O Thanks Unto The Lord
 SATB   Organ
 E. C. Schirmer (also found in Second Con-
      cord Anthem Book - Grey)

106:1-2, 4-5, 46
 Purcell, Henry (ed. Anthony Lewis and Nigel
      Fortune)
 O Give Thanks
 SATB   Organ and continuo
 Novello (1960) 46.0018.05

106:4
 Tomkins, Thomas
 Remember Me O Lord
 AATB   Organ
 Oxford (1965) (found in Anthems for Men's
      Voices, Volume I)

106:45-46
 Batten, Adrian
 Deliver Us, O Lord God
 SATB   Organ
 Oxford (1981) TCM 56

106:45, 46
 Batten, Adrian (ed. E. H. Fellowes)
 Deliver Us O Lord Our God
 SATB   kro
 Oxford (1981) TCM 56a (also found in
      Sixteenth Century Anthem Book)

106:45-46
 Gibbons, Orlando (ed. Mason Martens)
 Deliver Us, O Lord Our God
 SATB   kro
 Walton (1963) 2091

106:47
 Gibbons, Orlando (ed. Roy Harris)
 Deliver Us
 SATB   kro
 G. Schirmer (1943) 8983

106:47
 Newbury, Kent A.
 Save Us, O Lord
 SATB   kro
 G. Schirmer (1970) 11699

106:48
 Handel, G. F. (ed. John B. Haberlen)
 Alleluia, Amen (from Sing Unto God)
 SATB (T-solo)   Organ or Piano
 Kjos (1981) ED 5981

106:48   (Psalm 108:1-4)
 Nelson, Ronald A.
 Awake My Soul!
 SAB   Piano
 Augsburg (1973) 11-0650

107:00
 Diemer, Emma Lou
 O Give Thanks To The Lord
 SATB   Organ
 Columbo (1964) NY 2539

107:1 (Psalm 113:1, 5)
 Berger, Jean
 O Give Thanks Unto The Lord
 SATB   kro
 Augsburg (1979) 11-1982

107:1 (Psalm 136:25;   Psalm 147:9-11)
 Schütz, Heinrich
 Danket dem Herrn denn er ist sehr Freund-
      lich
 SATB   No accompaniment
 Merseburger (1977) (found in Motetten
      Alter Meister)

107:1   (and other)
 SEE: Psalm 118:14
 Couperin, Francois (arr. Kenneth W. Jewell)
 O Be Joyful In The Lord

107:1   (Psalm 108)
 Wapen, Francis A.
 Give Thanks To The Lord, Op. 20, #4
 SATB   Organ, Brass Quartet and Timpani
 Concordia (1975) 97-5309 (parts 97-5310)

107:1, 8
 Clatterbuck, Robert C.
 Psalm 107
 SATB   Keyboard
 Hope (1980) A-510

107:1-22, 43
 SEE: Psalm 96:1-3
 Zimmermann, Heinz Werner
 Psalm Konzert

107:2, 10, 20
 Butler, Eugene
 Let The Redeemed Of The Lord Say No!
 SATB   Keyboard
 Hinshaw (1976) HMC-168

107:8
 SEE: Psalm 113:3
 Wagner, Douglas
 From The Rising Of The Sun

107:20-21   (adapted)
 Kreutz, Robert E.
 Send Forth Your Word
 SATB   Organ
 GIA (1976) G-2048

107:23-26, 29
 Krenek, Ernst
 To The Sea In Ships   (Three Motets)
 SSA   kro
 Rongwen (1961) RM 3505

107:23-30
 Williamson, Malcolm
 Seafarer's Psalm (from Psalms of the
      Elements)
 Unison Choir   Congregation   Organ
 Boosey & Hawkes (1976) 5951

108:00
 Bortiniansky
 We Sing Thy Praise
 SATB   Piano ad lib.
 Kjos (1965) 6533

108:00
 Butler, Eugene
 My Heart Is Ready
 Unison   14 Handbells
 Abingdon (1964) APM-367 (found in Six
      Anthems for Junior Voices and Hand-
      bells)

108:00   (Watts)
    Gomolka, Mikolaj (arr. Johannes Riedel)
    Awake My Soul (Two Polish Psalms) (English/
        Polish)
    SATB   kro
    Schmitt, Hall, McCreary (1962) 1411

108:00
    SEE: Psalm 107:1
    Wapen, Francis
    Give Thanks To The Lord, Op. 20, #4

108:1   (based on)
    Johnson, Mark
    My Heart Is Ready
    Unison   Keyboard
    AMSI (1974) 258

108:1-2
    Wood, John
    God, My Heart Is Ready   (Two Introits)
    SATB   kro
    Novello (1961) 1388

108:1-2
    Wood, John
    O God My Heart Is Ready
    SATB   kro
    Novello (1978) (found in In Wonder, Love
        and Praise)

108:1-3
    Lekberg, Sven
    My Heart Is Ready O God
    SATB   kro
    Galaxy (1955) 2074

108:1, 3-5
    Newbury, Kent A.
    I Will Sing And Give Praise
    SATB   kro
    Shawnee (1966) A-816

108:1-4
    SEE: Psalm 106:48
    Nelson, Ronald A.
    Awake My Soul

108:1-4
    Young, Gordon
    Awake, Psaltry And Harp
    SATB   Organ
    Augsburg (1968) 11-0628

108:1-5
    Newbury, Kent A.
    Awake My Soul
    SATB   Organ or Piano
    The New Music Co. (1973) NM A-109

108:2   (Psalm 100)
    Bernstein, Leonard
    Chichester Psalms, Part I (Hebrew)
    SATB   Piano (Orchestra)
    G. Schirmer (1965) 2656

108:4
    SEE: Psalm 55:8
    Mendelssohn, Felix
    Cast Thy Burden Upon The Lord (Oxford -
        Church Anthem Book)

108:4
    SEE: Psalm 55:22
    Mendelssohn, Felix
    Cast Thy Burden Upon The Lord (Concordia)

108:5
    SEE: Psalm 61:1
    Kopyloff, Alexander
    Hear My Cry O God

108:5
    SEE: Psalm 48:5
    Lovelace, Austin
    God Is Gone Up

108:47, 48
    Croft, William (ed. Richard Peek)
    Deliver Us O Lord Our God
    SATB (A-T-B-solos)   Organ
    Concordia (1963) 98-1692

109:00
    LeJeune, Claude
    Psalm 109   (English/French)
    SAB   No accompaniment
    Mercury (1945) MC 56

109:1, 3
    Lahmer, Reuel
    First Mass At Christmas - Gradual and
        Alleluia
    Unison   Organ
    World Library (1967) EMP 1387

109:4
    Kreutz, Robert
    Tu es sacredos (Latin)
    SATB   Keyboard
    Summy Birchard (1962) 5208

109:21
    Morley, Thomas (ed. Hans T. David)
    A Prayer (Latin)
    SATB   No accompaniment
    Mercury (1944) MC 53

110:00
    Bernardi, Stefano
    Dixit Dominus Domino Meo
    SATB (S-solo)   Continuo
    Faber [G. Schirmer] (1968) 11731

110:00
    Galuppi, Baldassare (ed. David Larson)
    Dixit Dominus
    SATB   Piano or Strings
    Roger Dean (1977) CMC 109

110:00
    Galuppi, Baldassare
    Dixit Dominus
    SSA   Piano or Strings
    Roger Dean (1977) n.#.

110:00
    Mozart, W. A.
    Dixit Dominus (from Solemn Vespers, K. 339)
        (Latin/English)
    SATB   Piano
    Lawson Gould (1963) 51164

110:00
    Schütz, Heinrich
    Der Herr sprach zu meinem Herren
    Three Choirs   Organ continuo
    Barenreiter (1971) 4475

110:3
    SEE: Psalm 2:7
    Wetzler, Robert
    Offertory/Christmas Day

110:3a
    SEE: Psalm 48:5
    Lovelace, Austin
    God Is Gone Up

110:4
    Wesley, Samuel S. (ed. John Marsh)
    Tu es sacerdos (from Two Motets) (Latin)
    SATB   No accompaniment
    Novello (1974) NECM 28

111:00
    Proulx, Richard
    My Heart Is Full Today
    2 part children   Keyboard, 4 Handbells,
        Percussion
    Augsburg (1971) 11-0645

111:00
    Robertson, D.
    Psalm For A Festive Procession
    SATB   Brass Quartet
    Hinshaw (1976) HMC-172

111:00
    Schütz, Heinrich (ed. John F. Williamson)
    I Will Praise The Lord
    SATB   kro
    G. Schirmer (1931) 7556

111:1, 4, 7-9
    Wetzler, Robert
    Praise The Lord, All Ye People
    SATB   Organ
    AMSI (1977) AMSI 325

111:1, 9-10
    SEE: Psalm 56:12-13
    Lynn, George
    The Lord Is King

111:9 (Luke 24:26)
    Kreutz, Robert
    The Lord Has Sent Deliverance
    SATB   Organ
    GIA (1978) G-2152

111:10
    SEE: Psalm 94:1-7
    Baker, Robert
    O Lord God Unto Whom Vengance

111:10
    Schütz, Heinrich (ed. William Hermann)
    Fear The Almighty (Die Furcht des Herren)
        (English/German)
    SS   Organ
    Concordia (1966) 98-1854

112:00
    Carissimi, G.
    Beatus Vir (Latin)
    SSATB   Organ and Continuo
    Oxford (1975) A 311

112:00
    Monteverdi, Claudio (ed. John Steele)
    Beatus Vir
    SSATTB   Organ and Instruments
    Novello (1965)

112:00
    Perti, Giacomo A. (ed. Jean Berger)
    Beatus Vir (Latin)
    SATB   Organ
    Lawson Gould (1973) 51764

112:00 (paraphrased by John Patrick, 1679)
    Purcell, Henry (ed. Anthony Lewis and Nigel
        Fortune)
    O Happy Man
    SATB or SSAB   Organ continuo
    Novello (1966) PSR.12

112:00
    Vivaldi, Antonio (ed. Bruno Maderna)
    Beatus Vir
    SATB/SATB   Keyboard
    Ricordi (1969)

112:1
    Vivaldi, Antonio (ed. Douglas McEwen)
    Beatus Vir (Blessed Is The Man) (English/
        Latin)
    SATB/SATB   Keyboard
    Hinshaw (1976) HMC 177

112:6, 7
    Vivaldi, Antonio (ed. Douglas McEwen)
    In Memoria Aeterna (from Beatus Vir)
        (English/Latin)
    (S)ATB   Keyboard
    Hinshaw (1976) HMC-179

112:8, 9
    Vivaldi, Antonio (ed. Douglas McEwen)
    Paratum cor ejus (from Beatus Vir)
        (English/Latin)
    SATB/SATB   Keyboard
    Hinshaw (1976) HMC-180

113:00
    Berger, Jean
    The Lord Praise Ye (from Bay Psalm Book,
        Set II)
    SATB   No accompaniment
    Shawnee (1980) A-1597

113:00
    Butler, Eugene
    Praise Ye The Lord
    SATB   Keyboard
    Abingdon (1962) APM 212

113:00
    Hutmacher, Robert M.
    Praise You Servants Of The Lord
    3 part equal voices   Organ, percussion
    GIA (1978) G-2205

113:00
    Josquin des Prez
    Laudate pueri (All Ye Who Dwell On Earth)
        (Latin/English)
    SATB or STTB   kro
    Tetra [Alexander Broude] (1973) AB 720

113:00
    Lekberg, Sven
    Praise Ye
    SATB   kro
    Galaxy (1963) GMC 2254

113:00
    Mozart, W. A.
    Laudate pueri, K. 339 (Latin/English)
    SATB   Piano
    Arista (1981) AE 455

113:00
    Mozart, W. A.
    Laudate pueri, K. 339 (Latin/English)
    SATB   Piano
    G. Schirmer (1963) 51166

113:00
    Mozart, W. A.
    Laudate pueri (from Solemn Vespers, K. 339)
        (Latin/English)
    SATB   Piano
    Lawson Gould (1963) 51166

113:00
    Mozart, W. A. (ed. George Lynn)
    Psalm 113 (Laudate pueri from Solemn
        Vespers, K. 339) (English/Latin)
    SATB   Organ
    Golden Music (1964) G-16

113:00
    McCabe, Michael
    Praise Ye The Lord
    SATB   Organ
    Carl Fischer (1973) CM 7818

113:00
    Peek, Richard
    Praise The Lord, Ye Servants
    Unison mixed   Organ
    H. W. Gray (1973) CMR 3289

113:00
    Proulx, Richard
    Praise Ye The Lord Ye Children
    Unison   4 Handbells, Triangle
    Augsburg (1975) 11-0322

113:00
    Stroh, Virginia
    Praise Ye The Lord, Alleluia
    SATB   kro
    Broude Brothers (1965) BB 4008

113:00   (Psalter of 1912)
    Tallis, Thomas (arr. Robert Roesch)
    Praise God Ye Servants Of The Lord (Based
        on Tallis Canon)
    SATB   Organ or Piano
    Flammer (1975) A-5682

113:1
    Jackson, Francis
    Alleluia Laudate pueri Dominum
    SSAATTBB   kro
    Banks [F. Harris] (1978) ECS 42

113:1-2
    Blow, John (ed. Heathcote Statham)
    Praise The Lord Ye Servants
    SATB   Organ
    Oxford (1925) A 203

113:1, 2
    Blow, John
    Praise The Lord Ye Servants
    SATB   Organ
    Oxford (1973)   (found in Anthems For Choirs,
        Volume I)

113:1, 2
    Mendelssohn, Felix
    Ye Sons Of Israel (Laudate pueri Dominum)
    SSA   Piano
    E. C. Schirmer (1935) 1839

113:1-2
    Zimmermann, Heinz Werner
    Praise The Lord
    SATB   Keyboard
    Concordia (1973) 98-2176   (from Five Hymns,
        (1973) 97-5131)

113:1-2, 4-5
    Watters, Clarence
    Laudate pueri (O Praise the Lord)
    TTBB   Organ
    H. W. Gray (1939) 1559

113:1-3
    Tye, Christopher (ed. E. Stanley Roper and
        J. Dykes Bower)
    O Come, Ye Servants Of The Lord
    SATB   kro
    RSCM [Hinshaw] (1950) RSCM 508

113:1, 3
    Tye, Christopher
    Laudate Nomen Domini (Latin/English)
    SATB   Keyboard
    Novello (n.d.) 29.0219.02

113:1-3
    Young, Gordon
    Praise Ye The Lord
    SATB   Organ
    Oxford (1969) 94.207

113:1, 5
    SEE: Psalm 107:1
    Berger, Jean
    O Give Thanks Unto The Lord

113:1-6
    Pfohl, Henry
    Antiphonal Psalm
    2 unison choirs or SA/TB or ST/AB
        Piano or Organ
    Flammer (1963) A 5018

113:1-6, 8
    Tye, Christopher
    Praise Ye The Lord Ye Children
    SATB   kro
    Oxford (1967) TCM 58

113:3   (Psalm 107:8)
    Wagner, Douglas
    From The Rising Of The Sun
    Unison   Keyboard (optional Handbells)
    Choristers Guild (1980) A 223

113:4
    Pergolesi, G. P. (ed. C. Buell Agey)
    Excelsur super omnes gentes dominus
    SATB (S-A solos)   Keyboard
    G. Schirmer (1967)   11456

113:5-8
    Hillert, Richard
    Offertory/Annunciation (Verses and Offer-
        tories - Lesser Festivals)
    Unison   Organ
    Augsburg (1980) 11-9542

114:00
    Hassler, Hans Leo (ed. Abraham Kaplan)
    When Israel Went Out Of Egypt (Da Israel)
        (English/German)
    SATB   kro
    Lawson Gould (1977) 51983

114:00
    Hopkins, Francis (ed. Mason Martens)
    An Anthem From the 114th Psalm
    TTB   Keyboard
    McAfee (1975)   (found in Bicentennial Col-
        lection Of American Choral Music)

114:00
    Kraft, Leo
    When Israel Came Forth
    SATB   kro
    Presser (1963) 312-40558

114:1-3
    Byrd, William (ed. Edmund H. Fellowes)
    When Israel Came Out Of Egypt (free chant
        form)
    SATB   No accompaniment
    Stainer & Bell (1923) 2556

114:1-3
    Wesley, Samuel S. (ed. J. Barnby)
    In exita Israel (Latin only)
    SATB/SATB   Organ
    Novello (n.d.) n.#. (reprinted C. T. Wagner)

114:1-3
    Wesley, Samuel S.
    When Israel Came Out of Egypt
    SATB/SATB   Organ ad lib.
    Novello (n.d.) 786

114:1-8
    Kodaly, Zoltan
    Psalm 114 (English/French/German)
    SATB   Organ
    Boosey & Hawkes (1959) 5328

114:1-8
    Weisgall, Hugo
    When Israel Out Of Egypt Came (English/
        Hebrew)
    SATB   kro
    Presser (1961)   312-40509

115:00 (based on)
     Telemann, G. Philipp (ed. Ronald A. Nelson)
     O Not To Us, Good Lord
     Unison   Continuo and Flute
     Augsburg (1969) 11-0311

115:1
     Byrd, William (ed. David L. Weck)
     Non nobis Domine (Latin/English)
     3 part any combination   No accompaniment
     Somerset [Hope] (1980) SP-749

115:1
     Byrd, William
     Not Unto Us, O Lord (English/Latin)
     SAB   No accompaniment
     Concordia (1968) (found in A First Motet
          Book, 97-4845)

115:1 (I Chronicles 29)
     Gore, Richard T.
     Not Unto Us, Lord
     SATB (A or B solos)   Organ
     J. FIscher (1972) 10067

115:1
     Haydn, Franz J. (ed. Karl Geiringer)
     We Seek Not, God, Our Lord For Glory (Non
          nobis, Domine) (English/Latin)
     SATB   Organ
     Concordia (1960) 98-1515

115:1
     Purcell, Henry
     Lord Not To Us
     ATB   Continuo
     Oxford (1965) (found in Anthems For Men's
          Voices, Volume I)

115:1 (based on)
     Telemann, G. P. (arr. Ronald Nelson)
     O Not To Us Good Lord
     Unison   Continuo and Flute
     Augsburg (1969) 11-0311

115:1
     Walmisley, Thomas Attwood (arr. Vincent
          Knight)
     Not Unto Us, O Lord
     SAB   Organ
     Curwen (1963) 11200

115:1
     Walmisley, Thomas A.
     Not Unto Us O Lord
     SATB   Organ
     Novello (1976) 29.0374.01

115:1
     Walmisley, Thomas A.
     Not Unto Us O Lord
     SATB   Organ
     Oxford (1973) (found in Anthems For Choirs,
          Volume I)

115:1
     Pinkham, Daniel
     Non nobis, Domine (Three Motets) (Latin)
     SSA   Organ
     C. F. Peters (1979) 66709

115:1, 12-13, 16-18
     Ives, Elam, Jr. (ed. J. Heywood Alexander)
     Not Unto Us, O Lord
     SATB   Organ or Piano
     European American (1978) EA 373-11

115:1, 18
     SEE: Psalm 127:1
     Rubbra, Edmund
     Except The Lord Build The House

115:3-8, 12-15
     SEE: Psalm 96:2-3, 5, 7-10
     Wesley, Samuel S.
     Ascribe Unto The Lord

115:12 (II Timothy 2:9; Philippians 4:5)
     Mendelssohn, Felix
     But The Lord Is Mindful Of His Own
          (St. Paul)
     SATB   Organ
     Novello

115:12, 13
     Wesley, Samuel S.
     The Lord Hath Been Mindful Of Us
     SATB   Organ
     Novello (n.d.) 29.0118.08

115:13-15
     Bach, J. S. (ed. Paul Bunjes)
     The Lord Bless You (Der Herr segne euch)
          (Duet from Cantata 196)
     SA or TB   Organ
     Concordia (1959) 98-1474

116:00
     Glarum, L. Stanley
     I Love The Lord
     SATB   kro
     Bourne (1959) SG-3

116:00
     Goemanne, Noel
     Psalm 116 (Praise The Lord All Ye Nations)
     SATB   Organ
     McLaughlin & Reilly (1955) 2155

116:00 (Wesley)
     Lovelace, Austin C. (arr.)
     What Shall I Render To My God
     2 part   Keyboard
     Sacred Music Press (1976) S-179 (found in
          Service Music For Choir And Congrega-
          tion)

116:00
     Maudit, Jacques
     Psalm 116 (English/French)
     SATB   kro
     Schmitt, Hall, McCreary (1951) (found in
          Rare Choral Masterpieces)

116:00
     SEE: Daniel 6
     Pinkham, Daniel
     Daniel And The Lion's Den

116:00 (from A Century Of Select Psalms, by
          Patrick, 1684)
     Purcell, Henry
     Since God So Tender A Regard
     TTB   Keyboard
     Oxford (1965) (found in Anthems for Men's
          Voices, Volume II)

116:1-2, 5
     Powell, Robert J.
     My Delight Is In The Lord
     SAB   Organ
     Wood (1962) 815

116:1-4, 7-9
     Harvey, Johnathan
     I Love The Lord
     SSAATTBB   No accompaniment
     Novello (1977) 29.0437.03

116:1-5, 7
     Sleeper, H. D.
     I Love The Lord
     SATB   Keyboard
     Boston (1931) 8628

116:1-8, 17-19
   Schmutz, Albert D.
   I Love The Lord
   SATB   Piano or Organ
   Abingdon (1976) APM-439 (found in Anthems
      From The Psalms)

116:7
   SEE: Matthew 5:4
   Crandell, Robert
   The Second Beatitude

116:7, 12-14 (adapted)
   Pasquet, Jean
   Return Unto Thy Rest
   SATB   kro
   Elkan Vogel (1971) 362-01322

116:10-19
   Porpora, N. (ed. D. E. Hyde)
   Credidi
   SSA   Piano (or Strings)
   Novello (1972) 19923

116:12-13 (based on)
   Cromie, Marguerite Biggs
   What Return Shall I Make (Quid Retribuam)
     (English/Latin)
   SSAATB   kro
   Presser (1975) 312-41082

116:12-13, 18-19
   Norris, Kevin
   Offertory/Lent II (Verses and Offertories -
     Lent)
   Unison   Organ
   Augsburg (1980) 11-9545

117:00
   Bach, J. S.
   Praise The Lord All Ye Nations (Motet VI)
   SATB   Keyboard
   C. F. Peters (1962) 6106

117:00
   Bach, J. S.
   Praise The Lord All Ye Nations (Motet VI)
   SATB   No accompaniment
   University of Pennsylvania Series (n.d.)
     #35

117:00
   Batten, Adrian (ed. Walter Ehret)
   O Praise The Lord
   SATB   kro
   Chappell (1969) 6156

117:00
   Batten, Adrian (ed. S. Drummond Wolff)
   O Praise The Lord, All Ye People
   SATB   Keyboard ad lib.
   Concordia (1976) 98-2273

117:00
   Batten, Adrian
   O Praise The Lord
   SATB   Organ
   Oxford (1978) (found in Oxford Book Of
     Tudor Anthems)

117:00
   Berger, Jean
   All Nations Praise The Lord
   SATB   No accompaniment (optional per-
     cussion)
   Shawnee (1980) A-1597

117:00 (adapted)
   Bock, Fred
   Psalm 117
   SATB/SATB   kro
   Flammer (1959) 85495

117:00
   Charpentier, Marc-Antoine
   Laudate Dominum
   SSA or TTB   Organ or Piano, 2 Violins
   Marks (1973) MC 4603

117:00
   Cruft, Adrian
   O Praise The Lord (Two Psalms Of Praise)
     Op. 48
   Unison   Piano Duet
   Leeds (1969) n.#.

117:00 (adapted)
   Dressler, Gallus (ed. Matthew Lundquist)
   Let All The People Praise The Lord
   SATB   kro
   Schmitt, Hall & McCreary (found in Later
     Renaissance Motets)

117:00
   SEE: Ezekiel 47:12
   Ferris, William
   I Have Seen Water

117:00
   Ford, Virgil T.
   A Song Of Praise
   2 part children   Piano or Organ
   Abingdon (1975) APM-462

117:00
   Goldman, Maurice
   A Hymn Of Praise
   SATB   Piano
   Transcontinental (1969) TCL 671

117:00
   Goodman, James
   Laudate Dominum (Latin)
   SATB   kro
   Associated (1958) A-298 (also found in
     Contemporary Settings of Psalm Texts,
     APM-6910)

117:00
   Hahn, Harvey E.
   O Praise The Lord All Nations
   SATB   kro
   Concordia (1972) 98-2124

117:00
   Hassler, Hans Leo (ed. Carl Schalk)
   Laudate Dominum, Omnes Gentes (Praise Ye
     The Lord) (English/Latin)
   SSAB/ATTB   kro
   Concordia (1968) 97-4879

117:00
   Johns, Donald
   O Praise The Lord All Ye Nations
   SSAA   kro
   Augsburg (1966) 11-0648

117:00
   Jones, Robert W.
   A Psalm Of Praise
   SATB   Organ
   Lawson Gould (1969) 51354

117:00
   Kaderavek, Milan
   Psalm 117
   SATB   Organ
   Summy Birchard (1960) 5398

117:00
   Kay, Ulysses
   O Praise the Lord (part of A New Song)
   SATB
   C. F. Peters (n.d.) 6229a

117:00
Kirk, Theron
Praise The Lord All Ye Nations
SSCB   Keyboard (or 3 Trumpets, 2 Trom-
    bones, Tuba)
Cambiata Press (1976) C-117694

117:00   (adapted)
Kozinski, David
O Praise The Lord, All Ye Nations
SATB   kro
Presser (1958) 312-40382

117:00
Krapf, Gerhard
O Praise the Lord All Ye Nations
SAB   Organ
Abingdon (1975) APM-463

117:00
Laverty, John Timothy
Psalm 117
SATB   kro
Hall & McCreary (1955) 1727

117:00
SEE: Job 14:1-2
Lidholm, Inguar
Laudi

117:00
Lipkin, Malcolm
O Praise the Lord, All Ye Nations
SATB   kro
Novello (1969) 1522

117:00
Lockwood, Normand
Psalm 117
SATB   No accompaniment
Kjos (1966) ED. 18

117:00
Mason, Lowell (arr. G. Brandon)
Psalm 117
SATB   Keyboard
GIA (1973) G-1827

117:00   (Psalm 150)
McCabe, Michael
A Psalm Of Praise And Thanksgiving
SATB (S-solo)   Organ
H. W. Gray (1978) GCMR 3396

117:00
Monteverdi, Claudio
Laudate Dominum (Latin)
SSATTB   Continuo and 2 Violins
Eulenberg (1966) 1069

117:00
Mozart, W. A. (arr. Arthur S. Talmadge)
Laudate Dominum (from Vespers, K. 339)
    Latin/English)
SSAA (S-solo)   Organ or Piano
E. C. Schirmer (1949) 1958

117:00
Mozart, W. A.
Laudate Dominum (K. 339)
SATB (S-solo)   Piano
G. Schirmer (1968) 51165

117:00
Mozart, W. A.
Laudate Dominum (from Solemn Vespers, K.339)
    (Latin/English)
SATB (S-solo)   Piano
Lawson Gould (1963) 51165

117:00
Mozart, W. A. (arr. Lionel Lethbridge)
Laudate Dominum (from Vespers, K. 339)
    (Latin)
SSA   Piano
Oxford (1971) W. 90

117:00
Mozart, W. A. (ed. John B. Haberlen)
Laudate Dominum, K. 339 (Latin/English)
SATB (S-solo)   Organ and violin obligato
Kjos (1981) 5979

117:00
Mozart, W. A. (ed. George Lynn)
Praise Ye The Lord (K.V. 339)
SATB (S-solo)   Keyboard
Presser (1950) 312.40059

117:00
Mueller, Luise
O Praise The Lord
SATB   Keyboard
Abingdon (1962) APM-223

117:00
Murano, June
Psalm 117
SATB   Piano or Organ
Flammer (1971) A-5598

117:00   (Revelation 7:12)
Nagel, Robert
Triptych
SATB   Organ or Piano, or Brass (2 Trum-
    pets, 2 Trombones)
Marks (1972) 4595

117:00
Neff, James
Praise The Lord, All Nations
SATB   Keyboard
Augsburg (1972) 11-0644

117:00
Parks, Joe E.
O Praise The Lord
SATB   Keyboard
Broadman (1973) 4540-59

117:00
Petrich, Roger
O Praise The Lord All Ye Nations
SATB   No accompaniment
Augsburg (1964) PS 615

117:00
Porta, Costanzao (ed. Ralph Hunter)
Laudate Dominum (O Praise The Lord Our God)
    (Latin/English)
SATB/SATB   Organ continuo
Belwin (1981) OCT 2472

117:00
Powell, Robert J.
Praise The Lord All Ye Nations
SAB   Organ
B. F. Wood (1963) 819

117:00
Roman, Johann H. (ed. & arr. S. Drummond
    Wolff)
Praise The Lord, All Ye Nations
SATB   Organ (optional instruments)
Concordia (1973) 97-5160 (instruments 97-
    5226; Organ and Vocal 97-5206)

117:00
Scarlatti, Alessandro (ed. Jeanne E.
    Shaffer)
O Praise The Lord All Ye Nations (Latin/
    English)
SATTB   Strings and Continuo
Concordia (1970) 97-4973 (parts 97-4974)

117:00
Schlitternhard, Melody
Praise Ye The Lord
SATB   Piano
Mark Foster (1978) MF 184 (also found in
      Anthems, Book I, MF-211)

117:00   (adapted)
Schütz, Heinrich
O All Ye Nations
SATB   kro
Presser (1927) 332-13992

117:00
Schütz, Heinrich (ed. J. Meyerowitz)
Praise God With Sound (Lobt Gott mit Schall)
      English/German)
SATB   Keyboard
Broude Brothers (1967) 4067

117:00
Schütz, Heinrich
O Praise Our God
SATB   Organ
Concordia (1958) 98-2539

117:00
Selby, William
Psalm 117
SAB   Keyboard
J. Fischer (1970) FEC 9967

117:00
Sherman, Roger
Psalm 117
SATB or TTBB   Organ
GIA (1979) G-2194

117:00   (Psalm 118:1-4)
Silver, Mark
Praise The Lord
SATB (T-A solos)   Organ
Transcontinental (1941) TCL 223

117:00
Sowerby, Leo
O Praise The Lord, All Ye Nations
SATB   Organ
H. W. Gray (1962) 2743

117:00   (Psalm 118:1-4)
Staton, Kenneth W.
A Litany Of Praise and Thanksgiving
SATB (T-B-solos)   Piano
Music 70 (1975) M70-125

117:00
Sweelinck, J. P. (ed. Donald Colton)
Laudate Dominum (O Praise The Lord Our God)
      (English/Latin)
SSATB   kro
Concordia (1977) 97-5450

117:00
Telemann, Georg Philipp (ed. F. Oberdoerffer)
O Praise The Lord All Ye Nations (Latin/
      English)
SATB   Organ, 2 violins
Concordia (1967) 97-4838 (Parts 97-4842)

117:00
Telemann, G. P.
Lobet den Herrn, alle Heiden (English/German)
SSB or SS   Organ continuo, 2 violins
Hanssler   H. E. 39.007

117:00
Tomkins, Thomas (ed. Edmund Fellowes)
O Praise The Lord, All Ye Heathen
SSSAAATTTBBB   Optional Keyboard
Oxford (1964) TCM 100

117:00
Vivaldi, Antonio (ed. Keith D. Graumann)
Give Praise Unto The Lord
SATB   Continuo with 2 violins, 1 viola
Augsburg (1979) 11-1970 (parts 11-1871)

117:00
Victoria, Tomas (ed. Robert S. Hines)
Laudate Dominum (Oh Praise The Lord)
      (Latin/English)
SATB/SATB   Continuo
Concordia (1981) 98-2507

117:00
Vivaldi, Antonio
Laudate Dominum omnes gentes (O Praise The
      Lord) (English/Latin)
SATB   Continuo, violin, viola
Concordia (1974) (found in A Second Motet
      Book, 97-5205)

117:00   (Watts)
Walmisley, Thomas A. (ed. Gerald Knight)
From All That Dwell
SATB   Optional organ
RSCM (1957) 216

117:00   (based on)
Watson, Walter
Praise The Lord Alleluia
Unison   Keyboard
Choristers Guild (1973) A-133

117:00
SEE: Isaiah 60:1
Willan, Healey
Arise Shine For Thy Light Is Come

117:00
SEE: Psalm 135:1-3
Willan, Healey
O Praise The Lord

117:00
Willan, Healey
Oh, Praise The Lord, All Ye Nations
SSA   No accompaniment
Concordia (1953) (found in We Praise Thee,
      Volume I, 97-7564)

117:00   (Watts)
Wolff, S. Drummond (arr.)
From All That Dwell Below The Skies (Lasst
      uns erfreuen)
SATB/SATB or   SATB with Brass Quartet or
      Organ
Concordia (1975) 97-5290 (parts 97-5291)

117:00   (Watts)
Young, Gordon
From All That Dwell Below The Skies
SATB   Organ
Galaxy (1960) GMC 2186

117:00   (Psalm 150)
Young, Gordon
Praise
SATB   Organ
Presser (1964) 312-40591

117:00
Zimmermann, Heinz Werner
Psalm 117
SATB (S-solo)   Guitar, Organ, Bass
Carl Fischer (1973) CM 7826

117:1-2
SEE: Psalm 118:1
Felciano, Richard
Give Thanks To The Lord (from Songs For
      Darkness and Light)

117:2
    SEE: Psalm 95:1-3a
    Kimball, Jacob (ed. Mason Martens)
    O Come Sing Unto The Lord

118:00
    Beebe, Hank
    This Is The Day
    SATB   Keyboard
    Hinshaw (1977) HPC 7001

118:00
    Buxtehude, Dietrich (ed. Walter Buszin)
    Open To Me Gates Of Justice (English/Latin)
    ATB   Continuo, 2 strings
    C. F. Peters (1963) 6050

118:00
    Corina, John
    Psalm 118
    SATB   Organ, 2 Trumpets, 2 Trombones
    Abingdon (1971) APM-552 (Parts APM-917)

118:00 (taken from)
    Geoffray, Cesar
    Dextera Domini (Valiantly Doth The Lord's
        Right Hand) (English/Latin)
    SATB   kro
    Oxford (1958) X39

118:00
    Titcomb, Everitt
    The Lord Is My Strength
    SATB   Organ
    Flammer (1964) 84807

118:00
    Zimmermann, Heinz Werner
    The Lord Is All My Strength And My Song
    SSATB   Vibraphone, Harpsichord, Bass
    Barenreiter (1962) n.#.

118:1 (Psalm 117:1-2)
    Felciano, Richard
    Give Thanks To The Lord (Songs For Darkness
        And Light)
    Unison   Organ
    E. C. Schirmer (1971) 2804

118:1-2, 16-17, 22-23
    Peloquin, C. Alexander
    This Is The Day
    SATB   (solo)   Organ
    GIA (1971) G-1660 (also found in Songs Of
        Israel, G-1666)

118:1-2, 28
    Gardner, Tom
    O Give Thanks Unto The Lord
    SATB   Organ or Piano
    Flammer (1957) A-5103

118:1-4
    Bernstein, David (arr.)
    Hodu Ladonai (Give Thanks To The Lord)
        (English/Hebrew)
    SSA   Keyboard
    Lawson Gould (1978) LG 52038

118:1-4
    SEE: Psalm 117
    Silver, Mark
    Praise The Lord

118:1-4
    SEE: Psalm 117
    Staton, K. W.
    A Litany Of Praise And Thanksgiving

118:1-4
    Weisgall, Hugo
    Praise Be Unto God   (English/Hebrew)
    SATB   kro
    Presser (1961) 312-40508

118:1, 14, 19
    Younger, John B.
    The Lord Is My Strength And My Song
    SATB   Keyboard
    Harris (1973) HC 4044

118:1, 14, 23-24, 29
    Lewallen, James C.
    O Give Thanks Unto The Lord
    SATB   (T-solo)   Keyboard
    H. W. Gray (1961) GCMR 3445

118:1, 15-16, 22-24
    Proulx, Richard and J. Gelineau
    This Is The Day
    Unison With Descant   11 Handbells,
        Triangle, Tambourine, Organ
    GIA (1973) G 1964

118:1, 24
    Schroth, Godfrey
    This Is The Day
    SSATB   Organ (optional instruments)
    GIA (1971) G-2604

118:6, 14
    Blakenship, Mark
    The Lord Is On My Side
    SATB   3 Trumpets, 3 Trombones
    Broadman (1977) 4563-06

118:12-13 (Psalm 145:8-10; Psalm 65:14)
    Maunder, J. H.
    Praise The Lord Of Jerusalem
    SATB   Organ
    Novello (n.d.) 577

118:12-13 (Psalm 145:8-10; Psalm 65:14)
    Maunder, J. H. (arr. Rob Roy Perry)
    Praise The Lord Of Jerusalem
    SAB   Organ
    Presser (1957) 312-40533

118:14 (Psalm 107:1; and other)
    Couperin, Francois (arr. Kenneth W. Jewell)
    Be Joyful In The Lord
    SS   Keyboard
    Concordia (1964) 98-1734

118:14, 19-20
    Newbury, Kent
    The Lord Is My Strength And My Song
    SATB   Piano (optional Guitar, Bass,
        Drum)
    Flammer (1972) 1-5603

118:15
    SEE: Psalm 33:1
    Nares, James
    Rejoice In The Lord

118:15
    Nares, James (ed. Watkins Shaw)
    The Voice Of Joy
    Unison treble   Keyboard
    Novello (1970) NECM 16

118:17
    Luther, Martin
    Non moriar sed viram (Latin)
    SATB   No accompaniment
    Merseburger (1977) (found in Motetten Alter
        Meister)

118:19
    Pinkham, Daniel
    Open To Me The Gates Of Righteousness
    SATB   Organ ad lib.
    C. F. Peters (1966) 66037

118:19-20 (Psalm 100:4)
    Proulx, Richard
    Processional Psalm
    2 equal voices   4 Handbells
    GIA (1972) G-1750

118:19, 20, 24-26
    Buxtehude, Dietrich (ed. James Dunn)
    Aperite mihi portas justitiae (Open Wide
        The Gates Of Justice)
    SAB   Continuo, 2 Violins
    Concordia (1977) 97-5398 (Parts 97-5399)

118:24
    Anonymous (ed. Maurice Bevan)
    This Is The Day
    SATB   kro
    Oxford (1960) A-173 (also found in The
        Sixteenth Century Anthem Book)

118:24
    Arcadelt, Jacob
    Haec Dies (Latin only)
    SATB   kro
    J. & W. Chester (1977) JWC 55127 (found in
        Fifth Chester Book Of Motets)

118:24
    SEE: Psalm 57:9
    Barnby, J.
    Awake Up, My Glory

118:24
    Bengtson, F. Dale
    Rejoice, This Is The Day
    Speech Choir
    Fred Bock (1972) G 174

118:24
    Byrd, William
    Haec Dies
    SSATTB   kro
    H. W. Gray (1926) CMR 3093

118:24
    Byrd, William
    Haec Dies (This Is The Day) (Latin/English)
    Novello (n.d.) TM 24

118:24
    Byrd, William
    Haec Dies
    SSATTB   kro
    Oxford (1967) n.#. (also found in Oxford
        Book Of Tudor Anthems)

118:24
    Byrd, William   (ed. David Nott)
    Sing Praise To God This Holy Day (Haec
        Dies) (English/Latin)
    SSATBB   kro
    Concordia (1971) 98-2091

118:24
    Christiansen, Paul
    This Is The Day
    SATB   kro
    AMSI (1950) 300

118:24
    Copley, R. Evan
    This Is The Day
    SATB   kro
    Abingdon (1975) APM-388

118:24
    Copley, R. Evan
    This Is The Day
    Unison Treble   Organ
    Abingdon (1964) APM-341 (found in Seven
        General Anthems For Unison-Treble
        Choir)

118:24
    Fink, Michael
    This Is The Day
    SAB   Organ
    Mark Foster (1980) MF 196

118:24
    Ford, Virgil T.
    This Is The Day Which The Lord Hath Made
    SAB   Organ
    G. Schirmer (1968) 11503

118:24
    Ford, Virgil T.
    This Is The Day Which The Lord Hath Made
    SATB   Organ
    G. Schirmer (1965) 11272

118:24   (and additional)
    Friedell, Harold
    This Is The Day
    SATB (B-solo)   Organ
    H. W. Gray (1957) CMR 2457

118:24
    Gallus, Jacobus (ed. Paul Thomas)
    This Is The Day (Latin/English)
    SATB/SATB and Continuo; or SATB and Brass
    Concordia (1963) 98-1702

118:24   (Psalm 149:2)
    Geisler, J. C. (ed. E. Nolte)
    This Is The Day That The Lord Created
        (English/German)
    SSAB or SATB   Organ
    Boosey & Hawkes (1968) 5692

118:24
    Goemanne, Noel
    Be Glad And Rejoice
    SATB   Organ or Piano   (Optional chil-
        dren's voices, flute and Indian drum)
    Flammer (1974) A-5645

118:24
    Hampton, Calvin
    This Is The Day
    SATB   Organ, Percussion
    McAfee (1974) M 1046

118:24
    Handl, Jacob (ed. C. F. Simkin)
    Haec Dies (English/Latin)
    SATB/SATB   kro
    C. F. Peters (1958) 1523

118:24
    Ingegneri, Marc A.
    Haec Dies
    SATB   No accompaniment
    Arista (1978) AE 293

118:24
    Johnson, Ralph
    This Is The Day
    SATB   Keyboard and Flute
    Augsburg (1973) 11-1690

118:24
    Krenek, Ernst
    Easter (Haec Dies) (from Holiday Motets)
        (Latin)
    SSA Round   No accompaniment
    Broude Brothers (1967) BB-4069

118:24   (Proverbs 4:18)
    Leaf, Robert
    Awake, Arise, Go Forth And Rejoice
    Unison   Piano or Organ
    Augsburg (1969) 11-1580

118:24
    Leaf, Robert
    Let Us Be Happy
    SAB   Organ and Triangle
    Augsburg (1975) 11-0661

118:24
    SEE: Luke 24:6-7
    Lekberg, Sven
    He Is Risen

118:24 (and other)
    Lekberg, Sven
    This Is The Day Which The Lord Hath Made
    SATB   kro
    G. Schirmer (1976) 12064

118:24, 29
    Near, Gerald
    This Is The Day The Lord Hath Made
    SAB   Keyboard
    Augsburg (1971) 11-1620

118:24
    Newbury, Kent
    This Is The Day Which The Lord Has Made
    SATB   Organ
    Hope (1971) A-429

118:24
    Palestrina, G. P.
    Haec Dies (Latin)
    SSATTB   No accompaniment
    Arista (1968) AE 144

118:24
    Palestrina, G. P. (ed. Alec Harman)
    Haec Dies   (Latin/English)
    SATB   Optional keyboard
    Oxford (1964) (also found in Ten Four-Part
        Motets For The Church's Year)

118:24
    Palestrina, G. P.
    Haec Dies (Latin only)
    SSATTB   No accompaniment
    Oxford (1972) A 293

118:24
    Palestrina, G. P. (ed. C. A. Dower)
    Haec Dies (This Is The Day) (Latin/English)
    SATB   kro
    Tetra [Alexander Broude] (1975) AB 752

118:24
    Palestrina, G. P. (ed. Charles Marshall)
    This Glad Day   (English/Latin)
    SSATBB   kro
    Franck Music (1966) F 585

118:24
    Palestrina, G. P. (arr. David Pizarro)
    This Is The Day   (English/Latin)
    SATB   kro
    H. W. Gray (1961) CMR 2688

118:24
    Parker, Alice
    This Is The Day (part of Sunday Rounds)
    Three part round   No accompaniment
    Hinshaw (1975) HMC 106

118:24
    SEE: Romans 6:9
    Pelz, Walter
    Verse/The Resurrection Of Our Lord

118:24
    Pinkham, Daniel
    This Is The Day (Easter Cantata)
    SATB   Piano or Brass
    C. F. Peters (1962) 6393

118:24
    Rodgers, John
    This Is The Day (from Seven Choral Sen-
        tences)
    SATB   Organ
    H. W. Gray (1981) GCMR 3453

118:24
    Telemann, G. P.
    Dies ist der Tag, den der Herr macht
    SSB or SS   Organ continuo, 2 violins
    Hanssler (1972) HE 39.010

118:24
    Turle, James
    This Is The Day Which The Lord Hath Made
    SATB   Organ
    Novello (n.d.) #4

118:24
    Watson, Walter
    Rejoice
    Unison   Keyboard
    Choristers Guild (1971) A-102

118:24
    Wilson, John F.
    This Is The Day
    SATB   No accompaniment
    Hope (1981) A-523

118:24
    Zucchini, Gregorio (ed. Roger Wilhelm)
    This Is The Day (Haec Dies) (Latin/English)
    SATB   Organ
    Lawson Gould (1971) 51657

118:24, 29
    Titcomb, Everett
    This Is The Day
    SATB   kro
    Abingdon (1962) APM-208

118:26
    Herbst, Johannes (ed. & arr. Jeannine S.
        Ingram)
    How Blessed They (Wir segnen euch) (English/
    SATB   Keyboard
    Carl Fischer (1978) CM 8045

119:00
    Arnatt, Ronald
    Teach Me O Lord
    SATB (S-solo)   Organ
    H. W. Gray (1964) 2776

119:00
    Arnatt, Ronald
    Teach Me O Lord
    SSA   Organ
    H. W. Gray (1962) 2753

119:00
    Dieterich, Milton
    Great Is The Peace
    SATB   Accompaniment ad lib.
    Pro Art (1965) 2253

119:00 (based on)
    Gibbons, Orlando (setting by S. Drummond
        Wolff)
    My God Accept My Heart This Day
    SATB   Organ
    Lawson Gould (1970) 51528

119:00
    Lekberg, Sven
    With My Whole Heart Have I Sought Thee
    SATB   kro
    Galaxy (1963) GMC 2256

119:00 (Ainsworth Psalter)
    Malin, Don (arr.)
    A New England Psalm
    SATB   Piano
    C. C. Birchard (1954) 967

119:00
  Newbury, Kent
  Let My Prayer Come Before Thee
  SAB   kro
  G. Schirmer (1966) 11392

119:00   (Watts)
  Parker, Alice
  Prayer
  SATB/SATB   No accompaniment (Choir II
        may be instruments)
  Lawson Gould (1973) 51737

119:00   (adapted from)
  Rogers, Benjamin (ed. Elwyn Wienandt)
  Teach Me O Lord
  SATB   kro
  Flammer (1971) A 5552

119:1
  Greene, Maurice (ed. Melville Cook)
  Blessed Are Those That Are Undefiled
  2 trebles   Organ
  Hinrichsen [C. F. Peters] (1952) #51

119:1
  Stanford, C. F.
  Beati Quorum Via   Op. 38, #3
  SSATBB   kro
  Boosey & Hawkes (1905) Reprinted 1959

119:1-2
  Hassler, Hans Leo
  Ad Dominum cum tribularer
  SSATB   kro
  Mercury (1941) 2

119:1-2
  Victoria, Tomas (ed. Mason Martens)
  Beati Immaculati (Blessed Are The Undefiled)
        (English/Latin)
  SATB   kro
  Walton (1967) 6020

119:1-2, 33
  Willan, Healey
  Blessed Are The Undefiled
  SS   Keyboard
  Concordia (1953)   (found in We Praise Thee,
        Volume I, 97-7564)

119:1-6
  Tallis, Tomas (ed. Lowell Beveridge)
  Blessed Are Those
  SATTB   kro
  G. Schirmer (1946) 9567

119:1-8, 137
  Anders, Charles
  Psalm 119
  Unison   Organ
  Augsburg (1970) 11-0635

119:1-8
  Petrich, Roger
  Blessed Are Those Whose Way Is Blameless
  SAB   Keyboard
  Augsburg (1964) PS 614

119:18
  Persichetti, Vincent
  Scripture (from Hymns and Responses For the
        Church Year)
  SATB   No accompaniment
  Elkan-Vogel (1956) 463-00001

119:18-20
  SEE: Psalm 103:10-16
  Sowerby, Leo
  A Liturgy Of Hope

119:33
  Attwood, Thomas
  Teach Me, O Lord
  SATB   Organ
  Concordia   98-1343 (also found in The
        Parish Choir, 97-7574)

119:33
  Attwood, Thomas
  Teach Me O Lord
  SATB   Organ
  E. C. Schirmer (1952) ECS 169   (also found
        in Concord Anthem Book - Red)

119:33
  Attwood, Thomas
  Teach Me O Lord
  SATB   Organ
  Novello (n.d.) 29.0225.07

119:33, 145
  Attwood, Thomas (ed. & arr. Ivan Trusler)
  Teach Me, O Lord
  SATB   Keyboard ad lib.
  Plymouth (1963) TR 121   (also found in
        Anthems For The Church Year, Volume 1)

119:33
  Attwood, Thomas
  Teach Me O Lord
  SATB   Organ
  Oxford   (found in Anthems For Choirs)

119:33
  Franck, J. L. (arr. Elwood Coggin)
  Teach Me O Lord
  SAB   Accompaniment
  Pro Art [Belwin] (1981) PRO-CH 3014

119:33-40
  Hilton, John (the Younger) (ed. John
        Morehen)
  Teach Me O Lord
  SSATB   Organ
  Oxford (1963) A 196

119:33
  Young, Gordon
  Teach Me, O Lord
  SATB   No accompaniment
  Belwin (1980) DMC 8095

119:33-38
  Byrd, William
  Teach Me, O Lord
  SAATB or SSATB (S-T-solos)   Organ
  Oxford CMS-23 (also found in Oxford Book
        Of Tudor Anthems)

119:40-42, 45-46, **49**-50
  Lang, E.
  Meditation from Psalm 119
  SATB   Organ
  J. Fischer (1954) 8788

119:54
  Pinkham, Daniel
  Thy Statues Have Been My Song
  SAB   Organ
  E. C. Schirmer (1970) 2705

119:73, 77
  Wilkinson, Scott
  Psalm 119
  SATB   kro
  Carl Fischer (1964) CM 7436

119:92, 94
  Wesley, Samuel S. (ed. Watkins Shaw)
  I Am Thine, O Save Me
  SATTB   Organ
  Novello (1976) 29.0379.02

119:97
Croft, William
Lord, What Love Have I
SA   Organ
Oxford (1973) (found in Anthems For Choirs,
    Volume 2)

119:105
SEE: Job 3:3-4, 20-21, 23-24
Cook, Melville
Antiphon

119:105
Morgan, Haydn
Thy Word Is A Light
SATB   kro
Carl Fischer (1946) CM 6239

119:105
Pears, James R.
Thy Word Is A Lantern Unto My Feet
SATB   Organ
Flammer (1937) (found in Flammer Collection
    of Anthems, Volume 2)

119:105 (based on Scripture by Henry Chequer)
Talmadge, Charles
Be Thou A Lamp Unto Our Footsteps
SATB (S or T solo)   kro
H. W. Gray (1970) 3075

119:105-106, 109
Purvis, Richard
A Canticle Of Light
SATB   Organ
Flammer (1967) A-5076

119:105-107 (II Timothy 2:15)
Huntington, Ronald M.
Thy Word Is A Lamp
SATB   Organ
Mark Foster (1975) MF 143

119:105-108, 110, 111
Purcell, Henry
Thy Word Is A Lantern
SATB   Organ
Novello (1958) 29.0148.10

119:105-114
Powell, Robert J.
SATB   Organ
Abingdon (1963) APM 294

119:105, 114, 120, 125, 135, 144
Sowerby, Leo
Thy Word Is A Lantern Unto My Feet
SATB   kro
H. W. Gray (1964) 2868

119:130
SEE: Job 3:3-4, 20-21, 23-24
Cook, Melville
Antiphon

119:137-143 (adapted)
Vivaldi, Antonio (ed. & arr. Walter Ehret)
Righteous, O Lord, Art Thou
SAB (S-solo) Piano
Elkan-Vogel (1975) 362-03203

119:137-143 (adapted)
Vivaldi, Antonio (ed. & arr. Walter Ehret)
Righteous, O Lord, Art Thou
SATB (S-solo)   Piano
Elkan-Vogel (1975) 362-03119

119:145
Sullivan, Michael
I Call With My Whole Heart
SATB   Organ
GIA (1980) G-2323

119:145, 147-148, 150-151
Sowerby, Leo
I Will With My Whole Heart
SATB   kro
H. W. Gray (1957) 2459

119:169-170, 173-174 (paraphrase)
Wesley, Samuel S. (ed. Edward Baristow)
To My Request And Earnest Cry
SATB   Organ
Novello (1906) 758

119:169-172, 175
Batten, Adrian (ed. Maurice Bevan)
Let My Complaint Come Before Thee
SATB   kro
Oxford (1960) A 189 (also found in Sixteenth
    Century Anthem Book)

119:169-176
Morley, Thomas
Let My Complaint
ATBB   Organ
Oxford (1965) (found in Anthems for Men's
    Voices, Volume 1)

119:171-172
Greene, Maurice (ed. E. S. Roper)
My Lips Shall Speak Of Thy Praise
SS   Piano
Oxford (1928) 1421

119:174-175
Byrd, William (arr. Alfred Whitehead)
I Have Longed For Thy Saving Health
SATB   Keyboard
H. W. Gray (1940) 1679

119:175
SEE: Isaiah 26:3
Walker, Robert
Thou Wilt Keep Him In Perfect Peace

119:175
SEE: Isaiah 26:3
Wesley, Samuel S.
Thou Wilt Keep Him In Perfect Peace

119:175
SEE: Isaiah 26:3
Wesley, Samuel S. (ed. Basil Ramsey)
Thou Wilt Keep Him In Perfect Peace

119:175
SEE: Isaiah 26:3
Wesley, Samuel S.
Thou Wilt Keep Him In Perfect Peace
    (Novello)

120:00
Lunde, Lawson
Psalm 120, Op. 22
SATB   No accompaniment
Tetra [Alexander Broude] (1971) AB 711-5

120:1-2
Hassler, Hans Leo
Ad Dominum cum tribularer (Latin)
SAATB   No accompaniment
Presser (1941) 352.00002

120:1-5
Pratt, George
O Sing Unto The Lord A New Song (Four
    Anthems)
Unison   Organ
RSCM (1973) 251

120:4-5 (Psalm 55:6)
Amner, John (ed. Mason Martens)
Woe Is Me
SATB   kro
Leeds (1944) LCS 2005

120:5
   Tomkins, Thomas (ed. John McCarthy)
   Woe Is Me
   SSATBB   Piano
   Bourne (1970) 917

121:00
   Adler, Samuel
   Psalm 121   (Two Songs Of Hope)
   TTBB   Organ
   Mercury (1962) MC 430

121:00
   Bach, J. S.
   Psalm CXXI   (from Cantata 71)
   SATB   Organ
   Paterson's (1925) 1567

121:00
   Ben-Haim, Paul
   I Will Lift Up Mine Eyes
   SATB   kro
   Israeli Music (1951) L 400

121:00
   Berger, Jean
   I Lift Up My Eyes
   SATB   kro
   C. F. Peters (1961) 6251

121:00
   Berger, Jean
   I To The Hills Lift Up Mine Eyes
   SATB   kro
   Augsburg (1978) 11-0678

121:00
   Bode, Arnold G. H.
   I Will Lift Up Mine Eyes
   SATB   Piano or Organ
   Carl Fischer (1958) CM 6375

121:00
   Bourgeois, Louis (Claude Goudimel)
      (ed. A. Couper)
   Towards The Mountains I Lift Up My Eyes
      (English/French)
   SATB   kro
   Presser (1971) 352-00442

121:00
   Copes, V. Earle
   Psalm 121
   SATB   kro
   Abingdon (1965) APM-480

121:00
   Cowell, Henry
   Psalm 121
   SATB   kro
   Associated (1958) (also found in Contem-
      porary Settings Of The Psalms, APM-
      6910)

121:00
   DiLasso, Orlando (ed. C. Buell Agey)
   Levavi oculos meos (English/Latin)
   SATB/SATB   kro
   G. Schirmer (1965) 11269

121:00
   Finzi, Gerald
   Two Motets (Up To Those Hills and Glad-
      some Hills)
   SATB   Keyboard
   Stainer & Bell (1925) 3179

121:00
   Freed, Isadore
   I Will Lift Up Mine Eyes
   SATB   Optional accompaniment
   Transcontinental (1951) TCL 114

121:00 (metrical version by Rollin Pease)
   Fryxell, Regina Holmen
   To The Hills I Lift Mine Eyes
   SATB   kro
   Abingdon (1966) APM 475

121:00
   Gibbs, Alan
   I Will Lift Up Mine Eyes
   SATB   Organ
   RSCM (1974) (found in Five Anthems For
      Today)

121:00
   Glarum, L. Stanley
   I Will Lift Up Mine Eyes
   SSAATTBB   Keyboard
   Bourne (1958) SG-6

121:00
   Goldman, Edward A.
   I Will Lift Up Mine Eyes
   SATB   Piano or Organ
   Beckman (1967) MC 513

121:00
   Hanson, Howard
   The One Hundred Twenty-First Psalm
   SATB   Keyboard
   Carl Fischer (1968) CM 7700

121:00
   Hopson, Hal
   I Lift Up My Eyes To The Hills
   Unison   Organ (optional solo instrument)
   GIA (1980) G-2359

121:00
   Joubert, John
   I Will Lift Up Mine Eyes Unto The Hills,
      Op. 63
   SSAA   Piano
   Novello (1971) Chor. Series 125

121:00
   Kantor, Joseph
   Psalm 121
   SATB   No accompaniment
   Mercury (1962) MC 431

121:00
   Kechley, Gerald
   Psalm 121
   SATB   kro
   Presser (1968) 312-40710

121:00
   Kodaly, Zoltan
   Psalm 121   (English/German)
   SATTBB   kro
   Boosey & Hawkes (1959) 5330

121:00
   Laverty, John Timothy
   I Will Lift Up Mine Eyes
   SAB   Keyboard
   Broadman (1957) MF 449

121:00
   Ledger, Philip
   I Will Lift Up Mine Eyes
   SATB   No accompaniment
   Oxford (1963) A 192

121:00
   Lekberg, Sven
   I Will Lift Up Mine Eyes
   SATB   kro
   Galaxy (1962) GMC 2259

121:00
   Leslie, Robert
   I To The Hills
   2 part   Keyboard
   Flammer (1980) EA 5023

121:00
McAfee, Don
Psalm 121 (Three Psalm-Hymns for Juniors)
Unison   Keyboard
Canyon (1967) 6703

121:00   (taken from)
Marshall, Jane M.
Unto The Hills
SATB   Piano or Organ
Carl Fischer (1956) CM 6928

121:00
Mendelssohn, Felix (arr. Hal Hopson)
I To The Hills Will Lift Mine Eyes
2 part mixed   Organ
Agape [Hope] (1978) HH 3910

121:00
Milford, Robin
The One Hundred And Twenty-First Psalm
SATB (S-A-T-B--solos)   kro
Lengnick (1947) 3513

121:00
Milhaud, Darius
121 Psalm
TTBB   No accompaniment
Universal (1956) 9632

121:00
Moe, Daniel
I Lift Up My Eyes
SATB   Organ
Mercury (1955) MC 246

121:00   (adapted)
Morgan, Haydn
Mine Eyes Will I Lift Up
SATB   Optional accompaniment
Carl Fischer (1970) CM 7738

121:00
Mueller, Carl F.
I Will Lift Up Mine Eyes
SSAATTBB   kro
G. Schirmer (1934) 7804

121:00
Mueller, Carl F.
Psalm CXXI
SATB   Organ
G. Schirmer (1954) 10360

121:00 (Psalm 19:1;   Psalm 48:1)
Muro, Don
I Will Lift Up Mine Eyes
SATB   Organ and Tape
H. W. Gray (1976) CCS 25

121:00   (Psalm 122)
Nicholson, Sydney H. (arr.)
Psalm 121 (Processional Psalms)
SATB   No accompaniment
RSCM (1957) 331

121:00
Paul des Marais
Psalm 121
SATB   kro
Elkan-Vogel (1965) 1218

121:00
Pfautsch, Lloyd
I Will Lift Up Mine Eyes
SATB   kro
Abingdon (1965) APM-400

121:00
Porpora, Nicolai (ed. Hans David)
Laetatus sum (Latin)
SSAA   Keyboard and Strings
Marks (1971) 4542

121:00   (adapted)
Royse, Mildred Barnes
My Help Cometh From The Lord
SATB   Piano or Organ
Mercury (1971) 352-00454

121:00
Rutter, John
I Will Lift Up Mine Eyes
SATB   Organ
Oxford (1976) A 313

121:00
Schlittenhard, Melody
I Will Lift Up Mine Eyes
SATB (A-solo)   Keyboard
Mark Foster (1979) MF 187

121:00
Schütz, Heinrich (ed. Paul Boepple)
I Lift Mine Eyes (Four Psalms)
SATB   No accompaniment
Mercury (1941) 352-00006

121:00
Schütz, Heinrich
Ich hebe meine Augen auf zu den Bergen
SATB   Continuo
Barenreiter (1956) 1713

121:00
Schütz, Heinrich (ed. John Kingsbury)
Mine Eyes I Lift (Three Chorales) (English/
     German)
SATB   kro
Music 70 (1975) M70-153

121:00 (Becker Psalter)
Schütz, Heinrich (ed. George Lynn)
Psalm 121 (English/German)
SATB   kro
G. Schirmer (1972) 11900

121:00   (adapted)
Sinzheimer, Max
Psalm 121
Unison or 2 part or 4 part mixed
          Organ
Augsburg (1978) 11-0662

121:00
Sowerby, Leo
I Will Lift Up Mine Eyes
SATB (A-solo)   Organ
Boston Music (1920) 1385

121:00
Surplice, Alwyn
I Will Lift Up Mine Eyes
SATB   Organ
Boosey & Hawkes (1963) 5573

121:00
Thomas, Mansell
I Will Lift Up Mine Eyes
SATB   kro
Novello (1963) Anth. 1419

121:00   (adapted)
Upshur, Claire H.
Psalm 121
Unison with descant   Keyboard
Flammer (1960) (found in Unison Anthems
     With Descants)

121:00
Vaet, Jacobus
Laetatus sum (from Sechs Motetten)
     (Latin/German)
STTB   No accompaniment
Kalmus (n.d.) n.#.

121:00
Vick, Lloyd
Psalm 121
SATB   kro
Walton (1975) 2980

121:00
Wagner, Douglas E.
I To The Hills Lift Up My Eyes
SA   Piano, 2 octave Handbells
Belwin (1980) DMC 8087

121:00
Williamson, Malcolm
I Will Lift Up Mine Eyes
Unison Choir   Congregation, Organ
Weinberger [Boosey & Hawkes] (1970) W.001

121:00
Wright, Searle
Psalm CXXI
SATB (S or T solo)   kro
Witmark (1962) W 3694

121:00
Young, Gordon
I Will Lift Up Mine Eyes
SATB   Keyboard
Flammer (1973) A-5618

121:00
Zimmermann, Heinz Werner
Psalm 121
SATB   A cappella
Carl Fischer (n.d.) 7921

121:1-3
Haan, Raymond
I Will Lift Up Mine Eyes
SATB   Organ
AMSI (1974) 259

121:1-2
Matthew, Thomas
I Will Lift Up Mine Eyes
SATB   kro
H. T. Fitzsimons (1951) 2104

121:1-2, 5-6
Lutkin, Peter C.
I Will Lift Up Mine Eyes
SA   Organ
Fitzsimons (1932) 5010

121:1-3
Kreutz, Robert
I Lift Up My Eyes
SATB   No accompaniment
GIA 91978) G 2164

121:1-3
Wadley, G. W.
I Will Lift Up Mine Eyes
SATB   kro
Novello (1968) (also found in Sing To The
      Lord)

121:1-4
Dvorak, Anton (arr. K. K. Davis)
I Will Lift Up Mine Eyes
SATB   Piano or Organ
Carl Fischer (1970) CM 7729

121:1-4
Dvorak, Anton (arr. Charles Black)
I Will Lift Mine Eyes
SATB   Organ
H. W. Gray (1966) CMR 2960

121:1-4
Mendelssohn, F. (arr. Charles Kirby)
Lift Thine Eyes (Elijah)
S(A)CB   kro
Cambiata Press (1973) M-117322

121:1-4
Mendelssohn, Felix
Lift Thine Eyes (Elijah)
SSA   kro
Carl Fischer (n.d.) CM 618

121:1-4
Mendelssohn, Felix (arr. Jack Werner)
Lift Thine Eyes (not the version found in
      Elijah)
SA   Piano
Oxford (1958) OM 14

121:1-4
Walker, Ernest
I Will Lift Up Mine Eyes Op. 16, #1
ATB   Organ
Novello (1947) MV 127

121:1-4, 7-8
Newbury, Kent
I Lift Up My Eyes
SATB or SA   Keyboard with optional
      percussion
Flammer (1977) A-5766

121:4   (Psalm 138:7)
Mendelssohn, F. (ed. John Carlton)
He Watching Over Israel (Elijah)
SATB   Keyboard
Boosey & Hawkes (1958) 5177

121:4
Mendelssohn, Felix (arr. & adapted Don
      Collins)
He Watching Over Israel (Elijah)
SSCB   Keyboard
Cambiata (1975) M97557

121:4   (Psalm 138:7)
Mendelssohn, F.
He Watching Over Israel (Elijah)
SSA   Organ
E. C. Schirmer (1934) ECS 779

121:4   (Psalm 138:7)
Mendelssohn, F. (ed. Ivan Trusler)
He Watching Over Israel
SATB   Organ or Piano
Plymouth (1963) TR-119 (also found in
      Anthems For The Church Year, Volume 1)

121:5-6
Haan, Raymond
A Pilgrim's Song
SATB   Organ
GIA (1976) G-2041

121:5-7
Rose, Bernard
Dominus custodit te (from Three Introits)
      (Latin)
SATB   No accompaniment
Novello (1972) MT 1558

121:7-8
Hovhaness, Alan
The Lord Shall Preserve Thee From All Evil,
      Op. 93
SATB   Organ
C. F. Peters (1970) 66232B

121:7, 8
SEE: Proverbs 3:5, 6
Wetzler, Robert
He Shall Direct Your Paths

122:00
Beebe, Hank
And I Was Glad
2 part   Keyboard
Hinshaw (1977) HMC-7000

122:00
    Charpentier, Marc-Antoine (ed. James Dunn)
    Laetatus sum   (How Glad Was I)
    SATB (A-T-B-solos)   Organ, 2 violins
    Concordia (1965) 97-6425

122:00
    Davidson, Jerry F.
    I Was Glad
    Unison   Piano or Organ
    World Library (1980) 7622-1

122:00
    Hallock, Peter
    I Was Glad
    2 voices   7 Handbells
    GIA (1977) G-2079

122:00
    Monteverdi, Claudio
    Be Joyful (Laetatus sum)
    SATB   kro
    Mark Foster (1967) MF 109X

122:00
    SEE: Psalm 121
    Nicholson, Sydney H. (arr.)
    Psalm 122 (Processional Psalms)

122:00
    Pinkham, Daniel
    I Was Glad
    SATB   Optional Piano or Organ
    Associated (1963) A-426 (also found in The
        AMP Contemporary Choral Collection)

122:00
    Slack. Roy
    I Was Glad
    SATB   Organ
    Oxford (1964) E 105

122:00
    Sowerby, Leo
    I Was Glad When They Said Unto Me
    SATB   Organ
    H. W. Gray (1941) CMR 1787

122:00
    Sweelinck, J. P.
    Psalmus 122   (English/French/Dutch)
    SATB   kro
    Ed. Musico (1954) G 328

122:00
    Thompson, Alan
    I Was Glad When They Said Unto Me
    SATB   Organ or Piano
    BMI[Canada] (1956) 235

122:00
    Vivaldi, Antonio (ed. Keith Graumann)
    I Have Rejoice   (English/Latin)
    SATB   Strings and Continuo
    Augsburg (1978) 11-0669

122:00
    Vivaldi, Antonio (ed. Louis Pichierri)
    Laetatus   (Psalm 122)
    SATB   Piano or Organ
    Lawson Gould (1970) 51670

122:00
    Williamson, Malcolm
    O Jerusalem (Carols of King David)
    Unison   Organ
    Boosey & Hawkes (1972) W.002

122:1   (Psalm 84:2-5, 13)
    Arnatt, Ronald
    I Was Glad
    SATB   Organ
    Augsburg (1976) 11-0664

122:1
    Boberg, Robert
    I Was Glad (Introits, Benedictions and
        Amens)
    SATB   No accompaniment
    Boston Music (1981) 13959

122:1   (Habakkuk 2:20;   Genesis 28:17)
    Thompson, Randall
    The Gate of Heaven
    SATB   kro
    E. C. Schirmer (1961) 2490

122:1   (Habakkuk 2:20;   Genesis 28:17)
    Thompson, Randall
    The Gate of Heaven
    SSAA   kro
    E. C. Schirmer (n.d.) 2531

122:1   (Habakkuk 2:20;   Genesis 28:17)
    Thompson, Randall
    The Gate Of Heaven
    TTBB   kro
    E. C. Schirmer (n.d.) 2175

122:1   (Genesis 28:16-17)
    Young, Philip
    The House Of The Lord
    SATB   Organ
    Carl Fischer (1972) CM 7732

122:1, 2   (Psalm 127:1; Psalm 84:4, 10)
    Gustafson, Dwight
    The House Of Our Lord
    SATB   Organ
    Sacred Music Press (1975) S-176

122:1-2, 4-7
    Boyce, William (ed. Robert J. Bruce)
    I Was Glad
    SATB   Optional Organ
    Novello (1979) 29.0454.08

122:1-2, 6-7
    Simper, Caleb
    Pray For The Peace of Jerusalem
    SATB   Organ
    Weekes [Harris] (1902) n.#.

122:1-2, 6-9   (adapted)
    Verdi, Ralph C.
    Psalm 121
    Unison Choir, Cantor, Congregation, Organ
    GIA (1973) G-1793

122:1-2, 6-9
    SEE: Psalm 15:1-2
    Bliss, Arthur
    Lord, Who Shall Abide In Thy Tabernacle?

122:1-2, 7
    Willan, Healey
    I Was Glad
    SSA   No accompaniment
    Concordia (1962) 97-7160 (found in We
        Praise Thee, Volume 2)

122:1-2, 7
    Wolff, S. Drummond
    I Was Glad
    SATB   kro
    Concordia (1955) CH 1061

122:1-3, 6-7
    Parry, Hubert
    I Was Glad When They Said Unto Me
    SSATTB   Organ
    H. W. Gray (n.d.) CMR 2404

122:1-3, 6-7
    Parry, C. Hubert
    I Was Glad When They Said Unto Me
    SSATTB   Organ
    Novello (n.d.) 29.0122.06

122:1-3, 6-8
    Hallock, Peter
    I Was Glad
    2 part choir   Congregation, Percussion
    Walton (1971) 2197

122:1, 4-7
    Purcell, Henry (ed. Bruce Wood)
    I Was Glad
    SSATB   Optional organ
    Novello (1977) 29.0446.02

122:1, 6-7 (Psalm 123:1)
    Butler, Eugene
    I Was Glad
    SATB   Piano or Organ
    Agape [Hope] (1977) EB 9200

122:1-7
    Orr, Robin
    I Was Glad
    SATB   No accompaniment
    Hinrichsen (1957) 537

122:1, 7
    Wyton, Alec
    I Was Glad
    SATB   Organ
    Presser (1977) 312-41169

122:1, 7-9
    Hillert, Richard
    Offertory/Dedication (Verses and Offer-
        tories - Lesser Festivals)
    Unison   Organ
    Augsburg (1980) 11-9543

122:1-9
    Williamson, Malcolm
    O Jerusalem
    Unison   Organ
    Boosey & Hawkes

122:3, 6-7
    SEE: Psalm 16:7
    Phillips, John C.
    The Lot Is Fallen Unto Me

122:6 (Scottish Psalter, 1650)
    Stanford, C. F. (ed. Lionel Dakers)
    Pray That Jerusalem May Have Peace And
        Felicity
    SATB   Organ
    RSCM (1977) 256

122:6
    Tomkins, Thomas (ed. Robert Hickok)
    O Pray For The Peace Of Jerusalem
    SATB   kro
    Broude Brothers (1954) BB 901

122:6
    Tomkins, Thomas (ed. Ramsbotham)
    O Pray For The Peace Of Jerusalem
    SATB   kro
    Oxford (1921) (found in Sixteenth Century
        Anthem Book)

122:6
    Tomkins, Thomas (ed. Keith Clark)
    O Pray For The Peace Of Jerusalem
    SATB   kro
    Presser (1975) 312-41111

122:6, 7
    SEE: Psalm 102:16
    Cole, John (ed. Mason Martens)
    When The Lord Shall Build Up Zion

122:6, 7
    Howells, Herbert
    O Pray For The Peace Of Jerusalem
    SATB   Organ
    Oxford (1933) A-107

122:6-7
    Nocolson, Richard (ed. Cyril Simkins)
    O Pray For The Peace Of Jerusalem
    SAATB   kro
    Associated (1964) NYPMS 23

122:6-7
    Nicolson, Richard (ed. John Morehen)
    O Pray For The Peace Of Jerusalem
    SAATB   Organ ad lib.
    Oxford (1963) A 194

122:6-7
    Ossewaarde, Jack H.
    O Pray For The Peace Of Jerusalem (Two
        Motets)
    SATB   Organ
    H. W. Gray (1963) CMR 2777

122:6-7
    Taylor, Eric
    O Pray For The Peace Of Jerusalem
    SATB   Organ
    Novello (1955) (found in Into His Courts
        With Praise)

122:6-8
    Goss, John
    O Pray For The Peace Of Jerusalem
    SATB   Organ
    Oxford (found in Anthems For Choirs,
        Volume 1)

122:6-9
    Blow, John
    O Pray For The Peace Of Jerusalem
    SATB   (S-solo)   Organ
    Novello (1952) 29.0145.05 (also found in
        RSCM, Festival Service Book,
        Volume 2)

123:1
    SEE: Psalm 122:1, 6-7
    Butler, Eugene
    I Was Glad

123:1-4
    Williamson, Malcolm
    Thou That Dwelleth In The Heavens (from
        Psalms Of The Elements)
    Unison   Congregation   Organ
    Boosey & Hawkes (1976) 5948

123:3-4
    Palestrina, G. P.
    Miserere nostri
    SATB   kro
    E. C. Schirmer (1976) ECS 2986

124:00
    Bourgeois, L. (arr. C. Goudimel) (ed. A. B.
        Couper)
    Now Let Us Hear What Israel Hath Said
        (English/French)
    SATB   kro
    Presser (1971) 352.00437

124:00
    Parker, Alice and Robert Shaw (arr.)
    Psalm 124
    SATB   Keyboard
    G. Schirmer (n.d.) 583

124:00
    Sowerby, Leo
    Psalm 124
    TTBB   Organ
    H. W. Gray (1967) 2986

124:00
    West, Benjamin (ed. Gillian Anderson)
    Anthem! Psalm 124
    SATB   Keyboard
    C. T. Wagner Reprint (n.d.) C-062207

125:00
DiLasso, Orlando (arr. Matthew Lundquist)
All Who With Heart Confiding
SATB   kro
Elkan-Vogel (1956) 1111

125:00
Hartley, Walter S.
They That Put Their Trust
SSATB   Organ
MCA (1968)

125:00   (adapted)
Pooler, Frank
The Mountains Of God
SATB   Optional Accompaniment
Schmitt (1953) 852

125:1-2
Hallock, Peter
They Who Trust In The Lord
SATB   No accompaniment
GIA (1977) G-2081

125:1-2
Orr, Robin
They That Put Their Trust In The Lord
SATB   kro
Oxford (1948) n.#.

125:1-2
Zimmermann, Heinz Werner
Those Who Trust In The Lord
SATB   Organ
Concordia (1973) 98-2178 (also found in
Five Hymns (1973) 97-5131)

125:2
SEE: Psalm 16:7
Phillips, John C.
The Lot Is Fallen Unto Me

126:00
Billings, William (ed. Leonard Van Camp)
When The Lord Turned Again
SATB   kro
Concordia (1974) 98-2189

126:00
Krenek, Ernst
The 126th Psalm
SATB   Piano or Organ
Mills (1954) 60150

126:00
Marshall, Philip
When The Lord Turned Again
SATB   Organ
Oxford (1964) A 211

126:00
SEE: Psalm 96
Naylor, Peter
O Sing Unto The Lord

126:00
Peeters, Flor
In Convertendo Dominus (When God The Lord)
(English/Latin)
SATB   Organ ad lib.
McLaughlin & Reilly (1959) 2479

126:00
Rossi, Salomone
Shir Hama 'Alot B'shuv Adoni (Hebrew)
SATB   Organ
Lawson Gould (n.d.) 51909

126:00
Sherman, Roger
Psalm 126
SAB   Handbells
GIA (1979) G-2196

126:00
Willaert, Adriano (ed. Ralph Hunter)
In Convertendo Dominus (A Song of Thanks-
giving) (English/Latin)
SATB/SATB   Organ continuo
Belwin (1981) Oct. 2469

126:1-4
Batten, Adrian (ed. P. C. Buck)
When The Lord Turned Again
SATB   kro
Oxford (1960) (found in Sixteenth Century
Anthem Book)

126:3   (based on)
Konig, Johann (arr. Ronald A. Nelson)
Oh, That I Had A Thousand Voices
SAB   kro
Augsburg (1965) 1167

126:5-6
Antes, John (ed. & arr. Karl Kroeger)
Who With Weeping Soweth (English/German)
SATB   Organ
Boosey & Hawkes (1976) 5943

126:5-6
Bach, Johann Ludwig (ed. A. Owen)
They That Sow In Tears (English/German)
SATB   Organ
Concordia (1962) 97-6361

126:5-6
SEE: Matthew 5:4
Brahms, Johannes
Blessed Are They That Mourn (Requiem)

126:5-6
Peter, J. F. (ed. Hans T. David)
He Who Soweth Weeping (Die mit Tranen saen)
(English/German)
SATB   Organ and Instruments
C. F. Peters (1965) 6086

126:5-6
Schein, J. H.
Die mit Tränen saen   (German)
SSATB   Continuo
Barenreiter (1968) 2553

126:5-6
Schein, J. H. (ed. Norman Greyson)
They Who Grieving Soweth   (English/German)
SSATB   Piano
Bourne (1962)   ES 61

126:5-6
Schütz, Heinrich
Die mit Tränen saen   (German)
SATBB/SATBB   No accompaniment
Hanssler (n.d.) F 2636H

126:5-6
Schütz, Heinrich (ed. Robert Shaw and Klaus
Speer)
He Who With Weeping Soweth (Die mit Tranen
Saen (English/German)
SSATB   Organ ad lib.
Lawson Gould (1952) 10115

126:5-7
Byrd, William
Turn Our Captivity, O Lord
SSATBB   kro
Stainer & Bell (1964) MSP 78099

126:6-7
Schein, J. H.
Who With Grieving Soweth (English/German)
SSATB   No accompaniment
Mercury (1942) 352.00019

127:00
SEE: Isaiah 40
Beebe, Hank
I Wait For The Lord

127:00
Carissimi, Giacomo (ed. Janet Beat)
Nisi Dominus (Latin)
SSATB   Organ continuo
Novello (1974) NECM 29

127:00
Sowerby, Leo
Except The Lord Build The House
SATB   Organ
H. W. Gray (1965) 2906

127:1
SEE: Psalm 122:1-2
Gustafson, Dwight
The House Of Our God

127:1   (Psalm 115:1, 18)
Rubbra, Edmund
Except The Lord Build The House (Three
    Motets, Op. 76, #3)
SATB   No accompaniment
Lengnick (1952) 3767

128:00
Clark, Keith
A Gentle Psalm
SATB   kro
Presser (1971) 312-40932

128:00   (paraphrase)
Proulx, Richard
How Blest Are They
Unison   Keyboard with Flute
Augsburg (1973) 11-0654

128:00
Purcell, Henry
Blest Are All Who Fearfully Love The Lord
    (English/Latin)
SATB   Organ
Dartmouth (1965) n.#.

128:00
Sowerby, Leo
Blessed Are All They That Fear The Lord
SATB   Organ
H. W. Gray (1967) CMR 1573

128:00
Wetzler, Robert
Psalm 128
SATB   Piano or Organ
Augsburg (1972) 11-0646

128:1-2
Marshall, Jane
Happy Are You
SATB (B-solo)   No accompaniment
Augsburg (1980) 11-0686

128:1-5
Oliver, Stephen
How Blest Are They That Fear The Lord
    (from Wedding Anthem)
SS   Organ
Novello (1980) 29.0478.00

128:1-5
Purcell, Henry (ed. Philip Ledger and
    Imogen Holst)
How Blest Are They (Beati Omnes) (Latin/
    English)
SATB   Organ
Oxford (1968) A 245

128:1-6
Berger, Jean
Psalm 128
SATB (S-solo)   Piano
Broude Brothers (1965) BB-3054

128:1-7
Wetzler, Robert
Psalm 128
SATB   Keyboard
Augsburg (1972) 11-0646

129:00   (adapted)
Hokanson, Margrethe
The Lord Shall Bless Thee
SATB (B & S solos)   Keyboard
H. W. Gray (1962) CMR 2733

130:00
Alcock, John (ed. Robert Field)
Out Of The Deep
SATB   Keyboard
Presser (1977) 352-40133

130:00
Aldrich, Henry
Out Of The Deep
SATB   Organ
St. Mary's Press (1955) n.#.

130:00
Allanbrook, Douglas
Psalm 130
SATB   Organ
Boosey & Hawkes (1971) 5724

130:00
Batten, Adrian
Out Of The Deep
SATB (T-solo)   Organ
Schott (1957) 10573

130:00
SEE: Isaiah 40
Beebe, Hank
I Wait For The Lord

130:00
Bright, Houston
De Profundis (English/Latin)
SATB   kro
Shawnee (1963) A 682

130:00
Busarow, Donald
Out Of The Depths
SSATB   Flute (no accompaniment)
Concordia (1977) 98-2330

130:00
Carter, John
Psalm 130
SATB/SATB   No accompaniment
Augsburg (1975) 11-3014

130:00
Charpentier, Marc-Antoine (ed. & arr.
    Austin Lovelace)
Out Of The Depths
SATB   Organ
Concordia (1960) 98-1521

130:00
Chorbajian, John
De Profundis   (English)
SATB   kro
G. Schirmer (1970) 11740

130:00
Croft, William (arr. Austin Lovelace)
Out Of The Deep
SATB   Organ
Abingdon (1963) APM-309

130:00
DiLasso, Orlando
De Profundis
SATTB   No accompaniment
Arista (1975) AE 301

130:00   (paraphrase of Luther)
Distler, Hugo   (ed. Clifford Richter)
Aus Tiefer Not   (From Deepest Woe)
SSATB   kro
Boonin (1976) B 290

130:00   (metrical)
Dowland, John
Psalm 130
SATB   kro
Mark Foster (1964) MF 107

130:00
English Folk Melody (arr. Hal Hopson)
O Lord God, From The Depths I Cry Out
2 part   Keyboard
Agape [Hope] (1981) HH 3916

130:00
Giles, Nathaniel
Out Of The Deep
SSAATB   Organ
Oxford (1965) A 219

130:00
Gluck, Christoph   (ed. Mason Martens)
De Profundis (English/Latin)
SATB   kro
Walton (1962) 6007

130:00
Hancock, Gerre
Out Of The Deep
SATB   Organ
H. W. Gray (1964) CMR 2798

130:00
Handel, G. F. (arr. Hal Hopson)
Out Of The Depths I Cry (from Laudate Pueri
     Dominum)
SA or TB   Keyboard
Flammer (1980) EA 5025

130:00   (arranged)
Hoddinott, Alan
Out Of The Deep, Op. 74
SATB   No accompaniment
Oxford (1972) n.#.

130:00
Hovhaness, Alan
Out Of The Depths, Op. 142, #3
SATB (S-solo)   Organ
C. F. Peters (1961) 6270

130:00
Josquin des Pres (ed. Paul Boepple)
De Profundis (Latin)
SATB   No accompaniment
Mercury (1958) MC 43

130:00
Kelly, Brian
Out Of The Deep
SATB   Organ (brass band parts for hire)
Novello (1971) MW 13

130:00
Laster, James H.
De Profundis   (Latin)
SSAA   Piano, Percussion, Glockenspiel
Mark Foster (1979) MF 911

130:00
Latrobe, Christian (ed. Karl Kroeger)
Out Of The Deep
SATB (S-A-T-B-solos)   Organ or Piano
Boosey & Hawkes   6049

130:00
Lindusky, Eugene
From The Depths
SATB   kro
Walton (1971) 2952

130:00
Manz, Paul O.
Psalm 130
SATB   Organ
Summy Birchard (1955) 1547

130:00
Martin, Warren
Out Of The Depths
SATB   Organ ad lib.
Golden Music (1967) G 30

130:00   (paraphrase)
Mendelssohn, Felix (ed. David Nott)
In Deep Despair I Call On Thee, Op. 23, #1
SATB   Keyboard
Concordia (1968) 97-4857

130:00
Mitchell, David
Out Of The Depths
SATB   Organ
Augsburg (1979) 11-0680

130:00
Morley, Thomas (ed. Peter Le Huray)
Out Of The Deep
SAATB (A-solo)   Organ
Blandford Press [Alexander Broude] (1965)
     AB 708

130:00
Morley, Thomas (ed. William Palmer)
Out Of The Deep
SAATB   Organ
Novello (1959) 1365

130:00
Mozart, W. A. (ed. Don Smithers)
De Profundis, K.93   Latin
SATB   Organ or Piano
G. Schirmer (1966) 11322

130:00
Mozart, W. A.
De Profundis, K. 93   (English/Latin)
SATB   Organ
Schmitt, Hall, McCreary (1951) (found in
     Rare Choral Masterpieces)

130:00
Mozart, W. A. (ed. John F. Ohl)
De Profundis   (English/Latin)
SATB   Keyboard
Summy Birchard (1960) 5372

130:00
Mozart, W. A.
From The Depths Have I Called Unto Thee,
     K. 93   (Latin/English)
SATB   Keyboard
Concordia (1968) (found in A First Motet
     Book, 97-4845)

130:00
Mozart, W. A.
From The Depths Have I Called Unto Thee,
     K. 93   (Latin/English)
SATB   Keyboard
Concordia (1974) (found in A Mozart Anthem
     Book, Volume 1, 97-5230)

130:00
Nystedt, Knut
De Profundis, Op. 54   (Latin)
SATB   No accompaniment
Associated (1966) A-499 (also found in Con-
     temporary Settings of Psalm Texts)

130:00
   Peek, Richard
   Psalm 130
   2 part mixed   Organ
   Abingdon (1965) APM-477

130:00
   Peragallo, Mario
   De Profundis
   SATB   No accompaniment
   Universal (1953) 12131

130:00
   Proulx, Richard
   Processional Psalm For Lent
   2 mixed voices   5 Handbells
   GIA (1975) G-1966

130:00
   Purcell, Henry
   Plung'd In The Confines Of Despair
   TTB   Continuo
   Dartmouth College [Shawnee] (1967) n.#.

130:00   (adapted M. Luther)
   Schein, Johann H.
   From Depths Of Woe I Cry To Thee
   2 part   Keyboard
   Concordia (1966) 98-1866

130:00
   Schoenberg, Arnold
   De Profundis
   SSATBB   kro
   MCA (1953) 11193-062

130:00
   Schütz, Heinrich
   Aus der Tiefe ruf Ich   (German/English)
   SATB/SATB   Continuo
   Hanssler (1969) HE 20.025

130:00
   Schütz, Heinrich (ed. Elwood Coggin)
   Out Of The Depths We Cry, Lord
   SATB   kro
   Augsburg (1969) ACL1546

130:00
   Sessions, Roger
   Out Of The Depths   (Three Choruses On
        Biblical Texts)
   SATB   Piano
   Presser (1976) 342-40117

130:00
   Snow, Francis
   Out Of The Deep
   SATB   Piano or Organ
   Birchard (1955) 2106

130:00
   Thomson, Virgil
   Out Of The Deep
   SATB   kro
   Weintraub (1951) n.#.

130:00
   Vierra, M. L.
   Out Of The Depths
   SATB   kro
   Boosey & Hawkes (1959) 5302

130:00
   Walter, Johann (ed. Robert Wunderlich)
   From Depths Of Woe
   SATB   kro
   Augsburg (1963) 1356

130:00
   Wienhorst, Richard (arr.)
   Out Of The Depths
   SA(T)B   kro
   Associated (1961) A 344

130:00
   Williamson, Malcolm
   Out Of The Deep   (from Psalms Of The
        Elements)
   Unison choir   Congregation, Organ
   Boosey & Hawkes (1976) 5952

130:00
   Wyton, Alec
   Psalm 130
   SATB   (A-solo)   No accompaniment
   Augsburg (1974) 11-0547

130:00
   Zimmermann, Heinz Werner
   Psalm 130
   SATB (B-solo)   Guitar and Bass
   Carl Fischer (1977) CM 8028   (Parts 8028A)

130:1
   Goode, Jack C.
   Out Of The Depths (from Prayer Intonations)
   Unison   Organ
   Abingdon (1974) APM-516

130:1-2
   Krenek, Ernst
   Lent - De Profundis (from Holiday Motets)
        (Latin)
   SSA   Round   No accompaniment
   Broude Brothers (1967) BB 4069

130:1-2
   Tomkins, Thomas
   Out Of The Deep
   ATB   No accompaniment
   Oxford (1965) (found in Anthems For Men's
        Voices, Volume 1)

130:1-2
   Weelkes, Thomas
   Lord, To Thee I Make My Moan
   SAATB   Optional Organ
   Oxford (1964) TCM 89

130:1-2a, 5-6a
   Cassler, C. Winston
   My Soul Waiteth For The Lord
   SATB   kro
   Augsburg (1963) ACL 1343

130:1-4
   Aldrich, Henry
   Out Of The Deep
   SATB   Organ
   Music Press (1946) MP.61

130:1-4, 8
   Gluck, Christoph W. (arr. W. Williams)
   De Profundis (English/Latin)
   SATB   kro
   E. C. Schirmer (1932) ECS 617

130:1-4
   Latrobe, Christian (ed. Karl Kroeger)
   Out Of The Depths
   SATB (S-A-T-B-solos)   Organ or Piano
   Boosey & Hawkes (1981) 6049

130:1-4
   Lupo, Thomas (ed. John Morehen)
   Out Of The Deep
   SSATB   Optional Accompaniment
   Oxford (1964) A 216

130:3
   Wesley, Samuel S.
   Si iniquitates observaveris (Latin only)
   TTB   No accompaniment
   Oxford (1965) (found in Anthems for Men's
        Voices, Volume 2)

130:3-5
    Ferguson, Edwin E.
    If Thou, O Lord, Marked Our Iniquities
    SATB   Organ
    Lawson Gould (1979) 52035

130:4
    Lande, Michael de
    I Shall Find Forgiveness (from De Profun-
        dis)
    SAB   Organ or Piano
    Salabert (1976) n.#.

130:5, 6 (Psalm 143:8, 10)
    Slates, Philip
    I Wait For The Lord
    2 part mixed   Keyboard
    Abingdon (1965) APM-497

130:6
    Antes, John (ed. Karl Kroeger)
    Our Soul Doth Wait Upon The Lord (English/
        German)
    SATB   Organ
    Boosey & Hawkes (1976) 5941

130:6-7
    Wordsworth, William
    De Profundis (English)
    SATB   Organ
    Novello (1964) MT 1460

131:00
    Allanbrook, Douglas
    Psalm 131
    SATB   Organ
    Boosey & Hawkes (1971) 5725

131:00
    Anonymous
    Lord, I Am Not High Minded
    SAATB   Organ
    Novello (1969) NECM 4

131:00
    Beeson, Jack
    Psalm 131 (from Three Settings From The
        Bay Psalm Book)
    SATB   Optional Piano
    Oxford (1969) 92.332

131:00 (Psalm 133:1)
    Bernstein, Leonard
    Chichester Psalms - Third Movement
        (Hebrew)
    SATB   Piano (Orchestra)
    G. Schirmer (1965) 2656

131:00
    Chihara, Paul
    My Heart Is Not Haughty
    SATB   kro
    Elkan Vogel (1968) 1271

131:00
    Escovado, Robin
    Psalm 131
    SATB   kro
    Associated (1963) A-387 (also found in
        Contemporary Settings Of The Psalms,
        AMP-6910)

131:1-3
    Grantham, Donald
    O Lord, My Heart Is Not Lifted Up
    SATB   kro
    Mark Foster (1979) MF 169

132:00
    SEE: I Chronicles 28:20
    Oxley, Harrison
    Be Strong And Of Good Courage

132:8
    Hallock, Peter
    Antiphon On Psalm 132
    SATB   Trumpet
    GIA (1977) G 2082

132:8-9
    Weelkes, Thomas
    O Lord Arise
    SSAATBB   kro
    Oxford (1974)TCM 63 (also found in
        Oxford Book Of Tudor Anthems)

132:15
    SEE: Psalm 102:16
    Cole, John (ed. Mason Martens)
    When The Lord Shall Build Up Zion

132:16
    Peter, Johann F. (ed. Karl Kroeger)
    I Will Clothe Thy Priests With Salvation
    SATB   Keyboard
    Boosey & Hawkes (1978) 6004

133:00
    Clarke-Whitfeld, John
    Behold, How Good And Joyful
    SATB   Organ
    Oxford (found in Anthems For Choirs,
        Volume I)

133:00
    Hassler, Hans Leo (ed. M. Alfred Bichsel)
    Behold, How Good And Pleasant It Is
    SATBB   Keyboard
    Concordia (1967) 98-1874

133:00
    Hassler, Hans Leo (ed. George Lynn)
    Psalm 133
    SSATB   kro
    Golden Music (1963) W-3

133:00
    SEE: John 15:12
    Peloquin, C. Alexander
    Psalm 132

133:00
    Schalit, Heinrich
    Psalm Of Brotherhood
    SATB   Organ or Piano
    Transcontinental (1959) 125

133:00
    Sowerby, Leo
    Psalm 133
    TTBB   Organ
    H. W. Gray (1967) 2982

133:00
    White, John
    When Brothers Dwell In Unity
    SATB   Piano or Organ
    Lawson Gould (1965) 51209

133:1
    SEE: Psalm 131
    Bernstein, Leonard
    Chichester Psalms, Part III

133:1 (Psalm 134:1-4)
    Lewin, Frank
    Behold, How Good
    SATB   Piano
    Lawson Gould (1963) 51130

133:1
    Lock, Matthew
    Behold How Good And Joyful A Thing It Is
    SSA   Piano ad lib.
    Oxford (1937) JP-VIII

133:1 (and other)
McCabe, Michael
A Prayer For Peace
SATB or SAB or 2 part   Organ,
    optional Flute or Oboe
AMSI (1973) 238

133:1
Pinkham, Daniel
Behold, How Good, And How Pleasant
SATB   kro
C. F. Peters (1967) 66038

133:1-3
Rorem, Ned
Behold, How Good And Pleasant It Is
    (Two Psalms And A Proverb)
SATB   Piano or String Quartet
E. C. Schirmer (1965) 2674

133:1-3
Viadana, Ludovico
Exsultate justi (Latin only)
SATB   kro
J. & W. Chester (1977) JWC 55096 (found in
    First Chester Book Of Motets)

133:1-3
Williamson, Malcolm
Together In Unity (from Carols Of King
    David)
Unison   Organ
Boosey & Hawkes (1972) W.003

133:1-4
Rogers, Benjamin (ed. J. P. White)
Behold, How Good And Joyful
SATB   Organ
Concordia (1976) 98-2276

134:00
Fissinger, Edwin
Psalm 134
SATB   kro
Summy (1956) 1590

134:00 (adapted)
Floreen, John E.
Arise, Oh Ye Servants Of God
SATB   Organ
Oxford (1968) 94.204

134:00
Harris, William H.
Behold Now, Praise The Lord
2 part treble   Organ
Novello (1949) 87

134:00
LeJeune, Claude
Psalm 134 (English/French)
SAB   No accompaniment
Mercury (1945) MC 56

134:00
Parker, Alice
Blessings
SATB   kro
Lawson Gould (1971) 51592

134:00
Pinkham, Daniel
Chorale (from Prelude, Adagio and Chorale)
Unison   Brass Quintet
C. F. Peters (1969) 66294

134:00
Proulx, Richard
Psalm 134
2 part   Handbells and Tabor
GIA (1973) G-1821

134:00 (Psalm 150)
Schmutz, Albert D.
Behold, Bless Ye The Lord
SATB   Piano or Organ
Abingdon (1976) APM-439 (found in Anthems
    From The Psalms)

134:00
Sowerby, Leo
Psalm CXXXIV
SATB   Organ
Boston Music (1923) BMC 6798

134:00
Sweelinck, J. P.
Arise Ye Who Serve The Lord (English/French)
SSATBB   Piano or Organ
Mercury (1971) 352.00447

134:00
Sweelinck, J. P.
Psalm 134 (French)
SATB   Organ
E. C. Schirmer (1971) 2791

134:00
Wyton, Alec
Behold Now, Praise The Lord
Unison   Organ
Beekman [Mercury] (1964) MC 448

134:00
Zimmermann, Heinz Werner
Psalm 134
TBB   Harp or Organ
Carl Fischer (1976) CM 7957

134:1 (Psalm 135:1-3)
Newbury, Kent A.
Sing To His Name
SATB   Piano or Organ
Hope (1973) A-452

134:1-2
Titcomb, Everett
Behold Now, Praise The Lord
SATB   Organ
Mills (1938) 64133

134:1-2
Titcomb, Everett
Behold Now, Praise The Lord
TTBB   Organ
Mills (1938) 64158

134:1, 3
Glarum, L. Stanley
Behold, Bless Ye The Lord
SSATB   kro
Bourne (1959) SG-5

134:1-3
Lockwood, Normand
Psalm 134
SATB   No accompaniment
Kjos (1966) ED. 18

134:1-3
SEE: I Kings 8:13, 27-28
Milner, Anthony
I Have Surely Built Thee

134:1-3 (Psalm 135:1-4)
Pesich, Andy Anthony
Praise His Name
SATB   Organ
Lawson Gould (1979) 52080

134:1-4
Palestrina, G. P.
Ecce nunc benedicite dominum (Latin only)
TTBB   No accompaniment
Oxford (1965) (found in Anthems for Men's
    Voices, Volume 2)

134:1-4
    Wills, Arthur
    Behold Now, Praise The Lord
    SATB   Organ
    RSCM (1965) 234

135:00 (adapted)
    Hutchison, Warner
    Psalm 135
    SATB   Organ
    J. Fischer (1973) FEC 10082

135:00 (based on)
    Sweelinck, J. P. (ed. Arthur Hilton)
    Arise Ye Who Serve The Lord
    SSATBB   Keyboard
    Presser (1971) 352.00447

135:1 (Psalm 105:7; Psalm 68:20)
    Nares, James (ed. Peter Aston)
    O Praise The Lord
    SATB   Organ
    Novello (1973) MT 1564

135:1
    Shepherd, John
    O Give Thanks (Latin/English)
    TTBB   No accompaniment
    Novello   TM 8

135:1-3
    SEE: Psalm 134:1
    Newbury, Kent
    Sing To His Name

135:1-3 (Psalm 84:4; Psalm 145:18-19;
        Psalm 74:12; Habakkuk 2:14 and other)
    Willan, Healey
    O Praise The Lord
    SATB   Organ
    C. F. Peters (1963) 6464

135:1-3, 19-20
    Goss, John
    O Praise The Lord
    SATB   Organ
    G. Schirmer (1957) 10628

135:1-3, 19-20
    Perrin, Ronald
    O Praise The Lord
    SATB   Organ
    Oxford (1963) A 176

135:1-4
    Child, William (ed. Elwyn A. Wienandt)
    O Praise The Lord
    SSAATB   kro
    Lawson Gould (1973) 51667

135:1-4
    SEE: Psalm 134:1-3
    Pesich, Andy
    Praise His Name

135:3 (and other)
    Butler, Eugene
    Sing To His Name For He Is Gracious
    SAC(B)   kro
    Cambiata (1974) C 17429

135:3
    SEE: Psalm 105:1-3
    Geisler, Johann
    Thank Ye The Lord

135:3
    Manz, Paul
    Praise The Lord For He Is Good
    SATB/SATB or SSAB/SSAB   kro
    Concordia (1975) 98-2245

135:3, 6a
    Palestrina, G. P.
    Laudate Dominum (English/Latin)
    SATTB   kro
    Golden Music (1963) W-9

136:00 (Watts)
    Lovelace, Austin C. (arr.)
    Give To Our God Immortal Praise
    SAB   Keyboard
    Sacred Music (1976) S-179 (found in Service
        Music For Choir and Congregation)

136:00 (Bullough)
    Milner, Anthony
    Give Thanks Unto The Lord
    Unison   Organ
    Novello (1964) PCB 1413

136:00 (Milton paraphrase)
    Nicholson, Sydney H.
    Let Us With A Gladsome Mind
    SATB   Organ
    RSCM (n.d.) 243

136:00
    Parker, Alice
    Psalm 136
    SATB (B-solo)   No accompaniment
    Lawson Gould (1966) 51250

136:00 (Milton paraphrase)
    Ridout, Alan
    Let Us With A Gladsome Mind
    SATB   Organ
    Stainer & Bell (1969) 1.5077.1

136:00 (Milton paraphrase)
    Roesch, Robert A.
    Let Us With A Gladsome Mind
    SATB   Keyboard
    Broadman (1975) 4554-96

136:00 (Milton)
    Williams, David
    A Hymn Of Thanksgiving
    SA   Organ
    Summy-Birchard (1956) B-218

136:1 (Psalm 147:9-11)
    Berger, Jean
    Thank Ye The Lord
    SATB   kro
    Augsburg (1979) 11-0571

136:1
    Constantini, Alessandro
    Confitemini
    TTB   No accompaniment
    Oxford (1965) (found in Anthems for Men's
        Voices, Volume 2)

136:1
    Constantini, Alessandro (ed. Robert Field)
    Confitemini Domini
    SSA   kro
    Boosey & Hawkes (1964) 5543

136:1
    Constantini, Alessandro (ed. Theron Kirk)
    Confitemini Domino (Latin)
    SSA   kro
    Pro Art (1981) PRO CH 3002

136:1 (Psalm 105:14, 15)
    Krenek, Ernst
    Thanksgiving (Confitemini)(from Holiday
        Motets) (Latin)
    SSA in Canon   No accompaniment
    Broude Brothers (1967) BB 4069

136:1
Shepherd, John
Alleluia confitemino (O Give Thanks)
    (English/Latin)
TTBB   kro
H. W. Gray (n.d.) 1595

136:1
SEE: Ezekiel 36:28, 30, 34-35
Stainer, John
Ye Shall Dwell In The Land

136:1-2, 5, 9
Hopson, Hal
A Psalm Of Thanksgiving
SAB   Keyboard and Tambourine
Broadman (1971) 4562-29

136:1-2, 7-9, 25-27
Wood, John
O Give Thanks Unto The Lord
SAB   Organ
Novello (1972) 29.0259.01 (also found in
    With A Joyful Noise, 03.0137.10)

136:1-3
Palestrina, G. P.
Super flumina Babylonis
SATB   kro
J. Fischer (1937) 7259

136:1-9, 24-26
Peloquin, C. Alexander
Resurrection Psalm
SATB (solo)   Organ
GIA (1971) G-1659 (also found in Songs of
    Israel, G-1666)

136:1, 4, 7, 9
Frey, Richard
O Give Thanks To The Lord
SATB   Organ, Flute, Handbells
H. W. Gray (1973) CMR 3280

136:1, 4, 7-9, 13-16, 21, 25, 26
SEE: I Corinthians 13:13
Peloquin, C. Alexander
Faith, Hope and Love

136:1-5
Berger, Jean
Glory Be To God
SATB   kro
Kjos (1957) 5206A

136:1-5
Mechem, Kirke L.
Give Thanks Unto The Lord
SATB   No accompaniment
C. F. Peters (1960) 6213

136:1-9
Starer, Robert
Give Thanks Unto The Lord
SATB   kro
Galaxy (1960) 1.2196.1

136:1-9, 26
Berger, Jean
It Is Good To Give Thanks
SATB, Children's Voices   2 Flutes with
    Organ ad lib.
Augsburg (1971) 11-0643

136:1-9, 23-26
Sowerby, Leo
O Give Thanks Unto The Lord
SATB   Organ
H. W. Gray (1965) CMR 2890

136:25
SEE: Psalm 107:1
Schütz, Heinrich
Danket dem Herrn

137:00
Amram, David
By The Rivers Of Babylon
SSAA (S-solo)   kro
C. F. Peters (1969) 6983

137:00   (Peter Cornelius)
Bach, J. S. (Peter Cornelius)
By The Waters of Babylon, Op. 13, #2
SATB   kro
Broude Brothers (1952) BB 66

137:00
Coleridge-Taylor, Samuel
By The Waters Of Babylon
SATB   Organ
Novello (1899) n.#.

137:00
Cornelius, Peter (ed. George Lynn)
By The Waters Of Babylon
SATB   Organ
Golden Music (1963) W-8

137:00
Dalby, Martin
Ad flumina Babyloniae (Latin)
SSSAAATTBB   No accompaniment
Novello (1975) 29.0368.07

137:00   (paraphrase)
Gounod, Charles
By Babylon's Wave
SATB   Organ
Novello (n.d.) 279

137:00
Humphrey, Pelham (ed. Giles Bryant)
By The Waters Of Babylon
SATB (A-T-B-solos)   Organ continuo and
    2 violins
Concordia (1971) 97-5008

137:00
Loeffle, Charles M.
By The Rivers of Babylon
SSAA   Piano
G. Schirmer (1937) n.#.

137:00
Martin, Warren
Psalm 137
2 choruses of 2 parts   2 pianos
Hinshaw (1981) HMC 415

137:00
Mueller, Howard
By The Waters Of Babylon
SATB   kro
Mercury (1962) MC 418

137:00
Najera, Edmund
Ad flumina Babylonis (Latin)
SATB/SATB   No accompaniment
G. Schirmer (1972) 11873

137:00
Nares, James (ed. Derek Holman)
By The Waters Of Babylon
2 part treble   Organ or Piano
G. Schirmer (1962) 10931

137:00
Sumsion, Herbert
In Exile
SSAATTBB   Keyboard
Basil Ramsey (1980) n.#.

137:00   (Bay Psalm Book)
Williamson, Malcolm
Pilgrim's Water Psalm (from Psalms Of The
    Elements)
SATB and Congregation   Organ
Boosey & Hawkes (1976) 5955

137:00
   Wills, Arthur
   By The Waters Of Babylon (Two Anthems)
   ATB   Organ
   Novello (1966) MV 148

137:00
   Young, Gordon
   By The Waters Of Babylon
   SATB (S or T solo)   Organ
   Flammer (1970) A 5539

137:1
   DiLasso, Orlando
   Superflumina Babylonis (Latin)
   SATB   No accompaniment
   Arista (1981) AE 426

137:1
   Saminsky, Lazare
   By The Rivers Of Babylon, Op. 35, #1
   SATB (S or B solo)   Keyboard (optional
      instruments)
   Carl Fischer (1954) CM 265

137:1, 2
   Palestrina, G. P.
   Super Flumina (Latin only)
   SATB   kro
   J. & W. Chester (1977) JWC 55096 (found in
      First Chester Book Of Motets)

137:1-4
   Liebermann, Fredric
   By The Rivers Of Babylon
   SATB   Keyboard
   E. C. Schirmer (1971) ECS 2750

137:1-4
   Mawby, Colin
   By The Waters Of Babylon
   2 part treble   Organ
   Ascherberg [RSCM] (1964) PS 613

137:1-4
   Mawby, Colin
   By The Waters Of Babylon
   2 part treble   Organ
   GIA (1964) G-1098

137:1-4
   Pratt, George
   By The Waters Of Babylon
   Unison   Organ
   RSCM (1973) 251

137:1-5
   James, Philip
   By The Waters Of Babylon
   SATB   Organ
   H. W. Gray (1921) 636 (also available in
      SSAA edition)

137:1-5
   Milford, Robin
   By The Waters Of Babylon
   TB   Organ
   Oxford (1946) A 113

137:1-5
   Noble, T. Tertius
   By The Waters Of Babylon
   SATB   kro
   H. W. Gray (1949) 2082

137:1-5
   Palestrina, G. P. (transcribed C. Rossini)
   By The Waters Of Babylon
   SATB   kro
   J. Fischer (1937) 7259

137:1-5
   Wills, Arthur
   By The Waters Of Babylon (from Two Anthems)
   ATB   Organ
   Novello (1966) MU 148

137:1-6
   Ashworth, Caleb (ed. Elwyn Wienandt)
   By The Rivers Of Babylon
   SATB   Keyboard
   J. Fischer (1970) FE 10006

137:1-6
   Henning, Ervin
   By The Rivers Of Babylon
   SA   Piano
   E. C. Schirmer (1964) 2556

137:1-8
   Boyce, William
   By The Waters Of Babylon
   SATB   Organ
   Broude Brothers (1975) MGC 8

137:1-8
   Boyce, William (ed. Giles Bryant)
   By The Waters Of Babylon
   SATB (S-S-A-T-B-solos)   Organ
   Leeds (1968) #5

137:4
   SEE: Genesis 28:16-17
   Pfautsch, Lloyd
   The Lord Is In This Place

138:00   (Ainsworth Psalter)
   Finney, Ross Lee
   Psalm CXXXVIII (With Al My Hart I'le Thee
      Confess)
   SATB   kro
   Carl Fischer (1951) CM 6835

138:00
   Nystedt, Knut
   Psalm 138
   SATB/SATB   kro
   Summy Birchard (1963) 5628

138:00   (adapted)
   Washburn, Robert
   Praise Ye The Lord
   SATB   Organ (optional Brass)
   Skidmore Music (1963) SK 2081

138:00   (Dwight)
   Weaver, Powell
   I Love Thy Kingdom Lord
   SATB   Organ or Piano
   Galaxy (1950) 1799

138:00
   Wienhorst, Richard
   Psalm 138
   SATB   No accompaniment
   Concordia (1966) 98-1792

138:1-2
   Sweelinck, J. P. (ed. Richard Peek)
   Psalm 138
   SATB   kro
   Brodt Music (1965) 558

138:1-2, 7-9, 25-27
   Wood, John
   O Give Thanks Unto The Lord
   SAB   Organ
   Novello (1978) (found in With A Joyful
      Sound)

138:1-5
   SEE: Psalm 103:8, 10
   Martin, Reginald W.
   I Will Praise Thee

138:4-7
  Dyson, George
  I Will Worship
  Unison   Organ
  Novello (1954) MT 1337

138:7 (Psalm 18:28; Psalm 84:11)
  Fryxell, Regina Holmen
  The Lord Is My Light (from Seven Choral
     Service Settings)
  SATB or Unison   No accompaniment
  Abingdon (1963) APM-242

138:7
  SEE: Psalm 121:4
  Mendelssohn, Felix
  He Watching Over Israel

138:7
  SEE: Psalm 121:4
  Mendelssohn, Felix (ed. Trusler)
  He Watching Over Israel (SSA)

139:00 (versification)
  Bach, J. S.
  O Lord, Thou Hast Formed Me Every Part
  SATB   Keyboard ad lib.
  E. C. Schirmer (also found in Concord
     Anthem Book - Red)

139:00 (versification)
  Bach, J. S.
  O Lord, Thou Hast Formed Me Every Part
  SSA   Accompaniment ad lib.
  E. C. Schirmer (n.d.) 1049

139:00
  Clark, Keith (arr.)
  Lord Thou Hast Searched Me
  SATB   kro
  J. Fischer (1956) 9894

139:00 (based on)
  Cundick, Robert
  Lead Me By Thy Light
  SATB   Organ
  Sonos (1974) n.#.

139:00
  Geist, Susan Rowe
  Psalm 139: O God, Search Me
  SATB   Organ or Piano
  Shawnee (1966) A-817

139:00 (based on)
  Parker, Alice (arr.)
  Lord, Thou Hast Searched Me
  Unison   Keyboard
  Hinshaw (1980) HMC 456

139:00 (adapted)
  Posegate, Maxcine W.
  If I Should Ascend
  SATB   No accompaniment
  Broadman (1978) 4546-66

139:00
  Praetorius, Michael (ed. M. Lundquist)
  My Song Forever Shall Record
  SATB   kro
  Willis (1956) 6625

139:00
  Young, Carlton
  Psalm 139
  SATB (solo)   Oboe, Speaking Parts, No
     Accompaniment
  Hope (1969) CY 3332

139:1-2, 4-5, 9, 23
  Peninger, David
  O Lord, My Inmost Heart And Thought
  SATB   Keyboard
  Broadman (1975) 4551-89

139:1-2, 5b, 18b
  Martens, Edmund R.
  When I Awake (from Four Introits - Set I)
  Unison   Handbells
  Concordia (1976) 97-5384

139:1-2, 6-9, 12-13
  Walker, Robert
  O Lord Thou Hast Searched Me Out
  SATB   kro
  Novello (1977) 29.0377.06

139:1-2, 23
  Wolff, S. Drummond
  O Lord, Thou Hast Searched Me Out
  SATB   Accompaniment ad lib.
  Concordia (1952) CH-1023

139:1-3
  Neff, James
  O Lord Thou Hast Searched Me
  SATB   Keyboard
  Augsburg (n.d.) PA 601

139:1-6
  Slater, Richard W.
  O Lord Thou Hast Searched Me And Known Me
  SATB   kro
  Abingdon (1969) APM-714

139:1, 6, 8-11
  Willan, Healey
  Lord Thou Hast Searched Me Out And Known Me
  SATB   Organ
  Flammer (1967) A-5062

139:6-11
  Bouck, Marjorie
  Psalm (139)
  SATB or Unison   Piano
  Music 70 (1977) M70-210

139:6-11
  Williamson, Malcolm
  Whither Shall I Go (from Psalms Of The
     Elements)
  Unison Choir   Congregation   Organ
  Boosey & Hawkes (1976) 5947

139:7-12
  James, Allen
  Omnipresence
  SATB   Organ
  Abingdon (1971) APM-775

139:9-12 (Jerusalem Bible)
  Berger, Jean
  If I Flew To The Point Of Sunrise
  SATB   kro
  Kjos (1981) ED 5992

139:10
  SEE: Luke 24:6-7
  Lekberg, Sven
  He Is Risen

139:11
  SEE: Isaiah 26:3
  Walker, Robert
  Thou Wilt Keep Him In Perfect Peace

139:11
  SEE: Isaiah 26:3
  Wesley, Samuel S.
  Thou Wilt Keep Him In Perfect Peace
     (Abingdon)

139:11
  SEE: Isaiah 26:3
  Wesley, Samuel S.
  Thou Wilt Keep Him In Perfect Peace

139:11
     SEE: Isaiah 26:3
     Wesley, Samuel S. (ed. Basil Ramsey)
     Thou Wilt Keep Him

139:11
     SEE: Isaiah 26:3
     Williams, C. Lee
     Thou Wilt Keep Him In Perfect Peace

139:12
     SEE: Job 3:3-4, 20-21, 23-24
     Cook, Melville
     Antiphon

139:17, 23-24
     Crotch, William
     How Dear Are Thy Counsels
     SATB   Organ
     Novello (n.d.) MT 224

139:17-18, 23-24
     Fryxell, Regina Holmen
     How Precious Are Thy Thoughts (from Seven
          Choral Service Settings)
     SATB   No accompaniment
     Abingdon (1963) APM-242

139:23-24
     DiLasso, Orlando (ed. C. Buell Agey)
     Proba me Deus (Search Me O God)(English/
          Latin)
     SATB   kro
     G. Schirmer (1965) 11268

139:23-24
     Fritschel, James
     Search Me And Know My Heart
     SATB   No accompaniment
     Hinshaw (1977) HMC-200

139:23-24
     Greene, Maurice (ed. Mason Martens)
     Try Me, O God
     SSATB   Organ
     Walton (1971) 2181

139:23-24
     Herbeck, Raymond
     Search Me, O God And Know My Heart
     SATB   kro
     Flammer (1972) A-5604

139:23, 24
     Mueller, Carl F.
     Search Me O God
     SATB   kro
     G. Schirmer (1936) 7933

139:23-24
     Nares, James (ed. & arr. Paul Thomas)
     Search Me, O God
     SATB   Organ
     Concordia (1981) 97-5610 (found in Church
          Choir Book, Volume 2)

139:23-24
     Nares, James (ed. Watkins Shaw)
     Try Me O God
     SATB   Organ (manuals only)
     Novello (1970) 88.0019.07

139:23, 24
     Young, Carlton
     Psalm 139
     SATB (solo)   Oboe, No Accompaniment
     Hope (1969) CY 3332

139:23-24
     Young, Philip
     Search Me, O God
     SATB (S-solo)   kro
     Augsburg (1966) PS 621

140:00
     Berger, Jean
     Psalm 140
     SATB   String Orchestra
     Augsburg (n.d.) 11-9344

140:00
     Wickline, Homer
     Psalm 140 (Eripe Me, Domine)
     SATB   Organ
     H. W. Gray (1941) 1729

140:4
     DiLasso, Orlando
     Custodi Me, Domine (Guide and Keep Me O
          Lord) (English/Latin)
     SATB   kro
     G. Schirmer (1966) 11370

140:7   (Psalm 31:6)
     Brewer, A. Herbert
     O Lord God Thou Strength Of My Heart
     2 part   Organ
     RSCM (1971) 238

141:00
     Hughes, Howard
     Let My Prayer Rise Like Incense
     Unison (optional SATB)   Organ
     GIA (1978) G-2174

141:1   (Psalm 25:2, and other)
     Arcadelt, Jacob
     O Lord I Cry To Thee
     SATB   No accompaniment
     Concordia (1959) 98-1771 (also found in
          The Church Choir Book, 97-6320)

141:1-2
     Pooler, Frank
     Make Hast Unto Us
     SATB   kro
     Walton (1958) 2960

141:1, 3-4, 9
     Kirk, Theron
     Lord I Call Upon Thee   (Triptych Of Psalms)
     SATB   kro
     Kjos (1968) 5489B

141:2
     Binkerd, Gordon
     Let My Prayer Come Like Incense
     TB   Organ
     Boosey & Hawkes   5828

141:2
     Blow, John (ed. Walter Ehret)
     Let My Prayer Come Up
     SATB   kro
     Elkan Vogel (1971) 362-01321

141:2
     Blow, John
     Let My Prayer Come Up
     SATB   Optional Organ
     Stainer & Bell (1953) 5307

141:2
     Harris, William H.
     Let My Prayer
     SATB   Organ
     Novello (1953) 29.0440.03

141:2
     Martin, G. C.
     Let My Prayer Come Up
     SATB   kro
     Novello (1902) 116

141:2
     Near, Gerald
     Let My Prayer   (Three Introits)
     SATB   kro
     Calvary Press (1975) 1-009

141:2
Purcell, Henry
Let My Prayer Come Up Into Thy Presence
SSATB   kro
E. C. Schirmer (1952) (found in Concord
    Anthem Book - Red)

141:2
Purcell, Henry (ed. Arthur Hilton)
Let My Prayer Come Up
SSATB   Keyboard
Presser (1971) 352-00440

141:2-3, 5, 8 (paraphrase)
Hruby, Dolores
Let My Prayer Rise Like Incense
SATB   Keyboard, Orff Instruments or Hand-
    bells, C Instruments
Concordia (1980) 98-2481

141:8 (Psalm 143:8)
Haan, Raymond H.
Cause Me To Hear Thy Loving Kindness
SATB   Organ
H. W. Gray (1980) GCMR 3420

141:9
Handel, G. F.
O Lord We Trust Alone In Thee
SATB   Optional Keyboard
Novello (n.d.) 29.0219.02

142:00
Chajes, Julius
The 142nd Psalm
SATB (A-T-B-solos)   Organ
Transcontinental (1941) 215

143:00
Glarum, Stanley
Blessed Be The Lord
SATB   kro
Carl Fischer (1966) CM 7517

143:00 (adapted Blake)
Rochberg, George
Behold My Servant
SATB   kro
Presser (1974) 312-41062

143:00
Wyner, Yehudi
Psalm 143
SATB   kro
Associated (1973) A 675

143:1a, 2
Holyoke, Samuel
Hear Our Prayer O Lord Our God
SATB   Optional Keyboard
McAfee (1975) (found in Bicentennial Col-
    lection Of American Choral Music)

143:1-2
Lupo, Thomas (ed. John Morehen)
Hear My Prayer O Lord
SSATB   Optional Accompaniment
Oxford (1964) A 205

143:1-2, 6
Croce, Giovanni (ed. Maynard Kline)
Exaudi Deus (Latin/English)
SATB   kro
G. Schirmer (1973) 11985

143:1, 5
Hovhaness, Alan
Psalm 143 Hear My Prayer
SSATBB   Organ ad lib.
C. F. Peters (1962) 6444

143:5-6, 8-10
Holland, Ken
Cause Me To Know
SATB   Keyboard
Broadman (1981) 4563-61

143:7-12   (freely adapted)
Gibbons, Orlando (arr. Anna Mae Nichols)
O Lord I Meditate On Thee
SA(T)B   Keyboard
Canyon (1964) 6405

143:8
SEE: Psalm 141:8
Haan, Raymond
Cause Me To Hear Thy Loving Kindness

143:8, 10
SEE: Psalm 130:5-6
Slates, Philip
I Wait For The Lord

144:3-8
Williamson, Malcolm
Penitential Fire Psalm (from Psalms Of The
    Elements)
Unison Choir   Congregation   Organ
Boosey & Hawkes (1976) 5963

144:9-15
Williamson, Malcolm
David's House (from Psalms Of The Elements)
Unison Choir   Congregation   Organ
Boosey & Hawkes (1976) 5958

145:00 (versification)
Bach, J. S.
God My King, Thy Might Confessing
SATB   Keyboard
E. C. Schirmer (1952) 368 (also found in
    Concord Anthem Book - Red)

145:00 (Psalm 104)
Darke, Harold
A Psalm Of Thanksgiving
SATB   Organ
Oxford (1957) A 149

145:00 (based on)
Goemanne, Noel (arr.)
God My King Thy Might Confessing
SATB   Organ and 2 Trumpets
GIA (1979) G-2226

145:00
Gore, Richard T.
I Will Magnify Thee
SATB   Organ
Abingdon (1975) APM-957

145:00
Hamblen, Bernard
The Lord Is Gracious
SATB   Organ or Piano
Boosey & Hawkes (1949) 1768

145:00
SEE: I Chronicles 16:00
Huston, John
A Canticle Of Thanksgiving

145:00
Mathias, William
All Thy Works Shall Praise Thee (English/
    Welsh)
SATB   Organ
Oxford (1963) A-180

145:00
Webber, W. S. Lloyd
All Thy Works Praise Thee
SATB   Organ
Novello (1978) (found in In Wonder, Love
    And Praise)

145:1-2, 4
    Red, Buryl A.
    Psalm 145
    Unison   Keyboard
    Broadman (1963) (found in The Junior Choir
        Sings), #3)

145:1-2, 10-12
    Means, Claude
    I Will Magnify Thee, O God
    Unison   Organ
    H. W. Gray (1971) CMR 3227

145:1-3, 21
    Berger, Jean
    Great Is The Lord
    SATB   kro
    Augsburg (1976) 11-0668

145:1, 3, 8, 21
    Amner, John
    O God My King
    SATB   Organ
    Oxford (1973) (found in Anthems For Choirs,
        Volume 1)

145:1-3, 8-9, 21
    Moe, Daniel
    I Will Extol Thee
    TTBB   kro
    Augsburg (1966) 11-0623

145:1-3, 8-9, 13b, 14, 17-18, 21
    Folkemer, Stephen
    Psalm 145
    Unison (S-B-solos)   Organ and Trumpet
    GIA (1980) G 2337

145:1-4
    Berger, Jean
    I Will Extol Thee, My God
    SATB   2 Trumpets (kro)
    Associated (1967) A 558

145:1-4
    Butler, Eugene
    I Will Extol Thee
    SB   Keyboard
    Broadman (1970) 4562-17

145:1-4a, 6a, 7b
    Hallock, Peter
    I Will Exalt You
    SATB   Keyboard
    GIA (1978) G 2186

145:1-7 (Scottish Psalter 1564)
    Sateren, Leland (arr.)
    O Lord Thou Art My God And King
    SATB   Optional Keyboard
    Augsburg (1964) 11-0619

145:3
    SEE: Psalm 47:1-2, 5-7
    Steel, Christopher
    O Clap Your Hands

145:3-4
    Schütz, Heinrich (Der Herr ist Gross)
        (English/German)
    2 voices   Continuo
    Mercury (1942) n.#.

145:3-4, 8-13
    Lewis, John Leo
    Great Is The Lord
    SATB   Piano or Organ
    Presser (1962) 312-40534

145:8
    SEE: Psalm 96:4, 9
    Hollins, Alfred
    O Worship The Lord

145:8-10
    SEE: Psalm 118:12-13
    Maunder, J. H.
    Praise The Lord Of Jerusalem

145:8, 10
    Roff, Joseph
    The Lord Is Gracious
    SATB   Keyboard
    Augsburg (n.d.) 11-0612

145:9
    Berger, Jean
    The Lord Is Good To All
    SATB   kro   Finger cymbals, ad lib.
    Tetra [Alexander Broude] (1978) AB-448

145:10
    Smart, David
    Come Let Us Sing
    Unison   Keyboard
    Hope (1977) JR 204

145:10-11, 21
    Parker, Alice
    All Thy Works Shall Praise Thee (Psalms Of
        Praise)
    2 part men   Percussion
    Lawson Gould (1968) 51385

145:13
    SEE: Psalm 66:1-3, 7
    Willan, Healey
    O Be Joyful In God

145:15-16
    Berger, Jean
    The Eyes Of All Wait Upon Thee
    SATB   kro
    Augsburg (1959) 11-1264

145:15-16
    Felciano, Richard
    Motet
    SATB   kro
    E. C. Schirmer (1973) ECS 2280

145:15-16 (John 6:56-57)
    Schroth, Godfrey
    The Eyes Of All
    SATB   Organ
    J. Fischer (1974) FEC 10111

145:15-16
    Schütz, Heinrich
    Aller Augen warten auf dich Herre
        (German only)
    SATB   No accompaniment
    Merseburger (1977) (found in Motetten Alter
        Meister)

145:15-16
    Schütz, Heinrich (ed. John Kingsbury)
    Ev'ry Eye Waiteth Upon Thee (Three Chorales)
        (English/German)
    SATB   kro
    Music 70 (1975) M70-153

145:15-16
    Schütz, Heinrich (ed. Larry D. Wyatt)
    Oculi omnium in te sperant Domine (The Eyes
        Of All) (English/Latin)
    SATB   Optional Keyboard
    Plymouth (1981) SC-57

145:15-16
    Schütz, Heinrich
    Three Chorales
    SATB   No accompaniment
    Music 70 (1975) M70-153

145:15-16
    Schütz, Heinrich (ed. Charles G. Frischmann)
    To Thee We Turn Our Eyes (Latin/English)
    SATB   Keyboard
    Concordia (1967) 98-1885

145:15-16
    SEE: Psalm 146:1-2
    Sister Suzanne Toolan
    Keeping Festival

145:15-16
    Titcomb, Everett
    The Eyes Of All Wait Upon Thee
    SATB   kro
    Carl Fischer (1964) CM 7406

145:15-17
    SEE: Psalm 147:7-9, 12-14
    Harris, William H.
    O Sing Unto The Lord With Thanksgiving

145:15-18, 21
    Smith, Robert Edward
    The Eyes Of All Wait Upon Thee
    SSA   No accompaniment
    Continuo [Alexander Broude] (1978) AB 817

145:15-20
    Harris, William H.
    The Eyes Of All Wait Upon Thee, O Lord
    SATB   Organ
    Oxford (1956) A-142

145:17-18, 20
    Berger, Jean
    The Lord Is Righteous In All His Ways
    SATB   kro
    Alexander Broude (1980) AB 903

145:18-19
    Regnart, Jacob
    Prope est Dominus (Latin)
    SATB   kro
    J. & W. Chester (1977) JWC 55110 (found in
        Sixth Chester Book Of Motets)

145:18-19
    SEE: Psalm 135:1-3
    Willan, Healey
    O Praise The Lord

145:21
    SEE: Acts 13:32-33
    Baristow, Edward
    The Promise Which Was Made

145:21
    Handel, G. F. (ed. John Haberlen)
    Praise The Lord
    SATB   Organ or Piano
    Elkan Vogel (1978) 362-03262

146:00   (based on)
    Beck, Theodore (setting by)
    Praise The Almighty, My Soul Adore Him
    SATB   Organ and Trumpet
    Concordia (1979) 98-2401 (choir score and
        trumpet part, 98-2424)

146:00
    Berger, Jean
    Psalm 146
    SATB   String Orchestra
    Augsburg (n.d.) 11-1952

146:00
    Butler, Eugene
    Praise The Lord O My Soul
    SATB   Keyboard (Optional Guitar and
        Percussion)
    Abingdon (1978) APM-918

146:00
    Cornell, Garry A.
    Fantasia and Fugue
    SSAATTBB   No accompaniment
    Heritage (1977) H 154

146:00
    Diemer, Emma Lou
    Praise Ye The Lord
    SATB   2 Pianos (or 1 Piano)
    Flammer (1964) A-5021

146:00
    Pfautsch, Lloyd
    I'll Praise My Maker
    SATB   Organ or Brass Choir (3 Trumpets,
        2 Trombones, Tuba)
    Abingdon (1960) APM-110   (Parts APM-127)

146:00
    Powell, Robert J.
    Psalm 146
    SB   5 Handbells
    GIA (1977) G-2089

146:00
    Presser, William
    Psalm 146
    SATB   Piano or Organ
    Flammer (1964) 84798

146:00
    Rutter, John
    Praise The Lord, O My Soul
    SATB   Organ (optional Brass)
    Oxford (1981) A-330 (Brass parts on rental
        from publisher)

146:00   (based on)
    Wolff, S. Drummond
    Praise The Almighty, My Soul Adore Him!
    SATB   Organ
    Concordia (1981) 98-2513

146:1
    SEE: Psalm 103:1-3
    Tomkins, Thomas (ed. John Morehen)
    Praise The Lord O My Soul

146:1-2
    Rohlig, Harald
    Alleluia, Praise The Lord My Soul!
    Unison   Keyboard
    Concordia (1973) 97-5165 (found in Explode
        With Joy)

146:1-2   (Psalm 147:7-8, Psalm 145:15-16)
    Sister Suzanne Toolan
    Keeping Festival
    Unison   Keyboard
    Resource Publications (1979) n.#.

146:1-3
    DiLasso, Orlando (ed. C. Buell Agey)
    Lauda Anima Mea Dominum (English/Latin)
    SATB   kro
    G. Schirmer (1966) 11337

146:5
    Haan, Raymond
    A Song of Hope
    Unison   Keyboard
    AMSI (1975) 280

146:5-6
    Davis, Katherine K.
    He Is Our King
    SATB (S-solo)   Keyboard
    Flammer (1967) A 5007

147:00
    Porpora, Niccola (ed. Ralph Hunter)
    Lauda Jerusalem (Latin)
    SSAA   Keyboard and Strings
    Marks (1972) 4358

147:00 (Psalm 148;   Psalm 150)
  Sessions, Roger
  Praise Ye The Lord (Three Choruses On
       Biblical Texts)
  SATB   Piano
  Presser (1976) 342-40119

147:1
  Geisler, Johann C.
  Praise Ye The Lord   (English/German)
  SSAB or SATB   Organ
  Boosey & Hawkes (1968) 5655

147:1-2 (Psalm 148:2-4)
  Mechem, Kirke
  Praise Him Sun And Moon
  SSATBB   kro
  National Music (1971) WHC 21

147:1-3, 7-9, 12-14
  Sowerby, Leo
  O Praise The Lord For It Is A Good Thing
  SATB   Organ
  Flammer (1967) 84905

147:1, 5
  Weldon, James (ed. Mason Martens)
  O Praise The Lord
  SAB   Organ
  Concordia (1965) 98-1786

147:7, 8
  SEE: Psalm 146:1, 2
  Sister Suzanne Toolan
  Keeping Festival

147:7-9, 12-14   (Psalm 145:15-17)
  Harris, William H.
  O Sing Unto The Lord With Thanksgiving
  SATB   Organ
  Novello (1954) Anth. 1317

147:9-11
  SEE: Psalm 136:1
  Berger, Jean
  Thank Ye The Lord

147:9-11
  SEE: Psalm 107:11
  Schütz, Heinrich
  Danket dem Herren

147:12-13 (Psalm 145:8-10;   Psalm 65:14)
  Maunder, J. H.
  Praise The Lord O Jerusalem
  SATB   Organ
  Boston Music (1930) 1830

147:12-13 (Psalm 145:8-10;   Psalm 65:14)
  Maunder, J. H.
  Praise The Lord O Jerusalem
  SATB   Organ
  Novello (19897) 29.0119.06

147:12-20
  Williamson, Malcolm
  Praise The Lord O Jerusalem (from Psalms Of
       The Elements)
  Unison Choir and Congregation   Organ
  Boosey & Hawkes (1976) 5959

148:00 (adapted)
  Anderson, Muriel
  Alleluia! Praise The Lord
  Unison Treble with Descant   Organ
       Triangle and Drum
  J. Fischer (1972) FEC 10065

148:00 (based on)
  Arnatt, Ronald
  O Praise The Lord From The Heavens
  SATB   Organ
  Presser (1973) 312.40991

148:00
  SEE: Psalm 103
  Beck, John Ness
  Canticle Of Praise

148:00 (adapted)
  Billings, William (ed. Lawrence Bennett)
  An Anthem For Thanksgiving
  SATB   kro
  Broude Brothers (1976) WW.26

148:00
  Billings, William (ed. Leonard Van Camp)
  O Praise The Lord Of Heaven
  SATB   Keyboard
  Concordia (1974) 98-2196

148:00
  Bock, Fred
  Praise Hymn
  SATB and Junior Choir   Organ or Tape
  Fred Bock (1976) (found in Lord, Make My
       Life A Window)

148:00
  Butler, Eugene
  Praise Him
  Unison   12 Handbells
  Abingdon (1964) (found in Six Anthems For
       Junior Voices and Handbells)

148:00
  Charpentier, Marc-Antoine
  Laudate Dominum (Latin)
  TTB   Organ
  World Library

148:00
  Converse, Franck
  Laudate Dominum (Latin)
  TBB   Organ or Brass
  Boston Music (n.d.)   #228

148:00 (based on)
  Cromie, Marguerite Biggs
  Praise The Lord Forever And Ever (from
       American Songs For Worship)
  SATB   Organ or Piano or Guitar
  Presser (1975) 312-41093

148:00 (words from) (Psalm 29, words from)
  Fromm, Herbert
  Anthem Of Praise
  SATB (T-solo)   Organ
  Transcontinental (1961)

148:00
  Gelineau, Joseph
  Psalm 148
  SB   Organ
  GIA (1979) G-2245

148:00
  Glarum, L. Stanley
  Psalm 148
  SATB   kro
  G. Schirmer (1968) 11588

148:00
  Holst, Gustav
  Lord Who Hast Made Us For Thine Own
  SATB   Organ
  E. C. Schirmer (1927) 16662

148:00 (paraphrase)
  Holst, Gustav
  Psalm CXLVIII
  SATB   Organ or Brass
  Augener (1920) n.#.

148:00 (paraphrase)
  Holst, Gustav
  Psalm CXLVIII
  SATB   Organ or Brass
  Galaxy (n.d.) 1.5015.1

148:00   (based on Scripture adapted by C. York)
    Leaf, Robert
    Praise Hymn
    2 part or Unison   Keyboard
    AMSI (1981) 402

148:00
    Lewin, Frank
    Psalm 148
    SATB   Organ
    Presser (1966) 342-40017

148:00
    Nystedt, Knut
    Song Of Praise
    SSAATB   No accompaniment
    Augsburg (1974) 11-0656

148:00   (based on)
    Peek, Richard (arr.)
    Praise The Lord! Ye Heavens Adore Him
    SATB   Piano or Organ
    Carl Fischer (1959) CM 7113

148:00   (Psalm 150)
    Perera, Ronald
    Everything That Hath Breath
    2 part chorus   Tape
    E. C. Schirmer (1979) 3048

148:00
    Rameau, Jean P.
    Praise Ye The Lord My Soul, Adore Him
    Unison Soprano   Organ, 2 violins, cello
    Concordia (1973) 98-2121   (Parts 98-2122)

148:00
    Reese, Jan
    SATB   Keyboard
    Praise The Lord
    Flammer (n.d.) A 5947

148:00
    Rutter, John
    O Praise The Lord Of Heaven
    SATB/SATB   Keyboard (Brass: 3 Trumpets,
        3 Trombones, Tuba, Timpani, Organ)
    Hinshaw (1981) HMC 505 (Parts on Rental
        from Publisher)

148:00   SEE: Psalm 147
    Sessions, Roger
    Praise Ye The Lord

148:00
    Vaughan Williams, Ralph
    O Praise The Lord Of Heaven
    Double Chorus and Semi Chorus   kro
    Galaxy (1914) 1.5006.1

148:00
    Walker, George
    Praise Ye The Lord
    SATB   Organ
    General Music (1975) n.#.

148:00
    Wetherill, Edward H.
    Hymn Of Adoration
    SATB   Organ
    Flammer (1980) A-5925

148:00
    Wetzler, Robert
    Chorale (from Triology Of Praise)
    SATB   Organ
    G. Schirmer (1973) 11977

148:00
    Williamson, Malcolm
    A Psalm Of Praise
    Unison   Organ
    Boosey & Hawkes (1966) W.006

148:00
    Zaninelli, Luigi
    Psalm 148
    SATB   Optional Organ
    Shawnee (1960) A 584

148:00
    Zimmermann, Heinz Werner
    Psalm 148
    SMATB (S-T-solos)   Organ, Vibraphone, Bass
    Carl Fischer (n.d.) 04898 (chorus parts,
        04898A; instrumental parts 04898B)

148:1-2
    Hannahs, Roger C.
    O Praise The Lord From The Heavens
    SATB   Organ
    H. W. Gray (1973) CMR 3270

148:1-2   SEE: Revelation 7:12
    Wagner, C. C.
    Blessing, Glory, and Wisdom and Thanks

148:1-3, 7-12   (Psalm 150)
    Stark, Richard
    Praise The Lord
    Unison Chorus (solo)   Organ
    E. C. Schirmer (1959) 1704

148:1, 3, 5, 8, 12
    Butler, Eugene
    Praise Ye!
    SATB   Organ
    McAfee (1980) M 1198

148:1-4   SEE: Psalm 48:1
    Newbury, Kent A.
    Great Is The Lord

148:1-4, 7-13
    Hovhaness, Alan
    Psalm 148, Op. 160
    SATB (B-solo)   Organ
    C. F. Peters (1958) 6141

148:1-5
    Hurd, Michael
    Praise Ye The Lord
    SATB   Organ
    Novello (n.d.) 1464

148:1-5
    Mawby, Colin
    O Praise The Lord Of Heaven
    2 part treble   Organ
    GIA (1964) G-1098

148:1-5
    Pratt, George
    O Praise The Lord Of Heaven
    Unison   Organ
    RSCM (1973) 251

148:1-5, 8-13
    Bullard, Alan
    Praise The Lord Out Of Heaven
    SATB   Organ
    Banks (1979) ECS 69

148:1-5, 12
    Wills, Arthur
    O Praise The Lord Of Heaven
    SSA   kro
    Novello (1967) Ch. Ser. 121

148:1-6   (based on)
    Beck, Steven
    Praise The Lord From Heaven
    SATB   Organ
    Hope (1979) A 494

148:1-9   (Bay Psalm Book)
    Noss, Luther
    Psalm 148
    TBB   kro
    Associated (1956) AMP 95567

148:1-12
    Steel, Christopher
    O Praise The Lord Of Heaven
    SATB   Organ
    Novello (1969) 1480

148:2
    Kreutz, Robert
    Alleluia
    SATB   Organ
    GIA (1976) G-2047

148:3, 8-10, 12
    Grove, Jack Byron
    Shout Together, Shout For Joy!
    SATB   Organ, Brass Quartet, Handbells
    H. W. Gray (1980) GCMR 3433

148:5
    Hovhaness, Alan
    Let Them Praise The Name Of The Lord,
        Op. 160A
    SATB   Organ
    C. F. Peters (1962) 6450

148:9-13
    Hillert, Richard
    Offertory/Thanksgiving (Verses and
        Offertories - Lesser Feasts
    Unison   Organ
    Augsburg (1980) 11-9542

148:12
    SEE: Psalm 81:1-3
    Lefebvre, Channing
    Sing We Merrily

149:00
    Anerio, Giovanni F. (ed. Norris Stephen)
    Cantate Domino (O Sing Unto The Lord)
    SATB   No accompaniment
    G. Schirmer (n.d.) 11273

149:00
    Conte, David
    Cantate Dominum   (Latin)
    SATB/SATB kro
    Beckenhorst (1975) BP 1014

149:00
    Dvorak, Anton
    An Anthem Of Praise
    SATB   Organ
    E. C. Schirmer (also found in Second Con-
        cord Anthem Book - Grey)

149:00
    James, Philip
    Psalm 149
    SATB (S-solo)   Organ
    H. W. Gray (1960) 2676

149:00
    Manookin, Robert P.
    Psalm 149
    SATB   Organ
    Sonos (1976) TCS 106

149:00
    Nanino, Giovanni (ed. Walter Ehret)
    Sing Ye Unto The Lord (Cantate Domino)
        (English/Latin)
    SATB/SATB kro
    Shawnee (1976) A-1377 (Parts for Brass, or
        Woodwinds, or Strings available)

149:00
    Nicolson, Richard (ed. Cyril F. Simkins)
    Cantate Domino Canticum Novum (Latin)
    SSATB   kro
    Associated (1964) NYPMS 24

149:00
    Stanton, Kenneth
    Let The Saints Be Joyful
    SATB   kro
    Music 70 (1975) M70 124

149:00
    Sweelinck, J. P.
    Praise Ye The Lord (Chantez a Dieu Chanson
        Nouvelle) (English/French)
    SATB   kro
    Mark Foster (1971) MF 126

149:00
    Sweelinck, J. P. (ed. Donald Colton)
    Sing To The Lord (English/French)
    SATB   Optional Keyboard
    Concordia (1975) 98-2222

149:1
    Schütz, Heinrich (ed. Richard Peek)
    Cantate Domine (O Sing Ye To The Lord)
        (English/Latin)
    SATB   Organ
    Concordia (1969) 98-1974

149:1-2
    Byrd, William (ed. LeHuray & Willcocks)
    Cantate Domino (Latin only)
    SSATBB   kro
    Oxford (1969) TCM 27

149:1-2
    Kay, Ulysses
    Sing Unto The Lord (part of A New Song)
    SATB   No accompaniment
    C. F. Peters (1961) 6136a

149:1-2
    Pitoni, G. O. (ed. John Lee)
    Cantate Domino (English/Latin)
    SATB   kro
    GIA (1975) G-1949

149:1-2
    Pitoni, G. O.
    Cantate Domino (Latin only)
    SATB   No accompaniment
    Oxford (found in Anthems For Choirs,
        Volume 1)

149:1-2
    Pitoni, Giuseppi
    Sing To The Lord A New Song (Latin/English)
    SATB   kro
    Concordia (1968) (found in A First Motet
        Book, 97-4845)

149:1-2
    Tomkins, Thomas
    O Sing Unto The Lord A New Song
    SSAATBB   Organ ad lib.
    Schott (1958) 10610

149:1-3 (Psalm 98:7-10)
    Leighton, Kenneth
    O Sing Unto The Lord A New Song (from Three
        Psalms, Op. 54)
    TTBB   No accompaniment
    Novello (1974) NCM 34

149:1-3
    Schütz, Heinrich
    Cantate Domino (Latin)
    SATB   No accompaniment
    Arista (1978) AE 356

149:1-3
Schütz, Heinrich
Cantate Domino Canticum Novum (Latin/
    German)
SATB   No accompaniment
Barenreiter (n.d.) n.#.

149:1-3
Schütz, Heinrich (transcribed Lowell
    Bevenridge)
Cantate Domine (English/Latin)
SATB   Organ ad lib.
G. Schirmer (1941) 8678

149:1-3
SEE: Psalm 47:1-2, 5-7
Steel, Christopher
O Clap Your Hands

149:1-5
Diemer, Emma Lou
Praise The Lord
SATB   Keyboard (Brass Quintet with
    optional timpani)
Carl Fischer (1975) CM 7946 (parts 7946A)

149:2
SEE: Psalm 118:24
Geisler, J. C.
This Is The Day

150:00
Adler, Samuel
Psalm 150
Unison   Percussion
Choristers Guild (1966) A 39

150:00 (adapted Katherine Mahan)
Angell, Warren
Sing For Joy
SATB   Organ (optional brass - 3 Trumpets,
    3 Trombones, Tuba, Timpani)
H. W. Gray (1981) GCMR 3449

150:00
Arnold, Malcolm
Laudate Dominum
SATB   Organ
Lengnick (1950) 3717

150:00
Aston, Peter
Praise Ye The Lord
SATB   Organ (Optional brass: 3 Cornets,
    3 Trombones, Tuba)
Novello (1971) MW 14

150:00
Bender, Jan
Praise Ye The Lord
SSATB   3 Trumpets, 2 Trombones
Concordia (1957) 97-6278

150:00
Berger, Jean
Praise Ye The Lord (from Bay Psalm Book,
    Set I)
SATB   No accompaniment
Shawnee (1964) A 729

150:00
Butler, Eugene S.
Hallelujah
Unison   Keyboard
Broadman (1969) 4550-61

150:00
Cabena, Barrie
O Praise God, Op. 44
SATB   Keyboard
Jaymar [Oxford] (1971) n.#.

150:00
Carlson, Richard
Psalm 150
SATB   Organ
Canyon (1952) n.#.

150:00
Cooper, Rose Marie
Psalm 150
Unison or 2 part   Organ or Piano
Broadman (1964) (found in The Junior Choir
    Sings, Volume 3)

150:00
Cooper, Rose Marie
Psalm 150
Unison and two part   Keyboard
Broadman (1964) 4557-10

150:00
Copley, I. A.
The 150th Psalm
SATB and Unison   Piano
Lengnick (1964) 4167

150:00
Coutre, Jean Papineau
Laudate eum (Latin)
TTBB   3 Trumpets, 3 Trombones, Organ
BMI

150:00 (adapted)
Cram, James
Praise God In His Holiness
SATB   Keyboard
Broadman (1974) 4565-50

150:00
Curry, W. Lawrence
Psalm 150
SATB (Junior Choir ad lib.)   Organ,
    2 Trumpets, 2 Trombones
H. W. Gray (1950) CMR 2129

150:00
Deiss, Lucien
Let The Earth Shout With Gladness
SATB   Organ, 3 Trumpets, 1 Trombone
World Library (1980) 7602-8

150:00
SEE: Mark 11:9-11
Delmonte, Pauline
He Is Coming

150:00
Donato, Anthony
Praise Ye The Lord
SATB   kro
Boosey & Hawkes (1955) 5035

150:00
Englert, Eugene
Psalm 150! Praise The Lord!
SATB   Organ
GIA (1979) G-2227

150:00
Federlein, Gottfried
Psalm 150
SATB   Organ
Boston Music (1940) BMC 9668

150:00
Franck, Cesar
Psalm 150
SATB   Organ
Belwin (1970) n.#.

150:00
Franck, Cesar (arr. Edward S. Breck)
Psalm 150
SATB   Organ
Carl Fischer (1955) CM 6870

150:00
Franck, C. (ed. Norman Coke-Jephcott)
Psalm 150
SATB   Organ
H. W. Gray (1934) 1296 (also available in
     setting for men's voices)

150:00
Franck, Cesar (arr. Samuel R. Gaines)
Psalm 150
SATB   Organ
J. Fischer (1954) FEC 5470

150:00
Franck, Cesar (arr. Howard D. McKinney)
Psalm 150
SAB   Piano or Organ
J. Fischer (1960) 9207

150:00
Franck, Cesar (arr. Howard D. McKinney)
Psalm 150
SATB   Piano or Organ
J. Fischer (1960) 5670

150:00
Franck, Cesar (arr. Howard D. McKinney)
Psalm 150
SSA   Piano or Organ
J. Fischer (1960) 6822

150:00
Franck, Cesar (arr. Howard D. McKinney)
Psalm 150
SSAA   Piano or Organ
J. Fischer (1960) 5706

150:00
Franck, Cesar (arr. Howard D. McKinney)
Psalm 150
TTBB   Piano or Organ
J. Fischer (1960) 5707

150:00
Franck, Cesar (arr. H. A. Chambers)
Psalm 150
SATB   Organ
Novello (1969) 29.0143.09

150:00
Gibbs, C. Armstrong
Praise God In His Holiness
SA   Organ
Oxford (1953) 2230

150:00
Gibbs, C. Armstrong
Praise God In His Holiness
ST/AB   Organ
Oxford (found in Oxford Easy Anthem Book)

150:00
SEE: Psalm 103
Goemanne, Noel
Praise To The Lord

150:00
Goemanne, Noel
Psalm 150 Praise The Lord In His Sanctuary
SATB   Organ
McLaughlin & Reilly (1958) 2148

150:00
Goode, Jack C.
Psalm 150
SATB   Organ
Abingdon (1963) APM-263

150:00 (and others)
Gower, Robert
Joyfully, Sing Unto God
SATB   Keyboard
Belwin (1973) 2283

150:00
Hand, Colin
Praise Ye The Lord
SATB   Organ
Novello (1955) MT 1351

150:00
Hanson, Howard
The One-Hundred-Fiftieth Psalm
SATB   Piano
Carl Fischer (1968) CM 7699

150:00
Harbach, Barbara
Praise Him With The Trumpet
SATB   Keyboard
Agape [Hope] (1977) AG-7209

150:00
Harper, John
Psalm 150
2 part   Organ
Oxford (1974) E-135

150:00
Harris, Roy
Psalm 150
SATB   kro
Golden Music (1963) ACS 4

150:00
Heeble, Robert
Praise Ye The Lord
SATB   Organ
Bradley (1981) PRO 2

150:00
Hewitt-Jones, Tony
O Praise God In His Holiness
SATB   Organ
Novello (1964) 342

150:00
Hopson, Hal H.
Antiphonal Psalm
2-part Antiphonal Choirs   Organ
Hope (1976) HH 3901

150:00 (based on)
Hunnicutt, Judy
O Praise God In His Sanctuary
Unison   Organ
Augsburg (1971) 11-9285 (found in Music For
     Contemporary Choir, Volume 2)

150:00
Ives, Charles (ed. John Kirkpatrick and
     Gregg Smith)
Psalm 150
SSAA/SATB   Organ
Presser (1972) 342.40027

150:00
Jackson, Francis
Praise God In His Sanctuary
SATB   Organ
Banks (1978) ECS 84

150:00
Jones, David Hugh
Psalm 150
SATB   Organ
G. Schirmer (1931) 7494

150:00
Joubert, John
O Praise God In His Holiness, Op. 52
SATB   Organ
Novello (1968) 29.0428.04

150:00
Kelly, Bryan
Psalm 150
SA(T)B   Organ
RSCM (1981) A-12

150:00
    Kodaly, Zoltan
    Psalm 150
    SSA   No accompaniment
    Oxford (1966) 83.072 (also found in Anthems
        For Choirs, Volume 3)

150:00
    Krapf, Gerhard
    Psalm 150
    SSA (S-solo)   Organ or Piano, Flute
    Concordia (1972) 98-2134

150:00
    Langlais, Jean
    Praise Ye The Lord
    TTB   Organ
    McLaughlin & Reilly (1958) 2203

150:00
    Langstroth, Ivan
    Praise Ye The Lord, Op. 34, #2
    SATB   Organ
    Mills (1953) AMI 2301

150:00
    Lauridsen, Morten
    Praise Ye The Lord
    SATB   kro
    Augsburg (1967) PS 624

150:00
    Lekberg, Sven
    Praise Ye The Lord
    SATB   kro
    Galaxy (1963) 1.2261

150:00
    Lewandowski, Louis
    Hallelujah Praise Ye The Lord
    SAB   Organ
    G. Schirmer (n.d.) 10878

150:00
    Lewandowski, Louis
    Hallelujah Praise Ye The Lord (English/
        Hebrew)
    SATB   Organ
    G. Schirmer (n.d.) 7454

150:00
    Lewandowski, Louis
    Hallelujah Praise Ye The Lord
    SSA   Organ
    G. Schirmer (n.d.) 10874

150:00
    Lewandowski, Louis (arr. Lorrain Kingsley)
    Psalm 150
    SATB   Keyboard
    Carl Fischer (1954) CM 6753

150:00
    Lewandowski, Louis (arr. Wallingford
        Riegger)
    Psalm 150
    SATB (S-A-T-B-solos)   Organ
    Flammer (1956) A-5273

150:00
    Lewandowski, Louis
    Psalm 150 - Hallelujah Priase Ye The Lord
    SATB   Unaccompanied
    Hall McCreary (1947) n.#.

150:00
    Lockwood, Normand
    The Closing Doxology
    SATB   Band
    Broude Brothers (1952) BB 79

150:00 (Wesley)
    Lovelace, Austin
    Praise The Lord Who Reigns Above
    SATB   kro
    Abingdon (1966) APM-532

150:00 (Wesley)
    Lovelace, Austin
    Wesley's Psalm 150
    SATB   Optional Accompaniment
    Word (1973) CS 2680

150:00
    Lynn, George
    Praise The Lord!
    SSAATTBB   kro
    Presser (1971) 312-40747

150:00
    Marshall, Jane M.
    Praise The Lord
    SATB   Piano or Organ
    Carl Fischer (1969) CM 7722

150:00
    Mason, Lowell (ed. Leonard Van Camp)
    O Praise God In His Holiness
    SATB   kro
    Boonin (1976) B 267

150:00
    Mason, Lowell (ed. Mason Martens)
    O Praise God In His Holiness
    SATB   Keyboard
    McAfee (1975) (found in Bicentennial Col-
        lection of American Choral Music)

150:00
    Mathais, William
    Psalm 150, Op. 44
    SATB   Organ (optional orchestra)
    Oxford (1970) A 271

150:00
    Matthews, Thomas
    O Praise God In His Sanctuary
    SATB   kro
    H. T. Fitzsimons (1954) 2124

150:00
    Mauduit, Jacques (J. Meyerowitz)
    Psalm 150   (English/French)
    SSATB   kro
    Broude Brothers (1967) BB 4064

150:00
    SEE: Psalm 117
    McCabe, Michael
    A Psalm Of Praise And Thanksgiving

150:00
    Milner, Arthur
    O Praise God In His Holiness
    SAB   Organ
    Novello (1958) 1363

150:00
    SEE: Psalm 148:1-13
    Milner, Anthony
    Praise The Lord Of Heaven, Op. 13, #3

150:00
    McAfee, Don
    A Choric Psalm
    SATB   Percussion
    General Music (1968) CH 234

150:00
    Newbury, Kent
    Psalm 150
    SATB   kro
    G. Schirmer (1955) 638 (also available in
        TTBB arrangement)

150:00
    Nichols, Ted
    Praise Ye Him
    SATB   Organ, or Brass and Percussion
    Flammer (1971) A-5579

150:00 (Baker)
    Ossewaarde, Jack
    A Paean Of Praise
    SATB   Organ
    H. W. Gray (1965) CMR 2886

150:00 (Psalm 100)
    Ouchterlony, David
    A Psalm Of Praise
    SATB and Youth Choir   Organ
    F. Harris (1979) HC 4082

150:00 (Malachi 1:11)
    Ouchterlony, David
    Praise God!
    SATB   Organ
    F. Harris (1979) HC 4023

150:00
    Parker, Alice
    Praise Ye The Lord (Psalm of Praise)
    2 part male   Percussion
    Lawson Gould (1968) 51385

150:00
    Paul, Leslie
    O Praise God In His Holiness
    SATB   Organ
    Oxford (1965) A 230

150:00
    Pelz, Walter
    Psalm 150
    SAB   Congregation   Choir
    Augsburg (1978) (found in Seasonal Psalms
        For Congregation and Choir, 11-9376)

150:00
    SEE: Psalm 148
    Perera, Ronald
    Everything That Hath Breath

150:00 (paraphrase by Wesley)
    Pfautsch, Lloyd
    Praise The Lord Who Reigns Above
    SATB   No accompaniment
    Carl Fischer (1972) CM 7797

150:00
    Pfautsch- Lloyd
    Psalm 150
    SATB   Trumpet (No accompaniment)
    Flammer (1962) A 5143

150:00
    Pinkham, Daniel
    Psalm (from Fanfares)
    SATB   Organ (optional unison or con-
        gregation)
    Ione Press [E. C. Schirmer] (1975) ECS 3035

150:00
    Pitoni, Guiseppi
    Laudate Dominum
    SATB   No accompaniment
    Arista (1976) AE 323

150:00
    Pitoni, Guiseppi
    Laudate Dominum (Praise Ye The Lord) (Latin/
        English)
    SATB   Optional organ
    Concordia (1974) (found in The Second
        Motet Book, 97-5205)

150:00
    Poston, Elizabeth
    Antiphon and Psalm   Laude Dominum
    SATB   Organ
    Boosey & Hawkes (1956) 5122

150:00   (paraphrase)
    Purcell, Henry (arr. Hal Hopson)
    Sound The Trumpet
    2 part mixed   Keyboard
    Carl Fischer (1978) CM 8056

150:00 (Revised Standard Version)
    Ramsey, Dale E.
    Psalm 150
    SATB   Organ
    Kjos (1981) ED 5994

150:00
    Red, Buryl
    Praise Ye The Lord
    Unison   Keyboard and Percussion
    Broadman (1966) 4560-18

150:00
    Rochberg, George
    Psalm 150   (English/Hebrew)
    SATB   kro
    Presser (1956) 312-40299

150:00
    Rohlig, Harald
    Praise God In His Temple
    Unison   Keyboard
    Concordia (1973) 97-5165 (found in Explode
        With Joy)

150:00
    Rutter, John
    Praise Ye The Lord
    SATB (B-solo)   Organ
    Oxford (1969) 42.357 (also found in Anthems
        For Choirs, Volume 1)

150:00
    Schirrmann, Charles
    Praise Ye The Lord
    SAB   Piano
    J. Fischer (1956) 8975

150:00
    SEE: Psalm 134
    Schmutz, Albert D.
    Behold Bless Ye The Lord

150:00
    Schütz, Heinrich (ed. Theodore Marier)
    Psalm 150   (English/German)
    SATB/SATB   Organ and Brass
    Robert King (1958) 601

150:00
    Schütz, Heinrich (ed. Daniel Reuning)
    Sing Alleluia Praise The Lord (Five Psalms,
        Op. 5) (English/German)
    SATB   No accompaniment
    GIA (1973) G-1790

150:00
    SEE: Psalm 147
    Sessions, Roger
    Praise Ye The Lord

150:00
    Sewall, Maud
    Psalm 150
    SATB   Accompaniment ad lib.
    H. W. Gray (1951) 2203

150:00
    Shiner, C. J.
    O Praise God In His Holiness
    SATB   Organ
    Galliard (1963) n.#.

150:00
SEE: Psalm 148:1-3, 7-12
Stark, Richard
Praise The Lord

150:00 (from A Testament Of Life)
Stevens, Halsey
Psalm 150
SATB   Keyboard
Mark Foster (1975) MF 150D

150:00
Sweelinck, J. P. (ed. Thomas Dunn)
Psalm 150   (English/French)
SSAATTBB   Organ
E. C. Schirmer (1971) 2790

150:00
Tamblyn, William
Antiphon and Psalm 150
SATB   Cantor or Congregation   Organ
Boosey & Hawkes (1971) 5823

150:00
Walker, Robert
Psalm 150
SSATB   kro
Novello (1976) 29.0369.05

150:00
White, Robert (ed. Peter LeHuray)
O Praise God In His Holiness
SSAATTBB   Optional Organ
Oxford (1966) A 237

150:00
Whyte, Robert (ed. John West)
O Praise God In His Holiness
SATB   kro
Novello (n.d.) 1071

150:00
Wienhorst, Richard
Psalm 150
SATBB   No accompaniment
Concordia (1966) 98-1793

150:00 (Wesley)
Williams, David H.
Praise The Lord Who Reigns Above
SATB   Organ
Carl Fischer (1970) CM 7747

150:00
Williams, David H.
Praise Ye The Lord
SATB   Organ
Summy Birchard (1959) 5273

150:00 (Jerusalem Bible)
Williamson, Malcolm
Antiphons and Psalm 150
SATB   Organ
Boosey & Hawkes (1971) 5823

150:00 (Bay Psalm Book)
Williamson, Malcolm
Pilgrim's Earth Psalm
Unison Choir and Congregation   Organ
Boosey & Hawkes (1976) 5960

150:00
Wills, Arthur
O Praise God In His Holiness
SATB   Organ (optional Brass Quartet)
Novello (1964) MT 1452

150:00 (Baker)
Wood, Dale
O Praise Ye The Lord
SAB   Organ (optional percussion and
Brass)
Shawnee (1974) D 5222

150:00
York, David Stanley
Psalm 150
SATB   Keyboard
Presser (1968) 312-40683

150:00
SEE: Psalm 117
Young, Gordon
Praise

150:00
Young, Gordon
Praise Ye The Lord
SATB   Organ
Flammer (1966) A-5022

150:1-2
Crotch, William (arr. George Brandon)
Come Praise The Lord
TBB   Keyboard
Concordia (1977) 98-2320

150:1-2, 6
Martens, Edmund R.
Let Everything That Hath Breath (from Four
Introits, Set II)
Unison   Handbells
Concordia (1979) 97-5467

150:1-2, 6
Moe, Daniel
Psalm Concerto, Part I
SATB   2 Trumpets, 2 Trombones, Bass
Augsburg (1970) 11-0632

150:1-3, 5-6
Pitoni, Guiseppi (ed. Mason Martens)
Laudate Dominum   (English/Latin)
SATB   No accompaniment
Walton (1963) 2092

150:1-4, 6
Weldon, John (ed. Mason Martens)
O Praise God In His Holiness
SAB   Organ
Concordia (1965) 98-1787 (also found in
Sing For Joy, 97-5046)

150:3
SEE: Psalm 100:1
Ramsfield, Jerome K.
O Be Joyful

150:3
Nelhybel, Vaclav
Praise The Lord With The Sound Of Trumpet
(part of Four Motets)
SATB   2 Trumpets
European American   B-359

150:4 (Psalm 87:4)
Schütz, Heinrich
Jubilate Deo in Chordis   (Latin only)
TTB   Optional accompaniment
Oxford (1965) (found in Anthems For Men's
Voices, Volume 2)

P R O V E R B S

1:20-23, 33
SEE: Proverbs 3:19, 20
Spies, Claudio
Proverbs On Wisdom

2:1-6, 8
Sowerby, Leo
My Son, If Thou Wilt Receive
SATB   Organ
H. W. Gray (1963) 2792

2:1-15 (Proverbs 3:1-4)
   Nystedt, Knut
   If You Receive My Words
   SATTBB   No accompaniment
   Augsburg (1973) 11-9214

2:6-8
   Berger, Jean
   For The Lord Giveth Wisdom
   SATB   kro
   Kjos (1964) Ed. 5376

3:00
   Clark, Keith
   Happy Is The Man Who Finds Wisdom
   SATB   kro
   Lawson Gould (1973) 51679

3:1-2, 13-16
   Moe, Daniel
   Exhortation From Proverbs
   SATB   Keyboard or Brass (2 Trumpets,
      2 Trombones, Horn, Tuba)
   Carl Fischer (1978) CM 7983 (parts CP-28)

3:1-4
   Cram, James D.
   Favor And Good Understanding
   SATB   Keyboard
   Broadman (1974) 4545-81

3:1-4
   SEE: Proverbs 2:1-15
   Nystedt, Knut
   If You Receive My Words

3:1-6
   Effinger, Cecil
   Forget Not My Law
   TTBB   Organ
   H. W. Gray (1968) CMR 3006 (also available
      in SATB arrangement)

3:5, 6
   Brandon, George
   Trust In The Lord
   SATB   Keyboard
   GIA (1973) G-1797

3:5-6
   Davis, Katherine K.
   Trust In The Lord
   SATB   Organ or Piano
   Galaxy (1944) CM 1478

3:5-6
   Davis, Katherine K.
   Trust In The Lord
   SSA   Piano or Organ
   Galaxy (1946) CM 1566

3:5-6 (Job 22:21)
   Freestone, G. S.
   Trust In The Lord
   SATB   Piano or Organ
   Associated (1968) A 588

3:5, 6 (Psalm 121:7, 8)
   Wetzler, Robert
   He Shall Direct Your Paths
   SATB (B-solo)   Organ or Piano
   AMSI (1981) 414

3:5-7
   McCormick, Clifford
   Trust In The Lord
   SATB   Keyboard
   Shawnee (1960) (also found in Anthems From
      Scripture, G-34)

3:5-7
   Powell, Robert J.
   Trust In The Lord
   SATB   Organ
   J. Fischer (1964) 9489

3:5, 7, 13-14, 19
   Ford, Virgil T.
   Be Not Wise In Your Own Eyes
   SATB   Keyboard
   Abingdon (1974) APM-952

3:6
   Hutson, Wihla
   In All Thy Ways Acknowledge Him
   SATB   Organ
   Boston (1963) 12610

3:7, 8
   SEE: Proverbs 3:19-20
   Spies, Claudio
   Proverbs On Wisdom

3:9-10
   Powell, Robert J.
   Honor The Lord With Thy Substance
   SAB   kro
   Abingdon (1966) APM-535 (found in
      Festival Anthems For SAB)

3:13
   Wilkinson, Scott
   Happy The Man
   SATB   kro
   ZIA Music [Carl Fischer] (1968) ZCM-104

3:13-14
   Lassus, Orlandus
   Beatus Homo (Latin only)
   2 part   No accompaniment
   Mercury (1941) 325.00011 (found in Twelve
      Motets)

3:13-16
   Berger, Jean
   Happy Is The Man
   SATB   kro
   G. Schirmer (1962) 10910

3:16-17
   SEE: Proverbs 9:1-6
   Linn, Robert
   Anthem of Wisdom

3:19-20 (Proverbs 1:20-23, 33; Proverbs 3:7,
   8)
   Spies, Claudio
   Proverbs On Wisdom
   TTBB   Organ and Piano
   Elkan Vogel (1965) 131

4:1, 7-8
   Levy, Ernst
   Hear Ye Children
   SSA/SSA   No accompaniment
   Bennington College [Alexander Broude]
      (1957) BCS 1

4:5-6
   SEE: Proverbs 9:1-6
   Linn, Robert
   Anthem Of Wisdom

4:18
   SEE: Psalm 118:24
   Leaf, Robert
   Awake Arise Go Forth and Rejoice

4:18-23
   Nystedt, Knut
   The Path Of The Just
   SATB   No accompaniment
   Augsburg (1969) 11-9333

6:8-9
   Berger, Jean
   Go To The Ant, Thou Sluggard (from Of Wis-
      dom and Folly)
   SATB   kro
   John Sheppherd (1965) 1001

8:1-5
    SEE: Proverbs 9:1-6
    Linn, Robert
    Anthem Of Wisdom

9:1-6 (Proverbs 8:1-5; Proverbs 3:16-17;
        Proverbs 4:5-6)
    Linn, Robert
    Anthem Of Wisdom
    SATB   Piano Four Parts
    Lawson Gould (1965) 51207

9:13-18
    Milhaud, Darius
    The Women Folly (from Cantata From Proverbs)
    SSA   Piano (or Harp, Oboe, Cello)
    Mercury (1953) 352.00159

10:28-29
    Lassus, Orlandus
    Expectatio Justorum (Latin only)
    2 part   No accompaniment
    Mercury (1941) 352.00011 (found in Twelve
        Motets)

15:13, 15
    Berger, Jean
    All The Days Of The Afflicted (from Of Wis-
        dom And Folly)
    SATB   kro
    John Sheppherd (1965) 1001

16:2-9, 16-20
    Nystedt, Knut
    All The Ways Of A Man
    SATB   No accompaniment
    Augsburg (1971) 11-9004

16:9, 18-19
    Berger, Jean
    Better It Is To Be Of An Humble Spirit
    SATB   kro
    John Sheppherd (1965) 1001

16:17, 19
    Berger, Jean
    The Highway Of The Upright
    SATB   Organ ad lib.
    Kjos (1972) Ed. 5873

17:22
    Parker, Alice
    A Merry Heart (from Sunday Rounds)
    7 part round   No accompaniment
    Hinshaw (1975) HMC-106

20:29
    Collins, Don L.
    Be Strong And Wise In The Lord
    CBB   Keyboard
    Cambiata Press (1976) C-97689

22:17
    Parker, Alice
    Bow Down Thine Ear (from Sunday Rounds)
    5 part round   No accompaniment
    Hinshaw (1975) HMC 106

23:29-35
    Milhaud, Darius
    Who Crieth: "Woe"? (from Cantata From
        Proverbs)
    SSA   Piano (OR Harp, Oboe, Cello)
    Mercury (1953) 352.00159

23:29-35
    Rorem, Ned
    Wounds Without Cause (Two Psalms And A
        Proverb)
    SATB   Piano or String Quartet
    E.C. Schirmer (1965) 2674

30:4
    Wink, Sue Karen and Irma June Wink
    A Proverb
    SATB   Piano
    Broadman (1975) 4554-99

30:18-19
    Krenek, Ernst
    There Be Three Things
    SATB   kro
    Rongwen[Broude Brothers] (1973) RM 3523

30:24-28
    Krenek, Ernst
    There Be Four Things
    SATB   kro
    Rongwen [Broude Brothers] (1973) RM 3522

31:00 (taken from)
    Freed, Isadore
    A Woman Of Valor
    SATB   kro
    Transcontinental (1957) TCL 132

31:2, 6
    SEE: Lamentations 1:4
    Handel, G. F.
    Funeral Anthem On The Death Of Queen
        Caroline

31:10-31
    Milhaud, Darius
    A Woman Of Valour (from Cantata From Pro-
        verbs)
    SSA   Piano (OR Harp, Oboe, Cello)
    Mercury (1953) 352.00159

E C C L E S I A S T E S

1:3-7 (Ecclesiastes 3:1-8)
    Trythall, Gilbert
    A Time To Every Purpose
    SATB   Tape
    Marks (1972) 4586

1:4-5, 7
    Krenek, Ernst
    The Earth Abideth (Three Motets)
    SSA   kro
    Rongwen [Broude Brothers] (1961) RM 3504

1:18 (and other)
    Mechem, Kirke
    All Hath Been Heard - Recitative to A Song
        Of Praise   (from Songs of Wisdom)
    Bass solo   No accompaniment
    E. C. Schirmer (1970) 2741

3:00   (text taken from)
    Adler, Samuel
    Seasons Of Time
    Unison   Piano
    Choristers Guild (1972) A 45

3:1
    Fissinger, Edwin
    To Everything There Is A Season
    SATB   Narrator   No accompaniment
    Jenson (1979) 411.20024

3:1-2, 4, 8
    Patterson, Paul
    To Everything There Is A Season (from
        Requiem)
    SATB   kro
    Boosey & Hawkes (1975) W.153

3:1-2, 4, 8, 10
    Mailman, Martin
    To Everything There Is A Season
    SATB   kro
    Boonin (1976) B 273

3:1-8
  Goemanne, Noel
  A Time For Everything
  Unison   Organ
  GIA (1980) G-2380

3:1-8
  Mueller, Carl F.
  A Time For Everything
  SATB   kro
  Broadman (1973) 4565-46

3:1-8
  Orff, Carl
  Omnia tempus habent (from Sunt lacrimae
     rerum)   (Latin only)
  TTTBBB (T-B-B-solos)   kro
  Schott   #39534

3:1-8
  Starer, Robert
  To Everything There Is A Season (from On
     The Nature Of Things)
  SATB   kro
  MCA (1969)

3:1-8
  SEE: Ecclesiastes 1:3-7
  Trythall, Gilvert
  A Time For Every Purpose

3:1-10 (based on)
  Sleeth, Natalie
  It's All In The Hands Of God
  2 part   Keyboard
  AMSI (1981) 421

3:14
  Weinberger, Jaromir
  Of Divine Work
  SATB   Organ
  H. W. Gray (1950) CMR 2117

3:20
  SEE: Ecclesiastes 11:9
  Mechem, Kirke
  Recitative To The Protest Of Job

4:6
  London, Edwin
  Better Is
  SSA (or 9 solos)   No accompaniment
  Boonin (1974) B.178

4:11
  Red, Buryl
  Ecclesiastes 4:11
  SA(T)B   Keyboard
  Broadman (1971) 4565-29

4:11-12
  Nowak, Lionel
  Wisdom Exalteth Her Children
  SSA/SSA or TBB/TBB   No accompaniment
  Bennington College [Alexander Broude] (n.d.)
     #52

4:13
  SEE: Ecclesiastes 7:9, 16
  Mechem, Kirke
  Be Not Righteous - Recitative to A Song Of
     Comfort (from Songs Of Wisdom)

5:1-7
  Shaw, Christopher
  A Lesson From Ecclesiastes
  SATB   Organ
  Novello (1963) 1445

7:9, 16 (Ecclesiastes 4:13
  Mechem, Kirke
  Be Not Righteous - Recitative To A Song Of
     Comfort (from Songs Of Wisdom)
  Soprano Solo   No accompaniment
  E. C. Schirmer (1970) 2740

8:1 (Ecclesiastes 9:17-18)
  Hovhaness, Alan
  Wisdom (Three Motets) Op. 259, #3
  SATB   kro
  Rongwen [Broude Brothers] (1974) RM 3528

9:7-8
  Yeakle, Thomas
  Go Thy Way
  SATB   kro
  H. W. Gray (1976) CMR 3349

9:7, 9
  Mechem, Kirke
  Recitative To A Love Song (from Songs Of
     Wisdom)
  Alto Solo   No accompaniment
  E. C. Schirmer (1970) 2738

9:7, 9, 10
  Krenek, Ernst
  Go Thy Way (Three Sacred Pieces)
  SATB   kro
  Rongwen [Broude Brothers] (1973) RM 3521

9:11
  SEE: Ecclesiastes 11:9
  Mechem, Kirke
  Recitative To The Protest Of Job

9:17-18
  SEE: Ecclesiastes 8:1
  Hovhaness, Alan
  Wisdom

11:00 and 12:00 (taken from)
  Adler, Samuel
  Remember Your Creator
  Unison   Piano and Percussion
  Choristers Guild (1971) A 103

11:9 (and other)
  Beck, John Ness
  Hymn To David
  SSAATTBB   kro
  Buckeye Music (1968) n.#.

11:9
  Lewis, John Leo
  Rejoice
  SATB   kro
  Carl Fischer (1949) CM 6350

11:9 (Ecclesiastes 3:20; Ecclesiastes 9:11)
  Mechem, Kirke
  Recitative To The Protest Of Job (from
     Songs Of Wisdom)
  Tenor Solo   No accompaiment
  E. C. Schirmer (1970) 2739

12:00
  SEE: Ecclesiastes 11:00 and 12:00
  Adler, Samuel
  Remember Your Creator

12:1
  Lewis, John Leo
  Remember Now
  SATB   kro
  Carl Fischer (1949) CM 6349

12:1-2, 6-7
  Glarum, L. Stanley
  Remember Now Thy Creator
  SATB   kro
  Schmitt, Hall & McCreary (1950) 1790

12:1-7
  SEE: Psalm 38:21
  Mechem, Kirke
  Forsake Me Not, O Lord

12:1-7
   Playman, Gordon
   Remember Now Thy Creator
   SATB   Organ
   Augsburg (1947) 1045

12:1-8
   Krenek, Ernst
   Remember Now,   Op. 115a
   SSA   Piano
   Mobart Music (1976) M-102

12:4, 7-8
   Steggall, Charles
   Remember Now Thy Creator
   SATB   Organ
   Novello (n.d.) 38

43:16, 27 (Latin)   (Revelation 4:8, 11,
                English)
   Bruckner, Anton (ed. Richard Peek)
   Worthy Art Thou, O Lord God (English/Latin)
   SATB   3 Trombones   (or Organ)
   Augsburg (1969) 11-1564   (parts 11-9538)

S O N G   O F   S O N G S

1:2
   Josquin des Pres (ed. Maynard Klein)
   Ecce Tu Pulchra Es   (English/Latin)
   SATB   kro
   G. Schirmer (1973) 11988

1:2-3
   SEE: Song Of Songs 8:10
   Gregor, Christian (ed. E. Nolte)
   Lord In Thy Presence

1:2-3
   Handl, Jacob
   Trahe me post Te
   TTBBB   kro
   Mercury   #32

1:4, (5)   (Song Of Songs 2:10-12)
   Casals, Pablo
   Nigra Sum   (English/Latin)
   SA   Piano or Organ
   Tetra [Alexander Broude] (1966) AB-120

1:5-6
   Zarlion, G.
   Nigra Sum   (Latin only)
   SATTB   kro
   Flammer (1940) (found in Three Centuries Of
        Choral Music, Volume 2)

2:1-3, 7-11, 17
   Moss, Lawrence K.
   A Song Of Solomon
   SSA   Piano
   Beekman [Mercury] (1956) MC 284

2:1-5, 7-8, 10-11
   Billings, William (ed. Lawrence Bennett)
   I Am The Rose Of Sharon
   SATB   kro
   Broude Brothers (1975) WW 7

2:1-5, 7-8, 10-11
   Billings, William
   I Am The Rose Of Sharon
   SATB   kro
   G. Schirmer (1952) 42703

2:3, 4
   Baristow, Edward C.
   I Sat Down Under His Shadow
   SATB   Unaccompanied
   Oxford (1925) 43.002   (also found in
        Anthems For Choirs, Volume 1)

2:3-4
   Baristow, Edward (arr. Lawrence H. Davies)
   I Sat Under His Shadow
   2 part treble (S-solo)   Piano or Organ
   Oxford (1964) E 104

2:3-4
   SEE: Baruch 5:8-9
   West, John E.
   The Woods And Every Sweet Smelling Tree

2:3, 6
   Near, Gerald
   I Sat Down Under His Shadow
   SATB   kro
   Augsburg (1969) CS 527

2:5
   SEE: Song Of Songs 5:1-2, 6
   Billings, William
   I Am Come Into My Garden

2:5, 17
   SEE: Song Of Songs 5:1-2, 6
   Billings, William (ed. Mason Martens)
   I am Come Into My Garden

2:8-10   (Song Of Songs 3:5)
   Mechem, Kirke
   A Love Song   (from Song Of Wisdom)
   SSATB   kro
   E. C. Schirmer (1970) 2738

2:10-12
   SEE: Song Of Songs 1:5
   Casals, Pablo
   Nigra Sum

2:10-12
   Fried, Donovan R.
   Rise Up My Love, My Fair One
   SATB   kro
   Schmitt, Hall & McCreary (1963) 1183

2:10-12
   McCray, James
   Rise Up My Love My Fair One
   SSA (S-solo)   Piano and Flute
   National Music (1973) WHC 44

2:10-12
   Near, Gerald
   Arise My Love My Fair One
   SATB   kro
   Augsburg (1966) 11-0521

2:10-12   (Song Of Songs 6:1, 3)
   Pinkham, Daniel
   Rise Up My Love My Fair One (from Wedding
        Cantata)
   SATB   Piano (or Strings, 2 Horns, Celesta)
   C. F. Peters (1959) 66039

2:10-12
   Wade, Walter
   Arise, My Love
   SATB   kro
   Lawson Gould (1962) 51119

2:10-12   (selected)
   Wilkinson, Scott
   Rise Up My Love   (Two Songs From Solomon)
   SATB   kro
   ZIA [Carl Fischer] (1968) ZCM 104

2:10-12
   Willan, Healey
   Rise Up My Love My Fair One (from Liturgi-
        cal Motets, #5)
   SATB   kro
   Oxford (1929) 94 P306

2:10-12
Hadley, Patrick
My Beloved Spake
SATB   Piano or Organ
Curwen [G. Schirmer] (1938) 61345

2:10-13 (adapted)
Morgan, John G.
Arise My Love
SSA   Keyboard
Mark Foster (1981) MF 913

2:10-13
Wienandt, Elwyn A.
Song Of Solomon
SATB   Oboe
Agape [Hope] (1974) AG 7125

2:10-13, 16
Purcell, Henry (ed. Edward J. Dent)
My Beloved Spake
SATB   Organ
Novello (1952) 29.0447.00

2:11-12
SEE: Acts 13:32-33
Baristow, Edward
The Promise Which Was Made

2:11-12
Jordan, Alice
The Time Of Singing Has Come
Unison   Organ
Abingdon (1969) APM-799

2:11-13
SEE: Matthew 16:18-19
Beck, John Ness
Upon This Rock

3:00
Young, Gordon
Lament From A Song Of Solomon
SATB (B-solo) Piano or Organ (optional
    timpani)
Flammer (1962) 84734

3:1-2, 4-5
Berlinski, Herman
I Sought Him
SSA (S-solo)   Harp or Piano
Mercury (1949) C-21

3:5
SEE: Song Of Songs 2:8-10
Mechem, Kirke
A Love Song (from Songs Of Wisdom)

4:16
Pinkham, Daniel
Awake O North Wind (from Wedding Cantata)
SATB   Piano (or Strings, 2 Horns,
    Celesta)
C. F. Peters (1959) 66039

5:1-2, 6 (Song Of Songs 2:5;
        Song Of Songs 8:14)
Billings, William (ed. Lawrence Bennett)
I Am Come Into My Garden
SATB   kro
Broude Brothers (1974) WW 5

5:1-2, 6 (Song Of Songs 2:5, 17)
Billings, William (ed. Mason Martens)
I Am Come Into My Garden
SATB   Keyboard
McAfee (1975) (found in Bicentennial
    Collection Of American Choral Music)

5:6, 8
de Rivafrecha, Martin
Anima Mea (Latin only)
SATB   kro
J. & W. Chester (1977) JWC 55104 (found in
    Third Chester Book Of Motets)

5:8-12
SEE: Song Of Songs 8:4
Billings, William
I Charge You, O Ye Daughters

6:1-3
SEE: Song Of Songs 2:10-12
Pinkham, Daniel
Rise Up My Love   (Wedding Cantata)

7:1-2
Palestrina, G. P. (ed. Antal Ianscovies)
Quam Pulchri Sunt (Latin)
SSATB   No accompaniment
Presser (1976) 312-42024

7:4-7, 11-12
Dunstable, John (ed. Dennis Shrock)
Quam Pulchra Est
STB   No accompaniment
Hinshaw (1977) HMC 246

8:4 (Song Of Songs 5:8-12)
Billings, William (ed. Lawrence Bennett)
I Charge You, O Ye Daughters Of Jerusalem
SATB   kro
Broude Brothers (1974) WW 6

8:6
Adler, Samuel
Set Me As A Seal Upon Thy Heart
SATB   Organ
Mercury (1956) MC 267

8:6
Pinkham, Daniel
Set Me As A Seal (from Wedding Cantata)
SATB   Piano (or Strings, 2 Horns,
    Celesta)
C.F. Peters (1959) 66039

8:6-7 (Hosea 1:19-20)
Grieb, Herbert
Set Me As A Seal
SATB (B-solo)   Organ
G. Schirmer (1963) 11050

8:6, 7
Walton, William
Set Me As A Seal Upon Thine Heart
SATB   kro
Oxford (1938) A-86 (also found in Anthems
    For Choirs, Volume 4)

8:7 (John 15:13;   I Peter 2:24;
    I Corinthians 6:11; I Peter 2:9-20;
    Romans 12:1)
Ireland, John
Greater Love Hath No Man
SATB (B-solo)   Organ
Galaxy (1912) 1.5030.1

8:7
Pinkham, Daniel
Many Waters Cannot Quench Love (from
    Wedding Cantata)
SATB   Piano (or Strings, 2 Horns,
    Celesta)
C. F. Peters (1959) 66039

8:10 (Song Of Songs 1:2-3; Isaiah 53:3;
    Psalm 45:2, 8)
Gregor, Christian (ed. & arr. E. Nolte)
Lord In Thy Present (English/German)
SS or SA   Organ
Boosey & Hawkes (1969) 5700

8:14
SEE: Song Of Songs 5:1-2, 6
Billings, William
I Come Into My Garden

<u>I S A I A H</u>

1:00   (Isaiah 2:00)
    Sessions, Roger
    Ah Sinful Nation   (Three Choruses on
        Biblical Texts)
    SATB   Piano
    Presser (1976) 342-40118

1:2, 4, 11, 17-18
    Humphrey, Pelham (ed. William Bowie)
    Hear, O Heavens
    SATB   Organ
    Oxford (1964) A 213

2:00
    SEE: Isaiah 1:00
    Sessions, Roger
    Ah Sinful Nation

2:2-4
    Brant, Henry
    Credo For Peace
    SATB   Speaker, Trumpet in C   kro
    MCA (1972) 357-062

2:2-4
    Clokey, Joseph
    A Canticle Of Peace
    Unison   Keyboard
    Summy-Birchard (1945) SUMCO P 340

2:2-5
    Berger, Jean
    And It Shall Come To Pass
    SATB   kro
    Augsburg (1968) ACL 1519

2:2-5
    Hilty, Everett Jay
    Come Let Us Walk In The Light Of The Lord
    SATB   Optional Organ
    Golden Music (1970) G 40

2:3, 5 (Psalm 90:15;   Psalm 33:21)
    Crowe, John F.
    The Light Of The Lord
    SATB   Organ
    Augsburg (1965) 1443

2:3-5
    Naylor, Bernard
    Advent
    SSATB   No accompaniment
    Novello (1960) 1393

3:10-11   (Isaiah 65:14)
    Thompson, Randall
    Say Ye To The Righteous   (from Peaceable
        Kingdom)
    SATB   kro
    E. C. Schirmer (1936) 1730

5:1-2
    Felciano, Richard
    My Friend Had A Vineyard   (Songs For
        Darkness and Light)
    2 part mixed   No accompaniment
    E. C. Schirmer (1971) 2803

6:1-3
    Young, Gordon
    In The Year That King Uzziah Died
    SATB   Organ
    Abingdon (1967) APM-530

6:1-4
    Hughes, John
    Isaiah's Vision
    SATB   Organ or Piano
    Bourne (1967) 831

6:1-4
    Stainer, John
    I Saw The Lord
    SATB/SATB   Organ
    Novello (n.d.) 29.0110.02

6:1-4
    Vulpius, Melchoir
    Isaiah, Mighty Seer, In Days Of Old
    SATB   Organ
    Concordia (1961) 98-1533

6:1-5   (Luther)
    Luther, Martin (arr. Philip Dietterich)
    The Sanctus
    Unison and SATB   Keyboard
    Abingdon (1962) APM-191

6:1-8
    Moyer, J. Harold
    I Saw The Lord
    SATB   Organ and Percussion
    The New Music (1976) NM-A-126

6:1-8
    Naylor, Bernard
    Trinity Sunday
    SSATBB   No accompaniment
    Novello (1960) 1402

6:1-8
    Williams, David McK.
    In The Year That King Uzziah Died
    SATB   Organ
    H. W. Gray (1935) CMR 1356

6:1-8
    Wyton, Alec
    The Vision Of Isaiah
    SATB   Organ (Brass Quartet, Strings)
    Beekman [Mercury] (1966) MC 501

6:1-9
    Naylor, Bernard
    Motet For Trinity Sunday
    SSATB (S-A-T-B-solos)   No accompaniment
    Universal (1956) UE 12340

6:1-9
    Pinkham, Daniel
    The Call Of Isaiah
    Any Voicing   Organ, Tape, Percussion
    E. C. Schirmer (1971) 2911

6:2-3
    Dering, Richard (ed. Stanley Roper)
    Above Him Stood The Seraphim
    SS   Organ
    Oxford (1927) (found in <u>Oxford Easy Anthem
        Book</u>)

6:2-3
    Dering, Richard
    Duo Seraphim   (English/Latin)
    SS   Organ
    Oxford (1973) (found in <u>Anthems For Choirs</u>,
        Volume 2)

6:2-3
    Scheidt, Samuel
    Duo Seraphim Clamabant   (Latin)
    SSATT/ATBB   No accompaniment
    Barenreiter (1954) 2905

6:2-4   (Luther)
    Luther, M. (setting by Paul Bunjes)
    The Vision Of Isaiah
    Unison with Descant   Organ
    Concordia (1956) (found in <u>Lift Up Your
        Hearts</u>, 97-6219)

6:3
Bach, C. P. E. (ed. Karl Geiringer)
Holy Is God   (English/German)
SATB   Organ
Concordia (1956) 97-6223

6:3 (Matthew 21:9)
Beebe, Hank
Hosanna To The Lord   (from A Service Of
    Life)
2 part treble or 2 part mixed   Keyboard
    (optional guitar)
Pembroke [Carl Fischer] (1977) PC 1008

6:3 (Matthew 21:9)
Bortniansky, Demetrius
Sanctus With Hosanna   (Latin/English)
TTBB   No accompaniment
Carl Fischer (1928) CM 325

6:3 (Revelation 7:12)
Geisler, Johann (ed. E. Nolte)
The Seraphim On High (English/German)
SATB/SATB   Organ
Boosey & Hawkes (1965) 574

6:3
Hammerschmidt, Andreas (ed. Harold Mueller)
Holy Is The Lord   (English/German)
SSATB   Continuo, 2 violins
Concordia (1960) 97-6314

6:3
Handl, Jacob
Duo Seraphim   (Latin)
SATB/SATB   Organ
Arista (1978) AE 285

6:3
Pelz, Walter
Verse/Trinity (Verses and Offertories
     Easter - Trinity)
SATB   Organ
Augsburg (1980) 11-9546

6:3 (Revelation 5:12)
Posegate, Maxcine Woodbridge
Holy, Lord Of Hosts
SSATBB   Accompaniment ad lib.
Hope (1967) A-382

6:3 (I John 5:7)
Victoria, Tomas
Duo Seraphim   (Latin only)
SSAA   kro
J. & W. Chester [Alexander Broude] (1936)
     ABC 23

6:3
Walter, Samuel
Holy, Holy, Holy
SATB   No accompaniment
Abingdon (1961) APM-172

6:3a (Romans 11:36a;   Psalm 8:1a)
Martens, Edmund
Holy Is The Lord   (Four Introits, Set I)
Unison   Handbells
Concordia (1976) 97-5384

6:8
Berger, Jean
Whom Shall I Send?
SATB   kro
Augsburg (1962) 1338

7:14
Issac, Heinrich
Ecce Virgo Concipies   (Latin only)
SATB   kro
J. & W. Chester (1977) JWC 55110   (found in
     Sixth Chester Book Of Motets)

7:14 (Isaiah 9:6-7)
Morales, Cristobal (ed. Robert Goodale)
Ecce Virgo Concipiet   (Latin only)
SATB   kro
G. Schirmer (1965) 11233

7:14
Sweelinck, J. P. (ed. Percy Young)
Ecce Virgo Concipiet   (Behold A Virgin Shall
     Conceive)
SSATB   kro
Broude Brothers (1981) Series XI, #2

7:14
Sweelinck, J. P. (ed. Donald Colton)
Ecce Virgo Concipiet (Behold A Virgin Shall
     Conceive) (Latin/English)
SSATB   kro
Concordia (1978) 98-2347

9:2
SEE: Job 3:2-3, 20-21, 23-24
Cook, Melville
Antiphon

9:2 (Isaiah 60:3)
Couper, Alinda
Those Who Dwelt In A Land Of Darkness
     (Festival Introits)
SATB   kro
Abingdon (1969) APM-780

9:2
Fritschel, James
A Great Light
SATB   No accompaniment
Hinshaw (1976) HMC 147

9:2 (Isaiah 60:1)
Gieseke, Richard W.
The People Who Walked In Darkness
SAB   No accompaniment
Concordia (1978) 97-5481

9:2, 6
Naylor, Bernard
Christmas Day
SSAATTBB   No accompaniment
Novello (1960) 1394

9:2, 6
Wetzler, Robert
Offertory/Christma Midnight (Verses and
     Offertories - Advent I - The Baptism
     Of Our Lord)
SATB   Organ
Augsburg (1979) 11-9541

9:2-7 (based on)
Bach, J. S.
Break Forth, O Beauteous Heavenly Light
SATB   Piano
Novello (n.d.) 29.0309.01

9:2-7 (Rist)
Bodine, Willis
Break Forth, O Beauteous Heavenly Light
SATB   Organ
H. W. Gray (1966) CMR 2947

9:5-6
Franck, Melchior (ed. Walter Ehret)
Unto Us A Child Is Born
SATB/SATB   kro
Shawnee (1979) A-1522   (Parts LB-193)

9:6 (based on) (Psalm 97:1, based on)
Anonymous (ed. Albert Seay)
Born To Us Is The Christ Child
SATB   kro
Presser (1958) 312-40371

9:6 (based on)
    Caurroy, Eustache (ed. A. B. Couper)
    Rise From Your Bed Of Hay (English/French)
    SATB   kro
    Presser (1975) 312-41079

9:6
    SEE: Luke 2:10-11
    Gabrieli, Andrea (ed. C. Buell Agey)
    Lo, The Angel Said To The Shepherds

9:6
    Handel, G. F.
    For Unto Us A Child Is Born (Messiah)
    SATB   Organ
    F. Harris (n.d.) HC 4006

9:6
    Handel, G. F.
    For Unto Us A Child Is Born
    SATB   Keyboard
    Hall & McCreary (1941) 1902

9:6
    Handel, G. F. (ed. H. Watkins Shaw)
    For Unto Us A Child Is Born (Messiah)
    SATB   Keyboard
    Novello (n.d.) 29.0205.02

9:6
    Kuhnau, Johann (ed. Horace Fishback)
    For Unto Us A Child Is Born (found in How
        Brightly Shines, #3)
    SSATB   Organ
    H. W. Gray (1961) n.#.

9:6 (Psalm 98:1a)
    Martens, Edmund
    Unto Us A Child Is Born (from Four Introits,
        Set II)
    Unison   Handbells
    Concordia (1979) 97-5467

9:6 (John 1:14)
    Morales, Cristobal (ed. Kurt Stone)
    Puer natus est nobis (Latin/English)
    SAB   kro
    Broude Brothers (1967) BB 4071

9:6
    Roberts, Nancy M.
    Unto Us A Child Is Born
    SSAATTBB   kro
    Flammer (1971) A-5565

9:6
    Schütz, Heinrich (ed. R. E. Wunderlich)
    To Us A Child Is Born
    SATB   Organ
    Concordia (1960) 98-1494

9:6
    Willan, Healey
    Unto Us A Child Is Born
    SSA   No accompaniment
    Concordia (1953) (found in We Praise Thee,
        Volume I, 97-7564)

9:6-7
    Krieger, J. P. (ed. Harold E. Samuel)
    For Unto Us A Child Is Born (English/Ger-
        man)
    SAB (S-A-B-solos)   Continuo, 2 violins
    Concordia (1966) 97-4692   (Parts 97-4693)

9:6-7
    SEE: Isaiah 7:14
    Morales, Cristobal (ed. Robert Goodale)
    Ecce Virgo Concipiet

9:6-7
    Schütz, Heinrich (ed. Johann Riedel)
    To Us A Child Is Given (English/German)
    SSATTB   Optional Keyboard
    Summy Birchard (1961) 5507

10:9-11, 28-31
    Nystedt, Knut
    Get You Up
    SATB   No accompaniment
    Hinshaw (1980) HMC-439

11:1
    Distler, Hugo
    Lo! How A Rose E'er Blooming
    SATB   kro
    Concordia (1967) 98-1925

11:1 (based on)
    Distler, Hugo
    Lo! How A Rose (Chorale Motet from The
        Christmas Story, Op. 10)
    SATB   No accompaniment
    Concordia (1967) 97-4849

11:1 (based on)
    Houkom, Alf S. (arranger)
    Lo! How A Rose
    SATB or SAB   Organ, oboe or flute
    Concordia (1975) 98-2216

11:1
    Vulpius, Melchior
    Lo, How A Rose E'er Blooming
    SATB   No accompaniment
    Concordia (1960) 98-1519

11:1-2
    Aufdemberge, Edgar
    Behold A Branch Is Growing
    SAB   No accompaniment
    Concordia (1973) 98-2132

11:1-2 (Romans 15:12)
    Handl, Jacob
    Egre Dictur Virga
    SATB   No accompaniment
    Arista (1974) AE 244

11:5
    Handel, G. F. (ed. Carl F. Pfatteicher)
    And The Glory Of The Lord (Messiah)
    SATB   Keyboard
    Carl Fischer (1925) CM 174

11:5-6
    Roff, Joseph
    And A Little Child Shall Lead Them
    SATB   Keyboard
    Stony Chapel Press (1969) 137

11:6-9 (paraphrase)
    Hruby, Dolores
    The Peaceable Kingdom (Three Sacred Songs)
    Unison   Organ
    Concordia (1973) 98-2098

11:10
    SEE: Exodus 13:17
    Gregor, Christian (ed. & arr. E. Nolte)
    In Slumber, Peaceful Slumber

12:00
    Jacob, Gordon
    O Lord I Will Praise Thee
    SATB   Organ
    Oxford (found in Oxford Easy Anthem Book)

12:00
    Krapf, Gerhard
    O Lord I Will Praise Thee
    Unison   Organ
    Concordia (1966) 98-1853

12:00
    Nystedt, Knut
    Cry Out And Shout
    TTBB   kro
    Summy Birchard (1962) 5577

12:1, 2, 3-6
    Adler, Samuel
    God Is My Salvation   (Two Songs Of Hope)
    TTBB   Organ
    Mercury (1962) MC 430

12:2   (adapted)
    Palestrina, G. P.   (ed. & arr. Douglas E.
        Wagner)
    God Is My Strong Salvation
    SATB   kro
    Flammer (1980) A 5902

12:2, 4
    DuBois, Leon J.
    Behold God Is My Salvation
    SATB   kro
    J. Fischer (1964) 9484

12:2, 4   (based on)
    Powell, Robert J.
    Behold, God Is My Salvation
    SA   Piano or Organ
    McAfee [Belwin]   (1981) DMC 8106

12:2, 5
    Berger, Jean
    Behold! God Is My Salvation
    SATB   kro
    Augsburg (1966) 1464

12:2, 5-6
    Sowerby, Leo
    Behold God Is My Salvation
    SA   Organ
    H. W. Gray (1961) CMR 2712

12:2-6
    Proulx, Richard
    Song Of Isaiah
    SA or TB or ST or AB   2 Handbells,
        Percussion
    Art Master (1971) AMSI 189

12:2-6
    Rorem, Ned
    Ecce Deus (Canticles, Set II) (English)
    SATBB   No accompaniment
    Boosey & Hawkes (1972) 5841

12:2-6
    White, Jack Noble
    The First Song Of Isaiah
    SATB   Keyboard (optional Guitar, Hand-
        bells, Percussion, Choral Movement)
    H. W. Gray (1976) CMR 3347

12:2-6
    Wyton, Alec
    Surely It is God Who Saves Me
    SATB   Organ
    Hinshaw (1977) HMC 259

12:3, 6   (adapted)
    Nystedt, Knut
    Cry Out And Shout
    SSATB   kro
    Summy Birchard (1956) 1574

12:4-6
    Pelz, Walter
    Offertory/Fifth Sunday of Easter (Verses
        and Offertories - Easter - Trinity)
    SATB   Organan
    Augsburg (1980) 11-9546

12:6
    Ludlow, Ben
    Cry Out And Shout!
    Speech Choir and Snare Drum
    Flammer (1973) A-5628

13:00
    Young, Gordon
    Shout Ye
    SATB   Organ
    H. W. Gray (1970) CMR 3104

16:5
    SEE: Luke 1:31-33
    Handl, Jacob (ed. Cyril F. Simkins)
    Ecce Concipies (Behold Thou Shalt Conceive)

16:5
    SEE: Luke 1:31-33
    Handl, Jacob
    Ecce Concipies (Arista)

19:7
    Thompson, Randall
    The Paper Reeds By The Brooks (The Peaceable
        Kingdom)
    SATB   kro
    E. C. Schirmer (1936) 1035

25:1, 4
    Roff, Joseph
    O Lord Thou Art My God
    SATB   Organ
    Concordia (1966) 98-1857

25:1-9   (Exodus 12:2)
    Sisler, Hampson A.
    Let Us Exalt Him
    SATB   Organ (optional Trumpet and
        Percussion)
    World Library (1974) CA 2115 (Parts IN 2118)

25:8-9
    Pelz, Walter
    Day Of Rejoicing
    SATB   Organ   Trumpet
    Augsburg (1969) 11-1561

25:9
    Beattie, Herbert
    Lo This Is Our God (part of Six Choral
        Settings)
    SAB   Optional Organ
    G. Schirmer (1954) 510

25:9
    Busarow, Donald
    Verse/21st Sunday After Pentecost (Verses
        and Offertories - Pentecost 21 - Christ
        The King)
    2 part   Organ
    Augsburg (1979) 11-9540

25:9
    Wienhorst, Richard
    We Have Waited For The Lord   (Three Verse
        Settings, Set 2)
    SATB   Handbells or Keyboard
    Concordia (1979) 98-2441

26:00
    Young, Gordon
    Thou Wilt Keep Him In Perfect Peace
    SATB   No accompaniment
    Hope (1973) A 458

26:1, 3   (Scottish Paraphrase of 1781)
    Tye, Christopher (ed. Gerald Knight)
    How Glorious Sion's Courts Appear
    SATB   Unaccompanied
    RSCM (1956) 210

26:1-3   (metrical)
    Tye, Christopher (ed. Gerald Knight)
    How Glorious Sion's Court Appear
    SATB   kro
    RSCM [Hinshaw] (1955) RSCM 508

26:1-4
Mueller, Carl F.
Confidence In God
SATB   Organ
Carl Fischer (1952) CM 6642

26:1-4, 7-8
Gardner, John
We Have A Strong City
SATB   Organ
Oxford (1966) A 215

26:3   (Isaiah 30:15)
Beebe, Hank
Whose Minds Are Stayed
SATB   Organ
Hindon [Hinshaw] (1981) HPC 7022

26:3
Buck, Dudley (ed. Elwyn Wienandt and Robert
   Young)
Thou Wilt Keep Him In Perfect Peace
SATB   Keyboard
J. Fischer (1970) FE 10012

26:3
SEE: I Chronicles 29:11
Simper, Caleb
Shout For Joy

26:3   (Psalm 139:11; I John 1:5; Psalm 119:
   175)
Walker, Robert
Thou Wilt Keep Him In Perfect Peace
SATB   No accompaniment
Novello (1975) MT 1584

26:3
Wesley, Samuel S. (ed. Don Hinshaw)
Thou Wilt Keep Him In Perfect Peace
SA(A)TTB   Organ
Hindon [Hinshaw] (1981) HMC 506

26:3   (Psalm 139:11;   I John 1:5; Psalm
   119:175)
Wesley, Samuel S.
Thou Wilt Keep Him In Perfect Peace
SATBB   Organ
Abingdon (1963) APM-278   (found in Select
   Anthems For Mixed Voices, Volume I)

26:3   (Psalm 139:11   I John 1:5;   Psalm
   119:175)
Wesley, Samuel S.
Thou Wilt Keep Him In Perfect Peace
SATTB   Organ
Novello (1960) 29.0152.08   (also found in
   Church Anthem Book; and Short and Easy
   Anthems, Volume 2)

26:3   (Psalm 139:11;   I John 1:5;   Psalm
   119:175)
Wesley, Samuel S. (arr. Basil Ramsey)
Thou Wilt Keep Him In Perfect Peace
SATB   Organ
Novello (1962) 29.0104.08

26:3   (Psalm 139:11;   I John 1:5)
Williams, C. Lee
Thou Wilt Keep Him In Perfect Peace
SATB   kro
Novello (1950) 29.0114.05

26:3   (Psalm 139:11;   I John 1:5)
Williams, C. Lee
Thou Wilt Keep Him In Perfect Peace
SATB   kro
Presser (n.d.) 312-14785

26:3-4
Franck, Rene
Thou Wilt Keep Him In Perfect Peace
SATB   Organ or Piano
Hope (1962) A-337

26:3, 4
Fryxell, Regina H.
Thou Wilt Keep Him
SATB   Organ
Abingdon (1961) APM-121

26:3, 4
Redman, Reginald
Thou Wilt Keep Him In Perfect Peace
SATB   kro
Novello (1948) (also found in Short and
   Easy Anthems, Set 1)

26:3, 4
Young, Gordon
Thou Wilt Keep Him In Perfect Peace
SATB   No accompaniment
Hope (1973) A 458

26:3-4
Wienhorst, Richard
Thou Wilt Keep Him In Perfect Peace
Unison   Keyboard
Concordia (1979) 98-2427

26:4, 8
Redman, Reginald
Thou Wilt Keep Him In Perfect Peace
SATB   No accompaniment
Novello (1948) MT 1251   (also found in The
   Novello Anthem Book)

26:9   (Psalm 51:1-3, 6-10, 12, 15, 17-18;
   Ezekiel 18:31;   Zechariah 12:1)
Yardumian, Richard
Create In Me A Clean Heart
SATB (A or B solos)   kro
H. W. Gray (1963) CMR 2797

27:1-5
Smith, Michael
In That Day
SATB (B-solo)   No accompaniment
E. C. Schirmer (1971) 2749

27:3   (Hebrew Text)
Silvester, Philip
Israel   (Hebrew/English)
SATB   kro
Boosey & Hawkes   (1963)   5492

28:00
Bryan, Charles
Give Ear And Hear My Voice
SATB   Organ
Leeds (1948) 1-184

30:5
SEE: Isaiah 26:3
Beebe, Hank
Whose Minds Are Stayed

30:29
Thompson, Randall
Ye Shall Have A Song (Peaceable Kingdom)
SSAATTBB   kro
E. C. Schirmer (1936) 1107

33:20-21 (Psalm 87:3;   Exodus 13:22)
Kauffman, Ronald (arr.)
Glorious Things Of Thee Are Spoken
SATB   Organ
Mark Foster (1982) MF 228

33:22
Herbst, Johannes (ed. Karl Kroeger)
The Lord Our Mighty Sov'reign (Der Herr ist
   unser Koenig) (English/German)
SATB   Keyboard
Boosey & Hawkes (1973) 5863

35:1-2
    Pooler, Frank
    The Desert Shall Rejoice
    SATB   kro
    Walton (1963) 2959

35:1-2
    SEE: Isaiah 40:1-3
    Thalben-Ball, George
    Comfort Ye, My People

35:1-2, 4-6, 8, 10
    Wesley, Samuel S.
    The Wilderness
    SATB   Organ
    Novello (n.d.) Reprinted by C. T. Wagner
        C-567907

35:1, 4, 8, 10
    Jennings, Arthur
    Springs In The Desert
    SATB (T-solo)   Organ
    H. W. Gray (1948) CMR 580

35:1-6
    SEE: Ecclesiasticus 38:4, 6, 9, 10, 12
    Harris, William
    Strengthen Ye The Weak Hands

35:4
    DiLasso, Orlando (ed. John Craig)
    Confortamini (Be Ye Comforted) (English/
        Latin)
    SATB   kro
    Concordia (1979) 98-2422

35:4
    Newbury, Kent A.
    Behold Your God Will Come
    SATB   kro
    G. Schirmer (1969) 11650

35:4
    Titcomb, Everett
    Say To Them That Are Of A Fearful Heart
    SATB   kro
    Carl Fischer (n.d.) CM 436

35:4-6
    Westra, Everet
    The Lord Your God Will Come
    SATB   Organ ad lib.
    Chantry (1965) n.#.

38:1-6
    Krenek, Ernst
    The Deliverence Of Hezekiah
    SSA   Piano
    Mobart (1976) M 103

38:17-19
    SEE: Isaiah 53:4-5
    Bender, Jan
    A Little Lenten Cantata

39:6-7
    Berger, Jean
    All Men Are Grass (from Two Laments, chorus
        #2)
    SATB   kro
    Carl Fischer (1975) CM 7930

40:00   (selected)
    Beck, John Ness
    Have Ye Not Known
    SATB   Piano or Organ
    Beckenhorst (1975) BP 1008

40:00   (Psalm 130; Psalm 127: Psalm 25)
    Beebe, Hank
    I Wait For The Lord
    2 part   Keyboard
    Hinshaw (1980) HPC 7017

40:00
    Bortniansky, Dimitri (arr. Hal Hopson)
    Comfort, All My People
    SSATB   kro
    Flammer (1980) A-5926

40:00   (Olearius)
    Goudimel, Claude
    Comfort, Comfort Ye My People
    SATB   kro
    Concordia (1968) (found in A First Motet
        Book, 97-4845)

40:1
    Bruckner, Anton (ed. Roger Crandville)
    Locus iste   (Latin/English)
    SATB   kro
    Choral Art (1960) R 154

40:1   (Isaiah 49:13)
    Davis, Katherine K.
    Comfort Ye
    SATB   Piano or Organ
    Galaxy (1962) 2226

40:1   (Isaiah 55:1, 6-7)
    Faure, Gabriel (arr. Hal H. Hopson)
    Comfort, All Ye My People
    SATB   Keyboard
    Carl Fischer (1977) CM 8017

40:1-3   (based on)
    Bunjes, Paul (setting by)
    Comfort, Comfort Ye My People
    SATB   Keyboard
    Concordia (1956) 98-1388

40:1-3   (Isaiah 35:1-2; Isaiah 51:3; and
        Longfellow)
    Thalben-Ball, George
    Comfort Ye, My People
    SATB (B-solo)   Organ
    Novello (1953) ANTH. 1311

40:1-4a, 5a
    Babcock, Samuel (ed. Mason Martens)
    Comfort Ye My People
    SATB   kro
    McAfee (1975) (found in Bicentennial
        Collection Of American Choral Music)

40:1-5   (Olearius)
    Bach, J. S.
    Comfort, Comfort Ye My People (from Cantata
        #13)
    SATB (A-solo)   Continuo with 2 violins
        and Viola
    Concordia (1970) 98-2045

40:1, 5
    Schütz, Heinrich (ed. C. Buell Agey)
    Trostet, Trostet mein Volk (Comfort Ye My
        People) (English/Latin)
    SSATTB   Organ or Piano
    G. Schirmer (1966) 11423

40:1-9
    Hall, Henry (ed. Percy Young)
    Comfort Ye, My People
    SSATTB (A-T-T-solos)   Organ
    Broude Brothers (1977) MGC 23

40:3
    SEE: Joel 2:1
    Guerrero, F.
    Canite Tuba

40:3
    SEE: Joel 2:1
    Palestrina, G. P.
    Canite Tuba

40:3
  Powell, Robert J.
  Prepare Ye The Way Of The Lord
  SAB   kro
  Abingdon (1966) APM-535 (found in Festival
  Anthems For SAB)

40:3-5
  Pote, Allen
  Prepare Ye The Way
  SATB (or 2 part)   Piano
  Carl Fischer (1978) CM 8066

40:3-5
  Stevens, Halsey
  The Way Of Jehovah
  SATB   Organ or Piano
  Mark Foster (1966) MF 110

40:3-9
  Wise, Michael
  Prepare Ye The Way Of The Lord
  SATB (S-A-T-solos)   Organ
  Novello (n.d.) ANTH. 151

40:4-5
  Beck, John Ness
  Every Valley
  SATB   Piano or Organ
  Beckenhorst (1976) BP-1040

40:5
  Handel, G. F.
  And The Glory Of The Lord (Messiah)
  SATB   Organ
  F. Harris (n.d.) HC 4039

40:5
  Handel, G. F.
  And The Glory Of The Lord (Messiah)
  SATB   Organ
  G. Schirmer (n.d.) 3829

40:5
  Handel, G. F. (ed. H. Watkins Shaw)
  And The Glory Of The Lord (Messiah)
  SATB   Keyboard
  Novello (n.d.) 29.0204.04

40:5
  Handel, G. F. (ed. Ivan Trusler)
  And The Glory Of The Lord (Messiah)
  SATB   Piano Or Organ
  Plymouth (1963) TR 120 (also found in
  Anthems For The Church Year, Volume 1)

40:6
  SEE: Psalm 104:14-15
  Browne, Richmond
  Chortos I

40:6-8
  Berger, Jean
  All Flesh Is Grass
  SATB   kro
  Augsburg (1965) 1419

40:6-8
  Bliem, William
  All Flesh Is Grass
  SATB   Organ or Piano
  Lawson Gould (1973) 51788

40:6-11
  Naylor, E. W.
  Vox Dicentis Clama (Hark A Voice Is
     Calling) (English/Latin)
  SATB   No accompaniment
  Curwen (1919) 80581

40:9 (Habakkuk 2:3;   Hebrew 10:39)
  Gieseke, Richard
  Climb To The Top Of The Highest Mountain
  SAB   No accompaniment
  Concordia (1978) 97-5481

40:9
  Handel, G. F. (arr. Ernest Willoughby)
  O Thou That Tellest (Messiah)
  SSAA   Piano or Organ
  Carl Fischer (1939) CM 547

40:9
  Stainer, John
  O Zion That Bringest Good Tidings
  SATB   Organ
  Novello (n.d.) 381

40:9-11 (based on)
  Pethel, Stan
  Lift Up Your Voice
  SATB   Brass (3 Trumpets, 3 Trombones)
  Broadman (1982) 4563-73

40:9-11, 28-29
  Titcomb, Everett
  Herald Of Good Tidings
  SATB   Organ, 2 Trumpets
  C. F. Peters (1964) 6653

40:22-23
  SEE: Psalm 104:14-15
  Browne, Richmond
  Chortos I

40:24
  SEE: Psalm 104:14-15
  Browne, Richmond
  Chortos I

40:28-29   (Isaiah 41:10)
  Foster, Will
  Fear Not I Am With Thee
  SATB (S-solo)   Organ
  G. Schirmer (1941) 8711

40:28-31
  Banner, David
  Isaiah 40:28-31
  SATB   Keyboard or Woodwinds (2 Flutes;
     2 Clarinets in B-flat; 2 Bass
     Clarinets)
  Broadman (1978) 4562-55

40:28-31
  Bitgood, Roberta
  They Shall Walk
  SATB   Keyboard
  Lorenz (1966) E 63

40:28-31
  Clayton, Harold
  They Shall Rise Up As Eagles
  SATB   kro
  World Library (1959)

40:28-31
  Doig, Don
  Have Ye Not Known?
  SATB   Keyboard
  Hope (1980) A 525

40:28-31
  Jones, David Hugh
  Hast Thou Not Known?
  SATB   kro
  Carl Fischer (1938) CM 512

40:28-31
  Lewis, John Leo
  Hast Thou Not Known?
  SATB   Piano or Organ
  Broadman (1965) 451-617

40:28-31
  Templeton, Alec
  Hast Thou Not Known
  SATB   Piano
  Choral Press (1953) n.#.

40:28-31
    Weatherseed, John J.
    They Shall Mount Up With Signs
    SATB   Organ
    F. Harris (1956) 2965

40:30
    Colvin, Herbert
    They That Wait Upon The Lord
    SATB   Accompanied
    Word (1981) CS 2996

40:30
    SEE: Psalm 63:1, 3-4
    Handel, G. F.
    Blest Are They Whose Spirit

40:31
    Berger, Jean
    They That Wait Upon The Lord
    SATB   kro
    Augsburg (1966) 1467

40:31
    Bruckner, Anton (ed. Roger Granville)
    O How Blessed   (English/Latin)
    SATB   kro
    Choral Art (1960) R 154

40:31
    Near, Gerald
    Then They Wait Upon The Lord
    SATB   Organ
    Calvary Press (1974) 1-005

40:31
    Nelson, Ronald A.
    They That Wait Upon The Lord
    SATB   Piano or Organ
    Abingdon (1968) APM-596

40:31   (Psalm 27:14)
    Roff, Joseph
    Wait On The Lord
    SATB   Accompnaied
    Concordia (1960) 98-1493

40:31
    Walter, Samuel
    They That Wait Upon The Lord
    SATB   kro
    C. C. Birchard (1955) 2102

40:31
    Ward, William
    They Shall Mount Up With Wings
    SATB   Piano or Organ
    World Library (1980) 7620-8

41:10   (Isaiah 43:1)
    Bach, J. S.
    Be Not Afraid   (English/German)
    SATB/SATB   Continuo
    C. F. Peters (1959) 6104

41:10
    Bach, J. S.
    Be Not Afraid
    SATB/SATB   Piano
    H. W. Gray (n.d.) 1842

41:10
    SEE: Isaiah 40:28-29
    Foster, Will
    Fear Not I Am With Thee

41:10
    SEE: Luke 2:14
    Proulx, R.
    Christmas Procession

41:13, 17-20   (Isaiah 42:10-12)
    Nystedt, Knut
    Listen To Me
    SATB   No accompaniment
    Augsburg (1979) 11-0569

42:10-12
    Newbury, Kent A.
    Sing To The Lord A New Song
    SATB   kro
    Shawnee (1970) A-1032

42:10-12
    SEE: Isaiah 41:13, 17-20
    Nystedt, Knut
    Listen To Me

43:1
    SEE: Isaiah 41:10
    Bach, J. S.
    Be Not Afraid

44:2   (and other)
    Nystedt, Knut
    Thus Saith The Lord   (Three Motets)
    SATB   kro
    Augsburg (1958)

44:21-23
    Mathews, Peter
    Remember These Things
    SATB   Organ
    H. W. Gray (1980) GCMR 3432

44:22-24
    Beebe, Hank
    The Lord Hath Done It
    SATB   Keyboard
    Hindon [Hinshaw] (1981) HPC 7023

45:5-8
    Lekberg, Sven
    There Is No God Beside Me
    SATB   Keyboard
    Broadman (1964) 453-759

45:8   (Psalm 85:1)
    Byrd, William
    Rorate Caeli Desuper   (Drop Down Ye Heavens)
        (Latin/English)
    SAATB   kro
    Oxford (1972) TCM 31

45:8
    Guerrero, Francisco
    Rorate Caeli   (Latin only)
    SATB   kro
    J. & W. Chester (1977) JWC 55110   (found in
    Sixth Chester Book Of Motets)

45:8   (Psalm 85:10-11)
    Statham, Heathcote
    Drop, Down Ye Heavens
    2 part   Organ
    Oxford   (found in Oxford Easy Anthem Book)

45:8a   (Psalm 19:1)
    Cassler, G. Winston
    Drop Down Ye Heavens From Above
    SATB   kro
    Augsburg (1963) ACL 1342

48:10   (Isaiah 66:13; and other)
    Mechem, Kirke
    A Song Of Comfort   (from Songs Of Wisdom)
    SATB   kro
    E. C. Schirmer (1970) 2740

48:18
    SEE: Isaiah 54:10
    Wagner, Douglas
    For The Mountains Shall Depart

48:20b
  SEE: Psalm 66:1-2
  Jennings, Kenneth
  With A Voice Of Singing

49:00
  Diemer, Emma Lou
  Sing, O Heavens
  SATB   kro
  Carl Fischer (1975) CM 7923

49:3
  Johnson, David N.
  Verse/Epiphany II (Verses and Offertories -
      Epiphany II - The Transfiguration Of
      Our Lord)
  Unison   Organ
  Augsburg (1980) 11-9544

49:8-10
  Neff, James
  In An Acceptable Time
  SATB   kro
  Augsburg (1966) 1472

49:10
  Effinger, Cecil
  By The Springs Of Water
  SATB   Organ
  Augsburg (1975) 11-1747

49:13
  SEE: Isaiah 40:1
  Davis, Katherin K.
  Comfort Ye

49:13
  Tanner, J. Pater
  Sing For Joy
  SATB   Organ
  Lawson Gould (1966) LG 51266

49:13
  Warland, Dale
  O Be Joyful O Earth
  SATB   No accompaniment
  Augsburg (1963) ACL 1348

49:13   (Isaiah 51:3)
  Webber, Lloyd
  Sing, O Heaven
  SAB   Organ
  Novello (1957) MT 1372

49:13-15
  Amner, John
  Sing O Heavens
  SSAATBB   Keyboard
  Oxford (1969) A 270

49:13-15
  Roff, Joseph
  Sing For Joy O Heavens
  SATB   Organ or Piano
  Associated (1964) A 417

49:14-16
  Hammerschmidt, Andreas (ed. & arr. Walter
      Ehret)
  Zion Said
  SSATB   kro
  Abingdon (1974) APM-538

49:14-16
  Hammerschmidt, Andreas (ed. Theo. Hoelty-
      Nickel)
  Zion's Lament
  SSATB   kro
  Concordia (1960) 98-1487

49:14-16
  Schein, Johann H. (ed. John Scholten)
  Zion Speaks, I Am By God Forsaken
  SSATB   kro
  Concordia (1967) 98-1894

50:21
  Thompson, Randall
  Have Ye Now Known   (Peaceable Kingdom)
  SATB   kro
  E. C. Schirmer (1936) 1107

51:3
  SEE: Isaiah 40:1-3
  Thalben-Ball, George
  Comfort Ye My People

51:3
  SEE: Isaiah 49:13
  Webber, Lloyd
  Sing O Heaven

51:9-11
  Naylor, Bernard
  Easter Day
  SSATB   No accompaniment
  Novello (1960) 1398

51:9-11
  Warren, Elinor Remick
  Awake Put On Strength
  SATB   Organ
  Concordia (1967) 98-1875

52:00   (adapted)
  Moe, Daniel
  How Beautiful Upon The Mountains
  SAB   kro
  Presser (1955) 312-40230

52:1
  Powell, Robert J.
  Awake, Put On Thy Strength
  SAB   kro
  Abingdon (1966) APM-535   (found in Festival
      Anthems For SAB)

52:1-2, 7
  Wise, Michael   (ed. Giles Bryant)
  Awake, Awake, Put On Thy Strength
  SATB   Organ
  Leeds (Canada)   (1968) #3

52:1, 8   (adapted)
  Yardumian, Richard (Harmonized)
  Awake, Awake! Put On Thy Strength
  SATB   No accompaniment
  Elkan Vogel (1978) 362.03280

52:7
  Antes, John (ed. Ewald Nolte)
  How Beautiful Upon The Mountains
  SATB   Organ (Orchestra parts on rental)
  Boosey & Hawkes (1968) 5677

52:7
  Berger, Jean
  Quam Pulchri super Montes   (Latin)
  SATB   kro
  Concordia (1959) 98-1477

52:7
  Bradbury, William (ed. Leonard Van Camp)
  How Beautiful Upon The Mountains
  SATB   Keyboard
  Mark Foster (1977) MF 171

52:7
  Butler, Eugene
  How Beautiful Upon The Mountains
  SATB   Keyboard
  Carl Fischer (1981) CM 8130

52:7
  Carter, John
  How Beautiful Upon The Mountains
  SA or TB   Keyboard
  Hinshaw (1977) HMC 239

52:7
Handel, G. F.
How Beautiful Are The Feet Of Him (Messiah)
TTBB   Organ
E. C. Schirmer (1952) 912

52:7
Handel, G. F.
How Beautiful Are The Feet Of Him (Messiah)
SA   Organ
E. C. Schirmer (1952) 1834

52:7
Handel, G. F.
How Beautiful Are The Feet Of Him (Messiah)
SATB   Organ
E. C. Schirmer (1952) 1129 (also found in
Concord Anthem Book - Red)

52:7
Hillert, Richard
Verse/Common of Apostles, Evangelists
(Verses and Offertories - Lesser
Festivals)
Unison   Organ
Augsburg (1980) 11-9542

52:7
Jones, David Hugh
How Beautiful Upon The Mountains
TTBB   No accompaniment
C. C. Birchard (1950) 1541

52:7
Jones, David Hugh
How Beautiful Upon The Mountains
SATB   kro
Carl Fischer (1937) CM 491

52:7
Lora, Antonio
The Lord Shall Bless His People With Peace
SATB   Piano
Boosey & Hawkes (1964) 5562

52:7
Stainer, John
How Beautiful Upon The Mountains (from Awake,
Put On Thy Strength, O Zion)
SATB   Organ
Novello (n.d.) 29.0314.08 (also found in
Short And Easy Anthems, Set I)

52:7
SEE: Isaiah 61:1-4
Toolan, S.
Great Is The Lord

52:7-8
Moe, Daniel
How Beautiful Upon The Mountains
SAB   kro
Presser (1955) 312.40230

52:8 (based on)
SEE: Matthew 25:1-13
Nicolai, Philip (setting by Ludwig Lenel)
Wake, Awake For Night Is Flying

52:9 (adapted)
Yardumian, Richard (Harmonized)
Break Forth In Joy (from Eleven Easter
Chorales)
SATB   No accompaniment
Elkan Vogel (1978) 362.03280

52:13-15
Naylord, Bernard
Good Friday
SSATB   No accompaniment
Novello (1960) 1397

53:1-5 (adapted)
Yardumian, Richard (Harmonized)
Who Hath Believed Our Report (from Eleven
Easter Chorales)
SATB   No accompaniment
Elkan Vogel (1978) 362-03280

53:3
SEE: Song Of Songs 8:10
Gregor, Christian (ed. E. Nolte)
Lord In Thy Presence

53:3
Handel, G. F. (arr. Joyce Barthelson)
He Was Despised
SATB   Piano or Organ
Lawson Gould (1959) 814

53:3
Laverty, John Timothy
He Was Despised (Trilogy On The Passion Of
Christ)
SAB   Keyboard
Broadman (1967) 451-767

53:3
Stanton, Royal
He Was Despised
SATB   kro
Walton (1961) 2023

53:3-4 (John 14:6)
Hunnicutt, Judy
Surely He Has Borne Our Griefs
SATB   Keyboard
Augsburg (1971) 11-1643

53:3-5
Pooler, Frank
Man Of Sorrows
SAB   Optional Accompaniment
Augsburg (1950) 1082

53:3-10
Beebe, Hank
Isaiah's Song
2 part mixed   Keyboard
Pembroke [Carl Fischer] (1979) PC 1017

53:4
Graun, K. H. (ed. W. Buszin)
Surely He Hath Borne Our Griefs
SATB   kro
Concordia (1956) 98-1171

53:4
Graun, C. Heinrich (ed. Walter Ehret)
Surely He Hath Borne Our Griefs
SATB   kro
Lawson Gould (1956) 661

53:4
Laverty, John Timothy
Surely He Hath Borne Our Griefs (Trilogy
On The Passion Of Christ)
SAB   Keyboard
Broadman (1967) 451-767

53:4
Lotti, Antonio
Surely He Hath Borne Our Griefs
SATB   kro
E. C. Schirmer (1952) 136 (also found in
Concord Anthem Book - Red)

53:4
Lotti, Antonio (ed. Hunter)
Surely He Hath Borne Our Griefs (English/
Latin)
TTB   No accompaniment
Marks   #4458

53:4
Salathiel, Lyndon
Surely He Hath Borne Our Griefs
SATB   Optional Accompaniment
G. Schirmer (1959) 10651

53:4a
Victoria, T. (ed. Martin Banner)
Truly He Hath Borne Our Griefs (Latin)
SATB   Optional Accompaniment
Lawson Gould (1979) LA 52021

53:4-5
Antes, John (arr. C. Dickinson)
Go Congregation Go
SATB (S or T solo)   Organ
H. W. Gray (1954) MCM 6

53:4-5
Antes, John
Surely He Hath Borne Our Griefs (Go Con-
    gregation Go!)
SATB   Organ
Boosey & Hawkes (1959) 5303

53:4-5 (Isaiah 38:17-19;   Psalm 32:1-2;
        I John 1:8)
Bender, Jan
A Little Lenten Cantata, Op. 82
SATB   Organ (optional congregation)
Concordia (1981) 97-5672

53:4-5
Bender, Jan
Surely He Hath Borne Our Griefs
SS   Keyboard
Concordia (1959) 98-1640

53:4-5
Handel, G. F.
Surely He Hath Borne Our Griefs (Messiah)
SATB   Keyboard
Carl Fischer (1970) CM 518

53:4-5
Handel, G. F. (arr. Loy L. Beeal)
Surely He Hath Borne Our Griefs (Messiah)
SACB   Piano
Cambiata Press (1972) M 97201

53:4-5
Handel, G. F. (ed. T. Tertius Noble)
Surely He Hath Borne Our Griefs
SATB   Piano
G. Schirmer (1940) 6598

53:4-5
Hillert, Richard
Surely He Has Borne Our Griefs
SATB   No accompaniment
Concordia (1962) 98-1597 (also found in
    A First Motet Book, 97-4845)

53:4-5
SEE: Lamentations 1:12
Leo, Leonardo (ed. Denys Darlow)
Ecce Vidimus Eum

53:4-5
Leo, Leonard (ed. Paul Thomas)
Surely He Hath Borne Our Griefs
SA   Keyboard
Concordia (found in Second Morning Star
    Choir Book, 97-4702)

53:4-5
Nelson, Ronald A.
Surely He Hath Borne Our Griefs (Introits
    For Lent and Easter)
SAB   kro
Abingdon (1967) APM 598

53:4-5
Newbury, Kent A.
Surely He Hath Borne Our Griefs
SATB   kro
G. Schirmer (1966) 11349

53:4-5
Vittoria, Tomas
Surely He Bore Our Sorrows (Vere
    Languores)
SATB   No accompaniment
E. C. Schirmer (1943) 2217

53:4-5
Victoria, Tomas
Vere Languores Nostros (Latin)
SATB   No accompaniment
Arista (1978) AE 359

53:4-5
Victoria, Tomas (ed. Maynard Klein)
Vere Languores Nostros (Latin/English)
SATB   kro
G. Schirmer (1974) 12004

53:4-5
Victoria, Tomas (ed. Kurt Schindler)
Vere Languores (Surely He Hath Borne Our
    Griefs)
SATB   kro
Presser (1919) 332-13380

53:4-5
SEE: Matthew 1:29
Willan, Healey
Behold The Lamb Of God

53:4-6
Devidal, David
Surely He Bore Our Griefs
2 part mixed   Keyboard
Gentry (1970) G 129

53:4-6
Franck, Melchior
Fürwahr er trug unsre Krankheit
SATB   No accompaniment
Merseburger (1977) (found in Motetten
    Alter Meister)

53:4-6
Handel, G. F. (arr. & ed. Ivan Trusler)
Surely He Hath Borne Our Griefs
SATB   Organ or Piano
Plymouth (1963) (also found in Anthems
    For The Church Year, Volume 1)

53:4-6 (Lamentations 1:12;   Psalm 38:21-22)
Pasquet, Jean
A Lenten Meditation
SATB   Organ
H. W. Gray (1948) 2052

53:4-6
Willan, Healey
Surely He Hath Borne Our Griefs
SA   Keyboard
Concordia (1962) 97-1769 (also found in
    We Praise Thee, Volume 2, 97-7160)

53:4-6
Willan, Healey (arr. Dale Wood)
Surely He Hath Borne Our Griefs
SATB   Organ
Concordia (1981) 98-2520

53:5
Handel, G. F.
And With His Stripes We Are Healed
SATB   Piano
Carl Fischer (1938) CM 519

53:5
Laverty, John Timothy
He Was Wounded For Our Transgressions (from
    Trilogy On The Passion Of Christ)
SAB   Keyboard
Broadman (1967) 451-767

53:6
Handel, G. F.
All We Like Sheep Have Gone Astray (Messiah)
SATB   Keyboard
Carl Fischer (1938) CM 520

53:6
Handel, G. F. (ed. T. Tertius Noble)
All We Like Sheep (Messiah)
SATB   Piano
G. Schirmer (1912) 10235

53:6-7
Roff, Joseph
He Opened Not His Mouth
SATB   Organ
Concordia (1978) 98-2406

53:7-8
SEE: Isaiah 57:1
Ingegneri, Marc (ed. A. Payson)
See Then How The Holy Man Dieth

53:9-10
Simper, Caleb
Break Forth Into Joy
SATB   Organ
Boston Music (1910) 10792 (also found in
    The Parishional Choir, Volume 2)

53:10
Jaeschke, Christian David (ed. Karl Kroeger)
The Redeemed Of The Lord (English/German)
SATB   Organ
Boosey & Hawkes (1980) 6032

54:4-5
Victoria, Thomas L. (ed. Kurt Schindler)
Vere Languores (Surely He Hath Borne Our
    Griefs)
SATB   kro
Oliver Ditson (1919) 332-13380

54:6-7, 10
Beebe, Hank
For The Mountains Shall Depart
SATB (S-solo)   Keyboard
K. M. Music (1976) (found in Lord Make My
    Life A Window)

54:7-8
Yeakle, Thomas
For A Small Moment
SATB (B or A solo)   Organ
H. W. Gray (1974) CMR 3310

54:10
Sateren, Leland
The Abiding Presence
SATB   kro
Sacred Designs (1960) SD 6008

54:10 (Isaiah 48:18; Psalm 23:4)
Wagner, Douglas
For The Mountains Shall Depart
Unison   Keyboard
Augsburg (1980) 11-1962

54:13-14
SEE: Genesis 28:16-17
Fannon, David Stephen
Surely The Lord Is In This Place

55:1
Benion, Sebastian (ed. Martin Ellis)
Ho, Everyone That Thirsteth
SATB   Organ
Novello (1980) (found in Into His Courts
    With Praise)

55:1
Victoria, Tomas (ed. Pahissa-Vene)
Sitientes, Venite Ad Aquas (Latin/English)
SATB   kro
Ricordi (1957) NY 1854

55:1-2
Pulkingham, Betty Carr
Ho! Everyone That Thirsteth
SATB   Piano or Guitar
GIA (1972) G-1777

55:1-3, 7, 12-13
Martin, George
Ho! Everyone That Thirsteth
SATB (B-solo)   Organ
H. W. Gray (n.d.) 246

55:1-3, 11, 12   (Isaiah 58:11)
Sateren, Leland
You Shall Go Out In Joy
SATB   No accompaniment
Augsburg (1979) 11-0576

55:1, 6-7
SEE: Isaiah 40:1
Faure, Gabriel (ed. Hal H. Hopson)
Comfort, All Ye My People

55:3
Graun, Karl (ed. James Wilson)
He Was Despised
SATB   Organ
G. Schirmer (1966) 11391

55:3
Graun, Karl (ed. Arthur Hilton)
He Was Despised
SAB   Piano or Organ
Presser (1961) 352-00400

55:3
Graun, Karl (ed. Arthur Hilton)
He Was Despised
SAB   Piano or Organ
Presser (1961) MC 398

53:3
SEE: Song Of Songs 8:10
Gregor, Christian (ed. E. Nolte)
Lord In Thy Presence

55:3, 6, 9-11
SEE: John 1:14a
Wetzler, Robert
As The Rain And Snow From Heaven

55:6
Wetzler, Robert
Seek Ye The Lord
SATB   kro
Augsburg (1965) 1457

55:6-7
Bradbury, William B.
Seek Ye The Lord
SATB   Keyboard
McAfee (1975) (found in Bicentennial
    Collection Of American Choral Music)

55:6-7
Burns, William K.
Seek Ye The Lord
2 part mixed   Piano or Organ
Hope (1972) CF 144

55:6-7
Burroughs, Bob
Seek Ye The Lord
SATB   Piano
Sacred Music (1972) S-130

55:6-7
    Butler, Eugene
    Seek Ye The Lord
    SATB   Accompaniment ad lib.
    Flammer (1967) A-5063

55:6-7
    Nelson, Ronald A.
    Seek The Lord While He May Be Found
    SS   Organ
    Augsburg (1969) (found in Music For The
        Contemporary Choir, Volume 1)

55:6-7
    Roberts, J. Varley
    Seek Ye The Lord
    SATB (T-solo)   Organ
    Augsburg (1946) 1030

55:6-7
    Roberts, J. V.
    Seek Ye The Lord
    SATB (T-solo)   Organ
    Carl Fischer (1923) CM 143

55:6-7
    Roberts, J. Varley (ed. Noble Cain)
    Seek Ye The Lord
    SATB & Junior Choir   Organ
    Flammer (1955) 84457

55:6-7
    Roberts, J. Varley
    Seek Ye The Lord
    SATB (T-solo)   Organ
    G. Schirmer (n.d.) 3731

55:6-7
    Roberts, J. Varley
    Seek Ye The Lord
    SATB (T-solo)   Organ
    Novello (n.d.) 29.0112.09

55:6-7
    Roberts, J. Varley
    Seek Ye The Lord
    SATB (T-solo) Organ
    Presser (n.d.) 6245

55:6-7
    Roberts, J. Varley (ed. James McKelvy)
    Seek Ye The Lord
    SATB (T-solo)   Organ
    Mark Foster (1982) MF 227

55:6-7
    Young, Gordon
    Seek Ye The Lord
    SATB   kro
    Presser (1977) 312-41172

55:6-11
    Hall, Bradley
    Seek The Lord
    SATB   Organ
    Lawson Gould (1977) 51944

55:6-12
    Nystedt, Knut
    Seek Ye The Lord
    SSAA   No accompaniment
    Walton (1974) n.#.

55:8, 10-11
    Beck, John Ness
    As The Rain
    SATB   Organ or Piano
    Beckenhorst (1975) BP 1018

55:10-11
    Hopson, Hal
    For As The Rain And Snow Come Down
    SATB   kro
    Sacred Music (1980) S-254

55:10-13
    Lekberg, Sven
    For As The Rain Cometh Down
    SATB   kro
    G. Schirmer (1967) 11509

55:12   (Psalm 28:7)
    Diemer, Emma Lou
    For Ye Shall Go Out With Joy
    SATB   Piano
    Eastman School of Music [Carl Fischer]
        (1968) n.#.

55:12
    Hunnicutt, Judy
    Sing With Joy!
    Unison   Organ
    GIA (1980) G-2285

55:12
    Newbury, Kent A.
    For You Shall Go Out In Joy
    SATB   Piano
    G. Schirmer (1969) 11615

55:12
    Saliers, Donald E.
    Go In Joy
    4 groups   Rhythm Instruments
    Agape [Hope] (1980) (found in Choirbook For
        Saints and Sinners)

55:12-13
    Beebe, Hank
    Go Out With Joy
    SATB or Unison   Keyboard
    Hinshaw (1975) HMC 117

56:6-7
    Kohn, Karl
    Also The Sons
    SATB (S-A-T-B-solos)   Keyboard 4-hands
    Carl Fischer (1976) CM 7994

56:7   (Haggai 2:9)
    Howells, Herbert
    Coventry Antiphon
    SATB   Organ
    Novello (1962) 1420

57:1   (Isaiah 53:7-8)
    Ingegneri, Marc (ed. Arnold Payson)
    See Then, How The Holy Man Dieth (English/
        Latin)
    SATB   kro
    Franck (1963) F 447

57:1-2   (Psalm 75:3)
    Handl, Jacob
    Ecce Quomodo Moritur Justus   (Latin)
    SATB   No accompaniment
    Arista (1976) AE 283

57:1-2   (Psalm 76:2)
    Handl, Jacob
    Ecce Quomodo Moritur (English/Latin)
    SATB   kro
    E. C. Schirmer (1976) 2977 (also found in
        The Renaissance Singer)

57:1-2
    Handl, Jacob (Gallus)
    Ecce Quomodo Moritur Justus (Latin only)
    SATB   No accompaniment
    Oxford (1971) A 282

57:1-2
    Handl, Jacob (ed. Wallace Gillman)
    The Righteous Perisheth
    SATB   Organ
    Wallace (1966) 4009

57:1-2
    Krieger, Johann P. (ed. James Erb)
    For The Righteous Shall Be Swept Away From
        Misfortune   (English/German)
    SATB   Organ (optional strings)
    Lawson Gould (1957) 674

57:1-2
    Staden, Johann
    Die Gerechten werden Weggekrafft (German)
    SATB   No accompaniment
    Merseburger (1977)   (found in Motetten
        Alter Meister)

57:15 (Lamentations 4:2)
    Herbst, Johannes (ed. & arr. Karl Kroeger)
    Listen All Who Enter These Portals
    SATB   Keyboard
    Boosey & Hawkes (1974) 5889

58:00 (paraphrase)
    Darst, W. Glen
    A Lenten Carol
    Unison mixed   Organ
    H. W. Gray (1943) CMR 1847

58:1, 8   (Isaiah 60:18, 20)
    Beck, John Ness
    Cry Aloud (from Three Prophecies Of
        Isaiah)
    SATB   kro
    General Words & Music (1971) GC 24

58:5-8
    Brandon, George (arr.)
    True Fasting
    2 part mixed   Keyboard
    Abingdon (1968) APM 522

58:11
    SEE: Isaiah 55:1-3, 11-12
    Sateren, Leland
    You Shall Go Out In Joy

58:11-12
    SEE: Psalm 102: 25-27
    deTar, Gernon
    The Glory Of The Lord

59:20
    Beck, Theodore (arranger)
    Oh Come Oh Come Emmanuel
    SA   Organ
    Concordia (1975) (found in Seven Anthems
        For Treble Choir, Set II, 97-5163)

60:00
    Mathias, William
    Arise, Shine, For Your Light Has Come,
        Op 77, #2
    SATB   Organ
    Oxford (1978) A 327

60:1
    Byrd, William
    Surge Illuminare (Arise Shine Forth In
        Splendour) (Latin/English)
    SATB   kro
    Novello (n.d.) TM 6

60:1
    SEE: Isaiah 9:2
    Gieseke, Richard W.
    The People Who Walked In Darkness

60:1
    Martens, Edmund
    Behold The Lord Has Come (from Four
        Introits, Set II)
    Unison   Handbells
    Concordia (1979) 97-5467

60:1 (Matthew 2:2)
    Wetzler, Robert
    Offertory/Epiphany (Verses and Offertories -
        Advent I - The Baptism Of Our Lord)
    SATB   Organ
    Augsburg (1979) 11-9541

60:1 (Psalm 117)
    Willan, Healey
    Arise, Shine, For Thy Light Is Come
    SATB   Organ
    Concordia (1960) 98-1508

60:1-2
    Berger, Jean
    Arise, Shine
    SATB   kro
    Tetra [Alexander Broude] (1980) AB 901

60:1-3
    Elvey, George J.
    Arise, Shine For Thy Light Is Come
    SATB   Organ
    Novello (1951) (found in Short And Easy
        Anthems, Set 2)

60:1-3
    Jennings, Kenneth
    Arise, Shine, For Thy Light Has Come
    SATB   kro
    Augsburg (1967) ACL-1498

60:1-3
    Naylor, Bernard
    Epiphany (Nine Motets)
    SSATB   No accompaniment
    Novello (1960) 1395

60:1-3
    Nelson, Ronald A.
    For Your Light Has Come
    SATB   2 Trumpets and Cymbal (No
        accompaniment)
    Augsburg (1972) 11-1641

60:1, 3
    Ossewaarde, Jack
    Arise, Shine (Two Short Motets Or Introits)
    SATB   kro
    H. W. Gray (1965) CMR 2894

60:1-3
    Yardumian, Richard (Harmonized)
    Arise, Shine, Thy Light Is Come (Eleven
        Easter Chorales)
    SATB   No accompaniment
    Elkan Vogel (1978) 362-03280

60:1-3, 19   (Isaiah 61:10)
    Greene, Maurice (ed. C. Hylton Stewart)
    Arise, Shine, O Zion
    SATB   Organ
    Oxford (1952) C 7

60:1, 6b
    Powell, Robert J.
    All They From Saba Shall Come
    SATB/SATB   No accompaniment
    Concordia (1965) 98-1781

60:3
    SEE: Isaiah 9:2
    Couper, Alinda
    Those Who Dwell In A Land Of Darkness
        (Festival Introits)

60:3 (William Hurn)
    Pelz, Walter L.
    Arise, O God And Shine
    SATB   Organ
    Concordia (1964) 98-1718

60:3 (William Hurn)
     Wolff, S. Drummond
     Arise, O God And Shine (based on Darwall's
         148th)
     SATB   Organ   Solo Trumpet
     Concordia (1975) 98-2227

60:3, 19
     Greene, Maurice (transcribed and edited
         Christopher Dearnley)
     The Gentiles Shall Come (from Arise!
         Shine, O Zion)
     Unison   Organ
     RSCM (n.d.) 237

60:6
     Gallus, Jacobus (ed. Matthew Lundquist)
     All They From Saba
     SATTB   kro
     Willis (1939) 5797

60:6
     Handl, Jacob
     All They From Saba
     SATTB   kro
     Bosworth (1907) #3

60:6
     Handl, Jacob
     Omnes De Saba   (Latin)
     SATTB   No accompaniment
     Arista (1969) AE 147

60:6
     Handl, Jacob
     Omnes De Saba Venient
     SATTB   Organ
     E. C. Schirmer (1971) 2783

60:6 (translated 1879 by John, Marquess of
         Bude)
     Handel, Jacob
     Omnes De Saba Venient   (Latin)
     SATTB   No accompaniment
     Oxford (1974) A 302

60:6
     Sowerby, Leo
     All They From Saba Shall Come
     SATB (T-solo)   Organ
     H. W. Gray (1962) 1298

60:18
     SEE: Genesis 28:16-17
     Fannon, Daniel S.
     Surely The Lord Is In This Place

60:18, 20
     SEE: Isaiah 58:1, 8
     Beck, John Ness
     Cry Aloud

60:19
     Greene, Maurice
     The Sun Shall Be No More Thy Light
     Unison   Keyboard
     Concordia (found in Third Morning Star
         Choir Book, 97-4972)

60:19
     Greene, Maurice (ed. Richard Graves)
     The Sun Shall Be No More
     Unison   Piano
     Curwen [G. Schirmer] (1951) 72195

60:19
     SEE: Exodus 33:14
     Haan, Raymond H.
     My Presence Shall Go With Thee

60:20 (John 8:12;   Matthew 28:1, 5-6;
         Revelation 21:3, 10, 23-25)
     Gore, Richard T.
     The Sun Shall No More Go Down
     SATB   Organ
     J. Fischer (1954) 8782

61:1-3, 11
     SEE: Psalm 72:12
     Parry, C. Hubert
     He Delivered The Poor

61:1-4 (Isaiah 52:7)
     Toolan, Suzanne
     Great Is The Lord
     SATB   Organ and 2 Trumpets
     GIA (1966) G 2134

61:1-4, 11 (Luke 4:18-19)
     Elgar, Edward
     The Spirit Of The Lord Is Upon Me
     SATB   Piano or Organ
     Novello (1931) 29.0216.08

61:1, 6, 8 (John 20:22)
     Clokey, Joseph
     Men Of God
     SATB   Organ
     J. Fischer (1958) 9078

61:10
     SEE: Isaiah 60:1-3. 19
     Greene, Maurice (ed. C. Hylton Stewart)
     Arise, Shine, O Zion

61:10
     Rottermund, Donald
     I Will Greatly Rejoice
     SATB   No accompaniment
     Concordia (1967) 98-1877

61:10
     Van Vleck, Jacob (ed. & arr. Karl Kroeger)
     I Will Rejoice In The Lord
     SSAA   Piano
     Carl Fischer (1976) CM 7956

61:10-11
     Butler, Eugene
     I Will Greatly Rejoice
     SATB   Keyboard
     Carl Fischer (1980) CM 8118

61:10-11
     Joubert, John
     Let Me Rejoice, op. 94
     SATB   Organ
     Addington Press (1980) AP 209

61:10-11
     McLaughlin, Marian
     I Will Greatly Rejoice
     SSA   Organ
     J. Fischer (1974) FEC 10118

61:10-11
     Nystedt, Knut
     I Will Greatly Rejoice
     SATB   kro
     Hinshaw (1977) HMC 226

61:10-11
     Peck, Richard
     I Will Greatly Rejoice
     SATB (A or B solo)   Organ
     H. W. Gray (1981) GCMR 3441

61:10-11
     Young, Gordon
     A Canticle Of Celebration
     SATB   Organ   (optional brass)
     Carl Fischer (1972) CM 7792

61:11
    Wells, Dana F.
    Anthem For Springtime
    SATB   Organ
    Abingdon (1965) APM-501

61:11b
    SEE: John 1:1, 14a
    Wetzler, Robert
    As The Rain And Snow From Heaven

62:1, 6, 10-11 (paraphrase of J. Quarles)
    Brandon, George (arr.)
    Prepare The Way!
    SAB or SATB   Keyboard
    Concordia (1976) 98-2269

62:2
    SEE: Malachi 1:11
    West, John E.
    In Every Place Incense Shall Be Offered Up

63:00   (adapted)
    Sisler, Hampson C.
    Who Is This That Cometh
    SATB   Organ
    World Library (1974) CA 2116-8

63:7
    Antes, John (ed. Donald McCorkle)
    I Will Mention The Loving Kindness
    SA   Organ or Piano
    Boosey & Hawkes (1963) 5485

63:15
    Battishill, Jonathan (ed. Watkins Shaw)
    O Lord, Look Down From Heaven
    SATB   Organ
    Novello (1968) NECM 1

63:15
    Battishill, Jonathan
    O Lord, Look Down From Heaven
    SATB   Organ
    Novello (n.d.) ANTH 184

63:15
    SEE: Nehemiah 9:5-6
    Bliss, Arthur
    Stand Up And Bless The Lord

64:6-7
    Sateren, Leland
    None Call Upon Thy Name
    SATB   kro
    Augsburg (1948) 1061

64:9
    Byrd, William
    Ne Irascaris (O Lord Turn Thy Wrath)
        (English/Latin)
    SATTB   Organ
    Blandford Press [Alexander Broude] (1965)
        AB 216

65:13, 18 (based on)
    Geisler, Johann (ed. & arr. E. V. Nolte)
    Thus Saith The Lord (So Spricht der Herr)
        (English/German)
    SSTT   Organ
    Boosey & Hawkes (1965) 5604

65:14
    SEE: Isaiah 3:10-11
    Thompson, Randall
    Say Ye To The Righteous (from Peaceable
        Kingdom)

65:25   (Micah 4:4)
    Davidson, Charles
    Anthem For Peace
    SATB   Piano ad lib.
    Beekman (1967) MC 540

66:13   (and other)
    SEE: Isaiah 48:10
    Mechem, Kirke
    A Song Of Comfort (from Songs Of Wisdom)

71:1-3
    Marshall, Jane
    In Thee, O Lord
    SATB   No accompaniment
    Augsburg (1980) 11-0686

J E R E M I A H

4:00   (and other)
    Spicker, Max
    Fear Not, O Israel
    SATB (S-A-T-B-solos)   Organ
    G. Schirmer (1927) 4004

6:16
    Dett, R. Nathaniel
    Ask For The Old Paths
    SATB (T-solo)   kro
    Mills (1941) RD 1

7:14
    SEE: Psalm 6:3
    Victoria, Tomas
    Miserere mei Domine

8:9
    Sateren, Leland
    The Word Rejected
    SATB   kro
    Augsburg (1950) 1084

8:22
    Brandon, George (arr.)
    There Is A Balm In Gilead
    SAB   Organ ad lib.
    Hope (1964) A 362

8:22
    Davis, Frederick (arr.)
    There Is A Balm In Gilead
    SATB   kro
    Gentry [Presser] (1974) G-234

8:22
    Dawson, William
    There Is A Balm In Gilead
    SATB (S-solo)   kro
    Tuskegee Institute (1967) 105

8:22
    Owens, Sam Batt
    There Is A Balm In Gilead
    TTBB (A-solo)   No accompaniment
    Augsburg (1979) 11-1898

8:22
    Shaffer, Jeanne (arr.)
    Balm In Gilead
    SATB   Keyboard
    Broadman (1953) 4532-19

8:22
    Spiritual (arr. Irvin Cooper)
    Balm In Gilead
    SCB   Piano
    Cambiata Press (1978) 1978102

8:22
    Spiritual (arr. C. Harry Causey)
    There Is A Balm In Gilead
    SATB   Accompaniment
    AMSI (1979) 360

8:22
    Spiritual (arr. George Kemmer)
    There Is A Balm In Gilead
    SATB   Piano
    Galaxy (1954) 1991

9:1
    Clark, Keith
    O That My Head Were Waters
    SATB   kro
    Lawson Gould (1973) 51698

11:19   (Psalm 41:7)
    Victoria, Tomas
    Eram Quasi Agnum (I Was Like A Lamb)
        (English/Latin)
    SATB   kro
    E. C. Schirmer (1976) 2994

11:19   (Psalm 41:7)
    Vittoria, Tomas
    I Was Like An Innocent Lamb (Enam Quasi
        Agnus)
    SATB   No accompaniment
    E. C. Schirmer (1938) 726 (also found in
        The Renaissance Singer)

14:17-22
    Purcell, Henry (ed. Anthony Lewis & Nigel
        Fortune)
    Let Mine Eyes Run Down
    SSATB   Organ and Continuo
    Novello (1959) PSR 3

15:16
    Schalk, Carl
    Verse/Pentecost 15 (Verses and Offertories
        Pentecost 12 - 20)
    2 part   Organ
    Augsburg (1978) 11-9539

15:16
    Wienhorst, Richard
    Your Words Became A Joy (Three Verse
        Settings, Set I)
    SAB   No accompaniment
    Concordia (1979) 98-2430

17:7
    Hovhaness, Alan
    Blessed Is The Man That Trusteth In The
        Lord, Op.268, #1
    SATB   kro
    Associated (1973) A-691

17:7-8, 10
    Glarum, L. Stanley
    Blessed Is The Man
    SAB   kro
    G. Schirmer (1965) 11318

17:7-8, 10
    Glarum, L. Stanley
    Blessed Is The Man
    SSA   kro
    G. Schirmer (1965) 11317

17:7-8, 10
    Glarum, L. Stanley
    Blessed Is The Man
    SATB   kro
    G. Schirmer (1965) 11319

29:11-12, 14   (Psalm 85:1)
    Wienhorst, Richard
    I Know The Thoughts I Think
    SATB   No accompaniment
    Associated (1961) AMP 343 (also found in
        The AMP Contemporary Choral Collection)

31:13
    SEE: Matthew 5:4
    Crandell, Robert
    The Second Beatitude

31:15
    Breydert, F. M.
    Vox In Rama
    SATB   kro
    G. Schirmer (1947) 9623

31:15
    Clemens Non Papa
    Vox In Rama
    SATB   No accompaniment
    Arista (1974) AE 274

31:15
    Weinberg, Henry
    Vox In Rama   (Latin/Hebrew/English)
    SATB   kro
    Presser (1960) 312-40464

31:15
    Zielenska, Mikolaj (ed. J. A. Herter)
    Vox In Rama   (English/Latin)
    SATB   Organ
    GIA (1976) G-1972

31:31-34
    York, David Stanley
    The New Covenant
    SATB (T-solo)   Organ
    Presser (1966) 312-40640

31:33-34
    Berger, Jean
    This Is The Covenant
    SATB   Unaccompanied
    Augsburg (1973) 11-1677

31:33-35
    Mueller, Carl F.
    The New Covenant
    SATB   Piano or Organ
    Carl Fischer (1952) 6645

33:10-11
    Young, Carlton
    We Celebrate His Love
    SAB   Organ, Percussion, Dancers
    Agape [Hope] (1979) CY 3349

33:14-16
    Reger, Max (ed. Paul Thomas)
    Behold, The Days Come, Saith The Lord
    SATB   Organ
    Concordia (1981) 97-5610 (found in The
        Church Choir Book, Volume, 2)

50:4-5
    Norris, Kevin
    Offertory/Lent III (Verses and Offertories -
        Lent)
    Unison   Organ
    Augsburg (1980) 11-9545

51:27-29
    Telemann, G. P. (ed. Abram Kaplan)
    Wave All The Flags In The Country (English/
        German)
    SATB   kro
    Tetra [Alexander Broude] (1965) AB 102

L A M E N T A T I O N S

00:00
    Tallis, Thomas
    The Lamentations Of Jeremiah
    SATTB   kro
    Oxford (n.d.) Tudor Church Music n.#.

1:1-5
    Tallis, Thomas (ed. Philip Brett)
    The Lamentations Of Jeremiah (Latin)
    ATTBB   kro
    Oxford (1969) n.#.

1:1-5
    Tallis, Thomas
    The Lamentations Of Jeremiah (English/Latin)
    SATTB   kro
    Oxford (1925) TCM 47

1:4
    Handel, G. F. (ed. Max Seiffert)
    Funeral Anthem On The Death Of Queen
       Caroline
    SATB   Piano
    Broude Brothers (n.d.) BB 900

1:4
    Hilton, John (transcribed Paul Sweetman)
    The Lamentations Of Jeremiah
    SAB   Keyboard
    Waterloo (1973) n.#.

1:4-5, 11-12, 15-16
    Wise, Michael (ed. Daniel Pinkham)
    The Ways Of Zion Do Mourn
    SATB (S and B solos)   Organ
    E. C. Schirmer (1966) 2680

1:4-5, 11-12, 15-16
    Wise, Michael (ed. Christopher Dearnley)
    The Ways Of Zion Do Mourn
    SATB (S and B solos)   Organ
    RSCM (found in Festival Service Book,
       Volume 4)

1:7 (based on)
    Palestrina, G. P. (ed. Costellazzi-Vene)
    Recordata
    SSA   kro
    Ricordi (1958) NY 2033

1:10-14
    Couperin, Francois
    Troisieme Lecon De Tenebres (Latin only)
    SS   Continuo
    Mercury (1942) MC 14

1:12
    Averitt, William
    O Vos Omnes (Latin only)
    SATB   No accompaniment
    Hinshaw (1978) HMC 314

1:12
    Barlow, David
    Behold, And See
    SATB   kro
    Novello (1973) MW 31

1:12
    Berchem, Jachet
    O Vos Omnes (Latin only)
    SATB   No accompaniment
    Arista (1975) AE 259

1:12
    Casals, Pablo
    O Vos Omnes
    SSAATTBB   kro
    Tetra [Alexander Broude] (1965) AB 242-5

1:12
    Casals, Pablo (arr. Clifford Richter)
    O Vos Omnes (Latin/English)
    TTBB   kro
    Tetra [Alexander Broude] (1965) AB 128

1:12
    Compere, Loyset
    O Vos Omnes (Latin)
    SA(T)B   No accompaniment
    Annie Bank (1950) n.#.

1:12
    Couperin, Francois (ed. & arr. Robert S.
       Hines)
    O Vos Omnes (Latin/English)
    SA   Piano or Organ
    Elkan Vogel (1975) 362-03201

1:12
    Correa, Carlos
    O Vos Omnes (O My People)
    SATB   Optional Keyboard
    Oxford (1965) A 226 (also found in Anthems
       For Choirs, Volume 3)

1:12
    Croce, Giovanni (ed. & arr. Noble Cain)
    O Vos Omnes
    SATB   kro
    Flammer (1945) 84228

1:12
    Croce, Giovanni (arr. & ed. Walter Ehret)
    Is It Nothing To You (Latin/English)
    SATB   kro
    Tetra [Alexander Broude] (1980) AB 829

1:12
    Croce, Giovanni (ed. Schaller, Vene)
    O Vos Omnes (English/Latin)
    SATB   kro
    Ricordi (1957) NY 1884

1:12
    Dering, Richard (ed. C. F. Simkins)
    O Vos Omnes
    SSATTB   kro
    Oxford (1965) A-223

1:12
    Duron, Sebastian (ed. Walter Ehret)
    O Vos Omnes (Latin/English)
    SATB   Organ
    Colombo (1964) NY 2388

1:12
    Esquivel, Juan (ed. Robert Goodale)
    O Vos Omnes
    SATB   kro
    G. Schirmer (1965) 11231

1:12
    Farmer, Floyd
    All Ye That Pass By
    SATB   Optional Accompaniment
    Abingdon (1974) APM-872

1:12
    Gesualdo, Carlo (ed. William Harris)
    O Vos Omnes (Latin)
    SSATB   kro
    Novello (1948) Anth. 1271

1:12
    Ginastera, Alberto
    Lamentations Of Jeremiah (Latin only)
    SSAATTBB   kro
    Mercury (1947) 352-00103

1:12
    Haydn, Michael
    O Vos Omnes
    SATB   kro
    G. Schirmer (1967) 11517

1:12
    Jommelli, Niccolo (ed. Ralph Hunter)
    O Vos Omnes (Latin/English
    SATB   Organ
    Belwin (1981) OCT 2474

1:12 (Isaiah 53:4-5)
    Leo, Leonardo (ed. Denys Darlow)
    Ecce Vidimus Eum (Tenebrae 1st Nocturne)
       (Latin)
    SATB   kro
    Oxford (1964) n.#.

1:12
   Lotti, Antonio (ed. Walter Ehret)
   Ye Who Pass By   (Latin/English)
   SATB   kro
   Southern (1966) #6

1:12
   Martini, Padre (ed. & arr. Walter Ehret)
   Behold And See
   SATB   Optional Organ
   Tetra [Alexander Broude] (1978) AB 825

1:12
   Morales, Cristobal (ed. Charles Marshall)
   All Ye Who Pass By   (English/Latin)
   SATB   kro
   Franck (1965) F 544

1:12
   Ouseley, Frederick A. Gore
   Is It Nothing To You?
   SATB   No accompaniment
   Novello (1909) 155

1:12
   Ouseley, Frederick A. Gore
   Is It Nothing To You?
   SATB   No accompaniment
   Oxford (1933) (found in Church Anthem Book)

1:12
   SEE: Isaiah 53:4-6
   Pasquet, Jean
   A Lenten Meditation

1:12
   Palestrina, G. P.
   O Vos Omnes   (Latin only)
   TTBB   No accompaniment
   Oxford (1965) (found in Anthems For Men's
        Voices, Volume 2)

1:12
   Praetorius, Hieronymous
   O Ye People Who Pass Me By   (English/Latin)
   SATTB   kro
   Franck (1967) F-603

1:12
   Stanton, Royal
   Behold And See
   SATB   kro
   Walton (1961) 2024

1:12
   Vallotti, Francesco Antonio
   O Vos Omnes
   SATB   No accompaniment
   Arista (1981) AE 433

1:12
   Vaughan Williams, Ralph
   O Vos Omnes (Latin only)
   SSAATTBB (A-solo)   kro
   Curwen (1950) 80594

1:12
   Victoria, Tomas (ed. Walter Ehret)
   All Ye People   (English/Latin)
   SATB   kro
   Elkan Vogel (1970) 362-01314

1:12
   Victoria, Tomas
   O Vos Omnes (Latin)
   SATB   No accompaniment
   Arista (1969) AE 162

1:12
   Victoria, Tomas
   O Vos Omnes   (English/Latin)
   SATB   kro
   E. C. Schirmer (1976) 2997 (also found in
        The Renaissance Singer)

1:12
   Victoria, Tomas (ed. Lionel Benson)
   O Vos Omnes (Latin)
   SATB   kro
   H. W. Gray (n.d.) 1712

1:12
   Victoria, Tomas (ed. Bruno Turner)
   O Vos Omnes (Latin)
   SSAT   No accompaniment
   J. W. Chester (1960) JWC 8818

1:12
   Victoria, Tomas Luis
   O Vos Omnes   (Latin)
   SATB   kro
   J. & W. Chester (1977) JWC 55104 (found in
        Third Chester Book Of Motets)

1:12
   Vittoria, Ludovico-Tommaso (arr. James
        Reilly)
   O Vos Omnes (Latin only)
   SATB   kro
   McLaughlin & Reilly (n.d.) 828

1:12
   Victoria, Tomas Luis (ed. Joel Kramme)
   O Vos Omnes   (English/Latin)
   SATB   Piano
   Music 70 (1976) M70-162

1:12
   Victoria, Tomas (arr. Theodore Marier)
   O Vos Omnes
   TTBB   kro
   McLaughlin & Reilly (1954) 1965

1:12
   Victoria, Tomas Luis de
   O Vos Omnes (English/Latin)
   SSAA   No accompaniment
   Oxford (1973) (found in Anthems For Choirs,
        Volume 3)

1:12
   Wickens, Dennis
   O Vos Omnes
   SATB   No accompaniment
   Oxford (1965) A 227

1:12-14   (Hosea 14:1)
   Vaughan Williams, Ralph
   Is It Nothing To You?
   SSAATTBB (A-solo)   Unaccompanied
   Curwen (n.d.) 10582

1:12, 16
   Victoria, Tomas
   Caligaverunt oculi mea (Latin)
   SATB   kro
   Walton (1980) 12

1:12, 16
   Victoria, Tomas (ed. Carl Deis)
   Caligaverunt oculi mea (Latin/English)
   SATB   kro
   G. Schirmer (1939) 8409

1:13
   Schalk, Carl
   From Above He Hath Sent Fire (Four Choruses
        From The Lamentations)
   SATB   No accompaniment
   Concordia (1961) 98-1578

1:18
   Schalk, Carl
   The Lord Is Righteous (from Four Choruses
        From The Lamentations)
   SATB   No accompaniment
   Concordia (1961) 98-1578

2:8-9
Palestrina, G. P. (ed. Frank Damrosch)
In Parasceve (Lamentations On Good Friday)
SATTB   kro
G. Schirmer (1916) 6596

3:22
Johnson, David N.
Verse/Epiphany VIII (Verses and Offertories -
    Epiphany II - The Transfiguration Of
    Our Lord)
Unison   Organ
Augsburg (1980) 11-9544

3:22
SEE: I Peter 5:10-11
Gieseke, Richard
God Has Called You To Glory

3:22-23
Kohn, Karl
Sensus Spei   (Latin)
SSAATTBB   Piano
Carl Fischer (1967) CM 7553

3:22-26
Powell, Robert J.
It Is Of The Lord's Mercies
SATB   kro
Kjos (1963) 5365

3:22-26
Sateren, Leland
His Compassions Fail Not
SATB   kro
Schmitt, Hall, McCreary (1961) 878

3:41
SEE: Job 3:20-23
Brahms, Johannes
Why Then Has The Light

3:56, 58
Fervabosco I, Alphonso
Vocem meam audisti (Latin only)
ATTBB   No accompaniment
Oxford (1965) (found in Anthems For Men's
    Voices, Volume 1)

4:2
SEE: Isaiah 57:15
Herbst, Johannes (ed. Karl Kroeger)
Listen All Who Enter These Portals

4:13-15
Schalk, Carl
For The Sins Of Her Prophets (from Four
    Choruses From The Lamentations)
SATB   No accompaniment
Concordia (1961) 98-1578

5:1, 7, 15-16
Schalk, Carl
Remember, O Lord (from Four Choruses From
    The Lamentations)
SATB   No accompaniment
Concordia (1961) 98-1578

5:1-8
Phinot, Dominique (ed. Mason Martens)
Lamentationes Jeremiae (Latin)
SATB/SATB   No accompaniment
Brooklyn College [Leeds] (1961) BCS 5

E Z E K I E L

1:00
Vaughan Williams, Ralph
A Vision Of Aeroplane
SATB   Organ
Oxford (1956) 46.116

18:4-9
SEE: Psalm 46:10
Morgan, Haydn
Be Still And Know That I Am God

18:30-32
Norris, Kevin
Offertory/Lent I (Verses and Offertories -
    Lent)
Unison   Organ
Augsburg (1980) 11-9545

18:31
SEE: Isaiah 26:9
Yardumian, Richard
Create In Me A Clean Heart

34:11f
Pelz, Walter
Offertory/Fourth Sunday of Easter (Verses
    and Offertories - Easter - Trinity)
SAB   Organ
Augsburg (1980) 11-9546

34:13-16   (Genesis 49:25-26)
Parker, Tom
Lead Us On, Good Shepherd
SATB   Organ
GIA (1979) G-2220

36:28, 30, 34-35   (Psalm 136:1)
Stainer, John
Ye Shall Dwell In The Land
SATB   Organ
Novello (n.d.) 29.0232.10

39:26-27
Wetzler, Robert
Offertory/Advent III (Verses and Offertories
    Advent I - The Baptism Of Our Lord)
Unison   Organ, Handbells
Augsburg (1979) 11-9541

47:00   (based on)
Brandon, George (arr.)
Glad Tidings! Glad Tidings!
SAB   Organ
Concordia (1973) 98-2168

47:1-2   (Psalm 117)
Ferris, William
I Have Seen Water
Unison   Organ
GIA (1980) G-2352

D A N I E L

2:20-23
Butler, Eugene
Song Of David
SATB   Piano or Organ, Percussion
Carl Fischer (1971) CM 7766

6:00   (Psalm 116; Bel And The Dragon)
Pinkham, Daniel
Daniel In The Lion's Den
SATB (T-B-Baritone-solos) 2 Pianos,
    Percussion, Tape
E. C. Schirmer (1973) 2946

7:13-14
Naylor, Bernard
Ascension Day
SSATB   No accompaniment
Novello (1960) 1399

7:13-14
Pelz, Walter
Offertory/Ascension Of Our Lord (Verses
    And Offertories - Easter - Trinity
SATB   Organ
Augsburg (1980) 11-9546

H O S E A

1:19-20
SEE: Song Of Songs 8:6-7
Grieb, Herbert
Set Me As A Seal

6:1-2
Harris, David S.
Come And Let Us Return Unto The Lord
SAB   Organ
H. W. Gray (1976) CMR 3346

6:1-2
Norris, Kevin
Offertory/Lent IV (Verses and Offertories-
    Lent)
Unison   Organ
Augsburg (1980) 11-9545

6:1-4 (paraphrased)
Harter, Harry H. (arr.)
With Contrite Hearts Return
SATB   kro
Belwin (1968) 2212

6:3, 6 (I Samuel 15:22)
Dailey, William
As The Rain Of Early Spring
SATB   Piano
AMSI (1978) 356

14:1
SEE: Lamentations 1:12-14
Vaughan Williams, Ralph
Is It Nothing To You?

14:5-7
Pooler, Frank
I Will Be As The Dew
SATB   kro
Walton (1971) 2950

14:6
Peter, Simon (ed. & arr. Donald McCorkle)
I Will Be As The Morning Dew (English/
    German)
SSAB or SSA   Organ or Piano
Boosey & Hawkes (1963) 5484

J O E L

2:00 (adapted)
Butler, Eugene
The Prophecy Of Joel
SATB   Organ
Carl Fischer (1972) CM 7789

2:00
Harris, William H.
Fear Not, O Land
SATB   Organ
Oxford (1955) E 73

2:1 (Isaiah 40:3)
Guerrero, Francisco
Canite Tuba (Latin only)
SSATB   kro
J. & W. Chester (1977) JWC 55104 (found
    in Third Chester Book Of Motets)

2:1
Morley, Thomas (ed. Richard Proulx)
Sound Forth The Trumpet In Zion
SAB   kro
GIA (1974) G 1867

2:1 (Isaiah 40:3)
Palestrina, G. P.
Canite Tuba   (Latin only)
SSATB   kro
J. W. Chester [Alexander Broude] (1964)
    ABC-4

2:1-2, 15-17, 32
Jackson, Francis
Blow Ye The Trumpet In Zion
SATB   Organ
Oxford (1963) A-198

2:3
Gore, Richard T.
Blow The Trumpet
SATB   Organ
Abingdon (1975) APM-468

2:12-13
SEE: Job 14:1-2
Lidholm, Inguar
Laudi

2:13
SEE: Psalm 96
Butler, Eugene
Sing To The Lord A Marvelous Song (SSA)

2:13
SEE: Psalm 96
Butler, Eugene
Sing To The Lord A Marvelous Song (SATB)

2:13
Norris, Kevin
Verse/Ash Wednesday (Verses and Offertories
    Lent)
Unison   Organ
Augsburg (1980) 11-9545

2:15-17
Purcell, Henry (ed. Anthony Lewis and Nigel
    Fortune)
Blow Up The Trumpet In Zion
SSSAATTTBB   Keyboard
Novello (1959) PSR #17

2:17
Perti, Jacopo Antonio
Inter Vestibulum et Altare
SATB   No accompaniment
Arista (1978) AE 318

2:17 (paraphrased)
Perti, Giacomo Antonio
Inter Vestibulum (English/Latin)
SATB   kro
Schmitt, Hall, McCreary (1951) (found in
    Rare Choral Masterpieces)

2:17
Tallis, Thomas
In Ieiunio et Fleta   (Latin)
SAATB   Optional Organ
Oxford (1969) TCM 81

2:21-24, 26
Elgar, Edward
Fear Not, O Lord
SATB   Organ
Novello (1942) 03.0134.05 (found in Seven
    Anthems Of Edward Elgar)

2:21-24, 26
Sumsion, Herbert
Fear Not, O Land
SATB   Organ
Novello (1963) 29.0473.10

2:21-26
Goss, John
Fear Not, O Land; Be Glad And Rejoice
SATB   Organ
G. Schirmer (n.d.) 4494

2:28-32
   Naylor, Bernard
   Motet For Whitsunday
   SATB (S-S-solos)   No accompaniment
   Novello (1960) 1400

2:28-32
   Naylor, Bernard
   Motet For Whitsunday
   SATB (S-S-solos)   No accompaniment
   Universal (1956) UE 12339

9:21-24, 26
   Elgar, Edward
   Fear Not, O Lord
   SATB   Organ
   Novello (1914) 1050

A M O S

5:8
   Snyder, Wesley
   Seek Him That Maketh The Seven Stars And
        Orion
   SATB   kro
   Flammer (1964) 84786

5:24 (Micah 6:8)
   Darst, W. Glen
   Walk Humbly With Thy God
   SATB   Piano or Organ
   Carl Fischer (1964) CM 7422

M I C A H

4:4
   SEE: Isaiah 65:25
   Davidson, Charles
   Anthem For Peace

5:1 (Matthew 2:6)
   Franck, Melchior
   Und du Bethlehem in Judischen Lande
        (German only)
   SATB   No accompaniment
   Merseburger (1977) (found in Motetten
        Alter Meister)

6:1-2, 12
   Beversdorf, Thomas
   Mini Motet From Micah
   SATB   Organ or Harpsichord (optional
        bass)
   Southern (1972) SC 24

6:6-8
   Adler, Samuel
   God's Requirements
   Unison   Keyboard
   Choristers Guild (1964) A-28

6:8
   Berlinski, Herman
   It Hath Been Told Thee, O Man
   SATB   Organ
   Mercury (1967) MC 550

6:8
   SEE: Amos 5:24
   Darst, W. Glen
   Walk Humbly With Thy God

6:8
   SEE: Genesis 28:16-17
   Fannon, Daniel
   Surely The Lord Is In This Place

6:8
   Mueller, Carl F.
   Walk Humbly With Thy God
   SATB   Organ or Piano
   Abingdon (1978) APM-893

6:8 (freely adapted)
   SEE: I Corinthians 16:20 (freely adapted)
   Sleeth, Natalie
   Bought With A Price

7:18-20
   Lewis, John Leo
   Who Is A God Like Thee
   SATB   Organ
   Abingdon (1977) APM-590

N A H U M

3:17
   SEE: Psalm 104:14-15
   Browne, Richmond
   Chortos I

H A B A K K U K

2:3
   SEE: Isaiah 40:9
   Gieseke, Richard W.
   Climb To The Top Of The Highest Mountain

2:14
   SEE: Psalm 135:1-3
   Willan, Healey
   O Praise The Lord

2:14, 20
   Roff, Joseph
   The Earth Shall Be Filled
   2 part   Organ
   GIA (1970) G-2597

2:14, 20
   Roff, Joseph
   The Earth Shall Be Filled
   SATB   Organ
   GIA (1970) G-1598

2:20 (Psalm 96:2, 69)
   Simper, Caleb
   The Lord Is In His Holy Temple
   SATB   Organ
   A. Weekes [Galaxy] (n.d.) n.#.

2:20
   SEE: Psalm 122:1
   Thompson, Randall
   The Gate Of Heaven

3:00 (adapted)
   Demarest, Alison
   The Lord Is My Strength
   SATB   Piano or Organ
   Canyon (1950) n.#.

3:3, 6
   Steggall, Charles
   God Came From Teman
   SATB   Organ
   Novello (n.d.) Anth. 105

3:17-18
   SEE: James 1:17
   Williams, David McK.
   Every Good Gift

3:18
    SEE: Psalm 135:1-3
    Willan, Healey
    O Praise The Lord

3:18-19
    Hovhaness, Alan
    I Will Rejoice In The Lord, Op. 42
    SATB   Organ
    C. F. Peters (1969) 66200

Z E P H A N I A H

1:14   (Zephaniah 2:3)
    Martin, G. C.
    The Great Day Of The Lord Is Near
    SATB   Organ
    Novello (n.d.) (found in The Novello Anthem
        Book)

1:14   (Zephaniah 2:3)
    Stout, Alan
    The Great Day Of The Lord
    SATB   Organ
    C. F. Peters (1965) 6883

2:3
    SEE: Zephaniah 1:14
    Martin, G. C.
    The Great Day Of The Lord Is Near

2:3
    SEE: Zephaniah 1:14
    Stout, Alan
    The Great Day Of The Lord

3:9-17
    Trued, S. Clarence
    Sing Aloud!
    SATB   kro
    Abingdon (1980) APM-478

3:14   (Zechariah 9:9)
    Bender, Jan
    Sing, O Daughters Of Zion, Op. 43, #5
    SAB (S-solo)   No accompaniment
    Concordia (1981) 98-2517

3:14, 17
    Wetzler, Robert
    Offertory/Advent IV (Verses and Offertories
        Advent I - The Baptism Of Our Lord)
    SATB or Unison   Organ
    Augsburg (1979) 11-9541

H A G G A I

2:9
    SEE: Isaiah 56:7
    Howells, Herbert
    Coventry Antiphons

Z E C H A R I A H

00:00 (paraphrased)
    Hopson, Hal H.
    Song Of Zechariah
    Unison   Keyboard
    Flammer (1977) FA-5018

2:10
    Antes, John (ed. & arr. Karl Kroeger)
    Sing And Rejoice O Daughter Of Zion
    SATB   Organ
    Boosey & Hawkes (1976) 5942

2:10
    Geisler, Johann (ed. Ewald Nolte)
    Sing And Rejoice, O Zion (English/German)
    SSAB or SATB   Organ
    Boosey & Hawkes (1968) 5652

2:10
    Kirk, Theron
    Sing And Rejoice
    SATB   kro
    Ludwig (1969) L 1133

2:10-11
    Powell, Robert J.
    Sing And Rejoice O Zion!
    2 part mixed   Keyboard
    Flammer (1980) EA-5020

2:10-13
    Silk, Richard
    Sing And Rejoice
    SATB   Organ
    Oxford (1971) A-275

8:12
    SEE: Genesis 8:22
    Simper, Caleb
    While The Earth Remaineth

9:9
    SEE: Zephaniah 3:14
    Bender, Jan
    Sing O Daughters Of Zion

9:9
    Petzold, Johannes
    Rejoice Greatly
    Unison   Keyboard
    Augsburg (1969) 11-1651   (also found in
        Music For The Contemporary Choir,
        Volume 1)

9:9
    Powell, Robert J.
    Rejoice Thy King Cometh
    SAB   kro
    Abingdon (1966) APM-535 (found in Festival
        Anthems For SAB)

9:9
    Titcomb, Everett
    Be Joyful, O Daughters Of Zion
    SATB   kro
    Carl Fischer (1934) CM 437

9:9
    Willan, Healey
    Rejoice Greatly
    SA or TB   Keyboard
    Concordia (1956) 98-1113

12:1
    SEE: Isaiah 26:9
    Yardumian, Richard
    Create In Me A Clean Heart

14:00
    Anonymous (ed. Joseph A. Herter)
    Ecce Dominus Veniet (English/Latin)
    SATB   kro
    GIA (1976) G-2000

M A L A C H A I

1:11
    Ouseley, F. A. Gore
    From The Rising Of The Sun
    SATB   Organ
    Novello (n.d.) 29.0230.03

1:11
    Ouseley, F. A. Gore
    From The Rising Of The Sun
    SATB   Organ
    Oxford   (found in Anthems For Choirs,
        Volume 1)

1:11
    SEE: Psalm 150
    Ouchterlony, David
    Praise God!

1:11
    Powell, Robert J.
    From The Rising Of The Sun
    SATB   kro
    Abingdon (1960) APM-116

1:11   (Isaiah 62:2)
    West, John E.
    In Every Place Incense Shall Be Offered Up
    SATB   Organ
    Novello (1899) 619

2:2   (Malachai 3:7; Malachai 4:2)
    Sateren, Leland
    Return Unto Me
    SATB   kro
    Schmitt (1950) 843

3:7
    SEE: Malachai 2:2
    Sateren, Leland
    Return Unto Me

4:2   (Wesley)
    Angell, Warren M.
    Christ, Whose Glory Fills The Skies
    SATB   Piano
    Pro Art [Belwin] (1981) PRO CH 3009

4:2   (Wesley)
    Burroughs, Bob
    Christ Whose Glory Fills The Skies
    SATB   No accompaniment
    The New Music Company (1973) NM A-106

4:2   (Wesley)
    Candlyn, T. Frederick H.
    Christ, Whose Glory Fills The Skies
    SATB   Organ
    Carl Fischer (1942) CM 622

4:2   (Wesley)
    Darke, Harold
    Christ, Whose Glory Fills The Skies
    SATB   Organ
    RSCM (1967) (found in Festival Service
        Book, Volume 2)

4:2   (Wesley)
    Graves, John
    Christ Whose Glory Fills The Skies
    2 part treble   Organ
    Oxford (1961) E 93

4:2   (Wesley)
    Knight, Gerald H.
    Christ Whose Glory Fills The Skies
    Unison Treble   Organ
    RSCM (1957) 214

4:2
    SEE: Malachai 2:2
    Sateren, Leland
    Return Unto Me

4:2   (Wesley)
    Werner, Johann Gottlob (arr. Gerhard Krapf)
    Christ Whose Glory Fills The Skies
    2 part mixed   Organ
    Augsburg (1977) 11-1818

4:2   (Wesley)
    Willan, Healey
    Christ Whose Glory Fills The Skies
    SATB   Organ
    Concordia (1950) 98-2006

4:2   (Wesley)
    Wolff, S. Drummond
    Christ Whose Glory Fills The Skies
    SAB   kro
    Concordia (1967) 98-1905

THE APOCRYPHA *(Greek & Roman Catholic)*
(not Jewish or Protestant

II ESDRAS

16:35-36 (Romans 11:33, 36)
   Gieseke, Richard
   Now Listen You Servants Of God
   SAB   No accompaniment
   Concordia (1978) 97-5481

TOBIT

4:00
   Tye, Christopher
   Give Alms Of Thy Goods
   SATB   Organ
   Oxford (1972) (also found in Oxford Book
      Of Tudor Anthems)

4:7
   Tye, Christopher (ed. John Langdon)
   Give Alms Of Thy Goods
   SATB   Organ ad lib.
   Novello (1968) NECM 11

8:1, 11, 14-18
   Willan, Healey
   A Prayer Of Rejoicing
   SATB   Organ
   Novello (1953) 1302

13:11-18
   Chandler, Mary
   A Prayer For Rejoicing
   SATB   Organ
   Novello (1964) ANTH. 1431

JUDITH

9:14
   Berger, Jean
   Thou Alone Art Israel's Shield
   SATB   kro
   Augsburg (1975) 11-1714

15:10 (based on)
   Bruckner, Anton
   Antiphon (Latin)
   SATB   Organ
   C. F. Peters (1961) n.#.

16:2, 13-15
   Davis, Diane
   Praise God With The Tambourine
   SATB   Piano
   GIA (1973) G-2033

WISDOM OF SOLOMON

1:7a (Psalm 68:1, 3)
   Martens, Edmund R.
   The Spirit Of The Lord (from Four
      Introits, Set I)
   Unison   Handbells
   Concordia (1976) 97-5384

1:7 (Acts 2:1-4)
   Ridout, Alan
   Spiritus Domini: The Spirit Of The Lord
   SATB   Organ
   Stainer & Bell (1970) 704

1:14
   SEE: Wisdom 2:23-24
   Boe, John
   God Created Man To Be Immortal

2:23
   Young, Carlton
   God Created Man
   Unison   Piano or Organ
   Hope (1970) CY 3333

2:23-24 (Wisdom 1:14; Wisdom 11:24a-26;
       Wisdom 12:1)
   Boe, John
   God Created Man To Be Immortal
   SATB   Organ
   H. W. Gray (1953) 2306

3:1
   Nares, James
   The Souls Of The Righteous
   SS   Organ
   Oxford (1973) (found in Anthems For Choirs,
      Volume 2)

3:1
   Thiman, Eric
   The Souls Of The Righteous
   2 part   Organ
   Curwen (1940) 10594

3:1-2
   Marchant, Stanley
   The Souls Of The Righteous
   SATB   No accompaniment
   Novello (1936) (found in Oxford Easy
      Anthem Book)

3:1-3
   Byrd, William
   Justorum Animae (Latin/English)
   SATB   kro
   Arista (1981) AE 404

3:1-3
   Byrd, William
   Justorum Animae (The Souls Of The
      Righteous) (English/Latin)
   SSATB   kro
   H. W. Gray (n.d.) 1709

3:1-3
Byrd, William
Justorum Animae
SSATB
Oxford (1978) (found in Oxford Book Of
    Tudor Anthems)

3:1-3
Byrd, William
The Souls Of The Righteous (English/Latin)
SSATB   kro
E. C. Schirmer (1929) 327

3:1-3
Byrd, William (arr. Gwynn S. Bement)
Justorum Animae (The Souls Of The Righteous)
    (English/Latin)
SSAA   kro
E. C. Schirmer (1941) 1891

3:1-3
Davies, H. Walford
The Souls Of The Righteous
SATB (S-solo)   Organ
Oxford (1933) (found in The Church Anthem
    Book)

3:1-3
DiLasso, Orlando
Justorum Animae (Latin)
SSATB   No accompaniment
Arista (1969) AE 163

3:1-3
Ratcliffe, Desmond
The Souls Of The Righteous
TTBB   kro
Novello (1953) MV 130

3:1-3
Stanford, C. V.
Justorum Animae, Op. 38 (Latin)
SATB   kro
Boosey & Hawkes (1965) CCS-74

3:1-3
Stanford, C. V.
Justorum animae, Op. 51, #1
SATB   kro
C. T. Wagner Reprint Series (n.d.) C-067702

3:1-3
Titcomb, Everett
The Souls Of The Righteous
SATB (S-solo)   Organ
H. W. Gray (1964) 2866

3:1-3, 5
Woodman, R. Huntington
The Souls Of The Righteous
SATB   Organ
F. Harris (n.d.) FH 1341

3:1-5
Vaughan Williams, Ralph
The Souls Of The Righteous
SATB (A-T-B-solos)   No accompaniment
Oxford (1947) 42 L 800

3:1-8
Noble, T. Tertius
Souls Of The Righteous
SSAA   kro
G. Schirmer (1950) 9870

3:1-8
Noble, T. Tertius
Souls Of The Righteous, Op. 8, #1
SATB   kro
H. W. Gray (n.d.) CMR 69

3:1-8
Noble, T. Tertius
Souls Of The Righteous, Op. 8, #1
SATB   kro
Novello (1980) (found in In The Beauty Of
    Holiness)

3:1-8
Noble, T. Tertius
The Souls Of The Righteous
TTBB   Organ ad lib.
Oliver Ditson (1926) 13925

3:2-3
Nares, James (transcribed & edited by
    Christopher Dearnley)
In The Sight Of The Unwise (from The Souls
    Of The Righteous)
Unison   Organ
RSCM (n.d.) 237

5:15-16
Sowerby, Leo
The Righteous Live For Evermore
SA(T)B   Organ
Oxford (1960) A-166

7:29-30
Riegger, Wallingford
Evil Shall Not Prevail, Op. 48
SSA/SSA or SSA/TBB or TBB/TBB
    No accompaniment
Broude Brothers (1957) n.#.

10:12, 14
Handl, Jacob
Honestum Fecit (Latin only)
ATTB   No accompaniment
Oxford (1965) (found in Anthems For Men's
    Voices, Volume I)

10:17
Lassus, Orlandus
Sancti Mei (Latin only)
2 part   No accompaniment
Mercury (1941) 352.00011 (found in Twelve
    Motets)

10:19-20
Lassus, Orlandus
Justi Tulerunt Spolia (Latin only)
2 part   No accompaniment
Mercury (1941) 352.00011 (found in Twelve
    Motets)

11:24a-26
SEE: Wisdom 2:23-24
Boe, John
God Created Man To Be Immortal

12:1
SEE: Wisdom 2:23-24
Boe, John
God Created Man To Be Immortal

18:14-15
Lumsdaine, David
Dum Medium Silentium (Latin only)
SATB   No accompaniment
Novello (1976) 29.0370.09

18:14-15 (John 1:14)
Willan, Healey
While All Things Were In Quiet Silence
SATB   Organ
Novello (1907) 889

E C C L E S I A S T I C U S (or S I R A C H)

1:1-5, 8-10
    Joubert, John
    All Wisdom Cometh From The Lord, Op. 62
    SA   Organ
    Novello (1971) MT 1535

1:11-12
    Pinkham, Daniel
    The Fear Of The Lord (from Listen To Me)
    SA   No accompaniment
    E. C. Schirmer (1965) 2581

1:11-13
    Howells, Herbert
    The Fear Of The Lord
    SATB   Organ
    Oxford (1977) A 321

14:22
    Lassus, Orlandus
    Beatus Vir
    2 part   No accompaniment
    Mercury (1941) 352.00011 (found in Twelve
        Motets)

14:22
    Lassus, Orlandus
    Beatus Vir
    2 part   No accompaniment
    Oxford (1973) (found in Anthems For Choirs,
        Volume 2)

17:29-30, 32
    West, John
    How Great Is The Loving Kindness
    SATB   Organ
    Novello (1899)   615

18:8
    Jeppesen, Knud
    What Is Man? (Five Motets)
    SATB   kro
    Broude Brothers (1975) BB 5021

18:9-11
    Pinkham, Daniel
    The Number Of A Man's Days (from Listen To
        Me)
    SA   No accompaniment
    E. C. Schirmer (1965) 2581

32:3-9
    Pinkham, Daniel
    Hinder Not Music (from Listen To Me)
    SA   No accompaniment
    E. C. Schirmer (1965) 2581

38:00   (based on)
    Blake, Leonard
    Consecration
    2 part treble   Piano or Organ
    Oxford (1963) T-58

38:00   (based on)
    Blake, Leonard
    Consecration
    SATB   Piano or Organ
    Oxford (1963) E 52

38:4, 6, 9-10, 12   (Isaiah 35:1-6)
    Harris, William
    Strengthen Ye The Weak Hands
    SATB (T-solo)   Organ
    Novello (1950) 1275

39:6
    Lassus, Orlandus
    Justus cor sum tradet   (Latin only)
    2 part   No accompaniment
    Mercury (1941) 352.00011 (from Twelve
        Motets)

39:13-14
    Pinkham, Daniel
    Listen To Me (from Listen To Me)
    SA   No accompaniment
    E. C. Schirmer (1965) 2581

43:16, 27
    Bruckner, Anton
    Ecce Sacerdos (from Two Motets)
    SATB   3 Trombones
    C. F. Peters (1959) 6037

43:17-18
    Pinkham, Daniel
    He Scatters The Snow (from Listen To Me)
    SA   No accompaniment
    E. C. Schirmer (1965) 2581

44:00
    Engel, Lehman
    Let Us Now Praise Famous Men
    SATB   Piano
    Mercury (1954) MC 200

44:00
    Titcomb, Everett
    Let Us Now Praise Famous Men
    SATB   Piano or Organ
    B. F. Wood (1945) 646

44:00
    Wells, Dana F.
    Let Us Now Praise Famous Men
    SATB   kro
    Abingdon (1965) APM-483

44:1, 4-5, 9, 14
    Rubbra, Edmund
    Let Us Now Praise Famous Men, Op. 76, #2
        (Three Motets)
    SATB (S-solo)   No accompaniment
    Lengnick (1952) 3767

44:1-4, 7-15
    Wesley, Samuel S. (ed. J. West)
    Let Us Now Praise Famous Men
    SATB   Organ
    Novello (n.d.) 1145

44:1-5, 10, 14
    Sowerby, Leo
    Let Us Now Praise Famous Men
    SATB   Organ
    RSCM (1959)   223

44:1-15
    Pfautsch, Lloyd
    A Canticle Of Commemoration
    SATB   No accompaniment
    Abingdon (1962) APM-224

44:1-15
    Pfautsch, Lloyd
    A Canticle Of Commemoration
    TTBB   No accompaniment
    Abingdon (1962) APM-225

44:14
    Bitgood, Roberta
    Let Us Now Praise Famous Men
    SATB   Organ
    Stone Chapel Press (1970) 145

44:14
    Finzi, Gerald
    Let Us Now Praise Famous Men
    2 part   Piano
    Boosey & Hawkes (1980) 1919

44:14
    SEE: Lamentations 1:4
    Handel, G. F.
    Funeral Music On The Death of Queen
        Caroline

44:14
  Handel, G. F.
  Their Bodies Are Buried In Peace
  SATB   Organ
  E. C. Schirmer (1936) 1010   (also found in
    Second Concord Anthem Book - Grey)

44:14
  Handel, G. F.
  Their Bodies Are Buried In Peace
  SATB   Organ
  Oxford (found in Church Anthem Book)

44:14
  Handel, G. F. (ed. Don Craig and Harold
    Mason)
  Their Bodies Are Buried In Peace
  SATB   Piano or Organ
  Plymouth (1973) PCS-76

44:14
  Vaughan Williams, Ralph
  Let Us Now Praise Famous Men
  Unison   Organ
  Curwen [G. Schirmer] (1923) 8384

44:14
  Vaughan Williams, Ralph (arr. Maurice
    Jacobson)
  Let Us Now Praise Famous Men
  SATB   Keyboard
  G. Schirmer (1929) 11070   (also found in
    Five Centuries Of Choral Music)

44:14
  Vaughan Williams, Ralph
  Let Us Now Praise Famous Men
  Unison   Organ
  Oxford   (found in Church Anthem Book)

45:1, 3
  Pinkham, Daniel
  The Lord Brought Forth Moses (from Let Us
    Now Praise Famous Men)
  SA   No accompaniment
  E. C. Schirmer (1970) 2586

45:6-7, 9   (adapted)
  Pinkham, Daniel
  The Lord Exalted Aaron (from Let Us Now
    Praise Famous Men)
  SA   No accompaniment
  E. C. Schirmer (1970) 2586

47:3-5, 7-8, 11
  Pinkham, Daniel
  David Played With Lions (from Let Us Now
    Praise Famous Men)
  SA   No accompaniment
  E. C. Schirmer (1970) 2586

47:13-14, 16-17
  Pinkham, Daniel
  Solomon Reigned In Days Of Peace (from Let
    Us Now Praise Famous Men)
  SA   No accompaniment
  E. C. Schirmer (1970) 2586

48:1, 3, 9
  Pinkham, Daniel
  The Prophet Elijah Arose (from Let Us Now
    Praise Famous Men)
  SA   No accompaniment
  E. C. Schirmer (1970) 2586

50:22-24
  Bach, J. S. (ed. Joseph A. Herter)
  Now Thank We All Our God (from Cantata 79)
      (English/German)
  SATB   Keyboard (optional Brass)
  GIA (1975) G-1919

50:22-24   (paraphrase by Rinkart)
  Mendelssohn, Felix
  Now Thank We All Our God
  SATB   Keyboard
  Carl Fischer (1981) CM 8132

B A R U C H

4:36
  SEE: Baruch 5:5
  Issac, Heinrich
  Jerusalem Surge

4:36
  SEE: Luke 2:14
  Proulx, Richard
  Christmas Procession

5:1-5, 7-9
  Sowerby, Leo
  Put Off The Garment Of The Mourning
  SATB   Organ
  H. W. Gray (1963) CMR 2841

5:5   (Baruch 4:36)
  Issac, Heinrich
  Jerusalem Surge   (Latin only)
  SATB   kro
  J. & W. Chester (1977) JWC 55103 (found in
    Fifth Chester Book Of Motets)

5:5
  SEE: Luke 2:14
  Proulx, Richard
  Christmas Procession

5:8-9   (Song Of Songs 2:3-4)
  West, John E.
  The Woods And Every Sweet Smelling Tree
  SATB   Organ
  G. Schirmer (n.d.) 7297

P R A Y E R   O F   A Z A R I A H

1:28-64
  Vaughan Williams, Ralph
  Benedicite
  SATB (S-solo)   Keyboard
  Oxford (1958) n.#.

1:29-34
  Lassus, Orlandus (ed. Mason Martens)
  Benedicitus es, Domine (Blessed Art Thou)
  SATB   kro
  Concordia (1963) 98-1660

1:29-34
  Proulx, Richard
  Song Of The Three Young Men (Benedictus es,
    Domine)
  Unison or Two Parts   Organ
  GIA (1974) G-1863

1:29-34
  Shaw, Martin
  Blessed Art Thou, O Lord Of Our Fathers
  SATB   Organ
  Novello (1969) 85076

1:29-68
  Pinkham, Daniel
  Canticle Of Praise
  SATB (S-solo)   Brass, Percussion
  E. C. Schirmer (1965) 2694

1:35-65
    Wyton, Alec
    Glorify The Lord
    2 part   Organ, Flute, Handbells
    Hinshaw (1977) HMC-258

B E L   A N D   T H E   D R A G O N

00:00
    SEE: Daniel 6
    Pinkham, Daniel
    Daniel And The Lion's Den

P R A Y E R   O F   M A N A S S A H

00:7b
    Sowerby, Leo
    Prayer Of The King Manasses Of Juda
    SATB   Organ
    H. W. Gray (1964) 2849

T H E   N E W   T E S T A M E N T

M A T T H E W

1:21-23
  SEE: Luke 2:11-14
  Price, Milburn
  Hodie! Emmanuel!

1:23
  SEE: Galatians 4:4
  Gibbs, Allen Orton
  God Sent Forth His Son

1:23
  LaMontaine, John
  Behold, A Virgin Shall Be With Child (Songs
      Of The Nativity)
  SATB   kro
  H. W. Gray (1954) CMR-2374

1:23
  Wetzler, Robert
  Verse/Advent IV (Verses and Offertories
      Advent I - The Baptism Of Our Lord)
  SATB or 2 part   Organ
  Augsburg (1979) 11-9541

1:29   (Isaiah 53:4-5)
  Willan, Healey
  Behold The Lamb Of God
  2 part mixed   Organ
  Concordia (1960) 98-1509 (also found in
      Sing For Joy, 97-5046)

2:1-2
  Clemens Non Papa
  Magi Venirunt Ab Oriente (Latin)
  SATB   kro
  J. & W. Chester (1977) JWC 55110 (found in
      Sixth Chester Book Of Motets)

2:1-2 (Numbers 24:17;   Psalm 2:9)
  Mendelssohn, Felix
  Say Where Is He Born and There Shall Be A
      Star
  SATB   Organ
  H. W. Gray (n.d.) CMR 1695

2:1-2
  Mendelssohn, Felix (ed. Ivor Keys)
  There Shall A Star From Jacob Come Forth,
      Op. 97
  SATB (T-B-B-solos)   Organ
  Addington Press [Hinshaw] (1979) AP-206

2:1-2
  Mendelssohn, Felix
  When Jesus Our Lord (Christus)
  SATB (S-solo)   Organ
  Oxford (1933)   (found in Church Anthem Book)

2:1-2
  Williams, David H.
  Visit Of The Magi
  SATB (S-solo)   Organ
  H. W. Gray (1958) 2540

2:1-2
  Wuorinen, Charles
  An Anthem For Epiphany
  SATB   Organ, Trumpet
  C. F. Peters (1978) 66606

2:1, 11
  Gallus, Jacobus (Handl) (ed. Kurt Stone)
  Ab Oriente Venirunt Magi (From Eastern
      Lands) (English/Latin)
  SATB   kro
  Alexander Broude (1974) AB 271

2:1, 11 (based on)
  Handl, Jacob
  Ab Oriente   (Latin)
  SATB   Organ
  E. C. Schirmer (1971) ECS 2785

2:2
  Krenek, Ernst
  Epiphany (New Year) (from Holiday Motets)
      (Latin)
  SSA round   No accompaniment
  Broude Brothers (1967) BB 4069

2:2 (adapted)
  Mendelssohn, Felix
  Say, Where Is He That Is Born King Of Judah
  TTB   Organ
  E. C. Schirmer   #11

2:2
  Newbury, Kent A.
  We Have Seen His Star
  SATB   kro
  G. Schirmer (1968) 11533

2:2
  SEE: Isaiah 60:1
  Wetzler, Robert
  Offertory/Epiphany

2:2
  Wetzler, Robert
  Verse/Epiphany (Verses and Offertories
      Advent I - The Baptism Of Our Lord)
  SATB   Organ
  Augsburg (1979) 11-9541

2:2
  Titcomb, Everett
  We Have Seen His Star
  SATB   kro
  Carl Fischer (1934) CM 438

2:2, 5
  Hammerschmidt, Andreas (ed. Harold Mueller)
  Where Is The Newborn King? (English/
      German)
  SSATB   Continuo and 2 Violins
  Concordia (1972) 97-5038   (parts 97-5112)

2:6
SEE: Micah 5:1
Franck, Melchior
Und du Bethlehem in Judischer Lande

2:6
Hillert, Richard
And You, O Bethlehem
2 part mixed   Organ
Concordia (1962) 98-1632

2:9-10 (based on)
Victoria, Tomas
Videntes Stellam
SATB   kro
Shawnee (1976) A 1355

2:9-10
Willan, Healey
Lo, The Star Which They Saw
SSA   Keyboard
Concordia (1962) 97-7160 (found in We
      Praise Thee, Volume 2)

2:9-11
Newbury, Kent A.
And They Fell Down And Worshipped Him
SATB   Piano or Organ
Flammer (1972) A-5592

2:9-11
Petzhold, Johannes
And Lo, The Star
2 part treble   Keyboard, Instruments
      In C
Augsburg (1968) TI-305

2:10-11
Monteverdi, Claudio (ed. Maynard Klein)
Angelus Ad Pastores Ait (English/Latin)
SSA   kro
G. Schirmer (1971) 11785

2:10-11
Monteverdi, Claudio
Angelus Ad Pastores Ait
SSA   No accompaniment
Mercury (1944) 352.00024

2:10-11
Palestrina, G. P. (ed. Malcolm Sargent)
Videntes Stellam
SATB/SATB   No accompaniment
Oxford (1965) n.#.

2:10-11
Poulenc, Francis
Videntes Stellam (from Four Christmas
      Motets)
SATB   kro
Salabert (1962) SAL.14

2:11
Palestrina, G. P. (ed. Malcolm Sargent)
Videntes Stellam (Latin)
SATB/SATB   No accompaniment
Oxford (1965) 43.396

2:13-23
Bender, Jan
Three Prophecies, Op. 32, #5
3 part equal voices   Organ
Concordia (1973) 98-2133

3:11
Rubbra, Edmund
There Is A Spirit (from Three Motets),
      Op. 76, #2
SATB (S-solo)   No accompaniment
Lengnick (1952) n.#.

3:13-17 (based on)
SEE: Hebrews 10:7
Brandon, George (arr.)
Carol Of The Baptism

3:13-17
Hallstrom, Henry
The Baptism Of Jesus
SATB   Organ
Abingdon (1967) APM-581

4:1-11
Pfautsch, Lloyd
The Temptation Of Christ
SATB   No accompaniment
Abingdon (1961) APM-142

4:4
Moser, Rudolf
Man Shall Not Live By Bread Alone, Op. 94,
      #1a
Unison   Organ
Concordia (1955) CH-1082

4:10
Bender, Jan
Begone, Satan, Op. 32, #10
Unison   Organ
Concordia (1966) 98-1848 (also found in
      Third Morning Star Choir Book, 97-4972)

4:23
Johnson, David N.
Verse/Epiphany III (Verses and Offertories
      Epiphany II - The Transfiguration Of
      Our Lord)
Unison   Organ
Augsburg (1980) 11-9544

5:00 (based on)
Lovelace, Austin
The Beatitudes
Unison   Organ (optional congregation)
Augsburg (1979) 11-1867

5:1-2
Fetler, Paul
The Beatitudes
SATB   No accompaniment
Augsburg (1965) 1454

5:1-11 (based on)
Panchenko, Simon V. (arr. Peter J. Wilhousky)
The Promises
SATB   kro
Carl Fischer (1938) CM 515

5:1-12
Reynolds, William J.
The Beatitudes
SATB and Narrator   Keyboard
Broadman (1977) 4565-80

5:1-12
Smith, H. Hamilton
Three Beatitudes
SATB   Organ
World Library (1980) 7604-8

5:1-16
Simeone, Harry
The Beatitudes
SATB (S or T solo)   Organ
Shawnee (1951) A-178

5:2-12
Liszt, Franz
The Beatitudes (Latin)
SATB B-solo)   Organ
Arista (1969) AE-176

5:3, 5-6
  Johnson, David N.
  Offertory/Epiphany V (Verses and Offertories
     Epiphany II - The Transfiguration Of
     Our Lord)
  Unison   Organ
  Augsburg (1980) 11-9544

5:3-6
  Malotte, Albert Hay (arr. Bryceson Treharrne)
  The Beatitudes
  SATB   Organ or Piano
  G. Schirmer (1939) 8400

5:3-5, 7-9, 12
  Preston, John E.
  Blessed Are The Poor In Spirit
  SATB   Organ
  Flammer (1973) A 5615

5:3-5, 8
  Wilkinson, Scott
  Blessed Are They
  SATB (A-solo)   Organ
  Carl Fischer (1969) ZCM 105

5:3-10
  Avery, Richard and Donald Marsh
  The Beatitudes
  SATB   Organ or Piano
  Hope (1981) AM 6688

5:3-10
  Jordan, Alice
  The Beatitudes
  SATB   Organ
  Abingdon (1965) APM-464

5:3-10
  Tschesnokoff, P.
  The Beatitudes
  SATTBB (T-solo)   kro
  J. Fischer (1918) 4588

5:3-10, 12, 14, 16
  Arnatt, Ronald
  Blessed Are The Poor In Spirit
  SATB (S or T s.lo)   Organ
  H. W. Gray (1951) 2162

5:3-10, 14, 16
  Pfautsch, Lloyd
  The Beatitudes
  SATB   kro
  Flammer (1967) 84930

5:3-11
  Rubbra, Edmund
  The Beatitudes, Op. 109
  SSA   No accompaniment
  Lengnick (1960) 4052

5:3-11
  Rubbra, Edmund
  There Is A Spirit (Three Motets), Op. 76, #2
  SATB (S-solo)   No accompaniment
  Lengnick (1952) 3767

5:3-12
  Bender, Jan
  The Beatitudes, Op. 35
  2 part treble   Keyboard with Oboe, viola
    and cello
  Concordia (1966) 97-4742

5:3-12
  Glarum, L. Stanley
  The Beatitudes
  SSAATTBB   kro
  Hall & McCreary (1947) 1638 (also available
    in SSAA voicing)

5:3-12
  Gore, Richard T.
  The Beatitudes
  SATB   kro
  Chantry (1951) n.#.

5:3-12
  Grant, Micki
  Beatitudes (from Your Arms Too Short To
    Box With God)
  SATB   Piano
  Fiddleback (1978) V-101

5:3-12
  Joubert, John
  The Beatitudes, Op. 47
  SATB (S-T-solos)   No accompaniment
  Novello (1964) MT 1461

5:3-12
  Peloquin, Alexander
  Change Your Mind
  SATB   Cantor   Organ
  GIA (1978) G-2189

5:3-12
  Ridout, Alan
  The Beatitudes
  SSAA   No accompaniment
  Stainer & Bell (1969) 667

5:3-12
  Rubbra, Edmund
  The Beatitudes
  SSA   No accompaniment
  Lengnick (1960) 4052

5:3-12
  York, David Stanley
  The Beatitudes
  SSAATTBB   kro
  Mercury (1961) MC 389

5:3-16
  SEE: Luke 6:20-23
  Diemer, Emma Lou
  Blessed Are You

5:4 (Psalm 126:5-6)
  Brahms, Johannes (arr. C. Charlton Palmer)
  Blessed Are They That Mourn (Requiem)
  SATB   Organ
  Oxford (1933) (found in Church Anthem Book)

5:4 (Psalm 116:7; Deuteronomy 4:30-31;
    Jeremiah 31:13)
  Crandell, Robert
  The Second Beatitude
  SATB   Organ
  Canyon (1952) n.#.

5:5
  Wilson, Harry R.
  Blessed Are The Meek
  SATB (S or T solo)   Keyboard
  Carl Fischer (1945) CM 661

5:6-9
  Hillert, Richard
  Offertory/Renewers Of Society (Verses and
    Offertories - Lesser Festivals)
  Unison   Organ
  Augsburg (1980) 11-9543

5:7, 12
  Williams, David H.
  Blessed Are The Merciful
  2 part or Unison   Organ
  AMSI (1981) 416

5:8
  Davies, H. Walford
  Blessed Are The Pure In Heart
  SATB   Organ
  Oxford (1933) (found in Church Anthem Book)

5:8
    Herbst, Johannes (ed. & arr. Karl Kroeger)
    Blessed Are The Pure In Heart (English/
        German)
    SATB   Organ
    Boosey & Hawkes (1977) 5968

5:8
    SEE: Psalm 51:10
    Larson, Edward L.
    Invocation

5:8
    Walter, Samuel
    Blessed Are The Pure In Heart
    SATB   No accompaniment
    Abingdon (1961) APM-190

5:9
    Hillert, Richard
    Verse/Peace (Verses and Offertories - Lesser
        Festivals)
    Unison   Organ
    Augsburg (1980) 11-9543

5:10
    Hillert, Richard
    Verse/Common Of Martyrs (Verses and Offer-
        tories - Lesser Festivals)
    Unison   Organ
    Augsburg (1980) 11-9543

5:11-12
    Groce, Giovanni (ed. Mason Martens)
    Beati eritis (Yea Blessed Shall Ye Be)
        (English/Latin)
    SATB   kro
    Walton (1964) 2156

5:12
    SEE: Luke 11:28
    Stanley, F. B.
    Blessed Are They

5:13-14
    Avery, Richard and Donald Marsh
    You Are The Salt Of The Earth
    SATB   Accompaniment
    Hope (1981) AM 6687

5:13-16
    Butler, Eugene
    You Are The Salt Of The Earth
    SATB   Keyboard
    Word (1970) CS 2452

5:13-16
    Routley, Erik
    Light And Salt
    SATB   Organ
    GIA (1980) G-2300

5:14
    SEE: Mark 16:15
    Berridge, Arthur
    Go Ye Into All The World

5:14-16
    Cabena, Barrie
    Let Your Light So Shine Before Men
    SATB   Organ
    McKee[Associated] (1975) n.#.

5:14, 16   (based on)
    Lee, John
    Let Your Light Shine
    SATB   Keyboard
    Broadman (1980) 4566-21

5:14-18
    Mueller, Carl F.
    Ye Are The Light Of The World
    SATB   Keyboard
    Carl Fischer (1950) CM 6524

5:16
    Hillert, Richard
    Verse/Renewer of Society (Verses and
        Offertories - Lesser Festivals)
    Unison   Organ
    Augsburg (1980) 11-9543

5:16
    Whythbrooke, William (ed. Cvril F. Simkins)
    Let Your Light So Shine Before Men
    SATB   Keyboard
    Concordia (1976) 98-2278

6:00   (adapted)
    Bright, Houston
    Is Not The Life More Than Meat
    SATB   Keyboard
    Flammer (1971) A-5582

6:9-13
    Bingham, Seth
    The Lord's Prayer
    SATB   Organ
    Carl Fischer (1941) CM 607

6:9-13
    Blakley, Duane (Am Yisrael Chai)
    Our Father In Heaven
    SATB or Treble voices or Male voices
        Accompaniment is multiple options,
        plus bells
    Hinshaw (1978) HMC 430

6:9-13
    Clements, John
    The Lord's Prayer
    Unison   Keyboard
    Oxford (1960) 45 L 062

6:9-13
    Effinger, Cecil
    The Lord's Prayer
    SATB   kro
    Broadman (1975) 4546-10

6:9-13
    Farmer, John (arr. David Lumsden)
    The Lord's Prayer
    SSAA or ATTB   Optional keyboard
    Oxford (1967) A 231B

6:9-13
    SEE: John 16:23-24
    Hammerschmidt, Andrea (ed. Harold Mueller)
    Truly, Truly, I Say To You

6:9-13
    Helfer, William
    The Lord's Prayer
    SSA   kro   Timpani
    Carl Fischer (1941) CM 604

6:9-13
    Ley, Henry G.
    The Lord's Prayer
    Unison or SATB   No accompaniment
    Oxford (1925) 418

6:9-13
    Liszt, Franz
    Our Father (Pater Noster) (English/Latin)
    SSAATTBB   Optional Organ
    Concordia (1968) 97-4885

6:9-13
    Merbecke, John (arr. Everett Jay Hilty)
    The Lord's Prayer
    Unison   Piano or Organ
    Oxford (1971) 96.202

6:9-13
    Milford, Robin
    The Lord's Prayer
    2 equal voices   Organ
    Oxford (1939) 197

6:9-13
    Mueller, Carl F.
    The Lord's Prayer
    SSAATTBB   kro
    G. Schirmer (1941) 8680

6:9-13
    Schütz, Heinrich (ed. Fritz Sporn)
    Das Vater Unser   (German only)
    SATTB   Organ, 2 Violins
    Associated (1941) n.#.

6:9-13
    Schütz, Heinrich
    Das Vater Unser   (German)
    SATB   No accompaniment
    Merseburger (1977)   (found in Motetten
        Alter Meister)

6:9-13
    Schütz, Heinrich (ed. Larry D. Wyatt)
    Pater Noster (Our Father) (English/Latin)
    SATB   Optional Keyboard
    Plymouth (1981) SC-58

6:9-13
    Stone, Robert
    The Lord's Prayer
    SATB   No accompaniment
    Oxford (1973) A 305

6:9-13
    Strathdee, Jim
    Our Father
    2 Groups   Keyboard and Guitar
    Agape [Hope] (1980) (found in Choirbook For
        Saints and Sinners)

6:9-15
    Cain, Noble
    Our Father Who Art In Heaven
    SATB   kro
    Flammer (1972) A-5328   (also available in
        SAB, and in SSA voicings)

6:9-15
    Davies, Peter Maxwell
    The Lord's Prayer
    SATB   kro
    Schott (1962) 6480

6:9-15
    Donahue, Robert
    The Lord's Prayer
    SAB   No accompaniment
    Tetra [Alexander Broude] (1979) AB 836

6:9-15
    Fryxell, Regina Holmen
    Our Father   (found in Seven Choral Service
        Settings)
    SATB   Keyboard ad lib.
    Abingdon (1963) APM-242

6:9-15
    Handl, Jacob (ed. C. F. Simkins)
    Our Father   (Latin/English)
    SSAATTBB   No accompaniment
    Hinrichsen (1966) 1522

6:9-15
    Head, Michael
    The Lord's Prayer
    SATB   Organ
    Boosey & Hawkes (1966) 5347

6:9-15
    Hughes, Howard
    The Lord's Prayer
    SATB   Organ
    GIA (1978) G-2175

6:9-15
    Malotte, Albert Hay (arr. Carl Deis)
    The Lord's Prayer
    SATB   Organ
    G. Schirmer (1935) 7943

6:9-15
    Raymond, John
    The Lord's Prayer
    SATB   Organ
    Plymouth (1959) LC 100

6:9-15
    Raymond, John
    The Lord's Prayer
    SSAA   Piano
    Plymouth (1959) LC 200

6:9-15
    Raymond, John
    The Lord's Prayer
    TTBB   Piano
    Plymouth (1959) LC 300

6:9-15
    Robertson, Leroy
    The Lord's Prayer
    SATB   Piano or Organ
    Galaxy (1941) 1.1199.1

6:9-15
    Robertson, Leroy
    The Lord's Prayer
    SSA   Piano or Organ
    Galaxy (1961) 1.2208.1

6:9-15
    Schütz, Heinrich (ed. Kurt Stone)
    Our Father   (English/German)
    SATTB and SATB (T-solo)   Continuo
    Broude Brothers (1954) BB 131

6:9-15
    Solomin, G.
    The Lord's Prayer (from The Russian Liturgy)
    SATB   Piano ad lib.
    Boosey & Hawkes (1956) 5095

6:9-15
    Stravinsky, Igor
    Pater Noster   (Latin only)
    SATB   kro
    Boosey & Hawkes (1949) 1833

6:9-15
    Verdi, Giuseppi (ed. John Finley Williamson)
    Our Father   (English/Latin)
    SSATB   kro
    G. Schirmer (1936) 8001

6:9-15
    Villa-Lobos, Heitor
    The Lord's Prayer   (English/Portugese)
    SATB   kro
    Marks (1951) 30

6:9-15
    West Indian Spiritual (ed. Max Saunders)
    The Lord's Prayer
    SATB   Piano
    Boosey & Hawkes (1946) 1915

6:19-20
    Heath, John (transcribed & edited Hewitt
        Pantaleoni)
    Lay Not Up For Yourselves
    TTBB   No accompaniment
    Concordia (1963) 98-1683

6:19-21
    Bass, Claude
    Matthew 6:19-21
    SATB   Keyboard
    Broadman (1978) 4563012

6:19-21   (Matthew 7:7-8)
    Clokey, Joseph
    Treasures In Heaven
    SATB (S-solo)   Organ
    Summy Birchard (1941) SUMCO B-2010

6:19-21
    Jordahl, Robert
    Treasures
    SATB   kro
    Kjos (1981) ED 5971

6:19-21
    Neff, James
    Lay Up Treasures In Heaven
    2 part mixed   Keyboard
    Schmitt, Hall, McCreary (1965) SD 6210

6:25-26, 28-29
    Petzhold, Johannes
    More Than Raiment
    SATB   No accompaniment
    Augsburg (1973) 11-1682

6:28
    Willaert, Adrianus (ed. Zanon-Vene)
    Consider The Lilies (English/Latin)
    SATB   kro
    Ricordi (1958) NY 1898

6:28-29
    Winslow, R.
    Consider The Lilies
    SATB   kro
    Elkan Vogel (1965) 1217

6:28-29
    Young, Gordon
    Consider The Lilies
    SATB   No accompaniment
    Presser (1973) 312-41025

6:28-30
    McCormick, Clifford
    Consider The Lilies Of The Field
    SATB   No accompaniment
    Shawnee (1956) A-399   (also found in Anthems
        From Scripture, G-34)

6:31ff
    Schalk, Carl
    Offertory/Pentecost 14 (Verses and Offer-
        tories - Pentecost 12-20)
    Unison   Organ
    Augsburg (1978) 11-9539

6:31-33
    Glarum, L. Stanley
    Seek Ye First The Kingdom Of God
    SAB   kro
    H. T. Fitzsimons (1964) 2210

6:31-34
    Kirk, Theron
    Seek Ye First The Kingdom Of God
    2 part mixed   Piano
    Carl Fischer (1978) CM 8043

6:33
    Mozart, W. A.
    Quaerite Primum Regnum Dei (Seek Ye First),
        K. 86   (Latin/English)
    SATB   kro
    Concordia (1974) (found in Mozart Anthem
        Book, Volume I, 97-5230)

6:33
    Mozart, W. A. (ed. J. G. Smith)
    Seek First The Kingdom Of God, K.86
        (English/Latin)
    SATB   kro
    Mark Foster (1975) MF 157

7:7
    SEE: Matthew 11:28-30
    Cox, Michael
    Come Unto Me

7:7ff
    Pelz, Walter
    Offertory/Seventh Sunday of Easter (Verses
        And Offertories/Easter - Trinity
    SATB   Organ
    Augsburg (1980) 11-9546

7:7   (adapted)
    Sleeth, Natalie
    Seek And You Will Find
    2 part   Keyboard
    Hinshaw (1980) (found in Laudamus, HMB-126)

7:7-8
    Beebe, Hank
    Seek And Ye Shall Find
    2 part treble   Keyboard
    Pembroke [Carl Fischer] (1978) PC 1016

7:7-8
    SEE: Matthew 6:19-21
    Clokey, Joseph
    Treasures In Heaven

7:7-8
    Glarum, L. Stanley
    Ask, And It Shall Be Given You
    SATB   kro
    G. Schirmer (1963) 11033

7:7-12
    Mueller, Carl F.
    Do Ye Even So To Them
    SATB   Piano or Organ
    Carl Fischer (1950) CM-6525

7:16
    Wilkes, Jon
    By Their Fruits Ye Shall Know Them
    SATB   Piano or Guitar
    GIA (1972) G-1769

8:8
    Distler, Hugo (ed. Clifford Richter)
    Ach, Herr, Ich bin nicht wert (O Lord, I
        Have No Worth) (English/German)
    SATB   kro
    Boonin (1975) B 252

8:8
    Franck, Melchior (ed. Paul Thomas)
    O Lord, I Am Not Worthy
    SATB   Keyboard
    Concordia (1962) 98-1636

8:11-12
    Bender, Jan
    Many Shall Come From The East And The West
    SAB   Organ
    Concordia (1955) CH 1095

8:23-26
    Vulpius, Melchior (ed. Hans H. Eggebrecht)
    Ascendente Jesu in Naviculam
    SSATTB   kro
    Concordia (1961) MS 1028

8:25-27
    Bender, Jan
    Lord, Save Us
    SSA   kro
    Concordia (1956) 98-1160

8:25-27
    Vulpius, Melchior (ed. Hans H. Eggebrecht)
    Then Came The Disciples To Jesus (English/
        German)
    SATB   kro
    Concordia (1961) 98-1574

11:4-6 (based on)
    Pfautsch, Lloyd
    Go And Tell John
    3 part   Percussion
    Hope (1980) 939 (found in Choirbook For
        Saints and Sinners)

11:4-6
    Pfautsch, Lloyd
    Go And Tell John
    SATB   No accompaniment
    Hope (1970) CY 3334

11:9-10
    Frey, Richard E.
    Hosanna In The Highest
    SATB   No accompaniment
    Art Masters Studio (1970) AMS 177

11:10
    Wetzler, Robert
    Verse/Advent III (Verses and Offertories
        Advent I - The Baptism Of Our Lord)
    SATB   Organ, Handbells
    Augsburg (1979) 11-9541

11:10
    Willan, Healey
    Behold, I Send My Messenger
    SA   Keyboard
    Concordia (1962) 97-7160   (found in We
        Praise Thee, Volume 2)

11:28
    Cutler, Henry Stephen
    Come Unto Me
    SATB   Keyboard
    J. Fischer (1970) FE 10011

11:28
    SEE: Luke 14:27
    McCormack, Clifford
    Then Did Jesus Pray

11:28-29
    Atkinson, Thelma
    Come Unto Me
    SATB   Piano
    F. Harris (1951) FH 2821

11:28-29
    Phillips, J. G.
    Venite Ad Me (Latin)
    SATB   Organ
    McLaughlin & Reilly (1955) 2232

11:28-29
    Roff, Joseph
    Come To Me, All Ye That Labour
    SATB   Organ
    Shawnee (1953) n.#. (also available in
        SAB voicing)

11:28-30
    Blakenship, Mark
    Come Unto Me
    SATB   No accompaniment
    Broadman (1975) 4545-99

11:28-30
    Burroughs, Bob
    Come Unto Me
    SATB   kro
    New Music Company (1981) NM-A-135

11:28-30
    Christenius, Johann (ed. C. Buell Agey)
    Come Thou Unto Me
    SATB   kro
    Concordia (1978) 98-2353

11:28-30 (Matthew 7:7)
    Cox, Michael
    Come Unto Me
    SATB (solo)   Keyboard
    Chrismon [Hinshaw] (1980) CHC-5006

11:28-30
    Darst, W. Glen
    Come Unto Me
    SAB   Organ
    Concordia (1961) 98-1577

11:28-30
    diLasso, Orlando (ed. C. Buell Agey)
    Venite Ad Me Omnes (Come Unto Me) (English/
        Latin)
    SATTB   kro
    G. Schirmer (1966) 11399

11:28-30
    Glarum, L. Stanley
    Come Unto Me
    SATB   Optional accompaniment
    Boosey & Hawkes (1959) 5270

11:28-30
    Glarum, L. Stanley
    Come Unto Me
    SAB   Optional accompaniment
    Boosey & Hawkes (1963) 5480

11:28-30
    Glarum, L. Stanley
    Come Unto Me
    SSAA   Optional accompaniment
    Boosey & Hawkes (1959) 5474

11:28-30
    Hruby, Dolores
    Come To Me, All You Who Labor (from Three
        Sacred Songs)
    Unison   Organ
    Concordia (1973) 98-2098

11:28-30
    VanDyke, Paul C.
    Come Unto Me
    SATB   Piano or Organ
    Carl Fischer (1964) CM 7408

11:28-30
    Vick, Beryl
    Come Unto Me
    SACB   Piano
    Cambiata Press (1975) C 97559

11:28-30
    Willan, Healey
    Come Unto Me All Ye That Labor And Are
        Heavy Laden
    Unison   Organ
    Concordia (1958) 98-2359 (also found in
        Third Morning Star Choir Book, 97-4972)

11:29-30
    Palestrina, G. P. (ed. Paul Laubenstein)
    Tollite Jugum Meum (Latin)
    SATB   kro
    G. Schirmer (1949) 9702

13:3, 9
    McAfee, Don
    Parable Of The Sower (from Two Parables)
    SATB   kro
    General Music (1968) n.#.

13:39
  SEE: Revelation 14:14-15
  Willan, Healey
  I Looked And Behold A White Cloud

14:00 (adapted)
  Cain, Noble
  In The Night, Christ Came Walking
  SATB   kro
  G. Schirmer (1936) 7967

15:4-10
  Bender, Jan
  Begone, Satan
  2 equal voices   Organ
  Concordia   98-1834

15:22, 27-28
  Josquin Des Pres (ed. Robert Gronquist)
  O Jesu, Fili David (O Jesus, Son Of David)
  SA(T)B   Organ
  Tetra [Alexander Broude] (1968) AB 169

15:25-34
  Bender, Jan
  Come, O Blessed Of My Father
  2 equal voices   Organ
  Concordia   98-1834

15:26-28
  Bender, Jan
  It Is Not Fair, Op. 32, #13
  2 equal voices   Keyboard
  Concordia (1966) 98-1847

16:15
  Wetzler, Robert
  Go Ye Into All The World
  2 part mixed   Keyboard
  Augsburg (1962) 11-1346

16:18
  Durufle, Maurice
  Tu es Petrus (from Quatre Motets sur des
      Theme Gregoriens) (Latin only)
  SATB   No accompaniment
  Durand (1960)

16:18
  Hassler, Hans Leo
  Tu es Petrus (Latin only)
  SATB   kro
  J. & W. Chester (1977) JWC 55107 (found in
      Fourth Chester Book Of Motets)

16:18-19 (Song Of Songs 2:11-13)
  Beck, John Ness
  Upon This Rock
  SATB   Organ (optional brass sextet)
  G. Schirmer (1967) 11467

16:18-19
  Hewitt-Jones, Tony
  Thou Art Peter
  SATB   Organ ad lib.
  RSCM (1978) (found in Anthems From Addington,
      Volume 10)

16:18-19
  Monteverdi, Claudio
  Tu es Pastor
  SAB   No accompaniment
  Arista (1972) AE 208

16:18-19
  Morales, Cristobal
  Tu es Petrus
  SAB   No accompaniment
  Arista (1969) AE 168

16:18-19
  Palestrina, G. P.
  Tu es Petrus (Latin only)
  SSATBB   No accompaniment
  Breitkopf (1959) A 531

16:18-19
  Palestrina, G. P.
  Tu es Petrus (Latin)
  SSAATB   kro
  G. Schirmer (n.d.) 5603

16:18-19
  Palestrina, G. P.
  Tu es Petrus (Latin/English)
  SSAATB   kro
  G. Schirmer (1968) 11567

16:18-19
  Tambylyn, William
  You Are Peter
  SATB   Organ or Brass
  Boosey & Hawkes (1971) 5824

16:19, 24-25
  McCormick, Clifford
  The Keys Of The Kingdom
  SATB (B-solo)   Organ
  Shawnee (1958) A-472 (also found in Anthems
      From Scripture, G-34)

16:24
  Lassus, Orlandus
  Qui Vult Venire (Latin only)
  2 part   No accompaniment
  Mercury (1941) 352.00011 (found in Twelve
      Motets)

16:24-25
  York, David Stanley
  If Any Man Will Come After Me
  SATB (B-solo)   kro
  Mercury (1958) MC 313

17:5
  Nystedt, Knut
  This Is My Beloved Son
  SAB   Organ
  Concordia (1965) 98-1805 (also found in
      Sing For Joy, 97-5046)

17:7, 9
  Lenel, Ludwig
  Arise, And Be Not Afraid
  4 part round   Organ
  Concordia (1960) 98-1504

18:1-4
  McNair, Jacqueline Hanna
  Whosoever Shall Come To Me
  SATB (T-solo)   Keyboard
  Broadman (1967) 451-656

18:32-35
  Bender, Jan
  You Wicked Servant, Op. 32, #24
  3 equal voices   Keyboard
  Concordia (1974) 98-2085

19:13-15
  Lynn, George
  Suffer The Little Children
  SATB   Organ
  Mercury (1956) MC 270

20:1, 3-4
  Morales, Cristobal
  Simile est Regnum (Latin)
  SATB   kro
  J. & W. Chester (1977) JWC 55104 (found in
      Third Chester Book Of Motets)

20:26-28
  Nelson, Ronald A.
  Whoever Would Be Great Among You
  SAB   Guitar or Keyboard
  Augsburg (1971) 11-1638

21:5
   Wetzler, Robert
   Hark A Thrilling Voice Is Sounding
   SATB   kro
   Augsburg   11-1297

21:5, 9
   Couper, Alinda
   Tell The Daughters Of Zion   (Festival
       Introits)
   SATB   kro
   Abingdon (1969) APM-780

21:8-9
   SEE: Luke 9:51
   Friedell, Harold
   The Way To Jerusalem

21:8-9 (Matthew 11:8-10)
   Hancock, Eugene
   A Palm Sunday Anthem
   SATB, Youth Choir   Organ
   H. W. Gray (1971) CMR 3125

21:8-9
   Thompson, Randall
   Pueri Hebraeorum (Latin)
   SSAA/SSAA   kro
   E. C. Schirmer (1928) 492

21:8-9
   Victoria, Tomas
   Pueri Hebraeorum (Latin)
   SATB   No accompaniment
   Arista (1973) AE 228

21:8-9
   Victoria, Tomas Luis
   Pueri Hebraeorum (Latin only)
   SATB   kro
   J. & W. Chester (1977) JWC 55104 (found in
      Third Chester Book Of Motets)

21:8-9
   Victoria, Tomas (ed. Zanon-Vere)
   Pueri Hebraeorum (English/Latin)
   SATB   kro
   Ricordi (1957) NY 1879

21:8-19 (based on)
   George, Graham
   Ride On! Ride On!
   SATB   Organ
   H. W. Gray (1941) 1765

21:9
   SEE: Isaiah 6:3
   Beebe, Hank
   Hosanna To The Lord (Service Of Life)

21:9
   Bender, Jan
   Hosanna To The Son Of David, Op. 32, #6
   2 part equal voices   Keyboard
   Concordia (1969) 98-1964

21:9
   Bender, Jan
   Hosanna To The Son Of David, Op. 43, #1
   SAB   kro
   Concordia (1966) 98-1870

21:9
   SEE: Isaiah 6:3
   Bortniansky, Demetrius
   Sanctus and Hosanna

21:9 (L. S. Clark)
   Bristol, Lee Hastings, Jr.
   Could Jesus Hear The Sounds To Come?
   SATB, Junior Choir   Organ
   Canyon Press (1955) 5502

21:9
   Carter, John
   Hosanna To The Son Of David
   SATB, Junior Choir   Organ
   AMSI (1975) 271

21:9
   SEE: Psalm 3:8
   Copley, Evan
   Salvation Belongeth Unto The Lord

21:9
   Curry, L. Lawrence (arr.)
   Hosanna
   TTBB   Piano
   Flammer (1957) 85060

21:9
   Davis, Katherine K.
   Fanfare For Palm Sunday
   SATB   Piano
   B. F. Wood (1962) 44-804

21:9
   Davis, Katherine K.
   To The King Of Glory
   SATB   Keyboard
   Hinshaw (1978) HMC 281

21:9
   Dieterich, Milton
   Benedictus
   SATB   Keyboard ad lib.
   Boosey & Hawkes (1956) 5083

21:9
   Gesius, Bartholomaeus (ed. Paul Thomas)
   Hosanna To The Son Of David
   SATB   kro
   Concordia (1953) 98-1038 (also found in
      The Parish Choir Book, 97-7574)

21:9
   Gesius, Bartholomäus)
   Hosianna dem Sohne Davids   (German)
   SATB   No accompaniment
   Merseburger (1977) (found in Motetten Alter
      Meister)

21:9
   Gibbons, Orlando (ed. Granville Bantock)
   Hosanna To The Son Of David
   SSAATB   Organ ad lib.
   Curwen [G. Schirmer] (1913) 10321

21:9 (Mark 11:10; or Luke 19:38)
   Gibbons, Orlando (ed. H. Clough-Leighter)
   Hosanna To The Son Of David
   SSAATB   kro
   E. C. Schirmer (1932) ECS 574

21:9
   Gibbons, Orlando
   Hosanna To The Son Of David
   SSAATTB   kro
   Oxford (1976) (also found in Oxford Book
      Of Tudor Anthems)

21:9 (edited)
   Gibbons, Orlando
   Hosanna To The Son Of David
   SSAATTB   kro
   Oxford (1976) 43.079

21:9
   Gibbons, Orlando (ed. Ruth Heller)
   Hosanna To The Son Of David
   SSAATB   kro
   Summy Birchard (1960) 5396

21:9
   Gregor, Christian (arr. Benjamin Dunford)
   Hosanna!
   SATB/SATB   Organ (optional brass choir)
   Belwin (1972) FEC-10058

21:9
Gregor, Christian (arr. J. B. Lyle)
Hosanna
SA   and   SSCB   Piano
Cambiata Press (1979) M 979135

21:9
Gregor, Christian (arr. R. Bitgood)
Hosanna
SATB, Children's Choir   Organ
H. W. Gray (1963) GCMR 1345

21:9
Gregor, Christian (arr. Margaret J. Hoffmann)
Hosanna!
SAB   Piano or Organ
Presser (1956) 312-40928

21:9
Gumpeltzhaimer, Adam
Blessed Is He That Cometh
Canon for 2 equal voices   No accompaniment
Concordia (found in Second Morning Star
     Choir Book)

21:9
Hannahs, Roger
Hosannah To The Son Of David
SATB   Organ, 3 Trumpets
H. W. Gray (1960) 2631

21:9
Hutchings, Arthur
Hosanna To The Son Of David
SATB   kro
Novello (1964) 29.0358.10

21:9b
Lorenz, Ellen Jane
Hosanna To The Son Of David
2 antiphonal Unison Choirs   Handbells or
     Organ
Abingdon (1963) APM-266

21:9
Moe, Daniel
Hosanna To The Son Of David
SATB   Organ
Mercury (1956) MC 252

21:9
Mozart, W. A. (ed. Edward J. Dent)
He Is Blessed That Cometh (Benedictus from
     Requiem)
SATB (S-A-T-B-solos)   Organ
Oxford (1933) (found in Church Anthem Book)

21:9
Newbury, Kent A.
Blessed Is He That Cometh
TTBB   kro
Lawson Gould (1961) 51012

21:9
Palestrina, G. P. (ed. Bernard Rose)
Benedictus Qui Venit (from Missa Quarta -
     1583) (English/Latin)
SATB   kro
Oxford (1957) (found in Sixteenth Century
     Anthem Book)

21:9
Penhorwood, Edwin
Hosanna To The Son Of David
SATB (3 soprano solos)   Organ and
     string bass
Carl Fischer (1975) CM 7902

21:9
Pooler, Marie
Hosanna
2 part   Keyboard
Augsburg (1962) 11-1405

21:9
Pooler, Marie
Hosanna
Unison and 2 part   Keyboard
Augsburg (1962) 11-9517

21:9
Praetorius, Michael (ed. & arr. Robert
     Field)
Hosanna To The Son Of David
SSATB   keyboard ad lib.
Boosey & Hawkes (1964) 5528

21:9
Praetorius, Michael (arr. Isa McIlwraith)
Hosanna To The Son Of David
SSAAB   Accompaniment ad lib.
H. W. Gray (1946) CMR 1973

21:9
Praetorius, Michael (ed. Walter Buszin)
Hosanna To The Son Of David
SSATB   kro
Hall & McCreary (1939) 1516

21:9
Schreck, Gustav
Advent Motet - Entrance Scene
SATB   No accompaniment
Kjos (n.d.) 5083

21:9
Smith, Robert Edward
Hosanna To The Son Of David
SSATB   kro
Alexander Broude (1979) AB 834

21:9
Victoria, Tomas
Hosanna To The Son Of David
SATB   kro
Concordia (1970) 98-1993

21:9
Victoria, Tomas
Hosanna To The Son Of David (Latin/English)
SATB   kro
Concordia (1968) (found in A First Motet
     Book, 97-4845)

21:9
Voris, W. R.
Blessed Is He
SATB   Organ
H. W. Gray (1928) CMR 914

21:9
Vulpius, Melchior
Das Volk aber das vorging und nach folget
     (German)
SATB   No accompaniment
Merseburger (1977) (found in Motetten Alter
     Meister)

21:9
Weelkes, Thomas
Hosanna To The Son Of David
SSATBB   kro
Oxford (1968 TCM 9 (also found in Oxford
     Book Of Tudor Anthems)

21:9
Willan, Healey
Hosanna To The Son Of David
SATB   kro
Concordia (1952) 98-1016

21:9
Willan, Healey
Hosanna To The Son Of David
Unison   or   SSA   Keyboard
Concordia (1953) 98-1118 (also found in
     We Praise Thee, Volume 1)

21:9
    Williamson, Malcolm
    Procession of Palms
    SATB (S-A-solos)   Organ
    Weinberger [G. Schirmer] (1962) 11251

21:9-11 (Luke 19:38)
    Nelson, Ronald A.
    Hosanna
    SAB/SAB   Organ
    Augsburg (1967) ACL-1510

21:9-11 (based on)
    Tunder, Franz (ed. Leland A. Lillehaug)
    Scatter Palm Branches
    SSATB   Strings and Continuo
    Concordia (1963) 97-6406

21:22
    SEE: John 16:24
    Glarum, L. Stanley
    Ask And Ye Shall Receive

22:4
    Bender, Jan
    Tell Those Who Are Invited, Op. 32, #12
    2 part treble   Keyboard
    Concordia (1962) 98-1687

22:20-21
    Franck, Melchior (ed. Charles Frischmann)
    Jesus And The Pharisees! Tell Me Whose
            Likeness You See Thereon
    SATB   kro
    Concordia (1972) 98-2093

22:35-40
    Bristol, Lee H. Jr.
    God's Requirements
    2 part   Keyboard
    Choristers Guild (1965) A-33

22:38
    SEE: Matthew 28:19
    Butler, Eugene
    Go Ye Into All The World

23:37-38
    Bernhard, Christoph (ed. David Streetham)
    Jerusalem, Thou That Killest The Prophets
            (English/German)
    SSB   2 violins, continuo
    Concordia (1973) 97-5109

24:13
    Mendelssohn, Felix
    He That Shall Endure To The End
    SATB   Organ
    Oxford (1933) (found in Church Anthem Book

24:24-36   (based on)
    Roff, Joseph
    Listen, Christian
    SATB   Piano or Organ
    GIA (1975) G-1976

24:42
    Busarow, Donald
    Verse/26th Sunday After Pentecost (Verses
            And Offertories - Pentecost 21 -
            Christ The King)
    Unison   Organ
    Augsburg (1979) 11-9540

24:44
    SEE: Matthew 25:13
    Hammerschmidt, Andreas (ed. Harold Mueller)
    Therefore Watch That Ye Be Ready

25:1-13
    Buxtehude, Dietrich (ed. Clough-Leighter)
    Zion hört die Wächter singen (German)
    TB   Organ
    E. C. Schirmer   #538

25:1-13 (L. Laurenti)
    Gumpeltzhaimer, Adam (ed. Paul Thomas)
    Rejoice, Rejoice, Believers
    SATB   kro
    Concordia (1959) 98-1469

25:1-13
    Nicolai, Philip (setting by Harald Rohlig)
    Wake, Awake For Night Is Flying
    SAB   Congregation   Organ and Trumpet
    Concordia (1965) 97-4670

25:1-13
    Nicolai, Philip (setting by Friedrich Zipp)
    Wake, Awake For Night Is Flying
    SATB   Organ and/or Brass   Congregation
    Concordia (1956) 97-5389

25:1-13 (Revelation 19:6-9; Isaiah 52:8)
    Nicolai, Philip (setting by Ludwig Lenel)
    Wake, Awake For Night Is Flying
    Unison   Organ (brass ad lib.)
    Concordia (1958) 98-1453

25:6
    Tallis, Thomas (ed. R. R. Terry)
    Audivi, Media Nocte
    SSTB or AATB   Optional Keyboard
    Oxford (1963) TCM 2

25:6
    Taverner, John
    Audivi (Latin)
    SATB   kro
    J. & W. Chester (1977) JWC-5103 (found in
            Second Chester Book Of Motets)

25:11-13
    Bender, Jan
    Lord, Lord, Open To Us, Op. 32, #20
    Unison   Keyboard
    Concordia (1966) 98-1833

25:13 (Matthew 24:44)
    Hammerschmidt, Andreas (ed. Harold Mueller)
    Therefore Watch That Ye Be Ready
            (English/German)
    SSATB   Continuo and 2 Violins
    Concordia (1980) 97-6316

25:23
    Lassus, Orlandus
    Serve Bone   (Latin only)
    2 part   No accompaniment
    Mercury (1941) 352.00011 (found in Twelve
            Motets)

25:31
    Hoiby, Lee
    Inherit The Kingdom
    SATB (B-solo)   Organ
    Presser (1970) 312-40725

25:31-40
    Locke, Matthew
    When The Son Of Man Shall Come
    SSATB   Organ
    Oxford (n.d.) CMS Reprint, #7

25:32-33
    Nysted, Knut
    Before Him
    Unison   Organ
    Concordia (1965) 98-1894 (also found in
            Third Morning Star Choir Book)

25:32
    Bender, Jan
    Come, O Blessed Of My Father, Op. 32, #15
    2 part   Keyboard
    Concordia (1966) 98-1834

25:34
    Monteverdi, Claudio (ed. R. Vene)
    Come Thou Faithful Servant
    SSA   or   TTB   kro
    Ricordi (1950) 2032

25:34-36
    Haan, Raymond
    Come Ye Blessed
    SATB   Organ
    Broadman (1975) 4546-00

25:34-36
    Scott, John Prindle (arr. Carl Deis)
    Come Ye Blessed
    SATB   Organ
    G. Schirmer (1944) 7464

25:34-40
    Pelz, Walter L.
    Come, You Have My Father's Blessing
    SAB   Organ
    Augsburg (1973) 11-1761

25:33
    Proulx, Richard
    Look For Me In Lowly Men
    SATB   Organ   or   Brass (2 Trumpets,
        2 Trombones, Optional Timpani)
    GIA (1974) G-2145

25:35-40 (based on)
    Hruby, Dolores
    For The Least Of My Brothers
    2 part mixed   Keyboard
    Concordia (1976) 98-2296

26:00 (following)
    Victoria, Tomas (ed. Austin Lovelace)
    The Passion According to St. Matthew
    SATB   3 Readers   Keyboard
    Summy-Birchard (1956) SUMCO 4415

26:6, 10, 18, 20   (adapted)
    Yardumian, Richard (Harmonized)
    Our Lord Is Risen Today (Eleven Easter
        Chorales)
    SATB   No accompaniment
    Elkan Vogel (1978) 362.03280

26:17-30
    Donato, Anthony
    The Last Supper
    SATB   kro
    Southern (1958) MI 60

26:20, 26-28
    Newbury, Kent A.
    The Last Supper (from Three Short Holy
        Week Anthems)
    SATB   kro
    G. Schirmer (1966) 11349

26:23-24
    Victoria, Tomas
    Uns ex discipulis meis   (Latin)
    SATB   No accompaniment
    J. W. Chester (1960) 8813c

26:26-28
    SEE: Psalm 23:6
    Peloquin, Alexander
    Holy Communion

26:38
    Heussenstamm, George
    My Soul Is Exceeding Sorrowful
    SSATB   Keyboard
    Art Master (1970) AMS 173

26:38
    Kuhnau, Johann
    Tristes est anima mea   (Latin)
    SSATB   No accompaniment
    Arista (1981) AE 421

26:38
    Kuhnau, Johan (ed. Walter Buszin)
    Tristes est anima mea (Latin/English)
    SATB   No accompaniment
    Concordia (1952) 98-1971

26:38, 45
    Leo, Leonardo (ed. Denys Darlow)
    Tristes est anima mea (Tenebrae First
        Nocturne)
    SATB   kro
    Oxford (1964)n.#.

26:38-39
    Krenek, Ernst
    On Mount Olivet
    SATB   Organ or Piano
    Mills (1954) AMI 2317

26:38-39
    Pitoni, Giuseppi (arr. & ed. John Kingsbury)
    Tarry Here And Watch
    SATB   kro
    Tetra [Alexander Broude] (1977) AB 757

26:38, 41
    Neff, James
    My Soul Is Exceeding Sorrowful
    2 part mixed   Keyboard
    Augsburg (1964) 1396

26:38, 56 (paraphrase)
    Martini, G. B.
    Tristis anima mea   (Latin)
    TTB   kro
    Oratoriums Verlag (n.d.) (found in Geist-
        liche Gesang für Mannerchor

26:39, 41
    Croce, Giovanni (ed. F. Campbell Watson)
    In Monte Oliveti (On Mount Olive) (English/
        Latin)
    SATB   kro
    Witmark (1949) SW 3355

26:39, 41
    DiLasso, Orlando
    In Monte Oliveti (from Drei Passionsmotetten)
    SAATBB   No accompaniment
    Kalmus (n.d.) n.#.

26:39, 41
    Haydn, Michael (ed. Arthur Hilton)
    In Monti Oliveti   (English/Latin)
    SATB   Organ ad lib.
    Presser (1974) 352.00467

26:39, 41
    Ingegneri, Marc Antonio
    In Monte Oliveti (Latin only)
    SATB   kro
    J. & W. Chester (1977) JWC 55096 (found in
        First Chester Book Of Motets)

26:39-41
    Jommelli, Niccolo (ed. Ralph Hunter)
    In Monte Oliveti (Upon The Mount Of Olives)
        (Latin/English)
    SAB   Organ continuo
    Belwin (1981) Oct. 2470

26:39, 41
    Leo, Leonardo (ed. Denys Darlow)
    In Monte Oliveti (Tenebrae First Nocturne)
        (Latin only)
    SATB   Organ
    Oxford (1964) n.#.

26:39-41
    Martini, G. B.
    In Monte Oliveti   (Latin)
    SSA   kro
    E. C. Schirmer (1935) 933

26:39-41
  Martini, G. B.
  In Monte Oliveti (Latin)
  TTBB   No accompaniment
  E. C. Schirmer #1234

26:39, 41
  Palestrina, G. P.
  In Monte Oliveti (Latin/English)
  SATB   kro
  Hall & McCreary (1948) 1660

26:40
  Victoria, Tomas
  Una Hora
  SSAT   No accompaniment
  J. & W. Chester (1960) 8814b

26:47
  Victoria, Tomas
  Seniores Populi (Latin)
  SATB   No accompaniment
  J. & W. Chester (1960) JWC 8814

26:55
  Haydn, Michael
  Tanquam ad Lantronem existis (Latin/
      English)
  SATB   kro
  Schmitt, Hall, McCreary (1951) (found in
      Rare Choral Masterpieces)

26:55
  Victoria, Tomas (ed. Kurt Schindler)
  Tanquam ad Latronem (All Ye Come Out As
      Against A Thief) (English/Latin)
  SATB   kro
  Presser (1919) 332-13370

26:55
  Victoria, Tomas (ed. Bruno Turner)
  Tanquam Ad Latronem (Latin)
  SATB   No accompaniment
  J. & W. Chester (1960) JWC 8816

26:57-58
  Goodman, Joseph
  Jesum Tradidit (The Wicked Man Betrayed
      Jesus) (Three Responsories)
  SATB   kro
  Alexander Broude (1967) AB 148

27:1-2, 22-26
  Williams, David H.
  Jesus Before Pilate
  SATB   Organ
  Shawnee (1960) A 556

27:45 (Luke 23:46)
  Haydn, Michael (ed. William Ramsey)
  Tenebrae factae sunt (English/Latin)
  SATB   kro
  Boonin (1973) B 148

27:45-46
  Ingegneri, Marc A.
  Tenebrae factae sunt (Latin/English)
  SATB   kro
  E. C. Schirmer (1976) (found in The
      Renaissance Singer)

27:45, 46
  Jommelli, Niccolo (ed. Ralph Hunter)
  Tenebrae factae sunt (English/Latin)
  SATB   Organ continuo
  Belwin (1981) Oct. 2475

27:45-46 (Luke 23:24; John 19:30)
  Palestrina, G. P.
  Tenebrae factae sunt
  SATB   No accompaniment
  Merseburger (1977) (found in Motetten
      Alter Meister)

27:45-46
  Poulenc, Francis
  Tenebrae factae sunt (English/Latin)
  SAATBB   No accompaniment
  Salabert (1962) SAL. 18

27:45-46
  Victoria, Tomas (ed. Carolyn Bliss)
  And There Was Darkness (English/Latin)
  SSAT   kro
  Augsburg (1964) ACL 1407

27:45-46
  Victoria, Tomas (ed. Bruno Turner)
  Tenebrae Factae Sunt (Latin)
  SATB or TTBB   No accompaniment
  J. & W. Chester (1960) 8816b

27:45-47 (John 19:30; Luke 23:46)
  Haydn, Michael (ed. George Strickling)
  Tenebrae in E-flat (Latin/English)
  SATB   kro
  Hall & McCreary (1939) 1536

27:46 (Luke 23:46)
  Croce, Giovanni
  Tenebrae factae sunt (Latin)
  SATB   No accompaniment
  Arista (1970) AE 181

27:46 (Luke 23:46)
  Davye, John J.
  Tenebrae facta sunt (English/Latin)
  TTBB   kro
  Associated (1962) A 370

27:46 (Luke 23:46)
  Eberlin, Johann Ernest
  Tenebrae factae sunt (Latin only)
  SATB   No accompaniment
  Arista (1969) AE 167

27:46 (Luke 23:46)
  Haydn, Michael (transcribed Reinhard G.
      Pauly)
  Tenebrae factae sunt (English/Latin)
  SSA   Organ or Piano
  G. Schirmer (1958) 10532

27:46 (Luke 23:46)
  Ingegneri, Marc Antonio
  Tenebrae factae sunt (English/Latin)
  SATB   kro
  E. C. Schirmer (1976) ECS 2980

27:51-52 (Luke 23:42)
  Haydn, Michael
  Velum Templi Scissum Est
  SATB   Organ ad lib.
  G. Schirmer (1899) n.#.

27:60, 62
  Victoria, Tomas
  Sepulto Domino (Latin)
  SATB   No accompaniment
  J. & W. Chester (1960) JWC 8819

28:1, 5-6
  SEE: Isaiah 60:20
  Gore, Richard T.
  The Sun Shall No More Go Down

28:1
  Handl, Jacob
  Vespere Autem Sabbata
  SATB   No accompaniment
  Arista (1974) AE 246

28:1-6
  Speaks, Oley (arr. Lucien Chaffin)
  In The End Of The Sabbath
  SATB (A-solo)   Organ
  G. Schirmer (1918) 6795

28:1-10
Maeker, Nancy
Easter
Speech Choir   Narrator   Percussion
Augsburg (1979) 11-3505

28:1-2, 5-6   (Psalm 68:32)
Vincent, Charles
As It Began To Dawn
SATB (S-solo)   Organ
G. Schirmer (n.d.) 4500

28:2, 5-8
Anerio, Felice
Angelus Autem Domini   (English/Latin)
SATB   kro
E. C. Schirmer (1976) ECS 2975   (also found
     in The Renaissance Singer)

28:2, 5-7
Yardumian, Richard
From Heavens The Angel Came   (from Eleven
     Easter Chorales)
SATB   No accompaniment
Elkan Vogel (1978) 362-03280

28:2-3, 5-6
Krenek, Ernst
By The Sepulchre
SATB   Organ or Piano
Mills (1954) 2318

28:5-6
Rohlig, Harald
The Angel Said To The Woman
Unison or SA   Keyboard
Concordia (1973) 98-2287   (also found in
     Explode With Joy, 97-5156)

28:5b, 6a
Felciano, Richard
Sic Transit
SSA   Tape and Light
E. C. Schirmer (1971) 2807

28:5-7
Pinkham, Daniel
And The Angel Said   (from Easter Cantata)
SATB   Piano (Brass)
C. F. Peters (1962) 6393

28:6   (adapted)
SEE: Luke 24:1-5
Englert, Eugene
He Is Risen, Alleluia!

28:16-20   (Psalm 72)
Peek, Richard
Lo, I Am With You Always
SATB   Organ
Abingdon (1968) APM-755

28:18-20   (John 14:3)
Ingram, Ray   (arr. William J. Reynolds)
The Great Commission
SATB   Keyboard
Broadman (1956) 4533-68

28:18
Moe, Daniel
Lo, I Am With You
SATB   kro
Augsburg (1960) ACL 1270

28:18-20   (Mark 16:15)
York, David Stanley
Go Ye Into All The World
SATB   Organ
Presser (1962) 312-40538

28:19 (Matthew 22:38;   John 15:12-13;
     John 14:1)
Butler, Eugene
Go Ye Into All The World
SATB   Piano or Organ
Carl Fischer (1974) CM 7880

28:19
Gumpeltzhaimer, Adam
Go Ye Into All The World
Canon for 2 equal voices   No accompaniment
Concordia (1950) CTS 28   (also found in
     First Morning Star Choir Book)

28:19-20
Hancock, Gerre
Go Ye Therefore
SATB   Unison Chorus   Organ, Brass
H. W. Gray (1975) CMR 3331

28:19-20
Jordahl, Robert
Go Ye Therefore
SATB   Organ or Piano, 3 Trumpets
Kjos (1980) ED 5972   (Parts 5972X)

28:19-20
Sleeth, Natalie
Go Into All The World
Three Part: (SAB or SSA) or Two Part:
     (SA or Mixed)   Piano
Choristers Guild (1979) A-209

28:19-20
Wyton, Alec
Go Ye Therefore
SATB   Organ
H. W. Gray (1963) 2755

28:20
Hutson, Wihla
Lo I Am With You Alway
SATB   Organ
Shawnee (1965) A-801

28:20
SEE: Romans 6:9
Pelz, Walter
Verse/Ascension Of Our Lord

28:20b
SEE: John 20:21
Walter, Samuel
Peace Be Unto You

M A R K

1:3
Warren, William
Prepare Ye The Way Of The Lord
SATB   Keyboard and Clarinet
GIA (1975) G 1937

1:11
Wetzler, Robert
Verse/The Baptism Of Our Lord (Verses and
     Offertories - Advent I - The Baptism Of
     Our Lord)
2 part   Organ
Augsburg (1979) 11-9541

2:9-10
Harper, Marjorie
Blessed Is He
SATB   Organ or Piano
Beekman [Mercury] (1961) MC 381

2:9-10
  Harper, Marjorie
  Blessed Is He
  SSA   Organ or Piano
  Beekman [Mercury] (1961) MC 382

4:30-32
  Hopson, Hal H.
  Song Of The Mustard Seed
  Unison   Organ
  GIA (1979) G-2239

7:37
  Bender, Jan
  He Hath Done All Things Well
  SATB   kro
  Concordia (1955) 98-1067 (also found in A
       First Motet Book, 97-4845)

9:2-9
  Hovhaness, Alan
  Transfiguration, Op. 82
  SATB (T-solo)   No accompaniment
  C. F. Peters (1958) 6057

9:9
  Hovhaness, Alan
  And As They Came Down From The Mountain
  SATB   (T-solo)   No accompaniment
  C. F. Peters (1963) 6545

10:13-16
  Lovelace, Austin
  With Thankful Hearts (Two Baptismal
       Responses)
  Unison   Keyboard
  Augsburg (1979) 11-3015

10:14-15
  Roff, Joseph
  The Kingdom Of God
  Unison or 2 part   Keyboard
  H. W. Gray (1980) GCMR 3426

10:17-31
  Allen, Art
  Camel In The Eye
  Unison   Keyboard
  Agape (1975) (found in Choir Book For
       Saints And Sinners)

10:45
  Norris, Kevin
  Verse/Lent V (Verses and Offertories/Lent)
  Unison   Organ
  Augsburg (1980) 11-9545

11:8-10
  SEE: Matthew 21:8-9
  Hancock, Eugene
  A Palm Sunday Anthem

11:9
  Gregor, Christian (ed. E. A. Wienandt and
       Robert Young)
  Hosanna, Blessed Is He That Comes
  SATB   Keyboard
  J. Fischer (1970) 10007

11:9-10
  Frey, Richard E.
  Hosanna In The Highest!
  SATB   No accompaniment
  Art Masters Studio (1970) AMS 177

11:9-10
  Glarum, L. Stanley
  Lord, Hosanna In The Highest
  SAB   Optional accompaniment
  G. Schirmer (1968) 11548

11:9-10
  Glarum, L. Stanley
  Lord Hosanna In The Highest
  SATB   Optional accompaniment
  G. Schirmer (1962) 10903

11:9-10
  Harris, Jerry Weseley
  Hosanna To The Son Of David
  SATB   Piano (optional bongo drums)
  Flammer (1972) A-5597

11:9-10
  Hedges, Hazel
  Hosanna Blessed Is He That Cometh
  SATB (S-solo)   Organ
  Flammer (1956) A-5099

11:9-10
  Jommelli, Niccolo (ed. M. Lundquist)
  Hosanna David's Son
  SATB   Piano (ad lib.)
  Carl Fischer (1941) CM 559

11:9-10
  Means, Claude
  The King Rides Forth
  SATB (Bar. solo)   Organ
  H. W. Gray (1948) 2056

11:9-10
  Scheidt, Samuel (ed. Roger Granville)
  Hosanna To The Son Of David
  SSATB   Piano or Organ
  Sam Fox (1965) CM 14

11:9-11 (Psalm 150, based on)
  Delmonte, Pauline
  He Is Coming
  Unison   Keyboard   (triangle and
       finger cymbals)
  Choristers Guild (1973) A-142

11:10   (John 12:12-13)
  Newbury, Kent A.
  Hosanna
  SATB   Organ
  G. Schirmer (1966) 11350

11:17
  SEE: John 2:13
  Kodaly, Zoltan
  Jesus And The Traders

11:17   (Luke 11:10)
  Titcomb, Everett
  My House Shall Be Called Of All Nations
       (Eight Short Motets, #8)
  SATB   kro
  Carl Fischer (1934) CM 443

11:22-23
  Roff, Joseph
  Have Faith In God
  SATB   kro
  Abingdon (1974) APM-734

12:29-31
  Mueller, Carl F.
  The Great Commandments
  SATB   Organ
  Carl Fischer (1950) CM 6526

12:30-31
  Marshall, Jane
  The Great Commandment
  Unison   Keyboard
  Broadman (1966) 4560-17

12:30-31, 34
  McCormick, Clifford
  You Are Not Far From The Kingdom Of God
  SATB   kro
  Shawnee (1957) A-582 (also found in
       Anthems From Scripture, G-34)

14:32
    Young, Gordon
    Gethsemane
    SATB   Organ
    B. F. Wood (1963) 828

15:18-19
    Smith, Eric
    I Will Arise And Go To My Father
    SATB   Piano or Organ
    Mills (1955) 344

15:33-34
    Gounod, Charles (ed. & arr. Robert Hines)
    There Was Great Darkness
    SAB   Optional Keyboard
    Augsburg (1979) 11-1961

15:33-35
    Pinkham, Daniel
    The Seven Last Words Of Christ On The
        Cross (Word IV)
    SATB   (T-B-B-solo)   Organ and Tape
    E. C. Schirmer (1971) 2907

15:34   (Luke 23:46)
    Haydn, Michael (ed. George Lynn)
    Darkened Was All The Land (English/Latin)
    SATB   Organ
    Presser (1950) 312-40055

16:1
    Johnson, Robert
    Dum Transisset (Latin only)
    SATB   kro
    J. & W. Chester (1977) JWC 55103 (found in
        Second Chester Book Of Motets)

16:1
    Tallis, Thomas
    Dum Transisset Sabbatum
    SATTB   kro
    H. B. Collins (1925) #5

16:1-2
    Tallis, Thomas (ed. Richard Abram)
    Dum Transisset Sabbatum
    SATTB   Optional organ
    Novello (1979) 29.0455.01

16:1-2
    Taverner, John
    Dum Transisset Sabbatum (Latin/English)
    SATBB   kro
    Oxford (1975) A 310

16:1-2, 5-6, 8
    Williamson, Malcolm
    The Morning Of The Day Of Days
    SATB   (S-T-solos)   Organ
    Weinberger [G. Schirmer] (1963) 11247

16:1, 6   (based on)
    Van Iderstine, A. P.
    Early In The Morning
    SATB   No accompaniment
    AMSI (1974) 1240

16:1-7   (John 20:1-18)
    Hammerschmidt, Andrae (ed. Harold Mueller)
    Who Rolls Away The Stone (German/English)
    SSATB   2 violins and Continuo
    Concordia (1973) 97-5166

16:2-4
    McCormick, Clifford
    Early In The Morning
    SATB   kro
    Shawnee (1954) A-307 (also found in
        Anthems From Scripture, G-34)

16:6   (Luke 24:34)
    Powell, Robert J.
    He Is Risen
    SAB   kro
    Abingdon (1966) APM-535 (found in
        Festival Anthems For SAB)

16:6-7
    Bender, Jan
    Do Not Be Amazed, Op. 32, #1
    2 part equal voices   Keyboard
    Concordia (1969) 98-1966

16:6-7
    Vulpius, Melchior
    Entsetzet euch nicht   (German)
    SSAB   No accompaniment
    Merseburger (1977) (found in Motetten
        Alter Meister)

16:15   (Matthew 5:14)
    Berridge, Arthur
    Go Ye Into All The World
    SATB   Organ
    Banks (1929) 943 - York Series

16:15
    Wetzler, Robert
    Go Ye Into All The World
    2 part mixed   Organ
    Augsburg (1962) 11-1346

16:15
    SEE: Matthew 28:18-20
    York, David Stanley
    Go Ye Into All The World

16:15-16
    Bender, Jan
    Go Into All The World, Op. 32, #4
    2 part equal voices   Keyboard
    Concordia (1970) 98-1990

16:15-16   (adapted)
    Brubaker, Dale C. and James D. Cram
    Go Ye!!
    2 part mixed   Keyboard
    Signature [Carl Fischer] (1959) SS-131

16:15-16
    Ford, Virgil T.
    Go Ye Into All The World
    SATB   kro
    Carl Fischer (1965) CM 7463

16:15-16
    McCormick, Clifford
    Go Ye Into All The World
    SATB   kro
    Shawnee (1954) A-230 (also found in
        Anthems From Scripture, G-34)

L U K E

1:00
    Drayton, Paul
    Ecce Ancilla Domini (Anthem For The
        Annunciation) (Latin only)
    SATB   Organ
    Oxford (1972) A-290

1:7-8
    SEE: Galations 4:4
    Gibbs, Allen Orton
    God Sent Forth His Son

1:26 ff
    Christiansen, Paul
    The Annunciation
    SATB   kro
    Augsburg (1954) 1124

1:28-29
    Goodman, Joseph
    Behold The Handmaid Of The Lord
    SSA   kro
    Merrymount (1963) MC 440

1:28-33
    Kellam, Ian
    And The Angel Came In Unto Mary
    SATB   Organ
    Oxford (1968) CMSP 0.2

1:28-33
    Morales, Cristobal (ed. Robert L. Goodale)
    Missus est Gabriel
    SSAA   kro
    G. Schirmer (1964) 11147

1:28, 35
    Hillert, Richard
    Verse/Annunciation (Verses and Offertories
        Lesser Festivals)
    Unison   Organ
    Augsburg (1980) 11-9542

1:28-38
    Schütz, Heinrich (ed. Alfred Mann)
    The Annunciation
    SSATB (S and T solos)   Keyboard
        (3 Violins, Viola, Continuo)
    J. Fischer (1956) 8999

1:28, 42
    Verdonck, Cornelius
    Ave Maria (Latin only)
    SATB   kro
    J. & W. Chester (1977) JWC 55110 (found in
        Sixth Chester Book Of Motets)

1:30-31
    Victoria, Tomas
    In Venisti Enim Gratiam (You Have Been
        Acclaimed) (Latin/English)
    SATB   kro
    G. Schirmer (1973) 11966

1:30-31
    Victoria, Tomas (ed. Henry Washington)
    Netimeas Maria
    SATB   kro
    J. & W. Chester [Alexander Broude] (1957)
        ABC-6

1:31-32
    Victoria, Tomas
    Ne Timeas Maria (Latin only)
    SATB   kro
    J. & W. Chester (1977) JWC 55110 (found in
        Sixth Chester Book of Motets)

1:31-33 (Isaiah 16:5)
    Handl, Jacob
    Ecce Concipies
    SATB   No accompaniment
    Arista (1975) AE 243

1:31-33 (Isaiah 16:5)
    Handl, Jacob (ed. Cyril F. Simkins)
    Ecce Concipies (Behold, Thou Shalt Conceive)
        (Latin/English)
    SATB   kro
    Concordia (1975) 98-2244

1:31-33
    Handl, Jacob
    Ecce Concipies (Latin only)
    SATB   kro
    J. & W. Chester (1977) JWC 55107 (found in
        Fourth Chester Book Of Motets)

1:38
    Hassler, Hans Leo
    Dixit Maria (Latin)
    SATB   No accompaniment
    Arista (1978) AE 288

1:38
    Hassler, Hans Leo
    Dixit Maria (English/Latin)
    SATB   kro
    J. Fischer (1966) 9679

1:38
    Hassler, Hans Leo
    Dixit Maria (Latin only)
    SATB   kro
    J. & W. Chester (1977) JWC 55110 (found in
        Sixth Chester Book Of Motets)

1:38
    Hassler, Hans Leo (ed. M. A. Bichsel)
    And Mary Said To The Angel (Latin/English)
    SATB   kro
    Concordia (1969) 98-1960

1:39-50
    Eccard, Johann (ed. John A. Parkinson)
    Mary's Salutation (English/German)
    SSATB   kro
    Oxford (1968) A-254

1:42 (based on)
    Bruckner, Anton
    Ave Maria (Latin only)
    SAATTBB   No accompaniment
    C. F. Peters (1961) n.#.

1:46-57
    Baker, Richard
    Magnificat (Three Short Introits)
    SATB   kro
    F. Harris (1974) HC 4057

1:46-47, 68-69
    Wyton, Alec
    Tell Out My Soul
    2 part treble   Organ
    Beekman [Mercury] (1963) MC-435

1:46-48
    Prentice, Fred
    My Soul Doth Magnify The Lord
    SATB   kro
    Gentry (1973) G-211

1:46-55
    Beebe, Hank
    My Soul Doth Magnify The Lord
    SATB   Keyboard, Bass, Drums, 10 Brass
    Hinshaw (1979) HPC 7011

1:46-55
    Chepponis, James J.
    Magnificat
    2 voices   Organ and Flute
    GIA (1980) G-2302

1:46-55
    Crotch, William (ed. Robert Wetzler)
    Song Of Mary
    SATB   No accompaniment
    Art Master (1966) 126

1:46-55
    Gesius, Bartholomaus
    Das Magnificat (German)
    SATB   No accompaniment
    Merseburger (1977) (found in Motetten
        Alter Meister)

1:46-55
    Monnikendam, Marius
    Magnificat (Latin)
    TTBB (S-solo)   2 Pianos and Percussion
    Donemus (1967)

1:46-55
    Peeters, Flor
    Magnificat (Latin)
    TTB   Organ
    McLaughlin and Reilly   #2527

1:46-55
Pinelli, Giovanni B. (ed. D. G. Reuning)
Magnificat   (based on Tonus Peregrinus)
SATB   Piano
GIA (1974) G-1914

1:46-55
Purcell, Henry (ed. George Lynn)
Magnificat   (English)
SATB   No accompaniment
Westminster Choir College (1949) WCC 21

1:46-55
Schütz, Heinrich
Deutsches Magnificat   (German/English)
SATB/SATB   Continuo
Hanssler   HE 20.494/02 (Parts HE 20.404/
     09)

1:46-55 (and Doxology)
Schütz, Heinrich
Magnificat anima mea   (Latin/German)
SATB/SATB (S-A-T-B-solos) 2 Violins,
     3 Trombones, Continuo)
Hanssler (1968) HE 29.468

1:46-55
Schubert, Franz
Magnificat
SATB (S-A-T-B-solos)   Piano
Arista (1981) AE 450

1:46-55 (adapted)
Scott, Katheryne (arr. Kayron Lee Scott)
My Soul Praises The Lord
SATB   Accompanied
Gentry [Hinshaw] (1981) G-446

1:46-55
Stevens, Halsey
Magnificat
SATB   Piano (or organ) and Trumpet
Mark Foster (1965) MF 108

1:46-55
Telemann, G. P.
Meine Seele erhebt den Herrn (English/
     German)
SSB or SS   2 violins, Organ
Hanssler   39.015

1:46-55
Titcomb, Everett
Magnificat
3 equal voices   Organ
Boston Music   #12333

1:46-55
Wyton, Alec
Magnificat
SATB (S-solo)   No accompaniment
Agape (1973) AG-7127

1:46-55
Zimmermann, Heinz Werner
Magnificat   (Vespers)
SSATB   Harpsichord, Vibraphone, Bass
Barenreiter (1962) AG 7175

1:48-49
Hillert, Richard
Verse/Annunciation (Verses And Offertories -
     Lesser Festivals)
Unison   Organ
Augsburg (1980) 11-9542

1:48-49 (based on)
Prentice, Fred
For Behold
SSAATTBB   kro
Gentry (1978) G-393

1:54
Bach, J. S.
Suscepit Israel   (from Magnificat in D)
SSA   Keyboard
E. C. Schirmer

1:55
Bach, J. S. (ed. Gerald Mack & Martha
     Banghaf)
Sicut Locutus Est   (Sing Joyful Songs To
     God)   (English/Latin)
SSATB   Optional Keyboard
Carl Fischer (1980) CM 8111

1:63, 76-79
Naylor, Peter
His Name Is John
SATB   Organ
Novello (1965) 1450

1:68, 78-79
Scholz, Robert
Alleluia For Advent
SSATB   No accompaniment
Augsburg (1976) 11-3502

1:68-79
Cruft, Adrian
Benedictus, Op. 45
SATB   Organ (optional brass)
Boosey & Hawkes (1966) 5641

1:68-79
Gesius, Bartholomaus
Das Benedictus   (German)
SATB   No accompaniment
Merseburger (1977)   (found in Motetten
     Alter Meister)

1:68-79
Tallis, Thomas (ed. Cyril F. Simkins)
Blessed Be The Lord God Of Israel
SATB   Keyboard
Concordia (1976) 98-2277

1:68-79
Thalben-Ball, G. T.
Benedictus in C Major
SATB   kro
Boosey & Hawkes (1938) 5203

2:00 (based on)
Newbury, Kent A.
I Bring You Good Tidings
SATB   Piano (optional guitar and bass)
Shawnee (1972) A-1178

2:1-10
Petrich, Roger
Jesus Is Born
SATB   Handbells, Narrator
Augsburg (1980) 3507

2:1-14
Mayer, Martin (ed. & arr. Paul Thomas)
The Christmas Gospel
SATB (S and T solos)   Keyboard
Concordia (1972) 97-5100

2:1-14
Mayer, Martin
The Christmas Gospel
SATB   2 Violns and Continuo
Concordia (found in Third Morning Star
     Choir Book, 97-4972)

2:1-20
Beck, Theodore
The Christmas Story
SATB   kro
Concordia (1965) 97-6435

2:1-20
    Billings, William (ed. Leonard Van Camp)
    The Christmas Story
    SATB   Narrator   Keyboard
    Concordia (1974) 97-5258

2:1-20
    Dietrich, Fritz
    A Little Christmas Cantata
    SAB   Organ, 2 Violns, 2 Flutes
    Concordia (1957) 97-6277

2:1-20
    Maeker, Nancy
    Christmas
    Unison   Narration, Orff Instruments,
        Speech Choir
    Augsburg (1979) 11-3504

2:4-17   (based on)
    Van Hulse, Camil
    All The Way From Nazareth
    SATB   Organ
    AMSI (1972) 199

2:7
    Abbey, Harold
    No Room In The Inn
    SATB   Piano
    Mercury (1956) 269

2:8, 9, 14
    Powell, Robert J.
    Glory To God
    SATB   Junior Choir   Organ
    Abingdon (1974) APM 858

2:8-11, 13-14
    Statham, Heathcote
    There Were Shepherds Abiding In The Field
    SATB   Organ
    Novello (1958) MT 1388

2:8-11, 13-14
    Vincent, Charles
    There Were Shepherds
    SATB   Keyboard
    Carl Fischer (1947) CM 6252

2:8-11, 13-15
    Wyton, Alec
    There Were Shepherds
    SATB (S or T solo)   Organ
    Flammer (1967) A-5243

2:8-14   (paraphrase)
    Buxtehude, Dietrich (ed. James Boeringer)
    A Christmas Canon
    SSA   Keyboard
    Concordia (1965) 98-1780

2:8-14
    Hooper, William L.
    Glory To God
    SSCB   Keyboard
    Cambiata Press (1974) C97439

2:8-14   (based on)
    McCray, James
    The Shepherds
    2 part   Keyboard
    Augsburg (1979) 11-1877

2:8-14
    Richter, Willy
    The Birth Of Christ (Christmas Cantata)
    SATB (S-A-B--solos)   Piano or Organ
    Flammer (1961) A-5325 (also arrangements
        available for SAB, and for SSA)

2:8-15
    Scott, John P.
    There Were Shepherds
    SATB   Organ
    Flammer (1927) n.#.

2:8-16
    Charpentier, Marc Antoine
    Song Of The Birth Of Our Lord Jesus Christ
        (Latin/English)
    SSAATB (S-S-B-solos)   Continuo and
        2 Violins
    Concordia (1959) 97-6307   (parts separate)

2:9
    DiLasso, Orlando (ed. John Cramer)
    Angelus Ad Pastores Ait (Latin/English)
    SATBB   kro
    Marks (1964) 4298

2:9
    Sweelinck, J. P.
    Angelus Ad Pastores Ait (Latin only)
    SSATB   Keyboard
    St. Mary's Press (1955) n.#.

2:9-11
    Hassler, Hans Leo (ed. Roy Harris)
    Angelus Ad Pastores Ait (English/Latin)
    SATB   kro
    G. Schirmer (1940) 8600

2:9-11
    Hassler, Hans Leo
    Angelus Ad Pastores Ait (English/Latin)
    SATB   kro
    Walton (1962) 6002

2:9-11
    Sweelinck, J. P. (ed. & arr. Gerald Knight)
    Angelus Ad Pastores Ait (English/Latin)
    SSATB   kro
    Carl Fischer (1965) CM 7499

2:10-11
    Beyer, Johann S. (ed. Richard Peek)
    Christmas Cantata (Weihnachts Kantate)
        (English/German)
    SATB (extended S-solo)   Organ, 2 Violins
        Viola
    Concordia (1980) 97-5543 (Choir 98-2457;
        Instruments 97-5544)

2:10-11   (Isaiah 9:6)
    Gabrieli, Andrea (ed. C. Buell Agey)
    Lo, The Angel Said To The Shepherds
        (English/German)
    SATTBB   Organ ad lib.
    G. Schirmer (1961) 10865

2:10-11
    Goss, John
    Behold I Bring You Good Tidings
    SATB   Organ
    Novello (n.d.) 178

2:10-11   (plus poetry)
    Hagen, Francis F. (ed. Marilyn Gombosi)
    Fear Not, For Behold I Bring Good Tidings
    SATB (S-solo)   Organ or Piano
    Boosey & Hawkes (1963) 5482

2:10-11
    Hassler, Hans (ed. Clifford Richter)
    Angelus Ad Pastores Ait (Latin/English)
    SATB   kro
    Associated (1963) A-405

2:10-11
    Hassler, Hans leo
    Angelus Ad Pastores (English/Latin)
    SATB   kro
    E. C. Schirmer (1976) ECS 7978 (also
        found in The Renaissance Singer)

2:10-11
    Monteverdi, Claudio
    Angelus Ad Pastores   (Latin)
    3 equal voices   kro
    Mercury   #24

2:10-11
   Praetorius, Michael
   Der Engel sprach zu dem Hirten (German)
   SATB   No accompaniment
   Merseburger (1977) (found in Motetten
        Alter Meister)

2:10-11
   Scheidt, Samuel (ed. C. Buell Agey)
   Lo The Angels Said To The Shepherds
   SATB/SATB   kro
   Mercury (1963) MC 436

2:10-11
   Topoff, Johann (ed. Hugh Ross)
   The Angel To The Shepherds
   SSATB   No accompaniment
   Associated (1949) A 158

2:10-11
   Topoff, Johann
   Be Not Afraid
   SSATB   Keyboard ad lib.
   Golden Music (1963) W-5

2:10-11
   Vittoria, Tomas
   Behold I Bring You Good Tidings
   SATTB   Keyboard
   Novello (n.d.) 90

2:10-11, 14
   Corelli, Arcangelo (arr. Benjamin Stone)
   Glory To God In The Highest
   SAB   Organ/Piano
   Boston Music (1979) 13895

2:10-11, 14
   Gabrieli, Giovanni (ed. Paul Winter)
   Angelus Ad Pastores Ait   (Latin)
   12 voices in two choirs
   Litolff [C. F. Peters] (1967) 5930

2:10-12
   Beyer, Johann Samuel (ed. Richard Peek)
   Christmas Cantata (English/German)
   S or SATB with S-solo   Continuo and
        two treble instruments
   Concordia (1980) 97-5543 (choir - 97-2457;
        parts - 97-5544)

2:10-12
   Goodman, Joseph
   Alleluia! I Bring You Good Tidings (Three
        Alleluias For Christmas)
   SSA (A-solo)   No accompaniment
   Associated (1964) A-449

2:10-12, 14   (paraphrased)
   Burroughs, Bob
   A Joyful Greetings
   SAB   Piano
   Kjos (1981) ED GC 100

2:10-12, 14
   Hammerschmidt, Andreas (ed. Harold Mueller)
   O Beloved Shepherds (English/German)
   SATB   Continuo and 2 Violins
   Concordia (1960) 97-6332

2:10-12, 14-15b
   Beck, Theodore
   A Christmas Procession
   2 part equal voices   Keyboard (optional
        Handbells)
   Concordia (1977) 97-5395

2:10, 14
   Gabrieli, Giovanni (arr. & ed. Maynard Klein)
   Angelus Ad Pastores (Latin only)
   SSAATB/TTTBBB   2 Pianos Rehearsal only
   J. Fischer (1942) 7863

2:11
   Aston, Peter
   Hodie Christus Natus Est (On This Day
        Christ Is Born) (Latin/English)
   SATB   Organ
   Novello (1974) MW 44

2:11
   Wetzler, Robert
   Verse/Christmas Midnight (Verses And
        Offertories - Advent I - The Baptism
        Of Our Lord)
   Unison   Organ
   Augsburg (1979) 11-9541

2:11-14 (Matthew 1:21-23; John 1:14)
   Price, Milburn
   Hodie! Emmanuel! Gloria!
   SATB   Percussion
   Hinshaw (1976) HMC-157

2:11-14
   SEE: Job 38:7
   Steel, Christopher
   The Morning Stars Sang Together, Op. 31

2:14
   Bassano, Giovanni
   Hodie Christus Natus Est (Latin only)
   SSA/SATB   No accompaniment
   Oxford (1980) (found in Ten Venetian
        Motets)

2:14
   Copley, R. Evan
   Glory To God   (Three Anthems Based on
        Canon)
   2 part   Keyboard
   Abingdon (1974) APM-448

2:14
   Decius, Nikolas (arr. S. Drummond Wolff)
   All Glory Be To God On High
   SATB or SATB with Brass Quartet or
        Organ
   Concordia (1975) 97-5290 (Parts 97-5291)

2:14
   Distler, Hugo
   Glory To God In The Highest
   SSA   kro
   Concordia (1968) 97-4846 (found in Der
        Jahrkreis)

2:14
   Gabrieli, Giovanni
   Hodie Christus Natus Est (Latin)
   SATB/SATB   No accompaniment
   Oxford (1980) (found in Ten Venetian
        Motets)

2:14
   Geisler, Johann (ed. & arr. E. Nolte)
   Glory To God In The Highest (English/
        German)
   SSAB/SSAB or SATB/SATB   Organ
   Boosey & Hawkes (1968) 5660

2:14
   Hammerschmidt, Andreas (ed. Diethard Hell-
        mann)
   Glory To God In The Highest
   SSATB & TTB   Organ
   C. F. Peters (1970) 66305

2:14
   Hammerschmidt, Andreas (ed. Fritz Ober-
        doerffer)
   Glory To God In The Highest
   SATB/TTB   Keyboard and other instruments
   Concordia (1966) 98-1811

2:14
    Hammerschmidt, Andreas (ed. Walter Ehret)
    Glory To God In The Highest
    SATB/TBB   Piano or Organ
    Flammer (1972) A-5571

2:14
    Handel, G. F.
    Glory To God (Messiah)
    SATB   Keyboard
    G. Schirmer (n.d.) 7217

2:14
    Henderson, Raymond (ed. Charles Hirt)
    Glory To God
    SATB   kro
    Carl Fischer (1964) CM 7437

2:14
    Jordan, Alice
    Gloria (found in The Choral Music of Alice
        Jordan)
    SATB   No accompaniment
    Sacred Music Press (1978) S-217

2:14
    Leaf, Robert
    Glory, Glory To God
    Unison   Keyboard
    Choristers Guild (1979) A-212

2:14
    Mathias, William
    Gloria, Op. 52
    TTBB   Organ
    Oxford (1972) A-285

2:14
    Mozart, W. A. (arr. Don L. Collins)
    Gloria In Excelsis Deo (from Twelfth Mass)
        (Latin/English)
    SSCB   Keyboard
    Cambiata Press (1974) M97437

2:14
    Pergolesi, G. B. (ed. Barnes)
    Glory To God In The Highest
    SATB   Organ
    Ditson (n.d.) 332.14507

2:14
    Pergolesi, G. B. (arr. Wallingford
        Riegger)
    Glory To God In The Highest
    SATB   Organ
    Flammer (1946) 84265

2:14
    Pergolesi, G. B.
    Glory To God In The Highest
    SAB   Organ
    Lorenz (1979) 7380

2:14
    Pergolesi, G. B. (Organ part arr. Vincent
        Novello)
    Glory To God In The Highest
    SATB   Organ
    Lorenz (1979) 9658

2:14
    Pergolesi, G. B. (arr. Ivan Trussler)
    Glory To God In The Highest
    SATB   Organ or Piano
    Plymouth (1963) (also found in Anthems For
        The Church Year, Volume 1)

2:14
    Powell, Robert J.
    Glory To God
    SATB and Children's Choir   Organ
    Abingdon (1974) APM-858

2:14 (Isaiah 41:10;   Baruch 5:5;Baruch 4:36)
    Proulx, Richard
    Christmas Procession
    2 part Mixed   4 Handbells
    GIA (1972) G-1708

2:14 (II Corinthians 8:9;   John 1:11-14)
    Routley, Erik
    Of The Incarnation (Three Antiphonal
        Canticles)
    SATB   Organ
    Novello (1974) MW 24

2:14
    Schütz, Heinrich (ed. & arr. Walter Ehret)
    Glory To God
    SSATTB   Continuo
    Abingdon (1965) APM-416

2:14
    Thompson, Randall
    Glory To God In The Highest
    SATB   kro
    E. C. Schirmer (1958) 2470

2:14
    Vierdanck, Johann
    Glory To God In The Highest
    SA or TB   Keyboard and 2 Treble Instru-
        ments
    Concordia (1957) (found in Morning Star
        Choir Book, 97-6287)

2:14
    Vivaldi, Antonio (arr. Don L. Collins)
    Gloria
    SSCB   Piano
    Cambiata Press (1972) M117207

2:14
    Washburn, Robert
    Gloria In Excelsis (Latin)
    SATB   Organ or Brass (3 Trumpets, 2
        Horns, 3 Trombones, Tuba)
    Oxford (1971) 94.210 (also found in
        Anthems For Choirs, Volume 4)

2:14-15
    Moore, Undine Smith
    Glory To God
    SATB   kro
    Augsburg (1979) 11-1876)

2:15
    Victoria, Tomas (ed. Arnold Payson)
    The Shepherds Spoke One To Another
        (Pastores Loque Bantur) (English/
        Latin)
    SSATBB   kro
    Franck (1964) F 538

2:22-32
    Eccard, John
    Presentation Of Christ In The Temple
    SSATBB   kro
    G. Schirmer (1926) 2618

2:22-32 (based on)
    Goldschmidt, Otto
    Presentation Of Christ In The Temple
    SSATBB   No accompaniment
    Novello (n.d.) 29.0160.09

2:27-32
    Eccard, John (ed. O. Goldschmidt)
    Presentation Of Christ In The Temple
    SSATBB   Unaccompanied
    Novello (n.d.) 29.0160.09

2:29-32
   Bourgeois, Louis (Claude Goudimel) (arr.
      A. B. Couper)
   Song Of Simeon (Two Versions) (English/
      French)
   SATB   kro
   Presser (1975) 312-41097

2:29-32
   Gesius, Bartholomaus
   Das Nunc Dimittis (German)
   SATB   No accompaniment
   Merseburger (1977) (found in Motetten
      Alter Meister)

2:29-32
   Moe, Daniel
   Nunc Dimittis
   Unison   Keyboard
   Agape (1972) AG 7113

2:29-32
   Parker, Alice
   The Song Of Simeon
   SATB   Brass Quartet (or Keyboard)
   Hinshaw (1979) HMC-376

2:29-32
   Peloquin, Alexander
   The Canticle Of Simeon (English/French)
   SATB (B-solo)   Organ
   GIA (1978) G-2202

2:29-32
   Sherman, Roger
   Nunc Dimittis
   2 Voices   Handbells
   GIA (1979) G-2195

2:29-32
   Stevens, Halsey
   Nunc Dimittis
   SATB   No accompaniment
   Mark Foster (1972) MF 130

2:29-32
   Tallis, Thomas (arr. Arthur H. Egerton)
   Nunc Dimittis
   SSAA   kro
   Carl Fischer (1933) CM 402

2:29-32
   Tomkins, Thomas (ed. Keith Clark)
   Nunc Dimittis (from First Service)
   SATB   kro
   Presser (1975) 312-41112

2:29-32
   Wyton, Alec
   Nunc Dimittis
   SATB (B-solo)   No accompaniment
   Agape (1975) AG 7180

2:29-32
   Young, Carlton
   Nunc Dimittis
   2 part   Keyboard, Guitar (optional Bass)
   Agape (1973) AG-7129 (found in Fourteen
      Canticles And Responses)

2:29-32
   Young, Carlton
   Nunc Dimittis
   2 part   Organ or Piano (optional bass
      and drums)
   Agape (1973) (found in Choirbook For Saints
      And Sinners)

2:30
   Hillert, Richard
   Verse/Presentation (Verses And Offertories
      Lesser Festivals)
   Unison   Organ
   Augsburg (1980) 11-9543

2:30-31
   Victoria, Tomas (ed. Henry Washington)
   Ne Timeas Maria (Latin only)
   SATB   kro
   J. & W. Chester [Alexander Broude] (1957)
      ABC-6

2:34-35
   Schütz, Heinrich (ed. Denis Stevens)
   Behold This Child Is Set For The Fall
   SSATB   Organ and 2 Violins
   C. F. Peters (1966) 6594

2:48
   Bender, Jan
   Son, Why Have You Treated Us So? Op. 32, #8
   2 part treble   Keyboard
   Concordia (1969) 98-1963

2:48, 49   (Psalm 84:1, 2, 4)
   Schütz, Heinrich (ed. R. T. Gore)
   My Son, Wherefore Hast Thou Done This To
      Me? (English/German)
   SATB (S-A-B-solos)   2 Violins, 2 Violas,
      Continuo
   Concordia (1962) 97-9347

2:52
   Hahn, Harvey E.
   And Jesus Increased In Wisdom
   SAB   kro
   Concordia (1972) 98-2100

3:4, 6
   Wetzler, Robert
   Verse/Advent II (Verses And Offertories -
      Advent I - The Baptism Of Our Lord)
   SATB   Organ
   Augsburg (1979) 11-9541

3:4b-6
   Williams, David H.
   Advent Song
   SATB   Organ
   AMSI (1980) 390

4:1-4
   Gardner, Don
   Man Shall Not Live By Bread Alone
   SATB (S or T solo; B-solo)   Organ or
      Piano
   Flammer (1954) A-5061

4:16-19
   Marshall, Jane M.
   Good News
   SATB (B-solo)   Optional organ
   Carl Fischer (1970) CM 7758

4:18   (John 4:24)
   Curzon, Clara Jean
   The Spirit Of The Lord
   SATB   kro
   Pro Art (1981) PRO CH 3013

4:18
   Johnson, David N.
   Verse/Epiphany IV (Verses And Offertories -
      Epiphany II - The Transfiguration Of
      Our Lord)
   Unison   Organ
   Augsburg (1980) 11-9544

4:18-19
   Barnes, Norman J.
   The Spirit Of The Lord
   SATB   Organ
   Banks (1973) ECS 13

4:18-19
   SEE: Isaiah 61:1-4, 11
   Elgar, Edward
   The Spirit Of the Lord Is Upon Me

4:18-19
    Titcomb, Everett
    The Spirit Of The Lord
    TTBB   kro
    Abingdon (1962) APM-207

4:18-19
    Young, Carlton
    The Spirit Of The Lord
    SATB   Organ or Piano
    Hope (1981) F-967

5:1-11
    Krapf, Gerhard
    Master, We Toiled All Night
    Unison   Organ
    Concordia (1969) 98-1980

6:20-23   (Matthew 5:3-16)
    Diemer, Emma Lou
    Blessed Are You
    SATB   Organ or Piano
    Carl Fischer (1970) CM 7755

6:20-23
    Ford, Virgil T.
    The Beatitudes
    SATB   Keyboard
    Broadman (1971) 4562-27

6:24-26
    Ford, Virgil T.
    The Woes
    SATB   Keyboard
    Broadman (1971) 4562-26

6:27-31
    Ford, Virgil T.
    On Love Of One's Enemies
    SATB   Keyboard
    Broadman (1971) 4562-25

6:36-42
    Krapf, Gerhard
    Be Merciful, Even As Your Father Is Merci-
        ful
    Unison   Organ
    Concordia (1969) 98-1979

6:37-38
    Ford, Virgil T.
    On Judging
    SATB   Keyboard
    Broadman (1971) 4562-24

6:43-45
    Ford, Virgil T.
    A Test Of Goodness
    SATB   Keyboard
    Broadman (1971) 4562-23

6:47-48
    Ford, Virgil T.
    Hearers And Doers Of The Word
    SATB   Keyboard
    Broadman (1971) 4562-22

7:36
    Nicolson, Richard
    When Jesus Sat At Meat
    SSATB   Organ
    Oxford (1972) TCM 48

8:5-8
    Berger, Jean
    Parable Of The Sower
    SATB   Organ ad lib.
    Carl Fischer (1963) CM 7810

8:10
    Porta, Costanzo (ed. Percy Young)
    You Are Given To Know   (Latin/English)
    SATB   kro
    Broude Brothers (1975) MGC.11

8:10-14   (John 4:24)
    Martens, Warren
    The Pharisee And The Publican
    SATB   Organ
    Golden Music (1970) G-39

8:11, 15
    Vulpius, Melchior (ed. Margaret Dickinson)
    The Seed Is The Word Of God
    SATB   kro
    Concordia (1971) 98-2089

8:11, 15
    Willan, Healey
    The Seed Is The Word Of God
    Unison   Keyboard
    Concordia (1962) 97-7160   (found in We
        Praise Thee, Volume 2)

8:22-25
    Roberts, Myron J.
    The Storm On Lake Galilee
    SATB (B-solo)   Organ
    H. W. Gray (1946) 1976

9:51 (Matthew 21:8-9;   Luke 19:41-42;
        John 12:27-29)
    Friedell, Harold
    The Way To Jerusalem
    SATB (B-solo)   Organ
    H. W. Gray (1954) CMR 2328

10:27
    Glarum, L. Stanley
    Thou Shalt Love The Lord Thy God
    SATB   kro
    Bourne (1964) SG-7

10:27
    SEE: Luke 11:28
    Stanley, F. B.
    Blessed Are They

10:27-28   (John 14:15;   John 15:12)
    Ford, Virgil T.
    This Do, And Thou Shalt Live
    SATB   kro
    Lorenz (1961) C-179

10:30-36
    McAfee, Don
    The Good Samaritan   (from Two Parables)
    SATB   kro
    General Music (1968) n.#.

11:9-10
    Blankenship, Mark
    Ask, Seek, Knock
    SATB   No accompaniment
    Broadman (1978) 4565-89

11:10
    SEE: Mark 11:17
    Titcomb, Everett
    My House Shall Be Called Of All Nations

11:17, 21
    Brahms, Johannes
    When A Strong Man, Op. 109, #2 (English/
        German)
    SATB/SATB   kro
    C. F. Peters (1964) 6566

11:23
    Bender, Jan
    He Who Is Not With Me Is Against Me,
        Op. 32, #16
    2 part equal voices   Keyboard
    Concordia (1973) 98-2058

11:28 (Luke 10:27;   Matthew 5:12)
    Staley, F. Broadus
    Blessed Are They
    SATB and Junior Choir   Organ
    Flammer (1948) A-5164

12:32   (paraphrase)
    Amner, John (ed. Peter LeHuray)
    O Ye Little Flock
    SSAATB   Organ (optional instruments)
    Oxford (1964) CMS 47

12:32
    Zimmermann, Heinz Werner
    Have No Fear, Little Flock
    SATB   Keyboard
    Concordia (1973) 98-2175 (also found in
        Five Hymns, 97-5131)

12:37-38, 40
    Moeran, E. J.
    Blessed Are Those Servants
    SATB   No accompaniment
    Novello (1938) (found in The Novello
        Anthem Book)

13:29   (Luke 14:15)
    Wetzler, Robert
    Offertory/Advent II (Verses And Offertories
        Advent I - The Baptism Of Our Lord)
    SATB   Organ
    Augsburg (1979) 11-9541

14:15
    SEE: Luke 13:29
    Wetzler, Robert
    Offertory/Advent II

14:16-24
    Krapf, Gerhard
    At The Time Of The Banquet
    Unison   Organ
    Concordia (1969) 98-1977

16:19-31
    Krapf, Gerhard
    Father Abraham, Have Mercy On Me
    Unison   Organ
    Concordia (1969) 98-1976

16:24-26
    Bender, Jan
    Father Abraham, Have Mercy Upon Me, Op. 32,
        #23
    2 part equal voices   Keyboard
    Concordia (1976) 98-2084

16:24-31
    Schütz, Heinrich (ed. Richard T. Gore)
    Father Abraham, Have Mercy On Me (English/
        German)
    SSAT (T-B-solos)   2 Violins, Continuo
    Concordia (1962) 97-9348

17:1
    Loosemore, Henry
    O Lord Increase Our Faith
    SATB   kro
    J. & W. Chester [Alexander Broude] (1968)
        ABC 15

17:5   (II Corinthians 5:7; Hebrews 11:1, 3, 6)
    Mueller, Carl F.
    An Anthem Of Faith
    SATB   Piano or Organ
    G. Schirmer (1974) 12029

17:10-11
    Schütz, Heinrich (ed. John Finley Williamson)
    The Pharisee And The Publican
    SATB (T-B-solos)   Organ
    G. Schirmer (1931) 7473

17:11-19   (paraphrase)
    Sister Miriam Therese (arr. Joseph Roff)
    Ten Lepers
    SATB   Piano
    Vanguard (1965) V 516

18:10-14   (John 4:24)
    Martin, Warren
    The Pharisee And The Publican
    SATB   Organ
    Golden Music (1970) G-39

18:10-14
    Schütz, Heinrich (ed. R. T. Gore)
    Two Men Betook Themselves To Pray In The
        Temple   (English/German)
    SATB (S-A-solo)   Keyboard
    Concordia (1962) 98-1569

18:15-17
    Hilty, Everett Jay
    Suffer Little Children
    SATB   Organ
    J. Fischer (1953) 8745

18:15-17
    Owen, Cyril
    Suffer Little Children To Come Unto Me
    SATB and Junior Choir   No accompaniment
    Galaxy (1954) 2033

18:38-42
    Bender, Jan
    Jesus, Son Of David, Have Mercy On Me,
        Op. 32, #9
    2 part equal voices   Keyboard
    Concordia (1969) 98-1965

18:41-43
    Vulpius, Melchior (ed. Hans Eggebrecht)
    Jesus Said To The Blind Man
    SATB   kro
    Concordia (1953) 98-1027

18:41-43
    Vulpius, Melchior (ed. James McCullough)
    Jesus Said To The Blind Man (English/
        German)
    SATB   kro
    Lawson Gould (1972) 51702

19:9
    Haan, Raymond
    Today Is Salvation Come
    SATB   4 Handbells
    GIA (1977) G-2115

19:28
    Gregor, C. (ed. & arr. Ivan Trusler)
    Hosanna
    2 part   Organ or Piano
    Plymouth (1963) TR 106 (also found in
        Anthems For The Church Year, Volume 1)

19:38
    Dedekind, C. C. (realization by T. Ober-
        doerffer)
    Hosanna!   Blessed Is He Who Comes
    SAB   2 violins and Continuo
    Concordia (1976) 98-2307 (also found in
        The SAB Choir Goes Baroque, 97-5232)

19:38
    SEE: Matthew 21:9-11
    Nelson, Ronald A.
    Hosannas

19:41-42
    SEE: Luke 9:51
    Friedell, Harold
    The Way To Jerusalem

19:41-42
    Jeffreys, Gregor (ed. Peter Aston)
    He Beheld The City
    SATB   Keyboard
    Novello (1969) MT 1517

19:47
    SEE: John 2:13
    Kodaly, Zoltan
    Jesus And The Traders

20:38
    Harter, Harry H.
    Blessed Be The King
    SATB, Junior Choir   Organ
    Flammer (1956) 84502

21:00
    Schütz, Heinrich (arr. Carl Bowman)
    See The Fig Tree   (English/German)
    2 part mixed   Organ or Piano
    Lawson Gould (1959) 806

21:25   (Revelation 22:12, 20)
    Wadley, F. W.
    There Shall Be Signs In The Sun
    SATB   Organ
    Elkin   (1959) 2544

21:25-26, 33
    Bender, Jan
    And There Will Be Signs
    Unison   Organ
    Concordia (1971) 98-2082

21:34-36
    Schütz, Heinrich (ed. Denis Stevens)
    And Take Heed To Yourselves
    SSATTB   Organ, 2 Violins
    C. F. Peters (1966) 6595

21:36
    Busarow, Donald
    Verse/27th Sunday After Pentecost (Verses
        And Offertories - Pentecost 21 - Christ
        The King)
    2 part   Organ
    Augsburg (1979) 11-9540

22:47-48
    Wilkinson, Scott
    Easter Episodes (I-Betrayal, II-Trial)
    SATB   Organ or Piano
    Carl Fischer (1974) ZCM 109

23:24
    SEE: Matthew 27:45-46
    Palestrina, G. P.
    Tenebrae factae sunt

23:27-28, 33-34
    Wagner, Douglas
    This Dark Hour
    SATB   Narrator,   Handbells
    GIA (1979) G-2284

23:28-30
    Mendelssohn, Felix
    Daughters Of Zion (Christus)
    SATB   Organ
    Oxford (1933)   (found in Church Anthem
        Book)

23:33-34
    Pinkham, Daniel
    The Seven Last Words Of Christ On The Cross
    SATB (T-B-B-solos)   Organ and Tape
    E. C. Schirmer (1971) 2907

23:34   (John 14:27;   Matthew 11:28)
    McCormick, Clifford
    Then Did Jesus Say
    SATB   Organ
    Shawnee (1958) A-470   (also found in
        Anthems From Scripture, G-34)

23:34-39
    Skeat, William J.
    Calvary   (from The Son Of Man)
    SATB   Piano
    J. Fischer (1955) 8093

23:39-43
    Pinkham, Daniel
    The Seven Last Words Of Christ On The Cross
        (Third Word)
    SATB (T-B-B-solos)   Organ and Tape
    E. C. Schirmer (1971) 2907

23:42
    SEE: Matthew 27:51-52
    Haydn, Michael
    Velum Templi Scissum Est

23:42-43
    Back, Sven-Erik
    Dies Mortis Christi (Jesus Think Of Me)
        (English/Latin)
    SATB   No accompaniment
    W. Hansen [G. Schirmer] (1969) 11838

23:44-45
    Goodman, Joseph
    Tenebrae Factae Sunt   (Latin only)
    SATB   kro
    Marks (1950) 34

23:46
    SEE: Matthew 27:46
    Croce, Giovanni
    Tenebrae Factae Sunt

23:46
    SEE: Matthew 27:46
    Davye, John J.
    Tenebrae Factae Sunt

23:46
    SEE: Matthew 27:46
    Eberlin, J. E.
    Tenebrae Factae Sunt

23:46
    SEE: Mark 15:34
    Haydn, Michael
    Darkened Was All The Land

23:46
    SEE: Matthew 27:45
    Haydn, Michael (ed. William Ramsey)
    Tenebrae Factae Sunt   (Boonin)

23:46
    SEE: Matthew 27:45-47
    Haydn, Michael
    Tenebrae in E-flat

23:46
    SEE: Matthew 27:45
    Haydn, Michael (trans. R. Pauly)
    Tenebrae Factae Sunt   (G. Schirmer)

23:46
    SEE: Matthew 27:46
    Ingegneri, Marc-Antonio
    Tenebrae Factae Sunt

23:46
    Pinkham, Daniel
    The Seven Last Words Of Christ On The Cross
        (Seventh Word)
    SATB (T-B-B-solos)   Organ and Tape
    E. C. Schirmer (1971) 2907

23:46
    Shepherd, John
    In Manus Tuas   (Latin only)
    SATB   kro
    J. & W. Chester (1977) JWC 55103 (found in
        Second Chester Book Of Motets)

23:46
    Tallis, Thomas (ed. Walter Ehret)
    In Manus Tuas
    SATBB   kro
    Walton (1969) 6028

24:1-5   (Matthew 28:6, adapted)
    Englert, Eugene
    He Is Risen, Alleluia!
    2 part mixed   Organ
    GIA   G-1969

24:1-5
    Smith, Richard Harrison
    Early Easter Morning
    SATB   No accompaniment
    AMSI (1980) 395

24:1-6 (adapted)
    Yardumian, Richard   (harmonized)
    Hallelujah, Our Lord And God (from Eleven
          Easter Chorales)
    SATB   No accompaniment
    Elkan Vogel (1978) 362.03280

24:5-7   (Psalm 8:5-6
    Nelson, Ronald
    Introit For Easter
    SATB   Organ and Trumpet
    Abingdon (1969) APM-599

24:6-7 (Psalm 139:10;   Psalm 118:24)
    Lekberg, Sven
    He Is Risen
    SATB   kro
    Galaxy (1969) GMC 2406

24:26
    SEE: Psalm 111:9
    Kreutz, R.
    The Lord Has Sent Deliverance

24:27
    SEE: Romans 6:9
    Pelz, Walter
    Verse/Easter Evening

24:28-31
    Sowerby, Leo
    And They Drew Nigh
    SATB   Organ
    H. W. Gray (1960) 2625

24:29   (Psalm 91)
    Distler, Hugo (ed. Larry Palmer)
    Christ Who Alone Art Light Of Day
    SAB   Keyboard, 2 Violins
    Concordia (1972) 97-5066 (parts - 97-5127)

24:30-32
    Salathiel, Lyndon
    Did Not Our Heart Burn Within Us
    SATB (B-solo)   Organ or Piano
    G. Schirmer (1956) 10396

24:31 (paraphrase)   (John 6:55-56)
    Byrd, William
    Cognoverunt Discipuli (The Disciples With
          Wondering Eyes)   (English/Latin)
    SATB   kro
    Novello (n.d.) TM 18

24:32
    SEE: Romans
    Pelz, Walter
    Verse/Third Sunday Of Lent

24:34
    SEE: Mark 16:6
    Powell, Robert J.
    He Is Risen   (Festival Anthems For SAB)

24:34-35
    Pelz, Walter
    Offertory/Easter Evening (Verses and
          Offertories - Easter - Trinity)
    SATB   Organ
    Augsburg (1980) 11-9546

24:49
    SEE: Psalm 24:10
    Marenzio, Luca
    O Rex Gloriae

25:34
    Bender, Jan
    Come, O Blessed Of My Father, Op. 35, #15
    2 part equal voices   Keyboard
    Concordia (1966) 98-1834

J O H N

1:1, 3
    Wilson-Dickson, Andrew
    The Word
    SATB   Organ
    Banks (1973) ECS 9

1:1-4
    Felciano, Richard
    The Not-Yet Flower   (from Two Public Peaces)
    Unison   Tape
    E. C. Schirmer (1972) 2937

1:1-5
    SEE: Genesis 1:1-4
    Kauffman, Ronald
    In The Beginning

1:1-5
    Reynolds, William J.
    In The Beginning Was The Word
    SATB   kro
    Kjos (1978) 6303

1:1, 14   (adapted)
    Hovland, Egil (ed. Frank Pooler)
    The Glory Of The Father
    SSATB   kro
    Walton (1974) 2973

1:1, 14
    Reger, Max   (ed. Paul Thomas)
    The Word Was Made Flesh
    SATB   Organ
    Concordia (1979) 98-2389

1:1, 14a   (Isaiah 55:3, 6, 9-11a;   Isaiah 61:
          11b)
    Wetzler, Robert
    As The Rain And Snow From Heaven
    SATB   No accompaniment
    AMSI (1979) 366

1:1, 14
    Wetzler, Robert
    Offertory/Christmas I (Verses and Offertories
          Advent I - Baptism Of Our Lord)
    Unison   Organ
    Augsburg (1979) 11-9541

1:1-18
    Rogers, Bernard
    The Light Of Man
    SATB (S-A-B-solos)   Piano
    Presser (1964) 312-40608

1:4-5, 7 (John 3:19;   John 8:12;   John 12:35-36)
    Darst, W. Glen
    I Am The Light Of The World
    SATB   Keyboard
    Lorenz (1965) E-42

1:4, 8, 10
   Brandon, George
   The Word Became Flesh
   Unison   Organ
   Canyon Press (1952) n.#.

1:4-6
   Langlais, Jean
   Grace To You   (Three Anthems)
   SATB   No accompaniment
   Hinshaw (1980) HMC 423

1:5
   SEE: Isaiah 26:3
   Wesley, Samuel S.
   Thou Wilt Keep Him In Perfect Peace

1:11-13
   Young, Philip M.
   John 1:11-13
   SATB   Organ
   Broadman (1978) 4563-20

1:11-14
   SEE: Luke 2:14
   Routley, Erik
   Of The Incarnation

1:14
   Anonymous (ed. Abraham Kaplan)
   Verbum Caro Factum Est
   SATB   kro
   Tetra [Alexander Broude] (1967) AB-143

1:14
   Back, Sven-Erik
   Verbum Caro Factum Est   (English/Latin)
   SATB   No accompaniment
   H. Hansen [G. Schirmer] (1968) 11840

1:14
   Cary, Tristam
   Verbum Caro Factum Est   (from Two Nativity
       Songs)   (Latin only)
   SATB   (S & T solos)   Keyboard
   Oxford (1979) n.#.

1:14
   Compere, Loyset
   Verbum Caro Factum Est   (Latin only)
   SATB   kro
   J. & W. Chester (1977) JWC 55110 (found in
       Sixth Chester Book Of Motets)

1:14
   DiJulio, Max
   The Word Was Made Flesh
   SSA   Piano and Guitar
   Golden Music (1971) G-43

1:14
   Hassler, Hans Leo (ed. Roger Wilhelm)
   God Now Dwells Among Us   (Verbum Caro
       Factum Est)   (English/Latin)
   SAB or TTB   Keyboard
   Mark Foster (1972) MF 129

1:14
   Hassler, Hans Leo
   Verbum Caro Factum Est   (Latin)
   SSATTB   No accompaniment
   Arista (1976) AE 289

1:14
   Hassler, Hans Leo
   Verbum Caro Factum Est   (Latin/English)
   SSATTB   kro
   Tetra [Alexander Broude] (1967) AB 140-9

1:14
   Mauersberger, Erhard
   We Saw His Glory
   2 part   Keyboard
   Concordia 98-1914 (also found in Second
       Morning Star Choir Book, 97-4702)

1:14   (Wesley)
   Mauersberger, Erhard (ed. Paul Bunjes)
   We Saw His Glory
   SATB optional descant or instruments,
       Organ
   Concordia (1965) 97-5610 (found in The
       Church Choir Book, Volume 2)

1:14
   SEE: Isaiah 9:6
   Morales, C.
   Puer Natus Est Nobis

1:14
   SEE: Luke 2:11-14
   Price, Milburn
   Hodie! Emmanuel!

1:14
   Rohlig, Harald
   The Word Became Flesh
   Unison or SA   Keyboard
   Concordia (1973) 97-5165 (found in Explode
       With Joy)

1:14
   Schein, J. (ed. Roger Granville)
   Truly Was The Word Made Flesh (English/
       Latin)
   SSATBB   kro
   Sam Fox (1965) CM-8

1:14
   Walter, Johann
   Verum Caro Factum Est   (Latin only)
   SATB   kro
   J. & W. Chester (1977) JWC 55107 (found in
       Fourth Chester Book Of Motets)

1:14
   Wetzler, Robert
   Offertory/Christmas I (Verses and Offer-
       tories - Advent I - The Baptism Of Our
       Lord)
   2 part   Organ
   Augsburg (1979) 11-9541

1:14
   Willan, Healey
   The Word Was Made Flesh
   SA   Keyboard
   Concordia (1962) 97-7160 (found in We
       Praise Thee, Volume 2)

1:14
   SEE: Wisdom 18:14-15
   Willan, Healey
   While All Things Were In Quiet Silence

1:14
   Zimmermann, Heinz Werner
   And The Word Became Flesh
   SATB   Keyboard
   Concordia (1973) 98-2177 (also found in
       Five Hymns, 97-5131)

1:16-18
   Sinzheimer, Max
   The Great Light
   Unison   Organ
   Augsburg (1976) 11-1780

1:19
   Gibbons, Orlando
   This Is The Record Of John
   SAATB (A-solo)   Organ
   Oxford (1924) 42.676 (also found in
       Oxford Book Of Tudor Anthems)

1:19-23
   Gibbons, Orlando
   This Is The Record Of John
   SAATB (T-solo)   Organ
   Lawson Gould (1954) 550

1:19-23
 Gibbons, Orlando (ed. William Palmer)
 This Is The Record Of John
 SAATB Organ
 Novello (1957) 29.0147.01

1:23, 26-27
 Schütz, Heinrich (ed. Robert Shaw and
   Klaus Speer)
 Lo I Am The Voice Of One Crying In The
   Wilderness (English/German)
 SSATTB Organ ad lib.
 G. Schirmer (1952) 10116

1:23, 26-27
 Schütz, Heinrich (ed. C. Buell Agey)
 Lo, I Am The Voice Of One Crying In The
   Wilderness
 SSATTB Organ
 Mercury (1963) 437-13

1:29
 Beck, Theodore (arr.)
 Lamb Of God, Pure And Holy
 SSA No accompaniment
 Concordia (1975) (found in Seven Anthems
   For Treble Choirs, 97-5163)

1:29
 Bouman, Paul
 Behold The Lamb Of God
 SA Organ
 Concordia (1955) 98-1088 (also found in
   Morning Star Choir Book, 97-6287)

1:29 (based on)
 Bristol, Lee H. Jr.
 Lamb Of God
 SATB Organ
 Golden Music (1964) G-23

1:29
 Couper, Alinda
 Behold The Lamb Of God (Festival Introits)
 SATB Organ or Piano ad lib.
 Abingdon (1969) APM-780

1:29
 Handel, G. F. (arr. Loy L. Beal)
 Behold The Lamb Of God (Messiah)
 SACB Organ
 Cambiata Press (1974) M-17427

1:29
 Handel, G. F.
 Behold The Lamb Of God
 SATB Keyboard
 Ditson (n.d.) 332.00899

1:29
 Morley, Thomas (ed. Hans T. David)
 Agnus Dei (Latin)
 SATB No accompaniment
 Mercury (1944) MC 53

1:29
 Rohlig, Harald
 Behold The Lamb Of God
 Unison or SA Keyboard
 Concordia (1973) 98-2288 (also found in
   Explode With Joy, 97-5165)

1:29
 Rossini, Thomas D.
 O Lamb Of God
 SATB No accompaniment
 Concordia (1981) 98-2521

1:29 (Isaiah 53:4-5)
 Willan, Healey
 Behold The Lamb Of God
 SATB Organ
 Concordia (1960) 98-1509

2:10, 11
 Johnson, David N.
 Offertory/Epiphany II (Verses and Offer-
   tories - Epiphany II - The Trans-
   figuration Of Our Lord)
 Unison Organ
 Augsburg (1980) 11-9544

2:13 (Mark 11:17; Luke 19:47)
 Kodaly, Zoltan
 Jesus And The Traders
 SATB kro
 Boosey & Hawkes (n.d.) 1709

2:25-26
 Dressler, Gallus (ed. Matthew Lundquist)
 I Am The Resurrection
 SATB kro
 Schmitt, Hall, McCreary (found in Later
   Renaissance Motets)

3:1-15
 Krapf, Gerhard
 Truly, Truly I Say To You
 Unison Organ
 Concordia (1969) 98-1975

3:2
 Buch, P. C.
 Behold, Now Are We The Sons Of God
 ATB Keyboard
 Oxford (1943) A-103

3:3, 5-6, 8
 Bender, Jan
 Unless One Is Born Anew, Op. 32, #19
 Unison Keyboard
 Concordia (1974) 98-2056

3:14-15
 Norris, Kevin
 Verse/Lent III (Verses And Offertories -
   Lent)
 Unison Organ
 Augsburg (1980) 11-9545

3:14-15
 Schütz, Heinrich
 Sicut Moses Serpentem (English/Latin)
 SATB Organ or Piano
 Associated (1963) A-412

3:14-16 (John 12:32)
 Baristow, Edward C.
 As Moses Lifted Up The Serpent
 SATB Keyboard ad lib.
 Banks (1977) ECS 44

3:14-16 (John 12:32)
 Baristow, Edward C.
 As Moses Lifted Up The Serpent
 SATB Accompaniment ad lib.
 Oxford (1931) A-44

3:16
 Bender, Jan
 God So Loved The World
 SATB kro
 Concordia (1955) 98-1078

3:16
 Bender, Jan
 God So Loved The World
 SS Keyboard
 Concordia (1959) 98-1641

3:16
 Davis, Katherine K.
 God So Loved The World
 SATB kro
 Galaxy (1961) GMC 2214

3:16
Distler, Hugo
For God So Loved The World
SAB   kro
Concordia (1968) 98-2239

3:16
Distler, Hugo
For God So Loved The World
SAB   No accompaniment
Concordia (1968) 97-4846 (found in Der
    Jahrkreis)

3:16
Dressler, Gallus
Also hat Gott die Welt geliebet (German)
SATB   No accompaniment
Merseburger (1977) (found in Motetten
    Alter Meister)

3:16
Gibbons, Orlando (ed. Paul Vining)
So God Loved The World
SAATB   Organ
Novello (1969) NECM 15

3:16
Norris, Kevin
Verse/Lent IV (Verses And Offertories/Lent)
Unison   Organ
Augsburg (1980) 11-9545

3:16
Praetorius, H.   (ed. George Lynn)
God So Loved The World
SSATBB   Optional accompaniment
Golden Music (1963) W-4

3:16
Reynolds, William J.
God So Loved The World
SATB   Keyboard
Broadman (1977) 4565-79

3:16
Schütz, Heinrich
For God So Loved The World (English/German)
SATTB   Organ
Concordia (1959) 98-1472

3:16
Schütz, Heinrich (ed. C. Buell Agey)
For God So Loved The World (English/German)
SATTB   Continuo
Concordia (1974) (found in The Second
    Motet Book, 97-5205)

3:16
Schütz, Heinrich (ed. Kurt Stone)
Know All That God So Loved The World
    (English/German)
SAATB or SATTB   kro
Word (1971) CRS-16

3:16
Telemann, G. P.
God So Loved The World (English/German)
SAB   Continuo, 2 Violins, Viola
Concordia (1976) (found in The SAB Choir
    Goes Baroque, 97-5232)

3:16
Telemann, G. P.
Also hat Gott die Welt geliebet (English/
    German)
SSB or SS   Continuo, 2 Violins
Hanssler   HE 39.014

3:16
Tschesnokoff (ed. Noble Cain)
For God So Loved The World
SSAATTBB   kro
Boosey & Hawkes (1948) 1815

3:16 (based on)
Vulpius, Melchior (ed. & arr. Paul Thomas)
God So Loved The World
SATB   kro
Concordia (1981) 97-5610 (found in The
    Church Choir Book, Volume 2)

3:16-17
Goss, John
God So Loved The World
SATB   Organ
Novello (1976) 29.0374.01

3:16-17
Goss, John
God So Loved The World
SATB   No accompaniment
Oxford (1933) (found in Church Anthem
    Book)

3:16-17
Stainer, John
God So Loved The World (Crucifixion)
SATB   kro
Abingdon (1963) APM-278 (found in Select
    Anthems For Mixed Voices, Volume 1)

3:16-17
Stainer, John (ed. & arr. Harry R. Wilson
    and Walter Ehret)
God So Loved The World
SAB   Piano
Boosey & Hawkes (1956) 5110

3:16-17
Stainer, John (arr. C. H. Trevor)
God So Loved The World
SSAA   Unaccompanied
Novello (1970) Ch. Ser. 124

3:16-17
Stainer, John (ed. N. Clifford Page)
God So Loved The World (from The Cruci-
    fixion)
SATB   kro
Carl Fischer (1931) CM 283

3:16-17
Stainer, John
God So Loved The World (Crucifixion)
SATB   kro
G. Schirmer (n.d.) 6290

3:16-17
Stainer, John
God So Loved The World (Crucifixion)
SATB   kro
Novello (n.d.) 29.0234.06

3:16-17
Stainer, John (ed. Ivan Trusler)
God So Loved The World (Crucifixion)
SATB   kro
Plymouth (1963) (also found in Anthems For
    The Church Year, Volume 1)

3:19
SEE: John 1:4-5, 7
Darst, W. Glen
I Am The Light Of The World

4:13-14
Cain, Noble
Water Of Life
SATB   Reader   Keyboard
Flammer (1956) A-5210

4:16
Cruft, Adrian
May God Abide, Op. 20
TTBB   kro
Stainer & Bell   #5667

4:23b-24
    Bennett, William Sterndale
    God Is A Spirit
    SATB   kro
    Novello (n.d.) 29.0125.00

4:23-24
    Bennett, W. Sterndale
    God Is A Spirit
    SATB   No accompaniment
    Oxford (1933) (found in Church Anthem Book)

4:23-24
    Oncley, Paul B.
    God Is A Spirit
    SATB   kro
    Presser (1951) 312-40087

4:23-24
    Scholin, C. Albert
    God Is A Spirit
    SATB   kro
    Flammer (1937) A-5053 (also found in
        Flammer Collection Of Anthems, Volume
        2)

4:24
    Bennett, W. S. (revised & edited C. P.
        Scott)
    God Is A Spirit
    SATB   Organ
    Carl Fischer (1917) CM 39

4:24
    Bennett, W. S.
    God Is A Spirit
    SATB   kro
    G. Schirmer (n.d.) 2477

4:24
    Bennett, W. S.
    God Is A Spirit
    SATB   kro
    Novello (n.d.) ANTH. 967

4:24
    SEE: Luke 4:18
    Curzon, Clara Jean
    The Spirit Of The Lord

4:24
    Kopylov, Alexander
    God Is A Spirit
    SA   Keyboard
    E. C. Schirmer (1952) 1557

4:24
    Kopylov, Alexander
    God Is A Spirit
    SATB   kro
    E. C. Schirmer (1952) 147 (also found in
        Concord Anthem Book - Red)

4:24
    Kopylov, Alexander (arr. Arthur S. Talmadge)
    God Is A Spirit
    SSAA   kro
    E. C. Schirmer (1943) 1917

4:24
    SEE: Luke 18:10-14
    Martin, Warren
    The Pharisee And The Publican

4:24
    SEE: Psalm 102:25-27
    DeTar, Vernon
    The Glory Of The Lord

4:24-25
    McCormick, Clifford
    God Is A Spirit
    SATB   Organ
    Shawnee (1955) A-400 (also found in Anthems
        From Scripture, G-34)

4:35-36
    SEE: Revelation 14:14-15
    Willan, Healey
    I Looked And Behold A White Cloud

4:35-37 (adapted)
    Carley, Isabel McNeill
    Lift Up Your Eyes
    SSA   Orff Instruments (soprano recorder,
        soprano glockenspiel, etc.)
    Augsburg (1979) 11-0338

4:49-50
    Bender, Jan
    Sir, Come Down Before My Child Dies
    2 part treble   Keyboard
    Concordia (1966) 98-1835

5:25, 28-29
    Sateren, Leland
    The Hour Cometh
    SATBB   kro
    Summy Birchard (1958) 5182

6:14
    Bender, Jan
    This Is Indeed The Prophet, Op. 32, #17
    2 part equal voices   Keyboard
    Concordia (1972) 98-2054

6:20
    Philips, Peter
    Tristitia Vestra   (Latin)
    SSATB   Organ ad.lib.
    Oxford (1981) CMSR 56

6:27, 35, 50
    Brandt, William E.
    Communion Anthem
    SATB   Organ
    Hope (1974) CD-1601

6:32-35
    Lynn, George
    Jesus The Bread Of Life
    SSAATTBB   Organ
    Mercury (1962) MC 392

6:33-35
    Stainer, John
    Jesus Said Unto The People
    SATB   Organ
    G. Schirmer (n.d.) 4909

6:35
    Stainer, John
    I Am The Bread Of Life
    SATB   Organ
    Boston (1912) (found in The Parishonal
        Choir, Volume 2)

6:35-36
    Baek, Sven Erik
    Ego Sum Panis Vitae (I Am The Bread Of
        Heaven) (English/Latin)
    SATB   No accompaniment
    Wilhelm Hansen [G. Schirmer] (1967) 11837

6:35, 51
    Roff, Joseph
    I Am The Bread Of Life
    SATB   Keyboard
    Lorenz (1965) E-41

6:35, 51
    Schiavone, John
    I Am The Bread Of Life
    2 part   Organ
    GIA (1974) G-1855

6:35, 53 (John 11:25-27)
    Toolan, Suzanne
    I Am The Bread Of Life
    SATB   Organ
    GIA (1971) G-1693

6:37
    Welsh Hymn (arr. & ed. Walter Ehret)
    Come Unto Me, Ye Weary
    SATB   Organ
    Concordia (1977) 98-2310

6:48-50
    Palestrina, G. P.
    Ego Sum Panis Vivus (Latin only)
    SATB   kro
    J. & W. Chester (1977) JWC 55096 (found in
        First Chester Book Of Motets)

6:48-50
    Palestrina, G. P.
    Ego Sum Panis Vivus
    SATB   No accompaniment
    GIA (1954) 570

6:50-51
    Schalk, Carl
    Offertory/Pentecost 15 (Verses and
        Offertories - Pentecost 12-20)
    Unison   Organ
    Augsburg (1978) 11-9539

6:51
    Byrd, William
    Ego Sum Panis Vivus (Latin only)
    SATB   kro
    J.& W. Chester [Alexander Broude] (1929)
        ABC 30

6:51
    SEE: II Samuel 22:7, 17-18
    Gieseke, Richard
    I Call To My God For Help

6:51
    Harwood, Basil
    I Am The Living Bread
    SATB   Organ
    Oxford (1937) 75

6:51-57
    SEE: Psalm 23:6
    Peloquin, Alexander
    Holy Communion

6:53-56
    Tallis, Thomas
    Verily, Verily I Say Unto You
    SATB   Organ
    Oxford (1968) A-247 (also found in Anthems
        For Choirs, Volume 1)

6:55-56
    SEE: Luke 24:31 (paraphrase)
    Byrd, William
    Cognoverunt Discipuli

6:56-57
    SEE: Psalm 145:15-16
    Schroth, Godfrey
    The Eyes Of All

6:58
    Esquivel, Juan
    Ego Sum Panis Vivus (Latin)
    SATB   kro
    J. & W. Chester (1977) JWC 55104 (found in
        Third Chester Book Of Motets)

6:68
    Johnson, David N.
    Verse/Epiphany VI (Verses And Offertories -
        Epiphany II - The Transfiguration Of
        Our Lord)
    Unison   Organ
    Augsburg (1980) 11-9544

6:68
    Mudde, Willem
    Lord, To Whom Shall We Go?
    SATB   kro
    Augsburg (1969) 11-1569

8:12
    SEE: John 1:4-5, 7
    Darst, W. Glen
    I Am The Light Of The World

8:12
    SEE: Isaiah 60:20
    Gore, Richard T.
    The Sun Shall No More Go Down

8:12
    SEE: John 14:6
    Hurby, Dolores
    Your Holy Cross

8:12
    Johnson, David
    Verse/Epiphany V (Verses And Offertories -
        Epiphany II - The Transfiguration Of
        Our Lord)
    Unison   Organ
    Augsburg (1980) 11-9544

8:12   (Revelation 22:17, 20)
    Johnson, Ralph
    I Am The Light
    Unison   Keyboard
    Augsburg (1973) 11-1679

8:12
    Lassus, Orlandus
    Qui Sequitur Me (Latin only)
    2 part   No accompaniment
    Mercury (1941) 352.00011 (found in Twelve
        Motets)

8:12
    Wienhorst, Richard
    I Am The Light Of The World (Three Verse
        Settings, Set 1)
    SAB   No accompaniment
    Concordia (1979) 98-2430

8:31-32
    Hillert, Richard
    Verse/Reformation Day (Verses And
        Offertories/Lesser Festivals)
    Unison   Organ
    Augsburg (1980) 11-9543

8:51, 54-55b
    Bender, Jan
    If Anyone Keeps My Word, Op. 32, #18
    2 part equal voices   Organ
    Concordia (1976) 98-2057

9:7   (based on)
    Sowerby, Leo
    The Pool Of Bethesda
    SATB   Organ
    H. W. Gray (1964) CMR 2851

10:2, 7
    Hillert, Richard
    Verse/Common Of Saints Not Martyrs (Verses
        And Offertories - Lesser Festivals)
    Unison   Organ
    Augsburg (1980) 11-9542

10:7
    SEE: John 14:6
    Hurby, Dolores
    Your Holy Cross

10:7, 9 (adapted) (John 14:6, adapted)
Lewis, John Leo
I Am The Door
SATB   Keyboard
Lorenz (1965) E 43

10:11, 14-16, 28-30
Caldwell, Mary E.
I Am The Good Shepherd
SATB (S-solo)   Keyboard
Lorenz (1965) E-44

10:11-18
Englert, Eugene
I Am The Good Shepherd
SATB   Organ and Flute
GIA (1978) G-2117

10:14
SEE: Romans 6:9
Pelz, Walter
Verse/Fourth Sunday Of Easter

10:14-16
Bender, Jan
I Am The Good Shepherd, Op. 32, #2
2 part equal voices   Keyboard
Concordia (1970) 98-1992

10:14-16
Wood, Dale
I Am The Good Shepherd
Unison   Organ
Augsburg (1969) 11-1590 (also found in
    Music For The Contemporary Choir,
    Volume 1)

10:14-16
Woollen, Russell
One Fold, One Shepherd
2 equal or mixed voices   Organ
World Library (1962) ESA 660

10:14-16
Young, Philip M.
I Am The Good Shepherd
SATB   Organ
Carl Fischer (1970) CM 7759

10:14-16, 30
Morgan, Haydn
I Am The Good Shepherd
SATB   Piano
Kjos (1971) 5853

11:25
Caldwell, Mary E.
I Am The One
SATB   Organ
Fred Bock [Presser] (1971) G-153

11:25-26
Burroughs, Bob
I Am The Resurrection
SSATTB   No accompaniment
Carl Fischer (1973) CM 7834

11:25-26
Milton, John (ed. G. E. P. Arkwright)
I Am The Resurrection
SATTB   kro
Broude Brothers (n.d.) OEE 20

11:25-26
Morley, Thomas (ed. Cyril F. Simkins)
I Am The Resurrection
SATB   Optional Organ
Concordia (1978) 98-2393

11:25-26
Nelson, Ronald
I Am The Resurrection And The Life
SATB   kro
Augsburg (1967) ACL 1511

11:25-26
Schütz, Heinrich (ed. Dennis Stevens)
I Am The Resurrection And The Life
SATB/SATB   Organ ad lib.
C. F. Peters (1964) 6591

11:25-26
Willan, Healey
I Am The Resurrection And The Life
SA   Keyboard
Concordia (1962) 97-7610 (found in We
    Praise Thee, Volume 2)

11:25-26
Williams, David H.
I Am The Resurrection And The Life
SATB   Keyboard
Lorenz (1965) E-46

11:25-27
SEE: John 6:35, 53
Toolan, Suzanne
I Am The Bread Of Life

11:38-44 (based on)
Willaert, Adrian (ed. Zanon-Vene)
The Raising Of Lazarus (English/Latin)
SATB   kro
Ricordi (1957) 1873

12:13
Nystedt, Knut
Hosanna! Blessed Is He
SAB   Organ
Augsburg (1964) 1410

12:23
Norris, Kevin
Verse/Passion Sunday (Verses And Offer-
    tories - Lent)
Unison   Organ
Augsburg (1980) 11-9545

12:24, 26
Norris, Kevin
Offertory/Passion Sunday (Verses And
    Offertories - Lent)
Unison   Organ
Augsburg (1980) 11-9545

12:26
Hillert, Richard
Verse/Common Of Saints Not Martyrs (Verses
    And Offertories - Lesser Festivals)
Unison   Organ
Augsburg (1980) 11-9542

12:27-28, 30
SEE: Luke 9:51
Friedell, Harold
The Way To Jerusalem

12:32
SEE: John 3:14-16
Baristow, Edward C.
As Moses Lifted Up The Serpent (Oxford)

12:32
SEE: John 3:14-16
Baristow, Edward C.
As Moses Lifted Up The Serpent

12:32 (based on)
Blakenship, Mark
If I Be Lifted Up
SATB   Keyboard
Broadman (1975) 4565-68

12:35-36
Beebe, Hank
Walk, While You Have The Light
2 part choir   Keyboard
Hindon [Hinshaw] (1979) HPC 7013

12:35-36
    SEE: John 1:4-5, 7
    Darst, W. Glen
    I Am The Light Of The World

12:35-36
    Nystedt, Knut
    Yet A Little While
    SSATB   kro
    Summy Birchard (1959) 5350

13:34
    Shepherd, John (ed. Watkins Shaw)
    I Give You A New Commandment
    ATBB or TTBB   Organ ad lib.
    Oxford (1969) CMSR 18B

14:1
    SEE: Matthew 28:19
    Butler, Eugene
    Go Ye Into All The World

14:1-2, 27
    Dickey, Mark
    Let Not Your Heart Be Troubled
    SATB   Organ
    H. W. Gray (1932) 1191 (also available in
        SSA and in SAB voicings)

14:1-3
    Clark, Henry A.
    Let Not Your Heart Be Troubled
    SATB   kro
    F. Harris (1955) HC 4012

14:1, 3
    Burroughs, Bob
    I Will Come Again, Alleluia!
    SATB   Piano and 2 Flutes
    Broadman (1978) 4563-24

14:1-3
    Lepley, R. Benford
    A Scripture Response
    SAB   Keyboard
    Agape (1980) (found in Choirbook Of Saints
        And Sinners)

14:1-3
    Young, Gordon
    Let Not Your Heart Be Troubled
    SATB   Piano or Organ
    Presser (1973) 312-41024

14:1-3, 27
    MacFarlane, Will C.
    Peace I Leave With You
    SSA (S-A-solos)   Piano or Organ
    G. Schirmer (1945) 9472

14:1-4
    Mueller, Carl F.
    Let Not Your Heart Be Troubled
    SATB   Piano or Organ
    Carl Fischer (1950) CM 6521

14:1-7 (paraphrase)
    Harter, Harry H.
    Let Not Your Heart Be Troubled (based on
        Belmont)
    SATB   kro
    Shawnee (1958) A 566

14:1, 15-16, 27
    Wolff, S. Drummond
    Let Not Your Heart Be Troubled
    SATB   Optional accompaniment
    Concordia (1955) CH 1077

14:1, 27
    Burroughs, Bob
    Peace I Leave With You
    SATB   No accompaniment
    Broadman (1975) 4562-49

14:1, 27
    Speaks, Oley (arr. Lucien Chaffin)
    Let Not Your Heart Be Troubled
    SATB (S-solo)   Organ
    G. Schirmer (1919) 6915

14:2-3 (based on)
    Hawkins, Edwin R.
    In My Father's House
    SATB   Piano, Guitar, Bass
    United Artists (1971) 914/90

14:3
    SEE: Matthew 28:18-20
    Ingram, Ray
    The Great Commission

14:5-6
    Young, Gordon
    I Am The Way, The Truth And The Life
    SATB   Keyboard
    Lorenz (1965) E-40

14:5-7, 15-18
    Madsen, Florence J.
    If Ye Love Me, Keep My Commandments
    SSA   Organ or Piano
    Carl Fischer (1950) CM 6603

14:6
    SEE: Isaiah 53:3-4
    Hunnicutt, Judy
    Surely He Has Borne Our Griefs

14:6 (John 8:12; John 10:7)
    Hruby, Dolores
    Your Holy Cross
    3 equal voices   Organ
    GIA (1974) G-1894

14:6
    SEE: John 10:7, 9 (adapted)
    Lewis, John Leo
    I Am The Door

14:6
    SEE: Romans 6:9
    Pelz, Walter
    Verse/Fifth Sunday Of Easter

14:12-14
    Pelz, Walter
    Offertory/Sixth Sunday Of Easter (Verses
        And Offertories - Easter - Trinity)
    SATB   Organ
    Augsburg (1980) 11-9546

14:15
    SEE: Luke 10:27-28
    Ford, Virgil T.
    This Do, And Thou Shalt Live

14:15
    Willan, Healey
    If Ye Love Me
    SSA   No accompaniment
    Concordia (1953) (found in We Praise Thee,
        Volume 1, 97-7564)

14:15-17
    Combs, Francis
    If Ye Love Me, Keep My Commandments
    SATB   Organ
    Concordia (1942) 98-1215

14:15-17
    George, Graham
    If Ye Love Me, Keep My Commandments
    SATB   Organ
    H. W. Gray (1937) 1429

14:15-17
  Nevin, George
  If Ye Love Me, Keep My Commandments
  SATB   Organ
  Oliver Ditson (1914) 12590

14:15-17
  Tallis, Thomas
  If Ye Love Me
  SATB   Optional organ
  Boosey & Hawkes (1958) 5224

14:15-17
  Tallis, Thomas (ed. Hewitt Pantaleoni)
  If Ye Love Me
  TTBB   No accompaniment
  Concordia (1960) 98-1520

14:15-17
  Tallis, Thomas
  If Ye Love Me
  SATB   kro
  E. C. Schirmer (1976) 2992 (also found in
      The Renaissance Singer)

14:15-17
  Tallis, Thomas (ed. R. Proulx)
  If Ye Love Me
  SAB   No accompaniment
  GIA (1980) G 2290

14:15-17
  Tallis, Thomas
  If Ye Love Me
  SATB   Organ optional
  H. W. Gray (n.d.) 1629

14:15-17
  Tallis, Thomas
  If Ye Love Me
  SATB   Optional organ
  Novello (n.d.) 29.0227.03

14:15-17
  Tallis, Thomas (ed. Peter LeHuray)
  If Ye Love Me
  SATB   Optional organ
  Oxford (found in Oxford Book Of Tudor
      Anthems)

14:15-17
  Tallis, Thomas
  If Ye Love Me
  SATB   Optional organ
  Oxford (1965) TCM 43.50

14:15-17
  Tallis, Thomas (arr. Gerald Knight)
  If Ye Love Me
  SATB   Optional organ
  RSCM (found in Festival Service Book, 6)

14:15-17, 27
  Simper, Caleb
  If Ye Love Me
  SATB   Organ
  Presser (n.d.) 312-00100

14:15-17, 27
  Simper, Caleb
  If Ye Love Me
  SATB   Organ
  Weekes [Galaxy] (n.d.) W.4041

14:15-18, 21
  Pinkham, Daniel
  If Ye Love Me
  SSA   Organ
  E. C. Schirmer (1964) 2568

14:18
  Beattie, Herbert
  I Will Not Leave You Comfortless (part of
      Six Choral Settings)
  SAB   Organ optional
  G. Schirmer (1954) 510

14:18
  Byrd, William (ed. H. Clough-Leighter)
  I Will Not Leave You Comfortless
  SSATB   kro
  E. C. Schirmer (1935) 917

14:18
  Byrd, William (ed. W. M. McKie)
  I Will Not Leave You Comfortless
  SSATB   kro
  Novello (1953) AP 27

14:18
  SEE: Romans 6:9
  Pelz, Walter
  Verse/Seventh Sunday of Easter

14:18, 20
  Byrd, William (arr. A. T. Davison)
  Non Vos Relinquam Orphanos
  TTBB   kro
  E. C. Schirmer (1966) 2324

14:18, 28
  Byrd, William (ed. Edmund Fellowes)
  Non Vos Relinquam (I Will Not Leave You
      Comfortless) (English/Latin)
  SSATB   kro
  Stainer & Bell (1938) 539

14:18
  Donati, Ignazio (ed. Jerome Roche)
  Non Vos Relinquam Orphanos
  SSA or TTB   Organ
  Oxford (1973) A-296

14:18
  SEE: Psalm 24:10
  Marenzio, Luca
  O Rex Gloriae

14:18
  Nelson, Ron
  I Will Not Leave You Comfortless (Four
      Anthems For Young Choirs)
  2 part treble   Piano or Organ
  Boosey & Hawkes (1965) 5576

14:18
  Titcomb, Everett
  I Will Not Leave You Comfortless
  SATB   kro
  Carl Fischer (1934) CM 441

14:21
  Mundy, William
  He That Hath My Commandments
  AATB   kro
  Oxford (1965) (found in Anthems For Men's
      Voices, Volume 1)

14:23
  Bender, Jan
  If A Man Loves Me, Op. 32, #11
  Unison treble   Keyboard
  Concordia (1963) 98-1697

14:23
  SEE: Romans 6:9
  Pelz, Walter
  Verse/Sixth Sunday Of Easter

14:27
  Eddleman, David
  Peace I Leave With You
  SATB   Piano, 3 Trumpets
  Carl Fischer (1977) CM 8000

14:27
  Jergenson, Dale
  Peace
  SAB   kro
  GIA (1976) G-1984

14:27
 Lotti, Antonio (ed. & arr. Frank Pooler)
 My Peace I Give
 SATB   kro
 Schmidt (1957) 866

14:27
 Lovelace, Austin
 Peace I Leave With You
 SATB   Organ or Piano
 Canyon (1953) n.#.

14:27
 SEE: Luke 14:27
 McCormick, Clifford
 Then Did Jesus Pray

14:27   (John 16:33)
 Middleswarth, Jean Ewald
 Peace Unto Your Soul
 SATB   kro
 Broadman (1977) 4562-83

14:27
 McHugh, Charles R.
 Peace I Leave With You
 SATB   No accompaniment
 Augsburg (1979) 11-1872

14:27
 Nystedt, Knut
 Peace I Leave With You
 SSATB   kro
 Augsburg (1958) 1216

14:27
 Pelz, Walter
 Peace, I Leave With You
 SATB   kro
 Augsburg (1958) ACL-1364

14:27
 Turner, Ruth
 Peace, I Leave With You
 SATB   Organ
 H. W. Gray (1953) CMR 2298

14:27
 York, David Stanley
 Peace I Leave With You
 SATB   Organ
 Mercury (1957) MC 300

14:27
 Young, Gordon
 Peace I Leave With You
 SATB   Piano
 Presser (1977) 312-41167

15:1, 4-5
 Schalk, Carl
 Offertory/Pentecost 18 (Verses and
       Offertories - Pentecost 12-20)
 Unison   Organ
 Augsburg (1978) 11-9539

15:1-11   (adapted)
 Morgan, Haydn
 I Am The Vine
 SATB   Optional accompaniment
 Lorenz (1965) E-45

15:2, 4-5, 10
 SEE: Psalm 80:19
 Wyatt, Noel
 Turn Us Again O Lord God Of Hosts

15:5, 7
 McCormick, Clifford
 I Am The Vine
 SATB   No accompaniment
 Shawnee (1955) A-373 (also found in Anthems
       From Scripture, G-34)

15:10-12
 Heeley, Albert
 If Ye Keep My Commandments
 SATB   kro
 Novello (1938 (found in In Wonder, Love
       And Praise)

15:12
 SEE: Luke 27-28
 Ford, Virgil T.
 This Do And Thou Shalt Live

15:12   (Psalm 133)
 Peloquin, C. Alexander
 Psalm 132
 Unison or 2 part   No accompaniment
 GIA (1964) G-1141

15:12, 13
 SEE: Matthew 29:19
 Butler, Eugene
 Go Ye Into All The World

15:12-13
 Morgan, Haydn
 This Is My Commandment
 SATB   kro
 Flammer (1962) A-5075

15:12-13
 Tallis, Thomas
 This Is My Commandment
 AATB   Keyboard
 Oxford (1969) TCM 70A

15:12-14, 17
 Mueller, Carl F.
 Greater Love Hath No Man
 SATB   Piano or Organ
 Carl Fischer (1950) CM 6522

15:12-17
 Routley, Erik
 Of Divine Love (from Three Antiphonal
       Canticles)
 SATB   Organ
 Novello (1974) MW 24

15:13
 SEE: Song Of Songs 8:7
 Ireland, John
 Greater Love Hath No Man

15:16   (Philippians 4:6)
 Allen, Larry
 I Have Chosen You
 SATB   Brass (2 Trumpets, 2 Horns,
       2 Trombones, Tuba)
 Broadman (1978) 4562-56

15:26
 Nystedt, Knut
 The Spirit Of Truth
 SAB   Organ
 Concordia (1965) 98-1806

15:26-27
 Bender, Jan
 When The Counselor Comes, Op. 32, #5
 2 part equal voices   Keyboard
 Concordia (1973) 98-2055

16:13, 15, 17, 23
 McCormick, Clifford
 If I Go Not Away
 SATB   No accompaniment
 Shawnee (1960) A-548 (also found in
       Anthems From Scripture, G-34)

16:20
 Philips, Peter (ed. Lionel Pike)
 Tristita Vestra (from Two Motets) (Latin)
 SSATB   kro
 Oxford (1981) n.#.

16:20
    Vulpius, Melchior (ed. T. P. Klamner)
    Your Sorrow Shall Be Turned Into Joy
    SATB   kro
    Concordia (1950) MS 1002

16:23-24
    Bender, Jan
    If You Ask Anything Of The Father, Op. 32,
        #3
    SA   Keyboard
    Concordia (1970) 98-1991

16:23-24   (Matthew 6:9-13)
    Hammerschmidt, Andreas (ed. Harold Mueller)
    Truly, Truly, I Say To You   (English/
        German
    SSATB   Continuo, 2 Violins
    Concordia (1974) 97-5164 (parts - 97-5270)

16:23-24
    Willan, Healey
    Verily, Verily, I Say Unto You
    Unison   Keyboard
    Concordia (1962) 97-7160   (found in We
    Praise Thee, Volume 2)

16:24
    Burroughs, Bob
    Ask
    SATB   Keyboard
    Fred Bock (1971) G-152

16:24 (Matthew 21:22;   I John 5:14-15)
    Glarum, L. Stanley
    Ask And Ye Shall Receive
    SATB   kro
    H. T. Fitzsimons (1963) 2207

16:24-25
    Moser, Rudolf
    That Your Joy May Be Full, Op. 94, #5
    SATB   kro
    Concordia (1956) 98-1354

16:33
    Distler, Hugo
    In der Welt habt ihr Angst   (German only)
    SATB   No accompaniment
    Barenreiter (1967) 757

16:33
    Distler, Hugo
    In The World There Is Pain
    SATB   No accompaniment
    Arista (1971) AE 201

16:33
    Distler, Hugo (ed. Larry Palmer)
    In The World You Have Fear, Op. 12, #7
    SATB   kro
    Concordia (1972) 98-2146

16:33
    SEE: John 14:27
    Middlesworth, Jean Ewald
    Peace Unto Your Soul

17:17
    Johnson, David N.
    Verse/Epiphany VI (Verses and Offertories -
        Epiphany II - The Transfiguration Of
        Our Lord)
    Unison   Organ
    Augsburg (1980) 11-9544

17:21-22
    Mueller, Carl F.
    That They May All Be One
    SATB   Organ
    G. Schirmer (1968) 11594

18:00 (plus additional)
    Victoria, Tomas (ed. Austin Lovelace)
    The Passion According To St. John
    SATB   Readers   Unaccompanied
    Summy Birchard (1956) SUMCO 4867

18:1 - 19:30
    Victoria, Tomas   (ed. Austin Lovelace)
    Passion According To St. John
    SATB   kro
    Concordia (1977) 97-5430

19:25-27
    Pinkham, Daniel
    The Seven Last Words Of Christ On The Cross
        (Second Word)
    SATB (T-B-B-solos)   Organ and Tape
    E. C. Schirmer (1971) 2907

19:28-30
    Pinkham, Daniel
    The Seven Last Words Of Christ On The Cross
        (Fifth Word)
    SATB (T-B-B-solos)   Organ and Tape
    E. C. Schirmer (1971) 2907

19:29-30
    Pinkham, Daniel
    The Seven Last Words Of Christ On The Cross
        (Sixth Word)
    SATB (T-B-B-solos)   Organ and Tape
    E. C. Schirmer (1971) 2907

19:30
    SEE: Matthew 27:45-47
    Haydn, Michael
    Tenebrae In E-flat

19:30
    SEE: Matthew 27:45-46
    Palestrina, G. P.
    Tenebrae Factae Sunt

19:30
    Shaw, Robert and Alice Parker (arr.)
    'Tis Finished
    SA(T)B   No accompaniment
    Lawson Gould (1955) 9944

20:1
    Noble, T. Tertius
    That Easter Morn
    SATB   Organ
    J. Fischer (1945) 8086

20:1-18
    SEE: Mark 16:1-7
    Hammerschmidt, A. (ed. H. Mueller)
    Who Rolls Away The Stone

20:2
    Morley, Thomas (ed. Charles Marshall)
    Alas! They Have Taken Jesus (English/
        Latin)
    SATB   kro
    Franck (1965) F-552

20:2
    Morley, Thomas (ed. Hans T. David)
    Easter Motet   (Latin)
    SATB   No accompaniment
    Mercury (1944) MC 53

20:2
    Morley, Thomas
    Eheu, Sustulerunt Dominum   (English/Latin)
    SATB   kro
    Arista (1971) AE 194

20:2
    Morley, Thomas (ed. Thurston Dart)
    Eheu Sustulerunt Dominum   (English/Latin)
    SATB   kro
    Stainer & Bell (1959) 604

20:11
    Gabrieli, Andrea
    Maria Stabat   (Latin only)
    SAATBB   No accompaniment
    Oxford (1980) (found in Ten Venetian
        Motets)

20:11-16, 18
    Hovhaness, Alan
    I Have Seen The Lord, Op. 80
    SATB (S-solo)   Organ, Trumpet ad lib.
    C. F. Peters (1964) 6544   (part 6544a)

20:11-17 (adapted)
    Adolphe, Bruce
    Woman Why Do You Weep?
    SA   Piano
    Alexander Broude (1978) AB 831

20:13
    Pinkham, Daniel
    They Have Taken Away My Lord   (from Easter
        Cantata)
    SATB   Piano (Brass)
    C. F. Peters (1962) 6393

20:13-15
    Palestrina, G. P. (ed. John Finley
        Williamson)
    Alleluia!   Tulerunt Dominum
    SATTB   kro
    G. Schirmer (1932) 7663

20:13-16   (I Corinthians 15:55)
    Skeat, William J.
    The Resurrection   (from The Son Of Man)
    SATB   Keyboard
    J. Fischer (1955) 8094

20:13-16   (I Corinthians 15:55, 57)
    Stainer, John
    They Have Taken Away My Lord
    SATB   Organ
    Presser (n.d.) 10826

20:13-17
    Schütz, Heinrich (ed. Richard T. Gore)
    Woman Why Weepest Thou? (English/German)
    SATB   Organ
    Concordia (1961) 97-6369

20:16 (based on)
    Sateren, Leland
    Beside The Sepulchre
    SATB   kro
    Schmitt, Hall, McCreary (1960) 1793

20:17
    Handl, Jacob
    I Ascend Unto My Father
    SSATBB   kro
    Bosworth (n.d.) n.#.

20:17
    Handl, Jacob (ed. Walter Ehret)
    I Ascend Unto My Father (English/Latin)
    SSATBB   kro
    Elkan Vogel (1978) 362-03251

20:17
    Pfautsch, Lloyd
    I Ascend To My Father
    SATB   kro
    R. D. Row (1956) 6003

20:17
    Scheidt, Samuel
    Ascendo Ad Patrem Meum   (Latin)
    SATB/SATB   No accompaniment
    Arista (1974) AE 225

20:19-21
    Nystedt, Knut
    Peace Be Unto You
    SATB   Organ
    Augsburg (1965) 1455

20:19-22
    Wetzler, Robert
    Peace Be With You
    SATB   Organ
    Art Masters (1970) 178

20:19-31
    Bender, Jan
    Peace Be With You, Op. 32, #22
    2 part equal voices   Organ
    Concordia (1974) 98-2086

20:21   (Matthew 28:20)
    Walter, Samuel
    Peace Be Unto You
    SATB   Organ
    Abingdon (1963) APM-279

20:22
    SEE: Isaiah 61:1, 6, 8
    Clokey, Joseph
    Men Of God

20:22-23
    Hillert, Richard
    Receive The Holy Spirit
    SATB   Organ
    Concordia (1963) 98-1675

20:24-29
    Wetzler, Robert
    We Have Seen The Lord
    SATB   No accompaniment
    Augsburg (1975) 11-1705

20:29
    SEE: Job 23:3, 8-9
    Bennett, W. Sterndale
    O That I Knew Where I Might Find Him

20:29
    Hassler, Hans Leo (ed. Mason Martens)
    Quia Vidisti Me, Thoma (Because Thou Hast
        Seen Me)   (Latin/English)
    SATB   Keyboard
    Concordia (1964) 98-1741

20:29
    Pasquet, Jean
    Blessed Are They
    SATB   Optional accompaniment
    B. F. Wood (1959) 765

20:29
    Pasquet, John
    Blessed Are They
    SATB   Optional accompaniment
    Mills (1960) 44-765

29:29
    SEE: Romans 6:9
    Pelz, Walter
    Verse/Second Sunday Of Easter

21:15-19   (paraphrase)
    Sleeth, Natalie
    Feed My Lambs
    Unison   Keyboard, 2 Flutes
    Carl Fischer (1972) CM 7777

A C T S

1:8
  Hillert, Richard
  Verse/Common Of Apostles, Evangelists
      (Verses and Offertories - Lesser
      Festivals)
  Unison   Organ
  Augsburg (1980) 11-9542

1:10-11
  Hooper, William L.
  Acts 1:10-11
  SATB   Keyboard
  Broadman (1978) 4563-16

1:11
  Byrd, William
  Viri Galilaei
  AATBB   No accompaniment
  Oxford (1965) (found in Anthems For Men's
      Voices, Volume 1)

1:11 (Psalm 47:1)
  Martens, Edmund
  You Men Of Galilee (from Four Introits,
      Set 1)
  Unison   Handbells
  Concordia (1976) 97-5384

1:11
  SEE: Psalm 47:1, 4-5
  Titcomb, Everett
  God Is Gone Up

1:24
  SEE: Exodus 34:6-7
  Gregor, Christian (arr. E. V. Nolte)
  Lord God, Merciful And Gracious (from
      Two Anthems From The Moravians)

2:00
  Leaf, Robert (arr.)
  I Will Pour Out My Spirit
  SATB   Organ
  Augsburg (1972) 11-1674

2:00 (metrical version)
  Tye, Christopher (arr. Gerald Knight)
  Hail, Glorious Spirits Heirs Of Light
  SATB   kro
  RSCM (1959) 221

2:1 (and other material)
  Williamson, Malcolm
  Canticle Of Fire
  SATB   Keyboard
  Boosey & Hawkes (1973) W.109

2:1-2
  Palestrina, G. P.
  Dum Complerentur Dies Pentecostes (Latin)
  SAATTB   No accompaniment
  Arista (1968) AE 145

2:1-2
  Palestrina, G. P.
  Dum Ergo Essent (Latin/English)
  SAATTB   kro
  J. W. Chester (1967) JWC 8855

2:1-2
  Victoria, Tomas
  Dum Complerentur (English/Latin)
  SSATB   kro
  E. C. Schirmer (1976) ECS 2993 (also
      found in The Renaissance Singer)

2:1-4
  Coke-Jephcott, Norman
  When The Day Of Pentecost Was Fully Come
  SATB   Organ
  Galaxy (1943) 1371

2:1-4
  Palestrina, G. P. (ed. Henry G. Ley)
  Dum Complerentur Dies Pentecostes
      (English/Latin)
  SSATTB   kro
  Novello (n.d.) 1206

2:1-4
  SEE: Wisdom Of Solomon 1:7
  Ridout, Alan
  Spiritus Dominii

2:1-21
  Maeker, Nancy
  Pentecost
  Speech Choir   Narrator, Percussion
  Augsburg (1979) 11-3506

2:2 (Psalm 68:28-29)
  Aichinger, Gregor
  Factus Est Repente (Latin only)
  SATB   kro
  J. & W. Chester (1977) JWC 55107 (found
      in Fourth Chester Book Of Motets)

2:4
  Handl, Jakob (ed. Cyril F. Simkins)
  Repleti sunt omnes (And They Were All
      Filled) (English/Latin)
  SATB/SATB or SATB and Brass quartet
      kro
  Concordia (1978) 98-2394 (parts for
      choir II - 98-2396)

2:4, 11
  Handl, Jacob
  Replenti Sunt Omnes (Latin)
  2 choirs of 8 equal voices   No accompani-
      ment
  Mercury (1946) 352.00031

2:4, 11 (paraphrase)
  Palestrina, G. P. (ed. John E. West)
  In Divers Tongues
  SATB   kro
  Novello (n.d.) 913

2:32
  Hillert, Richard
  Verse/Common Of Apostles, Evangelists
      (Verses And Offertories - Lesser
      Festivals)
  Unison   Organ
  Augsburg (1980) 11-9542

2:46-47
  Landgrave, Phillip
  Acts 2:46-47
  SATB   Organ
  Broadman (1978) 4563-17

4:12
  Herbst, Johannes (ed. & arr. Karl Kroeger)
  No Other Way Is Given To Men (English/
      German)
  SATB   Organ
  Boosey & Hawkes (1977) 5967

6:00 (metrical)
  Tye, Christopher (ed. Gerald Knight)
  O Holy Spirit, Lord Of Grace
  SATB   kro
  RSCM [Hinshaw] (1955) HMC-487

7:00   (based on)
    Pfautsch, Lloyd (arr.)
    Knight Without A Sword
    SATB   Organ
    Abingdon (1968) APM-694

7:00   (metrical)
    Tye, Christopher (ed. Gerald Knight)
    The Eternal Gates Lift Up Their Heads
    SATB   kro
    RSCM [Hinshaw] (1956) 508

7:48-50
    SEE: I Kings 8:27-30
    Kirk, Theron
    The Temple Of The Living God

7:55-56
    Tomkins, Thomas
    Stephen Being Full Of The Holy Ghost
    SSAATBB   Organ
    Stainer & Bell (1965) #1

7:55-60
    Wyton, Alec
    Stephen
    SATB (T-solo)   Organ and/or Piano
    Flammer (1974) A-5676

8:1-47   (Acts 9:1-4)
    Hovland, Egil
    Saul
    SATB   Narrator   Organ
    Norsk Musikforlag (1972) M-126

9:1-4
    SEE: Acts 8:1-47
    Hovland, Egil
    Saul

13:32-33 (Song of Songs 2:11-12; Psalm 145:21)
    Baristow, Edward
    The Promise Which Was Made
    SATB   Organ
    Novello (n.d.) 1510

14:17   (and Psalms)
    Simper, Caleb
    Praise Him For His Goodness
    SATB   Organ
    A. Weekes [Harris] (1946) W.6750

16:14, 15   (based on)
    Burton, Daniel
    Lydia's Song: Lord, My Heart Is Open
        (found in Fire Children's Anthems)
    Unison   Keyboard
    Shawnee (1982) F-5015

16:36
    Parker, Alice
    Now Therefore Depart   (from Sunday Rounds)
    5 part round   No accompaniment
    Hinshaw (1975) HMC 106

17:24-28
    SEE: Job 23:3
    Baumgartner, H. Leroy
    In Him We Live

R O M A N S

5:15-16
    Mendelssohn, Felix
    How Lovely Are The Messengers
    SATB   Piano
    G. Schirmer (n.d.) 3741

5:19
    Norris, Kevin
    Verse/Lent I (Verses and Offertories - Lent)
    Unison   Organ
    Augsburg (1980) 11-9545

6:4-5 (Colossians 3:1-4)
    Baristow, Edward
    Know Ye Not
    SATB (S-solo)   Organ
    Novello (1906) 756

6:9   (Job 19:25)
    Diemer, Emma Lou
    Alleluia! Christ Is Risen
    SATB   Organ, Trumpet
    Flammer (1965) A-5373

6:9
    Ford, Virgil T.
    He Has Risen
    SATB   Brass Quartet
    Flammer (1966) A-5109

6:9
    Krapf, Gerhard
    Easter Antiphon
    SATB   Organ (Brass Quartet)
    Concordia (1964) 98-1751 (parts - 98-1752)

6:9 (Matthew 28:20)
    Pelz, Walter
    Verse/Ascension Of Our Lord (Verses And
        Offertories - Easter - Trinity)
    SAB   Organ
    Augsburg (1980) 11-9546

6:9 (Luke 24:27)
    Pelz, Walter
    Verse/Easter Evening (Verses And
        Offertories - Easter - Trinity)
    SATB   Organ
    Augsburg (1980) 11-9546

6:9   (John 14:6)
    Pelz, Walter
    Verse/Fifth Sunday Of Easter (Verses And
        Offertories - Easter - Trinity)
    SATB   Organ
    Augsburg (1980) 11-9546

6:9   (John 10:14)
    Pelz, Walter
    Verse/Fourth Sunday Of Easter (Verses And
        Offertories - Easter - Trinity)
    SATB   Organ
    Augsburg (1980) 11-9546

6:9   (Psalm 118:24)
    Pelz, Walter
    Verse/The Resurrection Of Our Lord (Verses
        And Offertories - Easter - Trinity)
    SATB   Organ
    Augsburg (1980) 11-9546

6:9   (John 20:29)
    Pelz, Walter
    Verse/Second Sunday Of Easter (Verses And
        Offertories - Easter - Trinity)
    SATB   Organ
    Augsburg (1980) 11-9546

6:9   (John 14:18)
    Pelz, Walter
    Verse/Seventh Sunday of Easter (Verses And
        Offertories - Easter - Trinity)
    SATB   Organ
    Augsburg (1980) 11-9546

6:9   (John 14:23)
    Pelz, Walter
    Verse/Sixth Sunday Of Easter (Verses And
        Offertories - Easter - Trinity)
    SATB   Organ
    Augsburg (1980) 11-9546

6:9 (Luke 24:32)
Pelz, Walter
Verse/Third Sunday Of Easter (Verses And
    Offertories - Easter - Trinity)
SATB   Organ
Augsburg (1980) 11-9546

6:9 (I Corinthians 15:22)
Stewart, C. Hylton
Christ Being Raised From The Dead
SATB   Organ
Oxford (1935) E-17

6:9 (Colossians 3:1)
Thiman, Eric
Christ Being Raised From The Dead
SATB   Organ
H. W. Gray (1962) CMR 2738

6:9-10
SEE: I Corinthians 5:7-8
Arnatt, Ronald
Easter Triumph

6:9-10
Sanborn, Jan
Christ Is Risen
SATB   Organ
Sacred Songs (1966) C5-669

6:9-10 (I Corinthians 15:21-22)
Shepherd, John
Christ Rising Again
TTBB   No accompaniment
Oxford (1965) (found in Anthems For Men's
    Voices, Volume 2)

6:9-10
Viadana, Lodovico (ed. Mason Martens)
Christus Resurges   (English/Latin)
SAB   Organ
MCA (1964) n.#.

6:9-10
Willan, Healey
Christ Being Raised From The Dead
SSA   No accompaniment
Concordia (1953) (found in We Praise Thee,
    Volume 1, 97-7564)

6:9-11 (I Corinthians 15:20-22)
Blow, John (ed. Mason Martens)
Christ Being Raised From The Dead
SATB   Organ
Concordia (1964) 98-1744

6:9-11 (I Corinthains 15:20-22)
Blow, John (ed. Beverly A. Ward)
Christ Being Raised From The Dead
SATB (S-A-T-B-solos)   Organ
H. W. Gray (1981) GCMR 3437

6:9-11
Byrd, William
Christ Rising Again
SSATTB   Organ (or String Quartet)
Lawson Gould (1955) 551

6:9-11
Byrd, William
Christ Rising Again (Part I)
SSATTB   Keyboard or Strings
Stainer & Bell (1949) 49

6:9-11
SEE: I Corinthians 5:7-8
Bodine, Willis
Christ Our Passover

6:9-11
SEE: I Corinthians 5:7-8
Dirksen, Richard
Christ Our Passover

6:9-11
SEE: I Corinthians 5:7-8
Harwood, Basil
Christ Our Passover

6:9-11
SEE: I Corinthians 5:7-8
Powell, Robert J.
Christ Our Passover

6:9-11
SEE: I Corinthians 5:7-8
Powers, G.
Christ Our Passover

6:9-11
SEE: I Corinthians 5:7-8
Roth, Robert
Christ Our Passover

6:9-11
SEE: I Corinthians 5:7-8
Stewart, C. Hylton
Christ Being Raised From The Dead
    [Curwen]

6:9-11 (I Corinthians 15:20-22)
Tomkins, Thomas (ed. Barry Rose)
Christ Rising Again From The Dead
SATB (A-T-B-solos)   Organ
Stainer & Bell (1965)

6:9-11
SEE: I Corinthians 5:7-8
Tours, Berthold
Christ Our Passover Is Sacrificed For Us

6:9-11   (I Corinthians 15:20-22)
Weelkes, Thomas
Christ Rising Again
SATB (S-S-A-A-solos)   Organ
Novello (1973) NECM 25

6:9-11 (I Corinthians 15:20-22)
Wise, Michael (ed. Michael J. Smith)
Christ Rising Again From The Dead
SSATB   Organ
Novello (1973) MT 1559

6:9-11
SEE: I Corinthians 5:7-8
Wyton, Alec
Christ Our Passover

6:9-11
SEE: I Corinthians 5:7-8
Wyton, Alec
Easter Canticle

6:10
SEE: I Corinthians 15:20
Noble, T. Tertius
The Risen Christ

6:11
SEE: Ephesians 5:4
Jackson, B.
Awake Thou That Sleepest

8:9-16 (I John 3:1-2)
Davies, H. Walford
If Any Man Hath Not The Spirit
SATB   Organ
H. W. Gray (n.d.) 1988

8:14, 16   (Romans 11:33, 36)
Williams, David McK.
As Many As Are Led By The Spirit
SATB   Organ
H. W. Gray (1956) 2413

8:18, 19
    Franck, Melchior (ed. Franklin Kinsman)
    The Sufferings Of The Present (English/
        German)
    SATB   kro
    Abingdon (1975) APM-560

8:28, 31 (adapted from)
    Burton, Daniel
    All Things Work Together (from Five
        Children's Anthems)
    Unison, Optional 2nd part   Keyboard
    Shawnee (1982) F 5015

8:28-32
    Kirk, Theron
    All Things
    SATB   Piano
    Elkan Vogel (1976) 362-03212

8:31
    Butler, Eugene
    If God Be For Us
    SATB   Piano
    Carl Fischer (1981) CM 8131

8:31-32, 35, 37
    Mueller, Carl F.
    If God Be For Us
    SATB   Piano or Organ
    Carl Fischer (1951) CM 6622

8:31b-32, 35, 37-39
    Young, Carlton (arr.)
    Canticle Of Affirmation
    SATB   Speaker   Organ
    Agape [Hope] (1978) CY 3348

8:31-34
    Franck, Melchior (ed. Matthew Lundquist)
    If God Is For Us
    SATB   Organ
    Mercury (1955) MC 233

8:31-34
    Franck, Melchior
    Ist Gott für uns wer mag wider uns sein
    SATB   No accompaniment
    Merserburger (1977) (found in Motetten
        Alter Meister)

8:31-34
    Franck, Melchior
    If God Be For Us
    SATB   kro
    Marks (1950) 12781

8:31-34
    Franck, Melchior (arr. Walter Ehret)
    If God Be For Us
    SATB   kro
    GIA (1978) G 2201

8:31-34
    Schütz, Heinrich (ed. C. Buell Agey)
    If God Be For Us, Who Can Be Against Us?
        (English/German)
    SATB   Organ
    G. Schirmer (1961) 10876

8:31-34
    Schütz, Heinrich
    Ist Gott für uns? (German)
    SATB   Continuo
    Barenreiter (1956) 1706

8:35, 37-39
    SEE: Ephesians 6:10-17
    Blakely, D. Duane
    Be Strong In The Lord

8:35, 38-39
    Doig, Don
    Who Shall Separate Us
    SATB   Keyboard
    Hope (1980) A-512

8:35, 38-39
    Schütz, Heinrich
    Wer will uns scheiden (German)
    SATB   Continuo
    Barenretier (1956) 1706

8:35, 38-39
    Schütz, Heinrich
    Who Shall Separate Us (German/English)
    SATB   Organ or Piano
    Sam Fox (1965) CM 11

8:35, 38-39
    Schütz, Heinrich (ed. C. Buell Agey)
    Who Shall Separate Us From The Love Of God
        (English/German)
    SATB   Organ
    G. Schirmer (1961) 10874

8:35-39
    Beck, John Ness
    Who Shall Separate Us?
    SATB   Organ
    AMSI (1974) 261

8:35-39 (adapted from)
    Burton, Daniel
    What Can Come Between Us? (from Five
        Children's Anthems)
    Unison, optional 2nd part   Keyboard
    Shawnee (1982) F-5015

8:35-39
    Schütz, Heinrich
    Who Shall Separate Us (German/English)
    SATB   Organ or Piano
    Chantry (1949)

8:37
    Caldwell, Mary F.
    Overwhelming Victory Is Ours
    SATB   Organ
    Fred Bock [Presser] (1971) G-151

9:10-11 (I Corinthians 15:20-22)
    Tye, Christopher (ed. John Langdon)
    Christ Rising Again
    SATTBB   kro
    Oxford (1970) A-267

9:11-13
    Stanford, C. V.
    If Thou Shalt Confess With Thy Mouth,
        Op. 37, #2
    SATB   Organ
    Novello (1978) (found in In Wonder, Love
        And Praise)

9:20-21 (based on, text by M. James)
    Lewis, John Leo
    Hath Not The Potter Power
    SATB   kro
    Carl Fischer (1955) CM 6800

10:4
    Schelle, Johann (ed. Karl Straube)
    Jesus Christ From The Law Hath Freed Us
        (English/German)
    SSAB/ATBB   Continuo
    Concordia (1958) 97-6297

10:9, 11-13
    Stanford, C. V.
    If Thou Shalt Confess With Thy Mouth
    SATB   Organ
    Novello (n.d.) 21

10:15
   Gounod, Charles
   Lovely, Appear   (from The Redemption)
   SATB (S-solo)   Organ
   G. Schirmer (n.d.) 2013

10:15 (paraphrased)
   Mendelssohn, Felix
   How Lovely Are The Messengers (St. Paul)
   SATB   Organ
   E. C. Schirmer (1940) 1134   (also found in
      Concord Anthem Book - Red)

10:15 (paraphrased)
   Mendelssohn, Felix
   How Lovely Are The Messengers (St. Paul)
   SA   Organ
   E. C. Schirmer   #1215

10:15
   Stafford, C.
   How Beauteous Are Their Feet
   SATB   Organ
   Novello (1951) 29.0240.00

10:15-16
   Mendelssohn, Felix
   How Lovely Are The Messengers (St. Paul)
   SATB   Piano
   Carl Fischer (1942) CM 620

11:33, 36
   SEE: Romans 8:14, 16
   Williams, David McK.
   As Many As Are Led By The Spirit

11:33-36
   Danner, David
   Romans 11:33-36
   SATB   Keyboard
   Broadman (1978) 4563-15

11:33, 36
   SEE: II Esdras 16:35-36
   Gieseke, Richard
   Now Listen You Servants Of God

11:33-36
   Nystedt, Knut
   O The Depth Of The Riches
   SATB   kro
   Walton (1968) 2902

11:33-36
   Pinkham, Daniel
   O Depth Of Wealth
   SATB   Organ and Tape
   E. C. Schirmer (1974) 2951

11:36a
   SEE: Isaiah 6:3a
   Martens, Edmund
   Holy Is The Lord   (from Four Introits -
      Set 1)

12:1
   SEE: Song Of Songs 8:7
   Ireland, John
   Greater Love Hath No Man

12:1
   Johnson, David N.
   Offertory/Epiphany VII (Verses And Offer-
      tories - Epiphany II - The Trans-
      figuration Of Our Lord)
   Unison   Organ
   Augsburg (1980) 11-9544

12:1, 2
   Hillert, Richard
   Offertory/Reformation Day (Verses And
      Offertories - Lesser Festivals)
   Unison   Organ
   Augsburg (1980) 11-9543

12:2   (Philippians 2:5-11)
   Landgrave, Phillip
   Do Not Be Conformed
   SATB   Organ or Piano
   Carl Fischer (1970) CM 7756

12:11-13
   Schalk, Carl
   Offertory/Pentecost (Verses and
      Offertories - Pentecost 12-20)
   Unison   Organ
   Augsburg (1978) 11-9539

13:11-12
   Nystedt, Knut
   The Night Is Far Spent
   SATB   Organ
   Augsburg (1966) 1463

13:12
   Back, Sven-Erik
   Dominica Prima Adventus (English/Latin)
   SATB   No accompaniment
   W. Hansen [G. Schirmer] (1968) 11839

13:12
   Willan, Healey
   Rejoice, O Jerusalem, Behold, Thy King
      Cometh
   SATB   Organ
   Concordia (1960) 98-1506   (also found in
      With High Delight, 97-5047)

13:12-14
   Roff, Joseph
   Put Ye On The Lord Jesus
   SATB   Optional Organ or Piano
   Columbo (1963) 2356

14:00
   SEE: Philippians 1:21
   Young, Philip
   What IS Life But Christ?

14:6-8
   Schalk, Carl
   Offertory/Pentecost 17 (Verses And
      Offertories - Pentecost 12-20)
   Unison   Organ
   Augsburg (1978) 11-9539

14:7-8
   Schütz, Heinrich
   No Man Liveth To Himself (English/German)
   SSATB   Optional Keyboard
   Summy (1956) 4696

15:4
   Schalk, Carl
   Verse/Pentecost 17 (Verses And
      Offertories - Pentecost 12-20)
   2 part   Organ
   Augsburg (1978) 11-9539

15:4
   Wienhorst, Richard
   Whatever Was Written In Former Days
      (Three Verse Settings, Set 2)
   SATB   No accompaniment
   Concordia (1979) 98-2441

15:12
   SEE: Isaiah 11:1-2
   Handl, Jacob
   Egre Dictur Virga

15:13
   Bitgood, Roberta
   May The God Of Hope   (Choral Benediction)
   SATB   No accompaniment
   Abingdon (1965) APM-470

15:19
    Rodgers, John
    Through Mighty Signs And Wonders (from
        Seven Choral Sentences)
    SATB (optional solo)   Organ
    H. W. Gray (1981) GCMR 3453

I C O R I N T H I A N S

1:18
    Hillert, Richard
    Verse/Common Of Apostles, Evangelists
        (Verses And Offertories - Lesser
        Festivals)
    Unison   Organ
    Augsburg (1980) 11-9542

1:18
    Hillert, Richard
    Verse/Renewers Of The Church (Verses
        And Offertories - Lesser Festivals)
    Unison   Organ
    Augsburg (1980) 11-9543

1:25
    Lovelace, Austin
    The Foolishness Carol
    SATB   kro
    Somerset (1971) CF 4326

2:9   (Isaiah 64:4)
    Lassus, Orlandus
    Oculus Non Vidit   (Latin only)
    2 part   No accompaniment
    Mercury (1941) 352.00011 (found in
        Twelve Motets)

2:9   (Isaiah 64:4)
    Lassus, Orlandus
    Oculus Non Vidit (Latin/English)
    2 part   No accompaniment
    Oxford (1973) (found in Anthems For
        Choirs, Volume 2)

2:9
    Wade, Walter
    Eye Hath Not Seen
    SATB   kro
    Abingdon (1961) APM-189

2:10-12   (based on)
    Zimmermann, Heinz Werner
    Now We Have Received
    SATB   Organ, Trumpet in C, or Oboe
    Carl Fischer (n.d.) CM 8101

3:00
    Nelson, Ronald A.
    Temples Of God
    2 part mixed   Organ
    Augsburg (1974) 11-1696

3:8-11, 13-14
    Hoddinott, Alan
    Every Man's Work Shall Be Made
    SATB   Organ
    Oxford (1964) A-209

3:9, 11, 16
    SEE: Psalm 102:25-27
    DeTar, Vernon
    The Glory Of The Lord

3:9, 16-17, 23   (Genesis 28:16-17)
    Sowerby, Leo
    For We Are Laborers Together With God
    SATB (B-solo)   Organ
    H. W. Gray (1963) CMR 2888

3:9-17
    Bohrnstedt, Wayne R.
    We Have Builded An House
    SATB   Organ, 2 Trumpets
    Apogee Press [World Library] (1970)
        CA 2088-8

3:10-11, 16-17
    Hilty, Everett Jay
    You Are The Temple Of God
    SA   Organ
    Oxford (1975) 94.405

3:16
    SEE: I Kings 8:27-30
    Kirk, Theron
    The Temple Of The Living God

5:7
    SEE: Psalm 66:1, 2
    Gieseke, Richard W.
    Sing Praise To The Lord

5:7-8   (Romans 6:9-10; I Corinthians 15:20,
        22)
    Arnatt, Ronald
    Easter Triumph (Christ Our Passover)
    SATB   Organ
    H. W. Gray (1957) 2451

5:7-8
    Bender, Jan
    Alleluia Christ Our Passover
    SSAB   kro
    Concordia (1973) 98-2207

5:7-8   (Romans 6:9-11; I Corinthians
        15:20-22)
    Bodine, Willis
    Christ Our Passover
    SATB   Organ   Brass Quartet
        Timpani
    H. W. Gray (1970) 3081

5:7-8   (free paraphrase)
    Diemente, Edward
    Alleluia 1973
    SAB   Tape
    Belwin (1974) GCCS 22

5:7-8   (Romans 6:9-11;
        I Corinthians 15:20-22)
    Dirksen, Richard
    Christ Our Passover
    SATB   Organ, Brass Quartet
    H. W. Gray (1965) CMR 2874

5:7-8
    Gibbs, Alan
    Christ Our Passover
    SATB   Organ
    Oxford (1968) A-248

5:7-8
    Goss, John (ed. N. Clifford Page)
    Christ Our Passover Is Sacrificed For Us
    SATB (S-solo)   Keyboard
    Carl Fischer (1931) CM 282

5:7-8   (Romans 6:9-11;
        I Corinthians 15:20-22)
    Harwood, Basil
    Christ Our Passover
    SATB   Organ
    H. W. Gray (n.d.) CMR 2638

5:7-8
    Marshall, Jane M.
    Canticle For Communion
    SATB   kro
    Carl Fischer (1964) CM 7434

5:7-8
Middleton, J. Roland
The Easter Anthems
SATB   Organ
Banks (1976) ECS 46

5:7-8
Pelz, Walter
Offertory/The Resurrection Of Our Lord
     (Verses And Offertories - Easter
       Trinity)
SATB   Organ
Augsburg (1980) 11-9546

5:7-8   (Romans 6:9-11;
          I Corinthians 15:20-22)
Powell, Robert J.
Christ Our Passover
2 part choir   Organ,   Handbells
Hinshaw (1980) HMC 380

5:7-8   (Romans 6:9-11)
Powers, George
Christ Our Passover
SATB   Organ
Abingdon (1975) APM 592

5:7-8   (and a hymn)
Proulx, Richard
Christ The Lord Is Risen Again
SATB   Organ,   Brass Quartet,   Timpani
GIA (1972) G-1709

5:7-8
Roff, Joseph
Christ Our Paschal Lamb
SATB   Keyboard
GIA (1970) G-1594

5:7-8
Roff, Joseph
Christ Our Paschal Lamb
2 part   Keyboard
GIA (1970) G-1595

5:7-8   (Romans 6:9-11;
          I Corinthians 15:20-22)
Roth, Robert
Christ Our Passover
Unison   Organ
Canyon (1961) 6101

5:7-8
Schütz, Heinrich (ed. Denis Stevens)
Purge Out The Old Leaven Therefore
SATB   Organ continuo, 2 Violins
C. F. Peters (1966) 6593

5:7-8
Shaw, Martin
The Easter Anthem (Christ Our Passover)
SATB   Organ (or orchestra)
Oxford (1935) A 68

5:7-8   (Romans 6:9-11;
          I Corinthians 15:20-22)
Stewart, C. Hylton
Christ Being Raised From The Dead
SATB   Organ
Oxford (1935) E 17

5:7-8
Titcomb, Everett
Christ Our Passover
SATB   kro
Carl Fischer (1934) CM 439

5:7-8   (Romans 6:9-11;
          I Corinthians 15:20-22)
Tours, Berthold
Christ Our Passover Is Sacrificed For Us
SATB   Organ
G. Schirmer (n.d.) 4403

5:7-8   (and other)
Wetzler, Robert
Triumphant Day
SATB   Organ   (optional brass)
AMSI (1980) 392

5:7-8   (Romans 6:9-11;
          I Corinthians 15:20-22)
Wyton, Alec
Christ Our Passover
SATB   Organ,   Brass Quartet
Alexander Broude (1978) GP 411

5:7-8   (Romans 6:9-11)
Wyton, Alec
Easter Canticle
SATB   Organ or Brass Quartet
H. W. Gray (1963) CMR 2786

5:8-9
Asola, Giovanni (adapted Edward Diemente)
Christ, Our Passover
SATB   Organ
Lawson Gould (1969) 51528

6:11
SEE: Song Of Songs 8:7
Ireland, John
Greater Love Hath No Man

6:20
Muller, George Gottfried (ed. & arr. Lou
     Carth and Karl Kroeger)
You Are Precious To Him   (English/German)
SSAB   Organ
Carl Fischer (1978) CM 8046

6:20
SEE: I John 2:28
Peter, J. F. (arr. Karl Kroeger)
Harken, Stay Close To Him

6:20   (Micah 6:8) (freely adapted)
Sleeth, Natalie
Bought With A Price
2 part mixed   (optional SATB)   Keyboard
Hinshaw (1981) HMC 542

10:16-17
Busarow, Donald
Offertory/22nd Sunday After Pentecost
     (Verses And Offertories - Pentecost 21
       Christ The King)
2 part   Organ
Augsburg (1980) 11-9540

11:24-26
Lovelace, Austin
This Do In Remembrance Of Me
SATB   Organ
Agape [Hope] (1975) AG 7189

11:26
Norris, Kevin
Verse/Maundy Thursday (Verses And
     Offertories - Lent)
Unison   Organ
Augsburg (1980) 11-9545

13:00   (based on)
Burton, Daniel
Love Is Forever (from Five Children's
     Anthems)
Unison   Keyboard, Optional Flute
Shawnee (1982) F 5015

13:00   (adapted)
Cox, Michael
Love Never Faileth
SATB   Keyboard
Hinshaw (1981) HMC 500

13:00
    Fitchett, Adios
    The Greatest Of These Is Love
    SATB   Keyboard
    Abingdon (1979) APM-622

13:00
    Goemanne, Noel
    Ode To Love - The Walk
    SATB (T or S solo)   Organ or Piano
    Mark Foster (1978) NME 148A

13:00 (based on)
    Hopson, Hal
    The Gift Of Love
    Unison or 2 part   Keyboard with
        optional Flute or Oboe
    Hope (1972) CF 148 (also found in Choir-
        Book For Saints And Sinners)

13:00
    Hopson, Hal
    Saint Paul's Letter On Love
    SATB   Narrator, Speaking Voices, No
        Accompaniment
    Gentry [Presser]) (1975) G 270

13:00
    Read, Gardner
    Though I Speak With The Tongues Of Men,
        Op. 109
    SATB   Organ
    Abingdon (1965) APM-386

13:00
    Ridout, Alan
    The Greatest Of These Is Love
    SATB (S-solo)   No accompaniment
    Stainer & Bell [Galaxy] (1967) 649

13:00
    Rorem, Ned
    The Corinthians
    SATB   Organ
    Henman [C. F. Peters] (1960) 6193

13:1-4, 7-9, 12-13
    Baristow, Edward C.
    Though I Speak With The Tongues Of Men
    SA(T)B   Organ
    Oxford (1934) A 63

13:4-8
    Clutterham, Lars T.
    Love Is Patient And Kind
    SATB   Organ Chimes or Handbells
    GIA (1977) G-2064

13:13 (Psalm 136:1, 4, 7-9, 13-16, 21, 23, 26)
    Peloquin, Alexander
    Faith, Hope And Love
    SATB   Cantor   Congregation   Organ
    GIA (1974) G-1899

14:20, 25
    Simper, Caleb (ed. Carl Deis)
    King Of Kings
    SATB   Organ
    G. Schirmer (1954) 7389 (also available
        in 2-part voicing)

15:00 (adapted) (Revelation-chapters 4-7,
        adapted)
    Pattinson, John
    He Is Risen, Forever
    SATB (B-solo; S or T solo)   Organ
    Carl Fischer (1923) CM 141

15:20
    Billings, William (ed. Leonard VanCamp)
    The Lord Is Risen
    SATB   kro
    Concordia (1974) 98-2292

15:20   (Romans 6:10)
    Noble, T. Tertius
    The Risen Christ
    SATB   Organ
    H. W. Gray (1915) 383

15:20ff (adapted)
    Rogers, Sharon F.
    Easter Triumph
    SATB   Piano or Organ (optional Brass
        Quartet)
    Flammer (1968) A 5209

15:20 (based on) (Revelation 7:12, based on)
    Roman, Johan H. (trans. & ed. S. Drummond
        Wolff)
    Christ The Lord Is Risen!   Alleluia!
    SATB   Keyboard (optional 2 Trumpets,
        2 Trombones, Strings)
    Concordia (1981) 98-2326

15:20-21
    Handel, G. F. (Spicker)
    Since By Man Came Death (Messiah)
    SATB   Piano or Organ
    G. Schirmer (1912) 9871

15:20-21
    Marshall, Jane
    Fanfare For Easter
    SATB   Organ, Brass Quartet, Timpani
    Carl Fischer (1959) CM 7090

15:20-22
    SEE: I Corinthians 5:7-8
    Arnatt, Ronald
    Easter Triumph

15:20-22
    SEE: Romans 6:9-11
    Blow, John (ed. Mason Martens)
    Christ Being Raised From The Dead

15:20-22
    SEE: Romans 6:9-11
    Blow, John (ed. Beverly A. Ward)
    Christ Being Raised From The Dead

15:20-22
    SEE: I Corinthians 5:7-8
    Bodine, Willis
    Christ Our Passover

15:20-22
    SEE: I Corinthians 5:7-8
    Dirksen, Richard
    Christ Our Passover

15:20-22
    SEE: I Corinthians 5:7-8
    Harwood, Basil
    Christ Our Passover

15:20-22
    Joubert, John
    Christ Is Risen, Op. 36
    SATB   Organ
    Novello (1961) 29.0420.09

15:20-22
    Nystedt, Knut
    Now Is Christ Risen
    SATB   Organ, Trumpet Or Flute, Bells
        or Chimes
    SATB   Organ
    Augsburg (1965) 1453

15:20-22
    Pizarro, David
    An Easter Laud
    SATB   Organ (optional brass)
    H. W. Gray (1958) 2508

15:20-22
SEE: I Corinthians 5:7-8
Powell, Robert J.
Christ Our Passover

15:20-22
SEE: I Corinthians 5:7-8
Roth, Robert
Christ Our Passover

15:20-22
SEE: I Corinthians 5:7-8
Stewart, C. Hylton
Christ Being Raised From The Dead

15:20-22
SEE: Romans 6:9-11
Tomkins, Thomas (ed. Barry Rose)
Christ Rising Again From The Dead

15:20-22
SEE: I Corinthians 5:7-8
Tours, Berthold
Christ Our Passover Is Sacrificed For Us

15:20-22
SEE: Romans 9:10-11
Tye, Christopher (ed. John Langdon)
Christ Rising Again

15:20-22
SEE: Romans 6:9-11
Weelkes, Thomas
Christ Rising Again

15:20-22
SEE: Romans 6:9-11
Wise, Michael (ed. Michael J. Smith)
Christ Rising Again From The Dead

15:20-22
SEE: I Corinthians 5:7-8
Wyton, Alec
Christ Our Passover

15:20-22
Zaninelli, Luigi
Now Is Christ Risen From The Dead
SATB   Organ
Shawnee (1965) A-782

15:20, 27
SEE: Psalm 57:9
Barnby, J.
Awake Up, My Glory

15:21
Handel, G. F.
Since By Man Came Death
SATB   Piano or Organ
G. Schirmer (1912) 9871

15:21, 22
SEE: Ephesians 5:4
Jackson, B.
Awake Thou That Sleepest

15:21-22
SEE: Romans 6:9-10
Shepherd, John
Christ Rising Again

15:21, 57
Couper, Alinda
God Who Giveth Us The Victory (Festival
    Introit)
SATB   Trumpet, kro
Abingdon (1969) APM-780

15:22
SEE: Romans 6:9
Stewart, C. Hylton
Christ Being Raised From The Dead

15:34, 51-53
Wesley, Samuel S. (ed. A. J. Pritchard)
For This Mortal Must Put On Immortality
SSATB   Organ
Oxford (1955) CMSR 33

15:37
Bouman, Paul
Thanks Be To God
2 part equal voices   Keyboard
Concordia (1977) 98-2342

15:51-52, 54-55, 57
McAfee, Don
Lo! I Tell You A Mystery
SATB   (T-solo)   Organ
Canyon (1963) 6302

15:54-56
Krapf, Gerhard
Easter Salutation
SATB   Organ or Brass Quartet
H. W. Gray (1980) GCMR 3424

15:55
SEE: John 20:13-16
Skeat, William J.
Resurrection

15:55-56
Martin, Gilbert
Praises From The Risen Christ
SATB   Organ, 3 Trumpets
Sacred Music Press (1971) S 93

15:55, 57
SEE: John 20:13-16
Stainer, John
They Have Taken Away My Lord

15:57-58
Blankenship, Mark
Thanks Be To God
SATB   Brass (3 Trumpets, 3 Horns,
        2 Trombones)   Timpani
Broadman (1982) 4563-76

16:13
SEE: Ephesians 6:10-11, 13-17
Nicholson, Sidney H.
Be Strong In The Lord

II C O R I N T H I A N S

1:20
SEE: II Corinthians 2:14-17
Matthews, Thomas
Thanks Be To God

2:4-6
Guerrero, Francisco (ed. Robert Goodale)
Ecce Nunc Tempus   (Latin)
SATB   kro
G. Schirmer (1965) 11230

2:14-17   (II Corinthians 4:5-6;
            II Corinthians 1:20)
Matthews, Thomas
Thanks Be To God
SATB   Organ
H. T. Fitzsimons (1964) 2215

4:5-6
SEE: II Corinthians 2:14-17
Matthews, Thomas
Thanks Be To God

5:7
     SEE: Luke 17:5
     Mueller, Carl F.
     An Anthem Of Faith

5:17
     Wilson
     A New Creation
     SATB   Piano or Organ
     Agape [Hope] (1973) AG 7135

5:17-19
     Pfautsch, Lloyd
     Reconciliation
     SATB   Trumpet   No accompaniment
     Abingdon (1964) APM-345

5:19
     Herbst, Johannes (ed. & arr. Karl Kroeger)
     God Was In Jesus   (English/German)
     SATB   Organ or Piano
     Boosey & Hawkes (1973) 5851

6:16
     SEE: I Kings 8:27-30
     Kirk, Theron
     The Temple Of The Living God

8:9
     SEE: Luke 2:14
     Routley, Erik
     Of The Incarnation

9:8
     Hillert, Richard
     Verse/Thanksgiving (Verses And Offertories-
          Lesser Festivals)
     Unison   Organ
     Augsburg (1980) 11-9542

9:15
     SEE: Galatians 4:4
     Gibbs, Allen Orton
     God Sent Forth His Son

13:11
     SEE: Colossians 3:12-15
     Barnes, Edward Shippens
     Put On Therefore, As God's Elect

13:14
     Willan, Healey
     The Apostolic Benediction
     SATB   Organ
     C. F. Peters (1958) 6099

G A L A T I A N S

1:3-5
     Mueller, Carl F.
     Grace Be To You And Peace
     SATB   Piano or Organ
     Carl Fischer (1953) CM 6715

2:16, 19-20
     Blankenship, Mark
     Galatians 2:16, 19-20
     SATB   Keyboard
     Broadman (1978) 4563-13

2:20
     Norris, Kevin
     Offertory/Monday, Tuesday, Wednesday In
          Holy Week (Verses And Offertories -
          Lent)
     Unison   Organ
     Augsburg (1980) 11-9545

4:4   (Titus 2:11;   Luke 1:7, 8;
          Matthew 1:23;   II Corinthians 9:13)
     Gibbs, Allen Orton
     God Sent Forth His Son
     SATB   Organ
     Abingdon (1977) APM-966

4:4
     Wetzler, Robert
     Verse/Christmas Eve (Verses and
          Offertories - Advent I - The Baptism
          Of Our Lord)
     Unison   Organ
     Augsburg (1979) 11-9541

5:22
     Geisler, J. Christian (ed. Karl Kroeger)
     The Fruit Of The Spirit Is Love   (English/
          German)
     SATB   Organ, Flute
     Boosey & Hawkes (1974) 5892

6:14   (Psalm 66:2-4)
     Anerio, Felice
     Nos Autem, Gloriari   (Latin)
     SATB   No accompaniment
     Arista (1976) AE 256

6:14 (based on)   (Psalm 66:2-4)
     Copes, Earle
     When I Survey The Wondrous Cross
     SATB   Organ or Piano
     G. Schirmer (1961) 10843

6:14   (based on Watts)
     Day, Edgar
     When I Survey The Wondrous Cross
     SSATB   Organ
     Basil Ramsey (1980)

6:14   (based on Watts)
     Eldridge, Guy
     When I Survey The Wondrous Cross
     SATB   Organ
     Novello (1973) 29.0026.02

6:14
     Hillert, Richard
     Verse/Holy Cross Day (Verses And
          Offertories - Lesser Festivals)
     Unison   Organ
     Augsburg (1980) 11-9542

6:14
     Norris, Kevin
     Verse/Monday, Tuesday, Wednesday in Holy
          Week (Verses And Offertories - Lent)
     Unison   Organ
     Augsburg (1980) 11-9545

6:14   (Watts)
     Mason, Lowell (arr. Gilbert Martin)
     When I Survey The Wondrous Cross
     SATB   Organ
     Presser (1970) 312-40785

6:14   (Watts)
     Vulpius, Melchior (setting by A. Strube)
     When I Survey The Wondrous Cross
     SAB   kro
     Concordia (1955) 98-1097

6:14   (Watts)
     Vulpius, Melchior (setting by A. Strube)
     When I Survey The Wondrous Cross
     SATB   kro
     Concordia (1955) 98-1094

EPHESIANS

1:2   (Ephesians 3:14)
      Kay, Ulysses
      Grace To You And Peace
      SATB   Organ
      H. W. Gray (1957) CMR 2467

1:2 (and other Pauline passages; Ephesians 4:1;
        Colossians 3:15, 16)
      Williams, David McK.
      Grace Be To You And Peace
      SATB   Organ
      H. W. Gray (1944) CMR 1914

1:3
      Christiansen, Paul
      Blessed Be The Father
      SATB   No accompaniment
      AMSI (1972) 200

1:3, 5, 7, 9-10   (Ephesians 6:11-18)
      Butler, Eugene
      Messenger To Ephesus
      SATB   Keyboard
      Agape [Hope] (1978) EB 9205

2:8-10
      Allen, Larry
      Ephesians 2:8-10
      SATB   Piano
      Broadman (1978) 4563-11

2:13-14, 17, 19
      Cruft, Adrian
      Ye Are No More Stranger, Op. 47
      SATB/SATB   kro
      Boosey & Hawkes (1966) 5640

2:14
      Avery, Richard and Donald Marsh
      My God Breaks Down Walls
      Unison   Keyboard (optional percussion
        and guitar)
      Agape (1980) (found in Choirbook For Saints
        And Sinners)

2:18
      Hurford, Peter
      Through Christ Jesus   (Two Sentences)
      SATB   Organ
      Novello (1972) MW 29

2:19b, 20-22
      Waters, Charles F.
      Ye Are Fellow Citizens With The Saints
      SATB   Organ
      Novello (1968) NCM 15

3:13-21
      Friedell, Harold
      For This Cause
      SATB   Organ
      H. W. Gray (1960) CMR 2622

3:14
      SEE: Ephesians 1:2
      Kay, Ulysses
      Grace To You And Peace

3:20-21
      Bender, Jan
      Now Unto Him That Is Able
      SATB   kro
      Concordia (1956) CH 1079

3:20-21
      Lovelace, Austin
      To Him Be Glory
      SATB   Organ
      H. W. Gray (1965) CMR 2914

3:20-21
      Marsh, Donald
      Response Of Praise For The Confession
        Of 1967
      SATB   Piano
      Proclamations Publications (1968) n.#.

4:00   (adapted)
      Beck, John Ness
      Anthem Of Unity
      SATB   Piano or Organ
      G. Schirmer (1971) 11872

4:1
      SEE: Ephesians 1:2
      Williams, David McK.
      Grace Be To You And Peace

4:1-3   (Ephesians 5:8, 9)
      Armstrong, Mimi
      Ye Were Sometimes Darkness
      Unison   Piano or Guitar
      GIA (1972) G-1781

4:1-4, 25-28   (Ephesians 5:19, 20)
      Gibbs, C. Armstrong,   Op. 108
      I Therefore, The Prisoner Of The Lord
      SATB   Organ
      Boosey & Hawkes (1957) 5192

4:1-6
      Mueller, Carl F.
      Walk Worthy
      SATB (B-solo)   Piano or Organ
      Carl Fischer (1953) CM 6714

4:4-6
      Hillert, Richard
      Verse/Unity (Verses And Offertories -
        Lesser Festivals)
      Unison   Organ
      Augsburg (1980) 11-9543

4:5
      Lorenz, Ellen Jane
      One O'er All The Earth
      SATB   Organ and Trumpet
      Abingdon (1974) APM-950

4:10
      SEE: Psalm 24:10
      Marenzio, Luca
      O Rex Gloriae

4:11-13
      Hillert, Richard
      Offertory/Renewers Of The Church (Verses
        And Offertories - Lesser Festivals)
      Unison   Organ
      Augsburg (1980) 11-9543

4:30-32
      Lloyd, Charles H.
      Grieve Not The Holy Spirit Of God
      2 part treble   Organ
      Yearbrook Press [RSCM] (1919) A-10

4:30-32
      Noble, T. Tertius
      Grieve Not The Holy Spirit Of God
      SATB (S or T solo)   Keyboard
      H. W. Gray (1943) CMR 409

4:30-32
      Stainer, John
      Grieve Not The Holy Spirit Of God
      SATB   Piano
      Novello (n.d.) 220

5:1, 2 (Ephesians 6:10, 13)
      Sowerby, Leo
      Be Ye Followers Of God
      SATB   Organ
      H. W. Gray (1963) 2790

5:1, 2, 6-8
    Roff, Joseph
    Walk As Children Of Light
    SATB (B-solo)   Piano or Organ
    Associated (1968) A 603

5:1-2, 8-9
    Moser, Rudolf
    Be Ye Therefore Followers Of God, Op. 94,
        #6
    Unison   Organ
    Concordia (1956) 98-1353

5:4   (Romans 6:11; I Corinthians 15:21, 22)
    Jackson, B.
    Awake Thou That Sleepest
    SATB   Organ
    G. Schirmer (1908) (found in The Parishonal
        Choir, Volume 2)

5:8-9
    SEE: Ephesians 4:1-3
    Armstrong, M.
    Ye Were Sometimes Darkness

5:8-9
    Willan, Healey
    Now Are Ye Light In The Lord
    Unison   Keyboard
    Concordia (1962) 97-7160 (found in We
        Praise Thee, Volume 2)

5:15, 18-20
    Pelz, Walter
    Offertory/The Day Of Pentecost (Verses
        And Offertories - Easter - Trinity)
    SATB   Organ
    Augsburg (1980) 11-9546

5:18-20
    Lenel, Ludwig
    Be Filled With The Spirit
    SATB   Organ
    Concordia (1956) CH 1157

5:18b-20
    Nelson, Ronald A.
    Be Filled With The Spirit
    2 part treble   Keyboard
    Choir School Guild (1962) n.#.

5:19, 20
    SEE: Ephesians 4:1-4, 25-28
    Gibbs, C. Armstrong
    I Therefore The Prisoner

5:19-21
    Shepherd, John
    Submit Yourselves
    AATB   No accompaniment
    Oxford (1965) (found in Anthems For Men's
        Voices, Volume 1)

5:30-32
    Stainer, John
    Grieve Not The Holy Spirit Of God
    SATB   keyboard ad lib.
    Hall McCreary (1945) 1914

6:00
    Warner, Richard
    Soldiers Of Christ Arise
    TTBB   Keyboard
    Abingdon (1963) APM-329

6:00
    Warner, Richard
    Soldiers Of Christ Arise
    SATB   Keyboard
    Abingdon (1964) APM-333

6:10-11, 13-17   (I Corinthians 16:13)
    Nicholson, Sydney H.
    Be Strong In The Lord
    2 part Treble   Organ
    Curwen [RSCM] (1919) 1528

6:10, 13
    SEE: Ephesians 5:1,2
    Sowerby, Leo
    Be Ye Followers Of God

6:10-17   (Romans 8:35, 37-39)
    Blakely, Duane
    Be Strong In The Lord
    SA(T)B or T(T)BB   Organ or Piano
        (Optional brass, percussion, and pre-
            pared tape)
    Flammer (1973) A-5637

6:10-20   (Wesley)
    Powell, Robert J.
    Soldiers Of Christ
    SATB   Keyboard
    Carl Fischer (1978) CM 8058

6:10-20   (Wesley)
    Wolff, S. Drummond (setting by)
    Soldiers Of Christ Arise
    SATB   Organ
    Concordia (1980) 98-2458

6:11-18
    SEE: Ephesians 1:1, 3, 5, 9-10
    Butler, Eugene
    Message To Ephesus

P H I L I P P I A N S

1:6
    Bender, Jan
    He Which Hath Begun A Good Work In You
    SAB   kro
    Concordia (1955) 98-1068

1:6-7, 9
    Danna, David
    Our Prayer
    SATB   Piano
    Broadman (1980) 4561-50

1:21   (Romans 14:00)
    Young, Philip
    What Is Life But Christ?
    SATB   Trumpets
    Broadman (1978) 4562-51

1:27
    Schalk, Carl
    Verse/Pentecost 18 (Verses And Offertories
        Pentecost 12 - 20)
    2 part   Organ
    Augsburg (1978) 11-9539

1:27
    Wienhorst, Richard
    Let Your Manner Of Life Be Worthy
    SATB   No accompaniment
    Concordia (1980) 98-2451

2:00
    Beck, John Ness
    Interpreted By Love
    SATB   Organ
    Beckenhorst (1976) BP-1010

2:5-6
    Lovelace, Austin
    Let This Mind Be In You
    SATB (A-solo)   Organ
    J. Fischer (1949) FEC 8458

2:5-11
    Burroughs, Bob
    Philippians 2:5-11
    SATB   Keyboard
    Broadman (1978) 4563-14

2:5-11
    Holman, Derek
    Let This Mind Be In You
    SATB   Organ
    Oxford (1967) n.#.

2:5-11
    SEE: Romans 12:2
    Landgrave, Phillip
    Do Not Be Confirmed

2:5-11
    Mueller, Carl F.
    Let This Mind Be In You
    SATB   Piano or Organ
    Carl Fischer (1953) CM 6713

2:5-11
    Wills, Arthur
    Let This Mind Be In You
    SATB   Organ
    Novello (1964) 1413

2:5-14
    Hoiby, Lee
    Let This Mind Be In You
    SAB   Organ
    Presser (1970) 312.40726

2:6-9
    Zingarelli, Niccolo (ed. Abraham Kaplan)
    Christus Factus Est   (English/Latin)
    SATB   kro
    Lawson Gould (1968) 51428

2:6-11
    Peloquin, Alexander
    Jesus Christ Is Lord
    SATB   Cantor   Organ
    GIA (1978) G-2130

2:2-8
    Anerio, Felice (ed. Walter Ehret)
    Christ Became Obedient   (English/Latin)
    SATB   kro
    GIA (1975) G-1967

2:7-11
    Hillert, Richard
    Offertory/Holy Cross Day (Verses And
        Offertories - Lesser Festivals)
    Unison   Organ
    Augsburg (1980) 11-9542

2:8
    Norris, Kevin
    Verse/Lent II (Verses and Offertories - Lent)
    Unison   Organ
    Augsburg (1980) 11-9545

2:8
    Robinson, McNeil
    Christus Factus Est   (Christ Became
        Obedient)
    SATB   kro
    Presser (1979) 312.41302

2:8-9
    Anerio, Felice
    Christus Factus Est
    SATB   kro
    J. & W. Chester (1977) JWC 55096 (found in
        First Chester Book Of Motets)

2:8-9
    Anerio, G. F.
    Christus Factus Est (Latin only)
    SATB   kro
    J. & W. Chester [Alexander Broude] (1938)
        ABC 32

2:8-9
    Bruckner, Anton
    Christus Factus Est (Latin)
    SATB   No accompaniment
    Arista (1969) AE-157

2:8-9
    Bruckner, Anton (ed. Stephen Barlow)
    Christus Factus Est
    SATB   kro
    Walton (1964) 2161

2:8-9
    Bruckner, Anton (ed. Maynard Klein)
    Christus Factus Est   (English/Latin)
    SATB   kro
    G. Schirmer (1966)

2:8-9
    Bruckner, Anton
    Christus Factus Est   (English/Latin)
    SATB   kro
    Summy Birchard (1959) 5249

2:8-9
    Comer, Juan Bautista (ed. Mason Martens)
    Christus Factus Est
    SATB   kro
    Leeds (1964) 2003

2:8-9
    Durante, Francesco
    Christus Factus Est
    SAB   No accompaniment
    Arista (1978) AE 275

2:8-9
    Leo, Leonardo
    Christus Factus Est   (Loving Savior)
        (English/Latin)
    SA   Organ
    GIA (1976) G-1974

2:8-9
    Palestrina, G. P.
    Christus Factus Est
    TTBB   kro
    Oratoriumsverlag (n.d.) (found in
        Geistliche Gesang Für Männerchor)

2:8-9
    Slater, Richard
    Christ Hath Humbled Himself
    SATB   kro
    Associated (1969) A-653

2:8-9
    Willan, Healey
    Christ Hath Humbled Himself
    2 part   Keyboard
    Concordia (1953) (found in We Praise Thee,
        Volume 1)

2:9, 10 (based on)
    Billingsley, Derrell
    Jesus! Precious Name
    SATB   Keyboard
    Broadman (1975) 4551-96

2:10
    Hillert, Richard
    Verse/At The Name Of Jesus (Verses And
        Offertories - Lesser Festivals)
    Unison   Organ
    Augsburg (1980) 11-9543

2:10f
    Schalk, Carl
    Verse/Pentecost 19 (Verses And Offertories
        Pentecost 12-20)
    2 part   Organ
    Augsburg (1978) 11-9539

2:10-11
    Gallus, Jacob (ed. John Cozens)
    At The Name Of Jesus (In Nomine Jesu)
        (English/Latin)
    SATB   kro
    Concordia (1954) 98-1051

2:10-11
    Gallus, Jacobus (ed. Walter Collins)
    In Nomine Jesu (English/Latin)
    TTBB   kro
    Lawson Gould (1965) 51203

2:10-11
    Handl, Jacob (ed. J. Herter)
    In Nomine Jesu (At Jesus' Holy Name)
        (English/Latin)
    SATB   kro
    GIA (1974) G-1860

2:10-11
    Langlais, Jean
    At The Name Of Jesus
    SATB   No accompaniment
    Hinshaw (1980) HMC 423

2:10-11
    Wienhorst, Richard
    At The Name Of Jesus Every Knee Should Bow
    SATB   Handbells or Keyboard
    Concordia (1980) 98-2451

2:10, 11
    Willan, Healey
    At The Name Of Jesus
    SA   Keyboard
    Concordia (1962) 97-7160 (found in We
        Praise Thee, Volume 2)

2:13 (and a hymn)
    Beckler, Johann Christian (ed. Karl Kroeger)
    It Is Our God (English/German)
    SATB   Keyboard (optional Strings, 2 Horns)
    Carl Fischer (1973) CM 7849

2:20, 21, 22
    Schütz, Heinrich (ed. C. Buell Agey)
    Wondrous Is The Life In Heaven
    SSATTB   Organ
    G. Schirmer (1961) 10875

4:4
    Goemanne, Noel
    Rejoice The Lord Is King
    SATB   Organ   1 or 2 Trumpets
    GIA (1979) G-2223

4:4 (based on - Wesley)
    Kelly, Brian
    Rejoice, The Lord Is King
    SATB   Organ
    Novello (1969) 29.0004.01

4:4
    SEE: Psalm 115:2
    Mendelssohn, Felix
    But The Lord Is Mindful Of His Own

4:4 (Psalm 100:5)
    Rickard, Jeffery (ed. and arr.)
    Rejoice In The Lord
    SATB   kro
    Augsburg (n.d.) 11-1631

4:4
    Schalk, Carl
    Verse/Pentecost 16 (Verses And
        Offertories - Pentecost 12 - 20)
    2 part   Organ
    Augsburg (1978) 11-9539

4:4
    Stanton, W. K.
    Rejoice The Lord Is King
    SATB   Organ
    Oxford (1957) (also found in RSCM Festival
        Service Book, 5)

4:4
    Wienhorst, Richard
    Rejoice In The Lord, Rejoice (Three Verse
        Settings, Set 1)
    SAB   No accompaniment
    Concordia (1979) 98-2430

4:4-5
    Willan, Healey
    Rejoice In The Lord Alway
    SA   Organ
    Concordia (1962) 98-1815

4:4-5
    Willan, Healey
    Rejoice In The Lord Alway
    SA   Keyboard
    Concordia (1962) 97-7160 (found in We
        Praise Thee, Volume 2)

4:4-6 (Psalm 85:2)
    Campbell-Watson, Franck
    Rejoice In The Lord Alway
    SATB   Organ
    Belwin (1974) CMR 3320

4:4-7
    Anonymous (Redford?)
    Rejoice In The Lord Alway
    SATB   Optional organ
    Oxford (1966) TEM 55 (also found in
        Sixteenth Century Anthem Book)

4:4-7
    Couston, Thomas (ed. Hewitt Pantaleoni)
    Rejoice In The Lord Alway
    TTBB   No accompaniment
    Concordia (1961) 98-1534

4:4-7
    Davis, Katherine K.
    Rejoice In The Lord
    SSA   kro
    E. C. Schirmer (1936) 1544

4:4-7
    Goemanne, Noel
    Rejoice In The Lord
    SATB   Organ
    GIA   G-2423

4:4-7
    Kirk, Theron
    Rejoice In The Lord Alway
    SATB   Piano or Organ
    Kjos (1971) 5864

4:4-7
    Ley, Henry G.
    Rejoice In The Lord Alway
    SS   Organ
    Oxford (1933) 44L 021 (also found in
        Church Anthem Book)

4:4-7
    Moe, Daniel
    Rejoice In The Lord Always
    SATB   Organ or Piano
    Abingdon (1960) APM-131

4:4-7
    Purcell, Henry (ed. Edward Dent)
    Rejoice In The Lord Alway
    SATB   Organ
    Novello (1957) 29.0150.01

4:4-7
    Purcell, Henry (ed. Edward J. Dent)
    Rejoice In The Lord (abridged edition)
    SATB   Organ
    Novello (1957) 29.0108.00

4:4-7
    Purcell, Henry
    Rejoice In The Lord Alway
    SATB (A-T-B-solos)   Piano or Organ
    Carl Fischer (1957) CM 6308

4:4-7
    Purcell, Henry
    Rejoice In The Lord
    SATB   Organ
    E. C. Schirmer (1952) 1101 (also found in
        Concord Anthem Book - Red)

4:4-7
    Purcell, Henry
    Rejoice In The Lord Alway (The Bell Anthem)
    SATB (A-T-B- solos)   Organ
    Oxford (1967) 50 (also found in the Church
        Anthem Book)

4:4-7
    Purcell, Henry (ed. Thomas Gieschen)
    Rejoice In The Lord Alway (The Bell Anthem)
    SATB   Organ or Strings and Continuo
    Concordia (1960) 97-6344

4:4-7
    Rathbone, George
    Rejoice In The Lord Alway
    SATB   Organ
    Novello (1959) 29.0138.02

4:4-7
    Redford, John
    Rejoice In The Lord Alway
    SATB   Optional organ
    Concordia (1974) (found in A Second Motet
        Book, 97-5205)

4:4-7
    Redford, John (attributed to)
    Rejoice In The Lord
    SATB   Keyboard ad lib.
    Novello (1958) 29.0113.07

4:4-7
    Westra, Evert
    Rejoice In The Lord Alway
    SATB   Organ ad lib.
    Chantry (1965) n.#.

4:4-8
    Cousins, M. Thomas
    Rejoice In The Lord Alway
    SATB   Organ
    Brodt Music (1965) 591

4:6b
    SEE: John 15:16
    Allen, Larry
    I Have Chosen You

4:8
    Burton, Daniel
    Think On These Things (from Five Children's
        Anthems)
    Unison   Keyboard
    Shawnee (1982) F 5015

4:8
    Mueller, Carl F.
    Think On These Things
    SATB   Keyboard
    Carl Fischer (1953) CM 6711

4:8
    Wilson, John
    Think On These Things
    SATB (divisi)   No accompaniment
    Hope (1981) A-523

4:8, 9
    Wills, Arthur
    Think On These Things
    SATB   Organ
    RSCM (1978) (found in Anthems From
        Addington, Volume 1)

4:13
    Krapf, Gerhard
    All Things In Him
    2 equal voices   Keyboard
    Concordia (1979) 98-2428

4:19
    Burroughs, Bob
    He Will Supply All Your Needs
    SATB   Keyboard
    Fred Bock [Presser] (1971) C-145

11:5-11
    Holman, Derek
    Let This Mind Be In You
    SATB   Organ
    Oxford (1967) n.#.

C O L O S S I A N S

1:12-14
    Good, Jack C.
    We Give Thanks (Prayer Intonation)
    Unison   Organ
    Abingdon (1974) APM 516

1:15-20
    Pelz, Walter
    Offertory/Third Sunday Of Easter (Verses
        And Offertories - Easter - Trinity)
    SATB   Organ
    Augsburg (1980) 11-9546

1:16
    SEE: Hebrews 1:8, 10
    Latrobe, Christian
    Thy Throne, O God, Is Forever And Ever

3:1
    SEE: Romans 6:9
    Thiman, Eric
    Christ Being Raised From The Dead

3:1
    Wadley, F. W.
    If Ye Then Be Risen With Christ
    2 part treble   Organ
    Novello (1946) Ch.Ser. 60

3:1-2
    Anonymous
    If Ye Be Risen Again
    TTBB   No accompaniment
    Oxford (1965) (found in Anthems For Men's
        Voices, Volume 2)

3:1-4
    SEE: Romans 6:4-5
    Baristow, Edward C.
    Know Ye Not

3:1-4
    Gibbons, Orlando (ed. Frederick Ouselay)
    If Ye Be Risen Again With Christ
    SATB (S-S-A-solos)   Organ
    Novello (1956) 1333

3:1-4
    Jennings, Kenneth
    If Ye Be Risen Again With Christ
    SATB   kro
    Concordia (1965) 98-1798

3:1-4
    Poole-Connor, David
    If Ye Then Be Risen
    SATB   Organ
    Novello (1946) 1237   (also found in Short
        And Easy Anthems, Set 2)

3:1-4   (Revelation 1:17-18)
    Williams, David McK.
    He Is Risen
    SATB (B-solo)   Organ
    H. W. Gray (1935) 1297

3:4
    Powell, Robert J.
    If Ye Then Be Risen
    SSATB   kro
    Abingdon (1964) APM-275

3:12-15   (II Corinthians 13:11)
    Barnes, Edward S.
    Put On Therefore, As God's Elect
    SATB   Organ
    H. W. Gray (1935) 1337

3:12-15
    Hillert, Richard
    Offertory/Unity (Verses And Offertories -
        Lesser Festivals)
    Unison   Organ
    Augsburg (1980) 11-9543

3:14
    Wetzler, Robert
    Verse/Christmas I (Verses And Offertories -
        Advent I - The Baptism Of Christ)
    SATB   Organ
    Augsburg (1979) 11-9541

3:15, 16
    SEE: Ephesians 1:2
    Williams, David McK.
    Grace Be To You And Peace

3:16-17
    Mueller, Carl F.
    Singing With Grace In Your Heart
    SATB (A-solo)   Piano or Organ
    Carl Fischer (1953) 6710

3:17   (first chorus)
    Buxtehude, Dietrich (ed. Paul Bunjes)
    Every Word And Thought   (English/German)
    SATB (S-A-T-B-solos)   Continuo with 2
        Violins, and Viola
    Concordia (1957) 97-6279

4:15
    Newbury, Kent A.
    Let The Word Of Christ
    SATB   kro
    G. Schirmer (1972) 11938

I THESSALONIANS

1:15-20
    Lovelace, Austin
    Begin Again
    Unison   Piano
    Augsburg   11-2085

3:3, 5, 16
    Roff, Joseph
    But The Lord Is Faithful
    SATB   Optional accompaniment
    Boosey & Hawkes (1963) 5477

4:14, 18
    Goss, John
    If We Believe
    SATB   Organ
    Novello (n.d.) 29.0233.08

4:14, 18
    Goss, John
    If We Believe That Jesus Died
    SATB   Organ
    Broude (1965) n.#.

4:14, 18
    Goss, John (ed. Dale Wood)
    If We Believe That Jesus Died
    SATB   Organ
    Sacred Music Press (1980) S-261

4:14, 18
    Goss, John
    If We Believe That Jesus Died
    SATB   Organ
    Oxford (1933) (found in Church Anthem
        Book)

4:16
    Black, James M. (arr. Sam Batt Owens)
    When The Roll Is Called Up Yonder
    SATB   Keyboard
    Augsburg (1979) 11-1903

5:9, 11-13, 16-18
    Pooler, Frank
    For This Is The Will Of God
    SATB   Organ
    Augsburg (1963)   1340

5:10
    Peter, Johan Frederich (ed. Karl Kroeger)
    Our Dear Lord Jesus Christ
    SATB   Organ
    Boosey & Hawkes (1978) 5919

5:23   (Andrew Reed)
    Gibbons, Orlando (setting by Richard Warner)
    Holy Ghost, With Light Divine
    SA   Keyboard
    Concordia (1956) 98-1363

5:23   (Andrew Reed)
    Gibbons, Orlando (setting by Richard
        Hillert)
    Holy Ghost, With Light Divine
    SATB   Organ
    Concordia (1962) 98-1590

5:23   (Andrew Reed)
    Gibbons, Orlando (setting by Theodore Beck)
    Holy Ghost, With Light Divine
    SA   2 Recorders
    Concordia (1974) 98-2354 (also found in
        Seven Anthems For Treble Choirs -
        97-5218)

II THESSALONIANS

3:1ff
    Busarow, Donald
    Verse/25th Sunday After Pentecost (Verses
        And Offertories - Pentecost 21 -
        Christ The King)
    2 part   Organ
    Augsburg (1979) 11-9540

I TIMOTHY

1:15-17
    Hammerschmidt, Andreas (ed. Roger Granville)
    This Is A Faithful Saying (English/German)
    SSATBB   kro
    Sam Fox (1967) CM 30

1:15-17
    Schütz, Heinrich
    Hear The Faithful Word Of God (English/
        German)
    SSATTB   Continuo
    Hanssler (1970) 20.388

1:17   (W. C. Smith)
    Lorenz, Ellen Jane
    Immortal, Invisible (Joanna)
    SATB   Organ
    Abingdon (1962) APM-222

1:17   (based on)
    Thiman, Eric
    Immortal, Invisible God Only Wise
    SATB   Organ
    Novello (1934) 29.0134.10

1:17   (based on)
    Welsh Melody (arr. Irvin Cooper)
    Immortal, Invisible
    SCB   Piano
    Cambiata Press (1980) T180140

1:17   (based on)
    Wolff, S. Drummond (setting by)
    Immortal, Invisible (St. Denio)
    SATB   Organ
    Concordia (1981) 98-2825

2:5-6a
    Geisler, Johann (ed. E. Nolte)
    There Is One God And One Savior (English/
        German)
    SSAB   Organ
    Boosey & Hawkes (1965) 5600

3:16
    Roff, Joseph
    Taken Up In Glory
    SATB (or SAB)   Piano or Organ
    GIA   G-1934

6:12
    Sowerby, Leo
    Fight The Good Fight
    SATB   kro
    H. W. Gray (1954) CMR 2334

II TIMOTHY

1:6-7 (adapted)
    Hancock, Gerre
    Kindle The Gift Of God
    SATB   Organ
    H. W. Gray (1974) CMR 3314

1:10
    Schalk, Carl
    Verse/Pentecost 14 (Verses And Offertories
        Pentecost 12 - 20)
    2 part   Organ
    Augsburg (1978) 11-9539

2:8-13
    Norris, Kevin
    Offertory/Lent V (Verses and Offertories -
        Lent)
    Unison   Organ
    Augsburg (1980) 11-9545

2:9
    SEE: Psalm 115:2
    Mendelssohn, Felix
    But The Lord Is Mindful Of His Own

2:15
    SEE: Psalm 119:105-107
    Hungtingdon, Ronald
    Thy Word Is A Lamp

4:6-8
    Busarow, Donald
    Offertory/26th Sunday After Pentecost
        (Verses And Offertories - Pentecost
        21 - Christ The King)
    Unison   Organ
    Augsburg (1979) 11-9540

4:18
    Busarow, Donald
    Verse/23rd Sunday After Pentecost
        (Verses And Offertories - Pentecost
        21 - Christ The King)
    2 part   Organ
    Augsburg (1979) 11-9540

TITUS

2:11
    SEE: Galatians 4:4
    Gibbs, Allen Orton
    God Sent Forth His Son

PHILEMON

1:3, 7, 20, 25
    Herrick, Kevin Jeff
    The Greeting Song
    SATB   Keyboard
    Broadman (1974) 4551-82

H E B R E W S

1:1-2
    Binkerd, Gordon
    Third Mass Of Christmas
    SATB   Organ
    Boosey & Hawkes (1967) 5829

1:1-12
    Powell, Robert J.
    Annointed Of God
    SATB   Piano or Organ
    Abingdon (1975) APM-460

1:8, 10   (Colossians 1:16)
    Latrobe, Christian (ed. Karl Kroeger)
    Thy Throne, O God, Is Forever And Ever
    SATB (S-A-T-B-solos)   Organ or Piano
    Boosey & Hawkes (1981) 6051

1:10-12
    Nystedt, Knut
    Thou, O Lord
    SATB   kro
    Walton (1968) 2900

2:9-10
    Brandon, George (arr.)
    The Head That Once Was Crowned
    SATB or SAB or Unison   Keyboard
    GIA (1973) G-1796

2:12
    Schalk, Carl
    Verse/Pentecost 20 (Verses And Offertories
        Pentecost 12-20)
    2 part   Organ
    Augsburg (1978) 11-9539

2:12
    Wienhorst, Richard
    I Will Proclaim Your Name
    SATB   No accompaniment
    Concordia (1980) 98-2451

3:6
    Gregor, Christian (ed. Nolte)
    The Lord's Temple (Das Haus Gottes)
        (English/German)
    SSAB   Organ
    Boosey & Hawkes (1965) 5609

4:12
    Schalk, Carl
    Verse/Pentecost 13 (Verses And Offertories
        Pentecost 12-20)
    2 part   Organ
    Augsburg (1978) 11-9539

4:12
    Wienhorst, Richard
    The Word Of God Is Living And Active
        (Three Verse Settings - Set 2)
    SATB   No accompaniment
    Concordia (1979) 98-2441

4:12, 13
    Langston, Paul
    Canticle For Modern Man
    SATB   Organ
    Broadman (1975) 4565-57

4:14, 16
    Powell, Robert J.
    Seeing That We Have A Great High Priest
    SAB   kro
    Abingdon (1966) APM-535   (from Festival
        Anthems for SAB)

4:16
    SEE: Hebrews 12:28, 29
    Brandon, George
    With Awe And Confidence

9:11-15
    Moser, Rudolf
    The Promise Of Eternal Inheritance,
        Op. 94, #2
    Unison   Organ
    Concordia (1955) CH 1093

10:7 (based on)   (Psalm 40:7; Matthew 3:13-17,
        based on)
    Brandon, George (arr.)
    Carol Of The Baptism
    SAB or 2 part mixed   Organ
    Concordia (1973) 98-2138

10:39
    SEE: Isaiah 40:9
    Gieseke, Richard W.
    Climb To The Top Of the Highest Mountain

Chapters 11 and 12
    Bowie, William
    Faith
    SATB   Organ
    Oxford (1969) A-268

11:1
    Schalk, Carl
    Verse/Pentecost 12 (Verses and Offertories
        Pentecost 12-20)
    2 part   Organ
    Augsburg (1978) 11-9539

11:1, 2, 4, 5, 7, 8   (Hebrews 12:1, 2)
    Bass, Claude
    Faith
    SATB   Organ
    Broadman (1980) 4561-54

11:1, 3-8, 23-31 (adapted)   (Psalm 33:6,
        adapted;   Psalm 39:13-14, adapted)
    Lockwood, Normand
    A Cloud Of Witnesses
    SATB (S-solo)   Organ
    H. W. Gray (1960) 2617

11:1, 3, 6
    SEE: Luke 17:5
    Mueller, Carl F.
    An Anthem Of Faith

12:1-2
    SEE: Hebrews 11:1, 2, 4, 5, 7, 8
    Bass, Claude
    Faith

12:1-2
    SEE: Psalm 102:25-27
    DeTar, Vernon
    The Glory Of The Lord

12:2b
    Graun, Carl H. (ed. Robert Wetzler)
    He Endured The Cross
    SATB   kro
    Augsburg (1964) ACL 1357

12:12
    Young, Philip M.
    Fanfare With Alleluia
    SATB   Organ (optional brass)
    Broadman (1967) 451-241 (brass - 451-240)

12:28, 29   (Hebrews 4:16)
    Brandon, George
    With Awe And Confidence
    SATB   Keyboard
    GIA (1944) G-1883

13:20, 21
    Bitgood, Roberta
    Now The God Of Peace (Choral Benediction)
    SATB   No accompaniment
    Abingdon (1956) APM-470

13:20, 21
    Knight, Gerald
    Now The God Of Peace
    SATB   Organ
    RSCM (n.d.) 257 (also found in Festival
         Service Book, 5)

13:20, 21
    McGlohan, Loomis
    Father Of Peace
    SATB   Keyboard
    Flammer (1980) A-5927

J A M E S

1:12 (paraphrase)
    Mendelssohn, Felix
    Happy And Blest Are They (St. Paul)
    SATB   Organ
    E. C. Schirmer (1952) 137 (also found in
         Concord Anthem Book - Red)

1:17
    Moser, Rudolf
    Every Good Gift And Every Perfect Gift Is
         From Above, Op. 94, #4
    SATB   kro
    Concordia (1956) 98-1352

1:17 (Psalm 92:1-4;   I Peter 4:10)
    Hancock, Gerre
    In Thanksgiving
    SATB   Organ
    H. W. Gray (1966) 2940

1:17 (Habakkuk 3:17-18)
    Williams, David H.
    Every Good Gift
    Unison treble   Keyboard
    H. W. Gray (1956) 2445

1:18
    Busarow, Donald
    Verse/22nd Sunday After Pentecost (Verses
         And Offertories - Pentecost 21 -
         Christ The King)
    Unison   Organ
    Augsburg (1980) 11-9540

1:27 (based on)
    Shaw, Geoffrey
    Worship
    SATB   Organ
    Novello (1955) ANTH. 1147

4:4, 8-10
    Lamb, Richard A.
    Wash Your Hands, You Sinners
    SATB   (optional 3 Trumpets, 2 Trombones)
    Fine Arts (1968) CM-1070

4:8-10
    Blakley, Duane
    Draw Near To God
    SATB   Organ
    Schmitt, Hall McCreary (1971) 15007

4:8-10
    Brandon, George
    Draw Nigh To God
    SATB   Organ
    Abingdon (1977) APM-703

4:8, 10
    Harwood, Basil
    Draw Nigh To God
    SATB   Organ
    Novello (1944) MT 1216

4:10 (Exodus 9:16)
    Pethel, Stan
    He Shall Lift You Up
    SATB   Keyboard
    Broadman (1978) 4563-08

4:14
    Berger, Jean
    A Sermon For Our Time
    SATB   kro
    Presser (1971) 312-40952

4:14
    Fritschel, James
    For You Are A Mist (from Four About Life
         And Death)
    SATB   No accompaniment
    Hinshaw (1975) HMC 122

5:11
    SEE: Job 3:20-23
    Brahms, Johannes
    Why Then Has The Light

I   P E T E R

1:00
    Butler, Eugene
    Praise Christ, Alleluia
    SATB   Keyboard
    Carl Fischer (1970) CM 7754

1:2
    Hovhaness, Alan, Op. 259, #1
    Peace Be Multiplied (Three Motets)
    SATB   kro
    Rongwen [Broude Brothers] (1974) RM 3526

1:3
    SEE: Psalm 66:1, 2
    Gieseke, Richard W.
    Sing Praise To The Lord

1:3-4
    Telemann, G. P.
    Gelobet sei Gott (English/German)
    SSB or SS   Continuo, 2 Violins
    Hanssler   H. E. 30.020

1:3-5, 15-17, 22-25
    Wesley, S. S.
    Blessed Be The God And Father
    SATB   Organ
    Oxford (found in Church Anthem Book)

1:3-5, 15-17, 22-25
    Wesley, S. S.
    Blessed Be The God And Father
    SATB   Organ
    Novello (n.d.) 29.0102.1

1:3-5, 15-17, 22-25
    Wesley, S. S.
    Blessed Be The God And Father
    SATB   Organ
    H. W. Gray (n.d.) GCMR 3166

1:3-5, 15-17, 22-25
    Wesley, S. S. (ed. Joseph Daltry)
    Blessed Be The God And Father
    TTBB   Organ
    B. F. Wood (1934) 342

1:3-9
  Davison, John
  Blessed Be The God
  SATB   Organ
  Elkan Vogel (1966) 1240

1:22
  Wesley, S. S.
  Love One Another (from Blessed Be The God
      And Father)
  Unison   Organ
  RSCM (n.d.) 245

1:22-25
  Roff, Joseph
  See That You Love One Another
  SATB (S-solo)   Organ
  H. W. Gray (1971) CMR 3224

2:1-3
  Pelz, Walter
  Offertory/Second Sunday Of Easter (Verses
      And Offertories - Easter - Trinity)
  SATB   Organ
  Augsburg (1980) 11-9546

2:1-9
  Felciano, Richard
  Words Of Saint Peter
  SATB   Organ, Tape
  World Library (1970) GA-2093-8

2:4, 5, 9, 10
  Marshall, Jane
  God's Own People
  SATB   Organ
  H. W. Gray (1965) CMR 2902

2:9
  Brown, Charles
  But Ye Are A Chosen Generation, Alleluia
  SATB (T-solo)   Keyboard, optional
      trumpet
  Broadman (1969) 4565-85

2:9-10
  SEE: Song Of Songs 8:2
  Ireland, John
  Greater Love Hath No Man

2:24
  SEE: Song Of Songs 8:7
  Ireland, John
  Greater Love Hath No Man

3:10-12
  Corina, John
  He That Would Love Life
  SATB   kro
  Abingdon (1971) APM-604

4:10
  SEE: James 1:17
  Hancock, Gerre
  In Thanksgiving

5:7 (paraphrase)
  Manuel, Ralph and Paul Williams
  Cast Your Care On Him
  SATB   Keyboard
  Shawnee (1982) A-5975

5:10-11   (Lamentations 3:22, 23)
  Gieseke, Richard
  God Has Called You To Glory (Seasonal
      Responses)
  SAB   No accompaniment
  Concordia (1978) 97-5481

II   P E T E R

3:18
  Telemann, G. P.
  Wachset in den Gnade
  SSB or SS   Organ, Continuo, 2 Violins
  Hanssler   HE39.003

I   J O H N

1:00   (based on)
  McCormick, Clifford
  If We Walk In The Light
  SATB   kro
  Shawnee (1954) A-581 (also found in
      Anthems From Scripture, G-34)

1:1-4 (based on)
  Ziegenhals, Harriet
  The Joy Of Us All
  SATB   Keyboard
  Hope (1980) A-517

1:5
  SEE: Job 3:3, 4, 20-21, 23-24
  Cook, Melville
  Antiphon

1:5
  SEE: Isaiah 26:3
  Walton, Robert
  Thou Wilt Keep Him In Perfect Peace

1:5
  SEE: Isaiah 26:3
  Wesley, S. S.
  Thou Wilt Keep Him In Perfect Peace

1:5
  SEE: Isaiah 26:3
  Wesley, S. S. (ed. Basil Ramsey)
  Thou Wilt Keep Him In Perfect Peace

1:5
  SEE: Isaiah 26:3
  Williams, C. Lee
  Thou Wilt Keep Him In Perfect Peace

1:5-7
  Wetzler, Robert
  Offertory/Christmas II (Verses And
      Offertories - Advent I - The Baptism
      Of Our Lord)
  Unison   Organ
  Augsburg (1979) 11-9541

1:7
  Schütz, Heinrich
  The Blood Of Jesus Christ, The Son Of God,
      Cleanse Us From Our Sin
  SAB   Continuo with 2 Violins
  Concordia (1976) (found in The SAB Choir
      Goes Baroque)

1:8
  SEE: Isaiah 53:4-5
  Bender, Jan
  A Little Lenten Cantata

2:1-2   (I John 3:1)
        Busarow, Donald
        Offertory/21st Sunday After Pentecost
              (Verses And Offertories - Pentecost
              21 - Christ The King)
        2 part   Organ
        Augsburg (1979) 11-9540

2:9-10
        Wells, Dana F.
        Abide In The Light   (Four Modern Anthems)
        SATB   (solo)   Piano
        Abingdon (1970) APM-619

2:28   (I Corinthians 6:20)
        Peter, J. F.   (arr. Karl Kroeger)
        Harken, Stay Close To Him
        2 equal voices   Keyboard
        Carl Fischer (1975) CM 7900

3:1
        SEE: I John 2:1-2
        Busarow, Donald
        Offertory/21st Sunday After Pentecost

3:1
        Homilius, Gottfried A. (Walter Wismar)
        What Great Affection!! (English/German)
        SATB   kro
        Hall & McCreary (1939) 1522

3:1
        Mendelssohn, Felix
        See What Love   (from St. Paul)
        SATB   Piano or Organ
        Augsburg (n.d.) 1281

3:1-2
        SEE: Romans 8:9-16
        Davies, H. Walford
        If Any Man Hath Not The Spirit

3:1-2
        Mueller, Carl F.
        Behold What Manner Of Love
        SATB   Keyboard
        Broadman (1972) 4563-31

3:1-2
        Mueller, Carl F.
        Behold What Manner Of Love
        SAB   Keyboard
        Broadman (1973) 4540-60

3:1-3
        Sowerby, Leo
        Behold, What Manner Of Love
        SSAA   Organ
        H. W. Gray (1961) 2699

3:2-3
        Busarow, Donald
        Offertory/Christ The King (Verses And
              Offertories - Pentecost 21 - Christ
              The King)
        Unison   Organ
        Augsburg (1979) 11-9540

3:2-3
        Johnson, David N.
        Offertory/The Transfiguration (Verses and
              Offertories - Epiphany II - The Trans-
              figuration Of Our Lord)
        Unison   Organ
        Augsburg (1980) 11-9544

3:4   (taken from)
        Benjamin, Tom
        The Message
        SATB   (T-solo)   kro
        Mark Foster (1982) MF 226

4:4
        Blankenship, Mark
        Great Is He
        SATB   Keyboard
        Broadman (1981) 4566-29

4:7-8, 10
        Langlais, Jean
        Beloved Let Us Love One Another (Three
              Short Anthems)
        Unison   Organ
        Hinshaw (1980) HMC 423

4:7-11
        Dailey, William
        Beloved Let Us Love One Another
        SATB   Keyboard
        Flammer (1979) A-5847

4:7-21
        York, David Stanley
        Beloved Let Us Love One Another
        SATB   (S-solo)   kro
        Golden Music (1964) G-22

4:16-19
        Mueller, Carl F.
        Because He First Loved Us
        SATB   Keyboard
        Broadman (1972) 4565-32

5:7
        SEE: Isaiah 6:3
        Victoria, Tomas
        Duo Seraphim

5:14-15
        SEE: John 16:24
        Glarum, L. Stanley
        Ask And Ye Shall Receive

J U D E

1:14-15
        Buxtehude, Dietrich (ed. R. T. Gore)
        Harken, Harken! The Lord Comes (chorus
              #3 of Good Christian Men) (English/
              German)
        SSATB   Organ (optional instruments)
        Concordia (1966) 97-4724

1:24, 25
        Marshall, Jane
        A Choral Ascription Of Praise
        SATB   No accompaniment
        Abingdon (1963) APM-273

R E V E L A T I O N

00:0   (adapted, John Bunyan)
        Vaughan Williams, Ralph
        The Song Of The Tree Of Life
        Unison or 2 part   . Keyboard
        Oxford (1952) T 37 (also found in Anthems
              For Choirs, Volume 2)

1:5, 6
        Vaughan Williams, Ralph
        Unto Him That Loved Us
        Unison   Keyboard
        Concordia (found in Morning Star Choir
              Book, Volume 1   97-6287)

1:7
    Christiansen, Paul
    He Cometh With Clouds (from The Revelation
        Of Saint John)
    SATB   kro
    Schmitt, Hall, McCreary (1967) 8033

1:8
    Stainer, John
    I Am Alpha And Omega
    SATB   Organ
    Presser (n.d.) 312-06099

1:8
    Stainer, John
    I Am Alpha And Omega
    SATB   Organ
    G. Schirmer (n.d.) 3897

1:8-9 (Revelation 10:6)
    Tchaikovsky, Peter (ed. Ivan Sokolov)
    I Am Alpha And Omega
    SATB   kro
    Bourne (1965) BL-3135

1:8-11 (adapted)
    Thiman, Eric
    I Am Alpha And Omega (Six Introductory
        Sentences)
    SATB   Organ
    Novello (1973) MW-25

1:17-18
    SEE: Colossians 3:1-4
    Williams, David McK.
    He Is Risen

2:7
    Franck, Melchior (ed. Roger Granville)
    Who Overcometh (English/German)
    SATB   kro
    Sam Fox (1967) CM 26

2:10
    Richter, Willy
    Be Thou Faithful Unto Death
    SATB (S-B-solos)   Organ
    G. Schirmer (1943) 9215

3:11, 15
    Telemann, G. P.
    Halt, was du hast (English/German)
    SATB/SATB   Organ ad lib.
    Hanssler   39.112

3:20 (Revelation 21:3)
    Burns, William K.
    Behold! I Stand At The Door
    SATB   Keyboard
    Abingdon (1961) APM-239

3:20
    Cain, Noble
    Behold! I Stand At The Door
    SATB   Keyboard optional
    Flammer (1948) A-5280

3:20
    McCormick, Clifford
    Behold! I Stand At The Door
    SATB (A or B solo)   Keyboard
    Shawnee (1958) A-471 (also found in
        Anthems From Scripture, G-34)

3:20-21
    Schalk, Carl
    Offertory/Pentecost 19 (Verses And
        Offertories - Pentecost 12 - 20)
    Unison   Organ
    Augsburg (1978) 11-9539

3:20-22
    Newbury, Kent A.
    Behold I Stand At The Door
    SATB   kro
    G. Schirmer (1971) 11812

4:1-11
    Felciano, Richard
    Three In One In Three
    Chorus   Organ   Tape
    E. C. Schirmer (1971) 2910

Chapters 4:00 - 7:00
    SEE: I Corinthians 15:00 (adapted)
    Pattison, John
    He Is Risen, Forevermore

4:8
    Handel, G. F. (adapted E. Baristow)
    Holy, Holy, Holy (from the aria,
        Dove Sei)
    SATB (S-solo)   Organ
    Oxford (1934) n.#.

4:8
    Powell, Robert J.
    Holy, Holy, Holy, Lord God Almighty
        (in Festival Anthems For SAB)
    SAB   kro
    Abingdon (1968) APM-585

4:8, 11 (English)
    SEE: Ecclesiastes 43:16, 27 (Latin)
    Bruckner, Anton (ed. Richard Peek)
    Worthy Art Thou, O Lord God (English/
        Latin)

4:11 (Revelation 5:9-10, 13)
    Hancock, Gerre
    A Song To The Lord
    SATB   Organ (2 Trumpets, 2 Trombones,
        Timpani)
    H. W. Gray (1973) CMR 3286

4:11
    SEE: Revelation 21:6-7
    Moe, Daniel
    I Am The Alpha And The Omega

4:11 (Revelation 7:12)
    Newbury, Kent
    Blessing And Glory
    Unison   Keyboard
    Flammer (1971) FA-5005

4:11
    Pooler, Frank
    Thou Art Worthy
    SATB   kro
    Augsburg (1957) 1187

4:11 (Revelation 5:9-10, 12)
    Weber, Paul O.
    To The Lamb Be Glory
    Unison choir   Organ or Brass Quartet,
        Congregation, Cymbal
    Concordia (1976) 98-2299

5:9-10, 12
    SEE: Revelation 4:11
    Weber, Paul O.
    To The Lamb Be Glory

5:9-10, 13
    SEE: Revelation 4:11
    Hancock, Gerre
    A Song To The Lord

5:11-12
    Hillert, Richard
    Offertory/St. Michael And All Angels
        (Verses And Offertories - Lesser
        Feasts)
    Unison   Organ
    Augsburg (1980) 11-9542

5:12   (Watts)
    Cruger, Johann (arr. Gerhard Krapf)
    Come, Let Us Join Our Cheerful Songs
    2 part mixed   Organ
    Augsburg (1977) 11-1822

5:12
    SEE: Isaiah 6:3
    Posegate, Maxcine W.
    Holy Lord Of Hosts

5:12, 13
    Handel, G. F. (ed. H. Watkins Shaw)
    Worthy Is The Lamb That Was Slain (Messiah)
    SATB   Keyboard
    Novello (1959) 29.0208.07

5:12, 13
    Hillert, Richard
    Festival Canticle: Worthy Is Christ
    Unison with Descant   Organ, 2 Trumpets,
        2 Trombones, Timpani
    Concordia (1976) 98-2305

5:12, 13
    Weelkes, Thomas
    Alleluia, I Heard A Voice
    SATBB or SSATB   Organ
    Oxford (1976) TCM 45

5:12-14
    Busarow, Donald
    Offertory/23rd Sunday After Pentecost
        (Verses And Offertories - Pentecost 21
        Christ The King)
    2 part   Organ
    Augsburg (1979) 11-9540

7:2-3, 9-10, 12
    Stanford, C. V.
    And I Saw Another Angel
    SATB   Organ
    Novello (n.d.) SH. ANTH. 20

7:2-3, 9-10, 12
    Stanford, C. V.
    And I Saw Another Angel, Op. 37, #1
    SATB (T-solo)   Organ
    B. F. Wood (1934) 324

7:9   (Revelation 14:4)
    Vaet, Jacobus (ed. David Pizarro)
    O Quam Gloriosum
    SATB   kro
    Sumco (1959) 5285

7:9, 10   (Revelation 21:3-5)
    Milner, Anthony
    I Looked And Behold
    SATB   Organ
    Novello (1969) NCM 26

7:9-10
    Powell, Robert J.
    O Quam Gloriosum
    SATB   kro
    Schmitt, Hall, McCreary (1962) SD 6203

7:9, 12
    Pullingham, Betty Carr
    Hallelujah!   Jesus Is Lord!
    Unison   Piano or Guitar
    GIA (1972) G-1768

7:9-15
    Blow, John (arr. & edited Watkins Shaw)
    I Beheld And Lo A Great Multitude
    TTBB   Organ
    Oxford (1953) n.#.

7:9-15
    Blow, John (arr. & edited Watkins Shaw)
    I Beheld And Lo A Great Multitude
    SATB (A-T-B-B-solos)   Organ
        (optional instruments)
    Oxford (1969) CMS 28

7:12
    Boyce, William (ed. John R. Van Nice)
    Blessing And Glory
    SATB   Organ
    Lawson Gould (1976) 51912

7:12
    SEE: Isaiah 6:3
    Geisler, Johann (ed. E. Nolte)
    The Seraphim On High

7:12
    Jackson, Francis
    Blessing And Glory, Op. 44, #1
    SATB   Organ
    RSCM (1974) (found in Five Anthems For
        Today)

7:12
    SEE: Psalm 117
    Nagel, R.
    Triptych

7:12
    SEE: Revelation 4:11
    Newbury, Kent
    Blessing And Glory

7:12
    Peloquin, C. Alexander
    Angelic Acclamations (English/Latin)
    SAB   Organ
    McLaughlin & Reilly (1964) 2501

7:12   (based on)
    SEE: I Corinthians 15:20 (based on)
    Roman, Johann
    Christ The Lord Is Risen! Alleluia!

7:12   (Psalm 148:1, 12; Psalm 66:1;
        Psalm 96:6)
    Wagner, C. G.
    Blessing, Glory, And Wisdom And Thanks
    SATB/SATB   Piano
    H. W. Gray (n.d.) 1502

7:13, 14
    Snow, Francis W.
    What Are These
    SATB   kro
    Carl Fischer (1969) CM 6488

7:13-17
    Franck, Melchior (ed. B. Henson)
    Revelation Motet (German)
    SATB   kro
    Jenson (1978) 413-18014

7:13-17
    Franck, Melchior (ed. J. Meyerowitz)
    Revelation Motet (English/German)
    SATB   kro
    Broude Brothers (1954) n.#.

7:14
    Bodycombe, Aneurin
    These Are They
    SATB   Organ
    Volkwein (1959) n.#.

7:15
    Hillert, Richard
    Verse/All Saints Day (Verses And
        Offertories - Lesser Festivals)
    Unison   Organ
    Augsburg (1980) 11-9543

8:1b (Revelation 12, based on;
        Revelation 19:2)
    Deering, Richard (transcribed and edited
        by C. F. Simkins)
    Factum Est Silentium   (Latin)
    SSATTB   kro
    Tetra [Alexander Broude] (1970) ABC 34

8:6-7
    SEE: Psalm 104:14-15
    Browne, Richmond
    Chortos I

8:10
    Spiritual (arr. H. T. Burleigh)
    My Lord What A Morning
    SATB   kro
    Ricordi (1929) 412

8:10
    Page, Sue Ellen   (arranger)
    My Lord What A Morning
    SSA   Keyboard
    Hinshaw (1978) HMC 266

9:3-4
    SEE: Psalm 104:14-15
    Browne, Richmond
    Chortos I

10:6
    SEE: Revelation 1:8-9
    Tchaikovsky, Peter (ed. Ivan Sokolov)
    I Am Alpha And Omega

11:15
    SEE: Revelation 19:6, 16
    Handel, G. F.
    Hallelujah (Messiah)   (Carl Fischer)

11:15
    SEE: Revelation 19:6, 16
    Handel, G. F. (ed. T. Tertius Noble)
    Hallelujah Chorus

11:15
    SEE: Revelation 19:6, 16
    Handel, G. F. (arr. Richison)
    Hallelujah

11:15
    SEE: Revelation 19:6, 16
    Handel, G. F. (ed. H. Watkins Shaw)
    Hallelujah Chorus

11:17 (Revelation 14:7)
    Busarow, Donald
    Offertory/27th Sunday After Pentecost
        (Verses And Offertories - Pentecost 21
        Christ The King)
    2 part   Organ
    Augsburg (1979) 11-9540

11:17
    Wetzler, Robert
    We Give Thee Thanks
    SATB   kro
    Augsburg (1963) 1359

12:00 (based on)
    SEE: Revelation 8:1b
    Deering, Richard
    Factum Est Silentium

12:7-8, 10-11
    Campbell, Sidney
    Fanfare For Michaelmas Day -- And There Was
        War In Heaven
    SATB (B-solo)   No accompaniment
    Novello (1961) MT 1422

14:4
    SEE: Revelation 7:9
    Vaet, Jacobus (ed. David Pizarro)
    O Quam Gloriosum

14:4, 5
    Goss, John
    These Are They Which Follow The Lamb
    SATB   Organ
    Oxford (1973) (found in Anthems For
        Choirs, Volume 1)

14:7
    SEE: Revelation 11:17
    Busarow, Donald
    Offertory/27th Sunday After Pentecost

14:13
    Billings, William (ed. Richard Peek)
    I Heard A Great Voice From Heaven
    SATB   kro
    Abingdon (1976) APM-726

14:13
    Billings, William (ed. Oliver Holden)
    I Heard A Great Voice
    SAATBB   kro
    C. F. Peters (1970) 66338

14:13
    Distler, Hugo
    Blessed Are The Dead
    SAB (S-solo)   kro
    Concordia (1968) 97-4846   (found in Der
        Jahrkreis)

14:13
    Goss, John
    I Heard A Voice From Heaven
    SATB   Accompaniment if necessary
    E. C. Schirmer (1936) 1009 (also in the
        Second Concord Anthem Book - Grey)

14:13
    Goss, John
    I Heard A Voice From Heaven
    SATB   Accompaniment if Necessary
    Oxford   (found in Church Anthem Book)

14:13
    Schütz, Heinrich (ed. Walter Ehret)
    Blessed Are The Dead (English/German)
    SSATBB   Optional accompaniment
    Abingdon (1980) APM-701

14:13
    Schütz, Heinrich (arr. Robert Shaw and
        Claus Speer)
    Blessed Are The Faithful (Selig sind die
        Toten) (English/German)
    SSATTBB   Organ ad lib.
    Lawson Gould (1952) 10114

14:13
    Tomkins, Thomas
    I Heard A Voice
    SATB   Organ
    Oxford (1978 (found in Oxford Book Of
        Tudor Anthems)

14:14, 15 (John 4:35, 36; Matthew 13:39)
    Willan, Healey
    I Looked And Behold A White Cloud
    SATB (T-solo)   Organ
    H. W. Gray (n.d.) CMR 1639

14:15-18 (Revelation 15:3-4)
    Wyton, Alec
    Put In Your Sickle
    SATB   Organ
    R. D. Row (1965) R-6136

15:3-4
    Dirksen, Richard
    The Song Of The Redeemer
    2 part (optional 3rd part)   Organ and
        Handbells
    Flammer (1976) A-5735

15:3-4
    Newbury, Kent A.
    King Of The Ages
    Unison   Piano
    Broadman (1975) 4555-01

15:3-4
    Pelz, Walter
    Offertory/Trinity (Verses And Offertories-
        Easter - Trinity)
    SATB   Organ
    Augsburg (1980) 11-9546

15:3-4
    Routley, Erik
    O Ruler Of The Universe
    Unison or 2 part   Organ
    Hinshaw (1977) HMC 240

15:3-4
    Sitton, Carl
    Song Of Praise
    SATB   Keyboard
    Galaxy (1960) GMC 2195

15:3-4
    Spayde, Luther
    Great And Marvelous Are Thy Works
    SATB   kro
    Flammer (1957) 84527

15:3-4
    SEE: Revelation 14:15-18
    Wyton, Alec
    Put In Your Sickle

19:00
    Clokey, Joseph
    King Of Kings
    SATB   Organ
    Birchard (1949) 2030

19:1b, 2, 6b, 7
    Newbury, Kent A.
    The Almighty Reigns
    SATB   No accompaniment
    Walton (1974) 2252

19:1, 6
    Weelkes, Thomas
    Alleluia, I Heard A Voice
    SATBB   Organ
    Oxford (1976) (also found in Oxford Book
        Of Tudor Anthems)

19:2
    SEE: Revelation 8:1b
    Deering, Richard
    Factum Est Silentium

19:6-7, 9
    Busarow, Donald
    Offertory/24th Sunday After Pentecost
        (Verses And Offertories - Pentecost 21
        Christ The King)
    Unison   Organ
    Augsburg (1979) 11-9540

19:6-9 (based on)
    SEE: Matthew 25:1-13
    Nicolai, Philipp (setting by Ludwig Lenel)
    Wake, Awake For Night Is Flying

19:6, 16   (Revelation 11:15)
    Handel, G. F.
    Hallelujah Chorus (Messiah)
    SATB   Piano
    Carl Fischer (1918) CM 86

19:6, 16   (Revelation 11:15)
    Handel, G. F. (arr. Stan Richison)
    Hallelujah (Messiah)
    SSCB   Piano
    Cambiata Press (1973) M 97317

19:6, 16   (Revelation 11:15)
    Handel, G. F. (ed. H. Watkins Shaw)
    Hallelujah Chorus (Messiah)
    SATB   Keyboard
    Novello (n.d.) 29.0206.00

19:6, 16
    Handel, G. F. (ed. T. Tertius Noble)
    Hallelujah Chorus (Messiah)
    SATB   Keyboard
    G. Schirmer (1912) 2020

19:7, 8
    Hillert, Richard
    Offertory/All Saints Day (Verses And
        Offertories - Lesser Feasts)
    Unison   Organ
    Augsburg (1980) 11-9543

21:1-4
    Aston, Peter
    And I Saw A New Heaven
    SATB (S-solo)   Optional Organ
    Novello (1971) MW 7

21:1-4
    Bainton, Edgar
    And I Saw A New Heaven
    SATB   Organ
    RSCM (found in Festival Service Book,
        Volume 4)

21:1-4
    Bainton, Edgar
    And I Saw A New Heaven
    SATB   Organ
    Novello (1956) 29.0342.03

21:1-4
    Kirk, Jerry
    God Shall Wipe Away All Tears
    SATB   Organ (also speaking parts)
    Lillenes [Belwin] (1976) AT 1140

21:1-6
    Ellsworth, A. Eugene
    I Saw A New Heaven And A New Earth
    SATB   Organ, 2 Trumpets
    Kjos (1981) ED 5993   (Trumpets - 5993X)

21:1-6a
    Bertelsen, Arne
    I Saw A New Heaven
    SSATTBB   No accompaniment
    Augsburg (1980) 0577

21:2-3
    Matthew, Thomas
    And I John Saw The Holy City
    SATB   Organ
    H. T. Fitzsimons (1965) 2216

21:3
    SEE: Revelation 3:20
    Burns, William K.
    Behold! I Stand At The Door

21:3   (Revelation 22:13; and other)
    Powell, Robert J.
    Of The Father's Love Begotten
    SATB (S & T solos)   Organ, 2 Flutes
    Concordia (1963) 97-6411

21:3-4
    Lorenz, Ellen Jane
    A New Heaven And A New Earth
    SATB   kro
    Carl Fischer (1951) CM 6614

21:3-5
    SEE: Revelation 7:9-10
    Milner, Anthony
    I Looked And Behold

21:3-5, 7
    Martin, Gilbert
    And God Shall Wipe Away All Tears
    SATB   Organ
    H. W. Gray (1975) CMR 3324

21:3, 10, 23-25
    SEE: Isaiah 60:20
    Gore, Richard T.
    The Sun Shall No More Go Down

21:6-7 (Revelation 4:11)
    Moe, Daniel
    I Am The Alpha And The Omega
    SATB   Organ
    Augsburg (1967) ACL 1483

21:6, 9-10, 18-19   (Revelation 22:1-5)
    Hamilton, Iain
    The Descent Of This Celestial City
      (Epithaph For This World And Time)
    SATB   Organ
    Presser (1973) 312-41004

22:1-5
    SEE: Revelation 21:6, 9-10, 18-19
    Hamilton, Iain
    The Descent Of This Celestial City

22:12, 20
    SEE: Luke 21:25
    Wadley, F. W.
    There Shall Be Signs In The Sun

22:13
    Busarow, Donald
    Verse/Christ The King (Verses And
        Offertories - Pentecost 21 - Christ
        The King)
    Unison   Organ
    Augsburg (1979) 11-9540

22:13
    SEE: Revelation 21:3
    Powell, Robert J.
    Of The Father's Love Begotten

22:16b, 20-21
    Schein, J. H. (ed. John Scholten)
    I Am The Root And The Branch Of David
    SSATB   kro
    Concordia (1968) 98-1895

22:17, 20
    SEE: John 8:12
    Johnson, Ralph
    I Am The Light

22:20
    Busarow, Donald
    Verse/24th Sunday After Pentecost (Verses
        And Offertories - Pentecost 21 -
        Christ The King)
    2 part   Organ
    Augsburg (1979) 11-9540

22:20 (adapted)
    Manz, Paul
    E'en So, Lord Jesus Quickly Come
    SA   Organ
    Concordia (1969) 98-2037

22:20 (adapted)
    Manz, Paul
    E'en So, Lord Jesus Quickly Come
    SSA   kro
    Concordia (1969) 98-2036

22:20 (adapted)
    Manz, Paul
    E'en So, Lord Jesus Quickly Come
    TTBB   kro
    Concordia (1969) 98-2038

22:20 (adapted)
    Manz, Paul
    E'en So Lord Jesus Quickly Come
    SATB   optional organ
    Concordia (1954) 98-1054

A D D E N D A

Listed below are items located after the main body of material had been
prepared for printing.

E X O D U S

13:3
 Herzogenberg, Heinrich
 Was habe ich dir getan, mein Volk
 SSAATTBB   No accompaniment
 Carus Verlag (1980) 40.193/10

15:1
 SEE: Psalm 98:4, 6
 Graun, Karl Heinrich
 Make A Joyful Noise

N U M B E R S

6:24-26
 Deen, Mark T.
 The Lord Bless You And Keep You
 SATB   Accompaniment
 Flammer   A-5940

6:24
 Rutter, John
 The Lord Bless You And Keep You
 SATB   Organ
 Oxford [Hinshaw] (1981) HMC 570

I   S A M U E L

2:00 (Luke 1:00, alt.)
 Jennings, Carol
 A New Magnificat
 SATB   Optional congregation   Organ
 Augsburg (1981) 11-2098

I I   C H R O N I C L E S

7:14
 McMurrin, Roger
 If My People (Enter Into His Gates)
 SATB   Organ
 Hinshaw (1982) HMC 566

J O B

1:21b
 SEE: John 11:25-26
 Croft, William (ed. Bruce Wood)
 Burial Sentences

14:1, 2
 SEE: John 11:25-26
 Croft, William (ed. Bruce Wood)
 Burial Sentences

19:25-27
 SEE: John 11:25-26
 Croft, William (ed. Bruce Wood)
 Burial Sentences

P S A L M S

4:9-10
 Lassus, Orlandus
 In pace (Latin)
 STB   kro
 J. & W. Chester (1979) 55222 (found in
   Seventh Chester Book Of Motets)

19:8-9, 10-11
 Isele, David Clark
 Lord, You Have The Words
 SATB   No accompaniment
 GIA (1979) G-2262 (found in Psalms For
   The Church Year)

22:00 (paraphrase)
 Handel, G. F. (arr. Hal H. Hopson)
 All You That Know God's Holy Name (from
   Alexander's Feast)
 SATB   Keyboard
 Coronet [Alexander Broude] (1981) CP 145

22:8-9, 17-18, 19-20, 23-24
 Isele, David Clark
 My God, My God
 SATB   Congregation   Organ
 GIA (1979) G-2262 (found in Psalms For
   The Church Year)

23:00
 Isele, David Clark
 The Lord Is My Shepherd
 SATB   No accompaniment
 GIA (1979) G-2262 (found in Psalms For
   The Church Year)

23:00
 Schubert, Franz
 Psalm 23, Op. 132   (English/German)
 SSAA   Keyboard
 Casus Verlag (1976) 40.149

24:1-5 (RSV)
 MacMillan, Alan
 The Earth Is The Lord's
 SATB   Organ   Optional Brass: 3 Trumpets,
   4 Horns, 3 Trombones, Tuba, Timpani
 Paraclete Press (1981) PPM 08108

25:00 (adapted)
 Beethoven, Ludwig (arr. Hal Hopson)
 My Soul Longs For You, O God
 SAB   Keyboard
 H. W. Gray (1981) GCMR 3442

25:4-5, 8-10, 14
 Isele, David Clark
 To You, O Lord
 SATB   Congregation   Organ
 GIA (1979) G-2262 (found in Psalms For
   The Church Year)

27:00
 Zimmermann, Heinz Werner
 The Lord Is My Light (Five Hymns)
 SATB   Organ
 Concordia (1973) 98-2174

PSALMS (continued)

27:1, 4, 6
   McMurrin, Roger
   The Lord Is My Light (Enter Into His Gates)
   SATB   Organ
   Hinshaw (1982) HMC 566

29:3-9
   Schütz, Heinrich
   Die Stimme des Herren, gehet auf den Wassern
   SATB   Continuo
   Barenreiter (1956) 1706

34:2-9
   Isele, David Clark
   O Taste And See
   SATB   No accompaniment
   GIA (1979) G-2262   (found in Psalms For The
       Church Year)

34:8
   Hancock, Eugene
   O Taste And See
   SATB   Organ
   H. W. Gray (1980) GCMR 3431

42:6
   Schütz, Heinrich
   Was betrübst du dich meine Seele (German)
   SSATB   Continuo
   Barenreiter (1956) 1706

46:00
   Wills, Arthur
   Psalm 46   (Three Psalms Of Celebration)
   Unison   Organ
   RSCM (1980) 269

47:2-3, 6-9
   Isele, David Clark
   God Mounts His Throne
   SATB   No accompaniment
   GIA (1979) G-2262   (found in Psalms For The
       Church Year)

51:00
   Pote, Allen
   Create In Me, A Clean Heart
   SATB   Keyboard
   Hinshaw (1982) HMC 557

51:3-6, 12-14, 17
   Isele, David Clark
   Be Merciful, O God
   SATB   Congregation   Organ
   GIA (1979) G-2262   (found in Psalms For The
       Church Year)

51:11-12, 17-18
   Wesley, Samuel Sebastian
   Cast Me Not Away From The Presence
   SSATB   Organ
   Novello (n.d.) n.#.

55:00 (Neumark)
   Burroughs, Bob
   If You Will Only Let God Guide Me
   SAB   Keyboard
   Coronet [Alexander Broude] (1982) CP 200

63:1, 2, 5
   Weelkes, Thomas (ed. Robert Gray)
   Early Will I Seek
   SATB   kro
   Tetra [Alexander Broude] (1981) AB 931

64:4
   SEE: Psalm 98:4, 6
   Graun, Karl Heinrich
   Make A Joyful Noise

66:00
   Hassler, Hans Leo (ed. Jerrold Fisher)
   O Praise The Lord
   SATB   Brass
   Flammer   A 5836   (Parts LB 5033)

66:1-7, 16, 20
   Isele, David Clark
   Let All The Earth
   SATB   Congregation   Organ
   GIA (1979) G-2262   (found in Psalms For The
       Church Year)

69:13-17 (metrical)
   Haydn, Franz J. (ed. H. C. Robbins Landon)
   O Let Me In The Accepted Hour
   SA(T)B   kro
   Broude Brothers (1980) CR 16

69:19-21
   Lassus, Orlandus
   Improperium   (Latin)
   SATB   kro
   J. & W. Chester (1977) 55127   (found in
       Fifth Chester Book Of Motets)

70:4 (based on) (Psalm 121:2, based on)
   Passerean (early 16th c.)
   Auxilius meum   (Latin)
   SATB   kro
   J. & W. Chester (1979) 55236 (found in
       Eighth Chester Book Of Motets)

72:1-2, 7-8, 10-13
   Isele, David Clark
   Lord, Every Nation
   SATB   Congregation   Organ
   GIA (1979) G-2262   (found in Psalms For The
       Church Year)

84:00
   Wills, Arthur
   Psalm 84   (Three Psalms Of Celebration)
   Unison   Organ
   RSCM (1980) 269

85:10-13 (Psalm 145:16)
   Gregor, Christian (ed. & arr. by Marilyn
       Gombosi)
   That In This Our Land There May Dwell Glory
       (chorus in Psalm of Joy - compiled by
       Johann Frederich Peter)
   SSAB or SATB   Organ
   Boosey & Hawkes (1975)

86:6-9
   Morales, C.
   In Die tribulationis
   STB   kro
   J. & W. Chester (1979) 55222   (found in
       Seventh Chester Book Of Motets)

90:1-5 (Watts)
   Thompson, Randall
   The Mirror of St. Anne
   SATB/SATB   No accompaniment
   E. C. Schirmer (1972) 2286

95:00 (adapted)
   Jothen, Michael
   The Lord Is A Mighty God
   4 parts, any combination   Keyboard
   Coronet [Alexander Broude] (1982) CP 210

95:1-2, 6-9
   Isele, David Clark
   If Today You Hear His Voice
   SATB   Keyboard
   GIA (1979) G-2262   (found in Psalms For The
       Church Year)

PSALMS   (continued)

96:00 (adapted) (Psalm 97, adapted)
    Brandon, George (setting by)
    The Lord Is King, Let The Earth Rejoice
    SAB   Organ
    Concordia (1980) 98-2477

96:00
    McMurrin, Roger
    Psalm 96   (Enter Into His Gates)
    SATB   Organ
    Hinshaw (1982) HMC 566

96:11, 12
    SEE: Psalm 98:4, 6
    Graun, Karl Heinrich
    Make A Joyful Noise

97:00 (adapted)
    SEE: Psalm 96:00 (adapted)
    Brandon, George
    The Lord Is King, Let The Earth Rejoice

98:1
    Crüger, Johann
    Cantate Domino (Latin)
    SSB   Continuo
    Hänssler (1967) HC 1366

98:1-6
    Isele, David Clark
    All The Ends Of The Earth
    SATB   Congregation   Organ
    GIA (1979) G-2262 (found in Psalms For The
        Church Year)

98:4, 6 (Psalm 103:20, 21; Psalm 96:11, 12;
        Psalm 64:4;   Exodus 15:1)

    Graun, Karl Heinrich (ed. & arr. Marilyn
        Gombosi)
    Make A Joyful Noise (chorus in Psalm of Joy
        compiled by Johann Frederick Peter
    SSAB or SATB   Organ
    Boosey & Hawkes (1975)

100: (Isaiah 64:8)
    Hopson, Hal H.
    Come, Make A Joyful Noise
    SATB   Organ
    Sacred Music Press (1982) S-287

100:1, 2 (John 1:14;   Psalm 111:1a;
        Psalm 145:4)
    Herzogenberg, Heinrich
    Jauchzet dem Herrn, alle Lande (English/
        German)
    SSATTB   No accompaniment
    Carus Verlag (1980) CV 40.192/10

100:4a
    McMurrin, Roger
    Enter Into His Gates (Enter Into His Gates)
    SATB   Organ
    Hinshaw (1982) HMC 566

103:00 (adapted)
    Owens, Sam Batt
    Bless The Lord, O My Soul
    SATB   No accompaniment
    GIA (1982) G-2510

103:1-4, 8-12
    Isele, David Clark
    The Lord Is Kind
    SATB   No accompaniment
    GIA (1979) G-2262 (found in Psalms For The
        Church Year)

103:1-3
    Claudin de Sermisy
    Benedic Anima Mea   (Latin)
    SATB   kro
    J. & W. Chester (1979) 52236 (found in
        Eighth Chester Book of Motets)

103:20, 21
    SEE: Psalm 98:4, 6
    Graun, Karl Heinrich
    Make A Joyful Noise

104:1-24, 29-31, 34
    Isele, David Clark
    Lord, Send Out Your Spirit
    SATB   No accompaniment
    GIA (1979) G-2262 (found in Psalms For The
        Church Year)

111:1a
    SEE: Psalm 100:1, 2
    Herzogenberg, Heinrich
    Jaudhzet dem Herrn, alle Lande

118:1-2, 16-17, 22-23
    Isele, David Clark
    This Is The Day
    SATB   No accompaniment
    GIA (1979) G-2262 (found in Psalms For The
        Church Year)

118:24
    Christiansen, Paul
    This Is The Day
    SATB   kro
    AMSI (1976) 300

118:24
    Hatch, Winnagene
    This Is The Day That The Lord Has Made
    2 part   Keyboard
    Coronet [Alexander Broude] (1982) CP 197

118:24
    Gregor, Christian (ed. & arr. Marilyn
        Gombosi)
    This Is The Day (English/German) (chorus
        from Psalm Of Joy, compiled by Johann
        Frederick Peter)
    SSAB or SATB   Organ
    Boosey & Hawkes (1975)

119:1-5
    SEE: Colossians 3:16
    Landgrave, Phillip
    The Word Of Christ In Song

119:117, 122, 124
    Conseil, Jean
    Adjuva me Domine (Latin)
    SATB   kro
    J. & W. Chester (1979) 55236 (found in
        Eighth Chester Book of Motets)

121:00
    Wills, Arthur
    Psalm 121 (Three Psalms Of Celebration)
    Unison   Organ
    RSCM (1980) 269

121:4
    SEE: Psalm 70:4
    Passereau
    Auxilium meum

122:00
    Hillert, Richard
    Psalm 122: I Was Glad When They Said Unto
        Me
    SATB   Organ, 2 Trumpets (optional Bells
        and Timpani)
    Concordia (1980) 97-5545

PSALMS (continued)

122:1-7
    Isele, David Clark
    Let Us God Rejoicing
    SATB   No accompaniment
    GIA (1979) G-2262   (found in Psalms For The
        Church Year)

125:00
    Willaert, Adriano (ed. Ralph Hunter)
    In Convertendo Dominus (Latin/English)
    SATB   Keyboard
    Belwin (1981) OCT 2469

130:1-8
    Isele, David Clark
    With The Lord There Is Mercy
    SATB   Congregation   Organ
    GIA (1979) G-2262   (found in Psalms For The
        Church Year)

134:00 (Milton)
    Thiman, Eric
    How Lovely Are Thy Dwellings Fair
    SS   Organ
    Novello (1939) 78

143:00 (paraphrase)
    Mendelssohn, Felix (arr. Hal H. Hopson)
    I Call To The Lord (Hör' mein Bitten, Herr)
    SATB   Keyboard
    Coronet [Alexander Broude] (1982) CP 196

144:9
    Asola, Giovanni M.
    Deus Canticum Novum
    SAB   kro
    J. & W. Chester (1979) 55222 (found in
        Seventh Chester Book Of Motets)

145:1-3
    Knapp, William (ed. Elwyn Wienandt and
        Robert Young)
    I Will Magnify Thee, O God
    SATB   Keyboard
    J. Fischer (1970) 10005

145:5
    SEE: Psalm 100:1, 2
    Herzogenberg, Heinrich
    Jauchzet dem Herrn, alle Lande

145:16
    SEE: Psalm 85:10-13
    Gregor, Christian
    That In This Our Land There May Dwell Glory

147:12 (Psalm 148:1-3, 12, 13; Psalm 150:2-6)
    Brau, C. L. (ed. & arr. Marilyn Gombosi)
    Praise, O Jerusalem, The Lord (chorus in
        Psalm of Joy compiled by Johann F.
        Peter)
    SSAB or SATB   Organ
    Boosey & Hawkes (1975)

147:14
    Anonymous (ed. & arr. Marilyn Gombosi)
    This Land Is Calm (found in Psalm of Joy
        compiled by Johann Frederich Peter)
    2 part   Organ
    Boosey & Hawkes (1975)

148:12, 13
    SEE: Psalm 147:12
    Brau, C. L.
    Praise, O Jerusalem, The Lord

148:1-13 (Psalm 150)
    Milner, Anthony
    Praise The Lord Of Heaven, Op. 13, #3
    SATB (A-T-B-solos)   Organ
    Novello (1960) 1407

150:00 (adapted)
    Anderson, Ronald
    Psalm Of Joy
    2 part   Keyboard
    AMSI (1982) 423

150:00
    SEE: Psalm 148:1-13
    Milner, Anthony
    Praise The Lord Of Heaven, Op. 13, #3

150:2-6
    SEE: Psalm 147:12
    Brau, C. L.
    Praise, O Jerusalem, The Lord

P R O V E R B S

3:13-20, 27-35 (Proverbs 4:1-13)
    Adolphe, Bruce
    She Is Thy Life
    SATB   Brass Quartet
    Cantata [Alexander Broude] (1982) AB 987

4:1-13
    SEE: Proverbs 3:13-20, 27-35
    Adolphe, Bruce
    She Is Thy Life

S O N G O F S O N G S

2:1-3
    Clemens Non Papa
    Ego flos campi (Latin)
    STB   kro
    J. & W. Chester (1979) 55222 (found in
        Seventh Chester Book Of Motets)

I S A I A H

1:2, 4, 16-18
    Humphreys, Pelham (ed. Daniel Pinkham)
    Hear, O Heaven
    SATB (A-T-B-solos)   Organ
    E. C. Schirmer (1972) 2679

3:1, 6
    SEE: John 1:29
    Albinoni, Tomaso (ed. Allen Petker)
    Behold The Lamb Of God

9:2-7 (based on - J. Rist)
    Young, Gordon
    Break Forth, O Beauteous Heavenly Light
    SATB   No accompaniment
    Coronet [Alexander Broude] (1982) GP 224

35:00
    Butler, Eugene
    The Desert Shall Rejoice
    SATB   Organ   2 Trumpets, 2 Trombones,
        Optional Timpani and Handbells
    Coronet [Alexander Broude] (1982) CP 202

53:4-5
    Willan, Healey (arr. Dale Wood)
    Surely He Hath Borne Our Griefs
    SATB   Organ
    Concordia (1981) 98-2520

55:10-12 (adapted from)
    Wagner, Douglas
    For As The Rains Come Down
    SAB   Keyboard
    Coronet [Alexander Broude] (1982) CP 193

ISAIAH (continued)

60:00 (based on)   (Matthew 2:00, based on)
    Mouton, Jean
    Reges Terrae   (Latin)
    SATB   kro
    J. & W. Chester (1979) 55236 (found in
        Eighth Chester Book Of Motets)

64:8
    SEE: Psalm 100
    Hopson, Hal H.
    Make A Joyful Noise

JEREMIAH

5:15-16
    Bach, J. C.
    Unsers Herzens Freude hat ein Ende
        (English/German)
    SATB/SATB   Organ
    Hänssler (1978) 30.562/02

LAMENTATIONS

1:12
    Asola, G. M.
    O Vos Omnes   (Latin)
    STB   kro
    J. & W. Chester (1979) 55222 (found in
        Seventh Chester Book Of Motets)

1:12
    Croce, Giovanni (arr. & ed. Rod Walker)
    O Vos Omnes   (English/Latin)
    SATB   kro
    Shawnee (1982) A-1661

1:12
    Jachet of Mantua
    O Vos Omnes   (Latin)
    SATB   kro
    J. & W. Chester (1979) 55236 (found in
        Eighth Chester Book Of Motets)

2:10
    Genet, E.
    Sederunt in Terra   (Latin)
    ATB   kro
    J. & W. Chester (1979)55222 (found in
        Seventh Chester Book Of Motets)

5:1
    Genet, E.
    Recordare Domine   (Latin)
    ATT   kro
    J. & W. Chester (1979) 5222 (found in
        Seventh Chester Book Of Motets)

TOBIAS

12:2
    Antoine de Longueval
    Benedicite deum caeli
    SATB   kro
    J. & W. Chester (1979) 55236 (found in
        Eighth Chester Book Of Motets)

ECCLESIASTICUS (or SIRACH)

50:22-24
    Cruger, J. (arr. Bob Burroughs)
    Now Thank We All Our God
    SATB   Keyboard (or Brass Quartet)
    Coronet [Alexander Broude] (1982) CP 182

MATTHEW

2:00 (based on)
    SEE: Isaiah 60:00 (based on)
    Mouton, Jean
    Reges Terrae

5:3-12a
    Schein, J.
    Selig sind, die da geistlich arm sind
        (German)
    SSATB   Organ continuo
    Hänssler (1980) HE 5.154/02

5:8 (Luke 13:29)
    Haan, Raymond H.
    The Pure In Heart
    SATB   Organ
    Coronet [Alexander Broude] (1981) CP 127

6:9-13
    Crosse, Gordon
    Pater Noster
    SSA or TBB or SSATBB   No accompaniment
    Oxford (1976) 55236 (found in Gaudeamus)

6:33
    SEE: John 14:15
    Eddlerman, David
    If You Love Me, Keep My Commandments

16:18-19
    Britten, Benjamin
    Hymn To St. Peter, Op. 56a
    SATB   Organ
    Boosey & Hawkes (1955)

21:9
    Scheidt, Samuel
    Hosianna filio David   (Latin)
    SSATB   Continuo
    Hänssler (1960) HE 1.139

MARK

16:1-2
    Dulot, Francois
    Maria Magdalene   (Latin)
    SATB   kro
    J. & W. Chester (1979) 55236 (found in
        Eighth Chester Book Of Motets)

LUKE

1:00 (alt.)
    SEE: I Samuel 2:00
    Jennings, Carol
    A New Magnificat

2:00 (adapted)
    Newbury, Kent
    Jesus Is Born In Bethlehem
    SSA (solo)   Keyboard
    Coronet [Alexander Broude] (1982) CP 226

LUKE (continued)

2:00 (adapted)
    Newbury, Kent
    Jesus Is Born In Bethlehem
    SATB (solo)   No accompaniment
    Coronet [Alexander Broude] (1982) CP 183

2:10-11
    Powell, Robert J.
    Behold I Bring You Good Tidings
    SAB   kro
    Abingdon (1966) APM 535 (found in Festival
        Anthems For SAB)

2:14
    Goudimel, Claude
    Gloria In Excelsis (Latin)
    SATB   kro
    J. & W. Chester (1979) 55236 (found in
        Eighth Chester Book Of Motets)

2:14
    Lotti, Antonio (ed. Ralph Hunter)
    In Terra Pax (Latin/English)
    SAAAATTTTBBBB   Organ
    Belwin (1981) 2471

2:14
    Norris, Kevin
    Glory To God
    SATB   Organ
    AMSI (1982) 429

13:29
    SEE: Matthew 5:8
    Haan, Raymond H.
    The Pure In Heart

JOHN

1:14
    SEE: Psalm 100:1, 2
    Herzogenberg, Heinrich
    Jauchzet dem Herrn, alle Lande

1:29 (Isaiah 3:1, 6)
    Albinoni, Tomaso (ed. Allen Petker)
    Behold The Lamb Of God
    SATB   Accompaniment
    Gentry (1982) G 468

6:56-58
    Cascogne, Mathieu
    Caro mea (Latin)
    SATB   kro
    J. & W. Chester (1979) 55236 (found in
        Eighth Chester Book Of Motets)

11:25-26 (Job 1:21b; Job 14:1, 2;
            Job 19:25-27; I Timothy 6:7)
    Croft, William (ed. Bruce Wood)
    Burial Sentences
    SATB   No accompaniment
    Oxford (1980) CMS Reprint 55

14:15 (Matthew 6:33)
    Eddlerman, David
    If You Love Me, Keep My Commandments
    SATB   Keyboard
    Coronet [Alexander Broude] (1982) CP 186

ACTS

1:11
    Couillart (early 16th century)
    Viri Galilaei (Latin)
    SATB   kro
    J. & W. Chester (1979) 55236 (found in
        Eighth Chester Book Of Motets)

PHILIPPIANS

2:10a
    Herzogenberg, Heinrich
    In Jesu Namen   (English/German)
    SSATTB   No accompaniment
    Carus Verlag (1980) CV 40.192/20

COLOSSIANS

3:16 (Psalm 119:105, and other)
    Landgave, Phillip
    The Word Of Christ In Song (based on
        tune, Munich)
    SATB   Keyboard
    Hinshaw (1982) HMC 552

I THESSALONIANS

5:23
    McMurrin, Roger
    Paul's Benediction (Enter Into His Gates)
    SATB   Organ
    Hinshaw (1982) HMC 566

I TIMOTHY

6:7
    SEE: John 11:25-26
    Croft, William (ed. Bruce Wood)
    Burial Sentences

REVELATION

5:12, 13
    Herzogenberg, Heinrich
    Das Lamm, das erwürget ist (Worthy Is The
        Lamb That Was Slain) (English/
        German)
    SSAATTBB   No accompaniment
    Carus Verlag (1980) 40.193/10

C O M P O S E R   I N D E X

Items marked [A] are found in the Addenda.

ABBEY, Harold - Luke 2:7.
ADLER, Samuel - Genesis 12:2, 3; Exodus
    15:1-6, 11, 18; Psalm 5:1-3, 11; Psalm
    24; Psalm 36:8-11; Psalm 40:1-5; Psalm
    44:23; Psalm 96:1-4, 9, 11-13; Psalm
    121; Psalm 150; Ecclesiastes 3; Eccle-
    siastes 11 and 12; Song of Songs 8:6;
    Isaiah 12:1, 2, 3-6; Micah 6:6-8.
ADOLPHE, Bruce - [A] Proverbs 3:13-20,
    27-35;   John 20:11-17.
AGAZZARI, Agostino - Psalm 100.
AICHINGER, Gregor - Genesis 4:9-10; Psalm
    68:28-29;   Acts 2:2.
ALBINONI, Thomas - [A] John 1:29.
ALCOCK, John - Psalm 130.
ALDRICH, Henry - Psalm 130;   Psalm 130:
    1-4.
ALEXANDER, Josef - Psalm 98.
ALLANBROOK, Douglas - Psalm 130;   Psalm
    131.
ALLEGRI, Gregorio - Psalm 51
ALLEN, Art - Mark 10:17-31.
ALLEN, Larry - John 15:16;   Ephesians 2:
    8-10.
ALLITSEN, Frances - Psalm 27:1, 3, 5.
ALLURED, Donald - Psalm 100.
ALTMAN, Ludwig - Psalm 13;   Psalm 19:14;
    Psalm 24;   Psalm 47.
AMNER, John - Psalm 24:7, 8a, 10b;   Psalm
    24:7-10; Psalm 66:14-18;   Psalm 72:18-
    19;   Psalm 104:33-35;   Psalm 120:4-5;
    Psalm 145:1, 3, 8, 21; Isaiah 49:13-15;
    Luke 12:32 (paraphrase).
AMRAM, David - Deuteronomy 6:5-9;   Psalm
    19:15;   Psalm 137.
ANDERS, Charles - Psalm 46:1-9; Psalm 119:
    1-8, 137.
ANDERSON, Muriel - Psalm 148.
ANDERSON, Ronald - [A] Psalm 150.
ANDERSON, William H. - Psalm 55:22.
ANDREWS, Mark - Psalm 103.
ANERIO, Felice - Psalm 75:9-10;   Matthew
    28:2, 5-8; Galatians 6:14; Philippians
    2:2-8; Philippians 2:8-9.
ANERIO, Giovanni F. - Psalm 149.
ANGELL, Warren - Psalm 23;   Psalm 150;
    Malachai 4:2 (Wesley).
ANONYMOUS - Psalm 51:12-14;   Psalm 118:24;
    [A] Psalm 147:14; Isaiah 9:6; Zechariah
    14; John 1:14; Philippians 4:4-7;
    Colossians 3:1-2.
ANTES, John - I Chronicles 17:36;   Psalm
    13:5-6;   Psalm 126:5-6;   Psalm 130:6;
    Isaiah 52:7; Isaiah 53:4-5; Isaiah 63:
    7;   Zechariah 2:10.
ANTIONE DE LONGUEVAL - [A] Tobias 12:2.
ARCADELT, J. - Psalm 4; Psalm 25:1; Psalm
    55:1-4;   Psalm 118:24;   Psalm 141:1.
ARCHER, Violet - Psalm 98.
ARENSKY, A. S. - Psalm 86:1, 3, 5.
ARMSTRONG, Mimi - Ephesians 4:1-3.
ARNATT, Ronald - Psalm 40:1-7, 10, 19-21;
    Psalm 67; Psalm 90:1, 2, 10, 17; Psalm
    100; Psalm 119; Psalm 122:1; Psalm 148;
    Matthew 5:3-10, 12, 14, 16;   I Corin-
    thians 5:7-8.

ARNOLD, Malcolm - Psalm 100; Psalm 150.
ASCHAFFENBURG, Walter - Psalm 23.
ASHWORTH, Caleb - Psalm 137:1-6.
ASOLA, Giovanni - Psalm 16:5-7; [A] Psalm
    144:9; [A] Lamentations 1:12; I Corin-
    thians 5:8-9.
ASTON, Peter - Psalm 42:4-7; Psalm 67;
    Psalm 96:1-4; Psalm 150; Luke 2:11;
    Revelation 21:1-4.
ATKINSON, Thelma - Matthew 11:28-29.
ATTWOOD, Thomas - Psalm 51:9, 10, 11;
    Psalm 51:10-12; Psalm 90:13; Psalm
    119:33; Psalm 119:33, 145.
AUFDEMBERGE, Edgar - Isaiah 11:1-2.
AULBACH, Francis E. - Psalm 25:1, 3-4;
    Psalm 55:23.
AVERITT, William - Lamentations 1:12.
AVERY, Richard and Donald Marsh -
    Matthew 5:3-10; Matthew 5:13-14;
    Ephesians 2:14.

BABCOCK, Samuel - Isaiah 40:1-4a, 5a.
BACH, C. P. E. - Isaiah 6:3.
BACH, J. C. - Job 14:1-2; [A] Jeremiah
    5:15-16.
BACH, Johann Ludwig - Psalm 126:5-6.
BACH, Johann Michael - Job 19:25-27.
BACH, J. S. - Psalm 46; Psalm 80:1;
    Psalm 84:11; Psalm 84:12; Psalm 88;
    Psalm 103; Psalm 103:1, 3, 6, 11;
    Psalm 115:13-15; Psalm 117; Psalm
    121; Psalm 137; Psalm 139; Psalm
    145; Isaiah 9:2-7; Isaiah 40:1-5;
    Isaiah 41:10; Ecclesiasticus 50:
    22-24; Luke 1:54; Luke 1:55.
BACK, Sven-Erik - Luke 23:42-43; John
    1:14; John 6:35-36; Romans 13:12.
BAIN, James Leith - Psalm 23.
BAINTON, Edgar - Revelation 21:1-4.
BAKER, Richard - Psalm 3:8; Psalm 30:
    4, 5, 12; Luke 1:46-57.
BAKER, Robert - Psalm 9:1, 2, 4, 19, 20;
    Psalm 94:1-7.
BALAKIREFF (BALAKIREV) M. A. - Psalm
    43:3, 5.
BALES, Gerald - Psalm 100.
BANCHIERI, Adriano - Psalm 33:1-3;
    Psalm 85:11.
BANNER, David - Isaiah 40:28-31.
BARD, Vivien - Psalm 46:1, 9, 10.
BARISTOW, E. C. - Exodus 15:4, 21;
    Psalm 94:7-10; Song of Songs 2:3, 4;
    John 3:14-16; Acts 13:32-33; Romans
    6:4-5; I Corinthians 13:1-4, 7-9,
    12-13.
BARKER, Ken - Job 38:4-7.
BARLOW, David - Lamentations 1:12.
BARNBY, J. - Psalm 57:9; Psalm 104:24.
BARNES, Edward Shippen - Colossians 3:
    12-15.
BARNES, Norman J. - Luke 4:18-19.
BARRETT-AYRES, Reginald - Psalm 9
    (adapted).
BASS, Claude - Psalm 23; Psalm 55:22;
    Matthew 6:19-21; Hebrews 11:1, 2, 4,
    5, 7-8.

BASSANO, Giovani - Luke 2:14.

BASSETT, Leslie - Psalm 64.

BATTEN, Adrian - Psalm 70:1-4; Psalm 81:
    1-4; Psalm 106:45-46; Psalm 117; Psalm
    119:169-172, 175; Psalm 126:1-4; Psalm
    130.

BATTISHILL, Jonathan 25:6; Psalm 26:7;
    Psalm 53:15; Isaiah 63:15.

BAUMGARTNER, H. Leroy - Job 23:3; Psalm 1.

BEATTIE, Herbert - Psalm 90:16-17; Psalm
    106:1; Isaiah 25:9; John 14:18.

BECK, John Ness - Psalm 8; Psalm 47; Psalm
    90; Psalm 98; Psalm 103:1; Psalm 104:16-
    18, 21-22, 24, 35; Ecclesiastes 11:9;
    Isaiah 40; Isaiah 40:4-5; Isaiah 55:8,
    10-11; Isaiah 58:1, 8; Matthew 16:18-19;
    Romans 8:35-39, Ephesians 4; Philippians
    2.

BECK, Steven - Psalm 148:1-6.

BECK, Theodore - Psalm 23; Psalm 24:7-10;
    Psalm 146; Isaiah 59:20; Luke 2:1-20;
    Luke 2:10-12, 14-15b; John 1:29.

BECKLER, Johann - Philippians 2:13.

BEEBE, Hank - Psalm 7:1, Psalm 24:1-2; Psalm
    24:3-5; Psalm 24:6; Psalm 24:7-9; Psalm
    24:10; Psalm 27; Psalm 46; Psalm 118;
    Psalm 122; Isaiah 6:3; Isaiah 26:3;
    Isaiah 40; Isaiah 44:22-24; Isaiah 53:3-
    10; Isaiah 54:6-7, 10; Isaiah 55:12-13;
    Matthew 7:7-8; Luke 1:46-55; John 12:35-
    36.

BEESON, Jack - Psalm 23; Psalm 47; Psalm
    131.

BEETHOVEN, Ludwig - Psalm 19 (paraphrase);
    [A] Psalm 25; Psalm 66:1-2, 4; Psalm 103.

BENDER, Jan - Psalm 27:1-2, 5, 7, 9, 13, 14;
    Psalm 31:1, 2, 3; Psalm 46; Psalm 73:25-
    26, 28; Psalm 96:1-3; Psalm 98:1-10;
    Psalm 150; Isaiah 53:4-5; Zephaniah 3:14;
    Matthew 2:13-23; Matthew 4:10; Matthew
    5:3-12; Matthew 8:11-12; Matthew 8:25-27;
    Matthew 15:4-10; Matthew 15:25-34;
    Matthew 15:26-28; Matthew 18:32-35;
    Matthew 21:9; Matthew 22:4; Matthew 25:
    11-13; Matthew 25:32; Mark 7:37; Mark
    16:6-7; Mark 16:15-16; Luke 2:48; Luke
    11:23; Luke 16:24-26; Luke 18:38-42;
    Luke 21:25-26, 33; John 3:3, 5-6, 8;
    John 3:16; John 4:49-50; John 6:14; John
    8:51, 54-55b; John 10:14-16; John 14:23;
    John 15:26-27; John 16:23-24; John 20:19-
    31; I Corinthians 5:7-8; Ephesians 3:20-
    21; Philippians 1:6.

BENGTSON, F. Dale - Psalm 118:24.

BEN-HAIM, Paul - Psalm 121.

BENION, Sebastian - Isaiah 55:1.

BENJAMIN, Tom - I John 3:4 (taken from).

BENNETT, Ronald C. - Psalm 8.

BENNETT, W. Sterndale - Job 23:3, 8-9; John
    4:23b-24; John 4:24.

BENSON, Warren - Psalm 24.

BERCHEM, Jachet - Lamentations 1:12.

BERGER, Jean - Exodus 15:11; Job 14:1-2;
    Job 14:7, 14; Psalm 9:1, 2, 3, 5; Psalm
    13; Psalm 23; Psalm 24:7-10; Psalm 24:9-
    10; Psalm 28:7; Psalm 43:5; Psalm 47;
    Psalm 67; Psalm 84; Psalm 84:4-8; Psalm
    86; Psalm 86:1-7; Psalm 86:8-13; Psalm
    86:14-17; Psalm 92:1-2; Psalm 95; Psalm
    95:1-7; Psalm 96:1-2; Psalm 100; Psalm
    105:1-3; Psalm 107:1; Psalm 113; Psalm
    117; Psalm 121; Psalm 128:1-6; Psalm
    136:1; Psalm 136:1-5; Psalm 136:1-9, 26;
    Psalm 139:9-12; Psalm 140; Psalm 145:1-3;
    21; Psalm 145:1-4; Psalm 145:9; Psalm
    145:15-16; Psalm 145:17-18, 20; Psalm
    146; Psalm 150; Proverbs 2:6-8; Proverbs
    3:13-16; Proverbs 6:8-9; Proverbs 15:
    13, 15; Proverbs 16:9, 18-19; Proverbs
    16:17, 19; Isaiah 2:2-5; Isaiah 6:8;
    Isaiah 12:2, 5; Isaiah 39:6-7; Isaiah 40:
    6-8;Isaiah 40:31; Isaiah 52:7; Isaiah 60:
    1-2; Jeremiah 31:33-34; Judith 9:14;
    Luke 8:5-8; James 4:14.

BERK, Adele - Psalm 100:1-4.

BERKELEY, Lennox - Psalm 23.

BERKELEY, Michael - Psalm 95:11, 13.

BERLINSKI, Herman - Ruth 1:16; Song of
    Songs 3:1-2, 4-5; Amos 6:8.

BERNARDI, Stefano - Psalm 110.

BERNHARD, Christopher - Psalm 37:1-6;
    Matthew 23:37-38.

BERNSTEIN, David - Psalm 118:1-4.

BERNSTEIN, Leonard - Psalm 23; Psalm
    108:2; Psalm 131.

BERRIDGE, Arthur - Mark 16:15.

BERTELSEN, Arne - Revelation 21:1-6a.

BESTON, Charles - Psalm 25:1, 4a.

BETTS, Donald - Psalm 42.

BEVANS, William - Psalm 24:1-2, 3-6,
    7-10.

BEVERSDORF, Thomas - Micah 6:1-2, 12.

BEVIN, Elway - Psalm 15:1-2.

BEYER, Johann S. - Luke 2:9-11; Luke
    2:10-12.

BILLINGS, William - II Samuel 18:33;
    Psalm 19; Psalm 23; Psalm 126; Psalm
    148; Song of Songs 2:1-5, 7-8, 10-
    11; Song of Songs 5:1-2, 6; Song of
    Songs 8:4; Luke 2:1-20; I Corinthians
    15:20; Revelation 14:13.

BILLINGSLEY, Derrell - Philippians 2:
    9, 10 (based on).

BINGHAM, Seth - Psalm 72; Matthew 6:
    9-13.

BINKERD, Gordon - Psalm 23; Psalm 25;
    Psalm 79:2; Psalm 91:4-5; Psalm
    93; Psalm 98:2, 3, 4; Psalm 141:2;
    Hebrews 1:1-2.

BITGOOD, Roberta - Psalm 57:7, 9; Psalm
    98; Isaiah 40:28-31; Ecclesiasticus
    44:14; Romans 15:13; Hebrews 13:20,
    21.

BLACK, James - I Thessalonians 4:16.

BLAIR, Dallas - Psalm 100.

BLAKE, Leonard - Psalm 65; Ecclesiasti-
    cus 38 (based on).

BLAKENSHIP, Mark - Psalm 118:6, 14;
    Matthew 11:28-30; John 12:32; I John
    4:4.

BLAKLEY, Duane - Psalm 9; Psalm 23;
    Matthew 6:9-13; Ephesians 6:10-17;
    James 4:8-10.

BLANKENSHIP, Mark - Luke 11:9-10;
    I Corinthians 15:57-58; Galatians 2:
    16, 19-20.

BLIEM, William - Isaiah 40:6-8.

BLISS, Arthur - Nehemiah 9:5, 6; Psalm
    15:1, 2; Psalm 106:1-3, 46.

BLOCH, Ernest - Psalm 19:14.

BLOW, John - Psalm 22:1; Psalm 24:7-10;
    Psalm 38:1-2, 21-22; Psalm 69:31, 34-
    36; Psalm 84:9; Psalm 86; Psalm 86:
    1-2, 5; Psalm 86:4, 5; Psalm 86:
    7-8, 10; Psalm 88:1, 2, 8; Psalm 89:
    14, 15; Psalm 102:11, 12, 13; Psalm
    113:1, 2; Psalm 122:6-9; Psalm 141:
    2; Romans 6:9-11; Revelation 7:9-15.

BOATWRIGHT, Howard - Psalm 61:1-4.

BOBERG, Robert - Psalm 11:4; Psalm 122:1.

BOCK, Fred - Psalm 117; Psalm 148.

BODE, Arnold G. H. - Psalm 121.

BODINE, Willis - Isaiah 9:2-7; I Corin-
    thians 5:7-8.

BODYCOMBE, Aneurin - Revelation 7:14.

BOE, John - Wisdom of Solomon 2:23-24.

BOHRNSTEDT, Wayne - I Corinthians 3:
    9-17.

BOLT, Conway A. - Psalm 96:1, 2.

BORTNIANSKY, Dimitri - Psalm 96; Psalm
    108; Isaiah 6:3; Isaiah 40.

BOUCK, Marjorie - Psalm 139:6-11.

BOULANGER, Lili - Psalm 24.

BOUMAN, Paul - Psalm 51:10, 11, 12;
    Psalm 67:1, 2, 3, 6-7; John 1:29;
    I Corinthians 15:37.

BOURGEOIS, Louis - Psalm 1; Psalm 42;
    Psalm 98; Psalm 121; Psalm 124; Luke

2:29-32.
BOWIE, William - Hebrews 11, and 12.
BOYCE, William - Job 28:12-13, 15, 23-28;
    Job 28:12, 15, 18, 20-28; Psalm 25:15-
    16, 19; Psalm 25:16-17; Psalm 26:2-3;
    Psalm 54:1-3; Psalm 122:1-2, 4-7; Psalm
    137:1-8; Revelation 7:12.
BRADBURY, William - Isaiah 52:7; Isaiah 55:
    6-7.
BRAHMS, Johannes - Deuteronomy 4:7, 9; Job
    3:20-23; Psalm 13; Psalm 22:5, 6; Psalm
    51:10; Psalm 51:10, 11, 12; Psalm 51:11;
    Psalm 51:11, 12, 13, 14; Psalm 51:12;
    Psalm 69:29; Psalm 84:1-2, 4; Matthew
    5:4; Luke 11:17, 21.
BRANDON, George - Psalm 91; [A] Psalm 96
    (adapted); Psalm 96; Psalm 96:4; Psalm
    103; Proverbs 3:5, 6; Isaiah 58:5-8;
    Isaiah 62:1, 6, 10-11 (paraphrase);
    Jeremiah 8:22; Ezekiel 47 (based on);
    John 1:4, 8, 10; Hebrews 2:9-10; Hebrews
    10:7 (based on); Hebrews 12:28, 29;
    James 4:8-10.
BRANDT, William S. - John 6:27, 35, 50.
BRANT, Henry - Isaiah 2:2-4.
BRAU, C. L. - [A] Psalm 147:12.
BREWER, A. Herbert - Psalm 140:7.
BREYDERT, F. M. - Jeremiah 31:15.
BRIGHT, Houston - Psalm 130; Matthew 6
    (adapted).
BRISTOL, Lee H. Jr. - Psalm 100; Matthew
    21:9; Matthew 22:35-40; John 1:29 (based
    on).
BRITTEN, Benjamin - Psalm 100; [A] Matthew
    16:18-19.
BROADHEAD, G. F. - Psalm 91:1-2.
BROWN, Charles - I Peter 2:9.
BROWNE, Richard - Psalm 104:14-15.
BRUBAKER, Dale C. and James D. Cram - Mark
    16:15-16 (adapted).
BRUCKNER, Anton - Psalm 37:30-31; Psalm 45:
    14-15; Psalm 45:15, 17; Psalm 89:20-21;
    Ecclesiastes 43:16, 27; Isaiah 40:1;
    Isaiah 40:31; Judith 15:10 (based on)
    Ecclesiasticus 43:16, 27; Luke 1:42
    (based on); Philippians 2:8-9.
BRYAN, Charles - Isaiah 28.
BUCH, P. C. - John 3:2.
BUCK, Dudley - Psalm 46; Psalm 46:1, 3;
    Psalm 72:6-8, 19; Psalm 77; Isaiah 26:3.
BULLARD, Alan - Psalm 148:1-5, 8-13.
BULLIS, Thomas - Psalm 47:1-3, 6.
BULLOCK, Ernest - Psalm 65:9, 11-13.
BUNJES, Paul - Psalm 103:1-6; Isaiah 40:1-3.
BURNELL, J. - Genesis 28:16, 17.
BURNS, William K. - Isaiah 55:6-7; Revelation
    3:20.
BURROUGHS, Bob - Genesis 28:16, 17; Psalm
    9:4, 20; Psalm 23; Psalm 40; Psalm 51:
    10, 11, 12; [A] Psalm 55; Psalm 67; Psalm
    71:8, 11; Psalm 103:1-4; Isaiah 55:6-7;
    Malachai 4:2 (Wesley); Matthew 11:28-30;
    Luke 2:10-12, 14 (paraphrase); John 11:
    25-26; John 14:1, 3; John 14:1, 27; John
    16:24; Philippians 2:5-11; Philippians
    4:19.
BURTON, Daniel - Acts 16:14, 15 (based on);
    Romans 8:28, 31 (adapted from); Romans
    8:35-39 (adapted from); I Corinthians 13
    (based on); Philippians 4:8.
BUSAROW, Donald - Psalm 130; Isaiah 25:9;
    Matthew 24:42; Luke 21:36; I Corinthians
    10:16-17; II Thessalonians 3:1ff;
    II Timothy 4:6-8; II Timothy 4:18; James
    1:18; I John 2:1-2; I John 3:2-3; Revela-
    tion 5:12-14; Revelation 11:17; Revela-
    tion 19:6-7, 9; Revelation 22:13; Reve-
    lation 22:20.
BUSH, Geoffrey - Psalm 24; Psalm 103:1-5,
    8-9, 14.
BUTLER, Eugene - Psalm 1; Psalm 5; Psalm 8
    (adapted); Psalm 9:1-2, 9; Psalm 20;
    Psalm 33; Psalm 43 (adapted); Psalm 57:
    5, 7-11; Psalm 92:12, 13; Psalm 96;

Psalm 107:2, 10, 20; Psalm 108;
    Psalm 113; Psalm 122:1, 6-7; Psalm
    135:3; Psalm 145:1-4; Psalm 146;
    Psalm 148; Psalm 148:1, 3, 5, 8, 12;
    Psalm 150; [A] Isaiah 35; Isaiah
    52:7; Isaiah 55:6-7; Isaiah 61:10-
    11;Daniel 2:20-23; Joel 2; Matthew
    5:13-16; Matthew 28:19; Romans 8:
    31; Ephesians 1:3, 5, 7, 9-10;
    I Peter 1.
BUTLER, J. Melvin - Psalm 27:4-6.
BUXTEHUDE, Dietrich - Psalm 31:1; Psalm
    96:1-4; Psalm 118; Psalm 118:19, 20,
    24-26; Matthew 25:1-13; Luke 2:18-
    24 (paraphrase); Colossians 3:17;
    Jude 1:14-15.
BYRD, William - I Chronicles 16:31;
    Psalm 6; Psalm 6:1-3; Psalm 44:23-
    24; Psalm 47:5; Psalm 51:1; Psalm
    51:1-2; Psalm 68:28, 29; Psalm 80:
    16; Psalm 81:1-4; Psalm 114:1-3;
    Psalm 115:1; Psalm 118:24; Psalm
    119:33-38; Psalm 119:174-175; Psalm
    126:5-7; Psalm 149:1-2; Isaiah 45:
    18; Isaiah 60:1; Isaiah 64:9; Wisdom
    of Solomon 3:1-3; John 6:51; John
    14:18; Acts 1:11; Romans 6:9-11.

CABENA, Barrie - Psalm 100; Psalm 150;
    Matthew 5:14-16.
CAIN, Noble - Psalm 23; Psalm 69:30-
    33; Psalm 100; Psalm 103; Matthew
    6:9-15; Matthew 14 (adapted); John
    4:13-14; Revelation 3:20.
CALDARA, Antonio - Psalm 6:6.
CALDWELL, Mary E. - Psalm 23; John 10:
    11, 14-16, 28-30; John 11:25; Romans
    8:37.
CALVIN, Susan - Psalm 1.
CAMPBELL, Sidney - I Chronicles 28:20;
    Psalm 81:1-4; Revelation 12:7-8, 10-
    11.
CAMPBELL-WATSON, Franck - Philippians
    4:4-6.
CAMPRA, Andre - Psalm 75; Psalm 84:1, 2.
CANDLYN, T. Frederick H. - Malachai
    4:2 (Wesley).
CAPELLO, Giovanni - Genesis 22:1-13.
CARISSIMI, G. - Judges 11:39; Judges
    11:40 (based on); Psalm 112; Psalm
    127.
CARLEY, Isabel M. - John 4:35-37
    (adapted).
CARLSON, Richard - Psalm 150.
CARPENTER, Adrian - Psalm 81:1-4.
CARTER, John - Psalm 95:1-6; Psalm 130;
    Isaiah 52:7; Matthew 21:9.
CARTFORD, Gerhard M. - Psalm 23;
    Psalm 29; Psalm 67.
CARY, Tristam - John 1:14.
CASALS, Pablo - Song of Songs 1:4,
    (5); Lamentations 1:12.
CASCIOLINI, Claudio - Psalm 50:3, 8;
    Psalm 51:9.
CASCOGNE, Mathieu - [A] John 6:56-
    58.
CASSELLS-BROWN, Alastair - Psalm 104:
    1-4, 32-35.
CASSLER, C. Winston - Psalm 33:1, 5b,
    6a; Psalm 65:1-2; Psalm 130:1-2a,
    5-6a.
CASTELNUOVO-TEDESCO, Mario - Ruth (based
    on); I Kings 10:1-13.
CAURROY, Eustache - Isaiah 9:6.
CAUSEY, C. Harry - Psalm 8:1-4; (arr.)
    Jeremiah 8:22.
CHAJES, Julius - Psalm 142.
CHANDLER, Mary - Tobit 13:11-18.
CHARPENTIER, Marc-Antoine - Psalm 117; Psalm
    122; Psalm 130; Psalm 148; Luke 2:8-16.
CHEPPONIS, James J. - Luke 1:46-55.
CHERUBINI, Luigi - Psalm 103:13.

CHIHARA, Paul - Psalm 131.

CHILD, William - Psalm 74:1, 2; Psalm 103;
PSALM 103:1-4, 22; Psalm 135:1-4.

CHORBAJIAN, John - II Samuel 18:33; Psalm
130.

CHRISTENIUS, Johann - Matthew 11:28-30.

CHRISTIANSEN, F. Melius - Psalm 50.

CHRISTIANSEN, Paul - Psalm 80; Psalm 92;
[A] Psalm 118:24; Psalm 118:24; Luke
1:26ff; Ephesians 1:3; Revelation 1:7.

CLARK, Henry - John 14:1-3.

CLARK, Jeremiah - Psalm 103:1-3.

CLARK, K. C. Psalm 98.

CLARK, Keith - Psalm 128; Psalm 139;
Proverbs 3; Jeremiah 9:1.

CLARKE, Thomas - Psalm 3:1-3.

CLARKE-WHITFELD, John - Psalm 133.

CLATTERBUCK, Robert C. - Psalm 103:1-4;
Psalm 107:1, 8.

CLAUDIN DE SERMISY - [A] Psalm 103:1-3.

CLAUSEN, Rene - Psalm 96; Psalm 96:1.

CLAWSON, Donald - Psalm 81:1-3.

CLAYTON, Harold - Isaiah 40:28-31.

CLEMENS NON PAPA - [A] Song of Songs 2:1-3;
Jeremiah 31:15; Matthew 2:1-2.

CLEMENT, Jacques - Psalm 47:5.

CLEMENTS, John - Matthew 6:9-13.

CLOKEY, Joseph - Genesis 28:16-17; Numbers
10:29; Isaiah 2:2-4; Isaiah 61:1, 6, 8;
Matthew 6:19-21; Revelation 19.

CLUTTERHAM, Lars T. - I Corinthians 13:4-8.

COCKSHOTT, Gerald - Psalm 69.

COGGIN, Elwood - Psalm 32:11.

COKE-JEPHCOTT, Norman - Acts 2:1-4.

COLE, John - Psalm 102:16.

COLERIDGE-TAYLOR, Samuel - Psalm 24:7-8;
Psalm 137.

COLLINS, Don L. - Proverbs 20:29.

COLVIN, Herbert - Isaiah 40:30.

COMBS, Francis - John 14:15-17.

COMER, Juan B. - Philippians 2:8-9.

COMPERE, Loyset - Lamentations 1:12; John
1:14.

CONSEIL, Jean - [A] Psalm 119: 117, 122,
124.

CONSTANTINI, Alessandro - Psalm 136:1.

CONVERSE, Franck - Psalm 148.

CONTE, David - Psalm 149.

COOK, Melville - Job 3:3, 4, 20-21, 23-24.

COOKE, Arnold - Psalm 96.

COOLEY, John C. - Psalm 10:1, 10, 17-18.

COOPER, Irvin - Psalm 19:16 (Tallis Canon);
Jeremiah 8:22; I Timothy 1:17 (based on).

COOPER, Rose Marie - Psalm 150.

COPE, Cecil - Psalm 100.

COPES, V. Earle - Psalm 51:10, 11, 12;
Psalm 96:1-3, 6, 9, 11-13; Psalm 121;
Galatians 6:14 (based on).

COPLAND, Aaron - Genesis 1:1 - 2:7.

COPLEY, I. A. - Psalm 150.

COPLEY, R. Evan - Psalm 3:8; Psalm 4:7;
Psalm 34:1; Psalm 72:18-19;
Psalm 96; Psalm 118:24; Luke 2:14.

CORELLI, Arcangelo - Psalm 103:1-4; Luke 2:
10-11, 14.

CORFE, Joseph - Psalm 5:3; Psalm 30:1;
Psalm 65:1.

CORIGLIANO, John - Psalm 8.

CORINA, John - Psalm 118; I Peter 3:10-12.

CORNELIUS, Peter - Psalm 137.

CORNELL, Garry A. - Psalm 146.

CORREA, Carlos - Lamentations 1:12.

COUILLART (early 16th century) - [A] Acts
1:11.

COUPER, Alinda - Psalm 67:5-7; Psalm 86;
Isaiah 9:2; Matthew 21:5, 9; John 1:29;
I Corinthians 15:21, 57.

COUPERIN, Francois - Psalm 47; Psalm 96:1-3;
Psalm 100; Psalm 118:14; Lamentations 1:
10-14; Lamentations 1:12.

COUSINS, M. Thomas - Psalm 47; Psalm 47:1-2,
6; Psalm 57:11, 14; Philippians 4:4-8

COUSTON, Thomas - Philippians 4:4-7.

COUTRE, Jean Papineau - Psalm 150.

COWELL, Henry - Psalm 121.

COX, Ainslee - Psalm 100.

COX, Michael - Matthew 11:28-30;
I Corinthians 13 (adapted).

CRAM, James D. - Psalm 8:1, 3, 4; Psalm 27:
1, 5; Psalm 34:1-9, 11-12, 14; Psalm 36:
5-9; Psalm 150; Proverbs 3:1-4.

CRANDELL, Robert - Psalm 98; Matthew 5:4.

CRAWFORD, John - Psalm 98.

CRESTON, Paul - Psalm 23.

CROCE, Giovanni - Psalm 95; Psalm 96:1-3;
Psalm 143:1-2, 6; Lamentations 1:12;
[A] Lamentations 1:12; Matthew 26:39,
41; Matthew 27:46.

CROFT, William - Psalm 6:4; Psalm 20:5-7;
Psalm 24:7-10; Psalm 47:5-7; Psalm 88:
1, 2, 3, 13; Psalm 90; Psalm 100; Psalm
105:1-2; Psalm 108:47, 48; Psalm 119:97;
Psalm 130; [A] John 11:25-26.

CROMIE, Marguerite Biggs - Psalm 116:12-13;
Psalm 148.

CROOK, Arthur - Psalm 68:11, 12.

CROSSE, Gordon - [A] Matthew 6:9-13.

CROTCH, William - Psalm 84:13; Psalm 86:4;
Psalm 139:17, 23-24; Psalm 150:1-2;
Luke 1:46-55.

CROWE, John F. - Isaiah 2:3, 5.

CRUFT, Adrian- Psalm 93; Psalm 100; Psalm
117; Luke 1:68-79; John 4:16; Ephesians
2:13-14, 17, 19.

CRUGER, Johann - [A] Psalm 98:1;   [A]
Ecclesiasticus 50:22-24; Revelation 5:
12 (Watts).

CUNDICK, Robert - Psalm 139.

CURRY, W. Lawrence - Psalm 150; Matthew
21:9.

CURZON, Clara Jean - Luke 4:18.

CUTLER, Henry Stephen - Matthew 11:28.

DACQUES, Pierre - Psalm 93.

DAILEY, William - Hosea 6:3, 6; I John 4:
7-11.

DALBY, Martin - Psalm 8:3-9; Psalm 137.

DANIELS, M. L. - Psalm 23; Psalm 29:1-4,
10-11; Psalm 96.

DANNER, David - Romans 11:33-36; Philippians 1:6-7, 9.

DARKE, Harold - Joshua 1:9; Psalm 145;
Malachai 4:2 (Wesley).

DARST, W. Glenn - Psalm 15:1-2; Isaiah 58
(paraphrase); Amos 5:24; Matthew 11:
28-30; John 1:4-5, 7.

DAVIDSON, Charles - Psalm 24; Isaiah 65:25.

DAVIDSON, Jerry F. - Psalm 122.

DAVIES, H. Walford - Wisdom of Solomon 3:
1-3; Matthew 5:8; Romans 8:9-16.

DAVIES, Peter Maxwell - Matthew 6:9-15.

DAVIS, Diane - Judith 16:2, 13-15.

DAVIS, Frederick - Jeremiah 8:22.

DAVIS, Katherine K. - Psalm 23; Psalm 51:
9-10; Psalm 146:5-6; Proverbs 3:5, 6;
Isaiah 40:1; Matthew 21:9; John 3:16;
Philippians 4:4-7.

DAVISON, John - I Peter 1:3-9.

DAVYE, John J. - Matthew 27:46.

DAWSON, William - Jeremiah 8:22.

DAY, Edgar - Galatians 6:14 (Watts).

DECIUS, Nikolas - Luke 2:14.

DEDEKIND, C. C. - Luke 19:38.

DEEN, Mark T. - [A] Numbers 6:24-26.

DEERING (Dering) Richard - II Samuel 18:33;
Isaiah 6:2-3; Revelation 8:1b.

DEISS, Lucien - Psalm 150.

DELLO JOIO, Norman - Psalm 98.

DELMONTE, Pauline - Mark 11:9-11.

DEMAREST, Alison - Habakkuk 3 (adapted).

DeMILLE, Robert - Psalm 99.

DERING, Richard - Lamentations 1:12.

de RIVAFRECHA, Martin - Song of Songs 5:6, 8.

DeTAR, Vernon - Psalm 102:25-27.
DETT, R. Nathaniel - Exodus 15:20-22 (based on); Jeremiah 6:16.
DEVIDAL, David - Isaiah 53:4-6.
DICKAU, David C. - Psalm 98.
DICKEY, Mark - John 14:1-2, 27.
DICKENSON, Clarence - Psalm 86:1, 3-7, 12.
DIEMENTE, Edward - I Corinthians 5:7-8 (free paraphrase).
DIEMER, Emma Lou - Psalm 8; Psalm 42; Psalm 57:1, 8-10; Psalm 67; Psalm 95:1-7; Psalm 101; Psalm 107; Psalm 146; Psalm 149:1-5; Isaiah 49; Isaiah 55:12; Luke 6:20-23; Romans 6:9.
DIERCKS, John - Psalm 2; Psalm 28:2; Psalm 47; Psalm 80.
DIERCKS, Louis H. - Psalm 24.
DIETERICH, Milton - Psalm 84; Psalm 119; Matthew 21:9.
DIETTERICH, Philip - Psalm 23; Psalm 85:6, 7.
DIETRICH, Fritz - Luke 2:1-20.
DIGGLE, Richard - Psalm 42.
DIGGLE, Roland - Psalm 15:1-3, 7.
DiJULIO, Max - John 1:14.
DiLASSO (Lassus),Orlando - Psalm 13:3-4; Psalm 36; Psalm 38:10; Psalm 39; Psalm 39:1; Psalm 42; Psalm 51; Psalm 69:20; Psalm 100; Psalm 100:1-3; Psalm 102:1; Psalm 102:13; Psalm 121; Psalm 125; Psalm 130; Psalm 137:1; Psalm 139:23-24; Psalm 140:4; Psalm 146:1-3; Isaiah 35:4; Wisdom of Solomon 3:1-3; Matthew 11:28-30; Matthew 26:39,41; Luke 2:9.
DIMEO, John J. - Psalm 102.
DINERSTEIN, Norman - II Samuel 18:33.
DIRKSEN, Richard - Psalm 92:1-4; Psalm 100; Psalm 103; Psalm 103:1; I Corinthians 5:7-8; Revelation 15:3-4.
DISTLER, Hugo - Psalm 46:1-2, 4; Psalm 98; Psalm 103:1-6; Psalm 130; Isaiah 11:1; Matthew 8:8; Luke 2:14; John 3:16; John 16:33; Revelation 14:13.
DOIG, Don - Isaiah 40:28-31; Romans 8:35, 38-39.
DONAHUE, Robert - Matthew 6:9-15.
DONATI, Ignazio - John 14:18.
DONATO, Anthony - Psalm 8; Psalm 100; Psalm 150; Matthew 26:17-30.
DORSTE, Doreen - Psalm 100.
DOWLAND, John - Psalm 68:21-22; Psalm 130.
DRAYTON, Paul - Luke 1.
DRESSLER, Gallus - Psalm 117; John 2:25-26; John 3:16.
DRESSLER, John - Psalm 72.
DROSTE, Doreen - Psalm 30:12-13.
DROZDOF, I. - Psalm 86:1, 6.
DuBOIS, Leon J. - Isaiah 12:2, 4.
DULOT, Francois - [A] Mark 16:1-2.
DUNFORD, Benjamin - Psalm 47.
DUNSTABLE, John - Song of Songs 7:4-7, 11-12.
DUPUIS, Thomas - Psalm 23.
DURANTE, Frances - Psalm 88:1.
DURANTE, Francesco - Philippians 2:8-9.
DURON, Sebastian - Lamentations 1:12.
DURUFLE, Maurice - Matthew 16:18.
DVORAK, Anton - Psalm 23; Psalm 23:1-4; Psalm 121:1-4; Psalm 149.
DYSON, George - Psalm 138:4-7.

EASTE, Michael - II Samuel 18:33.
EBERLIN, Johann Ernest - Matthew 27:46.
ECCARD, Johann - Luke 1:39-50; Luke 2:22-32; Luke 2:27-32.
EDDLEMAN, David - Psalm 47; Psalm 100; [A] John 14:15; John 14:27.
EFFINGER, Cecil - Psalm 81; Proverbs 3:1-6; Isaiah 49:10; Matthew 6:9-13.
EHRET, Walter (arranger) - John 6:37.

EIDSVOOG, John - Psalm 33:1-6, 8.
ELDRIDGE, Guy - Galatians 6:14 (Watts).
ELGAR, Edward - Psalm 5:2-3; Isaiah 61:1-4, 11; Joel 2:21-24, 26; Joel 9:21-24, 26.
ELLSWORTH, A. Eugene - Psalm 100; Revelation 21:1-6.
ELMORE, Robert - II Chronicles 7:1-3; Psalm 10:1-2, 7, 12; Psalm 23; Psalm 93.
ELVEY, George J. - Isaiah 60:1-3.
ELVEY, Stephen - Psalm 48:8.
EMIG, Lois Myers - Psalm 105.
ENGEL, Lehman - Ecclesiasticus 44.
ENGLERT, Eugene - Psalm 8:1, 3-6; Psalm 25: 1-2, 4-5; Psalm 27:1; Psalm 95; Psalm 150; John 10:11-18.
ENGLISH FOLK MELODY (Hopson) - Psalm 130.
ERBACH, Christian - Psalm 6:2-3; Psalm 30: 1-3.
ESCOVADO, Robin - Psalm 131.
ESQUIVEL, Juan - Lamentations 1:12; John 6:58.

FALLING, Wilfred - Psalm 47:1, 7.
FANNON, Daniel S. - Genesis 28:16-17.
FARMER, Floyd - Lamentations 1:12.
FARMER, John - Matthew 6:9-13.
FARRANT, Richard - Psalm 25:5, 6; Psalm 25:5, 6, 7; Psalm 25:6-7; Psalm 27:10.
FARRELL, Michael F. - Psalm 43:3-5.
FAURE, Gabriel - Psalm 84; Isaiah 40:1.
FAUSTINI, J. Wilson - Psalm 100.
FEDERLEIN, Gottfried - Psalm 150.
FELCIANO, Richard - Exodus 15:1-2; Deuteronomy 32:1-4; Psalm 42:2-4; Psalm 103: 30; Psalm 118:1; Psalm 145:15-16; Isaiah 5:1-2; Matthew 28:5b, 6a; John 1:1-4; I Peter 2:1-9; Revelation 4:1-11.
FERGUSON, Barry - Psalm 104:1, 10-11, 13-15, 24, 35.
FERGUSON, Edwin Earle - II Chronicles 6: 2, 18-20, 41; Psalm 130:3-5.
FERROBOSCO II, Alphonso - Psalm 42:3.
FERRIS, William - Psalm 2:7; Ezekiel 47: 1-2.
FERVABOSCO I, Alphonso - Lamentations 3: 56, 58.
FETLER, David - Psalm 95.
FETLER, Paul - Psalm 5:1; Psalm 66:1, 2, 4; Psalm 68:32, 33, 34; Psalm 100; Matthew 5:1-2.
FINK, Michael - Psalm 100; Psalm 118:24.
FINNEY, Ross Lee - Psalm 95; Psalm 138.
FINZI, Gerald - Psalm 121; Ecclesiasticus 44:14.
FISSINGER, Edwin - Psalm 66; Psalm 134; Ecclesiastes 3:1.
FITCHETT, Adios - I Corinthians 13.
FITSCHEL, James - Psalm 28:1; Psalm 46:10.
FITZGERALD, Mike - Psalm 42:1-7.
FLOREEN, John E. - Psalm 134.
FOLKEMER, Stephen - Psalm 145:1-3, 8-9, 13b, 14, 17-18, 21.
FORD, Virgil T. - I Kings 3:9; Psalm 25; Psalm 25:1, 3, 4; Psalm 34:8-10; Psalm 100; Psalm 117; Psalm 118:24; Proverbs 3:5, 7, 13-14, 19; Mark 16:15-16; Luke 6:20-23; Luke 6:24-26; Luke 6:27-31; Luke 6:37-38; Luke 6:43-45; Luke 6:47-48; Luke 10:27-28; Romans 6:9.
FOSTER, Will - Isaiah 40:28-29.
FOX, William - Psalm 86:11-12.
FRACKENPOHL, Arthur - Psalm 8:1-9; Psalm 89; Psalm 100.
FRANCK, Cesar - Psalm 23; Psalm 86; Psalm 150.
FRANCK, J. L. - Psalm 119:33.
FRANCK, Melchior - Isaiah 9:5-6; Isaiah 53:4-6; Micah 5:1; Matthew 8:8; Matthew 22:20-21; Romans 8:18-19; Romans 8:31-34; Revelation 2:7; Revelation 7:13-17.

FRANCK, Rene - Isaiah 26:3-4.

FRASER, Sheena - Psalm 67; Psalm 90.

FREED, Isadore - Psalm 100; Psalm 103; Psalm 121; Proverbs 31.

FREESTONE, G. S. - Psalm 6; Proverbs 3:5, 6.

FREUDENTHAL, Josef - Psalm 24.

FREY, Richard - Psalm 136:1, 4, 7, 9; Matthew 11:9-10; Mark 11:9-10.

FREYDT, Johann Ludwig - Psalm 52:11.

FREYLINGHAUSEN, J. A. - Psalm 43:3.

FRIED, Donovan R. - Song of Songs 2:10-12.

FRIEDELL, Harold - Psalm 118:24; Luke 9:51; Ephesians 3:13-21.

FRITH, Michael - Psalm 67:3, 6, 7; Psalm 103.

FRITSCHEL, James - Psalm 32:11; Psalm 139: 23-24; Isaiah 9:2; James 4:14.

FROMM, Herbert - Exodus 15:20-21; Psalm 23; Psalm 98; Psalm 148.

FRUCH, Armin Leberecht - Psalm 100.

FRYXELL, Regina Holmen - Numbers 6:24-26; Psalm 51:10-12; Psalm 67; Psalm 67:1-3, 7; Psalm 121; Psalm 138:7; Psalm 139: 17-18, 23-24; Isaiah 26:3, 4; Matthew 6:9-15.

FULLER, Jeanne Weaver - Psalm 32.

GABRIELI, Andrea - Psalm 6; Luke 2:10-11; John 20:11.

GABRIELI, Giovanni - Psalm 47; Psalm 85:1- 2; Psalm 96; Psalm 100; Psalm 100:1; Luke 2:10, 14; Luke 2:10-11, 14; Luke 2:14.

GABURO, Kenneth - Psalm 31:1.

GADSBY, Henry - Psalm 4:8.

GALLUS, Jacob - Psalm 96:1; Psalm 98; Psalm 118:24; Isaiah 60:6; Matthew 2:1, 11; Philippians 2:10-11.

GALUPPI, Baldassare - Psalm 110.

GARDINER, William - Psalm 23.

GARDNER, Don - Luke 4:1-4.

GARDNER, John - Psalm 84:1-2, 4; Psalm 100; Isaiah 26:1-4, 7-8.

GARDNER, Tom - Psalm 118:1-2, 28.

GATES, Crawford - I Samuel 15:22.

GAUL, A. R. - Psalm 92:5.

GEISLER, Johann - Deuteronomy 28:9-10; Psalm 14:7; Psalm 84:1-3; Psalm 84:5; Psalm 93:1; Psalm 96:1-2; Psalm 103:1-5; Psalm 103:13-14, 17-18; Psalm 105:1-3; Psalm 118:24; Psalm 147:1; Isaiah 6:3; Isaiah 65:13, 18 (based on); Zechariah 2:10; Luke 2:14; Galatians 5:22; I Timothy 2:5-6a.

GEIST, Susan Rowe - Psalm 139.

GELINEAU, Joseph - Psalm 23; Psalm 148.

GENET, Elzear - [A] Lamentations 2:10; [A] Lamentations 5:1.

GENEVA PSALTER TUNE - Psalm 98.

GEOFFRAY, Cesar - Psalm 118.

GEORGE, Graham - Matthew 21:8-19 (based on); John 14:15-17.

GERMAN TUNE - Psalm 23.

GESIUS, Bartholomaeus - Matthew 21:9; Luke 1:46-55; Luke 1:68-79; Luke 2:29-32.

GESUALDO, Carlo - Lamentations 1:12.

GIBBONS, Orlando - Psalm 6:1-4; Psalm 24:7- 8, 10; Psalm 42:5; Psalm 42:6; Psalm 47; Psalm 106:45-46; Psalm 106:47; Psalm 119; Psalm 143:7-12; Matthew 21:9; John 1:19-23; John 3:16; Colossians 3:1-4; I Thessalonians 5:23.

GIBBS, Alan - Psalm 50:1-4, 6, 23; Psalm 121; I Corinthians 5:7-8; Galatians 4:4.

GIBBS, C. Armstrong - Psalm 23; Psalm 104:1- 4, 10-12, 14, 15; Psalm 150; Ephesians 4:1-4, 25-28.

GIDEON, Miriam - Psalm 84.

GIESEKE, Richard W. - II Samuel 22:7, 17, 18; Psalm 66:1, 2; Isaiah 9:2; Isaiah 40:9; II Esdras 16:35-36; I Peter 5: 10-11.

GILBERT, Norman - Psalm 103.

GILES, Nathaniel - Psalm 130.

GINASTERA, Albert - Lamentations 1:12.

GLARUM, L. Stanley - Psalm 24:7-10; Psalm 31:1a, 2a, 3; Psalm 46:10; Psalm 47:6- 7; Psalm 50:14-15, 23; Psalm 51:10, 11, 12; Psalm 57:1, 3; Psalm 59:17; Psalm 75; Psalm 84:4, 5, 12; Psalm 91:1-4, 9, 11, 16; Psalm 96:1-2, 4, 9, 11; Psalm 100; Psalm 105; Psalm 116; Psalm 121; Psalm 134:1, 3; Psalm 143;Psalm 148; Ecclesiastes 12:1-2, 6-7; Jeremiah 17: 7-8, 10; Matthew 5:3-12; Matthew 6:31- 33; Matthew 7:7-8; Matthew 11:28-30; Mark 11:9-10; Luke 10:27; John 16:24.

GLASER, Carl - Psalm 98.

GLOVER, Robert F. - Psalm 47:1, 6-8.

GLUCK, Christoph - Psalm 130; Psalm 130: 1-4, 8.

GOEMANNE, Noel - Psalm 23; Psalm 99; Psalm 103; Psalm 116; Psalm 118:24; Psalm 145; Psalm 150; Ecclesiastes 3: 1-8; I Corinthians 13; Philippians 4: 4; Philippians 4:4-7.

GOLDMAN, Edward A. - Psalm 121.

GOLDMAN, Maurice - Ruth 1:16; Psalm 117.

GOLDSCHMIDT, Otto - Luke 2:22-32.

GOMOLKA, Mikolaj - Psalm 47; Psalm 108.

GOODE, Jack C. - Psalm 25:1, 4; Psalm 33: 3, 4; Psalm 47:1-2; Psalm 83:1; Psalm 104; Psalm 104:31-34; Psalm 130:1; Psalm 150; Colossians 1:12-14.

GOODMAN, Albert G. - Psalm 12.

GOODMAN, James - Psalm 117.

GOODMAN, Joseph - Psalm 16:1, 10-11; Matthew 26:57-58; Luke 1:28-29; Luke 2:10- 12; Luke 23:44-45.

GORCZYCKI, G. G. - Psalm 43:1-3.

GORDON, Philip - Psalm 67.

GORE, Richard - Psalm 115:1; Psalm 145; Isaiah 60:20; Joel 2:3; Matthew 5:3-12.

GOSS, John - Psalm 34:8-10; Psalm 104:31, 33-35; Psalm 122:6-8; Psalm 135:1-3, 19-20; Joel 2:21-26; Luke 2:10-11; John 3:16-17; I Corinthians 5:7-8; I Thessalonians 4:14, 18; Revelation 14:4, 5; Revelation 14:13.

GOTTLIEB, Jack - Genesis 2:1-3; Exodus 15: 11; Numbers 24:5; Psalm 19:15; Psalm 96.

GOUDIMEL, Claude - Psalm 23; Psalm 25; Psalm 42:1-2; Psalm 65; Isaiah 40; [A] Luke 2:14.

GOUNOD, Charles - Psalm 43:3, 5; Psalm 137; Mark 15:33-34; Romans 10:15.

GOWER, Robert - Psalm 150.

GRAM, James D. - Psalm 47:1-3, 6-7.

GRANT, David - Psalm 23.

GRANT, Micki - Matthew 5:3-12.

GRANTHAM, Donald - Psalm 131:1-3.

GRAUN, Karl H. - Psalm 5:11, 12; [A] Psalm 98:4, 6; Isaiah 53:4; Isaiah 55:3; Hebrews 12:2b.

GRAVES, John - Psalm 19; Malachai 4:2 (Wesley).

GREEN, Jane R. - Psalm 67.

GREENE, Maurice - Job 22:21-30 (free paraphrase); Psalm 22:1, 2, 7-8, 14, 17-19; Psalm 23:1-3; Psalm 39:5-8, 13, 15; Psalm 47:1-3, 6-7; Psalm 51:17; Psalm 55:1-6; Psalm 65:9-11; Psalm 65:9-12; Psalm 66:1, 8; Psalm 66:14, 17; Psalm 79:14; Psalm 81:1; Psalm 84; Psalm 84: 12; Psalm 93:1-2a; Psalm 103; Psalm 103:1-4; Psalm 119:1; Psalm 119:171- 172; Psalm 139:23-24; Isaiah 60:1-3, 19; Isaiah 60:3, 19; Isaiah 60:19.

GREENHILL, Harold - Psalm 100.

GREGOR, Christian - Exodus 13:17; Exodus 34:6, 7; [A] Psalm 85:10-13; Psalm 103: 2; [A] Psalm 118:24; Song of Songs 8:10; Matthew 21:9; Mark 11:9; Luke 19:28; Hebrews 3:6.

GRETCHANINOFF, A. - Psalm 104.

GRIEB, Herbert - Song of Songs 8:6-7.

GROCE, Giovanni - Matthew 5:11-12.

GROVE, Jack Byron - Psalm 148:3, 8-10, 12.

GUAMI, Giuseppi - Psalm 77:2.

GUERRERO, Francisco - Isaiah 45:8; Joel 2:1; II Corinthians 2:4-6.

GUMPELZHAIMER, Adam - Psalm 67; Matthew 21:9; Matthew 25:1-13; Matthew 28:19.

GUSTAFSON, Dwight - Psalm 100; Psalm 122: 1, 2.

HAAN, Raymond H. - Exodus 33:14; Psalm 5: 11; Psalm 36:7; Psalm 98:1-2; Psalm 98: 1, 5, 6; Psalm 121:1-3; Psalm 121:5-6; Psalm 141:8; Psalm 146:5; [A] Matthew 5:8; Matthew 25:34-36; Luke 19:9.

HACKENBERGER, Andreas - Psalm 81:1-3.

HADLEY, Patrick - Song of Songs 2:10-12.

HAGEN, Francis F. - Luke 2:10-11.

HAHN, Harvey E. - Psalm 117; Luke 2:52.

HAIL, King - Psalm 4:1, 7, 9.

HAINES, Edmund - Job 21:22-23, 25-26, 28-29.

HALL, Bradley - Isaiah 55:6-11.

HALL, Henry - Isaiah 40:1-9.

HALL, Kay H. - Psalm 63:1-5.   .

HALLOCK, Peter - Psalm 47:1, 5-8; Psalm 89: 1, 16-18; Psalm 100; Psalm 122; Psalm 122:1-3, 6-8; Psalm 125:1-2; Psalm 132: 8; Psalm 145:1-4a, 6a, 7b.

HALLSTROM, Henry - Psalm 67; Matthew 3: 13-17.

HALMOS, Laszlo - Psalm 66:1, 16.

HAMBLEN, Bernard - Psalm 145.

HAMILL, Paul - Psalm 23.

HAMILTON, Iain - Revelation 21:6, 9-10, 18-19.

HAMMERSCHMIDT, Andreas - Psalm 24:7-8; Psalm 24:7-10; Psalm 51:12-14; Psalm 67:4-7; Psalm 84; Isaiah 6:3; Isaiah 49:14-16; Matthew 2:2, 5;Matthew 25:13; Mark 16: 1-7; Luke 2:10-12, 14; Luke 2:14; John 16:23-24; I Timothy 1:15-17.

HAMPTON, Clavin - Psalm 118:24.

HAMSFIELD, Jerome K. - Psalm 100.

HANCOCK, Eugene - Matthew 21:8-9; [A] Psalm 34:8.

HANCOCK, Gerre - Psalm 130; Matthew 28:19-20; James 1:17; II Timothy 1:6-7 (adapted) Revelation 4:11.

HANCOCK, Vicki - Psalm 100.

HAND, Colin - Psalm 150.

HANDEL, G. F. - Exodus 15:2; I Kings 1:38-40; I Kings 1:39-40; Job 19:25-26; Psalm 8:1; Psalm 21:1; Psalm 21:1, 3, 5; [A] Psalm 22; Psalm 23; Psalm 31:1-2; Psalm 42:1-3; Psalm 42:4; Psalm 45:1, 9, 11; Psalm 51:2; Psalm 63:1, 3, 4; Psalm 86; Psalm 89:13; Psalm 89:13, 14; Psalm 89: 17; Psalm 96; Psalm 96:3; Psalm 96:3-4; Psalm 98; Psalm 100:2; Psalm 106:48; Psalm 130; Psalm 141:9; Psalm 145:21; Isaiah 9:6; Isaiah 11:5; Isaiah 40:5 Isaiah 40:9; Isaiah 52:7; Isaiah 53:3; Isaiah 53:4-5; Isaiah 53:4-6; Isaiah 53: 5; Isaiah 53:6; Lamentations 1:4; Ecclesiasticus 44:14; Luke 2:14; John 1:29; I Corinthians 15:20-21; I Corinthians 15: 21; Revelations 4:8; Revelations 5:12, 13; Revelation 19:6, 16.

HANDL, Jacob - Psalm 68:28-29; Song of Songs 1:2-3; Psalm 118:24; Isaiah 6:3; Isaiah 11:1-2; Isaiah 57:1-2; Isaiah 60:6; Wisdom of Solomon 10:12, 14; Matthew 2:1, 11; Matthew 6:9-15; Matthew 28:1; Luke 1:31-33; John 20:17; Acts 2:4, 11; Philippians 2:10-11.

HANLON, Kevin - Psalm 100:1, 4; Psalm 103: 1, 2.

HANNAHS, Roger - Psalm 148:1-2; Matthew 21:9.

HANSON, Howard - Psalm 8:1, 3-6; Psalm 121; Psalm 150.

HARBACH, Barbara - Psalm 150.

HARE, Ian - Psalm 65.

HARKER, F. Flaxington - Psalm 42:1-4.

HARPER, John - Psalm 150.

HARPER, Marjorie - I Chronicles 16:35; Mark 2:9-10.

HARRER, Johann Gottlob - Psalm 57:7.

HARRIS, David S. - Hosea 6:1-2.

HARRIS, Jerry W. - Psalm 47; Mark 11:9-10.

HARRIS, Roy - Psalm 150.

HARRIS, William H. - Psalm 23; Psalm 134; Psalm 141:2; Psalm 145:15-20; Psalm 147: 7-9, 12-14; Joel 2; Ecclesiasticus 38:4, 6, 9-10, 12.

HARRISON, Julius - Psalm 100.

HARTER, Harry H. - Psalm 23; Psalm 64; Psalm 66; Hosea 6:1-4 (paraphrased); Luke 20:38; John 14:1-7 (paraphrased).

HARTLEY, Walter S. - Psalm 98; Psalm 125.

HARVEY, Jonathan - Psalm 116:1-4, 7-9.

HARWOOD, Basil - Psalm 67:5-7; John 6:51; I Corinthians 5:7-8; James 4:8, 10.

HASSE, Johann A. - Psalm 51.

HASSLER, Hans Leo - Psalm 1:1, 2; [A] Psalm 66; Psalm 81; Psalm 95:11-13; Psalm 96; Psalm 96:1-3; Psalm 96:11-13; Psalm 100; Psalm 100:1-3; Psalm 105:1-5; Psalm 114; Psalm 117; Psalm 119:1-2; Psalm 120:1-2; Psalm 133: Matthew 16:18; Luke 1:38; Luke 2:9-11; Luke 2:10-11; John 1:14; John 20:29.

HASTINGS, Thomas - Psalm 34:8.

HATCH, Owen Andrews - Psalm 92:1-5.

HATCH, Winnagene - [A] Psalm 118:24.

HATTON, John - Psalm 72.

HAWKINS, Edwin R. - John 14:2-3 (based on).

HAWKINS, Gordon - Psalm 42.

HAYDN, F. J. - Exodus 20:2-17; Psalm 19 (adapted); Psalm 19:1-4; Psalm 19:1-6; Psalm 23:1-2; Psalm 26:5-8; Psalm 31: 21-24; Psalm 41:12-16; Psalm 50:1-6; Psalm 61:6-8; [A] Psalm 69:13-17; Psalm 115:1.

HAYDN, Michael - Psalm 96:1; Psalm 104; Lamentations 1:12; Matthew 26:39, 41; Matthew 26:55; Matthew 27:45; Matthew 27:45-47; Matthew 27:46; Matthew 27:51-52; Mark 15:34.

HAYDN, Thomas - Psalm 51:7.

HAYES, William - Psalm 86:1, 3, 5, 12.

HEAD, Michael - Matthew 6:9-15.

HEATH, John - Matthew 6:19-20.

HEDGES, Anthony - Psalm 81:1-3, 5, 13, 14-16, 18; Psalm 83:1-3, 5, 13-16, 18.

HEDGES, Hazel - Mark 11:9-10.

HEEBLE, Robert - Psalm 150.

HEELEY, Albert - John 15:10-12.

HELD, Wilbur - Psalm 24; Psalm 96.

HELFER, William - Matthew 6:9-13.

HEMINGWAY, Roger - Psalm 13:3-6.

HENDERSON, Raymond - Luke 2:14.

HENNAGIN, Michael - Psalm 23; Psalm 100:4.

HENNING, Ervin - Psalm 137:1-6.

HERBECK, Raymond - Psalm 139:23-24.

HERBST, Johannes - Psalm 105:4; Psalm 118: 26; Isaiah 33:22; Isaiah 57:15; Matthew 5:8; Acts 4:12; II Corinthians 5:19.

HERDER, Ronald - Job 3:11, 13, 18-21a (taken from); Psalm 23:1-4.

HERMAN, Nikolaus - Psalm 36.

HERRICK, Kevin - Philemon 1:3, 7, 20, 25.

HERZOGENBERG, Heinrich - [A] Exodus 13:3; [A] Psalm 100:1, 2; [A] Philippians 2: 10a; [A] Revelation 5:12, 13.

HEUSSENSTAMM, George - Psalm 33:20-22; Psalm 71; Matthew 26:38.

HEWITT-JONES, Tony - Psalm 47:1-6; Psalm 150; Matthew 16:18-19.

HILL, Nancy - Psalm 33.

HILLERT, Richard - II Chronicles 7:16; Psalm 8; Psalm 23; Psalm 23:3-6; Psalm 31:6-7, 16, 20; Psalm 50:14, 23; Psalm 85:10-12; Psalm 96:2-4, 6; Psalm 100; Psalm 103:20; Psalm 113:5-8; [A] Psalm 122; Psalm 122:1, 7-9; Psalm 148:9-13; Isaiah 52:7; Isaiah 53:4-5; Matthew 2: 6; Matthew 5:6-9; Matthew 5:9; Matthew 5:10; Matthew 5:16; Luke 1:28, 35; Luke 1:48-49; Luke 2:30; John 8:31-32; John 10:2, 7; John 12:26; John 20:22-23; Acts 1:8; Acts 2:32; Romans 12:1, 2; I Corinthians 1:18; II Corinthians 9:8; Galatians 6:14; Ephesians 4:4-6; Ephesians 4:11-13; Philippians 2:7-11; Philippians 2:10; Colossians 3:12-15; Revelation 5:11-12; Revelation 5:12-13; Revelation 7:15; Revelation 19:7, 8.

HILTON, John - Psalm 25:5-6; Psalm 119:33-40; Lamentations 1:4.

HILTY, Everett Jay - Isaiah 2:2-5; Luke 18: 15-17; I Corinthians 3:10-11, 16-17.

HOAG, Charles K. - Psalm 100.

HODDINOTT, Alan - Psalm 130; I Corinthians 3:8-11, 13-14.

HOFF, Erik - Psalm 100.

HOIBY, Lee - Matthew 25:31; Philippians 2: 5-14.

HOKANSON, Margrethe - Psalm 129.

HOLLAND, Ken - Psalm 143:5-6, 8-10.

HOLLINS, Alfred - Psalm 96:4, 9.

HOLMAN, Derek - Deuteronomy 33:13-16; Philippians 2:5-11; Philippians 11:5-11.

HOLMBOE, Vagn - Psalm 1:1-3.

HOLST, Gustav - Psalm 86; Psalm 100; Psalm 148.

HOLYOKE, Samuel - Psalm 143:1a, 2.

HOMILIUS, Gottfried August - Psalm 23; I John 3:1.

HOOPER, Edmund - Psalm 86:11-12.

HOOPER, William - Psalm 62:1; Luke 2:8-14; Acts 1:10-11.

HOPKINS, Francis - Psalm 114.

HOPSON, Hal - Exodus 15:2; Job 19:25 (based on); Psalm 8 (paraphrased); Psalm 19 (paraphrased); Psalm 24; Psalm 37:1, 5, 7; Psalm 47; Psalm 72; Psalm 95:1-6; Psalm 96; [A] Psalm 100; Psalm 121; Psalm 130; Psalm 136:1-2, 5, 9; Psalm 150; Isaiah 55:10-11; Zechariah (paraphrased); Mark 4:30-32; I Corinthians 13 (based on).

HORMAN, John - Genesis 31:49.

HOUKOM, Alf S. - Isaiah 11:1.

HOVDSVEN, E. A. - Psalm 33.

HOVHANESS, Alan - Psalm 12:1, 6; Psalm 14: 1-2; Psalm 15:1-2; Psalm 28; Psalm 29: 5, 7; Psalm 54:1-2; Psalm 54:1-2, 4, 6; Psalm 61:1-4; Psalm 67:1-7; Psalm 70:1; Psalm 74:1, 21; Psalm 75:1; Psalm 83:1; Psalm 86:11; Psalm 89:8-9, 11, 52; Psalm 106:1; Psalm 121:7-8; Psalm 130; Psalm 143:1, 5; Psalm 148:1-4, 7-13; Psalm 148:5; Ecclesiastes 8:1; Jeremiah 17:7; Mark 9:2-9; Mark 9:9; John 20:11-16, 18; I Peter 1:2.

HOVLAND, Egil - Psalm 18; Psalm 66:1-3; John 1:1, 14; Acts 8:1-47.

HOW, Martin - Psalm 23.

HOWE, Mary - Ruth 1:16-17.

HOWELLS, Herbert - Psalm 27:4-7; Psalm 42:1-3; Psalm 44:1-9; Psalm 81; Psalm 84:9-10; Psalm 100; Psalm 122:6, 7; Isaiah 56:7; Ecclesiasticus 1:11-13.

HRUBY, Dolores - Deuteronomy 32:1-10 (paraphrase); Psalm 9:1-2; Psalm 15:7-9; Psalm 72; Psalm 141:2-3, 5, 8; Isaiah 11:6-9; Matthew 11:28-30; Matthew 25:35-40; John 14:6.

HUGHES, Howard - Psalm 98; Psalm 141; Matthew 6:9-15.

HUGHES, John - Isaiah 6:1-4.

HUMFREY, Pelham - Psalm 33:1-4; Psalm 100; Psalm 137; Isaiah 1:2, 4, 11, 17-18; [A] Isaiah 1:2, 4, 16-18.

HUMPHREYS, Don - Psalm 106:1-4.

HUNNICUTT, Judy - Genesis 1:1-3; Psalm 19:1-4; Psalm 23; Psalm 47; Psalm 95: 1-7a; Psalm 100; Psalm 100:1, 2; Psalm 150; Isaiah 53:3-4; Isaiah 55:12.

HUNTER, Ralph - Psalm 84.

HUNTINGTON, Ronald M. - Psalm 119:105-107.

HURD, Michael - Psalm 92:1-4; Psalm 95:1-7; Psalm 148:1-5.

HURFORD, Peter - Genesis 28:16-17; Ephesians 2:18.

HUSTAD, Don - Psalm 23.

HUSTON, John - I Chronicles 16; Psalm 98; Psalm 100.

HUTCHESON, Charles - Psalm 23.

HUTCHINGS, Arthur - Psalm 47:5-6; Matthew 21:9.

HUTCHISON, Warner - Psalm 135.

HUTMACHER, Robert M. - Psalm 113.

HUTSON, Wihla - Proverbs 3:6; Matthew 28: 20.

IERLEY, Merritt - Psalm 80:1-2.

IMBRIE, Andrew - Psalm 42:1-2, 5, 7-8, 11.

INGEGNERI, Marc A. - Psalm 118:24; Isaiah 57:1; Matthew 26:39, 41; Matthew 27:45-46; Matthew 27:46.

INGRAM, Ray - Matthew 28:18-20.

IPPOLITOFF-IVANOFF, M. - Psalm 103; Psalm 103:1-2, 8, 13, 18.

IRELAND, John - Song of Songs 8:7.

ISELE, David Clare - [A] Psalm 19:8-9, 10-11; [A] Psalm 22:8-9, 17-18, 19-20, 23-24; [A] Psalm 23; [A] Psalm 25:4-5, 8-9, 10, 14; [A] Psalm 34:2-9; [A] Psalm 47: 2-3, 6-9; [A] Psalm 51:3-6, 12-14, 17; [A] Psalm 66:1-7, 16, 20; [A] Psalm 72: 1-2, 7-8, 10-13; [A] Psalm 95:1-2, 6-9; [A] Psalm 98:1-6; [A] Psalm 103:1-4, 8-12; [A] Psalm 104:1-24, 29-31, 34; [A] Psalm 118:1-2, 16-17, 22-23; [A] Psalm 122:1-7; [A] Psalm 130:1-8.

ISSAC, Heinrich - Psalm 34:8; Isaiah 7:14; Baruch 5:5.

ISSACSON, Michael - Psalm 30.

IVES, Charles - Psalm 24; Psalm 54; Psalm 67; Psalm 90; Psalm 150.

IVES, Elam, Jr. - Psalm 115:1, 12-13, 16-18.

IVES, Grayston - Psalm 81; Psalm 100.

JACHET OF MANTUA - [A] Lamentations 1:12.

JACKSON, B. - Ephesians 5:4.

JACKSON, Francis - Psalm 45; Psalm 131:1; Psalm 150; Joel 2:1-2, 15-17, 32; Revelation 7:12.

JACOB, Gordon - Psalm 23; Psalm 100; Isaiah 12.

JAESCHKE, Christian David - Isaiah 53:10.

JAMES, Allen - Psalm 34:1, 3-5; Psalm 139: 7-12.

JAMES, Philip - Psalm 23; Psalm 100; Psalm 137:1-5; Psalm 149.

JAMS-DE-FER, Philibert - Psalm 25.

JEFFREYS, George - Psalm 104:31-33.

JEFFREYS, Gregor - Luke 19:41-42.

JENKINS, Cyril - Psalm 23; Psalm 86:4, 5.

JENKINS, Joseph Willcox - Psalm 9:10-11, 19-20.

JENNI, Donald - Psalm 24:1; Psalm 25:1.

JENNINGS, Arthur - Isaiah 35:1, 4, 8, 10.

JENNINGS, Carol - [A] I Samuel 2.

JENNINGS, Kenneth - Psalm 66:1, 2; Psalm
    91:1, 11-12; Isaiah 60:1-3; Colossians
    3:1-4.
JEPPESEN, Knud - Psalm 3:1-4; Psalm 27:4;
    Psalm 55:1, 17, 19; Psalm 103:2-5; Ec-
    clesiasticus 18:8.
JERGENSON, Dale - Job 00:0; John 14:27.
JOHNS, Donald - Psalm 117.
JOHNSON, Allen - Psalm 100.
JOHNSON, David N. - Psalm 13:5-6; Psalm 23;
    Psalm 31:16, 19; Psalm 34:4-6; Psalm
    45:2; Psalm 54:4, 6-7; Isaiah 49:3;
    Lamentations 3:22; Matthew 4:23; Mat-
    thew 5:3, 5-6; Luke 4:18; John 2:10,
    11; John 6:68; John 8:12; John 17:17;
    Romans 12:1; I John 3:2-3.
JOHNSON, Mark - Psalm 108:1.
JOHNSON, Ralph - Psalm 118:24; John 8:12.
JOHNSON, Robert - Mark 16:1.
JOLLEY, Florence - Psalm 100.
JOMMELLI, Niccolo - Lamentations 1:12;
    Matthew 26:39-41; Matthew 27:45, 46;
    Mark 11:9-10.
JONES, David Hugh - Psalm 23; Psalm 150;
    Isaiah 40:28-31; Isaiah 52:7.
JONES, Howard - Psalm 81:1-4.
JONES, Robert W. - Psalm 117.
JONES, W. Bradwen - Psalm 100.
JORDAHL, Robert - Matthew 6:19-21; Matthew
    28:19-20.
JORDAN, Alice - Song of Songs 2:11-12;
    Matthew 5:3-13; Luke 2:14.
JOSQUIN DES PRES - II Samuel 18:33; Psalm
    51; Psalm 93:1, 2, 3; Psalm 113; Psalm
    130; Song of Songs 1:2; Matthew 15:22,
    27-28.
JOTHEN, Michael - [A] Psalm 95.
JOUBERT, John - Psalm 3; Psalm 8; Psalm
    90:1-7, 9, 13, 17; Psalm 100;Psalm 121;
    Psalm 150; Isaiah 61:10-11; Ecclesiasti-
    cus 1:1-5, 8-10; Matthew 5:3-12; I Co-
    rinthians 15:20-22.

KADERAVEK, Milan - Psalm 117.
KALMANOFF, Martin - Psalm 8.
KANTOR, Joseph - Psalm 121.
KARLIN, Robert - Deuteronomy 33:2-4.
KATZ, David - Psalm 51:10-12.
KAUFFMAN, Ronald - Genesis 1:1-4; Isaiah
    33:20-21.
KAY, Ulysses - Psalm 5:1-7; Psalm 13; Psalm
    103:13-16; Psalm 104; Psalm 117; Psalm
    149:1-2; Ephesians 1:2.
KECHLEY, Gerald - Psalm 121.
KELLAM, Ian - Luke 1:28-33.
KELLY, Brian - Psalm 100; Psalm 130;
    Philippians 4:4.
KELLY, Bryan - Psalm 5; Psalm 150.
KEMMER, George - Psalm 23; Jeremiah 8:22.
KEMP, John S. C. - Psalm 23.
KENNEDY, Mike and Ann Cadwallander - Exodus
    4:21-23; Joshua 6:1-21.
KENT, James - Psalm 3:6.
KENT, Richard - Psalm 42:1-5.
KIMBALL, Jacob - Psalm 95:1-3a.
KIMBERLING, Clark - Psalm 23.
KING, Alvin - Psalm 47; Psalm 67.
KING, Charles - Psalm 34:1.
KING, Gordon - Psalm 81:1-3.
KING, Robert - Psalm 34:1-3.
KIRK, Jerry - Revelation 21:1-4.
KIRK, Theron - II Samuel 22:2-3, 7; I Kings
    8:27-30; Psalm 24:1-4; Psalm 33:1-4;
    Psalm 48:1; Psalm 51:1-2, 10-12; Psalm
    81:1-3; Psalm 84; Psalm 95:1-7; Psalm
    96; Psalm 98:1; Psalm 98:4; Psalm 117;
    Psalm 141:1, 3-4, 9; Zechariah 2:10;
    Matthew 6:31-34; Romans 8:28-32; Philip-
    pians 4:4-7.

KIRKLAND, Terry - Psalm 1 (paraphrase).
KLUSMEIER, R. T. - Psalm 23.
KNIGHT, Clarence - Joshua 6:1-21.
KNIGHT, Clarice - Psalm 103.
KNIGHT, Gerald - Malachai 4:2 (Wesley);
    Hebrews 13:20-21.
KODALY, Zoltan - Psalm 114:1-8; Psalm 121;
    Psalm 150; John 2:13.
KOHN, Karl - Isaiah 56:6-7; Lamentations
    3:22-23.
KONIG, Johann - Psalm 126:3.
KOPYLOFF, Alexander - Psalm 61:1; Psalm
    102:1, 2; John 4:24.
KORTE, Karl - Psalm 13.
KOSAKOFF, Reuven - Ruth 1.
KOSHAT, Thomas - Psalm 23.
KOZINSKI, David - Psalm 117.
KRAFT, Leo - Psalm 40; Psalm 98; Psalm 114.
KRAPF, Gerhard - Exodus 3 (based on);
    Psalm 100; Psalm 103:1-6; Psalm 117;
    Psalm 150; Isaiah 12; Luke 5:1-11;
    Luke 6:36-42; Luke 14:16-24; Luke 16:
    19-31; John 3:1-15; Romans 6:9; I Co-
    rinthians 15:54-56; Philippians 4:13.
KNAPP, William - [A] Psalm 145:1-3.
KRAUSE, Ken - I Chronicles 16.
KRENEK, Ernst - Psalm 104:24-26; Psalm 107:
    23-26, 29; Psalm 118:24; Psalm 126;
    Psalm 130:1-2; Psalm 136:1; Proverbs
    30:18-19; Proverbs 30:24-28; Ecclesias-
    tes 1:4-5, 7; Ecclesiastes 9:7, 9, 10;
    Ecclesiastes 12:1-8; Isaiah 38:1-6;
    Matthew 2:2; Matthew 26:38-39; Matthew
    28:2-3, 5-6.
KREUTZ, Robert - Psalm 8; Psalm 9:3, 19;
    Psalm 34:8; Psalm 50:2-3, 5; Psalm 66:
    1-4; Psalm 96; Psalm 107:20-21 (adapted)
    Psalm 109:4; Psalm 111:9; Psalm 121:1-3;
    Psalm 148:2.
KRIEGER, Johann P. - Isaiah 9:6-7; Isaiah
    57:1-2.
KROEGER, Karl - Psalm 55:1-5, 22; Psalm
    100.
KUBIK, Gail - Psalm 84.
KUHNAU, Johann - Isaiah 9:6; Matthew 26:38.

LACEY, David T. - Psalm 100.
LAHMER, Reuel - Psalm 51:10, 11, 12; Psalm
    90:1, 2; Psalm 109:1, 3.
LALANDE, Michael de - Psalm 2:4; Psalm 54:
    1-2, 7; Psalm 70:2; Psalm 130:4.
LAMB, Richard A. - James 4:4, 8-10.
LaMONTAINE, John - Matthew 1:23.
LAND, Lois - Psalm 77:1, 2, 7, 9, 12, 13.
LANDGRAVE, Phillip - Psalm 29:1-3; Psalm
    103:1-4, 10, 12; Acts 2:46-47; Romans
    12:2; [A] Colossians 3:16.
LANG, C. S. - Psalm 91:1, 5, 11-12.
LANG, E. - Psalm 119:40-42; 45-46, 49-50.
LANGLAIS, Jean - Psalm 150; John 1:4-6;
    Philippians 2:10-11; I John 4:7-8, 10.
LANGSTON, Paul - Hebrews 4:12, 13.
LANGSTROTH, Ivan - Psalm 150.
LARSON, Edward L. - Psalm 51:10.
LASSUS, Orlandus (Orlando di Lasso) - Job
    19:25-27; Psalm 1 (based on); [A] Psalm
    4:9-10; Psalm 5; Psalm 24; Psalm 25;
    Psalm 26; Psalm 38:19; Psalm 43; Psalm
    44; [A] Psalm 69:19-21; Psalm 100:1-3;
    Proverbs 3:13-14; Proverbs 10:28-29;
    Wisdom of Solomon 10:17; Wisdom of Solo-
    mon 10:19-20; Ecclesiasticus 14:22; Ec-
    clesiasticus 39:6; Prayer of Azariah 1:
    29-34; Matthew 16:24; Matthew 25:23;
    John 8:12; I Corinthians 2:9.
LASSUS, Roland da - Psalm 38:19.
LASTER, James H. - Psalm 130.

LATROBE, Christian - Psalm 8; Psalm 43:3-4;
    Psalm 65:1-4; Psalm 84:1, 2; Psalm 130;
    Psalm 130:1-4; Hebrews 1:8, 10.
LAURIDSEN, Morten - Psalm 150.
LAVERTY, John Timothy - Psalm 100; Psalm
    117; Psalm 121; Isaiah 53:3; Isaiah
    53:4; Isaiah 53:5.
LAWES, William - Psalm 100.
LAWRENCE - Darlene - Psalm 23.
LEAF, Robert - Psalm 23; Psalm 29; Psalm
    95:1-7; Psalm 100; Psalm 118:24; Psalm
    148; Luke 2:14; Acts 2.
LEDGER, Philip - Psalm 121.
LEE, John - Matthew 5:14, 16 (based on).
LEE, T. Charles - Exodus 19:1, 16-17;
    Psalm 3.
LEEF, Henry Granville - Psalm 1.
LEFANU, Nicola - Psalm 65:9, 11; Psalm 90:
    1, 2, 4.
LeFEBVRE, Channing - Psalm 8:1-3.
LEIGHTON, Kenneth - Psalm 23; Psalm 24:9-
    10; Psalm 42:1-3, 6, 12-13, 15; Psalm
    84:1-9, 12, 13; Psalm 100; Psalm 149:
    1-3.
LeJEUNE, Claude - Psalm 9 (based on); Psalm
    9:11; Psalm 50; Psalm 100; Psalm 109;
    Psalm 134.
LEKBERG, Sven - Psalm 1; Psalm 13; Psalm
    23; Psalm 51; Psalm 55; Psalm 61:1-8;
    Psalm 63:1-8; Psalm 90:1-10, 17; Psalm
    92:1-4; Psalm 98; Psalm 100; Psalm 108:
    1-3; Psalm 113; Psalm 118:24; Psalm 119;
    Psalm 121; Psalm 150; Isaiah 45:5-8;
    Isaiah 55:10-13.
LeLACHEUR, Rex - Psalm 51:1, 10, 11, 12.
LENEL, Ludwig - Psalm 33; Psalm 45; Psalm
    53; Matthew 17:7, 9; Ephesians 5:18-20.
LEO, Leonardo - Psalm 51; Isaiah 53:4-5;
    Lamentations 1:12; Matthew 26:38, 45;
    Matthew 26:39, 41; Philippians 2:8-9.
LEPLEY, R. Benford - John 14:1-3.
LESLIE, Robert - Psalm 121.
LEVY, Ernst - Proverbs 4:1, 7-8.
LEVY, Marvin David - Psalm 9:15.
LEWALLEN, James C. - Psalm 118:1, 14, 23-
    24, 29.
LEWANDOWSKI, Louis - Psalm 150.
LEWIN, Frank - Psalm 133:1; Psalm 148.
LEWIS, Anthony - Psalm 19.
LEWIS, John Leo - Psalm 46:4-7; Psalm 54;
    Psalm 64:10; Psalm 68:32-35; Psalm 145:
    3-4, 8-13; Ecclesiastes 11:9; Ecclesi-
    astes 12:1; Isaiah 40:28-31; Micah 7:
    18-20; John 10:7, 9 (adapted); Romans
    9:20-21 (based on).
LEY, Henry G. - Psalm 100; Matthew 6:9-13;
    Philippians 4:4-7.
LIDDLE, Samuel - Psalm 84:1-3, 8, 10.
LIDHOLM, Ingvar - Job 14:1-2.
LIEBERMANN, Fredric - Psalm 137:1-4.
LIEBHOLD - Psalm 37:5.
LINDH, Jody - Psalm 47; Psalm 47:1-2, 6, 8.
LINDUSKY, Eugene - Psalm 130.
LINN, Robert - Proverbs 9:1-6.
LIPKIN, Malcolm - Psalm 117.
LISZT, Franz - Matthew 5:2-12; Matthew 6:
    9-13.
LIVINGSTON, Hugh, Jr. - Psalm 103.
LLOYD, Charles H. - Ephesians 4:30-32.
LOCKE, Matthew - Psalm 6:1-4; Psalm 39:5-8,
    12-15; Psalm 68:1, 3; Psalm 102:1, 2;
    Psalm 102:25-27; Psalm 133:1; Matthew
    25:31-40.
LOCKWOOD, Normand - Exodus 2 (based on);
    II Samuel 18:33 (based on); Psalm 9
    (based on); Psalm 23; Psalm 24; Psalm
    33:1, 3-4, 6, 13, 16-18; Psalm 93;
    Psalm 117; Psalm 134:1-3; Psalm 150;
    Hebrews 11:1, 3-8, 23-31 (adapted).
LOEFFLE, Charles M. - Psalm 137.
LOMBARDO, Robert - Psalm 42:1-2.

LONDON, Edwin - Psalm 13; Ecclesiastes
    4:6.
LONGTHORNE, Brian - Psalm 100.
LOOSEMORE, Henry - Psalm 43:5-6; Luke 17:1.
LORENZ, Ellen Jane - Genesis 28:16-17;
    Matthew 21:9b; Ephesians 4:5; I Timothy
    1:17 (W. C. Smith); Revelation 21:3-4.
LORO, Antonio - Isaiah 52:7.
LOTTI, Antonio - Psalm 103; Isaiah 53:4;
    Lamentations 1:12; [A] Luke 2:14; John
    14:27.
LOVELACE, Austin - Psalm 8 (paraphrase by
    Fred Kaan); Psalm 24:7-9; Psalm 48:5;
    Psalm 90:17; Psalm 100; Psalm 103:1-5;
    Psalm 116; Psalm 136; Psalm 150; Matthew
    5 (based on); Mark 10:13-16; John 14:27;
    Ephesians 3:20-21; I Corinthians 1:25;
    I Corinthians 11:24-26; Philippians 2:
    5-6; I Thessalonians 1:15-20.
LUCKY, Harrell C. - Psalm 27:4.
LUDLOW, Ben - Psalm 98:8; Isaiah 12:6.
LUDLOW, Joseph - Ruth 1:16.
LULLY, J. B. - Psalm 51:12; Psalm 86.
LUMSDAINE, David - Wisdom of Solomon 18:
    14-15.
LUNDE, Lawson - Psalm 120.
LUPO, Thomas - Psalm 130:1-4; Psalm 143:
    1-2.
LUTHER, Martin - Psalm 118:17; Isaiah 6:
    1-5; Isaiah 6:2-4.
LUTKIN, Peter - Numbers 6:24-26; Psalm
    121:1-2, 5-6.
LYNN, George - Psalm 19:7-9; Psalm 46:4-5,
    10; Psalm 47:1-2, 5-8; Psalm 56:12-13;
    Psalm 93; Psalm 98; Psalm 100; Psalm
    150; Matthew 19:13-15; John 6:32-35.

MacFARLANE, Will C. - John 14:1-3, 27.
MacFARREN, G. A. - Psalm 23:1-4, 6.
MacMILLAN, Alan - Psalm 8:1-5; [A] Psalm
    24:1-5 (RSV); Psalm 32.
MacMILLAN, Ernest - Psalm 21:1-7.
MacPHERSON, Charles - Psalm 65:1-2.
MADSEN, Florence - John 14:5-7, 15-18.
MAEKER, Nancy - Matthew 28:1-10; Luke 2:
    1-20; Acts 2:1-21.
MAILMAN, Martin - Ecclesiastes 3:1-2, 4,
    8, 10.
MALIN, Don - Psalm 46; Psalm 119.
MALOTTE, Albert Hay - Psalm 23; Psalm 26:
    1, 4-5; Matthew 5:3-6; Matthew 6:9-15.
MANOOKIN, Robert P. - Psalm 149.
MANUEL, Ralph and Paul Williams - I Peter
    5:7 (paraphrase).
MANZ, Paul O. - Psalm 16:1; Psalm 93:1a, 5;
    Psalm 103:1-6; Psalm 130; Psalm 135:3;
    Revelation 22:20 (adapted).
MARCELLO, Benedetto - Psalm 7:1-2; Psalm
    8:1; Psalm 8:1, 2; Psalm 8:9; Psalm
    13:6; Psalm 16:1; Psalm 17; Psalm 17:
    5; Psalm 19; Psalm 19:1; Psalm 19:1-4;
    Psalm 25:1; Psalm 36:5-7, 9; Psalm 42:
    1, 15; Psalm 46:4; Psalm 50:1, 3-4.
MARCHANT, Stanley - Wisdom of Solomon 3:
    1-2.
MARENZIO, Luca - Psalm 24:10.
MARSH, Donald - Ephesians 3:20-21.
MARSH, John - Psalm 81:1-3.
MARSHALL, Jack - Psalm 23.
MARSHALL, Jane - Psalm 1; Psalm 33; Psalm
    71:1-3; Psalm 73:25, 26; Psalm 92:
    Psalm 100; Psalm 103:1-5; Psalm 121;
    Psalm 128:1-2; Psalm 150; Isaiah 71:
    1-3; Mark 12:30-31; Luke 4:16-19;
    I Corinthians 5:7-8; I Corinthians
    15:20-21; I Peter 2:4, 5, 9, 10; Jude
    1:24, 25.
MARSHALL, Philip - Psalm 126.

MARTENS, Edmund - Psalm 77:18b; Psalm 139:
1-2, 5b, 18b; Psalm 150:1-2, 6; Isaiah
6:3a; Isaiah 9:6; Isaiah 60:1; Wisdom
of Solomon 1:7a; Acts 1:11.
MARTENS, Warren - Luke 8:10-14.
MARTIN, G. C. - Psalm 141:1; Zephaniah 1:14.
MARTIN, George - Isaiah 55:1-3, 7, 12-13.
MARTIN, Gilbert - Psalm 100; I Corinthians
15:55-56; Galatians 6:14 (Watts); Rev-
elation 21:3-5, 7.
MARTIN, Reginald W. - Psalm 103:8, 10.
MARTIN, Warren - Psalm 13; Psalm 23; Psalm
24; Psalm 67; Psalm 130; Psalm 137;
Luke 18:10-14.
MARTINI, G. B. - Psalm 70:1; Lamentations
1:12; Matthew 26:38, 56 (paraphrase);
Matthew 26:39-41.
MASLEN, Raymond - Psalm 84.
MASON, Lowell - Psalm 72:18-19; Psalm 84;
Psalm 117; Psalm 150; Galatians 6:14
(Watts).
MATHEWS, Peter - Isaiah 44:21-23.
MATHIAS, William - Psalm 19:7-8; Psalm 24:
7-10; Psalm 67; Psalm 96:1-4, 6, 8, 9;
Psalm 100; Psalm 104; Psalm 104:1-5;
Psalm 145; Psalm 150; Isaiah 60; Luke
2:14.
MATTHEWS, Thomas - II Chronicles 5:13;
Psalm 23; Psalm 121:1-2; Psalm 150;
II Corinthians 2:14-17; Revelation 21:
2-3.
MAUDIT, Jacques - Psalm 116; Psalm 150.
MAUERSBERGER, Erhard - John 1:14 (Wesley).
MAUNDER, J. H. - Psalm 118:12-13; Psalm 147:
12-13.
MAWBY, Colin - Psalm 95:1-5; Psalm 101:1-4;
Psalm 137:1-4; Psalm 148:1-5.
MAYER, Martin - Luke 2:1-14.
MAYFIELD, Larry - Psalm 100.
McAFEE, Don - Psalm 8; Psalm 51; Psalm 91:
1-2, 11; Psalm 104; Psalm 121; Psalm 150;
Matthew 13:3, 9; Luke 10:30-36; I Co-
rinthians 15:51-52, 54-55, 57.
McCABE, Michael - Psalm 113; Psalm 117;
Psalm 133:1.
McCORMICK, Clifford - Psalm 24:1-5, 7; Psalm
46:1, 2, 4, 10; Psalm 72:6, 11, 18;
Psalm 78:1-3; Psalm 82:2, 3; Psalm 92:1;
Proverbs 3:5-7; Matthew 6:28-30; Mat-
thew 16:19, 24-25; Mark 12:30-31, 34;
Mark 16:2-4; Mark 16:15-16; Luke 23:34;
John 4:24-25; John 15:5, 7; John 16:13,
15, 17, 23; I John 1 (based on); Revela-
tion 3:20.
McCRAY, James - Psalm 9:1, 2; Psalm 98;
Psalm 100; Song of Songs 2:10-12; Luke
2:8-14 (based on).
McGLOHON, Loomis - Psalm 67; Hebrews 13:20-
21.
McHUGH, Charles R. - John 14:27.
McLAUGHLIN, Marian - Psalm 86; Isaiah 61:10-
11.
McLELLAND, Young Thomas - Psalm 86:1-4.
McMURRIN, Roger - [A] II Chronicles 7:14;
[A] Psalm 27:1, 4, 6; [A] Psalm 96; [A]
Psalm 100:4a; [A] I Thessalonians 5:23.
McNAIR, Jacqueline H. - Matthew 18:1-4.
MEAD, Edward - I Chronicles 1:16, 23-25, 29-
31.
MEANS, Claude - Psalm 67; Psalm 145:1-2,
10-12; Mark 11:9-10.
MECHEM, Kirke - Deuteronomy 37:7-43; Job 3:
3, 23-26; Psalm 23; Psalm 38:21; Psalm
42; Psalm 92:1; Psalm 92:1-4; Psalm 98:
1, 4-6; Psalm 100; Psalm 136:1-5; Psalm
147:1-2; Ecclesiastes 1:18; Ecclesiastes
7:9, 16; Ecclesiastes 9:7, 9; Ecclesiastes 11:9; Song of Songs 2:8-10; Isaiah
48:10.
MENDELSSOHN, Felix - Numbers 24:17; I Kings
18:36-37; Psalm 2:1-12; Psalm 37:1, 5, 7;
Psalm 37:7; Psalm 40:1; Psalm 42; Psalm
42:5; Psalm 43; Psalm 51; Psalm 55:1-7;

Psalm 55:8; Psalm 55:22; Psalm 55:23;
Psalm 89:1; Psalm 90; Psalm 90:1, 2;
Psalm 91; Psalm 100; Psalm 113:1, 2;
Psalm 115:12; Psalm 121; Psalm 121:1-4;
Psalm 121:4; Psalm 130; [A] Psalm 143;
Ecclesiasticus 50:22-24 (paraphrase);
Matthew 2:1-2; Matthew 2:2; Matthew 24:
13; Luke 23:28-30; Romans 5:15-16;
Romans 10:15 (paraphrase); James 1:12
(paraphrase); I John 3:1.
MERBECKE, John - Matthew 6:9-13.
MEZZOGORRI, Giovanni - Psalm 100:1-2.
MICHAEL, Tobias - Psalm 24:7-10.
MIDDLESWARTH, Jean Ewald - John 14:27.
MIDDLETON, J. Roland - I Corinthians 5:7-
8.
MILFORD, Robin - Psalm 39; Psalm 121;
Psalm 137:1-5; Matthew 6:9-13.
MILHAUD, Darius - Psalm 121; Proverbs 9:
13-18; Proverbs 23:29-35; Proverbs
31:10-31.
MILLER, Thomas A. - II Chronicles 5:13;
Psalm 100.
MILNER, Anthony - I Kings 8:13, 27-28; Psalm
136; [A] Psalm 148:1-13; Revelation 7:9, 10.
MILNER, Arthur - Psalm 31:1, 3, 23; Psalm 47:
1-7; Psalm 66:1-4; Psalm 150.
MILTON, John - John 11:25-26.
MITCHELL, David - Psalm 130.
MOE, Daniel - Psalm 47:1, 7; Psalm 67;
Psalm 72:3, 18-19; Psalm 81; Psalm 91:
1, 11-12; Psalm 103:1, 2; Psalm 121;
Psalm 145:1-3, 8-9, 21; Psalm 150:
1-2, 6; Proverbs 3:1-2, 13-16; Isaiah
52; Isaiah 52:7-8; Matthew 21:9; Mat-
thew 28:18; Luke 2:29-32; Philippians
4:4-7; Revelation 21:6-7.
MOERAN, E. J. - Luke 12:37-38, 40.
MOEVS, Robert - Psalm 10:13.
MOIR, Franck - Psalm 86:12.
MONACO, Richard - Psalm 90; Psalm 90:1, 2.
MONHARDT, Maurice - Psalm 67.
MONNIKENDAM, Marius - Luke 1:46-55.
MONTEVERDI, Claudio - Psalm 112; Psalm 117;
Psalm 122; Matthew 2:10-11; Matthew 16:
18-19; Matthew 25:34; Luke 2:10-11.
MOORE, Philip - Psalm 91:1-2.
MOORE, Undine Smith - Leviticus 25:9; Luke
2:14-15.
MORALES, Cristobal - [A] Psalm 86:6-9;
Isaiah 7:14; Isaiah 9:6; Lamentations
1:12; Matthew 16:18-19; Matthew 20:1,
3-4; Luke 1:28-33.
MORGAN, Haydn - Psalm 8:1, 3-6; Psalm 23;
Psalm 37; Psalm 46:10; Psalm 51:10, 11,
12; Psalm 102:2; Psalm 119:105; Psalm
121; John 10:14-16, 30; John 15:1-11
(adapted); John 15:12-13.
MORGAN, Henry - Romans 8:37-39.
MORGAN, John G. - Song of Songs 2:10-13.
MORLEY, Thomas - Job 19:25-27; Psalm 96:
1-3; Psalm 109:21; Psalm 119:169-176;
Psalm 130; Joel 2:1; John 1:29; John
11:25, 26; John 20:2.
MOSER, Rudolf - Matthew 4:4; John 16:24-
25; Ephesians 5:1, 2, 8-9; Hebrews
9:11-15; James 1:17.
MOSS, Lawrence K. - Song of Songs 2:1-3,
7-11, 17.
MOUTON, Jean - [A] Isaiah 60.
MOYER, J. Harold - Isaiah 6:1-8.
MOZART, W. A. - Psalm 9:1, 9-11 (1912
Psalter); Psalm 46:1; Psalm 81:16;
Psalm 96; Psalm 100; Psalm 110;
Psalm 113; Psalm 117; Psalm 130;
Matthew 6:33; Matthew 21:9; Luke 2:
14.
MUDDE, William - John 6:68.
MUELLER, Carl F. - Numbers 6:24-26; Joshua
24:15; Psalm 23; Psalm 24:1-5; Psalm
34:3-4; Psalm 51:10, 11, 12, 13;
Psalm 55; Psalm 66:2, 4, 8; Psalm 86:
1-6; Psalm 100; Psalm 121; Psalm 139:

23, 24; Ecclesiastes 3:1-8; Isaiah 26:
1-4; Jeremiah 31:33-35; Micah 6:8; Matthew 5:14-18; Matthew 6:9-13; Matthew
7:7-12; Mark 12:29-31; Luke 17:5; John
14:1-4; John 15:12-14, 17; John 17:21-
22; Romans 8:31-32, 35, 37; Galatians
1:3-5; Ephesians 4:1-6; Philippians 2:
5-11; Philippians 4:8; Colossians 3:16-
17; I John 3:1-7; I John 4:16-19.
MUELLER, Howard - Psalm 137.
MUELLER, Luise - Psalm 92:1-4; Psalm 117.
MULLER, Georg - I Corinthians 6:20.
MUNDY, John - Psalm 81:1-4.
MUNDY, William - John 14:21.
MURANO, Jane - Psalm 117.
MURO, Don - Psalm 25; Psalm 121.
MUSKRAT, Nancy and Bruce - Psalm 51:10-13.

NAGEL, Robert - Psalm 117.
NAJERA, Edmund - Psalm 81; Psalm 137.
NANINO, Giovanni Maria - Psalm 45:2, 8;
    Psalm 149.
NARES, James - Psalm 33:1; Psalm 118:15;
    Psalm 135:1; Psalm 137; Psalm 139:23-24;
    Wisdom of Solomon 3:1; Wisdom of Solomon
    3:2-3.
NAYLOR, Bernard - Psalm 67; Psalm 100;
    Isaiah 2:3-5; Isaiah 6:1-8; Isaiah 6:1-
    9; Isaiah 9:2, 6; Isaiah 60:1-3; Isaiah
    51:9-11; Isaiah 52:13-15; Daniel 7:13-
    14; Joel 2:28-32.
NAYLOR, E. W. - Isaiah 40:6-11.
NAYLOR, Peter - Psalm 96; Luke 1:63, 76-79.
NEAR, Gerald - Psalm 22; Psalm 26:8; Psalm
    89; Psalm 89:1; Psalm 118:24; Psalm
    141:2; Song of Songs 2:3, 6; Song of
    Songs 2:10-12; Isaiah 40:31.
NEFF, James - Psalm 33; Psalm 104:33, 34;
    Psalm 117; Psalm 139:1-3; Isaiah 49:8-
    10; Matthew 6:19-21; Matthew 26:38, 41.
NELSON, Ron - Deuteronomy 6:4, 5; Psalm 100;
    John 14:18.
NELSON, Ronald A. - Psalm 24; Psalm 47;
    Psalm 62:1-8; Psalm 63:1-4; Psalm 98;
    Psalm 104:48; Isaiah 40:31; Isaiah 53:
    4-5; Isaiah 55:6-7; Isaiah 60:1-3;
    Matthew 20:26-28; Matthew 21:9-11;
    John 11:25-26; I Corinthians 3; Ephesians
    5:18b-20.
NELHYBEL, Vaclav - Psalm 150:3.
NEUMARK, Georg - Psalm 55.
NEVIN, George - John 14:15-17.
NEWBURY, Kent - Job 28:20-21, 23-28; Psalm
    24:1, 2, 7-10; Psalm 30:4-5; Psalm 47:1,
    5-8; Psalm 48:1; Psalm 69:30; Psalm 98:
    4-6; Psalm 102:1-2; Psalm 106:47; Psalm
    108:1, 3-5; Psalm 108:1-5; Psalm 118:14,
    19-20; Psalm 118:24; Psalm 119; Psalm
    121:1-4, 7-8; Psalm 134:1; Psalm 150;
    Isaiah 35:4; Isaiah 42:10-12; Isaiah 53:
    4-5; Isaiah 55:12; Matthew 2:2; Matthew
    2:9-11; Matthew 21:9; Matthew 26:20, 26-
    28; Mark 11:10; [A] Luke 2; Luke 2 (based
    on); Colossians 4:15; Revelation 3:20-22;
    Revelation 4:11; Revelation 15:3-4;
    Revelation 19:1b, 2, 6b, 7.
NICHOLS, Ted - Psalm 150.
NICHOLSON, Sydney H. - Psalm 121; Psalm 136;
    Ephesians 6:10-11, 13-17.
NICOLAI, Philip - Psalm 45; Matthew 25:1-13.
NICOLSON, Richard - Psalm 122:6-7; Psalm 149;
    Luke 7:36.
NIKOLSKY, A. - Psalm 34:8.
NOBLE, T. Tertius - Psalm 84; Psalm 137:1-5;
    Wisdom of Solomon 3:1-8; John 20:1;
    I Corinthians 15:20; Ephesians 4:30-32.
NOLTE, Ewald V. - Psalm 23.
NORDEN, Hugo - Psalm 90; Psalm 90:14, 16.
NORDEN, N. Lindsay - Psalm 92.

NORRIS, Kevin - Exodus 34:6-7; Psalm 51:
    10-12; Psalm 116:12-13, 18-19; Jeremiah
    50:4-5; Ezekiel 18:30-32; Hosea 6:1-2;
    Joel 2:13; Mark 10:45; John 3:14-15;
    John 3:16;   John 12:23; John 12:24, 26;
    [A] Luke 2:14; Romans 5:19; I Corinthians
    11:26; Galatians 2:20; Galatians 6:14;
    Philippians 2:8; II Timothy 2:8-13.
NOSS, Luther - Psalm 61:1-48; Psalm 70;
    Psalm 90; Psalm 148:1-9.
NOURSE, John - Psalm 100.
NOWAK, Lionel - Ecclesiastes 4:11-12.
NYSTEDT, Knut - Numbers 6:24-26; Psalm 9:1,
    2; Psalm 93; Psalm 130; Psalm 138;
    Psalm 148; Proverbs 2:1-15; Proverbs
    4:18-23; Proverbs 16:2-9, 16-20; Isaiah
    10:9-11, 28-31; Isaiah 12; Isaiah 12:3,
    6; Isaiah 41:13, 17-20; Isaiah 44:2;
    Isaiah 55:6-12; Isaiah 61:10-11; Mat-
    thew 17:5; Matthew 25:32-33; John 12:
    13; John 12:35, 36; John 14:27; John
    15:26; John 20:19-21; Romans 11:33-36;
    Romans 13:11-12; I Corinthians 15:20-
    22; Hebrews 1:10-12.

OLIVER, Stephen - Psalm 51:1-3, 4a; Psalm
    128:1-5.
ONCLEY, Paul B. - John 4:23-24.
ORFF, Carl - Ecclesiastes 3:1-8.
ORR, Robin - Psalm 81:1, 2, 3, 14, 15;
    Psalm 100; Psalm 122:1-7; Psalm 125:
    1-2.
OSSEWAARDE, Jack H. - Psalm 16:1-2, 12;
    Psalm 81:1-3; Psalm 97:1; Psalm 122:
    6-7; Psalm 150; Isaiah 60:1, 3.
OUCHTERLONY, David - Psalm 46:1-3, 5-7;
    Psalm 100; Psalm 150.
OUSELEY, F. A. Gore - Numbers 24:5; Num-
    bers 24:5-6; Psalm 97:10; Lamentations
    1:12; Malachai 1:11.
OWENS, Cyril - Luke 18:15-17
OWENS, Jimmy - Psalm 23.
OWENS, Sam Batt - [A] Psalm 103; Jeremiah
    8:22;   I Thessalonians 4:16.
OXLEY, Harrison - I Chronicles 28:20.

PACHELBEL, Johann - Psalm 46; Psalm 70:1;
    Psalm 96:1; Psalm 96:1-9; Psalm 98:
    1-3, 9; Psalm 99; Psalm 100.
PADILLA, Juan Gutierrez - Psalm 32:1-6.
PAGE, Robert - Psalm 95:1-3.
PAGE, Sue Ellen - Psalm 23; Revelation 8:
    10.
PALESTRINA, G. P. - Psalm 29:1-2; Psalm
    42:1;   Psalm 42:1-3; Psalm 80:1-3;
    Psalm 81:1; Psalm 86; Psalm 92:1;
    Psalm 95:6, 7; Psalm 118:24; Psalm
    123:3-4; Psalm 134:1-4; Psalm 135:3,
    6a; Psalm 136:1-3; Psalm 137:1, 2;
    Psalm 137:1-5; Song of Songs 7:1-2;
    Isaiah 12:2; Lamentations 1:7; Lam-
    entations 1:12; Lamentations 2:8-9;
    Joel 2:1; Matthew 2:10-11; Matthew
    2:11; Matthew 11:29-30; Matthew 16:
    18-19; Matthew 21:9; Matthew 26:39,
    41; Matthew 27:45-46; John 6:48-50;
    John 20:13-15; Acts 2:1-2; Acts 2:1-
    4; Acts 2:4, 11; Philippians 2:8-9.
PANCHENKO, Simon V. - Matthew 5:1-11
    (based on).
PARK, Chai Hoon - Psalm 15:1-2, 4-5.
PARKER, Alice - Psalm 30:10; Psalm 75:1;
    Psalm 84:11; Psalm 92:5; Psalm 118:
    24; Psalm 119; Psalm 134; Psalm 136;
    Psalm 139; Psalm 145:10-11, 21; Psalm
    150; Proverbs 17:22; Proverbs 22:17;
    Luke 2:29-32; Acts 16:36.

PRAETORIUS, Michael - Psalm 12 (Luther); Psalm 45; Psalm 46; Psalm 139; Matthew 21:9; Luke 2:10-11.

PRATT, George - Psalm 24:1-4, 9, 10; Psalm 120:1-5; Psalm 137:1-4; Psalm 148:1-5.

PRENTICE, Fred - Luke 1:46-48; Luke 1:48-49 (based on).

PRESSER, William - Psalm 146.

PRESTON, John E. - Matthew 5:3-5, 7-9, 12.

PRESTON, Simon - Psalm 46:1-2.

PRICE, Milburn - I Chronicles 16:8-12, 14, 23-25; Psalm 47; Luke 2:11-14.

PRITCHARD, Arthur J. - Psalm 100.

PROULX, Richard - Psalm 1 (based on); Psalm 19:8-11; Psalm 33:1, 5, 6a; Psalm 80:1-3; Psalm 81:1-4; Psalm 84; Psalm 92:1, 12, 13; Psalm 100; Psalm 100:4; Psalm 103; Psalm 111; Psalm 113; Psalm 118: 1, 15-16, 22-24; Psalm 118:19-20; Psalm 128; Psalm 130; Psalm 134; Isaiah 12: 2-6; Prayer of Azariah 1:29-34; Matthew 25:33; Luke 2:14; I Corinthians 5:7-8.

PULKINGHAM, Betty Carr - Exodus 15:1-6, 15; Isaiah 55:1-2; Revelation 7:9-12.

PULSIFER, Thomas R. - Psalm 67:1-7.

PURCELL, Henry - Job 14:1-2; Psalm 3; Psalm 4; Psalm 6; Psalm 8 (paraphrase by John Patrick); Psalm 19:14; Psalm 21:13; Psalm 43; Psalm 47; Psalm 54:1-7; Psalm 56:10, 11; Psalm 63; Psalm 63:1-5, 8; Psalm 74:4, 8-9, 14; Psalm 79:5, 8, 9, 13; Psalm 79:5, 8, 9, 14; Psalm 79:8; Psalm 80:4-7, 18; Psalm 96; Psalm 96:1; Psalm 96:3-6, 9-10; Psalm 96:6, 10; Psalm 100; Psalm 102:1; Psalm 106:1, 4, 48; Psalm 106:1-2, 4-5, 46; Psalm 112; Psalm 115:1; Psalm 116; Psalm 119:105-108, 110, 111; Psalm 122:1, 4-7; Psalm 128; Psalm 128:1-5; Psalm 130; Psalm 141:2; Psalm 150; Song of Songs 2:10-13, 16; Jeremiah 14:17-22; Joel 2:15-17; Luke 1:46-55; Philippians 4:4-7.

PURIFOY, John - Psalm 42.

PURVIS, Richard - Psalm 100; Psalm 119:105-106, 109.

RACHMANINOFF, S. - Psalm 25:1.

RAMEAU, Jean Philippe - Psalm 69:3; Psalm 148.

RAMSEY, Dale E. - Psalm 150.

RAMSFIELD, Jerome K. - Psalm 100.

RATCLIFFE, Desmond - Psalm 13; Wisdom of Solomon 3:1-3.

RATHBONE, George - Philippians 4:4-7.

RAYMOND, John - Matthew 6:9-15.

READ, Gardner - I Corinthians 13.

RED, Buryl A. - Psalm 145:1-2, 4; Psalm 150; Ecclesiastes 4:11.

REDFORD, John - Philippians 4:4-7.

REDMAN, Reginald - Isaiah 26:3, 4; Isaiah 26:4, 8.

REESE, Jan - Psalm 148.

REGER, Max - Jeremiah 33:14-16; John 1:1, 14.

REGNART, Jacob - Psalm 145:18-19.

REINAGLE, Alexander - Psalm 23.

REISBERG, Horace - Psalm 76:15, 16.

REYNOLDS, Gordon - Psalm 47.

REYNOLDS, John - Psalm 22:2.

REYNOLDS, William J. - Exodus 15:1-2, 11; Matthew 5:1-12; John 1:1-5; John 3:16.

RHEA, Arthur - Psalm 24.

RICHTER, Marga - Psalm 91.

RICHTER, Willy - Psalm 29; Luke 2:8-14; Revelation 2:10.

RICKARD, Jeffrey - Philippians 4:4.

RIDOUT, Alan - Psalm 46:1; Psalm 136; Wisdom of Solomon 1:7; Matthew 5:3-12; I Corinthians 13.

RIEGGER, Wallingford - Wisdom of Solomon 7:29-30.

RIMMER, Frederick - Psalm 81:1-4.

ROBERTS, J. Varley - Isaiah 55:6-7.

ROBERTS, Myron J. - Luke 8:22-25.

ROBERTS, Nancy M. - Psalm 47:1, 6; Psalm 100; Isaiah 9:6.

ROBERTSON, D. - Psalm 111.

ROBERTSON, Ed - Psalm 92.

ROBERTSON, Leroy - Matthew 6:9-15.

ROBINSON, McNeil - Philippians 2:8.

ROCHBERG, George - Psalm 23; Psalm 43; Psalm 143; Psalm 150.

ROCHEROLLE, Eugenie - Psalm 29:1-5.

RODBY, Walter and Joseph Roff - Psalm 23.

RODGERS, John - Psalm 19:14; Psalm 118:24; Romans 15:19.

ROESCH, Robert A. - II Chronicles 20:21; Psalm 67:3, 4; Psalm 136.

ROFF, Joseph - Psalm 13:3, 5, 6; Psalm 17: 6-8; Psalm 27:7-8; Psalm 31:1-3; Psalm 34:1-3; Psalm 37:3-6; Psalm 47; Psalm 57:5-11; Psalm 62:5-7; Psalm 68:32-33; Psalm 86:11-12; Psalm 100; Psalm 145: 8, 10; Isaiah 11:5-6; Isaiah 25:1, 4; Isaiah 40:31; Isaiah 49:13-15; Isaiah 53:6-7; Habakkuk 2:14, 20; Matthew 11: 28-29; Matthew 24:24-36 (based on); Mark 10:14-15; Mark 11:22-23; John 6: 35, 51; Romans 13:12-14; I Corinthians 5:7-8; Ephesians 5:1-2, 6-8; I Thessalonians 3:3, 5, 16; I Timothy 3:16; I Peter 1:22-25.

ROGERS, Benjamin - Psalm 54; Psalm 66:1, 4, 8; Psalm 67; Psalm 119; Psalm 133: 1-4.

ROGERS, Bernard - Psalm 18; Psalm 89; John 1:1-18.

ROGERS, James H. - Psalm 57:8-11.

ROGERS, Sharon - I Corinthians 15:20ff (adapted).

ROHLIG, Harald - Psalm 9:1-2; Psalm 25: 4-5; Psalm 33:1-3; Psalm 45; Psalm 47: 1; Psalm 47:1, 8; Psalm 96:1-3; Psalm 98; Psalm 100; Psalm 103:1-6; Psalm 146:1-2; Psalm 150; Matthew 28:5-6; John 1:14; John 1:29.

ROMAN, Johann Helmich - Psalm 100; Psalm 117; I Corinthians 15:20 (based on).

ROOT, Georg Frederick - Psalm 13:1-2a, 3, 5-6.

ROREM, Ned - Psalm 13:1-6; Psalm 70:1-6; Psalm 133:1-3; Proverbs 23:29-35; Isaiah 12:2-6; I Corinthians 13.

ROSE, Bernard - Psalm 121:5-7.

ROSSI, Salomone - Psalm 126.

ROSSINI, G. - Psalm 57:10, 11, 12.

ROSSINI, Thomas D. - John 1:29.

ROTERMUND, Donald - Psalm 98:1-3; Isaiah 61:10.

ROTH, Robert - Psalm 100; I Corinthians 5:7-8.

ROUTLEY, Erik - Genesis 32:24, 26-27, 29b-30; Matthew 5:13-16; Luke 2:14; John 15:12-17; Revelation 15:3-4.

ROWLEY, Alec - Deuteronomy 11:14; Psalm 65:9-10.

ROYSE, Mildred Barnes - Psalm 121.

ROZSA, Miklos - Psalm 23.

RUBBRA, Edmund - Genesis 28:17; Psalm 104; Psalm 127:1; Ecclesiasticus 44: 1, 4-5, 9, 14; Matthew 3:11; Matthew 5:3-11.

RUFFO, Vincenzo - Psalm 51:9-10.

RUSSELL, Carlton - Psalm 100.

RUSSIAN AIR - Psalm 103.

RUTTER, John - [A] Numbers 6:24; Psalm 23;

Psalm 47:1-7; Psalm 121; Psalm 146;
Psalm 148; Psalm 150.

SACCO, P. Peter - Psalm 62:1-8.
SALATHIEL, Lyndon - Isaiah 53:4.
SALIERS, Donald E. - Isaiah 55:12.
SALISBURY, Sonny - Psalm 19.
SAMINSKY, Lazare - Psalm 137:1.
SAMPSON, Godfrey - Psalm 89:1.
SANBORN, Jan - Romans 6:9-10.
SANDERS, Robert L. - II Samuel 18:24-27, 31-
    33; Psalm 62:1, 2, 7, 8.
SATEREN, Leland - Psalm 84:1-4; Psalm 102:
    12, 25-27; Psalm 145:1-7; Isaiah 54:10;
    Isaiah 55:1-3, 11, 12; Isaiah 64:6-7;
    Jeremiah 8:9; Lamentations 3:22-26;
    Malachai 2:2; John 5:25, 28-29; John
    20:16.
SATIE, Erik - Psalm 32.
SAUNDERS, Max - Matthew 6:9-15.
SAVAGE, Howard S. - Psalm 100:4-5.
SCANDRETT, Robert - Psalm 91.
SCARLATTI, Alessandro - Psalm 81:1; Psalm
    117.
SCARLATTI, Domenico - Psalm 105.
SCHACK, David - Psalm 23.
SCHALIT, Heinrich - Exodus 19:5-6; Psalm
    133.
SCHALK, Carl - I Chronicles 16:28-29, 34;
    Psalm 23; Psalm 34:8-10; Psalm 46;
    Psalm 51:10-12; Psalm 67; Psalm 104:13-
    15; Jeremiah 15:16; Lamentations 1:13;
    Lamentations 1:18; Lamentations 4:13-15;
    Lamentations 5:1, 7, 15-16; Matthew 6:
    31ff; John 6:50-51; John 15:1, 4-5;
    Romans 12:11-13; Romans 14:6-8; Romans
    15:4; Philippians 1:27; Philippians 2:
    10f; Philippians 4:4; II Timothy 1:10;
    Hebrews 2:12; Hebrews 4:12; Hebrews 11:
    1; Revelation 3:20-21;
SCHEIDT, Samuel - Isaiah 6:2-3; [A] Matthew
    21:9; Mark 11:9-10; Luke 2:10-11; John
    20:17.
SCHEIN, Johann H. - Psalm 42:11; Psalm 46;
    Psalm 96; Psalm 126:5-6; Psalm 126:6-
    7; Psalm 130; Isaiah 49:14-16; [A] Mat-
    thew 5:3-12a; John 1:14; Revelation 22:
    16b, 20-21.
SCHELLE, Johann - Romans 10:4.
SCHIAVONE, John - John 6:35, 51.
SCHIRRMANN, Charles - Psalm 150.
SCHLITTERNHARD, Melody - Psalm 117; Psalm
    121.
SCHMUTZ, Albert D. - Psalm 8; Psalm 33:1-5,
    20-22; Psalm 47; Psalm 57:1-2, 8-10;
    Psalm 67; Psalm 116:1-8, 17-19; Psalm
    134.
SCHOEN, Frank A. - Psalm 67.
SCHOENBERG, Arnold - Psalm 130.
SCHOLIN, C. Albert - John 4:23-24.
SCHOLZ, Robert - Luke 1:68, 78-79.
SCHRECK, Gustav - Matthew 21:9.
SCHREIBER, Frederick C. - Psalm 46.
SCHROTH, Godfrey - Psalm 118:1, 24;   Psalm
    145:15-16.
SCHUBERT, Franz - Psalm 5:1-3, 7-8, 11-12;
    [A] Psalm 23; Psalm 23; Psalm 92; Luke
    1:46-55.
SCHUFF, Albert - Psalm 16.
SCHUMANN, George - Psalm 23.
SCHUTZ, Heinrich - Genesis 49:10-11; Job 19:
    25-27; Psalm 1; Psalm 1:1-3; Psalm 4:1;
    Psalm 5:1; Psalm 5:1-2; Psalm 9:11-12;
    Psalm 9:12-13; Psalm 13:5-6; Psalm 19;
    Psalm 19:2-7 (and Doxology); Psalm 20;
    Psalm 20:1-4; Psalm 23; Psalm 26; Psalm
    27:1; Psalm 27:4; Psalm 29; Psalm 29:1-
    2; [A] Psalm 29:3-9; Psalm 30:4, 5;

Psalm 30:5, 6; Psalm 31:1-2; [A] Psalm
    42:6; Psalm 42:11; Psalm 51:10, 11, 12;
    Psalm 66; Psalm 67; Psalm 67:1; Psalm
    71:1-3a; Psalm 84; Psalm 96; Psalm 97;
    Psalm 98; Psalm 100; Psalm 103:1-4;
    Psalm 103:2-4; Psalm 105; Psalm 107:1;
    Psalm 110; Psalm 111; Psalm 111:10;
    Psalm 117; Psalm 121; Psalm 126:5-6;
    Psalm 130;Psalm 145:3-4; Psalm 145:15-
    16; Psalm 149:1; Psalm 149:1-3; Psalm
    150; Psalm 150:4; Isaiah 9:6; Isaiah
    9:6-7; Isaiah 40:1, 5; Matthew 6:9-13;
    Matthew 6:9-15; Luke 1:28-38; Luke 1:
    46-55; Luke 2:14; Luke 2:34-35; Luke 2:
    48, 49; Luke 16:24-31; Luke 17:10-11;
    Luke 18:10-14; Luke 21; Luke 21:34-36;
    John 1:23, 26-27; John 3:14-15; John 3:
    16; John 11:25-26; John 20:13-17; Ro-
    mans 8:31-34; Romans 8:35, 38-39; Ro-
    mans 14:7-8; I Corinthians 5:7-8;
    Philippians 2:20-22; I Timothy 1:15-
    17; I John 1:7; Revelation 14:13.
SCHWARTZ, Paul - Psalm 92:1-4.
SCHWEIZER, Rolf - Psalm 92.
SCHWOEBEL, David - Psalm 1.
SCOTT, John P. - Matthew 25:34-36; Luke
    2:8-15.
SCOTT, Katheryne - Luke 1:46-55.
SCOTT, Kayron Lee - Psalm 95:1-6.
SEAY, M. Berry - Psalm 29:1, 2, 3, 11.
SEELE, Thomas - Job 2:10; Psalm 33:2-3;
    Psalm 87:17.
SELBY, William - Psalm 117.
SELLERS, James - Psalm 100.
SELLEW, Donald - Psalm 18:1-2, 25-28.
SENFL, Ludwig - Genesis 37:33-35; Psalm
    70:1-3.
SESSIONS, Roger - Psalm 130; Psalm 147;
    Isaiah 1.
SEWALL, Maud - Psalm 150.
SHAFFER, Jeanne - Jeremiah 8:22.
SHAW, Christopher - Ecclesiastes 5:1-7.
SHAW, Geoffrey - Psalm 100; James 1:27
    (based on).
SHAW, Kirby - Numbers 6:24-26.
SHAW, Martin - Psalm 47; Psalm 47:1-2, 4-6;
    Psalm 67:5; Psalm 81:1-3; Psalm 104:24-
    28, 33; Prayer of Azariah 1:29-34;
    I Corinthians 5:7-8.
SHAW, Oliver - Psalm 23.
SHAW, Robert and Alice Parker - John 19:30.
SHELLY, Harry Rowe - Psalm 23.
SHEPHERD, Arthur - Psalm 42.
SHEPHERD, John - Psalm 40:13-17; Psalm 135:
    1; Psalm 136:1; Luke 23:46; John 13:34;
    Romans 6:9-10; Ephesians 5:19-21.
SHERMAN, Roger - Psalm 27:8-14; Psalm 117;
    Psalm 126; Luke 2:29-32.
SHIRFIN, Seymour - Deuteronomy 32:1-4.
SILK, Richard - Zechariah 2:10-13.
SILVER, Mark - Psalm 117.
SILVESTER, Frederick C. - Psalm 9:1-8;
    Psalm 57.
SILVESTER, Philip - Isaiah 27:3.
SIMEONE, Harry - Matthew 5:1-16.
SIMPER, Caleb - Genesis 8:22; I Chronicles
    29:11; Psalm 33:1-2, 4-5, 20; Psalm
    100; Psalm 122:1-2, 6-7; Isaiah 53:9-
    10; Habakkuk 2:20; John 14:15-17, 27;
    Acts 14:17; I Corinthians 14:20, 25.
SINDLINGER, Maureen - Psalm 98:4, 6, 7.
SINZHEIMER, Max - Psalm 98; Psalm 121;
    John 1:16-18.
SISLER, Hampson A. - Isaiah 25:1-9;
    Isaiah 63.
SISTER MIRIAM THERESE - Luke 17:11-19.
SISTER SUZANNE TOOLAN - Psalm 146:1-2.
SISTER THEOPHANE HYTREK - Psalm 23; Psalm
    33:1-8, 13-14.
SITTON, Carl - Revelation 15:3-4.
SJOSTRAND, Gene - Psalm 98.
SKEAT, William J. - Luke 23:34-39; John
    20:13-16.

SKINER, J. C. - Psalm 150.
SLACK, Roy - Psalm 122.
SLATER, Jean - Ruth 1:16.
SLATER, Richard W. - Psalm 139:1-6; Philippians 2:8-9.
SLATES, Philip - Psalm 130:5, 6.
SLATHAM, Heathcote - Isaiah 45:8.
SLEEPER, H. D. - Psalm 116:1-5, 7.
SLEETH, Natalie - Psalm 23; Psalm 92; Ecclesiastes 3:1-10; Matthew 7:7 (adapted); Matthew 28:19-20; John 21:15-19 (paraphrase); I Corinthians 6:20 (freely adapted).
SMART, David - Psalm 100; Psalm 145:10.
SMART, Henry - Psalm 23.
SMART, Richard - Psalm 103:1, 2.
SMIETON, J. More - Psalm 55:6, 7, 8.
SMITH, A. G. Warren - Psalm 67.
SMITH, Charles David - Psalm 9:1-2.
SMITH, Charles W. - Psalm 95:1, 6.
SMITH, Eric - Mark 15:18-19.
SMITH, Gregg - Numbers 6:24-26.
SMITH, H. Hamilton - Matthew 5:1-12.
SMITH, Larry A. - Psalm 42.
SMITH, Michael - Isaiah 27:1-5.
SMITH, Robert Edward - Psalm 145:15-18, 21; Matthew 21:9.
SMITH, Stanley - Psalm 96:1, 4.
SMITH, William - Psalm 67.
SNOW, Francis W. - Psalm 86:4-5; Psalm 130; Revelation 7:13, 14.
SNYDER, Wesley - Psalm 90:1, 2, 4, 12, 17; Amos 5:8.
SOLOMIN, G. - Matthew 6:9-15.
SOMARY, Johannes - Psalm 42:1, 2, 4.
SOWERBY, Leo - Deuteronomy 6:5-9; I Kings 8:27-30, 37-39; Psalm 18:1-2, 6-7, 17, 29, 47; Psalm 24; Psalm 48; Psalm 57:8; Psalm 70; Psalm 84; Psalm 84:8-12; Psalm 93; Psalm 103:10-16; Psalm 117; Psalm 119:105, 114, 120, 125, 135, 144; Psalm 119:145, 147-148, 150-151; Psalm 121; Psalm 122; Psalm 124; Psalm 127; Psalm 128; Psalm 133; Psalm 134; Psalm 136:1-9, 23-26; Psalm 147:1-3, 7-9, 12-14; Proverbs 2:1-6, 8; Isaiah 12:2, 5-6; Isaiah 60:6; Wisdom of Solomon 5:15-16; Ecclesiasticus 44:1-5, 10, 14; Baruch 5:1-5, 7-9; Prayer of Manassah 00:7b; John 9:7 (based on); I Corinthians 3:9, 16-17, 23; Ephesians 5:1, 2; I Timothy 6:12; I John 3:1-3.
SPAR, Otto - Psalm 103:1-6.
SPAYDE, Luther T. - Psalm 46; Revelation 15: 3-4.
SPEAKS, Oley - Psalm 27; Matthew 28:1-6; John 14:1, 27.
SPICKER, Max - Jeremiah 4.
SPIES, Claudio - Ruth 00; Proverbs 3:19-20.
SPIRITUAL - Jeremiah 8:22; Revelation 8:10.
SPORH, L. - Psalm 42:1-2.
STADEN, Johann - Psalm 96:1-2; Isaiah 57:1-2.
STAFFORD, C. - Romans 10:15.
STAINER, John - Isaiah 6:1-4; Isaiah 40:9; Isaiah 52:7; Ezekiel 36:28, 30, 34-35; John 3:16-17; John 6:33-35; John 6:35; John 20:13-16; Ephesians 4:30-32; Ephesians 5:30-32; Revelation 1:8.
STANDFORD, Patric - Psalm 84.
STANFORD, C. F. - Psalm 119:1; Psalm 122:6.
STANFORD, C. Villiers - Psalm 23; Wisdom of Solomon 3:1-3; Romans 9:11-13; Revelation 7:2-3, 9-10, 12.
STANLEY, F. Broadus - Psalm 67; Luke 11:28.
STANTON, Kenneth - Psalm 8:1a, 3-5; Psalm 149.
STANTON, Royal - Isaiah 53:3; Lamentations 1:12.
STANTON, W. K. - Philippians 4:4.
STARER, John - Psalm 19:14.

STARER, Robert - Psalm 13; Psalm 136:1-9; Ecclesiastes 3:1-8.
STARK, Richard - Psalm 148:1-3, 7-12.
STATHAM, Heathcote - Psalm 32:12; Luke 2: 8-11, 13-14.
STATON, Kenneth W. - Psalm 117.
STEEL, Christopher - Job 38:7; Psalm 47: 1-2, 5-7; Psalm 65; Psalm 65:1, 2, 5-14; Psalm 148:1-12.
STEFFANI, Agostino - Psalm 33:1; Psalm 34:11.
STEGGALL, Charles - Ecclesiastes 12:4, 7-8; Habakkuk 3:3, 6.
STEIN, Carl - Psalm 103:1-6.
STERN, Theodore - Psalm 96:1, 3, 10.
STEVENS, Halsey - Nehemiah 9:5-9, 11-12; Psalm 1; Psalm 24; Psalm 31:1-6, 17-18, 26-27; Psalm 150; Isaiah 40:3-5; Luke 1:46-55; Luke 2:29-32.
STEVENSON, Robert - Psalm 70.
STEWART, C. Hylton - Romans 6:9; I Corinthians 5:7-8.
STOLTZER, Thomas - Psalm 86.
STONARD, William - Psalm 50:1, 3, 22.
STONE, Robert - Matthew 6:9-13.
STOUT, Alan - Zephaniah 1:14.
STRATHDEE, Jim - Matthew 6:9-13.
STRAVINSKY, Igor - Matthew 6:9-15.
STRICKLING, George F. - Psalm 98.
STROH, Virginia - Psalm 113.
STUDEN, Johann - Psalm 92:1-2.
SULLIVAN, Arthur - Psalm 2:9-11; Psalm 34: 18; Psalm 44:1-5; Psalm 51:9-11; Psalm 51:10, 11.
SULLIVAN, Michael - Psalm 119:145.
SUMSION, Herbert - Psalm 84:4-8, 10, 11; Psalm 137; Joel 2:21-24, 26.
SURPLICE, Alwyn - Psalm 121.
SWEELINCK, J. P. - Psalm 17:1-2; Psalm 20: 1-2; Psalm 29; Psalm 44; Psalm 66; Psalm 75; Psalm 75:1, 9; Psalm 81; Psalm 90; Psalm 90:1, 2; Psalm 95:1-3; Psalm 96; Psalm 100; Psalm 102; Psalm 117; Psalm 122; Psalm 134; Psalm 135; Psalm 138:1-2; Psalm 149; Psalm 150; Isaiah 7:14; Luke 2:9; Luke 2:9-11.
SWENSON, Warren - Psalm 22:1-5.
SYMONS, Christopher - Psalm 81:1-3.

TALLIS CANON - Psalm 19:1-6.
TALLIS, Thomas - I Kings 8:28-30; Psalm 61:1; Psalm 100; Psalm 113; Psalm 119:1-6; Lamentations 00:0; Lamentations 1:1-5; Joel 2:1f; Matthew 25:6; Mark 16:1; Luke 1:68-79; Luke 2:29-32; John 6:53-56; John 14:15-17; John 15:12-13.
TALMADGE, Charles - Psalm 119:105.
TAMBYLYN, William - Psalm 150; Matthew 16:18-19.
TANNER, J. Pater - Isaiah 49:13.
TAVERNER, John - Psalm 20:1-2; Matthew 25:6; Mark 16:1-2.
TAYLOR, Clifford - Psalm 98.
TAYLOR, Eric - Psalm 122:6-7.
TAYLOR, Noxie - Psalm 23.
TCHAIKOVSKY, Peter - Revelation 1:8-9.
TCHESNOKOFF, Paul - Psalm 67.
TELEMANN, G. P. - Psalm 8:1; Psalm 13:6; Psalm 23:1b; Psalm 84:2-3; Psalm 115; Psalm 115:1; Psalm 117; Psalm 118:24; Jeremiah 51:27-29; Luke 1:46-55; John 3:16; I Peter 1:3-4; II Peter 3:18; Revelation 3:11, 15.
TEMPLETON, Alec - Isaiah 40:28-31.
THALBEN-BALL, George - Psalm 100; Isaiah 40:1-3; Luke 1:68-79.

THIMAN, Eric - Exodus 15 (based on); Psalm
    19:1; Psalm 21; Psalm 42; Psalm 72;
    Psalm 84; Psalm 84:5; Psalm 86:9; Psalm
    99:5; Psalm 102:24; [A] Psalm 134;
    Wisdom of Solomon 3:1; Romans 6:9;
    I Timothy 1:17 (based on); Revelation
    1:8, 11.
THOMAS, Mansell - Psalm 121.
THOMPSON, Alan - Psalm 122.
THOMPSON, Randall - II Samuel 23:3, 4; Psalm
    23; [A] Psalm 90:1-5; Psalm 122:1;
    Isaiah 3:10-11; Isaiah 19:7; Isaiah 30:
    29; Isaiah 50:21; Matthew 21:8-9; Luke
    2:14.
THOMSON, Virgil - Psalm 23; Psalm 130.
TITCOMB, Everett - Psalm 19:14; Psalm 23;
    Psalm 28:1; Psalm 33; Psalm 34:1, 3;
    Psalm 47:1, 4-5; Psalm 93; Psalm 100:1;
    Psalm 105:1-2; Psalm 118; Psalm 118:24,
    29; Psalm 134:1-2; Psalm 145:15-16;
    Isaiah 35:4; Isaiah 40:9-11, 28-29;
    Zechariah 9:9; Wisdom of Solomon 3:1-3;
    Ecclesiasticus 44; Matthew 2:2; Mark
    11:17; Luke 1:46-55; Luke 4:18-19; John
    14:18; I Corinthians 5:7-8.
TOMBLINGS, Philip - Psalm 100.
TOMKINS, Thomas - II Samuel 1:17; II Samuel
    18:33; Psalm 5:3; Psalm 19:1-4; Psalm
    23; Psalm 26:8-9, 12; Psalm 32:1, 2;
    Psalm 51:1; Psalm 51:1-2; Psalm 84:1-2;
    Psalm 102:1-2; Psalm 103:1-2; Psalm
    103:1-3; Psalm 105; Psalm 106:4; Psalm
    117; Psalm 120:5; Psalm 122:6; Psalm
    130:1-2; Psalm 149:1-2; Luke 2:29-32;
    Acts 7:55-56; Romans 6:9-11; Revelation
    14:13.
TOOLAN, Suzanne - Isaiah 61:1-4; John 6:35,
    53.
TOPOFF, Johann - Luke 2:10-11.
TOURS, Berthold - I Corinthians 5:7-8.
TRACK, Gerhard - Psalm 50:2-3, 5; Psalm 95:
    1-3a; Psalm 96:1.
TRAVERS, John - Psalm 96:7-13; Psalm 96:9.
TREW, Arthur - Psalm 23.
TRUED, S. Clarence - II Samuel 22 (adapted);
    Zephaniah 3:9-17
TRYTHALL, Gilbert - Ecclesiastes 1:3-7.
TSCHESNOKOFF, P. - Matthew 5:3-10; John 3:16.
TUFFS, A. - Psalm 104.
TUNDER, Franz - Matthew 21:9-11.
TURLE, James - Psalm 118:24.
TURNER, Ruth - John 14:27.
TUTHILL, Burnett - Psalm 3.
TYE, Christopher - Psalm 30; Psalm 30:1-4,
    11-13; Psalm 30:4, 11-13; Psalm 42;
    Psalm 67:1; Psalm 85:11, 13; Psalm 113:
    1-3; Psalm 113:1-6, 8; Isaiah 26:1, 3;
    Tobit 4; Tobit 4:7; Acts 2; Acts 6; Acts
    7; Romans 9:10-11.

UPSHUR, C. H. - Psalm 23; Psalm 27; Psalm 121.

VAET, Jacobus - Psalm 51:1, 2, 6; Psalm 121;
    Revelation 7:9.
VALLOTTI, Francesco Antonio - Lamentations
    1:12.
VAN DYKE, Paul C. - Psalm 67; Matthew 11:28-
    30.
VAN HULSE, Camil - Psalm 71; Luke 2:4-17.
VAN IDERSTINE, A. P. - Psalm 98; Mark 16:1, 6.
VAN VLECK, Jacob - Isaiah 61:10.
VAUGHN, Peter - Psalm 100.

VAUGHAN WILLIAMS, Ralph - Job 38:1-11, 16-
    17; Psalm 23; Psalm 33:1-4; Psalm 34:8;
    Psalm 34:8-10; Psalm 47; Psalm 47:1-7;
    Psalm 47:7; Psalm 84; Psalm 90:1-5;
    Psalm 90:1-17; Psalm 100; Psalm 148;
    Lamentations 1:12; Lamentations 1:12-14;
    Ezekiel 1; Wisdom of Solomon 3:1-5;
    Ecclesiasticus 44:14; Prayer of Azariah
    1:28-64; Revelation 00:0 (adapted);
    Revelation 1:5, 6.
VECCHI, Orazio - Psalm 96.
VERDI, Giuseppi - Matthew 6:9-15.
VERDI, Ralph - Psalm 122:1-2, 6-9.
VERDONCK, Cornelius - Luke 1:28, 42.
VERMULST, Jean - Psalm 23.
VIADANA, Lodovico - Psalm 33:1-2; Psalm 33:
    1-3; Psalm 96; Psalm 133:1-3; Romans 6:
    9-10.
VICK, Beryl - Matthew 11:28-30.
VICK, Lloyd - Psalm 121.
VICTORIA (Vittoria), Tomas - Psalm 6:3;
    Psalm 11:1-2; Psalm 117; Psalm 119:
    1-2; Isaiah 6:3; Isaiah 53:4a; Isaiah
    53:4-5; Isaiah 54:4-5; Isaiah 55:1;
    Jeremiah 11:19; Lamentations 1:12;
    Lamentations 1:12, 16; Matthew 2:9-10
    (based on); Matthew 21:8-9; Matthew
    21:9; Matthew 26; Matthew 26:23-24;
    Matthew 26:40; Matthew 26:47; Matthew
    26:55; Matthew 27:45-46; Matthew 27:
    60, 62; Luke 1:30-31; Luke 1:31-32;
    Luke 2:10-11; Luke 2:15; Luke 2:30-
    31; John 18; John 18:1--19:30; Acts
    2:1-2.
VIERDANCK, Johann - Luke 2:14.
VIERRA, M. L. - Psalm 130.
VILLA-LOBOS, Heitor - Matthew 6:9-15.
VINCENT, Charles - Matthew 28:1-2, 5-6;
    Luke 2:8-11, 13-14.
VIVALDI, Antonio - Psalm 112; Psalm 112:
    1; Psalm 112:6, 7; Psalm 112:8, 9;
    Psalm 117; Psalm 119:137-143; Psalm
    122; Luke 2:14.
VORIS, W. R. - Matthew 21:9.
VREE, Marion - Psalm 23.
VULPIUS, Melchior - Isaiah 6:1-4; Isaiah
    11:1; Matthew 8:23-26; Matthew 8:25-
    27; Matthew 21:9; Mark 16:6-7; Luke
    8:11, 15; Luke 18:41-43; John 3:16
    (based on); John 16:20; Galatians
    6:14 (Watts).

WADE, Walter - Song of Songs 2:10-12;
    I Corinthians 2:9.
WADLEY, F. W. - Luke 21:25; Colossians 3:1.
WADLEY, G. W. - Psalm 121:1-3.
WAGNER, C. G. - Revelation 7:12.
WAGNER, Douglas - Psalm 30 (adapted); Psalm
    113:3; Psalm 121; Isaiah 54:10; [A]
    Isaiah 55:10-12; Luke 23:27-28, 33-34.
WALKER, Alan - Psalm 24.
WALKER, Christopher - Psalm 99.
WALKER, David S. - Psalm 23.
WALKER, Ernest - Psalm 121:1-4.
WALKER, George - Psalm 148.
WALKER, Robert - Psalm 139:1-2, 6-9, 12-13;
    Psalm 150; Isaiah 26:3.
WALMISLEY, Thomas - Psalm 5:1-3, 7, 12-13;
    Psalm 115:1; Psalm 117.
WALTER, Johann - Psalm 130; John 1:14.
WALTER, Samuel - Psalm 93:1-5; Isaiah 6:3;
    Isaiah 40:31; Matthew 5:8; John 20:21.
WALTON, William - Psalm 100; Song of Songs
    8:6, 7.
WAPEN, Francis - Psalm 94:6-7; Psalm 97;
    Psalm 99; [A] Psalm 107:1.

WARD, William - Isaiah 40:31.
WARLAND, Dale - Isaiah 49:13.
WARING, Peter - Psalm 1; Psalm 67.
WARNER, Richard - Psalm 42; Ephesians 6.
WARREN, Elinor Remick - Psalm 89; Isaiah
    51:9-11.
WARREN, William - Mark 1:3.
WASHBURN, Robert - Psalm 138; Luke 2:14.
WATERMAN, Frances - Psalm 23.
WATERS, Charles F. - Ephesians 2:19b, 20-22.
WATERS, James - Psalm 25; Psalm 31.
WATSON, Walter - Psalm 96; Psalm 117; Psalm
    118:24.
WATTERS, Clarence - Psalm 113:1-2, 4-5.
WEATHERSEED, John J. - Isaiah 40:28-31.
WEAVER, John B. - Psalm 100.
WEAVER, Powell - Psalm 138.
WEBB, Charles H. - Psalm 47; Psalm 57.
WEBBER, W. S. Lloyd - Psalm 23; Psalm 103;
    Psalm 145; Isaiah 49:13.
WEBER, Paul - Psalm 32; Revelation 4:11.
WEELKES, Thomas - II Samuel 1:25-26; II Sam-
    uel 18:33; Psalm 47:1, 5-6; Psalm 61:6-8;
    [A] Psalm 63:1, 2, 5; Psalm 63:1, 2, 5;
    Psalm 84:1, 2, 13; Psalm 132:8-9; Psalm
    130:1-2; Matthew 21:9; Romans 6:9-11;
    Revelation 5:12, 13; Revelation 19:1, 6.
WEINBERG, Henry - Jeremiah 31:15.
WEINBERGER, Jaromir - Ecclesiastes 3:14.
WEINHORST, Richard - Psalm 98:1-3.
WEISGALL, Hugo - Exodus 15:11, 18; Psalm 19:
    14; Psalm 29; Psalm 114:1-8; Psalm 118:
    1-4.
WELDON, James - Psalm 147:1, 5.
WELDON, John - Psalm 61:1-2; Psalm 150:1-4, 6.
WELLS, Dana F. - Deuteronomy 30:15-16;
    I Chronicles 16:23-24; Job 28:1, 5, 12-
    13, 20, 23-28; Psalm 18:2; Isaiah 61:11;
    Ecclesiasticus 44; I John 2:9-10.
WELSH HYMN - John 6:37
WELSH MELODY - I Timothy 1:17 (based on).
WERNER, Johann G. - Malachai 4:2 (Wesley).
WESLEY, Charles - Psalm 33:21.
WESLEY, S. S. - I Kings 8 (words suggested
    by); I Kings 8:28, 30; Job 14:1, 2;
    Psalm 3 (adapted); Psalm 5:8; Psalm 23;
    Psalm 23:1-4, 6; Psalm 45:16-17; Psalm
    46:16-17; Psalm 51:2-3; Psalm 51:8, 11-
    12, 17; [A] Psalm 51:11-12, 17-18;
    Psalm 81:1-2; Psalm 96:2, 3, 5, 7-10;
    Psalm 110:4; Psalm 114:1-3; Psalm 115:
    12, 13; Psalm 119:92; Psalm 119:169-170,
    173-174; Psalm 130:3; Isaiah 26:3;
    Isaiah 35:1-2, 4-6, 8, 10; Ecclesiasti-
    cus 44:1-4, 7-15; I Corinthians 15:34,
    51, 53; I Peter 1:3-5, 15-17, 22-25;
    I Peter 1:22;
WEST, Benjamin - Psalm 124.
WEST INDIAN SPIRITUAL - Matthew 6:9-15.
WEST, John E. - Deuteronomy 33:2-3; Deuter-
    onomy 33:27-29; Psalm 84:1-3; Malachai
    1:11; Ecclesiasticus 17:29-30, 32;
    Baruch 5:8-9.
WESTRA, Evert - Psalm 24:7-10; Isaiah 35:4-
    5; Philippians 4:4-7.
WETERILL, Edward H. - Psalm 46:10-11; Psalm
    148.
WETZLER, Robert - Psalm 2:7-8; Psalm 3:1, 4,
    7-9; Psalm 22; Psalm 29:2-4; Psalm 85:7;
    Psalm 85:9, 12-13; Psalm 98:3; Psalm 111:
    1, 4, 7-9; Psalm 128; Psalm 128:1-7;
    Psalm 148; Proverbs 3:5, 6; Isaiah 9:2,
    6; Isaiah 55:6; Isaiah 60:1; Ezekiel 39:
    26-27; Zephaniah 3:14, 17; Matthew 1:23;
    Matthew 2:2; Matthew 11:15; Matthew 16:
    15; Matthew 21:5; Mark 1:11; Mark 16:15;
    Luke 2:11; Luke 3:4, 6; Luke 13:29; John
    1:1, 14; John 1:14; John 20:19-22; John
    20:24-29; I Corinthians 5:7-8; Galatians
    4:4; Colossians 3:14; I John 1:5-7;
    Revelation 11:17.

WHEELOCK, Larry L. - Psalm 24.
WHETTAM, Graham - I Kings 8:12-13.
WHITCOMB, Robert - Psalm 48.
WHITE, Jack Noble - Psalm 16:5-9, 11;
    Isaiah 12:2-6.
WHITE, John - Psalm 133.
WHITE, Louie L. - Psalm 100.
WHITE, Robert (See Whyte, Robert).
WHITEHEAD, Alfred - Psalm 23.
WHYTE, Robert - Psalm 15; Psalm 150.
WHYTHBROOKE, William - Matthew 5:16.
WICKENS, Dennis - Psalm 100; Lamentations
    1:12.
WICKLINE, Homer - Psalm 140.
WIDOR, Charles-Marie - Psalm 84.
WIENANDT, Elwyn A. - Song of Songs 2:10-13.
WIENHORST, Richard - Psalm 27; Psalm 74:2,
    4; Psalm 130; Psalm 138; Psalm 150;
    Isaiah 25:9; Isaiah 26:3-4; Jeremiah
    15:16; Jeremiah 29:11-12, 14; John 8:12;
    Romans 15:4; Philippians 1:27; Philip-
    pians 2:10-11; Philippians 4:4; Hebrews
    2:12; Hebrews 4:12.
WILBYE, John - Job 14:1-2.
WILKES, Jon - Matthew 7:16.
WILKINSON, Scott - Psalm 119:73, 77; Pro-
    verbs 3:13; Song of Songs 2:10-12;
    Matthew 5:3-5, 8; Luke 22:47-48.
WILLAERT, Adrianus - Psalm 25; [A] Psalm
    125; Psalm 126; Matthew 6:28; John 11:
    38-44.
WILLAN, Healey - Numbers 6:24-26; Psalm 4:
    9; Psalm 8:1; Psalm 13:5; Psalm 24:7-10;
    Psalm 33:11-12; Psalm 42:1-2; Psalm 43:
    3-4; Psalm 48:1; Psalm 51:10-12; Psalm
    62:1, 2, 7a; Psalm 66:1-3, 7; Psalm 67;
    Psalm 67:3-5; Psalm 84; Psalm 86:5-6;
    Psalm 98; Psalm 98:1, 2; Psalm 100;
    Psalm 100; Psalm 119:1-2, 33; Psalm
    122:1-2, 7; Psalm 135:1-3; Psalm 139:1,
    6, 8-11; Song of Songs 2:10-12; Isaiah
    9:6; [A] Isaiah 53:4-5; Isaiah 53:4-6;
    Isaiah 60:1; Zechariah 9:9; Malachai 4:
    2 (Wesley); Tobit 8:1, 11, 14-18; Wisdom
    of Solomon 18:14-15; Matthew 1:29; Mat-
    thew 2:9-10; Matthew 11:10; Matthew 11:
    28-30; Matthew 21:9; Luke 8:11, 15;
    John 1:14; John 1:29; John 11:25-26;
    John 14:15; John 16:23-24; Romans 6:
    9-10; Romans 13:12; II Corinthians 13:14;
    Ephesians 5:8-9; Philippians 2:8-9;
    Philippians 2:10, 11; Philippians 4:
    4-5; Revelation 14:14, 15.
WILLIAMS, C. Lee - Psalm 51:8, 11-12, 17;
    Isaiah 26:3.
WILLIAMS, David - Psalm 100; Psalm 136.
WILLIAMS, David H. - Deuteronomy 33:26-27;
    Psalm 23; Psalm 24; Psalm 84; Psalm
    150; Matthew 2:1-2; Matthew 5:7, 12;
    Matthew 27:1-2, 22-26; Luke 3:4b-6;
    John 11:25-26; James 1:17.
WILLIAMS, David McK. - Isaiah 6:1-8;
    Romans 8:14, 16; Ephesians 1:2;
    Colossians 3:1-4.
WILLIAMS, Frances - Psalm 1 (adapted);
    Psalm 43:4-5; Psalm 68:20.
WILLIAMS, Paul and Donna - Psalm 48:1.
WILLIAMS, Ralph - Psalm 51:11; Psalm 86:1-7.
WILLIAMSON, Malcolm - Genesis 32:24-26;
    Psalm 17:6-9; Psalm 18:6-18; Psalm 23;
    Psalm 24; Psalm 42:1-5; Psalm 65:1-8;
    Psalm 65:9-14; Psalm 66:7-13; Psalm 68:
    1-4; Psalm 84:1-13; Psalm 87:1-7;
    Psalm 89:45-51; Psalm 91; Psalm 98;
    Psalm 107:23-30; Psalm 121; Psalm 122;
    Psalm 122:1-9; Psalm 123:1-4; Psalm
    130; Psalm 133:1-3; Psalm 137; Psalm
    139:6-11; Psalm 144:3-8; Psalm 144:9-
    15; Psalm 147:12-20; Psalm 148; Psalm
    150; Matthew 21:9; Mark 16:1-2, 5-6,
    8; Acts 2:1.